The Railway Labor Act

Other BNA Books Authored by the ABA Section of Labor & Employment Law

The Developing Labor Law

Covenants Not to Compete: A State-by-State Survey

Employee Benefits Law

Employee Duty of Loyalty: A State-by-State Survey

Employment Discrimination Law

How Arbitration Works (Supplement)

Labor Arbitration: A Practical Guide for Advocates

Labor Arbitrator Development: A Handbook

Occupational Safety and Health Law

The Railway Labor Act

Editor in Chief

Douglas L. Leslie

Professor of Law
University of Virginia
Charlottesville

Senior Editors

Michael E. Abram
New York, NY

Dennis A. Arouca
Philadelphia, PA

Robert A. Bush
Burbank, CA

Michael H. Campbell
Atlanta, GA

John O'B. Clarke, Jr.
Washington, DC

Ronald M. Etters
Washington, DC

William E. Fredenberger, Jr.
Stafford, VA

Edgar N. James
Washington, DC

Tom A. Jerman
Los Angeles, CA

Joseph L. Manson III
Washington, DC

C. Richard Miserendino
Fairfax, VA

Stephen B. Moldof
New York, NY

Harry A. Rissetto
Washington, DC

Robert A. Siegel
Los Angeles, CA

Railway and Airline Labor Law Committee
Section of Labor and Employment Law
American Bar Association

The Bureau of National Affairs, Inc., Washington, DC

Library of Congress Cataloging-in-Publication Data

The Railway Labor Act / editor in chief. Douglas L. Leslie ; senior
editors, Michael E. Abram . . . [et al.].
    p.   cm.
    Chapters drafted and edited by members of the Airline and Railway
Labor Law Committee of the American Bar Association's Labor Section.
ISBN 0-87179-815-8
    1. Railroads—Employees—Legal status, laws, etc.—United States.
2. United States. Railway Labor Act. I. Leslie, Douglas L., 1942–
. II. American Bar Association. Airline and Railway Labor Law
Committee.
KF3448.R35   1995
344.73′01761385—dc20
[347.3041761385]   95-40435
                                                            CIP

Published by BNA Books
1250 23rd Street, N.W., Washington, D.C. 20037

International Standard Book Number 0-87179-815-8
Printed in the United States of America

31

CONTRIBUTING EDITORS

FOREWORD

Since 1945 the ABA Section of Labor and Employment Law has had as its stated purposes (1) to study and report upon continuing developments in the law affecting labor relations, (2) to assist the professional growth and development of practitioners in the field of employment and labor relations law, and (3) to promote justice, human welfare, industrial peace, and the recognition of the supremacy of law in labor-management relations. A significant part of the Section's pursuit of those stated goals has been the publication of a library of treatises devoted to the various component subspecialties that comprise the broad spectrum of labor and employment law in America.

Now, on the Fiftieth Anniversary of the Section, we are pleased *to provide an addition to that library,* the first definitive treatise dealing with the Railway Labor Act. For those of us who are from time to time called on to deal *in this esoteric arena,* this treatise exploring the oldest of our labor statutes is most welcome.

The Section wishes to express its appreciation to the Railway and Airline Labor Law Committee members who contributed their time, particularly to the editor in chief, Douglas A. Leslie of the University of Virginia School of Law, and to the editorial board members, Michael E. Abram, Dennis A. Arouca, Robert A. Bush, Michael H. Campbell, John O'B. Clark, Jr., Ronald M. Etters, William E. Fredenberger, Jr., Edgar N. James, Tom A. Jerman, Joseph L. Manson, III, C. Richard Miserendino, Stephen B. Moldof, Harry A. Rissetto, and Robert A. Siegel. Since 1991, this *diverse group of lawyers representing management, government, and unions* has labored successfully to produce a treatise that is balanced and nonpartisan, and one that is sure to be of great value to the practitioner, student, and sophisticated nonlawyer. *To them, the Section is indebted.*

The views expressed in the book do not necessarily represent the views of the American Bar Association or of its Section of Labor and Employment Law, or any other organization, but are the measured and collective views of the authors.

CHARLES A. POWELL III
Chair

DONALD P. MACDONALD
Chair-Elect

Section of Labor
and Employment Law
American Bar Association

July 1995

PREFACE

The Airline and Railway Labor Law Committee of the American Bar Association's Labor Section first discussed writing a book on the Railway Labor Act more than fifteen years ago. While the Committee recognized a compelling need, the project languished due to fears that the Committee could not produce a text that would be acceptable to union, management, and neutral Committee members. Eventually, in 1991, the then-chair of the Labor Section, Robert McCalla, asked the then-chairs of the Committee, Ronald Etters, Jay Roth, and Robert Siegel, whether the Committee would be interested in pursuing the project. This request proved to be an adequate catalyst. After retaining Professor Douglas A. Leslie as Editor-in-Chief, the work began.

Just as the Railway Labor Act itself is the product of negotiations between carrier and union representatives, so too is this book. Each chapter was drafted and edited by teams comprised of equal numbers of carrier, union, and neutral Committee members. The final version was prepared during a series of meetings conducted by the Senior Editorial Board, with Professor Leslie serving as interlocutor and, occasionally, as mediator.

While this was not an easy process, it has produced a book that the Committee members believe is a balanced, fair, and comprehensive discussion of the principal Railway Labor Act issues. While we have not attempted to resolve or opine on unsettled questions under the Act, hopefully we have identified most of them. We are most grateful for the efforts of all Committee members who contributed long and productive hours to this project.

xi

The case law under the Railway Labor Act continues to evolve. This edition of our book contains citations through the end of 1994. We plan to produce cumulative annual supplements, which will report on current developments concerning this unique statute.

SENIOR EDITORIAL BOARD

August 1995

CONTENTS

Chapter 1

INTRODUCTION

I. Overview of Dispute Resolution Procedures Under the Railway Labor Act

A defining feature of jurisprudence under the Railway Labor Act (RLA) is the necessity of characterizing the parties' dispute before determining how to resolve it. Virtually all disputes under the RLA fall into one of four recognized categories: representation disputes, major disputes, minor disputes, and statutory disputes. Each category is handled through a different statutory procedure, and the procedure that the parties are required to follow can control the ultimate outcome. Thus, the determination of which label to apply to the dispute is an important aspect of dispute resolution under the RLA.

A. Representation Disputes

Representation disputes are disputes over the selection of the representative for purposes of collective bargaining under the statute.[1] Exclusive jurisdiction to resolve representation disputes is vested in the National Mediation Board (NMB).[2] In resolving such disputes, the NMB may define the scope of the carrier, define the proper "craft or class" for

---

[1]Railway & Steamship Clerks v. Association for the Benefit of Non-contract Employees, 380 U.S. 650, 59 LRRM 2051 (1965); Switchmen's Union v. National Mediation Board, 320 U.S. 297, 13 LRRM 616 (1943).
[2]*Id.*

1

bargaining, specify the rules for conducting representation elections, and determine bargaining representatives. Chapter 2 discusses the treatment of representation disputes under the RLA, and Chapter 3 discusses representation issues in the context of claims of interference with self-organization.

B. Major/Minor Disputes

A central distinction in the administration of the RLA is that between major and minor disputes. Most litigation under the RLA requires courts to deal with this issue. This is understandable because whenever an employer takes an action to which the union objects, the determination of whether the resulting dispute is major or minor defines which dispute resolution procedure and status quo obligation applies. At the risk of oversimplification, the following is an introduction to the distinction, the subtleties of which recur often in this book.

Major disputes are disputes over the formation or modification of collective bargaining agreements.[3] Although there are statutory obligations that apply during major disputes, such as the duty under Section 2, First to "exert every reasonable effort" to make and maintain agreements;[4] the duty under Section 2, Seventh to serve written notice of proposed changes in agreements;[5] and the duty to maintain the status quo during the negotiation and mediation process,[6] the process of bargaining is largely unregulated. The NMB is obligated in major disputes to mediate if requested by the parties, but it has no statutory authority to regulate the bargaining process except to determine when to release the parties from mediation and thus free them to exercise self-help.[7] Chapter 4 discusses the treatment of major disputes under the RLA.

---

[3]Elgin, J. & E. Ry. v. Burley, 325 U.S. 711, 16 LRRM 749 (1945).
[4]Chicago & N.W. Ry. v. United Transp. Union, 402 U.S. 570, 77 LRRM 2337 (1971).
[5]Pittsburgh & L.E. R.R. v. Railway Labor Executives' Ass'n, 491 U.S. 490, 131 LRRM 2611 (1989).
[6]Detroit & T. Shore Line R.R. v. United Transp. Union, 396 U.S. 142, 72 LRRM 2838 (1969).
[7]Building Maintenance, Service & R.R. Workers, Local 808 v. NMB, 888 F2d 1428, 132 LRRM 2913 (CA DC, 1989).

Minor disputes, on the other hand, are disputes over "grievances" or "the interpretation or application of agreements" under the RLA."[8] The exclusive jurisdiction to resolve such disputes is vested in the appropriate Adjustment Board created under the statute, such as the National Railway Adjustment Board for railway disputes or the system Adjustment Boards used in the airline industry.[9] A decision of the appropriate Adjustment Board with respect to an issue of interpretation or application of a collective bargaining agreement is final and binding on the parties except in narrow circumstances.[10]

Although the distinction is long-standing, the RLA itself does not expressly differentiate between major and minor disputes. These terms were commonly used in the rail industry by the 1930s, and were introduced into the case law by the Supreme Court in *Elgin, Joliet & Eastern Railway v. Burley*,[11] where the Court wrote the following:

> The first relates to disputes over the formation of collective agreements or efforts to secure them. They arise where there is no . . . agreement or where it is sought to change the terms of one, and therefore the issue is not whether an existing agreement controls the controversy. They look to the acquisition of rights for the future, not to assertion of rights claimed to have vested in the past.
>
> The second class, however, contemplates the existence of a collective agreement already concluded or, at any rate, a situation in which no effort is made to bring about a formal change in terms or to create a new one. The dispute relates either to the meaning or proper application of a particular provision with reference to a specific situation or to an omitted case. In the latter event the claim is founded upon some incident of the employment relation, or asserted one, independent

---

[8]Consolidated Rail Corp. v. Railway Labor Executives' Ass'n, 491 U.S. 299, 131 LRRM 2601 (1989); Elgin, J. & E. Ry. v. Burley, 325 U.S. 711, 16 LRRM 749 (1945).

[9]Railroad Trainmen v. Chicago River & I. R.R., 353 U.S. 30, 39 LRRM 2578 (1957); Slocum v. Delaware, L. & W. R.R., 339 U.S. 239 (1950).

[10]*Id.* Chapter 5, "Enforcement of Collective Bargaining Agreements," discusses the processing of minor disputes under the RLA.

[11]325 U.S. 711, 16 LRRM 749 (1945).

of those covered by the collective agreement, e.g., claims on account of personal injuries. In either case the claim is to rights accrued, not merely to have new ones created for the future.

In general the difference is between what are regarded traditionally as the major and the minor disputes of the railway labor world.[12]

Thus, minor disputes are disputes over the interpretation and application of existing agreements, express and implied; major disputes are disputes over the making or modification of agreements.

Typically, the character of a dispute is obvious and the parties follow the requisite procedure, either bargaining or grievance arbitration. From time to time, however, disputes arise in which one party contends that the other's action modifies their collective bargaining agreement. The acting party, however, probably will respond that its conduct is allowed by the existing agreement in this situation. Thus, in practice, there is a tension between the command in Section 2, Seventh that no change be made except by agreement and the right of a party to apply its interpretation of the agreement. The Supreme Court, in *Consolidated Rail Corp. v. Railway Labor Executives' Ass'n (Conrail)*,[13] recognized this tension and concluded that a court must substitute its characterization of the dispute for that of the parties. The Court set out the standard for categorizing the dispute as follows:

> Where an employer asserts a contractual right to take the contested action, the ensuing dispute is minor if the action is arguably justified by the terms of the parties' collective bargaining agreement. Where, in contrast, the employer's claims are frivolous or obviously insubstantial, the dispute is major.[14]

The application of these principles to particular disputes is often difficult, particularly where the activity effects a change that is neither expressly allowed nor proscribed in the labor agreement. In these instances the party resisting

---

[12]325 U.S. at 723–24.

[13]491 U.S. 299, 302, 131 LRRM 2601 (1989). *See also* Hawaiian Airlines v. Norris, 146 LRRM 2577 (1994).

[14]491 U.S. at 307.

the conduct may assert that the dispute involves a change in an implied or express provision of agreement, and so the disagreement is a major dispute. This assertion permits the resisting party to seek an injunction in federal court requiring the other party to maintain the status quo until the initiating party exhausts the major dispute procedures under the Act.[15] The party engaged in the conduct will argue that its conduct is at least arguably permitted by the contract. If this characterization prevails, the changed condition generally may continue pending arbitration, and the federal and state courts have no jurisdiction over the dispute, except as may be necessary to protect the jurisdiction of the arbitration board.[16]

Courts have recognized that not all agreements about working conditions are reduced to writing. It is impossible to cover in a labor agreement every contingency that may arise. Some cannot be predicted; and even some predictable contingencies will carry such a low probability of occurrence or such a slight chance of having significant impact that they do not warrant specific expression in the agreement. Thus, there can be a minor dispute over a change in working conditions that is the subject of an implied agreement. On these occasions the absence of express contract language or clear past practice gives rise to opposing arguments over the impact of the language or practice on a particular situation. For example, the Seventh Circuit found that a carrier's subcontracting of engine repair work for leased engines was "arguably justified" under the collective bargaining agreement and thus a minor dispute, even though the agreement provided that union workers had the right to perform such repair work on all locomotives acquired by lease or purchase.[17] The subcontract could continue while the matters were grieved.

Difficult issues are presented when an agreement is silent about a particular activity. What is the legal implication of the parties' silence? The Tenth Circuit addressed this issue

---

[15]*See* Chapter 4, "Negotiation of Collective Bargaining Agreements," §§VIII, IX.

[16]*Id.*

[17]National Ry. Labor Conference v. Machinists, 830 F2d 741, 748–49, 126 LRRM 2615 (CA 7, 1987).

when it considered a carrier's decision to subcontract certain signal work.[18] The court noted that the agreement did not give the carrier the right to subcontract and that the carrier in the past unsuccessfully had served Section 6 notices to attain that right.[19] Therefore, the employer was seeking to gain a right it did not have, the dispute was major, and the employer had to negotiate the right to subcontract the work in dispute.

Another example is presented by *Consolidated Rail Corp. v. Railway Labor Executives' Ass'n.*[20] In that case, the Supreme Court considered whether a dispute over the carrier's addition of a drug test to its periodic and return-from-leave physicals was major or minor. The contract did not address drug testing directly, and the parties disagreed whether past practice had given rise to an implied contract term that permitted the carrier to conduct drug testing.[21] It was undisputed that Conrail had administered physicals on employees since its founding in 1976. The carrier argued that this long-standing practice constituted an implied agreement permitting it to establish unilaterally fitness-for-duty standards. The union argued that the past practice included urinalysis for some purposes, but for drug testing only in very limited circumstances involving particularized suspicion of drug abuse. The past practice was clear, but its characterization was not. The

[18]St. Louis S. Ry. v. Railroad Signalmen, 665 F2d 987, 108 LRRM 3239 (CA 10, 1981).

[19]665 F2d at 993.

[20]491 U.S. 299, 131 LRRM 2601 (1989).

[21]*Id.* The Court did not address the appropriate standard for determining whether a past practice arises to the level of an implied contractual term. *See* St. Louis S. Ry. v. Railroad and Signalmen, 665 F2d 987, 108 LRRM 3239. Among the factors normally considered by lower courts are intent of the parties, knowledge and acquiescence in the prior acts, and joint participation. United Transp. Union v. St. Paul Union Depot Co., 434 F2d 220, 223, 75 LRRM 2595 (CA 8, 1970), *cert. denied*, 401 U.S. 975, 76 LRRM 2779 (1971); Locomotive Eng'rs v. Boston & Maine Corp., 788 F2d 794, 799, 122 LRRM 2020 (CA 1), *cert. denied*, 479 U.S. 829, 123 LRRM 2592 (1986). Although past practice may clearly be relied upon to interpret language in an agreement (National Ry. Labor Conference v. Machinists, 830 F2d at 748–49), it is generally insufficient to contradict explicit terms in the agreement. Railway & Steamship Clerks v. Norfolk & W. Ry., 745 F2d 370, 377, 117 LRRM 2695 (CA 6, 1984); Airlines Stewards & Stewardesses Ass'n v. Caribbean Atl. Airlines, 412 F2d 289, 71 LRRM 2896 (CA 1, 1969).

Court found that the implied agreement arguably permitted the drug tests. The dispute was minor and the testing could continue pending arbitration.

C. Statutory Disputes

Statutory disputes are those disputes for which the statute creates an enforceable right or obligation but does not commit enforcement of the right or obligation exclusively to one of the administrative processes.[22] Statutory disputes fall within the jurisdiction of the courts.[23] In addition to the statutory obligations that apply during major disputes, discussed in Chapter 4, the principal category of statutory disputes involves employee rights arising under RLA Section 2, Third, Fourth, Eighth, and Eleventh. Chapter 3 discusses these statutory disputes.

D. Role of Courts in Defining Disputes

Unlike the National Labor Relations Act, the RLA does not establish an enforcement agency with powers to compel carriers and employees to make and maintain agreements in accord with the procedures of the Act. Where the parties to a dispute question whether compliance with the RLA is necessary, the courts act as gatekeepers and define and characterize the dispute in order to determine whether the court may exercise jurisdiction over the dispute, compel arbitration as a minor dispute, or direct the union to the NMB as a representation dispute. Thus, when a dispute arises about compliance with the RLA, the disputants resort to the federal courts. Almost inevitably, the courts are required to determine whether the dispute is major or minor as a predicate to identifying the status quo obligations that apply to the parties. Although the distinctions among the four categories of disputes are clear enough in principle, in practice the

---

[22]Chicago & N.W. Ry. v. United Transp. Union, 402 U.S. 570, 77 LRRM 2337 (1971); Virginian Ry. v. System Fed'n No. 40, 300 U.S. 515, 1 LRRM 743 (1943).
[23]*Id.*

boundaries are often blurred. For example, a union seeking to enforce a collective bargaining agreement may characterize the claim as a minor dispute, whereas a carrier that is resisting application of the agreement on the basis that the union no longer represents the majority of employees may characterize the case as a representation dispute within the exclusive jurisdiction of the NMB.[24] Similarly, a union may seek to characterize a carrier's unilateral action during bargaining as a violation of the status quo provisions of the statute, and thus as a major dispute, whereas the carrier may seek to defend on the basis that its conduct is sanctioned by the existing agreement, thus creating a minor dispute over interpretation of the agreement.[25] The federal court's characterization of the dispute as major or minor will determine not only where the dispute is decided, but also often how it is decided. As will be demonstrated in the following chapters, the majority of federal case law under the RLA involves determining the label properly applied to a particular dispute.

E. Court Jurisdiction Over Major Disputes

The mandatory procedures for the settlement of a collective bargaining major dispute consist of conference, mediation, nonmandatory arbitration, and intervention by Presidential Emergency Boards.[26] Compliance with these procedures is judicially enforced, and neither party may alter the status quo through self-help until these procedures are exhausted.[27] This major dispute process was devised with an eye toward the general purposes of the statute as set forth in Section 2, which include the avoidance of "any interruption to commerce or to the operation of any carrier engaged

---

[24]E.g. , Western Airlines v. Teamsters, 480 U.S. 1301, 124 LRRM 3139 (1987) (O'Connor, J., sitting as a single justice on a stay application).

[25]E.g., Consolidated Rail Corp. v. Railway Labor Executives' Ass'n, 491 U.S. 299, 131 LRRM 2601 (1989).

[26]§§2, Second; 5, First; 6; 7; 10.

[27]Chicago & N.W. Ry. Co. v. United Transp. Union, 402 U.S. 570, 581, 77 LRRM 2337 (1971); Railroad Telegraphers v. Chicago & N.W. Transp. Co., 362 U.S. 330 (1960) (employer action enjoined); Texas & N.O. R.R. v. Railway & Steamship Clerks, 281 U.S. 548 (1930).

therein." The Supreme Court has described the mandatory exhaustion of the major dispute settlement procedures as "an almost interminable process."[28] The Court in *Detroit & Toledo Shore Line Railroad v. United Transportation Union*[29] characterized it as follows:

> The Act's status quo requirement is central to its design. Its immediate effect is to prevent the union from striking and management from doing anything that would justify a strike. In the long run, delaying the time when the parties can resort to self-help provides time for tempers to cool, helps create an atmosphere in which rational bargaining can occur, and permits the forces of public opinion to be mobilized in favor of a settlement without a strike or lockout. Moreover, since disputes usually arise when one party wants to change the status quo without undue delay, the power which the Act gives the other party to preserve the status quo for a prolonged period will frequently make it worthwhile for the moving party to compromise with the interests of the other side and thus reach agreement without interruption to commerce.[30]

Thus, the Section 2, First duty to exert every reasonable effort to settle disputes, which has been likened to the duty to bargain in good faith under the National Labor Relations Act,[31] includes the good faith utilization of the mandatory major dispute settlement procedures by both parties to a dispute.

F. Role of NMB and Emergency Boards in Bargaining Process

The collective bargaining process commences with the service of a written notice of intended changes in an agreement. Section 6 of the RLA requires that both carriers and employee representatives provide at least 30 days' written notice of the intended changes. Within 10 days of the receipt

---

[28]Detroit & T. Shore Line R.R. v. United Transp. Union, 396 U.S. 142, 149, 72 LRRM 2838 (1969).

[29]396 U.S. 142, 72 LRRM 2838.

[30]396 U.S. at 150.

[31]49 Stat. 449 (1935) (codified at 29 USC §158(d) (1974)).

of a Section 6 notice, the parties must agree upon a time and place for conferring to discuss these intended changes. The conferences required by Section 2, Second must commence within the 30 days set forth in the Section 6 notice. If the conferences initiated by a Section 6 notice fail to resolve a dispute, either party to the dispute or the NMB itself may initiate mediation in accordance with Section 5, First of the RLA. If 10 days have elapsed after termination of the conferences and neither the NMB nor either of the parties has made a proffer of or request for the services of the Board, then the parties are allowed to exercise self-help to make the intended changes.

Once mediation commences, the NMB has substantial power to bring the parties together in order to resolve the dispute. The manner in which mediation is conducted, as well as its duration, is left to the judgment of the NMB and is subject to attack in only rare and unusual circumstances.[32] Section 5, First of the RLA further provides that if mediation fails to bring about a satisfactory resolution to the dispute, the NMB must offer the parties to the dispute the opportunity to submit to arbitration in accordance with Section 7 of the RLA. Since arbitration under Section 7 is not mandatory, and the refusal by either party to submit to arbitration is not a violation of the Act, the NMB has no power to compel the parties to consent to arbitration. If one or both of the parties to a dispute refuse arbitration, the NMB is required to give written notice that its mediation efforts have failed. The notice of failure of mediation also gives rise to a 30-day cooling off period during which the status quo must continue.

Section 10 of the RLA provides one final step to the major dispute process. If, at the conclusion of mediation, the NMB concludes that a dispute "threaten[s] substantially to interrupt interstate commerce to a degree such as to deprive any section of the country of essential transportation service," the NMB must notify the President, who may create an Emergency Board to investigate and report on the dispute. Section 10 further provides that after the President has created an

---

[32]Machinists v. NMB, 425 F2d 527, 73 LRRM 2278 (CA DC, 1970).

Emergency Board, and for an additional 30-day cooling off period following the Emergency Board's report to the President, the status quo must continue to be maintained. Only at the conclusion of this last 30-day cooling off period are the parties to a dispute free to resort to self-help.

G. Court Jurisdiction Relating to Minor Disputes

The procedures for settlement of a minor dispute involving a grievance, or a dispute involving the interpretation or application of a collective bargaining agreement, consist of conferences typically involving successively higher levels of employer and labor organization officials, and ultimately a final and binding decision by an Adjustment Board. The courts, both federal and state, lack jurisdiction to resolve the merits of a minor dispute.[33] Courts do, however, have jurisdiction to require a party to participate in a minor dispute procedure.[34] Further, some courts have issued injunctive relief to preserve the jurisdiction of an Adjustment Board to issue an effective remedy.[35] Except in these situations, the courts lack jurisdiction over minor disputes. In addition, the courts have jurisdiction to enjoin a union from striking a carrier while the minor dispute procedures are being exhausted.[36]

---

[33]Union P. R.R. v. Sheehan, 439 U.S. 89, 99 LRRM 3327 (1978).

[34]Missouri-K.-T. R.R. v. Railway & Steamship Clerks, 188 F2d 302 (CA 7, 1951); see Consolidated Rail Corp. v. Railway Labor Executives' Ass'n, 491 U.S. 299, 131 LRRM 2601 (1989) (leaving open the question of whether a federal court can require an employer to maintain the status quo during the pendency of a minor dispute if the union has not sought an injunction or based a claim for injunctive relief on irreparable injury); Machinists v. Central Airlines, 372 U.S. 682, 52 LRRM 2803 (1963) (federal courts have jurisdiction over suit filed to enforce NMB Adjustment Board award).

[35]Locomotive Eng'rs v. Missouri-K.-T. R.R., 363 U.S. 528 (1960); Railway & Steamship Clerks v. Railway Express Agency, 298 F Supp 523, 71 LRRM 3130 (WD NY), aff'd, 409 F2d 312, 70 LRRM 3295 (CA 2, 1969); Teamsters v. Southwest Airlines Co., 875 F2d 1129, 131 LRRM 2761 (CA 5, 1989), cert. denied, 493 U.S. 1043, 133 LRRM 2264 (1990); Machinists v. Eastern Air Lines, 847 F2d 1014, 128 LRRM 2225 (CA 2, 1969).

[36]Railroad Trainmen v. Chicago River & I. R.R., 353 U.S. 30, 39 LRRM 2578 (1957).

II. PRE–WORLD WAR I LEGISLATIVE EFFORTS

The RLA was enacted in 1926 to replace a labor relations regime for the rail industry that had failed to accomplish the amicable resolution of labor disputes.[37] As then enacted, the RLA was the product of an agreement by rail management and labor that Congress adopted, establishing a code of conduct by which labor and management pledged to "exert every reasonable effort to make and maintain agreements."[38] The Act's code of conduct, with enhancements, has remained essentially unchanged over the years. Although the RLA was novel in that it imposed definite, judicially enforceable obligations fostering collective bargaining, it was not without ties to the past. The agreement that labor and management presented to Congress in 1926 followed more than four decades of legislative efforts to prevent rail service from being disrupted by unresolved labor disputes. Although none of this legislation remains in effect, the major features of the 1926 legislation can be traced to these early laws.

A. Arbitration Act of 1888

Following the Great Railroad Strike of 1877, when federal troops were used to "maintain order,"[39] several states enacted legislation to provide a mechanism for the voluntary arbitration of disputes over wages and working conditions.[40] Congress also began to consider proposals to identify the

---

[37]Pub. L. No. 257, 44 Stat. 577 (1926) (codified at 45 USC §151 *et seq.* (1940)).
[38]RLA §2, First.
[39]FRANK N. WILNER, THE RAILWAY LABOR ACT AND THE DILEMMA OF LABOR RELATIONS 10 (1991); SHELTON STOMQUIST, A GENERATION OF BOOMERS: THE PATTERN OF RAILROAD LABOR CONFLICT IN NINETEENTH-CENTURY AMERICA 19, 23 (1987). This strike began in the summer of 1877 when the railroads cut wages by 10% during a depression that started in 1873 and caused massive unemployment. *Id.* at 249. During that strike, according to Wilner, approximately two-thirds of the country's rail mileage was out of service, and in the end, 200 people had been killed and 1000 injured. WILNER, *supra*, at 9–10.
[40]See THE RAILWAY LABOR ACT AT FIFTY 3 (Charles M. Rehmus, ed., 1976) [hereinafter RLA AT FIFTY]; JOSHUA BERNHARDT, THE RAILROAD LABOR BOARD: ITS HISTORY, ACTIVITIES AND ORGANIZATION 5–8 (1923).

causes for, and ways to prevent, strikes.[41] Finally, after several false starts,[42] Congress passed the Arbitration Act of 1888,[43] which authorized the arbitration of rail labor disputes that threatened to "hinder, impede, obstruct, interrupt, or affect" interstate rail transportation.[44] Arbitration was to be before a board of three "wholly impartial and disinterested [persons] in respect to such differences or controversies."[45] Arbitration, however, was entirely voluntary.[46] Moreover, the award was not binding on the parties; rather, it was to be enforced by public opinion, through filing with the Commissioner of Labor and subsequent release to the public.[47]

This Act also provided for the appointment of a temporary three-member Commission (the Commissioner of Labor and two others appointed for the particular dispute by the President), with subpoena and hearing powers similar to those given to the arbitrators, to "examin[e] the causes of the controversy, the conditions accompanying, and the best means for adjusting it."[48] After investigating the dispute, the Commission was to make a decision as to how to "adjust" the dispute; that decision was to be communicated to the disputants and made public.[49] Significantly, the Act provided that "[t]he services of the Commission . . . may be tendered by the President for the purpose of settling a controversy such as contemplated, either upon his own motion, or upon the application of one of the parties to the controversy, or upon the application of the executive of a State."[50]

---

[41]WILNER, *supra* note 39, at 33.

[42]See RLA AT FIFTY, *supra* note 40, at 3–4.

[43]Ch. 1063, 25 Stat. 501.

[44]*Id.* §1, 25 Stat. at 501.

[45]25 Stat. at 2502. Two of the three arbitrators were to be selected by the parties—one by the railroad and one by the employee or employees interested in the dispute. The two so selected were to select and appoint the third, who was to act as the president of the Board. 25 Stat. at 501–02. The three arbitrators, who were all to be paid by the government, were given the power to administer oaths, subpoena witnesses, preserve order during their sessions, and require the production of documents. §2, 25 Stat. at 502. Decisions could be made by majority vote. §3, 25 Stat. at 502.

[46]§1, 25 Stat. at 501.

[47]§3, 25 Stat. at 502.

[48]§6, 25 Stat. at 503.

[49]§8, 25 Stat. at 503.

[50]§6, 25 Stat. at 503.

The Arbitration Act did not achieve Congress's objectives. During the last quarter of the 19th century, strikes became more frequent in U.S. industries, but "in most years between 1877 and 1894 a higher percentage of railroad workers were on strike than was the case for industrial workers as a whole."[51] Each year between 1885 and the Pullman Dispute in 1894, there were at least 40 strikes.[52] Nevertheless, during the 10 years that the Arbitration Act of 1888 was in effect, "no attempt was made to use its arbitration features, and in only one instance, the Pullman strike of 1894, was a Commission appointed to make an investigation and report."[53] The report of that Commission was issued after a federal court injunction, followed by the deployment of federal troops, had restored rail service.[54] The report "recommended a more permanent framework for arbitration."[55] As the President's Commission observed, the Pullman Dispute highlighted the need to rethink the Arbitration Act. Congress began to undertake this task in 1895.

B. Erdman Act

In 1898, Congress enacted the Erdman Act,[56] which repealed the earlier legislation and attempted to make a more effective dispute resolution machinery available to the railroads and their operating employees. This legislation was more limited in scope than the Arbitration Act, for it applied only to employees "actually engaged in any capacity in train operation or train service of any description."[57] This included operating employees and telegraphers.[58] Unlike the Arbitra-

---

[51]STROMQUIST supra note 39, at 24.
[52]Id. at 26.
[53]HARRY D. WOLF, THE RAILROAD LABOR BOARD 6 (1927).
[54]See RLA AT FIFTY, supra note 40, at 4–5.
[55]STROMQUIST, supra note 39, at 260.
[56]Ch. 370, 30 Stat. 424 (1898).
[57]§1, 30 Stat. at 424.
[58]Railroad Labor Disputes: Hearings on H.R. 7180 Before the House Comm. on Interstate and Foreign Commerce, 69th Cong., 1st Sess. 198 (1926) [hereinafter Hearings on H.R. 7180] (statement of D.R. Richberg). Those crafts were the most organized in the late 1890s. STROMQUIST, supra note 39, at 263–66.

tion Act, the Erdman Act made the labor organizations that represented operating employees "parties" to the controversies and allowed them to select the employee member of the three-person arbitration panel.[59] Additionally, Section 10 of the Act contained provisions intended to strengthen the brotherhoods by making it a misdemeanor for any carrier to require employees, as a condition of employment, to promise not to join or remain a member of a union; to blacklist employees; or to "threaten any employee with loss of employment, or . . . unjustly discriminate against any employee because of his membership in such a labor" organization.[60]

In contrast to the Arbitration Act, the Erdman Act provided for the possibility of government involvement in rail labor disputes *before* the arbitration stage. Section 2 of the Act provided that whenever a labor dispute "seriously interrupt[ed] or threaten[ed] to interrupt the business" of the carrier, the Chairman of the Interstate Commerce Commission (ICC) and the Commissioner of Labor, "upon the request of either party to the controversy," were to "use their best efforts" to "amicably settle" the controversy "by mediation and conciliation."[61] If mediation failed, they were to "endeavor to bring about an arbitration of said controversy."[62] This voluntary arbitration was to be before a board of three

---

[59]§§2, 3, 30 Stat. at 425.

[60]§10, 30 Stat. at 428. Section 10 also made it a misdemeanor for any carrier to require as a condition of employment that an employee agree to contribute to "any fund for charitable, social, or beneficial purposes" and released the carrier from liability for personal injuries "by reason of any benefit received from such fund beyond the proportion of the benefit arising from the employer's contribution to such fund."

In 1908, the Supreme Court concluded that §10 deprived carriers of their freedom of contract in a manner repugnant to the Fifth Amendment to the U.S. Constitution, and was not justified by the Commerce Clause of the Constitution, art. I, §8, cl. 3. Adair v. United States, 208 U.S. 161 (1908).

[61]§2, 30 Stat. at 425. Congress made the provisions for mediation dependent on the *voluntary* action of the parties, and it did not incorporate into that Act the investigation features of the earlier Arbitration Act. Mediation depended upon the request of *one* party to the controversy (§2), but mediation would not be conducted unless *both* consented and cooperated. §6, 30 Stat. at 426–27.

[62]§2, 30 Stat. at 425.

arbitrators paid by the government;[63] one was to be chosen by the carrier "directly interested" in the controversy, one was to be chosen by the labor organization or organizations representing the employees,[64] and the two arbitrators chosen were to select the third "commissioner of arbitration."[65] If the two arbitrators were unable to select the third, the mediators were to select that person.[66] Significantly, however, their award was to be binding on the parties and was to "continue in force as between the parties for the period of one year after the same shall go into practical operation."[67] To make the award enforceable, Congress provided that it was to be filed with a federal trial court, and unless within 10 days either party filed "exceptions thereto for matter of law apparent upon the record," the court was to enter judgment upon the award.[68] However, although Congress provided that a court of equity could specifically enforce the award, it added that "no injunction or other legal process shall be issued which shall compel the performance by any laborer against his will of a contract for personal labor or service."[69]

Several other provisions of the Erdman Act have continuing relevance. Section 3, First of the Act[70] provided that "pending the arbitration the status existing immediately prior to the dispute shall not be changed: *Provided,* That no employee shall be compelled to render personal service without

---

[63]§11, 30 Stat. at 428. *Both* parties had to agree to arbitrate, and that agreement was to be in writing, acknowledged before a notary public or federal court clerk. §6, 30 Stat. at 426–27.

[64]If the employees were not represented, a majority of the employees could select a committee, which in turn was to select the employees' arbitrator. §3, 30 Stat. at 425.

[65]*Id.* Unlike the Arbitration Act, the Erdman Act did not provide that the arbitrators were to be "wholly impartial and disinterested." Arbitration Act, §1, 25 Stat. at 501. This resulted in the arbitrators selected by the parties being partisan. *See Hearings on S. 2306 Before the Senate Comm. on Interstate Commerce,* 69th Cong., 1st Sess. 183 (1926) [hereinafter *Hearings on S. 2306*] (statement of D.R. Richberg).

[66]§3, 30 Stat. at 425. Arbitrators were given the power to administer oaths and to issue subpoenas for witnesses and records; as was the case with the earlier Act, a majority of the arbitrators were "competent" to issue an award.

[67]§3, Fifth, 30 Stat. at 426.

[68]§4, 30 Stat. at 426.

[69]§3, Third, 30 Stat. at 426.

[70]30 Stat. at 425.

his consent,"[71] and strengthened this provision by providing as follows:

> [D]uring the pendency of arbitration under this Act it shall not be lawful for the employer, party to such arbitration, to discharge the employees, parties thereto, except for inefficiency, violation of law, or neglect of duty; nor for the organization representing such employees to order, nor for the employees to unite in, aid, or abet, strikes against said employer . . . .[72]

Section 7[73] provided that the ban on discharges and strikes was to continue for three months after the award was rendered unless 30 days' written notice was given. This ban, however, was qualified, for the Act further provided that "nothing herein contained shall be construed to prevent any employer, party to such arbitration, from reducing the number of its or his employees whenever in its or his judgment business necessities require such reduction."

Finally, Section 9 of the Act provided that employees, "through the officers and representatives of their associations," were given the right to be heard by federal courts supervising equity receivers in possession or control of railroads, and

> no reduction of wages shall be made by such receivers without the authority of the court therefor upon notice to such employees, said notice to be not less than twenty days before the hearing on the receivers' petition or application, and to be posted upon all customary bulletin boards along or upon the railway operated by such receiver or receivers.

A year after the Erdman Act was enacted, the employees attempted to use its provisions, "but the carriers refused to let the settlement of the controversy go out of their hands,"[74] and as a result, the Act's mediation machinery was not utilized. Assured of their bargaining strength, the carriers continued to insist for the first eight years of the Erdman Act's existence

---

[71] §7, 30 Stat. at 427.

[72] *Id.*

[73] 30 Stat. at 426.

[74] Harry D. Wolff, The Railroad Labor Board 7 (1927). *See also Hearings on S. 2306, supra* note 65, at 183 (statement of D.R. Richberg).

that the government not intervene in labor disputes, and consequently the Act's mediation and arbitration features lay unused between 1898 and 1906.[75] During that period, there were approximately 105 strikes.[76] The situation changed shortly after the operating employees began to exercise their economic power effectively through "multicarrier collective bargaining," which first occurred in a meaningful way in 1902. The first mediation effort under the Erdman Act occurred in 1906 when the Southern Pacific Railroad sought the aid of Judge Knapp and Commissioner Neill to mediate a dispute with the Brotherhood of Locomotive Firemen and Enginemen. Following that successful intervention, Judge Knapp and Commissioner Neill "were almost constantly engaged in the role of mediators."[77] Although arbitration was considered during the legislative process to be the Act's major feature, in practice, mediation by individuals trusted by the parties proved to be its most effective procedure.[78]

The success of the mediation procedure, however, was short lived. The operating brotherhoods expressed dissatisfaction with governmental intervention as the means to resolve wage and rule disputes.[79] Rail carriers also had reservations about the arbitration process, for they maintained that rail labor disputes were often too complicated for a single arbitrator to grasp.[80] This growing awareness that there were limitations to the usefulness of the Erdman Act's processes resulted in a threatened strike in 1913, which in turn led to

---

[75] WOLF, *supra* note 74, at 7.

[76] *Hearings on S. 2306, supra* note 65, at 183 (statement of D.R. Richberg).

[77] Between 1906 and the revision of the Erdman Act in 1913, Knapp and Neill resolved 61 controversies under the Act's framework—26 by mediation alone, 10 by mediation and arbitration, and 6 by arbitration alone. Of the remaining 19 cases, some were settled between the two parties themselves after appeal had been made to the Board of Mediation, whereas in others the second party refused to accept the offer of mediation by the Board. WOLF, *supra* note 74, at 7.

[78] See RLA AT FIFTY, *supra* note 40, at 5; WOLF, *supra* note 74, at 7.

[79] Laurence S. Zakson, *Railway Labor Legislation 1888 to 1930: A Legal History of Congressional Railway Labor Relations Policy*, 20 RUTGERS L.J. 317, 332 (1989); WOLF, *supra* note 74, at 8.

[80] WOLF, *supra* note 74, at 8. Although the Erdman Act provided for three arbitrators, two of whom were to be designated by the "interested parties," the practice soon developed that the arbitrators designated by the parties were partisan members. *Hearings on H.R. 7180, supra* note 58, at 95–96 (statement of D.R. Richberg).

the involvement of President Wilson and, shortly thereafter, congressional adoption of an "agreement" that the operating brotherhoods and the carriers negotiated to revise the Erdman Act.[81]

C. Newlands Act

Congress revised the Erdman Act through the Newlands Act,[82] which enhanced the Erdman Act's mediation features and modified its arbitration provisions to address some of the defects in the earlier provision that had caused both labor and management to reject its use. Like the Erdman Act, the Newlands Act applied solely to rail employees "actually engaged in any capacity in train operation or train service of any description."[83] It also provided that either party to a controversy "interrupting or threatening to interrupt the business" of the carrier could apply for mediation under the Act.[84] However, this mediation was to be conducted by a permanent Board of Mediation and Conciliation, which was to be made up of a full-time Commissioner, two other government officials designated to act with the Commissioner, and an Assistant Commissioner.[85] In addition, this Board, unlike the mediators under the Erdman Act, was given the power to "proffer its services" in "any case in which an interruption of traffic [was] imminent and fraught with serious detriment to the public interest."[86] It was also "to use its best efforts, by mediation and conciliation, to bring them to an agreement." If such efforts failed "to bring about an amicable adjustment" of the controversy, the Board was "at once [to] endeavor to

---

[81]Zakson, *supra* note 79, at 334 n.99, 380–81 n.350.

[82]Ch. 6, 38 Stat. 103 (1913).

[83]§1, 38 Stat. at 104.

[84]§2, 38 Stat. at 104.

[85]§11, 38 Stat. at 108.

[86]§2, 38 Stat. at 104. Under both the Erdman and Newlands Acts, the mediators took the position that "they had no jurisdiction to interfere until there was a dispute of such a nature as would in all probability interrupt transportation. And practically, in almost every case that was interpreted by the boards of mediation as not justifying their appearance until a strike vote had been taken." *Hearings on H.R. 7180, supra* note 58, at 114 (statement of Col. A.P. Thom).

induce the parties to submit their controversy to arbitration in accordance with the provisions of this Act."[87]

Newlands Act arbitration was similar to arbitration under the Erdman Act in that it was entirely voluntary and, if accepted, binding.[88] Arbitration awards were to be filed with the federal district courts and were to become a judgment of the court unless the court sustained exceptions to the award "for matter of law apparent upon the record."[89] But unlike under the Erdman Act, Newlands Act arbitrations were to be before a six-member board, unless the parties decided to use only three members. More importantly, the Act provided that the parties could agree to refer to the original arbitration board "any difference arising as to the meaning or the application of the provisions" of their award.[90] Similarly, the Board of Mediation and Conciliation was given the duty, upon request by "either party" to an agreement, to give its opinion "as to the meaning or application of such agreement."[91]

One feature absent from the Newlands Act revision of the Erdman Act's arbitration provision was the earlier Act's restriction on changes to the status quo both pending and for three months after the arbitration. However, the Newlands Act continued the earlier law's limitation on the use of the court's injunctive powers to "require an employee to render personal service without his consent, and no injunction" could "be issued which [compelled] the performance by any employee against his will of a contract for personal labor or service."[92]

---

[87]§2, 38 Stat. at 104.

[88]The arbitrators had the power to administer oaths, sign subpoenas, and "invoke the aid" of the federal courts to compel the attendance of witnesses and the production of records. §5, 38 Stat. at 106.

[89]§8, 38 Stat. at 107.

[90]§4, Twelfth, 38 Stat. at 105; see also §6, 38 Stat. at 106. This provision was to correct one of the objections the brotherhoods had to Erdman Act arbitrations, which was that since the carriers had to implement arbitration awards, the carriers could, and often did, modify the award by the manner in which they implemented that award. See Zakson, supra note 79, at 332.

[91]§2, 38 Stat. at 104.

[92]§8, 38 Stat. at 107. The Newlands Act reasserted the Erdman Act's equity receivership provisions, but did not reenact §10 of the Erdman Act, which the

Between 1913 and 1919, the Board of Mediation and Conciliation handled 148 disputes involving 586 railroads and 620,819 employees.[93] In only three of those cases did the carriers or the employees reject mediation,[94] and in none of the 148 cases did a strike occur. Mediation, however, was not always successful.[95] Nevertheless, mediation was considered to be the Act's most effective feature, and the statistics support that opinion. Seventy of the cases presented to the Board were resolved by mediation alone, and 21 by mediation and arbitration.[96] During the period between 1913 when the Newlands Act was enacted and December 1917 when the government took over control of the railroads and the Board ceased to function as an important force in the rail industry,[97] there were fewer than half a dozen rail strikes, "all of which were of limited extent and brief duration."[98] Moreover, each of those strikes "broke out suddenly, before the board was aware that they were impending, and in each case a settlement was quickly effected. In no instance [did] a strike [follow] the intervention of the board, some plan of adjustment having always been agreed to by the contending parties."[99] This stood in stark contrast with the labor relations situation in other industries during that same time period.[100] However, the Act's arbitration feature was not as successful.[101]

Supreme Court had declared unconstitutional in Adair v. United States, 208 U.S. 161 (1908).

[93]*Hearings on H.R. 7180, supra* note 58, at 198 (statement of W. Doak).

[94]*Id.*

[95]In one notable case, the eight-hour day movement in 1916, the President and Congress intervened to impose a settlement. Adamson Act, ch. 436, 39 Stat. 721 (1916).

[96]*Hearings on H.R. 7180, supra* note 58, at 198 (statement of W. Doak). The remaining cases were either withdrawn, settled by the parties, resolved once the government took control of the railroads, or dismissed for lack of jurisdiction. *Id.* In the first four years of its existence, 71 controversies were placed before the Board, and the Board was able to help resolve 58 of those controversies—52 by mediation alone and 6 by mediation and arbitration. Wolf, *supra* note 74, at 9.

[97]Wolf, *supra* note 74, at 9.

[98]*Hearings on H.R. 7180, supra* note 58, at 53 (statement of D.R. Richberg, quoting Report of Board of Mediation and Conciliation for 1917).

[99]*Id.*

[100]*Id.*

[101]Wolf, *supra* note 74, at 9–10; Zakson, *supra* note 79, at 335.

D. Adamson Act

In December 1915, the four operating brotherhoods began a concerted movement to obtain an eight-hour day and soon declared that the issue was not arbitrable. President Wilson called a conference of the parties and suggested that they arbitrate; the brotherhoods declined.[102] President Wilson then suggested that the carriers agree to the eight-hour day; this time the carriers declined.[103] On August 29, 1916, after the brotherhoods had set a strike date of September 4, 1916, President Wilson appeared before Congress and requested the enactment of a law that would impose an eight-hour day for all engine and train service employees. President Wilson also proposed both a prohibition against rail strikes pending investigation of the dispute and the promise of increased rail rates for the carriers, if investigation by a commission supported such an increase.[104] Congress passed the Adamson Act containing the eight-hour requirement, but not the strike prohibition or the guaranteed rate increase.[105]

The carriers opposed the eight-hour day legislation, and after it was enacted, they refused to implement it. Instead, they sought to have it declared unconstitutional. On March 19, 1917, the Supreme Court rejected the carriers' challenge to the constitutionality of that Act.[106] According to the Court, Congress had the power under the Commerce Clause of the Constitution to establish by legislation what labor and management had been unable to "fix by agreement"—i.e., "to compulsorily arbitrate the dispute."[107] Rail labor and management, the Court noted, had the "private right" to fix the wage rate by agreement, but where they were unable to agree, Congress had the power under the Commerce Clause to set that wage in order to avoid injury to commerce as a result of their dispute. The Court stated that "[t]he capacity to

---

[102]Wilson v. New, 243 U.S. 332, 342 (1917).
[103]*Id.*
[104]See WILNER, *supra* note 39, at 37.
[105]39 Stat. 721 (1916).
[106]Wilson v. New, 243 U.S. 332.
[107]*Id.* at 351–52.

exercise the private right free from legislative interference affords no ground for saying that legislative power does not exist to protect the public interest from injury resulting from a failure to exercise the private right."[108]

While the courts considered the Adamson Act's validity, the brotherhoods attempted to resolve the impasse by agreement. When this failed, they set a strike date. President Wilson again intervened and appointed a special committee in an attempt to bring about a settlement. This occurred against the backdrop of the German submarine campaign in early 1917 and the anticipated declaration of war. Finally, on March 19, 1917, when the Supreme Court issued its decision sustaining the Act's constitutionality, the carriers informed the President's committee that they would settle. That settlement included the establishment of the "Commission of Eight," which was "a bipartisan board consisting of four representatives of the roads [i.e., railroads] and four of the Brotherhoods, to decide disputed questions arising under the award [of the President's committee settling the dispute]."[109]

The brotherhoods' success was soon followed by the shop craft unions on the southeast railroads. Those unions were able to enter into an agreement with 31 railroads in that area.[110] By late 1917, the brotherhoods and nonoperating employee unions, encouraged by the success of concerted movements, were preparing to serve demands on the carriers to improve wages and working conditions.[111] Several factors, however, were combining to make the upcoming negotiations particularly contentious. First, the supply of labor available to the railroads, especially the number of journeymen shop craft employees, had dropped, for many employees had left the rail industry either to enter the military service or to take more lucrative jobs in war-related industries. Second, rail

---

[108]*Id.* at 353. The Court added that Congress's exercise of its Commerce Clause power was limited by "the beneficent and ever-present safeguards of the Constitution" such as the Fifth Amendment protections "against confiscation and against every act of arbitrary power." *Id.*

[109]WOLF, *supra* note 74, at 11.

[110]WALKER D. HINES, WAR HISTORY OF AMERICAN RAILROADS 176 (1928).

[111]WOLF, *supra* note 74, at 11–13.

employees were demanding that their wages be increased because of the rapidly rising cost of living and higher wages being paid in other industries. Thus, by the end of 1917, "[u]nrest and discontent were widespread among railroad employees and a number of small strikes had occurred and others were threatened."[112] That was the labor relations situation on the railroads when, on December 26, 1917, President Wilson ordered the railroads to be operated by the government as a war measure.[113]

III. 1918–20: FEDERAL CONTROL

When the United States declared war against the Imperial German Government on April 6, 1917, the U.S. rail system was not prepared to handle the increased traffic demanded by the war. Rail lines serviced most areas of the country, but they did not form a coordinated or integrated rail system.[114] Indeed, because the decisions as to where rail lines should be laid or continued had been driven by market forces without regulatory oversight,[115] there were redundant rail facilities in some parts of the country, and a shortage of facilities in other regions, especially in the Atlantic Coast port areas to which most of the troops and war-related materials were to move.[116] Immediately after war was declared, the

---

[112]*Id.* at 13.

[113]Zakson, *supra* note 79, at 340. It has been estimated that at the time the government took control over the railroads, approximately 80% of the operating employees and 30% of the other classes belonged to unions; at the conclusion of government control, those percentages had increased to 90% and not more than 80%, respectively. WOLF, *supra* note 74, at 59.

[114]The rail system in 1917 consisted of approximately 400,000 miles of track, employing almost two million workers. More than 300 railroads operated that trackage, and even though 77% of that trackage was operated by 32 rail systems, they did not operate as a coordinated system. HINES, *supra* note 110, at 1–8.

[115]Prior to 1920, the Interstate Commerce Act did not regulate entry into or exit from the rail industry. At the same time that Congress added this form of regulation, Congress drew upon its experience during the war and modified the Interstate Commerce Act to instruct the Interstate Commerce Commission to devise a plan to restructure the rail system to form a national system through consolidations and other unifications. Transportation Act of 1920, tit. IV, §§402, 407, 41 Stat. 456, 477–78, 480–83.

[116]HINES, *supra* note 110, at 1–8.

rail executives pledged to "coordinate their operations in a continental railway system,"[117] but they were unable to realize that goal.[118] This problem was exacerbated by the labor situation, where the disputes over wages and the acute shortage of skilled employees threatened further to impede the movement of troops and rail traffic. By December 1917, the traffic congestion at the key ports and terminals had become acute, and the prospects for improvement appeared to be nonexistent. The ICC issued a Special Report recommending either that the railroads be excused from the federal laws that restricted their cooperation with each other or that the President exercise the authority Congress gave him in August 1916 in the Army Appropriations Act "to assume control of" the railroads.[119]

Acting upon the Commission's report, President Wilson chose to exercise the powers given to him by the Army Appropriations Act, and on December 26, 1917, he issued a Proclamation to take possession of the railroads as of December 28, 1917.[120] He appointed Treasury Secretary William G.

---

[117]*Id.* at 11, quoting Railroad Executives Resolution (Apr. 11, 1917).

[118]Several factors made the achievement of that goal impossible. First, there was a legal impediment, for the antipooling provisions of the Interstate Commerce Act and the antitrust laws prohibited the necessary cooperation. Second, the earlier failure of many railroads to have invested in capital improvements, such as track, facilities, and equipment, meant that they did not have the physical capacity to handle the increased traffic caused by the war. And finally, the shortage of skilled employees to maintain the engines kept many engines out of service. HINES, *supra* note 110, at 12–16; Unification of Railroad Operations, 47 ICC 757, 758–60 (1917).

[119]Unification of Railroad Operations, 47 ICC 757 (1917). The Army Appropriations Act of 1916, 39 Stat. 619, included a provision that provided as follows:

The President in time of War is empowered . . . to take possession and assume control of any system or systems of transportation, or any part thereof, and to utilize the same, to the exclusion, as far as may be necessary, of other than war traffic thereon, for the transfer or transportation of troops, war material, and equipment therefor, and for other needful and desirable purposes connected with the prosecution of the war.

[120]Proclamation of December 26, 1917, quoted in HINES, *supra* note 110, at 245. President Wilson gave the following reason for the action:

This is a war of resources no less than of men, perhaps even more than of men, and it is necessary for the complete mobilization of our resources that the transportation systems of the country should be organized and employed under a single authority and a simplified method of coordination which have not proved possible under private management and control.

Statement accompanying Proclamation of December 26, 1917, quoted in HINES, *supra* note 110, at 245, 248.

McAdoo as Director General of Railroads with instructions to exercise control over the operation of the railroads.[121] The Proclamation further provided that "[u]ntil and except so far as said director shall from time to time otherwise by general or special orders determine," the railroads should continue to be operated by their officers and employees "in the names of their respective companies."[122] As a result of President Wilson's actions, the U.S. Railroad Administration became responsible for operating all of the nation's railroads until they were returned to private hands on March 1, 1920.

Director General McAdoo centralized the railroads' operations by dividing the overall responsibility for operations into seven divisions within the U.S. Railroad Adminstration, each of which was of equal rank.[123] Significantly, one of those divisions was the Division of Labor, which was created in February 1918.[124] This marked a radical change in the manner in which labor relations were handled on the railroads, for under the Director General's organizational structure, the Director of Labor was of a "coordinate rank" with the Director of Operations.[125] Additionally, in an effort to stabilize labor relations and establish credibility with rail labor, the Director General appointed the past president of the Brotherhood of Locomotive Firemen and Engineers, W.S. Carter, as the Director of the newly created Division of Labor. Carter in turn appointed former union officials and individuals who were acceptable to rail labor as officials in his division.[126] These developments gave rail unions a voice in the manner in which labor relations would be handled on the railroads. It placed labor relations on a par with railroad operational matters, with the expectation that there would be a consideration of the human factor when operational changes were made to improve service. Indeed, throughout the period of

---

[121]Proclamation of December 26, 1917, quoted in HINES, *supra* note 110, at 245.

[122]*Id.*

[123]HINES, *supra* note 110, at 24.

[124]*Id.* at 154.

[125]*Id.*

[126]*Id.* at 154–55.

federal control, the Director General often made important decisions affecting labor "with the concurrence of the directors of the Divisions of Operations and Labor."[127]

As a result of the Director General's actions, government control of labor relations during World War I had far-reaching effects for labor relations on the railroads, including general recognition of labor unions, central handling of grievances of employees, substantial increases in wage levels, uniform classification of work throughout the country, nationwide standardization of wages and hours of work and abolition of piece work.[128]

Shortly after being appointed, Director General McAdoo addressed the pending and potentially disruptive wage disputes by appointing a Commission[129] to study the wage situation and to give recommendations as to how those disputes should be resolved.[130] In April 1918, the Commission issued a report recommending wage increases on a national basis, decreasing in percentage as the base rate of the employee increased; additionally, the percentages were to be applied to the wages as they stood in December 1915, effectively discounting wage increases that had been obtained by organized employees through collective bargaining in 1917.[131] The disclosure and implementation of those changes through General Order No. 27 on April 30, 1918, "produced tremendous discontent throughout the country."[132] To reduce that

---

[127]*Id.* at 154.

[128]*Id.* at 153–54. *See also* LEONARD A. LECHT, EXPERIENCE UNDER RAILWAY LABOR LEGISLATION 31 (1955); P. HARVEY MIDDLETON, RAILWAYS AND ORGANIZED LABOR 63 (1941).

[129]This was a four-member body appointed "to make a general investigation of wages in the railroad industry and to make recommendations to the Director General." NMB, ADMINISTRATION OF THE RAILWAY LABOR ACT BY THE NMB 1934–1970, at 177 (1970).

[130]Gen. Order No. 5 (Jan. 18, 1918) created the Commission, and Gen. Order No. 8 (Feb. 21, 1918) announced that wage adjustments based on the Commission report would be retroactive to January 1, 1918. HINES, *supra* note 110, at 160.

[131]HINES, *supra* note 110, at 160–61. That report was leaked to the press before the Divisions of Operations and Labor had a chance to study it, effectively limiting the Railroad Administration's ability to revise the recommendations before implementing them. *Id.* at 162.

[132]*Id.* at 163; *see also* WOLF, *supra* note 74, at 11–13. Indeed, so great was the dissatisfaction that an unauthorized strike of shop craft employees occurred for two days at a shop in Alexandria, Virginia. *Id.* at 19–20.

discontent, the Director General created the Board of Railroad Wages and Working Conditions to address the problems "intensified" by the Commission's report.[133] That Board was composed of six people, three selected by the Director of the Division of Operations to represent railroad management, and three selected by the Director of the Division of Labor to represent rail labor.[134]

After receiving numerous protests to the adjustments implemented by General Order No. 27, the Director General invited those classes of employees who felt "that they [had] just ground for complaint under the wage decision" to submit their cases "promptly" to the Wage Board.[135] By June 1, 1918, all classes of employees had requested further consideration of their wage demands, and the Board then proceeded to consider the demands of the shop crafts, which was the first group to have submitted a request. After conducting extensive hearings on those demands, the Board recommended that those employees be given an increase in wages. Acting upon that recommendation, the Director General issued Supplement No. 4 to General Order No. 27 on July 25, 1918, increasing the wage rate of shop craft employees, and fixing a basic hourly rate for those employees.[136] This standardized the wages of shop craft employees throughout the country. Additionally, Supplement No. 4 "made elaborate provision for classification of the work of shop employees."[137] Those wage adjustments, however, did not satisfy the shop craft employees, and they continued to press for additional increases.[138]

Following consideration of the shop crafts' demands, the Wage Board began to address conditions in the other crafts,

---

[133]HINES, *supra* note 110, at 163.

[134]*Id.*

[135]Telegram from Director General McAdoo to labor leaders (May 30, 1918), quoted in WOLF, *supra* note 74, at 11–13.

[136]WOLF, *supra* note 74, at 11–13.

[137]HINES, *supra* note 110, at 166. Those classifications "represented as to many railroads a splitting up of a particular job among many employees in a manner entirely new to those railroads. On others the classifications fixed by the order approximated those already in effect." *Id.*

[138]WOLF, *supra* note 74, at 11–13.

and proposed that their rates be increased as well.[139] The Director General granted those increases through additional Supplemental Orders to General Order No. 4, and included important rules improving the employees' working conditions.[140] The employees considered those increases to be inadequate also.[141] Nevertheless, the Supplemental Orders had the effect of standardizing the employees' working conditions by promulgating rules concerning discipline, seniority, and the establishment of the eight-hour day.[142]

In the meantime, the Director General had taken steps to guarantee the right of rail employees to organize without interference by management. In February 1918, the Director General issued General Order No. 8, which mandated that "no discrimination will be made in the employment, retention, or conditions of employment of employees because of membership or nonmembership in labor organizations."[143] Consequently, labor union influence significantly increased in crafts and classes that had been largely unorganized before the takeover.[144]

That influence was further enhanced by the actions of the unions in obtaining wage increases, improving the employees' working conditions and, as discussed later, establishing machinery for the resolution of disputes over discipline and grievances. Capitalizing upon their new influence, the shop craft organizations and four of the organizations representing nonoperating employees sought to enter into agreements with the Railroad Administration setting out rules and working conditions. In September 1919, the Director General entered into an agreement with the shop craft organizations. In late 1919 and early 1920, he entered into agreements with the organizations representing maintenance of way employees, clerks, firefighters and oilers, and finally the signalmen. Those agreements set forth in written form, for all railroads

---

[139]*Id.* at 24–29.
[140]HINES, *supra* note 110, at 165–69.
[141]*Id.* at 165–66.
[142]*Id.*; WOLF, *supra* note 74, at 33–39.
[143]Gen. Order No. 8 (Feb. 21, 1918).
[144]NMB, *supra* note 129, at 177.

under federal control, basic rules and working conditions for employees represented by those organizations.[145] Rules, hours of service, working conditions, and provisions for the incorporation of awards as wage schedules were covered in these agreements.[146] The effect of these agreements was to extend to the entire transportation system the rules and working conditions that had formerly been made on an individual carrier basis.[147]

In addition to extending to rail employees the right to organize and providing a method to resolve disputes over changes to working conditions, the Director General implemented an organizational structure to settle disputes arising from the agreements that were in existence when the government assumed control of the railroads. He did this by accepting agreements that had been negotiated by the unions and management officials acting as Regional Directors under the Railroad Administration structure. Drawing upon their experiences with the "Committee of Eight," which was a partisan board of equal membership formed to resolve disputes arising from implementation of the Adamson Act, the operating brotherhoods and the railroads' Regional Directors entered into an agreement in March 1918 to create an Adjustment Board, to be known as "Railway Board of Adjustment No. 1." That Board was to consider "all controversies growing out of the interpretation or application of the provisions of the wage schedule or agreements which [were] not promptly adjusted by the officials and the employees on any one of the railroads operated by the Government."[148] The Director General gave his approval to that agreement and subsequently approved identical agreements creating two other Adjustment Boards to hear unresolved controversies growing out of the interpretation or application of the provisions of the wage schedules or agreements covering shop craft employees (Railway Board of Adjustment No. 2)[149] and then most other

---

[145]WOLF, *supra* note 74, at 40–45.
[146]NMB, *supra* note 129, at 177.
[147]*Id.*
[148]Memorandum of Understanding, accompanying Gen. Order No. 13 (Mar. 22, 1918). *See also* HINES, *supra* note 110, at 156–57.
[149]Gen. Order No. 29 (May 31, 1918).

organized rail employees (Railway Board of Adjustment No. 3).[150]

Each of the three Boards was composed of an equal number of carrier and employee representatives who were considered to be knowledgeable of the operations of the railroads and "experts in the settlement of railroad labor disputes."[151] The Railroad Administration selected the carrier representatives, who were then paid by the carriers.[152] The unions selected and paid the employee representatives.[153] In the event of a deadlock, the controversy could be referred to the Director General for a decision.[154]

Originally, the Adjustment Boards were to deal with controversies arising out of the interpretation or application of wage schedules or agreements that were in existence when those Boards were formed, but in practice "each board handled controversies for all its classes of labor on all of the railroads under Federal Control."[155] Any dispute or grievance had to be "handled in the usual manner by general committees of the employees up to and including the chief operating officer of the railroad."[156] If the controversy could not be settled through the usual manner, the chief executive of the

---

[150]Gen. Order No. 53 (Nov. 12, 1918).

[151]WOLF, *supra* note 74, at 55.

[152]LECHT, *supra* note 128, at 32 (citing HINES, *supra* note 110, at 155).

[153]LECHT, *supra* note 128, at 32.

[154]*Id.* A dispute resolution procedure was also established for unrepresented employees. An Assistant Director of the Division of Labor was assigned to attempt to "adjust" those disputes locally up to the chief operating official of the carrier, and if that failed, the dispute was to be investigated by the Division of Labor. If an agreement was not reached after that investigation, it was to be referred to the Director General for decision. WOLF, *supra* note 74, at 53.

[155]HINES, *supra* note 110, at 157. Hines explained that the Boards considered discipline and other grievances where there were no agreements because

> even if . . . there was no agreement between the management and a union representing the particular class of employees, nevertheless any unsettled controversy could be presented by the appropriate national union representative to the Railroad Administration's Division of Labor, whereupon the appropriate board of adjustment would be asked for its recommendation and this would generally be adopted by the Railroad Administration through the concurrent action of the Divisions of Labor and Operation.

Id. at 157–58.

[156]Memorandum of Understanding §10, accompanying Gen. Order No. 13 (Mar. 22, 1918).

employees' organization had to decide whether to proceed further. If the chief executive officer of the organization agreed with the general committee's contention, that officer and the chief operating officer of the railroad were required to refer the matter to the Division of Labor, which in turn presented the case to the appropriate Adjustment Board for a hearing and decision, if possible.[157] If a majority of the Adjustment Board was unable to reach a decision, either the employee or carrier members of the Board could elect to refer the controversy to the Director General "for a final decision."[158]

Those Boards proved to be very successful. The three Boards considered more than 3500 cases with but a handful of deadlocks: Board No. 1 was able to reach a decision in each case presented to it, Board No. 2 reached a decision in all but nine cases, and Board No. 3 reached a decision in all but one case.[159]

During the second year of government operation, the cost of living was increasing rapidly, more than outdistancing the increases that the employees had won in their wages. Consequently, the employees continued to press their demands for wage increases.[160] This demand for wage hikes to offset the increased cost of living "came to a head in unauthorized shopcraft strikes in August, 1919."[161] Although shop craft employees received a raise after that strike, that raise was considered to be necessary to bring them to the level of the other crafts, thus completing the "war cycle."[162] The other employee groups were also seeking wage increases, "but their demands had been refused by the Director-General in the hope that prices would soon fall."[163] Unfortunately, the cost of living continued to rise.[164] When it was announced that their wage demands would not be addressed until after the

---

[157]*Id.* at §§10, 11.
[158]*Id.* at §16.
[159]HINES, *supra* note 110, at 158; *see also* WOLF, *supra* note 74, at 54.
[160]LECHT, *supra* note 128, at 36.
[161]*Id.* at 37.
[162]*Id.*
[163]HINES, *supra* note 110, at 158.
[164]*Id.*

railroads were returned to private operations, the employees felt that they had been treated unfairly, and sporadic strikes occurred throughout the country.[165] As the end of federal control approached, President Wilson agreed "'to use his influence to expedite . . . consideration [of wage demands] . . . immediately after the expiration of Federal control.'"[166]

Although federal control had significantly advanced the organization of the employees and the position of the standard rail unions, the carriers were not as pleased with the results of the government's control. In particular, a common complaint voiced by the railroad executives was that the machinery that the Railroad Administration set up for the adjustment of disputes tended to undermine the authority of the local managers and thus undermined discipline.[167] The executives also complained that the rules and working conditions that the Director General had established were too liberal—in effect, bribes to assure labor peace.[168] "Finally, the action of the Director-General in entering into the national agreements was condemned as hasty and ill-advised, especially in view of the fact that three of the five agreements were entered into after the President had definitely announced that the roads would be returned to private operation on March 1, 1920."[169]

IV. 1920–24: TRANSPORTATION ACT OF 1920

Once the armistice was signed in November 1918, the President and Congress began to consider what to do with the railroads.[170] President Wilson outlined three alternatives: (1) the return of the railroads to private management, "with unrestricted competition and multiform regulation by both

---

[165]*Id.*

[166]LECHT, *supra* note 128, at 37 (quoting U.S. RAILROAD ADMIN., ANNUAL REPORT OF THE DIRECTOR GENERAL FOR 1920, at 19).

[167]WOLF, *supra* note 74, at 64; *see also* HINES, *supra* note 110, at 158.

[168]WOLF, *supra* note 74, at 64–65.

[169]*Id.* at 65.

[170]*Id.* at 73. The Federal Control Act of 1918 stipulated that the railroads would be released by the government within 21 months of the declaration of peace. *Id.* (citing 405 Stat. 451, 458 (1918)).

state and federal authorities that existed before the government assumed control; (2) the establishment of government control, with government ownership if necessary; or (3) the adoption of "an intermediate course of modified private control, providing a more unified and affirmative public regulation, together with such alterations of the law as would avoid wasteful competition by promoting a greater degree of unification."[171] These three alternatives generated substantial debate in Congress. It became apparent that it would be "impracticable" to return the railroads to the private owners "to be operated in the future as they had been under the old system."[172] Thus, Congress initially considered government ownership, such as that advocated by rail labor in the Plumb Plan,[173] or a modified form of private control with greater government regulation than before the war.

While Congress was debating what to do with the railroads, President Wilson announced that the railroads would be returned to private ownership at the end of 1919.[174] That decision, plus the mood of the country against government ownership, essentially doomed any thought that the government would nationalize the railroads.[175] Finally, as 1919 came

---

[171]WOLF, *supra* note 74, at 73–74.

[172]*Id.*

[173]This plan, which was sponsored by the railway brotherhoods, was named after its author, Glenn E. Plumb, counsel for the rail labor organization. WOLF, *supra* note 74, at 77.

[174]*Id.* at 75 (citing 58 CONG. REC. 40–42 (1919). The House Report to accompany H.R. 10453, H.R. Rep. No. 456, 66th Cong., 1st Sess. 2–3 (1919) [hereinafter H.R. REP. No. 456], stated as follows with respect to the rejection of government ownership:

In view of the fact that the President early this year delivered to the Houses in joint session a message in which he expressed his intention to return the roads to private ownership and control by the end of the current year, and in view of the desire on the part of the carriers to be so returned and the widespread demand among the people that Federal control cease as soon as suitable legislation could be enacted, your committee has not recommended Government ownership as a solution for the railroad problem. . . .

[175]H.R. REP. No. 456, *supra* note 174, at 2–3. Nevertheless, proponents of government ownership—the Plumb Plan—particularly rail labor, were not discouraged by President Wilson's announcement that the railroads would be returned to private ownership, and they continued to advocate government ownership. WOLF, *supra* note 74, at 79. Congress did conduct limited hearings on the Plumb Plan, but at the conclusion of those hearings in 1919 it was clear that the Plumb Plan would never be enacted. *See* H.R. REP. No. 456, *supra*, at 3.

to a close, Congress began to draft bills to return the railroads to private ownership, but with substantial regulation by the ICC so as to create a unified rail system. Various proposals were considered, including one creating a Transportation Board to "better coordinat[e] . . . all forms of transportation—rail, highway and water."[176] Eventually, in late February 1920, Congress passed the Transportation Act of 1920, which President Wilson signed on February 28, 1920.[177] That Act gave the ICC greater control over the economic affairs of railroads by subjecting decisions of railroads to enter markets, or to exit from those markets, to regulation by the Commission.[178] Additionally, the Commission was to prepare a plan for the consolidation of all railroads into a few systems, and only mergers or consolidations consistent with that plan could be approved by the Commission.[179]

Congress was also concerned with rail labor–management relations issues, and each version of what eventually became the Transportation Act of 1920 contained provisions to aid the settlement of rail labor disputes. The House considered this issue first and rejected a plan to provide for the compulsory arbitration of disputes through various governmental boards.[180] Instead, it adopted a plan calling for the resolution of disputes through direct negotiation and, if that was unsuccessful, through partisan Adjustment Boards (similar to those adopted by the Railroad Administration) and through arbitration, but only if by mutual agreement.[181] That bill, however, also provided that carriers or labor organizations could be sued for damages if they breached any contract reached by negotiations or arbitration.[182] The Senate disagreed with the House and adopted a bill that provided for the compulsory resolution of disputes before various boards, including the Transportation Board that the House had re-

---

[176]H.R. REP. No. 456, *supra* note 174, at 4.
[177]41 Stat. 456. *See* WOLF, *supra* note 74, at 87.
[178]Transportation Act of 1920, tit. IV, §402, 41 Stat. 456, 477–78.
[179]*Id.* §407, 41 Stat. at 480–82.
[180]WOLF, *supra* note 74, at 81–82.
[181]H.R. REP. No. 456, *supra* note 174, at 15–16.
[182]*Id.*

jected. That bill also included a provision making it a criminal offense to strike.[183]

When the two bills were considered in conference, the Conference Committee adopted a substitute bill. The substitute bill imposed the "duty" upon labor and management "to exert every reasonable effort . . . to avoid any interruption" in the carrier's services arising out of a labor dispute.[184] However, the substitute did not provide for the enforcement of that duty through the courts or an administrative agency. Rather, Congress established several mechanisms in title III to facilitate the resolution of any labor dispute that might arise on a rail carrier and then relied upon public pressure to compel compliance with the Act's directives.

The predominant dispute resolution mechanism was direct conferences between representatives of the employer and the employees, including subordinate officials.[185] During those face-to-face meetings, the parties were to address any problem involving wages and salaries, rules, and working conditions, as well as any grievances arising under labor agreements. Additionally, the parties were permitted to establish Adjustment Boards by "agreement between any carrier, group of carriers, or the carriers as a whole, and any employees or subordinate officials of carriers, or organization or group of organizations thereof"[186] to consider any dispute

---

[183]WOLF, *supra* note 74, at 83–86. The labor provisions of the bill proposed in the Senate caused considerable controversy and were "hotly debated." *Id.* at 85. Initially, the Senate was almost evenly divided over the issue of compulsory arbitration, but that changed in late 1919. "The steel strike, which began in September 1919, the strike of the bituminous coal miners, beginning in October, and the several strikes of the longshoremen which tied up the harbor of New York during the summer of 1919 swung the balance of sentiment in favor of compulsory arbitration, and the Cummins bill [i.e., the Senate substitute for the House bill], with its antistrike provisions, was passed by the Senate on December 20 by a vote of 46 to 30." *Id.* at 85 (footnote omitted).

[184]Transportation Act of 1920, tit. III, §301, 41 Stat. 456, 469, which provided in part as follows:

It shall be the duty of all carriers and their officers, employees, and agents to exert every reasonable effort and adopt every available means to avoid any interruption to the operation of any carrier growing out of any dispute between the carrier and the employees or subordinate officials thereof.

[185]*Id.*

[186]*Id.* §302, 41 Stat. at 469.

"involving only grievances, rules or working conditions, not decided as provided in section 301" (i.e., through negotiation).[187]

If conferences failed to produce a settlement, the statute provided for referral of disputes "with respect to the wages or salaries of employees" to a newly created federal agency, the U.S. Railroad Labor Board (RLB).[188] Additionally, the RLB was to hear and decide any dispute that had been referred to an Adjustment Board if (1) the Adjustment Board failed to reach a decision, (2) the Adjustment Board referred the dispute to the RLB, or (3) the RLB on its own motion removed a dispute from an Adjustment Board for decision.[189] Finally, any dispute referable to an Adjustment Board could be referred directly to the RLB if the appropriate Adjustment Board had not been established.[190] In all disputes referred to it, the RLB was authorized to hold hearings and issue decisions that would provide for "just and reasonable" wages, salaries, and working conditions.[191] Title III did not require that the parties adhere to RLB decisions, and the only power of the RLB was the "moral constraint . . . of publication of its decision."[192] This was a

---

[187]*Id.* §303, 41 Stat. at 470.
[188]*Id.* §307(b), 41 Stat. at 471.
[189]*Id.* §§303, 307(a), 41 Stat. at 469–71.
[190]*Id.* §307(a), 41 Stat. at 471.
[191]*Id.* §307, 41 Stat. at 471, provided in part as follows:
In determining the justness and reasonableness of such wages and salaries or working conditions the Board shall, so far as applicable, take into consideration, among other relevant circumstances:
    (1) [t]he scale of wages paid for similar kinds of work in other industries;
    (2) [t]he relation between wages and the cost of living;
    (3) [t]he hazards of employment;
    (4) [t]he training and skill required;
    (5) [t]he degree of responsibility;
    (6) [t]he character and regularity of employment; and
    (7) [i]nequalities of increases in wages or of treatment, the result of previous wage orders or adjustments.
Additionally, §307(c), 41 Stat. at 471, provided that RLB decisions required the agreement of at least five members, but in wage disputes, one of the members had to be a public representative.
[192]Pennsylvania R.R. v. RLB, 261 U.S. 72, 84 (1923). The Supreme Court decided that title III left "to the two sides to accept or reject the decision" of the RLB. *Id.* at 85. Thus, compliance with the Transportation Act was "wholly at the volition of either party." WOLF, *supra* note 74, at 326.

major shortcoming of the statute and one of the factors leading to its ultimate repeal.[193]

Two of the early tasks faced by the RLB were determining the future status of the national labor agreements entered into by the Director General during the period of federal control and deciding on the demands of the employees for increased wages. Shortly after the RLB was formed, representatives of the employees asked the Board to grant a wage increase and to rule that the national agreements negotiated with the Railroad Administration should continue in effect. The carriers, however, objected to having the two issues considered in one proceeding.[194] In July 1920, the RLB announced its decision, concluding that a wage increase was appropriate, but that it needed additional time to consider the national agreement question. It stated that until it addressed the issue further, the rules and working conditions, including agreements, established while under federal control should remain in effect unless changed by agreement.[195]

Beginning on January 10, 1921, the Board conducted hearings to consider the national agreement issue.[196] Before the conclusion of these hearings, the RLB announced, on April 14, 1921, that the national agreements were to be terminated on July 1, 1921.[197] Prior to this date, the "[c]arriers and

---

[193]Although rail labor objected to the Transportation Act and had asked President Wilson to veto it, labor initially agreed to abide by RLB decisions. However, several large carriers, notably the Pennsylvania Railroad, ignored adverse RLB decisions, seemingly with impunity. WOLF, *supra* note 74, at 295–329. In April 1924, Representative Barkley summed up the feelings of rail labor as follows:

[U]p until November, 1923, there had been 148 violations of the decisions of the Railroad Labor Board by the carriers. . . . If an employee or group of employees is dissatisfied with the decision of the Railroad Labor Board all they can do is to quit work. They either must abide by the decision or subject themselves to discharge by their employer, or quit work. In other words, the carrier has the means of enforcing the law against the employee by compelling him either to quit or to go on strike, while the employee has no remedy either legal or economic against the carrier who disobeys the orders of the commission except to strike.

CONG. REC. 6382 (1924) (statement of Rep. Barkley).

[194]WOLF, *supra* note 74, at 108–11.

[195]*Id.* at 127.

[196]*Id.* at 167 (citing MINUTES OF THE RAILROAD LABOR BOARD (Dec. 17, 1920)).

[197]*Id.* at 183; Decision No. 119, 2 R.L.B. Dec. 87 (1921).

the employees were to negotiate new agreements and if no agreements were reached, the Board itself [was to] 'promulgate such rules as it determined just and reasonable.' "[198] Because the carriers and the unions were unable to negotiate new agreements, the RLB in June 1921, seeking to provide "a uniform policy to be pursued on all roads," decided that the Railroad Administration rules, with the exception of the overtime rule, would remain in effect until it could render a decision.[199]

In August 1921, the RLB began substituting new rules for the Railroad Administration's national agreement with the shop craft employees. By November 1921, the RLB had completed the implementation of new rules for the shop craft employees and abrogated the national agreement.[200] By March 1922, the RLB had substituted new agreements to replace the national agreements covering the remaining organizations with which the Director General had reached agreements (i.e., the Brotherhood of Railway & Steamship Clerks, the Brotherhood of Railway Signalmen, and the International Brotherhood of Firemen and Oilers).[201]

While the RLB was considering what to do about the national agreements, the Board was also considering requests by the carriers that wages should be decreased because of a

---

[198]Lecht, *supra* note 128, at 42 (quoting Decision No. 119, 2 R.L.B. Dec. 91 (1921)). The RLB attached to Decision No. 119 an exhibit listing 16 "principles" with which it expected the parties to comply when they adopted new rules. Those principles included the right of employees to organize without carrier interference or obstruction (2 R.L.B. Dec. at 96, ¶5), and the right of "[t]he majority of any craft or class of employees . . . to determine what organization shall represent members of such craft or class." *Id.* ¶15. Point 15 further provided that the organization selected by the majority "shall have the right to make an agreement which shall apply to all employees in such craft or class." *Id.* Additionally, Point 7 provided that "[t]he right of employees to be consulted prior to a decision of management adversely affecting their wages or working conditions shall be agreed to by management. This right of participation shall be deemed adequately complied with if and when the representatives of a majority of the employees of each of the several classes directly affected shall have conferred with the management." *Id.*

[199]Wolf, *supra* note 74, at 190 (citing Addendum No. 2 to Decision No. 119, 2 R.L.B. Dec. 535 (1921)).

[200]*Id.* at 191 (citing Addendum No. 6 to Decision No. 222, 2 R.L.B. Dec. 567 (1921)).

[201]*Id.* at 207 (citing each respective decision).

decline in the cost of living. In May 1921, the RLB, relying on the decrease in both the cost of living and the wage scale in other industries, ordered a reduction in wages effective July 1, 1921, which averaged 12.2 percent and eliminated approximately 60 percent of the increase that had been obtained through its earlier decision.[202] In 1922, the RLB, citing the continued decline of the cost of living, the continued general depression, and "the resulting bad financial condition of the railroads," authorized further reductions in wages.[203] These decreases, when coupled with the rulings abrogating the national agreements, caused much dissension among rail employees.[204]

The shop craft unions were concerned with their inability to insert their own work rules into these new agreements, and this factor, coupled with the 1922 wage reductions, precipitated what became the largest national railroad strike to that date.[205] The RLB considered the national strike to be directed against its decisions, and it issued a resolution "out-

---

[202]LECHT, *supra* note 128, at 41 (citing Decision No. 147, 2 R.L.B. Dec. 133 (1921)). In response to labor leaders' request for increased wages, the RLB granted a wage increase in 1920 that amounted to a 22% average increase for all employees. As the basis for the increase, the RLB cited the continued increases in the cost of living that had reduced railroad "wages below the pre-war standards of these employees." *Id.* at 40 (quoting Decision No. 2, 1 R.L.B. Dec. 17 (1920)).

[203]MIDDLETON, *supra* note 128, at 70 (1941) (noting Decision No. 1028, 3 R.L.B. Dec. 383 (1922), Decision No. 1036, 3 R.L.B. Dec. 423 (1922), and Decision No. 1074 3 R.L.B. Dec. 486 (1922)). The labor members of the RLB were strongly opposed to the wage reductions. "An important consequence of the 1922 decision was the revelation that the Railroad Labor Board was seriously split." LECHT, *supra* note 128, at 42.

[204]Labor relations on the railroads had become strained after the return of the railroads to private control because of actions that several carriers had taken to reduce costs, such as laying off approximately 300,000 employees between September 1920 and March 1921, and contracting out the work of employees, without any relief from the RLB. WOLFF, *supra* note 74, at 141. The wage decrease decisions further aggravated the perception of the railroad employees that the RLB was a form of protection for carriers, and in October 1921, several of the operating brotherhoods threatened to strike. After the strike threat was resolved, the RLB stated that if the employees had gone on strike, they would have forfeited their rights to their contracts "and the employees so striking [would] have voluntarily removed themselves from the classes entitled to appeal to this Board for relief and protection." *Id.* at 164 (quoting Decision No. 299, 2 R.L.B. Dec. 328 (1921)).

[205]*Id.* at 205, 238.

lawing" the strike on July 3, 1922.[206] The Department of Justice obtained an injunction that prohibited the shop craft unions from interfering with railroad operations in interstate commerce.[207] This injunction was "widely criticized, both in the press and in Congress."[208] The manner in which the RLB responded to the shop craft employees' strike caused the rail unions to boycott the RLB. This boycott, along with the clear perception that the RLB's decisions were unenforceable, effectively ended the RLB's influence on railroad labor relations. First labor, beginning in 1922, and then finally the carriers in 1925, began to call for the repeal of title III of the Transportation Act.[209]

Title III's ineffectiveness was further demonstrated by the manner in which the parties implemented the Act's grievance machinery. Both versions of the Transportation Act being considered by the Conference Committee made the creation of Adjustment Boards mandatory, but the bill that emerged from the Conference gave the carriers and the employees the option of establishing local, regional, or national Railroad Boards of Adjustment to hear those minor disputes that were not settled in conference.[210] Significantly, unlike the wartime Adjustment Boards that provided for the Director General to resolve deadlocks, title III did not include a provi-

---

[206]LECHT, *supra* note 128, at 42–43. The RLB's "outlaw resolution" declared that the shop craft organizations' members were "no longer employees of" railroads and that "the employees remaining in the service and the new employees succeeding those who have left the service [were] to take steps as soon as practicable to perfect on each carrier such organizations as may be necessary for the purposes above mentioned [i.e., to function in the representation of said employees before the RLB and in conference with the carriers]." WOLF, *supra* note 74, at 239–40 (quoting 3 R.L.B. Dec. 1139 (1922)). It became clear to employees that they should advocate the repeal of the RLB in view of this RLB resolution, Chairman Ben Hooper's actions in urging the resolution's adoption and in condemning the strike, and the unequal manner in which Board decisions were enforced. *Id.* at 363–82.

[207]LECHT, *supra* note 128, at 43 (citing 73 RAILWAY AGE 469 (1922)). The shop crafts lost the representation on many carriers as a result of that strike. *Id.*

[208]MIDDLETON, *supra* note 128, at 72. Labor's opposition to the injunction "was a definite factor in the elimination of the Railroad Labor Board." *Id.*

[209]LECHT, *supra* note 128, at 43; WOLF, *supra* note 74, at 362–73.

[210]Transportation Act, tit. III, §302, 41 Stat. 456, 469 (1920).

sion for the compulsory resolution of deadlocks.[211] Rather, any deadlock could be referred to the RLB for decision.

Because the unions desired national Adjustment Boards, whereas the carriers preferred systemwide Boards,[212] no Adjustment Boards were established for several years after the enactment of the Transportation Act. Eventually, in 1922 and 1923, the operating brotherhoods began to establish regional Adjustment Boards.[213] Some carriers, such as the Pennsylvania Railroad, established "Joint Reviewing Committees," which were a form of company-dominated union, to resolve disputes arising from grievances and contracts.[214] The failure to achieve a broader proliferation of Adjustment Boards resulted in a greater number of minor cases coming before the RLB so that it "was fairly swamped with work during the critical period of its existence."[215]

Finally, title III also weakened the legal status of unions.[216] Title III did not include the provisions of General

---

[211]If an Adjustment Board certified that it failed, or would have failed, to reach a decision, or if the RLB determined that an Adjustment Board had failed either to use due diligence or to reach a decision, the RLB was to hear and decide the dispute. If an Adjustment Board had not been established, the RLB had the authority to resolve the dispute under the following circumstances:

(1) upon the application of the chief executive of any carrier or any organization of employees or subordinate officials whose members [were] directly interested in the dispute,

(2) upon written petition signed by not less than 100 unorganized employees or subordinate officials whose members [were] directly interested in the dispute, or

(3) upon the Labor Board's own motion if it [was] of the opinion that the dispute [was] likely substantially to interrupt commerce.

Transportation Act of 1920, tit. III, §307(a), 41 Stat. at 470–71.

[212]W.W. Atterbury, The Railroad Labor Situation 24–25, Address Before the National Industrial Conference Board (Nov. 18, 1920).

[213]LECHT, *supra* note 128, at 45. The regional train service Adjustment Boards were primarily for train and engine service employees. "[T]he other crafts or classes of employees either were not organized by the standard labor organizations on many properties, or, if they were, they were not strong enough to compel the carrier to establish a board of adjustment." Jacob Seidenberg, *Grievance Adjustment in the Railroad Industry*, in RLA AT FIFTY, *supra* note 40, at 211. One study of the Labor Board period asserted that the initial agreement to establish system boards was the result of W.W. Atterbury's efforts to break the impasse between the American Federation of Labor (AFL) unions and the railroads over national boards. LOUIS A. WOOD, UNION-MANAGEMENT COOPERATION ON THE RAILROADS 71–72 (1931).

[241]J. DOUGLAS BROWN, RAILWAY LABOR SURVEY 28 (1933).

[215]WOLF, *supra* note 74, at 273.

[216]LECHT, *supra* note 128, at 39.

Order No. 8, which guaranteed employees the right to join a union. Whereas the RLB considered those "guarantees" to be essential principles of collective bargaining,[217] the actions of the Pennsylvania Railroad in creating company unions showed that the Act contained no effective method to enforce those principles.[218] Other railroads followed the example of the Pennsylvania, and company unions surfaced on virtually all the major railroads, further diminishing the effectiveness of the national independent labor organizations.[219]

The demise of the RLB, and title III itself, was a foregone conclusion after the national shop craft strike in 1922 and the boycott of RLB procedures that followed.[220] The fact that RLB decisions were not enforceable did not engender any popular support for maintaining its operations. These shortcomings led to the enactment of the RLA in 1926.

V. 1924–26: RLA OF 1926

As a result of the ineffectiveness of the Transportation Act of 1920, there were widespread calls for change. President Coolidge, in his congressional message of December 6, 1923, stated, "The Labor board is not altogether satisfactory to the public, the employees, or the companies. If a substantial agreement can be reached among the groups interested, there should be no hesitation in enacting such agreement into law."[221] In the 1924 election year, both the Republican[222] and

---

[217]Decision No. 119, 2 R.L.B. Dec. 87, 96, ¶¶4, 5, 6, 15 (1921).

[218]*See* Pennsylvania R.R. v. RLB, 261 U.S. 72 (1923).

[219]WOOD, *supra* note 213, at 71–78.

[220]The spokesperson for rail labor, D.B. Robertson, summed up labor perception as follows: "The Labor Board is clearly not a two-edged sword which cuts impartially in either direction. It has a blunt edge when used against the employers. Its blows have no force; but when this sword is turned against the employees it is sharp and cuts deep." Wolf, *supra* note 74, at 373, quoting *Hearings on S. 2646 Before the Senate Comm. on Interstate Commerce*, 68th Cong., 1st Sess. 233 (1924) (statement of D.B. Robertson).

[221]LECHT, *supra* note 128, at 48 (citing statement of President Coolidge).

[222]The Republican Party Platform of 1924 provided as follows:
Collective bargaining, voluntary mediation and arbitration are the most important steps in maintaining peaceful labor relations. We do not believe in compulsory action at any time. Public opinion must be the final arbiter in any crisis

Democratic party platforms[223] called for change to the Transportation Act of 1920. Finally, in the same year, a legislative attempt was made to replace the Act.

The Howell-Barkley bill, introduced in Congress in 1924, resulted from a proposal made by the railway unions after discussions with the Secretaries of Labor and Commerce.[224] The bill proposed replacing title III of the Transportation Act of 1920 with provisions for mediation, voluntary arbitration, and nationwide Adjustment Boards. Although the Senate Committee on Interstate Commerce gave the bill a favorable report,[225] it did not become law.[226]

In 1925, industry and labor leaders met to draft a bill that would replace the Transportation Act of 1920. The Howell-Barkley bill was used as the starting point for their discussions, and by the end of 1925 they had reached an agreement;[227] the result of those discussions became the RLA of 1926. This collaborative effort was considered a momentous event in the labor legislative process. In his statement to the House

---

which so vitally affects public welfare as the suspension of transportation. Therefore, the interests of the public require the maintenance of an impartial tribunal which can in an emergency make an investigation of the fact and publish its conclusions. This is accepted as a basis of popular judgment. 1 NATIONAL PARTY PLATFORMS 263 (Donald B. Johnson ed., Univ. of Ill. Press, rev. ed. 1978).

[223] The Democratic Party Platform of 1924 provided as follows:

We are in accord with those announced purposes [of the Transportation Act of 1920] but contend that the act has failed to accomplish them. . . . The labor provisions of the act have proven unsatisfactory in settling differences between employer and employee. . . . It must, therefore, be rewritten so that the high purposes which the public welfare demands may be accomplished.

1 NATIONAL PARTY PLATFORMS 246 (Donald B. Johnson ed., Univ. of Ill. Press, rev. ed. 1978).

[224] LECHT, *supra* note 128, at 48.

[225] *Id.* at 49. As initially proposed, the Howell-Barkley bill did not contain an Emergency Board provision, but that feature was added by the Senate Committee on Interstate Commerce when it reported the bill. *See* WOLF, *supra* note 74, at 413.

[226] Congress adjourned before a vote was taken. LECHT, *supra* note 128, at 49. In February 1925, Representative Barkley "definitely abandoned the bill, declaring that it would be futile and unwise to bring it before the House for consideration at that time. He announced, however, that efforts were being made to secure the cooperation of the railroad executives in securing an amendment to the Transportation Act." WOLF, *supra* note 74, at 414 (footnote omitted).

[227] *Id.* at 415.

regarding the bill, Donald R. Richberg, a principal attorney for the railway labor organizations, stated:[228]

> I want to emphasize again that this bill is the product of a negotiation between employers and employees. . . .
>
> For the first time representatives of a great majority of all the employers and all the employees in one industry conferred for several months for the purpose of creating by agreement a machinery for the peaceful and prompt adjustment of both major and minor disagreements that might impair the efficiency of operations or interrupt the service they render to the community. . . .

The railroads supported the bill for several reasons. First, the industry was experiencing a period of profitability. In 1926 the railroad industry as a whole had a net income of $883 million dollars.[229] The railroads were prepared to exchange economic improvements for an extended period without strikes. Second, the railroads knew that some type of legislation would inevitably be passed, and they believed it was better to take part in drafting the legislation, and to ensure recognition of the employers' interests.[230] The rail unions supported the bill because of their intense dislike of the RLB.[231] Public opinion also favored the bill. A *New York Times* editorial stated that the "great virtue" of the bill was that it sought to resolve disputes through mediation and voluntary arbitration rather than by compulsory means.[232]

---

[228]*Hearings on H.R. 7180, supra* note 58, at 9, 21 (statement of D.R. Richberg).

[229]LECHT, *supra* note 128, at 55 (citing STATISTICS OF RAILWAYS IN THE UNITED STATES, 1927, tab. XV, at xv).

[230]*Hearing on H.R. 7180, supra* note 58, at 7 (statement of Ben Hopper, Chair of the RLB).

[231]The unions, in order to come to agreement with the railroads on the bill, were even willing to sacrifice their demand for nationwide Adjustment Boards (WOLF, *supra* note 74, at 418) and to agree to forgo their right to strike until the processes of the Act had been complied with. *Hearings on S. 2306, supra* note 65, at 167, 182 (statement of D.R. Richberg).

[232]LECHT, *supra* note 128, at 56 (quoting N.Y. TIMES, Mar. 17, 1926, at 24). The only opposition to the bill came from a few shipper organizations that wanted more protection from possible rate increases. The shipper organizations feared that wage increases that could not be vetoed would be passed along to customers in the form of higher prices. *Id.* However, this opposition was not strong enough to overcome the wide support for the bill.

The bill, sponsored by the Senate and House Chairs of the Commerce Committees, was passed by an overwhelming majority.[233] The decision to pass the bill was relatively noncontroversial because it was supported by both the railroads and the unions.[234]

The RLA embodied several important principles.[235] First, it established a duty to "exert every reasonable effort to make and maintain agreements concerning rates of pay, rules, and working conditions."[236] Second, it established the right of each party to select its representatives without interference from the other.[237] Third, the Act established procedures relating to the resolution of collective bargaining disputes over changes in rates of pay, rules, and working conditions, as well as disputes arising from grievances and the interpretation or application of agreements. The Act stressed reliance on the voluntary resolution of disputes, and to assist in this purpose, it established separate procedures through which each type of dispute must pass.

For disputes over intended changes to an existing agreement, the Act established a process that relied upon collective bargaining to bring about an agreement.[238] First, the parties were required to give at least 30 days' written notice of any "intended change affecting rates of pay, rules, or working conditions."[239] The parties were then required to exert every reasonable effort to resolve the dispute through direct negotiations.[240] Those initial conferences were to be without the

---

[233]The vote in the House was 381 in favor and 13 opposed. The vote in the Senate was 69 in favor and 13 opposed. RLA AT FIFTY, *supra* note 40, at 8.

[234]*Id.*

[235]RLA, Pub. L. No. 257, 44 Stat. 577 (1926).

[236]*Id.* §2, First, 44 Stat. at 577.

[237]*Id.* §2, Third, 44 Stat. at 578. Section 2, Third of the 1926 Act provided as follows:

Representatives, for purposes of this Act, shall be designated by the respective parties in such manner as may be provided in their corporate organization or unincorporated association, or by other means of collective action, without interference, influence, or coercion exercised by either party over the self-organization or designation of representatives by the other.

[238]*Id.* §5, First; §6, 44 Stat. at 580, 582.

[239]*Id.* §6, 44 Stat. at 582.

[240]*Id.* §2, First, Second, 44 Stat. at 577–78.

interference of the government. If this was unsuccessful, then the government could intercede in an attempt to assist the settlement of the dispute through mediation by the Board of Mediation, then through voluntary arbitration, or if such arbitration was rejected by either party, through investigation by an Emergency Board. While the dispute was working its way through the Act's processes, and for 30 days after the Emergency Board had issued its report, neither party was to change the "conditions out of which the dispute arose."[241]

For disputes growing out of grievances or out of the interpretation or application of agreements concerning rates of pay, rules, or working conditions, the statute also relied upon conferences, but added an additional step. Such disputes were first to be handled in the "usual manner up to and including the chief operating officer of the carrier designated to handle such disputes."[242] If the dispute remained unsettled, it was to be referred to a Board of Adjustment, which was to be established by agreement of the parties.[243] Those Boards could be established on a national basis, but the Act allowed an individual railroad and its employees to settle disputes through local, system, or regional boards, depending on the agreement of the parties.[244] The Boards of Adjustment were to be made up of an equal number of management and employee representatives. Additionally, all decisions, which were to be by majority vote, would be final and conclusive on the parties.[245] However, in the event that the Board of Adjustment deadlocked, and therefore was unable to resolve the dispute, the dispute could be referred by either party to the Board of Mediation. There it would be subject

---

[241]*Id.* §10, 44 Stat. at 587; *see also id.* §6. Section 5, First of the Act as enacted in 1926 did not contain a similar status quo provision. 44 Stat. at 580.

[242]*Id.* §3, First (c), 44 Stat. at 578.

[243]§3, 44 Stat. at 578–79.

[244]Section 3 of the Act, 44 Stat. at 578, provided that "[b]oards of adjustment shall be created by agreement between any carrier or group of carriers, or the carriers as a whole, and its or their employees." Additionally, §3, Second, 44 Stat. at 579, provided that "[n]othing in this Act shall be construed to prohibit an individual carrier and its employees from agreeing upon the settlement of disputes through such machinery of contract and adjustment as they may mutually establish."

[245]*Id.* §3, First, 44 Stat. at 578–79.

to the same processes of mediation and voluntary arbitration that were applicable to disputes involving proposed changes to agreements.[246]

The Board of Mediation was a government agency composed of five members nominated by the President and confirmed by the Senate.[247] The purpose of the Board of Mediation was to assist the parties in coming to an agreement in both types of disputes. Either of the parties, or the Board itself, could invoke its procedures to mediate disputes over changes to agreements or arising out of grievances or contract interpretation issues not resolved by the Adjustment Boards.[248] However, if the Board of Mediation was unable to bring about a settlement, it was required to "endeavor" as its final act to "induce" the parties to submit the dispute to voluntary arbitration.[249] Arbitration under the RLA was purely voluntary, for the Act provided that "the failure or refusal of either party to submit a controversy to arbitration shall not be construed as a violation of any legal obligation imposed upon such party by the terms of this Act or otherwise."[250]

Although arbitration of disputes over the formation of agreements was purely voluntary, it was nevertheless subject to requirements similar to those set forth in the Newlands Act.[251] Arbitration panels were to consist of three or six members, with each party choosing either one or two partisan members. The partisan members were to chose the third or fifth and sixth members.[252] Arbitration agreements were to (1) be in writing, (2) specify the questions to be submitted to arbitration, and (3) specify the court in which the award was to be filed.[253] Additionally, Arbitration Board awards were

---

[246]*Id.* §5, First (a), 44 Stat. at 580.

[247]*Id.* §4.

[248]*Id.* §§4–6.

[249]*Id.* §5.

[250]*Id.* §7, First, 44 Stat. at 582.

[251]Ch. 6, 38 Stat. 103 (1913).

[252]RLA §7, Second, 44 Stat. 482–83. However, if the chosen arbitrators were not able to agree on the neutral arbitrator or arbitrators within five days, the Board of Mediation would appoint the neutral or neutrals. §7, Second (a), (b).

[253]*Id.* §8, 44 Stat. at 584–85. That provision was modeled after §4 of the Newlands Act, 38 Stat. 103, 105–06 (1913).

to be "conclusive" on the parties.[254] If all else failed, and the unresolved dispute "in the judgment of the Board of Mediation, threaten[ed] substantially to interrupt interstate commerce to a degree such as to deprive any section of the country of essential transportation service,"[255] the Board of Mediation was required to notify the President of the potential crisis.[256] The President could then, in the exercise of discretion, convene an Emergency Board.[257]

The Emergency Board would investigate the situation and within 30 days from the date of its creation give a report to the President. That report was to be made public. The Act further provided that once the Emergency Board was created and for 30 days after it issued its report, "no change, except by agreement, [could] be made by the parties to the controversy in the conditions out of which the dispute arose."[258] However, since the Emergency Board had no powers other than to investigate the dispute, its report was not to be binding on the parties, and if the dispute remained unresolved at the end of the 30-day cooling off period, either party was free to exercise self-help.

In 1930, the Supreme Court upheld the constitutionality of the RLA in *Texas & New Orleans Railroad v. Railway & Steamship Clerks*.[259] The Court stated that it "entertain[ed] no doubt of the constitutional authority of Congress to enact the prohibition. The power to regulate commerce is the power

---

[254]RLA §9, Second, 44 Stat. at 585. Such awards could be impeached on only three grounds:

> (a) That the award plainly does not conform to the substantive requirements laid down by this Act for such awards, or that the proceedings were not substantially in conformity with this Act;
> (b) That the award does not conform, nor confine itself, to the stipulations of the agreement to arbitrate; or
> (c) That a member of the board of arbitration rendering the award was guilty of fraud or corruption which fraud or corruption affected the result of the arbitration. . . .

§9, Third, 44 Stat. at 585–86.

[255]*Id.* §10, 44 Stat. at 586.

[256]*Id.*

[257]*Id.*

[258]*Id.* §10, 44 Stat. at 587.

[259]281 U.S. 548 (1930).

to enact 'all appropriate legislation' for its 'protection and advancement'. . . ."[260]

VI. 1934 AND 1936 AMENDMENTS

A. 1934 Amendments

Despite the overall success of the RLA of 1926, several partisan issues arose during the next eight years that led representatives of the railroads and employees to agree that the Act needed "improvement."[261] First, despite the requirement in Section 3, First of the 1926 Act that the parties were to establish Adjustment Boards, the disagreement over national versus local Boards once again prevented the establishment of those Boards.[262] Second, the Act's provisions calling for complete independence in the selection of representatives needed strengthening. Even though the 1926 Act had prohibited either party from interfering with the other's choice of representatives, that prohibition did not eliminate company-dominated unions, which continued to flourish.[263] Nor did the 1926 Act provide a method to resolve a dispute as to who was the representative of a craft or class of employees when the carriers questioned a union's representative status. And finally, rail labor asserted that the 1926 Act needed explicitly to prohibit unilateral changes in rates of pay, rules, and working conditions. This recognition that the Act needed improvement led to its amendment in 1934.[264]

Prior to 1934, the rail unions urged Congress to enhance the Act's enforcement provisions to prohibit by express provi-

---

[260]*Id.* at 570 (quoting The Daniel Ball, 10 Wall. 557, 564 (1870)).

[261]S. REP. No. 1065, 73rd Cong., 2d Sess. 1 (1934).

[262]The railroads wanted a system of local Adjustment Boards and the unions wanted national Adjustment Boards. *To Amend the Railway Labor Act: Hearings on S. 3266 Before the Senate Comm. on Interstate Commerce,* 73rd Cong., 2d Sess. 15 (1934) [hereinafter *Hearings on S. 3266*] (statement of Hon. Joseph B. Eastman, Federal Coordinator of Transportation). Additionally, some railroads used existing grievance procedures with their company-dominated unions, and thereby excluded the standard unions. Aaron, *supra* note 233, at 10.

[263]Aaron, *supra* note 233, at 9.

[264]Pub. L. No. 442, 48 Stat. 1185 (1934).

sions unilateral changes in wages or working conditions and any interference with the right of employees to join labor organizations. Congress first prohibited the "yellow dog" contract[265] in 1932 when it enacted the Norris-LaGuardia Act.[266] In March 1933, Congress enacted the Railroad Reorganization provisions of the Bankruptcy Act[267] and prohibited any judge or trustee operating a railroad in reorganization from "chang[ing] the wages or working conditions of railroad employees, except in the manner prescribed in the Railroad Labor Act, or as set forth" in a certain agreement entered into in 1932 in Chicago.[268] It prohibited the judge or trustee from "deny[ing] or in any way question[ing] the right of employees . . . to join a labor organization of their choice" or from "interfer[ing] in any way with the organizations of employees,"[269] and it prohibited the judge or trustee from requiring any prospective employee to enter into a yellow dog contract or from enforcing such an agreement.[270] Later that year, Congress passed the Emergency Railroad Transportation Act of 1933, which extended the labor prohibitions of the Bankruptcy Act Amendments to all carriers.[271]

     In 1934, Federal Transportation Coordinator Joseph B. Eastman[272] sponsored an amendment to the 1926 Act[273] that was enacted by Congress and then signed by the President

---

[265]"Yellow dog" contracts referred to contracts that employers required employees or prospective employees to enter into by which the employee agreed, as a condition of employment or continued employment, not to join a union. *See* FELIX FRANKFURTER & NATHAN GREENE, THE LABOR INJUNCTION 37 (1930).

[266]Pub. L. No. 65, §3, 47 Stat. 70 (1932).

[267]Pub. L. No. 420, 47 Stat. 1467 (1933).

[268]*Id.* adding §77(o), 47 Stat. at 1481. The "Chicago Agreement" had provided for a 10% reduction in wages for one year beginning on February 1, 1932, and had provided that it would "terminate automatically January 31st, 1933." NMB Files, Memorandum Agreement (Jan. 31, 1932).

[269]Pub. L. No. 420, adding §77(p), 47 Stat. at 1481.

[270]*Id.* adding §77(q), 47 Stat. at 1481.

[271]Pub. L. No. 68, §7(e), 48 Stat. 211, 214 (1933).

[272]Commissioner Eastman was a member of the ICC and the Federal Coordinator of Transportation created by the Emergency Railroad Transportation Act of 1933. As the Supreme Court has stated, Commissioner Eastman was "one of the weightiest voices before Congress on railroad matters." St. Joe Paper Co. v. Atlantic Coast Line R.R., 347 U.S. 298, 304 (1954).

[273]The railway unions also sponsored the amendment. MIDDLETON, *supra* note 128, at 73.

on June 21, 1934.[274] The amendment made several major changes to the 1926 Act. First, the amendment provided for the creation of national Adjustment Boards and provided for the arbitration of deadlocks of the partisan members.[275] Second, the amendment expressly prohibited interference with the freedom of association of the employees and provided a method to resolve disputes among employees as to who were their representatives for purposes of the Act.[276] And third, the amendment incorporated into the RLA the Bankruptcy Act's and Emergency Railroad Transportation Act's prohibition against unilateral changes. It also made other changes to correct some of the loopholes in the 1926 Act's coverage.

Accepting rail labor's request for national Adjustment Boards, the amendment created a new National Railroad Adjustment Board (NRAB), consisting of four divisions with a total of 36 partisan members.[277] The NRAB had jurisdiction over all disputes "growing out of grievances or out of the interpretation or application of agreements concerning rates of pay, rules, or working conditions" that could not be resolved after being "handled in the usual manner up to and including the chief operating officer of the carrier designated to handle such disputes."[278] If the partisan members of the division were unable to reach a decision, the NRAB was to select a referee to sit with the division to "make" the award.[279] Either party could ask the NRAB to resolve a dispute, and the Board's orders were enforceable in court.[280]

Congress strengthened the Act's protections of the right of employees to organize freely and choose their representatives by modifying the language in Section 2, Third of the

---

[274]Pub. L. No. 442, 48 Stat. 1185 (1934).

[275]REPORT OF HOUSE COMM. ON INTERSTATE AND FOREIGN COMMERCE, WITH AMENDMENTS ON H.R. 9861, H.R. REP. No. 1944, 73d Cong., 2d Sess. 2 (1934).

[276]Id. at 1–2.

[277]Fifty percent of the Board were to represent the railroads, and the other 50% were to represent the employees.

[278]Pub. L. No. 442, §3, First (i), 48 Stat. 1185, 1191 (1934).

[279]Id. §3, First (I), 48 Stat. at 1191.

[280]Id. §3, First (i), (p), 48 Stat. at 1191, 1192.

Act;[281] by including a provision specifically stating that employees had the right to organize and bargain collectively; and by including a method to determine that choice if there was a dispute among employees over the issue. In particular, Congress provided in Section 2, Fourth that the "majority of any craft or class of employees shall have the right to determine who shall be the representative of the craft or class for the purposes of this Act."[282] Section 2, Fourth further provided that no carrier "shall deny or in any way question the right of its employees to join, organize, or assist in organizing the labor organization of their choice."[283] Section 2, Ninth of the Act imposed upon the newly reformed Mediation Board the duty "to investigate," upon request of either party, a dispute "among a carrier's employees as to who are the representatives of such employees" for purposes of the Act.[284] In exercising that jurisdiction, the Mediation Board had the power to hold elections or utilize other means to ascertain the employees' choice of representative, to determine what rules would apply, and to determine who was eligible to vote. The amendments once again outlawed yellow dog contracts.[285] Unlike the 1926 Act, however, the amendment included both express civil and criminal means to enforce these provisions.[286]

Whereas the 1926 Act's "machinery for mediation and possible arbitration and for the final appointment of a fact-

---

[281]*Id.* §2, Third, 48 Stat. at 1187. As amended, §2, Third provides as follows: Representatives, for the purposes of this Act, shall be designated by the respective parties without interference, influence, or coercion by either party over the designation of representatives by the other; and neither party shall in any way interfere with, influence, or coerce the other in its choice of representatives. Representatives of employees for the purposes of this Act need not be persons in the employ of the carrier, and no carrier shall, by interference, influence, or coercion seek in any manner to prevent the designation by its employees as their representatives of those who or which are not employees of the carrier.

[282]*Id.* §2, Fourth, 48 Stat. at 1187.

[283]*Id.*

[284]*Id.* §2, Ninth, 48 Stat. at 1188–89.

[285]*Id.* §2, Fifth, 48 Stat. at 1188.

[286]*Id.* §2, Tenth, 48 Stat. at 1189. The amendment provides that a willful failure to comply with §2, Third, Fourth, Fifth, Seventh, or Eighth will be a misdemeanor subject to a fine of between $1000 and $20,000 and imprisonment for up to six months.

finding board [was] . . . left largely unchanged,"[287] the amendments modified several of those provisions. For example, they included as Section 2, Seventh the prohibitions against unilateral changes that had been enacted first in the Bankruptcy Act Amendments and then in the Emergency Railroad Transportation Act.[288] Also, a "status quo" provision was included in Section 5, First, prohibiting any change "in rates of pay, rules, or working conditions or established practices" for 30 days after the Board released the parties from its mediatory jurisdiction.[289] That provision was added to correct a loophole that a railroad had used in 1931 to implement its proposed changes before an Emergency Board could be created.[290] Additionally, the coverage of the Act was expanded to "bring within the scope of the act operations which form an integral part of railroad transportation, but which are performed by companies which are not now subject to the Railway Labor Act."[291] To accomplish this, Section 1, First of the Act was amended to broaden the definition of "carrier."[292]

Finally, the amendment replaced the Board of Mediation with a new National Mediation Board, which consisted of three rather than five members as under the 1926 Act.[293] The President was to appoint the three members with the consent of the Senate, and no more than two of the three could be from the same political party.[294] The Board was given powers similar to, but broader than, those of the old Mediation Board.

---

[287]*Hearings on S. 3266, supra* note 262, at 21 (statement of Commissioner Eastman).

[288]Pub. L. No. 442, §2, Seventh, 48 Stat. 1185, 1188 (1934). That amendment modified the comparable provision in both the Bankruptcy Act and the Emergency Railroad Transportation Act by inserting the phrase "as embodied in agreements." *See Hearings on S. 3266, supra* note 262, at 65 (statement of W.M. Clement). A similar change was made to §6. *Id.* at 73.

[289]Pub. L. No. 442, §5, First, 48 Stat. at 1195.

[290]*See Hearings on S. 3266, supra* note 262, at 21 (statement of Commissioner Eastman); REPORT OF EMERGENCY BOARD RE LOUISIANA & ARKANSAS RY., (May 5, 1931).

[291]*See Hearings on S. 3266, supra* note 262, at 10 (statement of Commissioner Eastman).

[292]Pub. L. No. 442, §1, First, 48 Stat. 1185, 1185–86 (1934).

[293]*Id.* §§4–5.

[294]*Id.* §4, First, 48 Stat. at 1193–94.

It could select employees as mediators, and it had the freedom to delegate its work to staff members.[295]

The 1934 amendments strengthened the procedures of the 1926 Act and created a labor–management framework that continues to the present. Subsequent amendments expanded the Act's jurisdiction to the emerging airline industry and refined the procedures of the Act in an effort to have them apply more efficiently.

B. 1936 Amendments

The 1936 amendments extended the RLA's coverage to the airline industry. The amendments were passed as the result of the lobbying efforts of the Air Line Pilots Association. Beginning in 1932, bills were introduced in Congress that sought to bring the airline industry under the RLA.[296] While the Air Line Pilots Association lobbied Congress to include the airline industry in the RLA's coverage, Congress passed the National Industrial Recovery Act of 1933 (NIRA), creating the National Labor Board.[297] In order to avert an airline strike in September 1933, the National Labor Board asserted jurisdiction over a wage dispute between the Air Line Pilots Association and five major air carriers.[298] The Air Mail Act of 1934 required carriers to conform to the decisions of the National Labor Board as a condition of receiving air mail

---

[295]*Id.* §4, Third, Fourth, 48 Stat. at 1194–95.

[296]S. REP. No. 713, 72d Cong., 1st Sess. 1 (1932). In the 1930s the infant airline industry was heavily subsidized by the federal government and the U.S. Postal Service was expanding its use of air carriers to speed mail delivery. As a result of opposition by the airline carriers and the Post Office, the early bills did not reach a vote. Herbert R. Northrup, *Collective Bargaining by Air Line Pilots*, 61 Q. J. ECON. 533, 534 (1947).

[297]The NIRA was ultimately found unconstitutional and replaced by the NLRA in 1935. A.L.A. Schlechter Poultry Corp. v. United States, 295 U.S. 495 (1935).

[298]For a history of this dispute, *see* LEVINSON, ET AL., COLLECTIVE BARGAINING AND TECHNOLOGICAL CHANGE IN AMERICAN TRANSPORTATION 462–64 (1971). On May 10, 1934, the National Labor Board issued a decision "setting forth its views regarding a fair wage scale for air pilots." *In re* Air Line Pilots Ass'n's Wage Dispute, NLB Decision No. 83, at 20-11, 1 LRRM 224 (May 10, 1934). Although the carriers had agreed to accept Decision No. 83 to avoid a strike by the Air Line Pilots Association, no carrier voluntarily adopted its recommendations. RLA AT FIFTY, *supra* note 40, at 3.

contracts.[299] The resulting wage scale created by National Labor Board Decision No. 83 gave pilots "the highest minimum wage and lowest maximum hours legislation in the United States."[300] In 1935, Congress amended the Air Mail Act of 1934 and again required air carriers to conform to the decisions of the National Labor Board or its successors.[301]

After Decision No. 83, the Air Line Pilots Association renewed attempts to include the airline industry in the scope of the RLA. The Senate held hearings in May and June 1935.[302] Although the carriers did not support the Air Line Pilots Association's proposal, they did not actively oppose the legislation.

With no significant opposition, title II of the RLA was signed into law on April 10, 1936. Title II extended the RLA, except Section 3, to "every common carrier by air engaged in interstate or foreign commerce, and every carrier by air transporting mail for or under contract with the United States Government." Although the definitions listed in Section 1 apply to the airline industry, Section 201 defines further an airline industry employee as "every air pilot or other person who performs any work as an employee or subordinate official of such carrier or carriers, subject to its or their continuing authority to supervise and direct the manner of rendition of his service."[303]

Section 202 requires that all of the same "duties, requirements, penalties, benefits and privileges," except those in Section 3 of the RLA, apply to air carriers and their employees in the same way they apply to rail carriers and their employees. The only significant difference between the RLA's application to the airline and railroad industries was the procedure used to resolve grievances in the railroad industry.[304]

---

[299]Air Mail Act of 1934, Public Law No. 308, 48 Stat. 933, 937.

[300]*In re* Air Line Pilots Ass'n's Wage Dispute, NLB Decision No. 83, at 20-11, 1 LRRM 224 (May 10, 1934).

[301]Pub. L. No. 270, 49 Stat. 614 (1935).

[302]*A Bill to Amend the Railway Labor Act: Hearing on S. 2497 Before the Senate Comm. on Interstate Commerce*, 74th Cong., 1st Sess. 1–30 (1935).

[303]RLA §201.

[304]In testimony before a subcommittee of the Senate Committee on Interstate Commerce, George Cook, then Secretary of the NMB, expressed concern that the bill

Instead of establishing the airline equivalent of the NRAB, Section 204 required the carriers and labor organizations to create single- or multicarrier Adjustment Boards to resolve disputes involving the interpretation or application of agreements concerning rates of pay, rules, or working conditions. Title II also authorized the creation of a National Air Transport Adjustment Board when the NMB determined it necessary to have a "permanent national board of adjustment."[305] To date, the NMB has not established a National Air Transport Adjustment Board. Rather, the system Adjustment Boards created by the carriers and labor organizations pursuant to Section 204 continue to function independently.

VII. POST–WORLD WAR II AMENDMENTS

The RLA has been amended five times since World War II, in 1951, 1964, 1966, 1970, and 1981.

A. 1951 Amendments

The 1934 amendments to the RLA had made it unlawful for a carrier to (1) influence or coerce employees to join a labor organization, (2) deduct dues or other contributions to unions from employee wages, or (3) require that a person seeking employment sign an agreement promising to join or not to join a labor organization.[306] These prohibitions of carrier actions had the effect of forbidding union shop and dues checkoff agreements between carriers and labor organizations.[307]

---

then before the Senate would require the NMB to resolve the individual grievances of the employees of air carriers in the same manner as the NRAB handles railroad employee grievances. Because the proposal was a departure from the dispute resolution scheme in the RLA, Cook offered alternate language that is now included in RLA §§ 203 and 204.

[305]RLA §205.

[306]Act of June 21, 1934, Pub. L. No. 73-422, 48 Stat. 1185 (codified at RLA §2, Fourth, Fifth).

[307]H.R. 2811, 81st Cong., 2d Sess. 4 (1950).

Efforts to legalize union shop agreements began in 1942.[308] After World War II, union membership declined substantially and company unions virtually disappeared.[309] Bills to legalize the union shop and checkoff were introduced in Congress in 1950.[310] Congress passed the legislation on the last legislative day of the 81st Congress, and the President signed it on January 10, 1951.[311] Codified as Section 2, Eleventh, the amendments provided that carriers and labor organizations could make agreements requiring, as a condition of continued employment, that all employees become members of the labor organization representing their craft or class within 60 days of either their date of hire or the effective date of the agreement, whichever was later.[312]

B. 1964 Amendments

Congress has made a number of additional changes to the RLA since the union shop amendments of 1951. In 1964, Congress amended Section 4, First to delete provisions about the first term of office for NMB members and to clarify that the terms of Board members in office on January 1, 1965, would expire on July 1 of the year in which their term would otherwise expire.[313] A member of the NMB whose term had expired could continue in office until a successor was appointed and confirmed.

C. 1966 Amendments

In 1966, Congress amended Section 3, Second to address two separate but related issues: (1) the large backlog of claims pending before the NRAB and (2) the effect and enforcement

---

[308]LECHT, *supra* note 128, at 177.
[309]S. REP. NO. 2262, 81st Cong., 2d Ses. 3 (1950), *reprinted in* 1950 U.S. CODE CONG. & ADMIN. NEWS 4319.
[310]LECHT, *supra* note 128, at 227.
[311]Pub. L. No. 81-914, 64 Stat. 1238 (1951).
[312]RLA §2, Eleventh (a).
[313]Act of Aug. 31, 1964, Pub. L. No. 88-542, 78 Stat. 748.

of NRAB awards.[314] With respect to the first issue, Congress authorized the creation of special Adjustment Boards, at the request of carriers or employee representatives, to hear and render final decisions in minor disputes otherwise referable to the NRAB.[315] These special Adjustment Boards have become known as the Public Law Boards. They consist of one person designated by the carrier and one designated by the employees.[316] If the Board deadlocks, the dispute is resolved by a neutral member designated by the parties or by the NMB. In most respects the Public Law Board's procedures are the same as the NRAB's.

The legislation also addressed the second issue, the effect and enforcement of grievance awards, which arose out of the several provisions of the law in effect prior to 1966. Section 3, First (m), added in 1934, provided that NRAB awards would be "final and binding upon both parties to the dispute, except insofar as they shall contain a money award." Section 3, First (p) provided that if the carrier did not comply with a monetary award, the petitioner or another person could file a petition to enforce the award in federal district court. The findings of the Adjustment Board were "to be prima facie evidence of the facts stated therein." Thus, carriers could refuse to comply with monetary awards, forcing employees and labor organizations to engage in litigation in which the courts would undertake a de novo review of the merits of the award.[317] Employees had no recourse other than the

---

[314]Act of June 20, 1966, Pub. L. No. 89-456, 80 Stat. 208; *see Railway Labor Act Amendments Relating to NRAB: Hearings Before the Subcomm. on Transportation and Aeronautics of the House Comm. on Interstate and Foreign Commerce on H.R. 701, 704 and 706,* 89th Cong., 1st Sess. 1 (1965); *Amend the Railway Labor Act: Hearing Before the Subcomm. on Labor of the Senate Comm. on Labor and Public Welfare on H.R. 706,* 89th Cong., 2d Sess. 8 (1966).

[315]J. Seidenberg, *Grievance Adjustment in the Railroad Industry,* in RLA AT FIFTY, *supra* note 40, at 229–35.

[316]Railway & Steamship Clerks v. St. Louis S. Ry., 676 F2d 132, 111 LRRM 2391 (CA 5, 1982); O'Neill v. Public Law Bd. No. 550, 581 F2d 692, 99 LRRM 2204 (CA 7, 1978); Cole v. Erie L. Ry., 541 F2d 528 93 LRRM 2077 (CA 6, 1976), *cert. denied,* 433 U.S. 914, 95 LRRM 2765 (1977).

[317]*See Railway Labor Act Amendments Relating to NRAB: Hearings Before the Subcomm. on Transportation and Aeronautics of the House Comm. on Interstate and Foreign Commerce on H.R. 701, 704 and 706,* 89th Cong., 1st Sess. 12–13 (1965); *Amend the Railway Labor Act: Hearing Before the Subcomm. on Labor of the Senate Comm. on Labor and Public Welfare on H.R. 706,* 89th Cong., 2d Sess. 53 (1966).

courts for a carrier's refusal to comply, for under the Supreme Court's opinions in *Railroad Trainmen v. Chicago River & Indiana Railroad*,[318] and *Locomotive Engineers v. Louisville & Nashville Railroad*,[319] employees could not strike to enforce their claims. The Act lacked provisions and standards for the review of Adjustment Board awards.

In the 1966 amendments to the RLA, Congress deleted the exception of monetary awards from the finality provision of subsection (m) and substituted the phrase "conclusive on the parties" for language making the award "prima facie evidence of the facts herein."[320] In addition, the amendments added a new subsection (q) to provide for judicial review of NRAB (and Public Law Board) awards limited to whether (1) the Board had jurisdiction over the subject matter of the dispute, (2) statutory requirements had been complied with, or (3) a member of the Board had engaged in fraud or corruption. The same standard was added to subsection (p) as a limited qualification to the "conclusive" character of Board orders that are the subject of petitions for enforcement.[321]

D. 1970 Amendments

In 1970, the NRAB was again the subject of congressional action.[322] Amendments to Section 3, First, which were supported by the affected unions and the railroads, reduced the membership of the NRAB from 36 to 34 members, 17 to be selected by carriers and 17 to be selected by labor organiza-

---

[318]353 U.S. 30, 39 LRRM 2578 (1957).

[319]373 U.S. 33, 52 LRRM 2944 (1963).

[320]For judicial interpretation and application of the provision addressing the finality of money awards, *see* Northwest Airlines v. Air Line Pilots Ass'n, 373 F2d 136, 64 LRRM 248 (CA 8, 1967), *cert. denied*, 389 U.S. 827, 66 LRRM 2307 (1967); Hanson v. Chesapeake & O. Ry., 412 F2d 631, 71 LRRM 2649 (CA 4, 1969); Railroad Trainmen v. Denver & R. G. W. R.R., 370 F2d 833, 64 LRRM 215 (CA 10, 1966), *cert. denied*, 386 U.S. 1018, 65 LRRM 2059 (1967).

[321]Union P. R.R. v. Sheehan, 439 U.S. 89, 99 LRRM 3327 (1978); Seidenberg, *supra* note 315, at 234; Railroad Trainmen v. Central of Ga. Ry., 415 F2d 403, 71 LRRM 3042 (CA 5, 1969), *cert. denied*, 396 U.S. 1008, 73 LRRM 2120 (1970). *See also* Murray v. Consolidated Rail Corp., 736 F2d 372, 116 LRRM 2810 (CA 6, 1984) (a Public Law Board award may not be collaterally attacked before the NRAB).

[322]Act of April 23, 1970, Pub. L. No. 91-234, 84 Stat. 199.

tions. Membership of the First Division accordingly was reduced to 4 representatives of the carriers and 2 from each of the national operating labor organizations. This adjustment reflected the merger of unions representing four of the five operating crafts (trainmen, firemen, conductors, and switchmen) into a new organization, the United Transportation Union.[323] The amendment was necessary because Section 3, First (c) provided that no organization could have more than one representative on any division of the Board.

Also in 1970, a minor amendment deleted a provision of Section 7, Third (h) authorizing interest Arbitration Boards to invoke the powers of the federal courts to compel witnesses to attend and testify at Board hearings and to produce documents to the extent provided for by the Interstate Commerce Act (ICA).[324]

E. 1981 Amendments

Congress most recently amended the RLA in 1981, adding Section 9a to establish special Emergency Board procedures for certain publicly funded and operated carriers providing rail commuter service.[325] This amendment arose within the context of the demand for alternate dispute resolution procedures in response to the June–July 1980 PATH strike by the Transportation Communications Union-Railway–Carmen in the New York metropolitan area,[326] as well as the debate over whether the RLA would apply to commuter railroads taking over passenger service formerly provided by Conrail. Section 9a expressly subjected Amtrak Commuter Services Corporation and the commuter authorities contracting with Amtrak Commuter to the RLA.

---

[323]H.R. REP. No. 901, 91st Cong., 2d Sess. 1–2 (1970).

[324]Act of October 15, 1970, Pub. L. No. 91-452, §238, 84 Stat. 922, 930.

[325]Act of August 31, 1981, Pub. L. No. 97-35, §§1157, 1158, 95 Stat. 357, 681.

[326]*Conrail Commuter Service in the Northeast: Hearings Before the Subcomm. on Commerce, Transportation, and Tourism of the House Comm. on Energy and Commerce.* 97th Cong., 1st Sess. 48–50 (1981) (statement of Raymond Schwartz, President, Path Commuter Organization).

The Emergency Board procedures for commuter railroads are different from those set forth in Section 10 in several respects. First, under Section 9a, a party to the dispute or the governor of any state may compel the President to create an Emergency Board to investigate and report on the dispute, whereas under Section 10, the decision whether to create a Board is left to the President's discretion. Second, under Section 9a a party or the governor of any state can request the President to establish a second Emergency Board. This second Board will review the final settlement offers submitted by the parties and will select the most reasonable offer. Under Section 9a (as under Section 10), the parties are not required to accept the award. However, employees who strike after the Board chooses the carrier's offer will not be eligible for Railroad Unemployment Insurance benefits, and a carrier that refuses to accept the Board's choice of the union's final offer may not participate in any agreement designed to provide benefits to a carrier during a strike.

VIII. Defining the Carrier

Section 1 of the ICA defines a "carrier" by railroad for purposes of determining coverage of the RLA.[327] Either the NMB or the ICC may determine whether an employer associated with the rail industry is a carrier for the purposes of the RLA.[328] In either forum, the central inquiry is whether the employer is subject to the ICA. The ICC will decide the question directly, whereas the NMB will consider the question usually as part of a jurisdictional inquiry in connection with a representation dispute.[329]

Determinations of carrier status for employers associated with the airline industry are ordinarily made by the NMB.[330]

---

[327]49 USC §10102(22), (23) (1994).

[328]Id. §10102(21); UTDC Transp. Servs., Inc., 17 NMB 343, 355 (1990); O/O Truck Sales, 21 NMB 258 (1994); Pacific S.W. Airlines, 4 NMB 124 (1967); Pan Am. Airlines, 3 NMB 41 (1957); Union Stock Yard, 3 NMB 149 (1953).

[329]Chesapeake & O. Ry. Co., 4 NMB 215 (1962); TDC Transit Serv., Inc., 17 NMB 343 (1990).

[330]Pacific S.W. Airlines, 4 NMB 124 (1967); Pan Am. Airlines, 3 NMB 41.

Definitional terms in Sections 181 and 151, First provide the standards for those determinations.

This section will focus on the standards used to determine whether an employer is subject to the RLA as a direct air or rail carrier. The following section will describe the standards used to determine whether an entity is a "derivative carrier" covered by the RLA because it performs transportation-related activities and is owned or controlled by or is under common control with an air or rail carrier.

The Act applies with certain exceptions to all employees employed by the carrier. A series of decisions in the 1950s and 1960s suggested a disagreement as to whether the RLA applies to individuals employed by a carrier who do not perform services for the carrier's rail or air operations. The NMB took the position that the RLA covered individuals who performed any work as an employee of the carrier.[331] However, two appellate courts held that the RLA was inapplicable to individuals employed by a carrier if they did not perform work related to the carrier's rail or air operations.[332]

A. Carrier by Air

Section 201 makes the RLA applicable to carriers by air in interstate or foreign commerce.[333] An airline is also subject to the Act if it transports the mail for or under contract with the U.S. government.[334] Ordinarily, the NMB and the courts rely exclusively on Section 201 when making air carrier determinations. Nevertheless, the NMB refers to Section 151, First in determining whether an entity is covered by the Act be-

---

[331]NMB File No. C-2202, *quoted in* Pan Am. World Airways v. Carpenters, 324 F2d 217 (CA 9, 1963), *cert. denied*, 376 U.S. 964 (1964). *See also* Biswanger v. Boyd, 324 LRRM 2267 (D DC, 1957).

[332]Northwest Airlines v. Jackson, 185 F2d 74 (CA 8, 1950); Pan Am. World Airways v. Carpenters, 324 F2d 217.

[333]Flight Attendants (UFA) v. Pan Am. World Airways, 923 F2d 678, 136 LRRM 2217, 2220 (CA 9, 1991), *opinion withdrawn on reh'g*, 966 F2d 457, 140 LRRM 2110 (CA 9, 1992); *see* Air Florida, 7 NMB 162 (1979); Southwest Airlines, 239 NLRB 1253, 100 LRRM 1146 (1979); Pacific S.W. Airlines, 233 NLRB 1, 97 LRRM 1329 (1977).

[334]45 USC §181 (1936).

cause the entity is owned or controlled by, or under common control with, an air carrier.[335] Occasionally, courts and the NMB will define an air carrier in terms of Section 151, First.[336] Typically, the certifications issued by the U.S. government, along with the employer's actual operations, establish whether the entity is operating as a common carrier in interstate or foreign commerce.[337]

Foreign airlines are carriers under the Act with respect to their ground-based employees in the United States.[338] The Act does not apply to airlines whose operations originate and terminate in a foreign jurisdiction and whose transportation of passengers and goods does not cause them to enter U.S. airspace.[339] The NMB has taken the position that "interline activities"[340] by a foreign carrier into the United States through agreement with other carriers could be the basis for carrier status provided the percentage of interline operations is more than de minimis.[341]

A "fixed-based" operator that is not controlled directly or indirectly by a carrier, but that performs maintenance and other services at an airport for private and commercial aircraft, is not subject to the Act if it does not engage in the transportation of passengers or baggage by air, has no mail contract, provides no substitute air service, and does not inter-

---

[335]TNT Skypak, 20 NMB 153 (1993).

[336]See Regional Airline Pilots Ass'n v. Wings W. Airlines, 915 F2d 1399, 135 LRRM 2735 (CA 9, 1990); Airline Stewards & Stewardesses Ass'n v. Northwest Airlines, 267 F2d 170 (CA 8), cert. denied, 361 U.S. 901 (1959); In re Overseas Nat'l Airways, 238 F Supp 359 (ED NY, 1965); Airline Stewards & Stewardesses Ass'n v. Trans World Airlines, 173 F Supp 369 (SD NY), aff'd, 273 F2d 69 (CA 2, 1959), cert. denied, 362 U.S. 988 (1960); America W. Airlines, 21 NMB 362 (1994).

[337]See Friiedkin Aeronautics, Inc., 2 NMB 13 (1954); Air Florida, 6 NMB 777 (1979); Evergreen Int'l Airlines, 6 NMB 609 (1978) (reliance on Civil Aeronautics Board); Southwest Airlines, 6 NMB 774 (1979); Zantop Int'l Airlines, 6 NMB 7401 (1979).

[338]Ruby v. TACA Int'l Airlines, 439 F2d 1359, 77 LRRM 2089 (CA 5, 1971); see, e.g., Aerovias de Mexico, 20 NMB 584 (1993); Egypt Air, 19 NMB 166 (1992).

[339]Airline Dispatchers Ass'n v. NMB, 189 F2d 685 (CA DC), cert. denied, 342 U.S. 849 (1951).

[340]An interline agreement is a commercial arrangement between two or more carriers that coordinates and supplies the ticketing of passengers whose itinerary involves more than one carrier. Typically, a single fare is charged and the carrier allocates the revenue by segment.

[341]Kuwait Airways, 5 NMB 232 (1975).

line or contract with other carriers.[342] However, fixed-based operators may be covered by the RLA by virtue of providing maintenance and refueling services for common carriers.[343]

The NMB has held that air freight forwarders are not subject to the Act if they do not engage directly in the operation of aircraft and thereby do not meet the definition of a carrier in Section 201.[344] Employers engaged in travel and publishing ventures have been excluded if they do not engage in direct common carrier activities, transport mail, interline, or provide a substitute air service for carriers covered by the Act.[345] Section 1, First's express exclusion of entities in receivership or bankruptcy is equally applicable to air carriers.[346]

B. Carrier by Railroad

The RLA definition of a carrier includes a carrier by railroad "subject to subtitle IV of Title 49."[347] Title 49 codifies the ICA and provides a principal basis for determining whether an entity is directly covered by the RLA.[348]

---

[342]Skyway Aviation, Inc., 6 NMB 541 (1978); Beckett Aviation Corp., Cleveland, 8 NMB 47 (1980) (insignificant relationship to common carriage by air); York Aero, Inc., 17 NMB 498 (1990) (employer engaged in charter and a taxi service is a carrier); Jimsair Aviation Serv., 15 NMB 85 (1988) (air taxi and charter operator is carrier); C&E Aero Serv., 10 NMB 62 (1982) (de minimis air taxi and charter activities; not a carrier); United Jet Ctr., 18 NMB 354 (1991) (charter operator is a carrier); Miami Aircraft Support, 21 NMB 78 (1993); TNT Skypak, 20 NMB 153 (1993); Federal Express, 6 NMB 442 (1978); Novo Int'l Airfreight, 5 NMB 191 (1975).

[343]See infra note 434.

[344]Novo Int'l Airfreight Corp., 5 NMB 191.

[345]Arthur Frommer Enters., 6 NMB 750 (1979).

[346]See, e.g., In re Continental Airlines Corp., 50 Bankr. 342, 119 LRRM 1752, 2756 (D Tex, 1985), aff'd, 790 F2d 35 (CA 5, 1986) (Congress's inclusion of "receiver, trustee" clause in definition of carrier demonstrates intent to prevent debtors in possession from interfering in employee conduct).

[347]RLA §1, First. RLA also defines carriers as including express companies and sleeping car companies subject to the jurisdiction of the ICC. An "express carrier" is defined as a "person providing express transportation for compensation." See REA Express, Inc., 4 NMB 253 (1965) (express business provided cartage pickup and delivery services to customers and, typically, carriage by rail and air carriers). A "sleeping-car carrier" is a "person providing sleeping-car transportation for compensation." 49 USC §10102(25) (1994).

[348]See Tri-County Community Rail Org., 17 NMB 321, 322 (1990). But see infra §IX for a discussion of entities controlled by carriers.

C. ICA Definitions

Section 1 of the ICA defines a rail carrier as a person currently providing railroad transportation for compensation. The statute defines railroad transportation by providing that the term "railroad" includes

(A) a bridge, car float, lighter, and ferry used by or in connection with a railroad;
(B) the road used by a rail carrier and owned by it or operated under an agreement; and
(C) a switch, spur, track, terminal, terminal facility, and a freight depot, yard, and ground, used or necessary for transportation.[349]

The term "transportation" used in the coverage provision of the ICA means more than the dictionary definition of that term. An ICC doctrine applicable to all of the coverage provisions requires that the entity must *currently* provide railroad transportation for compensation to qualify as a carrier for ICA purposes.[350] The entity need not actually provide rail transportation at the current time; the requirement will be deemed satisfied if the entity currently has a residual obligation to furnish adequate rail service.[351] Consequently, the entity's present obligation to maintain a rail line in order to permit common carriage of freight, coupled with the entity's duty to furnish adequate freight service in interstate commerce—a duty that the ICC found to be implicit and that remained latent while a wholly separate carrier provided that

---

[349]49 USC §10102(23) (1994).

[350]Railway Labor Executives' Ass'n v. Wheeling Acquisition Corp., 736 F Supp 1397, 135 LRRM 23545 (ED Va, 1990); Alabama S. R.R. Co. —Acquisitions, Operations and Traffic Rights—Exemption, 1 ICC2d 298 (1984). Once an entity abandons its connection to the interstate rail system, it ceases to qualify as a carrier under the ICA. Railway Labor Executives' Ass'n v. ICC, 859 F2d 996, 999, 129 LRRM 2778, 2780 (CA DC, 1988).

[351]Locomotive Eng'rs v. Staten Island Rapid Transit Operating Auth., 360 ICC 464 (1979); Smith v. Hoboken R.R. Warehouse & S.S. Connecting Co., 328 U.S. 123 (1946).

service—was sufficient to establish the entity as a carrier by railroad subject to the ICA.[352]

To determine whether an entity is a carrier by railroad, the ICC employs a "facts and circumstances test" in which it examines the operations of each entity in question.[353] The two predominant factors of this test are (1) whether any of the indicia of transportation provided in 49 USC § 10102(26) are present[354] and (2) whether the performance of such transportation is for compensation.[355] For the entity to be found to be a carrier by railroad, both factors must be present.[356]

The ICC has elaborated on the meaning of compensation by holding that an entity does not provide transportation for compensation by carrying its own property by rail between two sites.[357] This is true even if the entity will tender traffic to and receive traffic from carriers by railroad at those sites,

---

[352]*Id.* The presence of residual common carrier status may eliminate the need for the current performance of transportation services. Winona Bridge Ry.—Trackage Rights—Burlington N. R.R., No. 31163, 1987 WL 100161 (ICC Dec. 23, 1987). Thus, the ICC found that an entity was a carrier when the entity had operated approximately 1 mile of track as a switching carrier prior to acquiring trackage rights over an additional 1860 miles of track. Despite the absence of evidence that the entity currently performed transportation services, the ICC held that the entity was subject to the ICA because it could have been found to have residual common carrier obligations with respect to the operation of its track. *Id.*

[353]Locomotive Eng'rs v. Interstate R.R., No. 31078, 1978 WL 99928 (ICC Nov. 20, 1987); Boeing Co.—Acquisition and Operation Exemption—Chehalis W. Ry., No. 31916, 1991 WL 212940 (ICC Oct. 10, 1991) (whether or not ICC has jurisdiction is determined by nature of transaction and service that entity holds itself out to provide).

[354]Section 1 of the ICA provides that the term "transportation" includes

(A) a locomotive, car, vehicle, motor vehicle, vessel, warehouse, wharf, pier, dock, yard, property, facility, instrumentality, or equipment of any kind related to the movement of passengers or property, or both, regardless of ownership or an agreement concerning use; and

(B) services related to that movement, including receipt, delivery, elevation, transfer in transit, refrigeration, icing, ventilation, storage, handling, and interchange of passengers and property.

49 USC § 10102(28) (1994).

[355]Locomotive Eng'rs v. Interstate R.R., 1987 WL 99928 (ICC 1987).

[356]Applying this test, the ICC found that an entity did not qualify as a carrier by railroad because it was not paid to receive, deliver, store in transit, handle, or interchange any railroad traffic. *Id.*

[357]Boeing Co.—Acquisition and Operation Exemption—Chehalis W. Ry., 1991 WL 212940 (ICC 1991).

so long as the traffic being shipped and received is made up of its own goods.[358]

The ICC has found that an entity does not need to operate any rail engines or rail cars or employ any employees to fall within the statutory definition of a carrier by railroad.[359] Consequently, where an entity owned approximately 2000 feet of trackage that served the site of a major milling plant and connected with major carriers by railroad, and the entity leased the track to operating railroads that agreed to maintain the track, the ICC found the entity to be a carrier by railroad.[360] The fact that an entity owns a carrier by railroad is not enough, standing alone, to support a finding that it is a railroad carrier under the ICA.[361]

As part of its responsibilities under the ICA, the ICC has the authority to exempt "a person, [or] class of persons . . . [from] the application of a provision" of the Act.[362] Additionally, "persons" acquiring a line of railroad under the "feeder line" provisions of the ICA may "elect to be exempt from any of the provisions of this title," except certain rate provisions.[363] These ICC determinations may have an impact on whether an entity is found to be a carrier under the RLA.[364]

Neither the NMB nor the courts have been called upon to determine if either of the exemptions affects whether the "person" so exempted is a "carrier" within the meaning of

---

[358]*Id.*

[359]*See, e.g.,* CPC Int'l, Inc.—Control Exemption—BHL Transp., Inc., 1987 WL 100186 (ICC 1987).

[360]*Id.*

[361]*Id.*

[362]49 USC §10505(a) (1994). Section 10505 applies solely to "a matter related to a rail carrier providing transportation subject to the jurisdiction of the Interstate Commerce Commission," and, subsection (g) further provides that "[t]he Commission may not exercise its authority under this section . . . (2) to relieve a carrier of its obligation to protect the interests of employees as required by this subtitle."

[363]49 USC §10910(g)(1) (1994). Another provision of the ICA, *id.* §10504, provides that the Commission does not have jurisdiction over certain forms of "rail mass transportation," but §10504 expressly provides that such exempt mass transportation "is subject to applicable laws of the United States related to . . . (2) the representation of employees for collective bargaining."

[364]New York C. R.R., 1 NMB 303, 308–09 (1945); *cf.* Conrail Abandonment, 366 ICC 384 (1982); Pocono N.E. Ry.—Acquisition and Operation Exemption—Certain Property of Air Prods. and Chems., Inc., 1989 WL 239708 (ICC 1989).

Section 1, First of the RLA. The NMB will make an independent coverage inquiry where an entity's employees are not reported to the ICC and the Commission has not determined that those employees are excluded from coverage under the ICA.[365] On the other hand, the courts have always deferred to the determinations of the ICC.[366]

State-owned railroads that otherwise meet the definition of a carrier may be found to be a carrier for purposes of the RLA.[367] Rail operations conducted by local public bodies are excluded from the ICA,[368] but they are included under the RLA if the ICA would have otherwise applied except for the public body exclusion.[369] The ICA also excludes from carrier status entities engaged solely in intrastate transportation. The courts and the NMB have accepted this exclusion under the RLA only where the transportation is not a link in the interstate transportation of goods or passengers.[370]

---

[365]*See* Canadian Nat'l Marine Corp., 6 NMB 480, 481 (1978).

[366]From the cases involving disputes over the extent of the ICA's jurisdiction, the following holdings have emerged: CSX Transp. v. United Transp. Union, 879 F2d 990, 131 LRRM 2681 (CA 2, 1989), *cert. denied*, 493 U.S. 1020, 133 LRRM 2192 (1990) (a Class 1 railroad subject to the jurisdiction of the ICC is also a carrier under the RLA); Locomotive Eng'rs v. Consolidated Rail Corp., 844 F2d 1218, 1219, 128 LRRM 2103 (CA 6, 1988) (an entity operating a freight railroad system in 14 states and the District of Columbia is a carrier under the RLA); California v. Taylor, 353 U.S. 553 (1957) (a state-owned common carrier by rail engaged in interstate transportation that filed tariffs with the ICC is subject to the RLA).

[367]United Transp. Union v. Long Island R.R., 455 U.S. 678, 109 LRRM 3017 (1982); Garcia v. San Antonio Metro. Transit Auth., 469 U.S. 528 (1985). When the Alaska Railroad was an operating division of the Federal Railway Administration within the Department of Transportation, it was not a carrier within the meaning of the RLA. Alaska R.R., 6 NMB 8 (1979). When it was subsequently transferred to the State of Alaska, it was expressly excluded from coverage under the RLA. Alaska Railroad Transfer Act of 1982, Pub. L. No. 97-468 (codified as 45 USC §1207 (1983)).

[368]49 USC § 10504(b) (1994). *See* New Jersey Transit Policemen's Benevolent Ass'n Local 304 v. New Jersey Transit Corp., 806 F2d 451 (CA 3, 1986), *cert. denied*, 483 U.S. 1006 (1987); UTDC Transit Servs., Inc., 17 NMB 343 (1990).

[369]*See* RLA §159(a) establishing special collective bargaining procedures for commuter authorities. This section does not confer jurisdiction on the RLA to an entity that otherwise is not covered as a carrier. Tri-County Community Rail Org., 17 NMB 321 (1990). Section 591 of the Rail Passenger Service Act is limited in its grant of RLA jurisdiction to commuter authorities that assumed service from Conrail. *Id.*

[370]Staten Island Rapid Transit Operating Auth. v. ICC, 718 F2d 533, 114 LRRM 3007 (CA 2, 1983) (Commuter Rail Authority's commuter rail is not in

The RLA covers a carrier by railroad in bankruptcy or receivership. Section 151, First of the RLA provides that the term "carrier" includes "any receiver, trustee, or other individual or body, judicial or otherwise, when in possession of the business of any such carrier."[371]

In drafting the definition of carrier found in the RLA, Congress made the RLA expressly reliant on the ICC to oversee the electric railway exclusion:

> Provided, however, that the term "carrier" shall not include any street, interurban, or suburban electric railway, unless such railway is operating as a part of a general steam-railroad system of transportation, but shall not exclude any part of the general steam-railroad system of transportation now or hereafter operated by any other motive power. The Interstate Commerce Commission is authorized and directed upon request by the [NMB] or upon complaint of any party interested to determine after hearing whether any line operated by electric power falls within the terms of this proviso.[372]

Courts have held that Congress committed the determination of the scope of the electric railroad proviso to the ICC.[373] Neither the RLA nor the ICA defines the term "interurban."

---

interstate commerce); United States v. Union Stockyard Transp. Co., 226 U.S. 286 (1912).

[371]*See also* Burke v. Morphy, 109 F2d 572, 575, 5 LRRM 906 (CA 2), *cert. denied*, 310 U.S. 635, 6 LRRM 708 (1940) ("[T]he RLA applies to every interstate carrier, including a carrier that is being operated by a receiver.").

[372]RLA §1, First.

[373]Railway Labor Executives' Ass'n v. ICC, 859 F2d 996, 998, 129 LRRM, 2778, 2779 (CA DC, 1988); Chicago, S.S. & S. B. R.R. v. Fleming, 109 F2d 419 (CA 7, 1940); Shields v. Utah I.C. R.R., 305 U.S. 177, 3 LRRM 669 (1938); Texas Elec. Ry. v. Eastus, 25 F Supp 825, 3 LRRM 748 (ND Tex, 1938), *affd*, 308 U.S. 512, 5 LRRM 694 (1939); Sprague v. Woll, 124 F2d 767 (CA 7, 1941). The process by which the ICC determines whether or not a railroad is exempt from the RLA under the electric railway proviso is not fixed by statute. The ICC has discretion to employ its own process, provided that such process is reasonable and in accordance with the RLA. Texas Elec. Ry. v. Eastus, 25 F Supp at 825, 3 LRRM at 748. The ICC has the right to reopen, on its own motion, its determination of the issue of whether a railroad is exempt from the RLA under the electric railway proviso, Sprague v. Woll, 124 F2d at 767, and judicial review of the ICC's findings is limited to a determination of whether the ICC departed from applicable law or was arbitrary and capricious. Railway Labor Executives' Ass'n v. ICC, 859 F2d at 998, 129 LRRM at 2779; Staten Island Rapid Transit Operating Auth. v. ICC, 718 F2d at 539; Chicago, S.S. & S. B. R.R. v. Fleming, 109 F2d 419; Shields v. Utah I.C. R.R., 305 U.S. 177, 3 LRRM 669; Texas Elec. Ry. v. Eastus, 25 F Supp 825, 3 LRRM 748.

This particular exclusion is limited to an electrified railroad line, if the line so operated is not otherwise used directly or indirectly in the movement of freight and passengers associated with a general system of transportation subject to the ICA. Where a line connects with a general rail system and is used to connect with service over that system, then the proviso would not apply. In the *Staten Island* cases, the ICC and later the court considered whether there was freight service on the line in question and whether the line connected with a railroad that is a carrier under the ICA.[374] The court also took into account the railroad's Staten Island Rapid Transit Operating Authority (SIRTOA) obligations to maintain the line to freight standards, the regular use by SIRTOA for movement of interstate freight, the physical connection of the line to an interstate system of transportation, and the contractual understandings of the parties to conclude that the SIRTOA is not exempted by the electric railway provision.[375]

An entity that owns a carrier is not itself a carrier by virtue of that ownership interest unless it exercises direct control over the carrier on a day-to-day basis, or independently meets the test of carrier status.[376]

IX. Eɴᴛɪᴛɪᴇs Cᴏɴᴛʀᴏʟʟᴇᴅ ʙʏ Cᴀʀʀɪᴇʀs

The RLA covers not only traditional carriers, but also certain enterprises that are directly or indirectly "controlled by" a rail or air carrier.[377] The NMB applies a two-part test

---

[374]*See* Staten Island Rapid Transit Operating Auth. v. ICC, 718 F2d 533; Railway Labor Executives' Ass'n v. ICC, 859 F2d 996, 129 LRRM 2778.

[375]The ICC later reached the contrary conclusion based on the discontinuance of interstate freight traffic and the absence of a person with the right to carry such freight over the line. Staten Island Rapid Transit Operating Auth., 1987 ICC LEXIS 123 (1987); Railway Labor Executives' Ass'n v. ICC, 859 F2d 996, 729 LRRM 2778. *See also* Texas Elec. Ry. v. Eastus, 25 F Supp 825, 3 LRRM 748 (the district court stresses the notion of physical connection as a determining factor).

[376]Metropolitan Transp. Auth., 8 NMB 1 (1980); TNT Skypak, Inc., 20 NMB 153 (1993).

[377]RLA §1, First.

to determine whether a common carrier or carriers exercise direct or indirect control over the enterprise:[378] (1) whether there is common ownership and control between the entity and an RLA carrier (the "ownership or control" prong of the test)[379] and (2) whether the nature of the enterprise's operations is work traditionally performed by rail or air carrier employees (the "function" prong of the test).[380] Both components must be satisfied for the NMB to conclude that the entity is covered by the RLA.[381]

Determining the scope of the function component of the "controlled by" test has proven simpler with respect to rail carriers than to air carriers. The RLA specifically sets forth the kinds of operations that can bring a company under the control of a carrier by rail, but it provides less direct guidance with respect to the kinds of operations that can bring a company under the control of a carrier by air.[382] That guidance has instead come on an ad hoc, case-by-case basis as the NMB has issued decisions.

---

[378]*See, e.g.,* Delpro Co. v. Railway & Steamship Clerks, 519 F Supp 842, 108 LRRM 2123 (D Del, 1981), *aff'd,* 676 F2d 960, 110 LRRM 2132 (CA 3), *cert. denied,* 459 U.S. 98, 111 LRRM 2856 (1982); Longshoremen (ILA) v. NMB, 870 F2d 733, 130 LRRM 3085 (CA DC, 1989); Bankhead Enters., 17 NMB 153 (1990); Inter Mobile Co., 17 NMB 223 (1990); Glenway, Inc., 17 NMB 257 (1990); C.W.S., Inc., 17 NMB 371 (1990); Ohio Barge Line, 11 NMB 290 (1984); Cybernetics & Sys., Inc., 10 NMB 334 (1983); UTDC Transit Servs., Inc., 17 NMB 343 (1990); Pacific Rail Servs. d/b/a Intermodal Mgmt. Servs., 16 NMB 468 (1989); Florida Express Carrier, Inc., 16 NMB 407 (1989).

[379]*Id.*

[380] *See, e.g.,* Delpro Co. v. Railway & Steamship Clerks, 519 F Supp 842, 108 LRRM 2123 (railroad functions listed in RLA §151 are nonexclusive). The NMB describes the function test as whether the work is that "traditionally performed" by carrier employees. O/O Truck Sales, 21 NMB 258, 266 (1994).

[381]Ohio Barge Line, 11 NMB 290; Delpro Co. v. Railway & Steamship Clerks, 519 F Supp 842, 108 LRRM 2123; Machinists v. NMB, 870 F2d 733, 130 LRRM 3085; Bankhead Enters., 17 NMB 153; Inter Mobile Co., 17 NMB 223; Glenway, Inc., 17 NMB 257; C.W.S., Inc., 17 NMB 371; Cybernetics & Sys., Inc., 10 NMB 334; UTDC Transit Servs., Inc., 17 NMB 343; Pacific Rail Servs. d/b/a Intermodal Mgmt. Servs., 16 NMB 468; Florida Express Carrier, Inc., 16 NMB 407.

[382]This enumeration of railroad operations has been held to be nonexclusive for purposes of RLA coverage. Delpro Co. v. 676 F2d 960, 110 LRRM 2132 (CA 3), *cert. denied,* 459 U.S. 989, 111 LRRM 2856 (1982).

A. Decisions Involving Entities Controlled by Railroad Carriers

The RLA provides some guidance as to which entities will be deemed carriers solely because of their operational relationship with a rail carrier. The Act includes the following type of enterprise in the definition of the term "carrier":

> any company which is directly or indirectly owned or controlled by or under common control with any carrier by railroad and which operates any equipment or facilities or performs any service (other than trucking service) in connection with the transportation, receipt, delivery, elevation, transfer in transit, refrigeration or icing, storage, and handling of property transported by railroad.[383]

1. Ownership or Control Requirement. The ownership or control requirement is a disjunctive test.[384] In determining the issue of ownership, entities that are owned either by a carrier by rail or by a subsidiary of a carrier by rail will be found to have met this part of the test.[385]

In determining whether the ownership or control requirement is satisfied in the context of entities not owned directly by carriers, the courts and the NMB have focused on the substance of the relationship between the carrier and the entity in question. In so doing, courts have found entities to be controlled by carriers even though the carriers were a step removed in the chain of ownership.[386] Accordingly, an entity was found to be controlled by a carrier even though the company that owned it was not a carrier, because a group of carriers owned the company that owned the entity in ques-

---

[383]RLA §1, First.

[384]Thus the requirement is met if the carrier owns the entity in question, whether or not the carrier controls it, or if the carrier controls the entity in question, notwithstanding whether the carrier owns it. *See* Delpro Co. v. Railway & Steamship Clerks, 676 F2d at 964, 110 LRRM at 2135.

[385]Florida Express Carrier, Inc., 16 NMB 407 (1989); Cybernetics & Sys., Inc., 10 NMB 334 (1983); O/O Truck Sales, 21 NMB at 272.

[386]Delpro Co. v. Railway & Steamship Clerks, 519 F Supp 842, 108 LRRM 2123 (D Del, 1981), *aff'd*, 676 F2d 960, 110 LRRM 2132 (CA 3), *cert. denied*, 459 U.S. 989, 111 LRRM 2856 (1982); Longshoremen (ILA) v. NMB, 870 F2d 733, 130 LRRM 3085.

tion.[387] Another entity was found to be potentially subject to the jurisdiction of the RLA because its parent corporation, which was not a carrier itself, also owned a carrier that was a sister company to the entity in question.[388] Other decisions have held that common ownership of a carrier and a noncarrier by a noncarrier holding company may be insufficient to satisfy the ownership or control requirement.[389]

Whether an entity is directly or indirectly owned by a rail carrier is a relatively straightforward inquiry that has not inspired a great deal of precedent.[390] In contrast, whether a rail carrier exercises control over an entity has been a subject of more controversy. There are two contexts. In the first, it is alleged that the entity is controlled by a carrier. In the second, the allegation is that the entity and a carrier are under the common control of another company.[391]

Resolution of the first scenario typically involves an inquiry into whether the rail carrier exercises direct supervision of the other company's day-to-day business operations or employment policies.[392] In the second scenario, the entity may be found to have satisfied the ownership or control test if the rail carrier and the entity in question are sufficiently similar to justify a finding that the entity in question is under common control with the rail carrier.[393]

Under each analysis the rail carrier must exercise meaningful control or a material degree of control over the entity

---

[387]Delpro Co. v. Railway & Steamship Clerks, 676 F2d at 963–64, 110 LRRM at 2135–36.
[388]Longshoremen (ILA) v. NMB, 870 F2d 733, 130 LRRM 3085 (CA DC, 1989).
[389]TNT Skypak, 20 NMB 153, 158 (1993); Eastern Aviation Serv., 5 NMB 53, 55 (1970); Mercury Refueling, 9 NMB 451, 455–56 (1982).
[390]See generally O/O Truck Sales, 21 NMB 258 (1994).
[391]Longshoremen (ILA) v. NMB, 870 F2d at 737, 130 LRRM at 3088.
[392]Bankhead Enters., 17 NMB 153, 157 (1990); Inter Mobile Co., 17 NMB 223, 225 (1990); C.W.S., Inc., 17 NMB 371, 374 (1990); Pacific Rail Servs. d/b/a Intermodal Mgmt. Servs., 16 NMB 468, 471 (1989).
[393]Delpro Co. v. Railway & Steamship Clerks, 519 F Supp 842, 848, 108 LRRM 2123 (D Del, 1981), aff'd, 676 F2d 960, 110 LRRM 2132 (CA 3), cert. denied, 459 U.S. 989, 111 LRRM 2856 (1982); Longshoremen (ILA) v. NMB, 870 F2d 733, 737, 130 LRRM 3085, 3088 (CA DC, 1989).

in question for the latter to be deemed a carrier.[394] To make such a finding, the NMB examines the extent of carrier control over the manner in which the entity does business and the carrier's access to the entity's operations and records.[395] Significant factors include (1) whether the entity's employees are supervised by railroad employees,[396] (2) whether employees of the entity in question acted as the rail carriers' agents in certain matters,[397] (3) whether officials of the rail carrier have the ability to make effective recommendations regarding the hiring and firing of the entity's employees,[398] (4) whether the entity in question uses equipment owned by the rail carrier to perform its duties,[399] (5) whether the carrier has a significant degree of control over the training of the entity's employees,[400] and (6) whether the entity performs work for more than one company and retains control over its operations.[401]

2. Function Requirement. In determining whether the function requirement has been met, the courts and the NMB inquire into the entity's activities respecting rail transportation to determine whether the nature of the services rendered is that traditionally performed by employees of rail carriers.[402] Because of the detailed definition provided in the RLA, there are relatively few contested decisions on this issue. The decisions that have ben reported establish the following types of services as traditional railroad work: (1) repair of railroad

---

[394]C.W.S., Inc., 17 NMB at 374; Inter Mobile Co., 17 NMB at 225; Bankhead Enters., 17 NMB 153; Glenway, Inc., 17 NMB 257, 259 (1990); Pacific Rail Servs. d/b/a Intermodal Mgmt. Servs., 16 NMB at 471.

[395]Bankhead Enters., 17 NMB 153.

[396]*Id.*; Inter Mobile Co., 17 NMB at 225; C.W.S., Inc., 17 NMB at 374; Pacific Rail Servs., d/b/a Intermodal Mgmt. Servs., 16 NMB at 471.

[397]*Id.*

[398]*Id.*

[399]*Id.*

[400]Bankhead Enters., 17 NMB 153 (1990).

[401]Track Maintenance, Inc., 8 NMB 86 (1980); Cincinnati, N.O. & T.-P. R.R., 4 NMB 280 (1966).

[402]Delpro Co. v. Railway & Steamship Clerks, 676 F2d 960, 963–64, 110 LRRM 2132, 2135–36 (CA 3), *cert. denied*, 459 U.S. 989, 111 LRRM 2856 (1982); Ohio Barge Line, 11 NMB 290, 293 (1984); Inter Mobile Co., 17 NMB 223, 224 (1990); Bankhead Enters., 17 NMB 153; Glenway, Inc., 17 NMB 257, 258 (1990).

cars,[403] (2) loading and unloading containers on and off rail-cars,[404] (3) maintenance of train yard facilities,[405] (4) mainte-nance of equipment required to provide train service,[406] and (5) data processing services.[407]

B. Decisions Involving Entities Controlled by Carriers by Air

Entities controlled by air carriers are subject to the juris-diction of the NMB under Section 201. The legal principles outlined in the previous subsection have been applied in cases involving air carriers.

1. Ownership or Control Requirement. The NMB em-ploys the two-part test previously described for determining whether an entity is controlled by an air carrier.[408] In evaluat-ing the ownership or control requirement, the NMB focuses upon the carrier's role in the entity's daily operations and

---

[403]Delpro Co. v. Railway & Steamship Clerks, 519 F Supp 842, 848, 108 LRRM 2123 (D Del, 1981), aff'd, 676 F2d 960, 110 LRRM 2132 (CA 3), cert. denied, 459 U.S. 989, 111 LRRM 2856 (1982).

[404]Glenway, Inc., 17 NMB at 258; Bankhead Enters., 17 NMB 153; Inter Mobile Co., 17 NMB at 224; Pacific Rail Servs. d/b/a Intermodal Mgmt. Servs., 16 NMB 468, 471 (1989).

[405]Pacific Rail Servs. d/b/a Intermodal Mgmt Servs., 16 NMB at 471; Bankhead Enters., 17 NMB 153 (1990).

[406]UTDC Transit Servs., Inc., 17 NMB 343, 351 (1990).

[407]Cybernetics Sys., Inc., 10 NMB 334 (1983).

[408]Eastern Air Lines, 17 NMB 432 (1990); Jimsair Aviation Servs., Inc., 15 NMB 85 (1988); Eagle Aviation, Inc., 15 NMB 285 (1988); York Aero, Inc., 17 NMB 498 (1990); Stanley Smith Sec., 16 NMB 379 (1989); Flight Terminal Sec. Co., 16 NMB 387 (1989); Sky Valet, 17 NMB 250 (1990); E G & G Special Projects, Inc., 17 NMB 457 (1990); Intertec Aviation, LP, 17 NMB 487 (1990); Panorama Air, 15 NMB 181 (1988); Energy Support Servs., Inc., 14 NMB 326 (1987); Allied Maintenance Corp., 13 NMB 255 (1986); Ebon Servs. Int'l, Inc., 13 NMB 3 (1985); CFS Air Cargo, 13 NMB 369 (1986); Huntleigh Corp., 14 NMB 149 (1987); Dynamic Science, Inc., 14 NMB 206 (1987); Olympic Sec. Servs., Inc., 16 NMB 277 (1989); Globe Sec. Sys. Co., 16 NMB 208 (1989); ARA Ground Servs., Inc. (BWI), 13 NMB 175 (1986); Sky Cap, Inc., 13 NMB 292 (1986); Ground Handling, Inc., 13 NMB 116 (1986); Tampa Airways d/b/a Top Air, Inc., 14 NMB 331 (1987); ARA Envtl. Servs., Inc., 9 NMB 37 (1981); International Total Servs./Servs. & Sys., Ltd., 9 NMB 392 (1982); Elliot Flying Serv., Inc., 9 NMB 146 (1981); Tri-State Aero, Inc., 9 NMB 356 (1982); New York Interstate Serv., Inc., 14 NMB 439 (1987); International Total Servs., Inc., 16 NMB 44 (1988); Aircraft Eng'g & Maintenance Co., 3 NMB 45 (1958).

the effect that the carrier's policies have on the manner in which the entity's employees perform their jobs.[409] In the absence of actual ownership, factors that may guide the Board in determining whether an entity is controlled directly or indirectly by an air carrier include (1) the carrier's role in hiring and terminating employees,[410] (2) the degree to which the carrier affects the conditions of employment of the entity's employees,[411] (3) whether the entity's employees are held out to the public as carrier employees (including the use of carrier uniforms by employees of the entity),[412] (4) the degree of influence that the carrier exercises over training received by the entity's employees,[413] and (5) whether the carrier exercises control over the entity's employees in the performance of their job duties (including supervision).[414]

The test is multifactored, and the NMB has not stated whether any one factor is more probative than the others. However, in the cases where the NMB has found the ownership or control requirement missing and thus has found the entity to be not subject to the RLA's jurisdiction, one or more of these factors has been conspicuously absent.[415]

---

[409]Air BP, Div. of BP Oil, 19 NMB 90, 92 (1991); SAPADO I, 18 NMB 525, 530 (1991); TNT Skypak, 20 NMB 153 (1993).

[410]SAPADO I, 18 NMB at 530; International Total Servs., Inc., 16 NMB 44; Tampa Airways d/b/a Top Air, Inc., 14 NMB 331; Ground Handling, Inc., 13 NMB 116; Sky Cap, Inc., 13 NMB 292; ARA Ground Servs., Inc. (BWI), 13 NMB 175; International Total Servs./Servs. & Sys., Ltd., 9 NMB 392; Ground Servs., Inc., 8 NMB 112 (1980); New York Interstate Serv., Inc., 14 NMB 439; ARA Envtl. Servs., Inc., 9 NMB 37 (1981); Sky Valet, 18 NMB 482 (1991); International Total Servs., Inc., 11 NMB 67 (1983); TNT Skypak, 20 NMB 153, Miami Aircraft, 21 NMB 78 (1993); Peatross Servs., 21 NMB 139 (1994); Caribbean Airlines Servs., 19 NMB 242 (1942); Pacific Rail Servs., 16 NMB 468 (1989); Inter Mobile, 17 NMB 223 (1990).

[411]SAPADO I, 18 NMB at 530.

[412]Id.

[413]Id.

[414]Id.

[415]Air BP, Div. of BP Oil, 19 NMB 90 (1991) (entity in question had sole authority over its employees); Combined Contract Serv., 18 NMB 163 (1991) (entity in question trained its own employees, had its own employee policy manual, and supervised its own employees); Stanley Smith Sec., 16 NMB 379 (1989) (entity in question remained in control of its workforce by inter alia, hiring, firing, training, and paying its workforce); Flight Terminal Sec. Co., 16 NMB 387 (1989) (entity in question performed functions relating to, inter alia, hiring, firing, paying, disciplining, training, evaluating, and supervising its employees); Energy Support Servs.,

2. Function Requirement. Evaluating the function requirement once again involves an inquiry into whether the services rendered by the entity's employees are of a type traditionally performed by employees of air carriers. No single case lists the services that qualify as traditional airline work or the factors that support the conclusion that an entity's employees provide such services. The NMB has fashioned the rules through case-by-case analyses of the airline industry. In each case, the NMB examines the entire scope of services in which an entity is engaged.[416]

From these cases, the following types of ancillary activity have emerged as work traditionally performed by employees of air carriers for purposes of applying the functional test: (1) air taxi service and charter operations, other than those that are negligible or sporadic,[417] (2) refueling, maintenance,

---

Inc., 14 NMB 326 (1987) (entity in question performed functions relating to, inter alia, hiring, firing, disciplining, scheduling, compensating, and supervising its own employees); Allied Maintenance Corp., 13 NMB 255 (1986) (entity in question performed functions relative to, inter alia, hiring, firing, disciplining, scheduling, screening, compensating, and promoting its employees); Ebon Servs. Int'l, Inc., 13 NMB 3 (1985) (entity in question had control over functions such as hiring, firing, promoting, and disciplining its employees); CFS Air Cargo, 13 NMB 369 (1986) (entity in question had control over, inter alia, hiring, firing, training, and compensating its employees); Huntleigh Corp., 14 NMB 149 (1987) (entity in question had control over, inter alia, hiring, supervising, compensating, disciplining, and training its employees); Dynamic Science, Inc., 14 NMB 206 (1987) (entity in question had control over, inter alia, hiring, firing, supervising, disciplining, and compensating its employees); Olympic Sec. Servs., Inc., 16 NMB 277 (1989) (entity in question had control over, inter alia, hiring, firing, disciplining, establishing pay rates, and establishing benefits); Globe Sec. Sys. Co., 16 NMB 208 (1989) (entity in question had control over, inter alia, hiring and firing its employees).

[416]International Air Serv. Co., 18 NMB 492, 498 (1991).

[417]AMR Combs-Memphis, Inc., 18 NMB 380, 381 (1991) (12% of gross income derived from air taxi service); York Aero, Inc., 17 NMB 498, 500 (1990) (air taxi service of seven flights per week); Eagle Aviation, Inc., 15 NMB 285, 287 (1988); Jimsair Aviation Servs., Inc., 15 NMB 85, 86 (1985) (air taxi service of 25 flights per week); Tampa Airways d/b/a Top Air, Inc., 14 NMB 331, 332 (1987); Tri-State Aero, Inc., 9 NMB 356 (1982); Elliot Flying Serv., Inc., 9 NMB 146, 147 (1981). *But see* CRE Aero Servs., Inc., 10 NMB 62 (1982) (air taxi service generating mere 3% of entity's gross income held negligible and sporadic). Although the NMB employs the same two-part test in examining the status of entities that provide air taxi service, once the Board finds that the entity provides significant air taxi service, the ownership or control requirement becomes moot. Jimsair Aviation Servs., Inc. 15 NMB at 87; Eagle Aviation, Inc., 15 NMB at 287; General Aviation Group of Piedmont Aviation, 15 NMB 256 (1988); Tri-State Aero, Inc., 9 NMB 146 (1981).

and servicing of airline ground equipment or aircraft,[418] (3) predeparture screening and checkpoint security service;[419] (4) in-flight food catering services;[420] (5) sky cap services (including curbside baggage check-in, baggage claim area monitoring, and passenger assistance);[421] (6) piloting and flight engineering;[422] (7) ground services (including directing, parking, starting and towing aircraft, transporting cargo or baggage between aircraft and airport terminals, and cleaning aircraft);[423] and (8) several miscellaneous functions such as escorting disabled passengers to and from planes, loading irregular baggage, sorting unclaimed luggage, operating parking lot booths at airports, and air traffic control.[424]

Finally, on several occasions the NMB has confronted situations where entities have conducted business operations in various cities throughout the country. These cases generally come before the NMB on referral from the National Labor Relations Board (NLRB). As a result of a limited re-

---

[418]Air BP, Div. of BP Oil, 19 NMB at 92; International Air Serv. Co., 18 NMB 492, 497 (1991); AMR Combs-Memphis, Inc., 18 NMB at 381; York Aero, Inc., 17 NMB at 500; Intertec Aviation L.P., 17 NMB 487, 490 (1990); Cross Continent Aircraft Serv., Inc., 17 NMB 107 (1990); Dalfort Corp., 16 NMB 275 (1989); Eagle Aviation, Inc., 15 NMB at 287; Jimsair Aviation Servs., Inc., 15 NMB at 86; Energy Support Servs., Inc., 14 NMB 326; Dynamic Science, Inc., 14 NMB 206 (1987); Memorandum re: Airline Industry Hearings, 5 NMB 2, 4 (1972).

[419]Combined Contract Serv., 18 NMB at 168 (1991); Stanley Smith Sec., 16 NMB 379; Olympic Sec. Servs., Inc., 16 NMB 277; Globe Sec. Sys. Co., 16 NMB 208 (1989); Total Servs., 16 NMB 44 (1988); New York Interstate Serv., Inc., 14 NMB 439, 441 (1987); Flight Terminal Sec. Co., 16 NMB at 395; Dynamic Science, Inc., 14 NMB 206; Allied Maintenance Corp., 13 NMB 255; Ground Handling, Inc., 13 NMB 116, 117 (1986); Total Servs., 9 NMB 392 (1982); ARA Envtl. Servs., 9 NMB 37, 39 (1981).

[420]SAPADO I, 18 NMB 525, 530 (1991); Sky Chefs, Inc., 15 NMB 397 (1988).

[421]Sky Valet, 18 NMB 482 (1991); Sky Valet, 17 NMB 250, 255 (1990); Sky Cap, Inc., 13 NMB 292 (1986); Huntleigh Corp., 14 NMB 149 (1987); Allied Maintenance Corp., 13 NMB 255.

[422]International Air Serv. Co., 18 NMB 492; E G & G Special Projects, Inc., 17 NMB 457, 458 (1990).

[423]Energy Support Servs., Inc., 14 NMB 326 (1987); CFS Air Cargo, Inc., 13 NMB 369 (1986); ARA Ground Servs., Inc. (BWI), 13 NMB 175, 176 (1986); ARA Envtl. Servs., Inc., 9 NMB 37; Ground Servs., Inc. (W. Palm Beach), 12 NMB 266 (1985).

[424]Flight Terminal Sec. Co., 16 NMB 387, 395 (1989); Allied Maintenance Corp., 13 NMB 255 (1986); Dynamic Science, Inc., 14 NMB 206 (1987); Huntleigh Corp., 14 NMB 149.

cord, the NMB tends to decide the issues on a case-by-case approach that is limited to the location in dispute before the NLRB.[425]

C. RLA Exclusions

In defining "carrier," the RLA contains the following language respecting trucking services:

> When used in this chapter and for the purposes of this chapter—First. The term "carrier" includes any express company, sleeping-car company, carrier by railroad, subject to subtitle IV of Title 49, and any company which is directly or indirectly owned or controlled by or under common control with any carrier by railroad and which operates any equipment or facilities or performs any service (*other than trucking service*) in connection with the transportation, receipt, delivery, elevation, transfer in transit, refrigeration or icing, storage, and handling of property transported by railroad. . . .[426]

The NMB initially took the position that an entity holding a certificate as a motor carrier under the ICA was excluded from RLA coverage,[427] but subsequently determined that that factor was not conclusive on an entity's carrier status.[428] Where a trucking company "performs services almost exclusively for" a rail carrier, the NMB takes the position that the trucking exclusion is inapplicable.[429]

---

[425]Allen Servs., Co., 314 NLRB No. 176 (Sept. 9, 1994); Caribbean Airline Servs., 307 NLRB 361 (1992); United Jet Ctr., 304 NLRB 177 (1991); Intertec Aviation, L.P., 300 NLRB 555 (1990); Ground Handling, Inc., 278 NLRB 946 (1986); Henson Aviation, Inc., 10 NMB No. 36, at 99 (1983).

[426]RLA §1, First (italics supplied).

[427]Southern Region Motor Transp., 5 NMB 298 (1975).

[428]Florida Express Carrier, Inc., 16 NMB 407 (1989); O/O Truck Sales, 21 NMB 258 (1994).

[429]O/O Truck Sales, 21 NMB at 272; Florida Express Carrier, Inc., 16 NMB at 410 (trucking company "integrally related" to rail carrier where the entity's services were performed predominantly for the rail carrier and the entity was "organized for the purpose" of serving the rail carrier, which was also its corporate parent). The NMB has suggested that the "trucking exclusion" would be applicable if the "nature of the work done" by a trucking company's employees was not principally for an RLA carrier. O/O Truck Sales, 21 NMB at 271. *See also* Chicago Truck Drivers, Helpers & Warehouse Workers Union v. NLRB, 599 F2d 816, 101 LRRM 2624 (CA 7, 1979) (holding that court lacked jurisdiction to review NLRB deermina-

Congress also excluded another type of entity from coverage under the RLA. At the very end of Section 151, First, the RLA provides that the term "carrier" does not include "any company by reason of its being engaged in the mining of coal, the supplying of coal to a carrier where delivery is not beyond the mine tipple, and the operation of equipment or facilities therefor, or in any of such activities." Neither the courts, the ICC, nor the NMB has had occasion to speak to this exclusion.

X. Common Carrier and Private Carriage

A. Definition of Common Carrier

In order for a rail or air employer to be covered by the RLA, it must be a "common carrier." The RLA provides some definitional guidance as to its coverage with respect to rail carriers, but none with respect to common carriers by air. As a result, the NMB, following judicial lead, has resorted to common law concepts for aid in applying the Act to putative carriers.[430] The standards that determine that status have developed in a common manner for both industries.

In order for the entity to be deemed a common carrier, as opposed to a private carrier, either it must have an affirmative duty to serve the public or the public must have a right to demand service of the carrier.[431] The actual extent of public

---

tion that RLA applied to Federal Express truck drivers, and declining to decide on the merits which statute applied); Chicago Truck Drivers, Helpers & Warehouse Workers Union v. NMB, 670 F2d 665, 109 LRRM 3284 (CA 7, 1981) (court lacked jurisdiction to review NMB refusal to consider petition to decline jurisdiction over Federal Express truck drivers because there was no pending application for an NMB investigation of a representation dispute); *but see* Missouri Pac. Trucking Lines v. United States, 3 Cl. Ct. 14 (1983), *adopted on appeal*, 736 F2d 706 (CA Fed, 1984) (in case under the Railroad Retirement Act, on a detailed review of the legislative history of the RLA, the court found that the RLA exclusion applied to trucking companies even if owned by and integrated with a railroad).

[430]Southern Air Transp. 8, NMB 31 (1980) (citing, inter alia, National Ass'n of Regulatory Util. Comm'rs v. FCC, 525 F2d 630 (CA DC, 1976)); Las Vegas Hacienda, Inc. v. CAB, 298 F2d 430, 434 (CA 9), *cert. denied*, 369 U.S. 885 (1962).

[431]United States v. Louisiana & P. R.R. (Tap Line Cases), 234 U.S. 1, 24 (1914); Southern Air Transp., 8 NMB 31 (citing, inter alia, National Ass'n of Regulatory Util. Comm'rs v. FCC, 525 F2d 630); Las Vegas Hacienda, Inc. v. CAB, 298 F2d at 434.

use or demand of the services is not determinative; rather, the fundamental question is the public character of the carrier as manifested by the activities it performs.[432]

Even where a carrier has no affirmative duty to serve the public, if it holds itself out as available for public service indiscriminately, it will be deemed a common carrier.[433] Where a carrier's practice is to make individualized decisions in particular cases whether and on what terms to serve, it is not a common carrier.[434] The NMB has defined "holding out" as "any conduct which communicates that a service is available to those who wish to use it."[435]

B. Factors

Advertising and soliciting are the most obvious and visible examples of "holding oneself out" to the public,[436] "but a carrier may also hold itself out by conduct that naturally induces a belief in the minds of the public that service is

---

[432]Id. See also National Ass'n of Regulatory Util. Commr's v. FCC, 533 F2d 601, 608 (CA DC, 1976) (citing Washington v. Kuykendall, 275 U.S. 207, 211–12 (1927)) (common carrier is deemed to be such by actual activities it carries on); Las Vegas Hacienda, Inc. v. CAB, 298 F2d at 434–35 (entity that was primarily in hotel business and furnished air transportation incidentally thereto properly deemed common carrier by Civil Aeronautics Board); cf. Cooperative Shippers, Inc. v. Atchison, T. & S.F. Ry., 613 F Supp 788, 792 (ND Ill., 1985).

To be deemed a carrier, the transportation service must be currently provided. Railway Labor Executives' Ass'n v. Wheeling Acquisition Corp., 736 F Supp 1397, 1402–03, 135 LRRM 2345 (ED Va, 1990).

[433]See, e.g., Computer & Communications Indus. Ass'n, v. FCC, 693 F2d 198, 209–10 (CA DC, 1982), cert. denied, 461 U.S. 938 (1983); Delta Air Lines v. CAB, 543 F2d 247, 259 (CA DC, 1976); Cox Cable Communications, Inc. v. Simpson, 569 F Supp 507, 519 (D Neb, 1983).

[434]National Ass'n of Regulatory Util. Commr's v. FCC, 533 F2d at 608 (citing Semon v. Royal Indem. Co., 279 F2d 737, 739–40 (CA 5, 1960)).

[435]Southern Air Transp., 8 NMB 31, 34 (1980). As will be noted infra, that service may be specialized and directed at only a fraction of the population, but the offering entity will still be deemed a common carrier if the service is offered indifferently among those who may seek to use it. National Ass'n of Regulatory Util. Comm'rs v. FCC, 533 F2d at 608; California v. FCC, 905 F2d 1217, 1240 n.32 (CA 9, 1990).

[436]Alaska Air Transp., Inc. v. Alaska Airplane Charter Co., 72 F Supp 609, 610 (D Alaska, 1947).

available."[437] However, lack of advertising does not compel the conclusion that there has not been a holding out.[438]

The essential question is whether the carrier is competing commercially in the market for the patronage of some portion of the general public.[439] Indeed, the mere practice of engaging in the business of carriage for hire may be deemed to be holding out to the public.[440]

An entity's self-characterization is not definitive of its status as a common carrier. Thus, an "air travel club," which owned large aircraft, served its members exclusively, solicited membership, and operated flights that were announced and booked months in advance, was deemed a common carrier.[441] The club was determined to have held itself out as "ready and willing to undertake for hire the transportation of passengers or property from place to place, and so invite(d) the patronage of the public."[442]

The fact that a carrier may operate pursuant to contracts with customers, including government contracts, does not exempt it from common carrier status.[443] The tribunals ad-

---

[437]*Id.*

[438]*See, e.g.,* Voyager 1000 v. CAB, 489 F2d 792, 800 (CA 7), *cert. denied,* 416 U.S. 982 (1973); Alaska Air Transp., Inc. v. Alaska Airplane Charter Co., 72 F Supp at 610.

[439]Las Vegas Hacienda, Inc. v. CAB, 298 F2d 430, 434 (CA 9), *cert. denied,* 369 U.S. 885 (1962).

[440]*See, e.g.,* Arrow Aviation, Inc. v. Moore, 266 F2d 488, 490 (CA 8, 1959) (and authorities cited therein); Southern Air Transp., 8 NMB 31, 34 (1980) (and cases cited therein).

[441]Voyager 1000 v. CAB, 489 F2d at 802. *See also* Alaska Air Transp., Inc. v. Alaska Airplane Charter Co., 72 F Supp 609, 611 (D Alaska, 1947); Southern Air Transp., 8 NMB at 34; Monarch Travel Servs., Inc. v. Associated Cultural Clubs, Inc., 466 F2d 552 (CA 9, 1972), *cert. denied,* 410 U.S. 967 (1973).

[442]Voyager 1000 v. CAB, 489 F2d 792, 799 (CA 7), *cert. denied,* 416 U.S. 982 (1973) (quoting Transocean Air Lines Enforcement Proceedings, 11 CAB 350, 352 (1950)). *See also* Las Vegas Hacienda, Inc. v. CAB, 298 F2d at 434, in which the carrier's initial contention that its flights were free and thus not travel "for hire" was rejected.

[443]45 USC §181 (1936); *see also* Ross Aviation, Inc., 9 NMB 193, 194–97 (1982) (common carrier despite contract with Department of Energy to transport government cargo); Southern Air Transp., 8 NMB at 35 (and cases cited therein); Pacific N. Airlines v. Alaska Airlines, 80 F Supp 592, 601 (D Alaska, 1948) (citing Alaska Air Transp., Inc. v. Alaska Airplane Charter Co., 72 F Supp at 611).

dressing the contention that providing transportation per contract is not "public" in character view contracts as simply a vehicle by which a carrier in the business assures itself of continuing commerce.[444] In fact, the existence of such contracts detracts from any claim that the transportation in question is occasional, infrequent, or casual, and hence not indicative of common carrier status.[445]

The service offered by the carrier need not be extended to the entire population; it may extend only to a fraction thereof, so long as the potential users of the service are provided offers in an indiscriminate fashion.[446] One court declared that "the essential element is the offer to transport anything for anyone within the limitations specified."[447] Another court observed that "[a] service provided on a common carrier basis is one that is offered to the public on standard terms."[448] One court defined this element in terms of what it is not: "[A] carrier will not be a common carrier where its practice is to make individualized decisions in particular cases whether and on what terms to serve."[449] Finally, the NMB declared that "[a]s long as a carrier serves indiscriminately to the limit of its facilities those who fall into the class which the carrier has determined to be the subject of its business, it is a common carrier."[450]

XI. EMPLOYEE OR SUBORDINATE OFFICIAL

Section 151, Fifth of the RLA defines "employees" as every person "in the service of a carrier (subject to its continuing authority to supervise and direct the manner of rendition of his service) who performs any work defined as that of an

---

[444]*Id.*

[445]*Id .*

[446]Southern Air Transp., 8 NMB 31, 35 (1980).

[447]Delta Air Lines v. CAB, 543 F2d 247, 259 (CA DC, 1976) (airlines that serve only certain class of shippers and carry only limited cargo are nonetheless common carriers).

[448]California v. FCC, 905 F2d 1217, 1240 n.32 (CA 9, 1990).

[449]National Ass'n of Regulatory Util. Commr's v. FCC, 533 F2d 601, 608–09 (CA DC, 1976).

[450]Southern Air Transp. 8 NMB at 35.

employee or subordinate official." In addition, Section 181 defines employees of air carriers as "every air pilot or other person who performs work as an employee or subordinate official of such carrier."[451] Both the courts and the NMB have determined employee status. For example, courts have decided whether an individual in training is an employee entitled to the protections of the Act.[452] The NMB has jurisdiction in representation cases to determine employee status in connection with voting eligibility findings and craft or class determinations.[453]

The NMB and the courts have taken a somewhat restrictive view of the meaning of working "in the service of" a

---

[451]Congress added a separate definition of "employee" for air carriers. RLA tit. II, §202.

[452]*See, e.g.,* Air Line Pilots v. United Air Lines, 802 F2d 886, 123 LRRM 2617 (CA 7, 1986), *cert. denied,* 480 U.S. 946, 124 LRRM 3192 (1987).

[453]RLA §2, Ninth; Northwest Airlines, 2 NMB 19 (1948). In United States v. Feaster, 330 F2d 671, 56 LRRM 2018, 2021 (CA 5, 1964), *cert. denied,* 389 U.S. 920 (1967), the court described the jurisdictional boundaries between the ICC and the NMB with respect to one aspect of employee status. The RLA explicitly gives the ICC exclusive authority to define whether certain railroad work is work of employees or subordinate officials. However, the NMB has the authority to determine whether a particular individual or job classification performs work that the ICC has designated as work of an employee or of a subordinate official. *Ex parte* 72 (Sub. No. 1), 259 ICC 443 (1945), is an ICC determination pursuant to the Transportation Act of 1920 that determined whether work performed by individuals or job classifications is work of an employee or a subordinate official of a rail carrier. Although §181 defines employees of air carriers as "every air pilot or other person who performs work as an employee or subordinate official of such carrier," there are no ICC standards binding on the NMB when it determines whether individuals or job classifications perform work that is work of an employee or subordinate official of an air carrier. Guilford Rail Div., 19 NMB 32 (1991); Guilford Rail Div., 19 NMB 24 (1991); Birmingham S. Ry., 16 NMB 55 (1988); Long Island Ry., 9 NMB 551 (1982); Chicago, M., St. P. and P. R.R., 6 NMB 383 (1978); Penn Centr. Transp. Co., 5 NMB 335 (1975); REA Express, 4 NMB 253 (1965); Pennsylvania R.R., 4 NMB 234 (1965); Chesapeake & O. Ry., P.I.D., 4 NMB 206 (1962); Grand Truck W. R.R., 3 NMB 216 (1961); Houston Belt & Terminal Ry., 3 NMB 197 (1955); International Great N. R.R., 3 NMB 134 (1953); Erie R.R., 2 NMB 202 (1951); Atlantic Coast Line R.R., 2 NMB 197 (1951); Chesapeake & O. Ry., 2 NMB 184 (1951); Pullman, 2 NMB 120 (1949); Erie R.R., 2 NMB 102 (1949); Lake Front Dock & R.R. Terminal Co., 2 NMB 101 (1948); Western P. R.R., 1 NMB 356 (1947); Texas & P. Ry., 1 NMB 341 (1947); Chicago & N.W. Ry., 1 NMB 352 (1947); Seaboard Airline Ry., 1 NMB 167 (1940); Robinson v. Pan Am. World Airways, 597 F Supp 1063, 1066 (SD NY, 1984), *rev'd on other grounds,* 777 F2d 84 (CA 2, 1985) (finding NMB determination of employee status controlling).

carrier,[454] while generally adopting rules similar to those used by the NLRB in determining coverage of employees after they have actually performed on-line service. In order to achieve employee status, the individual must have completed training and actually commenced work for the carrier.[455]

In the representation context, the Board has declared that "performance of line functions as part of a training program is not sufficient to qualify as a member of the craft or class."[456] Rather,

> [f]or the Board to find trainees eligible, the Board must be presented with evidence that the individuals in question *have performed* line functions in the craft or class as of the cut-off date. *Factors such as accrual of seniority and receiving pay and benefits are not determinative of employee status absent substantive evidence of line work in the craft or class.*[457]

Job applicants are excluded from RLA coverage except for the specific prohibition contained in Section 2, Fifth against a carrier requiring an employee to sign an agreement promising to join or not to join a labor organization.[458]

Individuals working for a carrier's subcontractor are not necessarily employees of the carrier.[459] The Board has looked to NLRA precedent for guidance on this issue and has adopted a "right-to-control" test to determine independent contractor status.[460] That is, if the carrier retains the right to control the manner and means by which the workers accom-

---

[454]RLA §2, Fifth defines "employee" as "every person in the service of a carrier . . . who performs any work defined as that of an employee." The Board has focused on the word "performs" as the definitive factor.

[455]Air Line Pilots Ass'n v. United Air Lines, 802 F2d 886, 911–14, 123 LRRM 2617 (CA 7, 1986); Eastern Airlines v. Air Line Pilots Ass'n, 920 F2d 722, 727, 136 LRRM 2082 (CA 11, 1990); Flight Attendants (IFFA) v. Trans World Airlines, 819 F2d 839, 845–47, 125 LRRM 2544 (CA 8, 1987). Striking employees are "employees" covered by the RLA. Professional Cabin Crew Ass'n v. NMB, 872 F2d 456, 460, 131 LRRM 2034 (CA DC, 1989).

[456]United Air Lines, 18 NMB 181, 184 (1991).

[457]*Id.* (quoting Simmons Airlines, 15 NMB 228 (1988)).

[458]Nelson v. Piedmont Aviation, Inc., 750 F2d 1234, 1236, 118 LRRM 2138 (CA 4, 1984), *cert. denied,* 471 U.S. 1116, 119 LRRM 2376 (1985); Railway Labor Executives' Ass'n v. Wheeling Acquisition Corp., 736 F Supp. 1397, 1403–04, 135 LRRM 2345 (ED Va, 1990).

[459]NMB REPRESENTATION MANUAL §4.309 (1995).

[460]Eastern Air Lines, 9 NMB 285, 296 (1982).

plish their tasks, the workers will be deemed employees of the carrier; if the carrier retains control only as to the final result, the workers will be independent contractor employees.[461] In a case raising the issue of whether truck drivers were independent contractors, the Board stated that it would consider the following factors in making the contractor status determination: "ownership and maintenance of the vehicle, freedom to accept other work, opportunity for entrepreneurial risk taking and profit, government regulation, pay and fringe benefits, tax status, and supervision."[462]

Courts have held that the RLA does not apply to employees based outside the United States and U.S. territories who perform activities wholly outside the United States.[463] The only court to have considered the matter of foreign-based flight crew members who work on international flights into and out of the United States held that the RLA does apply to such employees.[464]

Where an employee for a foreign carrier is based in the United States and has a "reasonable expectation of continued employment," that employee will be covered by the Act.[465]

---

[461]*Id.*

[462]*Id.*

[463]Airline Dispatchers Ass'n v. NMB, 189 F2d 685 (CA DC), *cert. denied,* 342 U.S. 849 (1951), Air Line Stewards & Stewardesses Ass'n v. Northwest Airlines, 267 F2d 170, 44 LRRM 2189 (CA 8), *cert. denied,* 361 U.S. 901, 45 LRRM 2163 (1959); Flight Attendants (UFA) v. Pan Am. World Airways, 923 F2d 678, 136 LRRM 2217 (CA 9, 1991), *vacated as moot,* 966 F2d 457, 140 LRRM 2110 (CA 9, 1992) (the courts' presumption against extraterritoriality and Congress's definition of commerce requires a finding that the RLA does not govern with respect to purely foreign flights); Flight Attendants (UFA) v. Pan Am. World Airways, 810 F Supp 263 (ND Cal, 1992) (denying motion to vacate prior decision); Airline Stewards & Stewardesses Ass'n v. Trans World Airlines, 173 F Supp 369 (SD NY), *aff'd,* 273 F2d 69 (CA 2, 1959), *cert. denied,* 362 U.S. 988 (1960) (court has no subject matter jurisdiction in a dispute involving flight attendants flying wholly outside the United States); United Transp. Union, General Comm. of Adjustment v. Burlington N. R.R., 620 F2d 161, 103 LRRM 2990 (CA DC), *cert. denied,* 449 U.S. 826 (1980); Allen v. CSX Transp., Inc., 22 F3d 1180, 146 LRRM 2566 (CA DC, 1994). *See also* NMB REPRESENTATION MANUAL §4.310 (1995).

[464]Transport Workers Local 553 v. Eastern Air Lines, 544 F Supp 1315, 111 LRRM 2402 (ED NY), *aff'd with modification,* 695 F2d 668, 112 LRRM 2482 (CA 2, 1982). *See* NMB REPRESENTATION MANUAL §4.310 (1995) (for purposes of determining eligibility to participate in representation elections, NMB considers foreign-based employees not to be covered by the RLA).

[465]*See, e.g.,* Swissair, 16 NMB 146 (1989); El Al Is. Airlines, 12 NMB 238 (1985); Japan Air Lines, 4 NMB 112 (1967).

XII. RELATION TO OTHER STATUTES

As discussed earlier,[466] the RLA relies on ICA decisions in determining whether a rail entity is covered by the RLA and in determining whether certain work performed by railroad employees is work of management officials or of subordinate officials covered by the Act.

Chapter 7 details the relationship between railroad and airline labor protective legislation and NMB findings of carrier status,[467] and discusses the extent to which the RLA preempts state regulation.

Under the National Labor Relations Act, NLRB jurisdiction does not extend to an entity that is a carrier subject to the RLA."[468] By practice, the NLRB ordinarily permits the NMB's review of the jurisdiction question.[469] In the typical case, if the coverage issue is raised during an NLRB proceeding, the NLRB will collect the facts and solicit the views of the NMB.[470]

---

[466]*See supra* note 453.

[467]*See* Chapter 7, "Accommodating the RLA to Other Laws," §III.

[468]29 USC §152(2), (3) (1978).

[469]On occasion the NLRB makes the initial coverage decision. It is not required first to seek the opinion of the NMB. Dobbs House, Inc. v. NLRB, 443 F2d 1066, 77 LRRM 2429 (CA 6, 1971); *see also* Pan Am. World Airways, 115 NLRB 493, 37 LRRM 1336 (1956) (NLRB will not assert jurisdiction unless NMB declines jurisdiction).

[470]*See* NLRB FIELD MANUAL ¶17,020 (1990); Allen Servs. Co., 314 NLRB No. 176 (Sept. 9, 1994); Caribbean Airline Servs., 307 NLRB 361 (1992); United Jet Ctr., 304 NLRB 177 (1991); Intertec Aviation, L.P., 300 NLRB 555 (1990); Ground Handling, Inc., 278 NLRB 946 (1986); Henson Aviation, Inc., 10 NMB No. 36, at 99 (1983).

CHAPTER 2

SELECTING A BARGAINING REPRESENTATIVE

I. EXCLUSIVE JURISDICTION OF NATIONAL MEDIATION BOARD TO MAKE CRAFT OR CLASS DETERMINATIONS

In a group of cases known collectively as the *Switchmen's Trilogy*,[1] the Supreme Court established that the National Mediation Board (NMB) has exclusive jurisdiction over disputes regarding the selection and identity of employee representatives pursuant to Section 2, Ninth of the Act. The Court found that Congress "fashioned an administrative remedy" for representational disputes and "did not select the courts to resolve" such controversies.[2] "Representational disputes" may also raise questions as to the appropriate craft or class.[3]

---

[1]Switchmen's Union v. NMB, 320 U.S. 297, 13 LRRM 616 (1943); General Comm. of Adjustment v. Missouri-K.-T. R.R., 320 U.S. 323, 13 LRRM 627 (1943); General Comm. of Adjustment v. Southern P. Co., 320 U.S. 338, 13 LRRM 635 (1943).

[2]General Comm. of Adjustment v. Missouri-K.-T. R.R., 320 U.S. at 336, 13 LRRM at 636.

[3]Switchmen's Union v. NMB, 320 U.S. 297, 13 LRRM 616; Railway & Steamship Clerks v. Atlantic Coast Line R.R., 201 F2d 36, 31 LRRM 2264 (CA 4), *cert. denied*, 345 U.S. 992, 32 LRRM 2246 (1953). *See also* Steele v. Louisville & N. R.R., 323 U.S. 192, 15 LRRM 708 (1944). The term "craft or class" is not defined in the Act because the term was well known at the time the Act was passed. *See* Machinists v. Alitalia Airlines, 600 F Supp 268, 270 n.2, 116 LRRM 3214, 3216 (SD NY, 1984), *aff'd*, 753 F2d 3, 118 LRRM 2237 (CA 2, 1985).

Courts have held that the NMB has exclusive jurisdiction to determine crafts and classes,[4] and that such determinations are virtually nonreviewable.[5] In rejecting an attempt to seek judicial determination of a representation matter, the Supreme Court stated that "[i]n view of the pattern of this legislation and its history the command of the Act should be explicit and the purpose to afford a judicial remedy plain before an obligation enforceable in the courts should be implied."[6]

II. POLICY OF SYSTEMWIDE REPRESENTATION

The 1934 amendments to the RLA of 1926 were drafted by Joseph B. Eastman, then Federal Coordinator of Transportation.[7] In including the provision that the "majority of any craft or class" should determine representation, Commissioner Eastman was guided by a rule of decision laid down by the Railroad Labor Board in the early 1920s.[8] The Railroad Labor Board, later eliminated by the 1926 Act, had been

---

[4]Railroad Trainmen v. Howard, 343 U.S. 768, 30 LRRM 2258 (1952); Steele v. Louisville & N. R.R., 323 U.S. at 205, 15 LRRM at 713; Teamsters v. Texas Int'l Airlines, 717 F2d 157, 114 LRRM 3091 (CA 5, 1983); Reynolds v. Machinists Local 244, 87 LRRM 2123 (MD NC, 1973), aff'd mem., 498 F2d 1397, 87 LRRM 2125 (CA 4, 1974); Howard v. St. Louis-S.F. Ry., 361 F2d 905, 62 LRRM 2531 (CA 8), cert. denied, 385 U.S. 986, 63 LRRM 2559 (1966); Flight Eng'rs v. NMB, 294 F2d 905, 48 LRRM 2620 (CA DC, 1961), cert. denied, 368 U.S. 956, 49 LRRM 2359 (1962); Railway Conductors & Brakemen v. Switchmen's Union, 269 F2d 726, 44 LRRM 2432 (CA 5), cert. denied, 361 U.S. 899, 45 LRRM 2163 (1959); Railway & Steamship Clerks v. Atlantic Coast Line R.R., 201 F2d 36, 31 LRRM 2264; Hester v. Railroad Trainmen, 206 F2d 279, 32 LRRM 2568 (CA 8, 1953); Rose v. Railway & Steamship Clerks, 181 F2d 944, 26 LRRM 2133 (CA 4), cert. denied, 340 U.S. 85, 26 LRRM 2644 (1950); United Transp. Serv. Employees ex rel. Washington v. NMB, 179 F2d 446, 24 LRRM 2589 (CA DC, 1949).

[5]Railway & Steamship Clerks v. Association for the Benefit of Non-Contract Employees, 380 U.S. 650, 59 LRRM 2051 (1965); Switchmen's Union v. NMB, 320 U.S. 297, 13 LRRM 616; Howard v. St. Louis-S.F. Ry., 361 F2d 905, 62 LRRM at 2534; Air Canada v. NMB, 478 F Supp 615, 107 LRRM 2028 (SD NY, 1980), aff'd mem., 659 F2d 1057, 107 LRRM 2049 (CA 2), cert. denied, 454 U.S. 965, 108 LRRM 2923 (1981).

[6]General Comm. of Adjustment v. Missouri-K.-T. R.R., 320 U.S. 323, 337, 13 LRRM 627, 632–33 (1943).

[7]Senate Debate, 78 CONG. REC. 954 (1934).

[8]Hearings Before the House Comm. on Interstate and Foreign Commerce on H.R. 7650, 73d Cong., 2d Sess. 44 (1934) [hereinafter Hearings on H.R. 7650].

established by the Transportation Act of 1920 to deal with disputes on the railroads. It drafted rules of decision about the procedures it intended to follow to settle representation disputes. One provided that "[t]he majority of any craft or class of employees shall have the right to determine what organization shall represent members of such craft or class."[9] Commissioner Eastman intended Section 2, Fourth to mandate representation on a systemwide basis:

> Well, my understanding of the way in which the words "craft" or "class" have been defined in the past, is that they would cover the entire service of any particular carrier. That is, it would not be a class of employees, to pick out those that did work in a particular shop, but it would be all of the employees of the carrier, no matter in what shop they were located, who did that particular kind of work.[10]

Commissioner Eastman's view was incorporated into the RLA, which provides that "[t]he majority of any craft or class of employees shall have the right to determine who shall be the representative of the craft or class for the purposes of this Act."[11]

The NMB has consistently interpreted this provision as a mandate that a union may be certified by the NMB only on a systemwide basis.[12] Systemwide representation is possible only when the craft or class to be certified includes all the employees who are eligible to belong to that craft or class, regardless of their work locations.[13] The Board will dismiss

---

[9]Pennsylvania R.R. v. Railroad Labor Bd., 261 U.S. 72, 74 (1923).

[10]*Hearings on H.R. 7650, supra* note 8, at 57. It is also clear that opponents of the amendments understood the amendments to mandate systemwide representation, and both the House and the Senate were asked to include language allowing for less then systemwide representation. *See, e.g., id.* at 126–28 (statement of M.W. Clement, Chairman of the Committee of the Railroads).

[11]RLA §2, Fourth.

[12]*See, e.g.,* American Airlines, 19 NMB 113, 126 (1991) ("The Board has long held that representation elections must include a carrier's entire system. . . . As a consequence of this policy, when an election results in a certification for a craft or class, the certification is issued carrier-wide.").

[13]*See, e.g.,* Henson Aviation, 18 NMB 441, 443 (1991); America W. Airlines, 16 NMB 135, 141 (1989); Atchison, T. & S.F. Ry., 12 NMB 95, 110 (1985); Grand Trunk W. R.R., 12 NMB 228, 234 (1985); Offshore Logistics, Aviation Servs. Div., 11 NMB 144, 152 (1984); Air Cargo, 10 NMB 166, 172 (1983); Alia Royal Jordanian

any petition that seeks to certify less than a systemwide craft or class.[14]

Employers and employee representatives may, without the Board's involvement, agree to less than systemwide representation. However, once the services of the Board are invoked to resolve a representation dispute, such arrangements do not bind the Board in its determination of the proper craft or class.[15]

The Board's authority to identify which union represents the majority extends only to identifying the certified representative and not the people who may act for that representative. In *Grand Trunk Western Railroad*,[16] a number of locals represented different groups of employees around the system, as a result of a past series of railroad mergers. There was systemwide representation, however, in that each craft or class was represented by one international union. The employer asked the Board to identify a spokesperson for each craft or class, because the employer found it burdensome to bargain with so many different groups. The Board refused to grant the request on grounds that it was not within the Board's purview to designate spokespeople because the Act authorized it only to identify "the labor organization which represents the crafts or classes on a system-wide basis."[17]

A. Requests for Less Than Systemwide Representation

The Board will not process an application by a group of employees to be represented by the union of their choice where that group seeks representation of less than a full craft

---

Airlines, 10 NMB 389, 390 (1983); KLM Royal Dutch Airlines, 3 NMB 1, 4 (1953); New York C. R.R., 1 NMB 303, 312 (1945); Pennsylvania R.R., 1 NMB 23, 24 (1937).

[14]New York C. R.R., 1 NMB 197, 209 (1941). *See also* Galveston Wharves, 4 NMB 200, 203 (1962); Pan Am. Airways, 1 NMB 388, 390 (1945); Varig Airlines, 10 NMB 223 (1983); Delaware, L. & W. R.R., 2 NMB 98 (1952); Pennsylvania R.R., 1 NMB 467 (1937).

[15]*See infra* §IV.

[16]17 NMB 282 (1990).

[17]*Id.*

or class.[18] Similarly, where employees divide themselves, for representation purposes, into groupings that do not correspond to traditional crafts or classes, such as by department or work location, the Board will, if its services are properly invoked, invalidate such representation and order an election along traditional craft or class lines.[19] Where an unrepresented group of employees seeks to be represented, the Board will consider the wishes of the entire craft or class, even if the employees seeking representation are in a separate and distinct geographical unit.[20]

The Board adheres to the principle of systemwide representation even where a carrier has operations that are functionally unrelated to each other, so long as employees at each location perform similar work.[21]

B. Employees Who Work Under the Joint Control of Several Carriers

Although joint employer cases are relatively rare in the RLA context, on at least three occasions the Board has deter-

---

[18]In Pennsylvania R.R., 1 NMB 23 (1937), the Board dismissed the petition submitted by the Longshoremen (ILA) on behalf of 21 out of 25 freight handlers employed by the company at one location. The company had recently recognized another union as the representative of all its clerical, station, and freighthouse employees, totaling about 21,000 employees. The Board held that the 25 employees were not a craft or class, because there were other employees performing similar work elsewhere on the railroad line. See also Norfolk S., 16 NMB 355, 356 (1989); Northwest Airlines, 6 NMB 105 (1977); Seaboard Coast Line R.R., 6 NMB 63, 64 (1976).

[19]In Pullman Co., 1 NMB 503, 510 (1946), the Board rejected the grouping of employees into shop and yard employees for representation purposes, and ordered elections along six craft or class lines.

[20]The clerical employees of one airline who were responsible for operations at the only U.S. airport to which that airline flew at that time, and who were geographically and departmentally removed from the clerical staff in the sales and general office, could not select a representative on their own. KLM Royal Dutch Airlines, 3 NMB 1 (1953).

[21]In Pan Am. World Airways, 3 NMB 27 (1956), the ground maintenance and plant service employees at Pan American's Guided Missiles Range Division in Florida were placed in the same craft or class as ground maintenance and plant service employees on the carrier's commercial air transportation operation, even though there was no dispute that the operations at the Guided Missiles Range Division bore no relationship to the company's regular business as an air carrier. Id. at 30. In a similar vein, the Board refused to permit Amtrak to carve out a

mined the scope of a system for employees who were under the joint control of several carriers.[22] For example, in *Ground Services, Inc.*,[23] the employer performed operations at 15 airports under contract with various airlines. Those contracts gave the airlines substantial control over the personnel of Ground Services. Four unions represented employees at a total of six of those airports, whereas employees at the other nine airports were unrepresented. The Board found that Ground Services and the airline or airlines with which it contracted constituted a joint employer at each location. The Board thus concluded that each location was its own system. This is to be distinguished from single-carrier situations, where separate or merged entities are deemed to be a single carrier or single transportation system.[24]

Conversely, in *International Total Services*,[25] the Board dismissed an application seeking to represent employees stationed at one airport because that location did not constitute a separate system. The company's centralized management system and its use of core agreements with several airlines indicated that the system included employees working at the 110 company stations throughout the country.

III. DEFINING CRAFTS AND CLASSES

Among the factors that the Board has considered in making craft or class determinations over the years are the following:[26]

---

separate piece of an existing system, even where the new subdivision had been set up by an act of Congress. National R.R. Passenger Corp., 12 NMB 80 (1985).

[22]Donora S. R.R., 2 NMB 80 (1952); Ground Servs., Inc., 8 NMB 112, (1980); Air Cargo, 10 NMB 166 (1983).

[23]8 NMB 112 (1980).

[24]*See infra* §XIII.

[25]20 NMB 537 (1993).

[26]*See, e.g.*, Seaboard Air Line Ry., 1 NMB 167 (1940); New York, N. H. & H. R.R., 1 NMB 260, 266 (1942); Chicago M., St. P. & P. R.R., 3 NMB 120, 126 (1955); REA Express, Inc., 4 NMB 253, 267 (1965); *see* NMB REPRESENTATION MANUAL §5.1 (1995) [hereinafter REPRESENTATION MANUAL].

The Board is not necessarily bound by precedents (Chicago, M., St. P. & P. R.R., 3 NMB at 132), nor are there meaningful expressions of congressional intent on which it can rely. Pan Am. Airways, 1 NMB 381 (1945).

- Historical patterns of representation[27]
- The nature and extent of the work-related communities of interest between the employees[28]
- The similarity of job functions and the interchange of jobs between the employees in question[29]
- The desires of the employees[30]
- The present duties of the employees and their similarity to the duties of other employees[31]
- Usual practices of promotion, demotion, and seniority observed or developed for the employees concerned[32]
- The recognized boundaries of a given craft or class in the industry generally[33]

Because the Board's craft or class determinations are almost entirely fact-specific, employees with the same job title may be grouped in different crafts on different carriers.[34]

---

[27]Erie-L. R.R., 4 NMB 296 (1967); Ontario Midland R.R., 10 NMB 18 (1982); Northwest Airlines, 22 NMB 29 (1994); United Air Lines, 22 NMB 12 (1994); cf. Northwest Airlines, 14 NMB 173, 179 (1987) ("collective bargaining history alone is an insufficient basis for finding a craft or class to be appropriate").

[28]Challenge Air Cargo, 17 NMB 501 (1990).

[29]Mercury Servs., Inc., 9 NMB 104 (1981).

[30]Florida E. C. Ry., 18 NMB 460 (1991); Georgia Ports Auth., 5 NMB 269 (1970); New York Cent. Sys., 4 NMB 181 (1959); New York, N. H. & H. R.R., 2 NMB 88, 97 (1948); see also Pacific Elec. Ry., 1 NMB 289, 299–300 (1944). Whether those employees are presently represented is not a relevant consideration. Long Island R.R., 7 NMB 303 (1980).

[31]The Board typically examines both the mechanical aspects of the job and the general purpose of the work performed. For example, it has considered whether the employees use similar tools (Wabash Ry., 1 NMB 90, 93 (1938)) and whether the employees are all primarily employed to serve food and drink to passengers (Erie-L. R.R., 4 NMB 296 (1967)). Where it finds the duties of employees have changed since prior determinations, the Board may reclassify the relevant positions. Galveston Wharves, 1 NMB 274 (1943); see also Grand Trunk W. R.R., 3 NMB 216, 217 (1961); Chicago, M., St. P. & P. R.R., 3 NMB 120, 127 (1955).

[32]Long Island R.R., 9 NMB 551 (1982); Tennessee, A. & G. Ry., 2 NMB 174 (1950). Employees in the same craft or class need not have identical skill levels. Boston & A. R.R., 1 NMB 157, 160–61 (1940); Norfolk & W. Ry., 1 NMB 68, 73 (1938).

[33]Chicago & N.W. Ry., 1 NMB 327, 332–34 (1946). For example, whether and how often a certain group, such as waiters, are included with another group, such as dining car employees, may be considered.

[34]For example, the Board has in some cases recognized patrolmen as a separate craft or class. See Duluth, M. & I. R. Ry., 16 NMB 495; Texas P.-M. P. T. R.R., 4 NMB 302 (1967); Northern Pac. Terminal Co., 2 NMB 190 (1951); Galveston

The manner in which an employer groups its employees—for example, by department or for payroll purposes—is not necessarily a consideration in the craft or class determination. Whereas voluntary recognition agreements between an employer and a union do not control craft or class determinations,[35] jurisdictional agreements between national unions may be relevant to craft or class determinations.[36]

Unlike the National Labor Relations Act, which grants no representation rights to supervisory personnel, the RLA applies to those supervisors who are considered "employees or subordinate officials."[37] Consequently, the Board occasionally decides cases involving crafts or classes composed entirely of supervisory employees.[38] Supervisory employees who qualify as subordinate officials may be included for representation purposes with employees whom they supervise where those supervisory employees work along with those whose work they direct, using the tools and equipment of such employees, and working similar hours.[39] Where, however, supervisors perform work consisting exclusively of supervisory duties, those supervisors have normally been grouped in a separate craft or class.[40]

A. Applications in the Railway Industry

At the time of the 1934 amendments to the RLA, the craft or class structure in the railroad industry was the product of a history of collective bargaining relationships. Many of the crafts or classes in existence at that time, and that exist

---

Wharves, 1 NMB 274. In others, the Board found them to be part of the craft or class of Clerical, Office, Station and Storehouse Employees. See REA Express, Inc., 4 NMB 253 (1965); Norfolk & W. Ry., 1 NMB 68 (1938).

[35]National R.R. Passenger Corp., 12 NMB 80 (1985); Metro-N. Commuter Ry., 12 NMB 38 (1984); Chesapeake & O. Ry., 9 NMB 362 (1982); Union P. R.R., 8 NMB 434, 448 (1981); Chicago & N.W. Ry., 4 NMB 240, 251 (1965); Galveston Wharves, 1 NMB 274; Pacific Elec. Ry., 1 NMB 289 (1944).

[36]Union R.R., 1 NMB 336, 339 (1946).

[37]See also infra §VII.A.

[38]See, e.g., Detroit, T. & I. R.R., 6 NMB 429 (1978); but see Aerorias de Mexico, 20 NMB 584 (1993); Union P. R.R., 8 NMB 434 (1981).

[39]Seaboard Air Line Ry., 1 NMB at 177. See, e.g., Long Island R.R., 9 NMB 551 (1982).

[40]Seaboard Air Line Ry., 1 NMB at 177.

today, evolved from 19th-century rail brotherhoods, organizations of particular or generally related railroad occupations.[41] These organizations were further shaped by the collective bargaining process. For example, union agreements established rules of apprenticeship and lines of advancement among various occupations,[42] and managements recognized and dealt with certain groups as a craft or a class.[43] After 1934, these factors remained the foundation of the Board's craft or class determinations.

The Board has on many occasions stated that historical patterns of representation in the railroad industry provide the basis for its craft or class determinations.[44] The Board has generally adhered to traditional railroad craft or class distinctions, even in the face of changing technology and economics. Employer arguments that composite crafts or classes should be formed on the basis of economic necessity or changed conditions have generally been rejected,[45] even if the employer has negotiated a collective bargaining agreement covering multiple crafts or classes.[46] Small short-line railroads have been held to the same craft or class determinations applicable to large railroads,[47] even where the railroad employs as few as eight employees.[48] In fact, a craft or class under the RLA need not be comprised of more than one person.[49]

The Board has also been reluctant to reconfigure crafts or classes merely to accommodate the change from steam to electric railroads,[50] or because of differences between passen-

---

[41]American Airlines, 1 NMB 394, 399 (1945).

[42]Delaware, L. & W. R.R., 1 NMB 43 (1937).

[43]*Id.*

[44]*See, e.g.,* Ontario Midland R.R., 10 NMB 18, 21 (1982); Chicago, M., St. P. & P. R.R., 3 NMB 120 (1955); Delaware, L. & W. R.R., 1 NMB 43.

[45] Kiamchi R.R., 20 NMB 449 (1993); Dakota, M. & E. R.R., 16 NMB 126 (1989); Genesee & W. R.R., 12 NMB 261 (1985); Metro-N. Commuter R.R., 12 NMB 38 (1984); *but see* Florida E. C. Ry., 21 NMB 35 (1993) (departing from historic craft or class designations because of changed conditions).

[46]Metro-N. Commuter R.R., 12 NMB 38; Chicago, A. & E. Ry., 1 NMB 282 (1943).

[47]Dakota, M. & E. R.R., 16 NMB 126 (1989); Ontario Midland R.R., 10 NMB 18; Tennessee, A. & G. Ry., 2 NMB 174 (1950).

[48]White City Terminal & Util. Ry., 9 NMB 23 (1981).

[49]Pend Oreille Valley R.R., 10 NMB 402 (1983); Maryland & P. R.R., 9 NMB 251 (1982).

[50]Chicago, N. S. & M. Ry., 1 NMB 215 (1942).

ger subways and freight railroads.[51] However, in a few cases where the duties characteristically performed by a craft or class have become obsolete (for example, telegraphers[52] or blacksmiths[53]), the Board has refused to continue to treat those employees as belonging to a separate craft or class.

The Board has likewise been disinclined to break up or subdivide generally recognized railroad crafts or classes,[54] despite the Board's apparent authority to restructure and splinter historic bargaining groups in response to changed conditions.[55]

The following are well-recognized crafts or classes in the railroad industry:[56] Locomotive Engineers;[57] Locomotive Firemen and Hostlers;[58] Conductors (Road);[59] Brakemen, Flagmen and Baggagemen (Trainmen);[60] Yard Service Employees (Yardmen);[61] Yardmasters;[62] Clerical, Office, Station and Store Employees;[63]

---

[51]Hudson & M. R.R., 2 NMB 132, 138–39 (1949).

[52]National R.R. Passenger Corp., 10 NMB 510 (1983) (functions formerly performed by telegraphers merged into functions performed by clerks); New York & L. B. R.R., 5 NMB 331 (1974) (same holding).

[53]Railway Express Agency, 4 NMB 227 (1964) (blacksmithing duties evolved into automotive maintenance).

[54]Union P. R.R., 8 NMB 434, 447–48 (1981); Railway Express Agency, 4 NMB 227; Chicago & N.W. Ry., 4 NMB 240, 249 (1965); Union R.R., 1 NMB 323 (1945).

[55]See Arouca & Perritt, Transportation Labor Law and Policy for a Deregulated Industry, 1 LAB. LAW. 617, 645 (1985); Flight Eng'rs v. NMB, 294 F2d 905, 908, 48 LRRM 2620 (CA DC, 1961), cert. denied, 368 U.S. 956, 49 LRRM 2359 (1962); Pittsburgh & L. E. R.R., 1 NMB 115, 122 (1938).

[56]See generally NMB, FIRST ANNUAL REPORT (1935).

[57]National R.R. Passenger Corp., 12 NMB 80 (1985); Long Island R.R., 9 NMB 551 (1982).

[58]Erie R.R., 3 NMB 187, 189 (1955); Union R.R., 1 NMB 323 (1945).

[59]Chicago & N.W. Ry., 4 NMB 240 (1965); Spokane, P. & S. Ry., 3 NMB 159 (1954); Maine C. Ry., 1 NMB 111 (1938); Norfolk & W. Ry., 1 NMB 68 (1938); Norfolk & W. Ry., 1 NMB 101 (1935).

[60]New York C. R.R., 1 NMB 303 (1945); Maine C. Ry., 1 NMB 111 (1938); Norfolk & W. Ry., 1 NMB 68 (1938).

[61]Chicago & N.W. Ry., 4 NMB 240; Spokane, P. & S. Ry., 3 NMB 159 (1954); Union R.R., 1 NMB 336 (1946); Pittsburgh & L. E. R.R., 1 NMB 115 (1938); Indiana Harbor Belt R.R., 1 NMB 28 (1937).

[62]Wheeling & L. E. Ry., 17 NMB 460 (1990); Richmond, F. & P. R.R., 3 NMB 222, 224 (1960).

[63]Union P. R.R., 8 NMB 434 (1981); REA Express, 4 NMB 253 (1965); Northern P. T. Co., 3 NMB 112 (1953); Hudson & M. R.R., 2 NMB 132, 138 (1949); Chicago, A. & E. Ry., 1 NMB 282 (1943); Chicago, N. S. & M.R.R., 1 NMB 276 (1943); St. Paul Union Depot Co., 1 NMB 181 (1940); Norfolk & W. Ry., 1 NMB at 69; Delaware, L. & W. R.R., 1 NMB 43, 51 (1937).

Telegraph Workers;[64] Dispatchers;[65] Signalmen;[66] Maintenance of Way Employees;[67] Machinists;[68] Boilermakers and Blacksmiths;[69] Sheet Metal Workers;[70] Electrical Workers;[71] Dining Car Attendants;[72] Carmen and Coach Cleaners;[73] and Powerhouse Employees and Shop Laborers.[74] In addition to these well-established crafts or classes, the Board in special circumstances has held that the following occupations constitute a separate craft or class: Patrolmen,[75] Claim Agents and District Claim Agents,[76] Concession Clerks and Dishwashers,[77] and Technical Engineers, Architects, Draftsmen, and Allied Workers.[78]

---

[64]Grand Trunk W. R.R., 3 NMB 216 (1961); Union R.R., 1 NMB 336 (1946); Indiana Harbor Belt R.R., 1 NMB 28 (1937). *But see* National R.R. Passenger Corp., 10 NMB 510 (1983); New York & L. B. R.R., 5 NMB 331 (1974).

[65]Nashville Terminals, 1 NMB 361, 364 (1947); Nashville, C. & St. L. Ry., 1 NMB 285 (1944).

[66]Kansas City Terminal Co., 2 NMB 238 (1953); Southern P. Lines, 1 NMB 96 (1938).

[67]Consolidated Rail Corp., 13 NMB 298 (1966); Delpro Co., 9 NMB 85, 88 (1981); Chicago N.W. Ry., 4 NMB 187 (1960); Hudson & M. R.R., 2 NMB 132 (1949); Texas & P. Ry., 1 NMB 341 (1947); New York, N. H. & H. R.R., 1 NMB 260 (1942).

[68]Seaboard Coast Line R.R., 8 NMB 374 (1981); Seaboard Coast Line R.R., 6 NMB 63 (1976); Pullman Co., 1 NMB 503 (1946).

[69]Railway Express Agency, 4 NMB 227 (1964).

[70]Chicago, M., St. P. & P. R.R., 3 NMB 120 (1955); Wabash Ry., 1 NMB 90 (1938).

[71]Florida E. C. Ry., 18 NMB 460 (1991); Chesapeake & O. Ry., 9 NMB 362 (1982); Southern P. Lines, 1 NMB 96 (1938).

[72]Erie-L. R.R., 4 NMB 296 (1967); Colorado & S. Ry., 2 NMB 186 (1951); New York, N. H. & H. R.R., 2 NMB 88 (1948); Chicago & N.W. Ry., 1 NMB 327 (1946).

[73]Chicago, M., St. P. & P. R.R., 3 NMB 120; Pullman Co., 1 NMB 503 (1946).

[74]Pullman Co., 1 NMB at 505; Boston & A. R.R., 1 NMB 157, 159 (1940); Great N. Ry., 3 NMB 144 (1953).

[75]Duluth, M. & I. R. Ry., 16 NMB 495 (1989); National R.R. Passenger Corp., 6 NMB 216 (1977); Texas P.-M. P. T. R.R., 4 NMB 302 (1967); Northern Pac. Terminal Co., 2 NMB 190 (1951); Galveston Wharves, 1 NMB 274 (1943); *but see* REA Express, Inc., 4 NMB 253 (1965); Norfolk & W. Ry., 1 NMB 68 (1938) (patrolmen part of craft or class of Clerical, Office, Station and Storehouse Employees).

[76]Consolidated Rail Corp., 13 NMB 298 (1986); Penn Cent. Transp. Co., 5 NMB 335 (1975).

[77]Chicago, N. S. & M. Ry., 1 NMB 276 (1943).

[78]Texas & P. Ry., 1 NMB 341 (1947).

The appropriate classification of marine and waterfront employees of carriers has presented special issues for the Board, because the duties and bargaining history of these employees differ from their entirely land-based counterparts. Although it has consistently assumed jurisdiction over these employees,[79] the Board's treatment of marine employees has not been uniform. In some cases, all such employees have been treated as one craft or class,[80] whereas in others they have been divided into two separate crafts or classes: Licensed Captains and Unlicensed Deck Personnel.[81] In still others, Engine Room Personnel have been separated from Unlicensed Deck Personnel.[82]

B. Applications in the Airline Industry

1. Historical Overview. The airline industry was relatively new when coverage under the Act was extended to air carriers in 1936. Thus, whereas the NMB was able to pattern its craft or class determinations for railroads on historical industrywide groupings of employees that had a "high degree of crystallization," no similar uniform patterns were available for airlines.[83] In fact, well-defined craft or class lines had not yet been developed for some categories of employees as late as 1961.[84]

The NMB made its first reported determination of an airline craft or class in 1943[85] and its next a year later.[86] In 1945, the NMB conducted the first of its industrywide hearings into the appropriate groupings of airline employees, inviting "interested organizations" as well as management of "the 19 principal air carriers of the United States . . . to

---

[79]Georgia Ports Auth., 5 NMB 269, 274–75 (1970); Norfolk & W. Ry., 1 NMB 68.
[80]Erie R.R., 1 NMB 488 (1947); Delaware, L. & W. R.R., 1 NMB 481 (1943).
[81]Erie R.R., 2 NMB 102 (1949); Delaware, L. & W. R.R., 1 NMB 481. *See also* Erie-L.R.R., 4 NMB 193 (1961).
[82]Delaware, L. & W. R.R., 1 NMB 481.
[83]*See* United Air Lines, 3 NMB 56, 64 (1961).
[84]*Id.*
[85]Transcontinental & W. Air, 1 NMB 367 (1943) (radio operators).
[86]American Airlines, 1 NMB 371 (1944) (flight engineers).

participate."[87] As the NMB ultimately found in this first industrywide proceeding,

> [t]he most striking fact emerging from the mass of evidence presented at the hearings, and from a study of occupational representation and association for collective bargaining purposes in the air industry[,] is the almost complete lack of uniformity in these respects among all but a very few rather well-defined occupational groups.[88]

Since then, the NMB has conducted additional industrywide proceedings on a variety of craft or class issues.[89]

2. Development of Specific Craft or Class Lines. When the NMB first addressed craft or class issues in the new airline industry, it drew upon the model of its railroad experience. Thus, the NMB's first efforts to establish airline crafts or classes centered on what had worked for a different transportation industry. In the first industrywide hearings on airline craft or class issues, the NMB drew a distinction between "operating" and "nonoperating" employees.[90] Operating employees were responsible for the actual transportation of passengers and cargo using the carrier's equipment. All others were nonoperating employees.

3. Avoidance of Undue Splintering of Crafts or Classes. As is the Board's practice in the rail industry, "[i]t is a long-standing Board policy [in the airline industry] not to fragment traditional employee crafts or classes into smaller subgroups,"[91] even where other factors might support a discrete craft or class for a small group of employees. Thus, the NMB

---

[87] American Airlines, 1 NMB 394, 397 (1945) (airline mechanics, fleet service personnel, stores department personnel, and plant maintenance personnel).
[88] *Id.* at 400.
[89] National Airlines, 1 NMB 423 (1947) (radio operators and teletype operators; clerical, office, stores, fleet, and passenger service employees); Pan Am.-Grace Airways, 2 NMB 44 (1949) (flight dispatchers); Eastern Airlines, 4 NMB 54 (1965) (airline mechanics and related employees); Airline Indus. Hearings, 5 NMB 2 (1972) (considering segregation of fleet service employees from broad craft or class of clerical, office, fleet, and passenger service employees).
[90] American Airlines, 1 NMB 394, 402–03 (1945).
[91] Eastern Air Lines, 12 NMB 29, 34 (1984).

has declined to recognize a separate craft or class for crew schedulers, holding to its consistent practice of including crew schedulers in the traditional clerical, office, fleet, and passenger service craft or class, or recognizing them as part of a more limited office clerical craft or class.[92] The NMB has also refused to recognize a separate craft or class for network coordinators (individuals performing troubleshooting on communications network systems), including them instead in the office clerical, fleet, and passenger service craft or class.[93] The NMB has similarly refused to segregate data processing and communication services employees or airport operations agents from the traditional office clerical craft or class.[94]

4. Cross-Utilization of Employees. Some air carriers have cross-trained and cross-utilized employees in various job categories, extending across traditional craft or class lines. When this occurs, an issue may be raised as to the practicability of the NMB's traditional craft or class determinations. The NMB has demonstrated a strong reluctance to allow cross-utilization to interfere with or blur long-standing craft or class groupings.[95] The NMB applied a "preponderance of work" test or a "principal duties and functions" test to place cross-utilized employees into separate fleet service and passenger service crafts or classes,[96] and to find that cross-utilized ramp service employees, storekeepers, and customer service agents should not be included in the craft or class of mechanics and related employees.[97]

---

[92]*Id.; accord,* Eastern Air Lines, 5 NMB 133 (1973); Wien Air Alaska, 7 NMB 326 (1980) (airline crew schedulers); Capitol Int'l Airways, 7 NMB 234 (1980) (crew schedulers).

[93]Republic Airlines, 11 NMB 57 (1983).

[94]American Airlines, 10 NMB 26 (1982).

[95]*See* America W. Airlines, 16 NMB 135 (1989) (combined customer service representative position encompassing flight attendant duties as well as traditional passenger service duties; NMB used preponderance test to determine to which craft or class employees belonged); USAir, 15 NMB 369 (1988) (customer service agents who performed both fleet service and customer service duties).

[96]Continental Airlines, 10 NMB 433 (1983).

[97]United Air Lines, 6 NMB 134 (1977); Air Canada, 6 NMB 779, 785 (1979) ("principal duty" test applied to segregate office clerical from fleet and passenger service employees).

5. Ground Personnel. In 1945, the NMB determined that the airline craft or class of mechanics and related employees would encompass all employees responsible for the maintenance of equipment. Thus, in what came to be known as the *R-1447* craft or class,[98] airline mechanics (including radio mechanics), ground service personnel, plant maintenance personnel, and fleet service personnel (including cargo handlers) were combined. However, the NMB noted that one organization was already contending that fleet service personnel should more appropriately be placed in a single clerical, office, station, and storehouse employees craft or class.

Just 15 months later, the NMB rendered its second determination after industrywide hearings. In what has become known as the *R-1706* determination, the NMB held that the traditional railroad grouping of clerical, office, station, and storehouse employees was also an appropriate airline grouping and should include fleet and passenger service employees.[99] *R-1706* established an extremely broad craft or class of employees covering office, payroll, and accounting employees, as well as baggage and freight handlers and ticket, reservation, and operation agents. *R-1706* thus included nearly all airline classifications other than flight personnel and mechanics and related employees.

Not long after the NMB issued the *R-1706* determination, discrete subclasses of employees began to seek separate treatment. The industry was expanding rapidly, and the number of employees in the *R-1706* craft or class on the larger carriers was growing. After public hearings into the matter, the NMB held that the general purpose of the Act would better be served by recognizing the stocks and stores employees of Trans-Texas Airways and of North Central Airlines as a distinct craft or class on each carrier.[100] The NMB reached similar results in a line of subsequent cases.[101]

The breakup of the *R-1706* craft or class continued in other areas as well. In 1966, the NMB recognized a separate

---

[98]American Airlines, 1 NMB 394, 404 (1945). *R-1447* refers to the NMB's docket number in the case.

[99]National Airlines, 1 NMB 423, 438–39 (1947).

[100]Trans-Texas Airways/N. Cent. Airlines, 3 NMB 16 (1956).

[101]Western Air Lines, 4 NMB 74 (1965); Frontier Airlines, 4 NMB 174 (1968).

fleet and passenger service craft or class, although it denied that the certification necessarily constituted a determination of the appropriateness of such a grouping for future cases.[102] In 1977, however, the NMB determined that the passenger service employees of United Airlines would constitute a more appropriate craft or class than the traditional *R-1706* grouping.[103] In 1978, the NMB determined that Eastern Air Lines' passenger service employees constituted an appropriate, distinct craft or class.[104] The same year, the NMB determined that China Airlines' office clerical employees, on the one hand, and its customer service employees, on the other, constituted separate crafts or classes.[105] Finally, in 1980, the NMB established that fleet service employees and passenger service employees would presumptively constitute separate crafts or classes, and that this presumption could be overcome only by proof of overlapping duties or composite jobs.[106]

In 1982, the NMB held that an existing *R-1706* craft or class over which the Machinists had held a certification since 1952 would be divided in order to allow the Office & Professional Employees to pursue a representation application covering only Alitalia Airlines' office clerical employees.[107] According to the NMB, the 1952 certification over an *R-1706* craft or class had made sense in its time because the carrier then had a small operation, but by 1982, the craft or class had grown to more than 450 employees. The NMB stated that "[t]his growth by the carrier brings into serious question the appropriateness of the original craft or class determination."[10]

By 1982, then, the *R-1706* grouping had been replaced by separate craft or class groupings for the job classifications

---

[102]Lake Cent. Airlines, 4 NMB 100, 101 (1966).

[103]United Air Lines, 6 NMB 180 (1977).

[104]Eastern Air Lines, 6 NMB 561 (1978); American Airlines, 6 NMB 661 (1978).

[105]China Airlines, 6 NMB 434 (1978); Air Canada, 6 NMB 779 (1979).

[106]Japan Air Lines, 7 NMB 217, 222 (1980).

[107]Alitalia Airlines, 9 NMB 200 (1982).

[108]*Id.* at 223; *see also* Continental Airlines, 10 NMB 433 (1983); *but cf.* Britt Airways, 10 NMB 137 (1983) (combining cross-utilized passenger service and fleet service employees on small carrier).

originally included in the integrated clerical, office, stock, and storehouse employees and fleet and passenger service employees craft or class. The NMB has resisted most new applications of the *R-1706* grouping, even in cases where planned cross-training and cross-utilization of employees has suggested a possible need for a broader grouping.[109]

6. Flight Personnel. The Board's craft or class determinations concerning flight personnel have long separated flight deck crew members from cabin crew members. The latter group included flight stewardesses, stewards, and pursers, who were regarded as part of the same craft or class.[110] Today, this grouping is described as the flight attendant craft or class.[111]

With respect to flight deck crew members—those who serve in the aircraft cockpit—pilots and copilots were from the early years established as a single craft or class.[112] So, too, the groupings of navigators and flight radio officers were each recognized as separate crafts or classes.[113]

The position of flight engineers, who originally served as aircraft mechanics during flight and at stations, was more problematic. The Board initially placed flight engineers in the craft or class of mechanics and related employees.[114] Soon thereafter, the Board found that flight engineers performed little mechanical work but were primarily operating personnel responsible for aircraft systems control while in flight.[115] As a result, the Board placed flight engineers in a separate craft or class.[116]

The advent of commercial turbojet aircraft prompted further review of the question of flight engineer placement.

---

[109]*See* Continental Airlines, 10 NMB 433 (1983).

[110]Northwest Airlines, 2 NMB 16 (1947) (adding flight pursers to certified craft of flight stewardesses); American Airlines, 1 NMB 394, 402 (1945) ("flight stewards" comprise a "definitely established" craft or class).

[111]*See, e.g.,* Business Express, Inc., 20 NMB 324 (1993); America W. Airlines, 16 NMB 135 (1989).

[112]American Airlines, 1 NMB 394, 401 (1945).

[113]*Id.* at 402.

[114]American Airlines, 1 NMB 371 (1944).

[115]Transcontinental & W. Air, 1 NMB 412 (1945).

[116]*Id.*

In 1959, the NMB appointed a committee of three neutrals to determine whether all flight deck crew members (i.e., pilots, copilots, and flight engineers) would constitute a single craft or class or whether flight engineers would constitute a separate craft or class. Based upon the committee's work, the NMB found the determinative factor to be whether the flight engineers are required by their carrier to hold a pilot's certification; if so, they are placed in the pilot craft or class.[117] In applying this conclusion, the NMB has held that it is the carrier's requirement of licensing or certification that controls, not whether many, or even most, flight engineers happen to have pilot certificates.[118]

Other significant craft or class issues among flight personnel concerned the status of flight instructors and check airmen. The NMB originally considered flight instructors to be management officials, and thus excluded them from coverage under the Act.[119] Eventually the NMB deemed them subordinate officials, who were within the reach of the Act.[120] Instead of placing them in an existing craft or class, however, the NMB determined that they should have their own.[121] In other cases, the Board determined that check airmen—employees who conduct Federal Aviation Administration–mandated proficiency checks on flight deck personnel—should be included in the same craft or class as flight deck personnel.[122]

7. Licensing Requirements. The NMB also recognized the appropriateness of separate crafts or classes for employees who are required to have specialized education or to hold special licenses or certificates. Thus, the NMB has determined that meteorologists,[123] link trainer instructors,[124] dispatchers

---

[117]United Air Lines, 3 NMB 56 (1961).
[118]Zantop Int'l Airlines, 8 NMB 596 (1981).
[119]Pan Am. World Airways, 2 NMB 7 (1953).
[120]United Air Lines, 4 NMB 30 (1965).
[121]Id.
[122]American Airlines, 19 NMB 113 (1991); Executive Airlines, 19 NMB 455 (1992).
[123]Braniff Int'l Airways, 1 NMB 448, 453 (1947).
[124]Northwest Airlines, 2 NMB 13 (1953).

and dispatch clerks,[125] flight instructors,[126] and nurses[127] each should constitute a separate craft or class.

IV. EFFECT OF VOLUNTARY RECOGNITION ON NMB CRAFT OR CLASS DETERMINATIONS

The NMB has declared that whereas the Act does not preclude a carrier from "voluntarily recognizing a particular union as a representative of a group or groups of employees which may not constitute a generally recognized craft or class,"[128] voluntary recognition agreements do not control the Board's determination in a later representation dispute over the covered employees. "[L]egislative procedures take precedent [sic], and the craft or class must be the controlling factor in [the Board's] determination."[129]

Applying these principles, the Board refused to give "decisional cognizance" to a voluntary recognition agreement covering only mechanics and helpers in one facility of a railroad when an organization sought to represent a traditional craft or class of mechanics or related employees systemwide.[130] As the Board stated the governing principle, "[t]he Board has historically denied acknowledgement of such private agreements as regards their impact on craft or class configuration."[131] In another case, a voluntary recognition agreement covering employees in charge of locomotive engine service on a part of a larger railroad system was rejected in favor of a traditional craft or class covering those employees on the whole system where an organization sought to represent employees in the traditional craft or class.[132] The Board has also set aside a voluntary recognition agreement covering

---

[125]United Air Lines, 3 NMB 35 (1957).
[126]United Air Lines, 4 NMB 47 (1965); Pan Am. World Airways, 4 NMB 129 (1967).
[127]Pan Am. World Airways, 4 NMB 90 (1965).
[128]Galveston Wharves, 4 NMB 200, 203 (1962).
[129]Id.
[130]Seaboard Coast Line R.R., 6 NMB 63, 64 (1976).
[131]Id.
[132]Amtrak, 12 NMB 80 (1985).

a narrow classification of employees when a rival organization sought to represent a broader, traditional craft or class.[133]

Voluntary recognition agreements may be given weight in determining the craft or class, however, when they are consistent with a traditional craft or class grouping. Thus, the Board has stated that craft or class determinations may be made along the lines of voluntary recognition agreements when "the agreement . . . does not contravene Board policy regarding craft or class determinations."[134] Apparently, the Board will consider the parties' collective bargaining history in cases where voluntary recognition agreements encompass traditional crafts or classes.[135]

The Representation Manual expressly recognizes the validity of voluntary recognition agreements. Section 8.0 of that manual states that voluntary recognition can dispose of a pending representation dispute and stop the election process. In order for this to occur, (1) the carrier must be willing to recognize the petitioning organization voluntarily, (2) the group of employees at issue must be unrepresented, (3) there must be no contesting organization (or organizations), and (4) the petitioning organization must be willing to accept voluntary recognition and withdraw its application rather than complete the statutory proceedings required for certification by the Board.

V. SHOWING OF INTEREST

A. Authorization Cards

If a representation dispute arises among a carrier's employees, the RLA requires the Board to "investigate such

---

[133]Missouri P. R.R., 14 NMB 168 (1987).

[134]Union P. R.R., 8 NMB 434, 449 (1981).

[135]In Varig Airlines, 10 NMB 223, 224 (1983), the Board processed an organization's application to represent a broad, traditional craft or class of employees despite the carrier's attempt to limit the dispute to a narrower group of employees covered by the carrier's long-standing voluntary recognition agreement with the same organization. In AirCal, 17 NMB 33, 42–43 (1986), the Board processed an application to represent only a carrier's mechanics and related employees despite a voluntary collective bargaining history treating them as part of a larger employee complement.

dispute" and, following the investigation, certify the union or individual chosen to represent the employees.[136] In order to trigger the Board's investigatory powers under this provision of the Act, the Board generally requires that, where the craft or class is unrepresented, a union submit an application to investigate the dispute (Form NMB-3) accompanied by authorization cards signed by at least 35 percent of the employees in the craft or class involved in the dispute.[137] If the craft or class described in the application is already represented, the application must be supported by authorization cards from a majority of the craft or class.[138] The authorization cards constitute evidence that a representation dispute exists.[139]

The Act does not expressly require the submission of authorization cards to satisfy the showing of interest requirement.[140] Rather, the NMB requires a minimum showing of interest to authorize an election. The regulations governing treatment of authorization cards exist for the Board's own convenience[141] and may be waived if circumstances warrant. For example, the Board has dispensed with the showing of interest when the carrier's refusal to provide the required documentation made it impossible to verify that the requisite number of cards had been received.[142] The Board does not,

---

[136]RLA §2, Ninth.

[137]29 CFR §1206.2(b) (1993).

[138]*Id.* §1206.2(a). For a discussion of representation procedures following an employer restructuring, such as a merger, see *infra* §XIII.

[139]REPRESENTATION MANUAL, *supra* note 26, §6.0.

[140]American Airlines v. NMB, 588 F2d 863, 866, 99 LRRM 3450 (CA 2, 1978). *See also* Atchison, T. & S.F. Ry., 4 NMB 189, 191 (1961).

[141]Air Fla., 8 NMB 571, 575 (1981).

[142]Air Fla., 10 NMB 326 (1983). *See also* Air Can. v. NMB, 107 LRRM 2028, 2030 (SD NY, 1980), *aff'd mem.*, 659 F2d 1057, 107 LRRM 2049 (CA 2), *cert. denied*, 454 U.S. 965, 108 LRRM 2923 (1981) ("Since none of these guidelines are mandated by the RLA . . . [t]he NMB may properly assert jurisdiction without strict adherence to the regulations."); Continental Airlines, 17 NMB 432, 436 (1990) ("[S]ince the showing of interest requirement is meant to conserve administrative resources, it is a matter solely of concern to the Board and to no one else."); Air Can., 7 NMB 71, 72 (1979) ("The showing of interest requirement is designed to minimize the burden placed upon the Board's resources in conducting an investigation. . . . [I]f the circumstances warrant, the Board may dispense with the use of authorization cards as a method of establishing the showing of interest.")

however, dispense with this requirement lightly. In a case where the NMB-3 and accompanying authorization cards were apparently lost in the mail, the Board dismissed the union's application, without prejudice, even though the union submitted copies of the lost application and the certified mail receipt.[143]

Although the Board does not require a specific format for authorization cards, it has established guidelines. Each card must indicate that the employee is interested in being represented by the applicant union or desires an election,[144] although the cards need not mention the RLA.[145] The employees may sign their nicknames, abbreviated names, or maiden names on the cards,[146] and each card must be individually signed and dated in the employee's handwriting or witnessed mark.[147] The Board has dismissed applications where dates were typed or missing altogether.[148] Petitions are not acceptable as authorizations, because "collection of signatures on petitions exerts an undue influence over employees, and interferes with their ability to select a representative."[149]

The regulations provide that "[n]o authorizations will be accepted by the National Mediation Board . . . which bear a date prior to one year before the date of the application for the investigation of such dispute."[150] Once the Board determines that a sufficient showing of interest has been made, the cards originally submitted in a dispute will continue to be valid, regardless of how long the dispute continues.[151]

---

[143]Consolidated Rail Corp., 6 NMB 691 (1979).

[144]REPRESENTATION MANUAL, *supra* note 26, §6.1

[145]Duluth, M. & I. R. Ry., 16 NMB 495, 500 (1989).

[146]United Air Lines, 8 NMB 642, 647 (1981).

[147]*Id.;* 29 CFR §1206.2 (1994).

[148]Atchison, T. & S.F. Ry., 13 NMB 76 (1985).

[149]Air Fla., 9 NMB 524, 525 (1982). Cards submitted to the Board by any union or individual must be organized alphabetically. REPRESENTATION MANUAL, *supra* note 26, §5.1.

[150]29 CFR §1206.3 (1994). *See also* Air Can. v. NMB, 107 LRRM 2028, 2031 (SD NY, 1980), *aff'd mem.*, 659 F2d 1057, 107 LRRM 2049 (CA 2), *cert. denied*, 454 U.S. 965, 108 LRRM 2923 (1981) ("[A]uthorization cards must be dated within one year of the date of application of investigation, not of the date a case is docketed."); Air Fla., 8 NMB 571, 577 (1981).

[151]In one case, cards submitted in 1965 continued the dispute into 1968, despite the carrier's claim that there had been a substantial personnel turnover and

Once the Board receives an NMB-3 application for investigation and accompanying authorization cards, a mediator is appointed to investigate the dispute. The mediator's task is to determine whether there is a sufficient showing of interest to hold an election, and if so, to check the validity of the cards submitted. In order to help determine the sufficiency of showing of interest, the carrier is required to submit an alphabetical list of all employees eligible to vote in an election.[152] The list must contain all eligible employees who were on the carrier payroll on the last day of the last payroll period prior to the receipt of the NMB-3 application by the Board.[153] A list based on a payroll period that ended on the day that the application was received by the NMB was considered invalid.[154]

The carrier may not place any limitations on the Board's use of the list; the "Board is entitled to have access to and to copy all carrier records required in fulfilling its obligations under Section 2, Ninth, without condition."[155]

The list also generally acts as a cutoff for the receipt of additional authorization cards by the Board. A union may continue submitting cards to the Board until 5 P.M. of the day on which the Board receives the list of eligible employees from the employer. The union may not know, however, on which day the employer will submit its list to the Board. This is also true for an intervening union, which must intervene before this deadline. A list received from the employer by

---

an increase in the size of the craft or class in that time. Teamsters v. Railway & Steamship Clerks, 402 F2d 196, 201 n.11, 68 LRRM 2651 (CA DC), *cert. denied*, 393 U.S. 848, 69 LRRM 2435 (1968). *See also* Pan Am. World Airways, 5 NMB 34, 35 (1967) ("The Board does not require that the showing of interest in these investigations be reinvigorated because a long period has elapsed during the course of its investigation.")

[152]REPRESENTATION MANUAL, *supra* note 26, §3.6.

[153]*Id.* §3.5.

[154]Wisconsin Cent. Ltd., 18 NMB 26 (1990). On the other hand, where the employer interfered with organizing efforts by threatening, bribing, and dismissing employees, the Board allowed the cutoff date for eligibility to fall on the day before the employer learned of the organizing drive, rather than two weeks later, which would otherwise have been the proper date. Sea Airmotive, Inc., 11 NMB 87 (1983).

[155]Air Fla., 8 NMB 571, 578 (1981). *See also* South Afr. Airways, 7 NMB 352 (1980).

the Board after 3 P.M. is treated as if it had been received on the following day, and cards may continue to be submitted until 5 P.M. on the following day.[156] Once the list is received, however, the Board will not accept additional authorization cards.[157]

The mediator uses the list of eligible employees to check whether the required percentage of authorization cards has been submitted. If this initial check reveals that an insufficient number of cards has been submitted, the case is dismissed.[158] If enough cards have been submitted, the mediator must check the validity of the cards received against copies of employees' signatures, which must be provided by the carrier.[159] If a carrier refuses to provide copies of employees' signatures, the Board may dispense with the showing of interest requirement.[160]

The Board deems employees unrepresented for purposes of the requisite showing of interest if an incumbent union represents only part of a craft or class.[161] Since the Board will not certify unions representing only part of a craft or class, partial representation occurs when an employer voluntarily recognizes a union to represent a group of employees that is not a "traditional" craft or class under the RLA.[162] Thus, another union seeking to organize in these circumstances need only show authorization cards from 35 percent of eligible employees. If an incumbent union wishes to take part in the election, it must file a timely application to intervene and must also make a 35 percent showing of interest.[163] The incumbent union's showing of interest may be evidenced by a dues checkoff list.[164]

---

[156]REPRESENTATION MANUAL, *supra* note 26, §6.3.

[157]Wheeling & L. E. R.R., 17 NMB 477 (1990); Iberia Int'l Airlines, 16 NMB 490 (1989); United Air Lines, 10 NMB 508 (1983); Eastern Airlines, 9 NMB 411 (1982); British Airways, 7 NMB 441 (1980).

[158]REPRESENTATION MANUAL, *supra* note 26, §6.6.

[159]*Id.* §§3.7, 6.6.

[160]Air Fla., 10 NMB 326, 327 (1983).

[161]REPRESENTATION MANUAL, *supra* note 26, §6.601. *See also* British Airways, 7 NMB 457, 460 (1980).

[162]Air Fla., 8 NMB 571, 575 (1981).

[163]*See infra* §V.C.

[164]*See infra* §V.B.

A 35 percent showing of interest by an outside union may be sufficient where a certified incumbent union does not have a valid existing contract.[165]

Once authorization cards are filed with the Board, the Board will not accept attempts by employee-signers to revoke their authorizations.[166] The Board has refused to disregard authorizations that were allegedly obtained through threat or coercion.[167] However, employees who signed cards remain free not to vote in favor of union representation in an election.

Individuals who wish to revoke their cards must direct their requests to the union representatives to whom the authorizations were originally given.[168] The union is not obliged to act upon the revocations, but the Board has explained that the applicant organization may wish to determine whether, based on the revocations, it wishes the Board to proceed with the investigation.[169] "The free choice of the individual employees cannot be determined where revocations obtained under unknown circumstances are weighed against authorization cards similarly obtained."[170]

Because the showing of interest is not a statutory requirement, judicial challenges to the Board's treatment of showing of interest issues have been unsuccessful.[171]

All evidence submitted to the Board "in connection with a representation dispute" is confidential.[172] Consequently, authorization cards themselves and information about them are

---

[165]Representation Manual, *supra* note 26, §6.601; Simmons Airlines, 16 NMB 479, 480 (1989).

[166]Representation Manual, *supra* note 26, §6.4.

[167]*See* Singapore Airlines, 9 NMB 304 (1982); Rich Int'l Airways, 14 NMB 66, 69–70 (1986); Pend Oreille Valley R.R., 10 NMB 402, 406 (1983).

[168]*Id.*

[169]Air Fla., 8 NMB 634, 638 (1981) (citing Houston Belt & Terminal R.R., 2 NMB 226 (1951)). *See also* Western Air Lines, 4 NMB 74, 85 (1965).

[170]Air Fla., 8 NMB 571, 575 (1981).

[171]Air Can. v. NMB, 478 F Supp 615, 618 (SD NY, 1980) ("The courts have uniformly held that 'the validity of the showing of interest is for administrative determination and may not be litigated by the parties, either Employer or Union.'" (quoting NLRB v. P.A.F. Equip. Co., 528 F2d 286, 287, 91 LRRM 2204 (CA 10, 1976)); Teamsters Local 732 v. NMB, 438 F Supp 1357, 1364, 96 LRRM 2927 (SD NY, 1977); Machinists v. NMB, 409 F Supp 113, 114, 91 LRRM 2813 (D DC, 1976) (citing Switchmen's Union v. NMB, 320 U.S. 297, 13 LRRM 616 (1943)).

[172]29 CFR §1208.4(b) (1994). Guilford Rail Div., 19 NMB 32 (1991).

protected by the Board from disclosure. Indeed, the Board will not even disclose the number of authorization cards submitted by an applicant, aside from informing the parties whether a sufficient showing of interest has been made. Courts have held that all evidence relating to showing of interest is confidential commercial information, and thus exempt under the Freedom of Information Act (FOIA).[173]

B. Other Methods of Showing Interest

Authorization cards are generally the only form of showing of interest that the Board will accept before it schedules an election among employees who are unrepresented. Where, however, the processes of the Board are invoked by a union that already represents at least some of the employees among whom it desires an election, the Board has accepted other documentation as evidence of interest in representation, such as dues checkoff lists[174] or valid collective bargaining agreements.[175] Whereas a dues checkoff list has, by itself, been regarded as a "sufficient form of authorization,"[176] where a union seeks to represent a broader class the union can, if necessary for a sufficient showing of interest, supplement the

---

[173]American Airlines v. NMB, 588 F2d 863, 871, 99 LRRM 3450 (CA 2, 1978); Eastern Air Lines, 17 NMB 432, 436 (1990). *See also* Teamsters v. NMB, 712 F2d 1495, 113 LRRM 3757 (CA DC, 1983) (Board's transitory possession of address labels for ballot preparation derived from list of eligible voters were not agency records subject to disclosure under FOIA).

[174]Under the NMB's Airline and Railroad Merger Procedures, incumbent representatives of a carrier undergoing a merger, acquisition, or consolidation may file applications for representation investigations supported by other than authorization cards. In those circumstances, the NMB will also accept dues checkoff authorizations or seniority lists covering employees at any of the carriers involved in the merger or related transaction. The showing of interest for incumbent applicants in these instances will be 35% for 60 days following the NMB's determination of the effect of the merger on existing NMB certifications. After the 60-day period, absent unusual or extraordinary circumstances, the showing of interest will revert to the standard majority requirement for represented crafts or classes with an agreement in effect. For a discussion of the status of the Merger Procedures, *see infra* §XIII.

[175]*See* British Airways, 7 NMB 457, 459–60 (1980).

[176]*Id.* at 460; *but see* National R.R. Passenger Corp., 21 NMB 306–08 (1994) (incumbent on part of system not permitted to support its applications with dues checkoff list).

dues checkoff list with authorization cards signed by employees it does not yet represent.[177]

C. Participation in Election by Nonpetitioning Union

Once a petitioning organization has filed an application for investigation of a representation dispute, another organization may intervene and place itself on the ballot by presenting authorization cards signed by at least 35 percent of the employees in the craft or class.[178]

The deadline for submission of authorization cards by an intervenor is the same as that for a petitioning union. Thus, an intervenor may file its application and submit authorization cards until the cutoff date for submission of cards by the petitioning union.[179]

An intervenor is treated as a full party to a representation dispute. Where an intervenor is the only party remaining in the dispute after the original applicant withdraws, the Board continues with its investigation and, if warranted, conducts an election with the intervenor as the sole union on the ballot.[180]

---

[177]*Id.; see also* Pacific S.W. Airlines, 7 NMB 277 (1980); Varig Brasilian Airlines, 10 NMB 121 (1983). *Cf.* Northwest Airlines, 2 NMB 16 (1947) (where the union was certified to represent flight stewardesses, but sought also to represent flight pursers as part of the same craft or class, the Board used signed authorizations from the pursers, together with the certification issued to the stewardesses, to determine a sufficient showing of interest).

Where the NLRB certified a union to represent employees of a carrier that subsequently became subject to the RLA as a result of an act of Congress, the NMB refused to recognize the NLRB certification, but the NMB did accept a copy of a current and valid collective bargaining agreement in lieu of authorization cards. Air Fla., 7 NMB 162 (1979).

[178]29 CFR §1206.5 (1994).

[179]The deadline is 5 p.m. of the day on which the carrier submits the list of eligible employees to the Board, unless the list is received by the board representative after 3 p.m., in which case the intervenor has until 5 p.m. the next business day. Representation Manual, *supra* note 26, §6.3. *See also* United Air Lines, 10 NMB 508 (1983); Consolidated Rail Corp., 7 NMB 206 (1980); Puerto Rico Int'l Airlines, 7 NMB 56 (1979); Northwest Airlines, 5 NMB 250 (1976).

[180]American Inter-Island, 8 NMB 423 (1981); *see* Teamsters v. Railway & Steamship Clerks, 402 F2d 196, 202–03, 68 LRRM 2651 (CA DC) (upholding Board policy requiring incumbent union either to appear on the ballot or to forswear further representation of employees), *cert. denied*, 393 U.S. 848, 69 LRRM 2435 (1968).

VI. ELECTION BARS

A. Prior Election Bar

Where a prior representation election has been held, the Board may recognize a "qualified bar." Section 1206.4 of Board's Rules states that absent "unusual or extraordinary circumstances," the Board will not accept an application for investigation of a representation dispute among employees of a carrier for a period of one year from the date on which

1. the Board dismissed a docketed application after having conducted an election, among the same craft or class of employees on the same carrier, in which less than a majority of eligible voters participated in the election;[181]

2. the Board dismissed a docketed application covering the same craft or class of employees on the same carrier because no dispute existed as defined in 29 CFR §1206.2 of the Board's Rules;[182] or

3. the Board dismissed a docketed application after the applicant withdrew an application covering the same craft or class of employees on the same carrier after the application was docketed by the Board.[183]

The craft or class of employees and the carrier must be the same for a prior application to act as a bar.[184] Also, an application dismissed by the Board because it was found not to encompass an appropriate craft or class does not trigger the bar rule.[185]

---

[181] In cases where the petitioner union fails to obtain a majority in an election and alleges carrier interference, the Board generally does not dismiss the docketed application until it issues its decision overruling the objections. Continental Airlines/ Continental Express, 21 NMB 229 (1994).

[182] 29 CFR §1206.4(b)(2) (1994); §1206.2 contains the Board's requirement for a percentage of valid authorizations necessary to determine the existence of a representation dispute.

[183] 29 CFR §1206.4(b)(3) (1994); Lehigh Valley R.R., 3 NMB 225, 227 (1960). REPRESENTATION MANUAL, *supra* note 26, §17.1.

[184] 29 CFR §1206.4 (1994).

[185] Airborne Express, 9 NMB 151 (1981); Central R.R., 16 NMB 5 (1988).

B. Certification Bar

The Board also applies a "certification bar," meaning that an application for investigation of a representation dispute will not be accepted for two years from the date of issuance of a certification of representative covering the same craft or class of employees on the same carrier.[186] The Board's justification for the certification bar rule is that "labor stability is enhanced by providing labor and management with a reasonable period of time to establish a collective bargaining relationship."[187]

Voluntary recognition of a bargaining representative by a carrier does not bar applications for investigation of a representation dispute. The Board will investigate and conduct an election upon proper application despite a voluntary recognition of a labor organization by the carrier.[188]

C. Contract Bar

Under the National Labor Relations Act, the existence of a collective bargaining agreement in some situations bars a representation election in that bargaining unit for the duration of the agreement.[189] The NMB does not recognize any similar kind of "contract bar" rule.[190]

D. Extraordinary or Unusual Circumstances

The Board may make an exception to its bar rules in "unusual or extraordinary circumstances."[191] Situations

---

[186]29 CFR §1206.4(a) (1994); REPRESENTATION MANUAL, *supra* note 26, §17.1; Amtrak Police Ass'n, 6 NMB 216, 221 (1977); Pennsylvania R.R. Co., 2 NMB 204, 207 (1951).

[187]National R.R. Passenger Corp., 13 NMB 412, 416 (1986) (citing Jet Am., 11 NMB 173 (1984)).

[188]Trump Shuttle, 17 NMB 142, 152 (1990); Aspen Airways, 8 NMB 123, 126 (1980); Amtrak Police Ass'n, 6 NMB at 221.

[189]Avco Mfg. Corp., 106 NLRB 1104, 32 LRRM 1618 (1953).

[190]Teamsters, 10 NMB 345, 348 (1983); Oklahoma Ry., 1 NMB 35 (1937); 29 CFR §1206.4 (1994).

[191]NLRB, 39TH ANNUAL REPORT 54–55 (1974).

where this exception has been applied to shorten the periods include mergers, consolidations, acquisitions, carrier election misconduct, Board mistake, and interaction of the Act with other laws.[192] The period can be extended because of a carrier's refusal to bargain.[193]

VII. ELIGIBILITY TO VOTE

Eligibility to vote in elections conducted under the RLA is limited to individuals considered to be "employees and subordinate officials" as defined in the Act.[194] Title I of the RLA defines "employee" to include "every person in the service of a carrier (subject to its continuing authority to supervise and direct a manner of rendition of a service) who performs any work defined as that of an employee or subordinate official in the orders of the Interstate Commerce Commission."[195] Title II of the RLA extends coverage to "every air pilot or other person who performs any work as an employee or subordinate official of [common carriers by air]."[196]

A. Subordinate Officials

Although management officials are excluded from elections, subordinate officials are covered by the Act and are

---

[192]*See* Transworld Airline/Ozark Airlines, 14 NMB 218 (1987) (merger); Key Airlines, 16 NMB 473, 475 (1989); Sea Airmotive, 11 NMB 207 (1984) (carrier interference); Aspen Airways, 8 NMB 123 (1980) (Board's erroneous dismissal of Teamsters application caused Board to disregard requirements of §§1206.2(a) and 1206.4(a) of Board's Rules); Amtrak Police Ass'n, 6 NMB 216 (1977) (Regional Rail Reorganization Act of 1973 (Public Law 93-236) resulted in Board's waiver of §1206.4). For examples of situations where the Board found that unusual or extraordinary circumstances did not exist within the meaning of §1206.4 of the Board's Rules, *see* Aviation Assocs., 15 NMB 276 (1988) (organization filing application sought waiver of §1206.4(a)(3) one-year bar because organization unaware of systemwide requirement for organization of craft or class); National R.R. Passenger Corp., 13 NMB, 412 (1986) (barring accretion election because of certification within prior two-year period).
[193]Virgin Atl. Airways, 21 NMB 183, 198 (1994).
[194]RLA §§1, Fifth, 201; *see* Pan Am. World Airways, 5 NMB 112 (1973).
[195]RLA §1, Fifth. The term "employee" specifically excludes any individual engaged in the physical operation of mining, preparation, or handling of coal.
[196]RLA §201.

eligible to vote in elections conducted in their particular crafts or classes. Thus, individuals with supervisory authority may be eligible to participate in elections conducted under the RLA.

The Board has used a case-by-case approach in determining who is a subordinate official. Among the factors the Board considers in determining whether an employee is a subordinate official are (1) whether the individual has the authority to discharge or discipline employees or effectively recommend the same, (2) the extent of supervisory authority, (3) the ability to authorize and grant overtime, (4) the authority to transfer or establish assignments, (5) the authority to create carrier policy, (6) the existence and extent of authority to commit carrier funds, and (7) whether the authority is circumscribed by operating policy manuals.[197] The greater the employee's authority, the more likely the Board is to find the individual to be a management official, as opposed to a subordinate official. The Board also considers the placement of the individual in the organizational hierarchy of the carrier and any other relevant factors regarding the individual's duties and responsibilities.[198]

B. Dismissed Employees

A dismissed employee whose request for reinstatement on account of wrongful dismissal is pending before proper authorities is eligible to participate in an election among the craft or class of employees in which the employee was employed at the time of dismissal.[199] However, discharged employees who are seeking reinstatement solely on a leniency basis are not eligible to vote.[200]

---

[197]REPRESENTATION MANUAL, *supra* note 26, §5.312; Grand Trunk W. R.R., 12 NMB 228, 235 (1985); Pan Am. World Airways, 9 NMB 229 (1982); Pan Am. World Airways, 4 NMB 124, 131 (1967).

[198]*See supra* §III (subordinate officials as a separate class or craft).

[199]29 CFR §1206.6 (1994); REPRESENTATION MANUAL, *supra* note 26, §5.304; Emery Air Charter, 18 NMB 387, 388 (1991); Air Canada v. NMB, 478 F Supp 615, 616 (SD NY, 1980).

[200]29 CFR §1206.6 (1994).

C. Part-Time Employees

Part-time employees may be eligible to participate in elections, but casual employees are not. The Board has stated that "if the individual's employment is casual, that is, where the employee has no regular employee–employer relationship or scheduled work assignment, then the employee should be considered ineligible."[201]

In determining the eligibility of a part-time employee, the Board considers (1) whether the employee works an identifiable schedule during a specified time period, (2) whether the employee regularly relieves other employees, (3) what benefits the employee receives, (4) deductions taken from the employee's pay, and (5) any other relevant facts that would indicate whether the employee has a regular part-time or a casual part-time employer–employee relationship.[202]

D. Temporary Employees

Temporary employees—those who have no reasonable expectation of continued employment or reemployment in the craft or class—are not eligible to vote.[203]

E. Employees Regularly Working in Another Craft or Class

Employees who regularly work in a craft or class on and after the cut-off date are eligible unless they leave the craft or class prior to the ballot count.[204] For example, employees on permanent assignment in a separate class or craft on the election date are ineligible even if they have retained recall rights in the craft or class involved in the election.[205]

---

[201]Emery Air Charter, 18 NMB at 390.
[202]REPRESENTATION MANUAL, *supra* note 26, §5.301.
[203]*Id.* §5.302; Swissair, 16 NMB 146 (1989).
[204]REPRESENTATION MANUAL, *supra* note 26, §5.303.
[205]Trans World Airways, 8 NMB 663 (1981), REPRESENTATION MANUAL, *supra* note 26, §5.305.

F. Furloughed Employees

Furloughed employees are eligible to vote in an election in the craft or class in which they last worked, provided they retain an employer–employee relationship and have a reasonable expectation of returning to work.[206] However, a furloughed employee regularly working in another craft or class is ineligible in the craft or class from which the employee is furloughed.

G. Employees on Leaves of Absence and Probationary Employees

Employees on authorized leaves of absence are eligible unless employed by the same carrier in another craft or class or in any official capacity, or in any capacity by another carrier.[207] Employees who are receiving physical disability payments and who retain an employer-employee relationship and have a reasonable expectation of returning to work are eligible,[208] as are probationary employees.[209]

H. Trainees

Trainees are not eligible to vote unless they "have performed line functions in the craft or class as of the cut-off date."[210] Trainees who perform some line functions as part of their training program but who have not worked in the craft or class are not eligible,[211] even if the trainees are paid, receive full benefits, and are guaranteed employment by the carrier.[212]

---

[206]Representation Manual, *supra* note 26, §5.305; USAir, Inc., 21 NMB 281 (1994); Union P. R.R., 18 NMB 516, 523 (1991).

[207]Representation Manual, *supra* note 26, §5.306; Express Airlines 1, 15 NMB 311 (1988).

[208]Representation Manual, *supra* note 26, §5.311; Bangor & A. R.R., 18 NMB 404 (1991).

[209]Representation Manual, *supra* note 26, §5.307.

[210]Simmons Airlines, 15 NMB 228, 230 (1988); *accord* WestAir Commuter Airlines, 15 NMB 213 (1988); Midway Commuter, 15 NMB 278 (1988); Rosenbalm Aviation, 15 NMB 313 (1988); Horizon Air, 14 NMB 406 (1987); *see also* Air Line Pilots Ass'n v. United Air Lines, 802 F2d 886, 123 LRRM 2617 (CA 7, 1986), *cert. denied*, 480 US 946, 124 LRRM 3192 (1987) (pilot trainees not employees under the RLA).

[211]America W. Airlines, 18 NMB 140 (1991).

[212]United Air Lines, 18 NMB 181 (1991).

I. Employees Working in More Than One Craft or Class

Employees regularly assigned on the election cutoff date to an extra board or bulletined position within the craft or class involved are eligible to participate in the election.[213] Employees performing emergency services in the craft or class are not automatically eligible.[214]

J. Other Eligibility Issues

The Board has found that the following categories of workers are not eligible to vote: (1) employees otherwise eligible to vote who are working for a carrier other than the carrier involved in the dispute,[215] (2) employees of an independent contractor that is not part of the transportation system,[216] (3) employees based outside the United States or its possessions,[217] and (4) retired employees.[218]

Employees not otherwise eligible by virtue of their assignment on the cutoff date may become eligible based on what is referred to as a "preponderance" check. Where the employee has worked a preponderance of a specified time period in the craft or class covered by the application, the employee may be added to the list of eligible voters.[219]

The election eligibility cutoff date is established by the last payroll period before the NMB received the application. "[A]ll individuals with employee–employer relationships as of the last day of the last payroll period prior to the date of receipt at the NMB's offices of the 'application for investigation of representation dispute' (Form NMB-3) are eligible."[220]

---

[213]REPRESENTATION MANUAL, *supra* note 26, §5.313.

[214]*Id.*

[215]REPRESENTATION MANUAL, *supra* note 26, §5.308; Egyptair, 18 NMB 173, 176 (1991); Express Airlines I, 15 NMB 311 (1988).

[216]REPRESENTATION MANUAL, *supra* note 26, §5.309; United Air Lines, 12 NMB 218 (1985).

[217]REPRESENTATION MANUAL, *supra* note 26, §5.310; Offshore Logistics Aviation Servs., 11 NMB 144 (1984).

[218]REPRESENTATION MANUAL, *supra* note 26, §5.311.

[219]*Id.* §5.313.

[220]*Id.* §3.5.

After an election has been authorized, the Board determines whether the list of eligible voters should be updated by deleting employees who left the craft or class after the original list was prepared. The list of potential eligible voters as revised constitutes the official eligibility list following an election authorization.[221] The parties are furnished with a list of potential eligible employees and must thereafter file any objections or challenges to the list.

In the event of a rerun election, the cutoff date for the initial election will, in most cases, continue to govern voter eligibility.[222] An employee eligible to vote at the conclusion of the first election is eligible to vote in any rerun election unless the employee is no longer employed in the craft or class,[223] but an employee hired after the first election is generally not eligible to vote in a rerun. The Board may move the cutoff date in cases involving unusual circumstances, however.[224] Judicial challenges to the Board's refusal to change cutoff dates for rerun elections have been unsuccessful.[225]

VIII.   Voting Procedures

A. Preballoting Procedures

Once the NMB determines that a representation dispute exists, the RLA empowers the NMB to resolve the dispute, either by means of a secret ballot election or through "any other appropriate method."[226] The NMB usually chooses the former alternative, but it may determine the majority status

---

[221]*Id.* §11.1.

[222]USAir, 16 NMB 63 (1988); America W., 17 NMB 226 (1990).

[223]29 CFR §1206.1(c) (1994).

[224]USAir, 10 NMB 495 (1983) (complete turnover in craft or class); Piedmont Airlines, 9 NMB 41 (1981) (five-year delay between original and rerun elections); *but see* Federal Express, 20 NMB 7 (1992) (changing cutoff date without mention of any unusual circumstances).

[225]British Airways Bd. v. NMB, 533 F Supp 150, 109 LRRM 2527 (ED NY), *aff'd,* 685 F2d 52, 110 LRRM 3364 (CA 2, 1982); Air Canada v. NMB, 478 F Supp 615 (SD NY, 1980).

[226]RLA §2, Ninth.

of the party seeking representation through other means, such as a check of authorizations.[227]

Normally the NMB conducts elections by mail ballot,[228] but it may authorize a ballot box election either as the sole means of determining certification or in conjunction with a supplemental mail ballot election.[229] The mediator conducting the election is responsible for timely notifying the employees of the rules governing the election.[230] This responsibility includes requiring the carrier (1) to post notices at appropriate stations prior to the election and (2) to update the list of employees eligible to vote in the election.[231] To facilitate mail balloting, the carrier must furnish the NMB representative with the eligible voters' home addresses and corresponding address labels or compatible computer tape containing this information.[232]

B. Balloting Procedures

The NMB has discretion to decide the time period for voting. When making this decision, the NMB considers the size of the electorate, the number of stations involved, and

---

[227]See REPRESENTATION MANUAL, supra note 26, §10.3; ADMINISTRATION OF THE RAILWAY LABOR ACT BY THE NATIONAL MEDIATION BOARD 1934–1957, at 44 (1958) (During fiscal years 1935 through 1957, 619 certifications were issued based on checking employee authorization cards; card checks were used "in many cases where there [was] only one organization seeking representation of a group of employees." Id. During that same time period, 1954 certifications were based on elections). Also see Railway & Steamship Clerks v. Virginian Ry., 125 F2d 853, 10 LRRM 316 (CA 4, 1942) (NMB card check certification with two contesting unions upheld); International In-Flight Catering Co. v. NMB, 555 F2d 712, 95 LRRM 2675 (CA 9, 1977) (card check certification vacated where cards were solicited with written assurances that they would be used solely to trigger an election).

[228]REPRESENTATION MANUAL, supra note 26, §12.2.

[229]In some cases, for example, the NMB may send supplemental mail ballots to small outlying stations to condense the voting period. REPRESENTATION MANUAL, supra note 26, Appendix. In at least one case, the Board ordered a ballot box election to remedy the employer's unlawful conduct during the original election, including soliciting employees to return ballots to the employer. Laker Airways, 8 NMB 236, 255–56 (1981).

[230]REPRESENTATION MANUAL, supra note 26, §12.101-1.

[231]Id. §12.101-2.

[232]Id. §11.2.

the geographical distribution of the voting employees.[233] The Board's procedures provide that the time period should not be shorter than 28 calendar days.[234]

To ensure the integrity and security of the mail balloting process, each ballot bears a key number. This number eliminates the risk of unauthorized ballots while maintaining voter secrecy.[235] Ballots for which a challenge or objection is pending are marked accordingly.[236]

Ballot box elections pose several concerns not present in mail ballot elections. In a ballot box election, the NMB determines where the ballot box will be located, taking into consideration factors such as accessibility by voting employees and the preservation of secrecy.[237] The NMB forbids electioneering around the polling place, and agents and officers of the parties and of management are excluded from areas near the polling area.[238] In cases in which the NMB has authorized supplemental mail ballots, the NMB sends mail ballots to each employee who did not cast a ballot, including those employees who failed to appear and vote during the ballot box election,[239] after the last ballot box voting session.[240]

C. Majority Requirement

Under the ordinary NMB balloting procedures, a majority of all eligible employees must cast valid ballots in the election in order for a representative to be certified. Absent such a majority, the NMB will dismiss the representation petition.[241] If a majority of eligible employees cast valid ballots

---

[233]*Id.* §12.201.

[234]*Id.*

[235]*Id.* §12.203.

[236]*Id.* §12.205.

[237]*Id.* Appendix.

[238]*Id.*

[239]If an employee has expressed a desire to refrain from voting, the NMB should heed this wish and not send the individual a mail ballot. *Id.* Appendix.

[240]*Id.*

[241] *See* Zantop Int'l Airlines, v. NMB, 544 F Supp 504, 506, 110 LRRM 3165 (ED Mich, 1982), *aff'd*, 732 F2d 517, 116 LRRM 2030 (CA 6, 1984) ("If a majority of eligible voters does favor some representation, the NMB certifies the representative receiving a majority among valid ballots cast."); *cf.* Laker Airways, 8 NMB 236, 257 (Board required only majority of employees actually voting to certify the representative because of employer's egregious violations of the RLA in prior election).

in the election, the NMB will certify the representative that receives a majority of votes cast.[242] Integrally related to this majority rule requirement is the form of the NMB election ballot, which does not contain a space for the entry of a "no union" vote.[243] If an employee attempts to vote against a union by writing another name in the space for write-ins, the ballot nevertheless contributes to the majority rule requirement. An employee desiring no representation by any union can refrain from participating in the election by not returning a valid ballot,[244] or by clearly indicating a "no union" preference across the ballot's face.[245]

The RLA provides that "[t]he majority of any craft or class of employees shall have the right to determine who shall be the representative of the craft or class for the purposes of this Act."[246] Although this language does not specify whether certification requires a majority of all eligible voters or a majority of voting employees, the NMB has adopted the latter construction, so long as the majority of eligible voters cast ballots in favor of some representative.[247]

In an election conducted among two or more representatives, if a majority of eligible voters participated in the election but no single representative received a majority of votes cast, the NMB may authorize a runoff election provided that "an individual or organization entitled to appear on the run-off ballot" so requests in writing within 10 days of the report of

---

[242]See Zantop Int'l Airlines v. NMB, 544 F Supp at 505.

[243]See REPRESENTATION MANUAL, supra note 26, §12.102-2. In Railway & Steamship Clerks v. Association for the Benefit of Non-Contract Employees, 380 U.S. 650, 59 LRRM 2051 (1965), the Supreme Court upheld the use of elections ballots that did not contain a "no union" box. See also Zantop Int'l Airlines v. NMB, 544 F Supp at 506 (ballot did not contain space for "no union" vote).

[244]See Railway & Steamship Clerks v. Association for the Benefit of Non-Contract Employees, 380 U.S. at 669 n.5 (abstention from voting is considered a vote against representative); Laker Airways, 8 NMB at 248.

[245]See Zantop Int'l Airlines v. NMB, 732 F2d 517, 116 LRRM 2030 (CA 6, 1984); Teamsters v. Railway & Steamship Clerks, 402 F2d 196, 199 n.6 (CA DC), cert. denied, 393 U.S. 848 (1968).

[246]RLA §2, Fourth.

[247]Zantop Int'l Airlines v. NMB, 544 F Supp 504, 506, 110 LRRM 3165 (ED Mich. 1982), aff'd, 732 F2d 517, 116 LRRM 2030 (CA 6, 1984) (NMB has statutory authority to construe language of statute to permit certification based only on a majority of employees actually voting for certification).

the election results.[248] In a runoff election, the ballot includes only the two representatives receiving the greater number of votes cast in the initial election, and does not include a space for write-in votes. The representative receiving the higher number of votes in the runoff is declared the winner even if fewer than a majority of the eligible employees cast runoff ballots.[249]

IX. Postballoting Procedures

Before tabulating the results of an election, the NMB representative responsible for conducting the election must review the eligibility list and file in order to resolve all timely outstanding challenges or objections to eligibility.[250] In some instances, for example, although an employee's eligibility to vote is challenged, the employee is permitted to vote pending a determination of the challenge.[251] An NMB representative's decision on a challenge or objection that has not been timely appealed to the NMB is final.[252]

After resolving all challenges and objections to eligibility, the NMB representative combines the ballots submitted in the ballot box and by return mail, as well as challenged ballots that are held to be eligible.[253] If a ballot is returned in an envelope lacking a properly executed attest, the ballot is invalid.[254] Likewise, a returned mail ballot of an employee who voted in person or by a duplicate mail ballot is invalid.[255] "Void" ballots are also inadmissible, including those cast for

---

[248]29 CFR §1206.1(a) (1994). An NMB representative may not proceed with a runoff election without authorization from the NMB. Representation Manual, *supra* note 26, §16.0.

[249]Notice, 14 NMB 155 (1987).

[250]Representation Manual, *supra* note 26, §12.303-1. Challenges and objections to eligibility must be made in writing to the NMB supported by substantive evidence and argument. *Id.* §4.1.

[251]*See id.* §12.205.

[252]Generally, a party must file an appeal within 10 calendar days of the date of the decision letter. *Id.* §4.6.

[253]*See id.* Appendix.

[254]*Id.* §12.401-1.

[255]*Id.* §12.401-3.

a carrier or carrier official, those marked negatively (indicating no desire for representation), blank ballots, and signed ballots.[256] A write-in ballot that clearly indicates an employee's desire for representation is valid.[257]

After assessing the validity of the ballots, the NMB representative tabulates the ballots. A reasonable number of observers may witness the ballot count with permission from the NMB. Upon completion of the ballot count, the representative prepares a final report of the election results for the NMB and the participants in the election.[258]

X. JUDICIAL REVIEW OF NMB REPRESENTATION DECISIONS

A. Standard of Review

The Supreme Court in *Switchmen's Union v. NMB*[259] held that NMB representation decisions generally are not subject to judicial review. Unlike Section 3 of the RLA, which expressly authorizes judicial review of Adjustment Board awards under specified circumstances, Section 2, Ninth sets forth no basis for review of representation decisions.

Switchmen's did not foreclose all types of judicial review, however. It expressly reserved the question of "[w]hat is open when a court of equity is asked for its affirmative help by

---

[256]*Id.* §§12.402-1, 12.402-3, and 12.402-4. *See* Zantop Int'l Airlines v. NMB, 544 F Supp 504, 505 n.1, 110 LRRM 3165 (ED Mich, 1982), *aff'd*, 732 F2d 517, 116 LRRM 2030 (CA 6, 1984) ("A void ballot is one with 'No' or 'No union' written across the face of the ballot."). *See also* Buffalo & P. R.R., 19 NMB 276 (1992).

[257]*Id.* §12.403-1.

[258]REPRESENTATION MANUAL, *supra* note 26, §13.0.

[259]320 U.S. 297, 13 LRRM 616 (1943). Two companion cases were General Comm. of Adjustment v. Missouri-K.-T. R.R., 320 U.S. 323, 13 LRRM 627 (1943) (whether agreement regarding jurisdictional dispute between two unions, mediated by NMB, was contrary to RLA involved nonreviewable functions of NMB), and General Comm. of Adjustment v. Southern Pac. Co., 320 U.S. 338, 13 LRRM 635 (1943) (validity of agreement of carrier and one union regarding jurisdictional dispute that could affect work of another union's members did not present justiciable controversy because it raised representation issue within exclusive jurisdiction of NMB).

granting a decree for the enforcement of a certificate."[260] Although federal courts have jurisdiction to order a carrier to bargain with a certified union,[261] a carrier is not necessarily entitled to judicial review of an NMB certification in a union's suit to compel bargaining.[262]

In *Railway & Steamship Clerks v. Association for the Benefit of Non-Contract Employees*,[263] the Supreme Court addressed a challenge to the NMB's choice of the form of the ballot and its failure to conduct a hearing before making a craft or class determination. The Court held the Board's action was reviewable only "to the extent that it bears on the question of whether [the NMB] performed its statutory duty to 'investigate' the dispute."[264] The "failure to investigate" avenue to judicial review is narrow, however, because the Court concluded that the Section 2, Ninth command to investigate is as "broad and sweeping . . . as the nature of the case requires."[265] The Court continued that "Congress has simply told the Board to investigate and has left to it the task of selecting the methods and procedures which it should employ in each case."[266]

Accordingly, the courts have generally denied review to challenges to particular facets of a representation proceeding within the NMB's authority, such as the sufficiency of a showing of interest,[267] eligibility of particular voters,[268] procedures

---

[260]320 U.S. at 307.

[261]Virginian Ry v System Fed'n No. 40, 300 U.S. 515, 1 LRRM 743 (1937).

[262]Aeronautical Radio, Inc. v. NMB, 380 F2d 624, 65 LRRM 2522 (CA DC), *cert. denied*, 389 U.S. 912, 66 LRRM 2370 (1967). *See* Machinists v. Trans World Airlines, 839 F2d 809, 127 LRRM 2854 (CA DC, 1988), *cert. denied*, 488 U.S. 820, 129 LRRM 2464 (1988).

[263]380 U.S. 650, 59 LRRM 2051 (1965).

[264]380 U.S. at 661; *see also* United States v. Feaster, 410 F2d 1354, 71 LRRM 2218 (CA 5), *cert. denied*, 396 U.S. 962, 72 LRRM 2866 (1969).

[265]380 U.S. at 662.

[266]*Id.*

[267]Varig Brasilian Airlines v. NMB, 112 LRRM 3348 (ED NY, 1983) (allowing union to submit dues checkoff cards rather than authorization cards).

[268]Virgin Atl. Airways v. NMB, 956 F2d 1245, 139 LRRM 2541 (CA 2), *cert. denied*, 141 LRRM 2408 (1992) (proper to count votes of several dismissed employees); Professional Cabin Crew Ass'n v. NMB, 872 F2d 456, 131 LRRM 2034 (CA DC), *cert. denied*, 493 U.S. 974, 132 LRRM 2960 (1989) (unreinstated strikers remain eligible to vote); USAir, Inc. v. NMB, 711 F Supp 285, 132 LRRM 2395 (ED Va), *aff'd without opinion*, 894 F2d 403, 133 LRRM 2072 (CA 4, 1989) (excluding employees

for determining whether a majority desires union representation,[269] and the procedures used in conducting an investigation.[270] The NMB is not required to explain the reasons for its decisions.[271]

In two cases, however, an NMB decision has been overturned based on the failure of the Board to satisfy its statutory obligation to investigate representation disputes. In *Russell v. NMB*,[272] the NMB refused to process a representation application filed by an individual who stated that if elected he would decline to represent the employees and who thereby sought to decertify an incumbent union. The Fifth Circuit ruled that employees had the right under the RLA to be unrepresented

---

who transferred into craft after cutoff date); British Airways Bd. v. NMB, 685 F2d 52, 110 LRRM 3364 (CA 2, 1982) (use of eligibility cutoff date two years earlier than date of NMB decision); *but see* Washington C. R.R. v. NMB, 830 F Supp 1343, 143 LRRM 2871 (ED Wash, 1993) (NMB's action in allowing 13 former employees to vote constituted gross violation of RLA).

[269]USAir, Inc. v. NMB, 711 F Supp 285, 132 LRRM 2395 (counting write-in votes for another union toward majority of certified union); Zantop Int'l Airlines v. NMB, 544 F Supp 504, 110 LRRM 3165 (ED Mich, 1982) (same holding), *aff'd*, 732 F2d 517, 116 LRRM 2030 (CA 6, 1984); (Aeronautical Radio, Inc. v. NMB, 380 F2d 624, 65 LRRM 2522 (CA DC) (same holding), *cert. denied*, 389 U.S. 912, 66 LRRM 2370 (1967).

[270]Flight Eng'rs v. NMB, 294 F2d 905, 48 LRRM 2620 (CA DC, 1961), *cert. denied*, 368 U.S. 956, 49 LRRM 2359 (1962) (union's challenge to craft or class determination that was contrary to dominant bargaining pattern in the industry); Machinists v. Alitalia Airlines, 600 F Supp 268, 116 LRRM 3214 (SD NY, 1984), *aff'd*, 753 F2d 3, 118 LRRM 2237 (CA 2, 1985) (NMB could split single certification into three certificates without specifically deciding whether employees in new units actually supported union since no employees in new unit invoked NMB's services). A challenge to the validity of some aspects of these procedures was successful in the D.C. Circuit. *See* Railway Labor Executives' Ass'n v. NMB, 29 F3d 655, 146 LRRM 2897 (CA DC, 1994) (5–4 en banc decision), *cert. denied*, 148 LRRM 2832 (1995), discussed *infra* §XIII.

[271]British Airways Bd. v. NMB, 533 F Supp 150, 109 LRRM 2527 (ED NY), *aff'd*, 685 F2d 52, 110 LRRM 3364 (CA 2, 1982). Courts have also held that the NMB's failure to follow its own rules is not grounds for judicial review. Air Can. v. NMB, 478 F Supp 615, 107 LRRM 2028 (SD NY, 1980), *aff'd mem.*, 659 F2d 1057, 107 LRRM 2049 (CA 2), *cert. denied*, 454 U.S. 965, 108 LRRM 2923 (1981) (NMB's published rules on timeliness of authorization cards need not be followed); Hawaiian Airlines v. NMB, 107 LRRM 3322 (D Haw, 1979), *aff'd mem.*, 659 F2d 1088, 107 LRRM 3352 (CA 9), *opinion replaced*, 109 LRRM 2936 (CA 9, 1981), *cert. denied*, 456 U.S. 929, 110 LRRM 2120 (1982) (Representation Manual not binding on Board).

[272]714 F2d 1332, 114 LRRM 2800 (CA 5, 1983), *cert. denied*, 467 U.S. 1204, 116 LRRM 2393 (1984).

and that the NMB violated its duty to investigate the representation dispute. In *International In-Flight Catering Co. v. NMB*,[273] the NMB certified a union based on authorization cards without conducting an election even though the employees had been informed in writing that signing cards was only to obtain an election. The Ninth Circuit held the NMB had not performed its statutory duty to investigate the representation dispute and set aside the certification.

B. Timing and Standing

Challenges to NMB decisions may be brought by losing unions and employees. A carrier also may challenge an NMB determination in court, even though it is not considered a party to NMB representation proceedings.[274]

A judicial challenge to NMB procedures raised prior to the completion of the investigation will be considered premature if there is no actual injury.[275] For instance, the NMB's decision to conduct an investigation generally does not give rise to any claim until the investigation is complete.[276]

It has been held that NMB action must be final in order to be subject to review.[277] In one case, however, prior to completion of the NMB investigation, a carrier obtained a preliminary injunction against a particular notice the Board had directed involving findings of interference in the election

---

[273]555 F2d 712, 95 LRRM 2675 (CA 9, 1977).

[274]Railway & Steamship Clerks v. Association for the Benefit of Non-Contract Employees, 380 U.S. 650, 59 LRRM 2051 (1965); British Airways Bd. v. NMB, 685 F2d 52, 110 LRRM 3364 (CA 2, 1982).

[275]Air Fla. v. NMB, 534 F Supp 1, 109 LRRM 2924 (SD Fla, 1982), *dismissed*, 720 F2d 686, 114 LRRM 3640 (CA 11, 1983); *see also* Leedom v. Kyne, 358 U.S. 184, 43 LRRM 2222 (1958) (NLRA).

[276]*See* United States v. Feaster, 410 F2d 1354, 71 LRRM 2218 (CA 5), *cert. denied*, 396 U.S. 962, 72 LRRM 2866 (1969); Air Fla. v. NMB, 534 F Supp 1, 109 LRRM 2924.

[277]Hunter v. NMB, 754 F2d 1496, 118 LRRM 2993 (CA 9, 1985) (only final agency action if reviewable, not preliminary actions where NMB acted with one-member instead of two-member quorum); Railroad Yardmasters v. Harris, 721 F2d 1332, 114 LRRM 3214 (CA DC, 1983) (delegation to one member); Chicago Truck Drivers v. NMB, 670 F2d 665, 668–69, 109 LRRM 3284 (CA 7, 1981).

process.[278] A court may exercise plenary review of NMB determinations regarding whether an entity is a carrier subject to the RLA.[279]

XI. MODIFICATION OF CERTIFICATION

A. Amending a Certification

Unlike the National Labor Relations Board, which regularly entertains petitions to clarify or amend a certification, the NMB appears not to recognize those types of petitions. The NMB has issued no relevant regulations, and on at least one occasion the NMB explicitly refused to hear a petition to clarify a certification.[280] In that case, the NMB ruled that the petition was a request for an advisory opinion, which the NMB does not entertain.[281]

B. Accretion

In an accretion procedure, generally "an organization seeks to adjust its certification to incorporate employees in a new job classification not present at the time of the original election."[282] On occasion the Board has ordered an accretion

---

[278]America W. Airlines v. NMB, 743 F Supp 693, 135 LRRM 2064 (D Ariz, 1990), aff'd, 969 F2d 777, 140 LRRM 2765 (CA 9, 1992), modified, 986 F2d 1252, 142 LRRM 2639 (CA 9, 1993).

[279]See Longshoremen (ILA) v. NMB, 870 F2d 733, 130 LRRM 3085 (CA DC, 1989); Longshoremen (ILA) v. North Carolina Ports Auth., 463 F2d 1, 3, 80 LRRM 2930 (CA 4), cert. denied, 409 U.S. 982, 81 LRRM 2609 (1972); Delpro Co. v. NMB, 509 F Supp 468, 108 LRRM 2116 (D Del, 1981), aff'd, 676 F2d 960, 110 LRRM 2132 (CA 3, 1982), cert. denied, 459 U.S. 989, 111 LRRM 2856 (1983); Longshoremen (ILA) v. North Carolina Ports Auth., 370 F Supp 33, 86 LRRM 2774 (ED NC, 1974), aff'd, 511 F2d 1007, 88 LRRM 2863 (CA 4, 1975).

[280]Consolidated Rail Corp., 15 NMB 80 (1988).

[281]Clarification rulings have been sought from the NMB by filing an NMB-3 application alleging a representation dispute among the target employees. If the NMB declares the target group to be already represented by the applicant (or someone else), the application is dismissed. If the NMB declares that the target employees are not yet represented, the applicant may also dismiss its application; in either case the applicant has, in effect, clarified the status of the target group. See National R.R. Passenger Corp., 13 NMB 412 (1986).

[282]Hawaiian Airlines, 15 NMB 193, 195 (1988). See also Braniff Int'l Airlines, 7 NMB 96 (1979); United Airlines, 6 NMB 252 (1977); Penn Cent. Transp. Co., 5 NMB 348 (1976); American Airlines, 5 NMB 248 (1976).

procedure with respect to a job classification that may have existed at the time of the original certification but that was not included in the original craft or class determination.[283]

An accretion procedure is initiated by an organization that holds the certification for the underlying craft or class and that wishes to include the target classification within the certification. The organization must file a showing of interest among the employees in the target classification.[284] If the Board determines that the target classification is properly included in the underlying craft or class, the Board generally orders an accretion election among the target employees to determine if they wish to be represented by the applicant organization.[285] The Board has also ordered an accretion election with respect to a grouping that previously voted against representation as a separate craft or class, based upon a determination that the grouping should have been included in a larger craft or class.[286] In one case the Board accreted the target classification to the underlying craft or class on the basis of a check of authorization cards, on the ground that "[n]o organization other than the applicant claimed representation."[287]

In an accretion procedure, the Board determines the wishes of the employees in the target classification even where the Board has determined that this classification is part of the underlying craft or class, on the theory that this classification did not express its wishes in the original election.[288] The Board does not hold a representation election among the entire craft or class, even if a substantial period of time has elapsed since the original certification,[289] because the appli-

---

[283]Pacific S.W. Airlines, 14 NMB 10, 12 (1986); Piedmont Airlines, 10 NMB 504 (1983).

[284]Hawaiian Airlines, 15 NMB 193 (1988); Pacific S.W. Airlines, 14 NMB 10 (1986).

[285]*Id.*

[286]British Overseas Airways, 5 NMB 207, 209 (1975).

[287]Penn Cent. Transp. Co., 5 NMB 348, 348 (1976).

[288]Hawaiian Airlines, 15 NMB 193; Braniff Int'l Airlines, 7 NMB 96 (1979); United Airlines, 6 NMB 252 (1977); American Airlines, 5 NMB 248 (1976).

[289]*See, e.g.,* Braniff Int'l Airlines, 7 NMB 96 (accretion election ordered among target employees; certification of underlying craft or class took place in 1957).

cant was previously designated as representative by the majority of that craft or class.[290]

If the Board determines to hold an accretion election but the majority of the target employees do not choose to be represented by the applicant organization, then those employees remain unrepresented; this result obtains even though the Board has determined that their job classification belongs to the craft or class for which the applicant organization is the certified representative.[291] In a sense, this results in a splitting of the craft, but leaves the splinter group in a position where it cannot obtain separate certification because it is not a craft or class. If the Board determines that the target classification should be included in a craft or class for which an organization other than the applicant is the certified representative, the target employees nonetheless remain unrepresented unless the representing organization files an accretion application of its own with an appropriate showing of interest.[292] The Board also will dismiss an accretion application if it determines that the target classification belongs to a craft or class that is unrepresented.[293]

The Board also will dismiss an accretion application if it determines that the target classification is *already included* in the underlying craft or class for which the applicant is the certified representative.[294] The effect of the application in that case is to clarify the existing certification as including the target classification without an additional election among the target employees. The Board reached this result where it was clear that the target employees were simply new hires in the existing craft or class,[295] and where the carrier merely changed the title of employees in the target classification without substantially changing their duties.[296] On the other

---

[290]National R.R. Passenger Corp. (Amtrak), 13 NMB 412 (1986).

[291]American Airlines, 5 NMB 248.

[292]British Overseas Airways, 5 NMB 207, 209 (1975); United Airlines, 9 NMB 266, 282–83 (1982).

[293]American Airlines, 10 NMB 26, 43 (1982).

[294]Executive Airlines d/b/a American Eagle, 19 NMB 455 (1992); American Airlines, 19 NMB 113, 126 (1991); National R.R. Passenger Corp. (Amtrak), 13 NMB 412, 418 (1986).

[295]National R.R. Passenger Corp. (Amtrak), 13 NMB at 418.

[296]Florida E.C. Ry., 18 NMB 460, 464 (1991).

hand, in one case, where the target group performed the same duties as a predecessor job classification but the Board could not determine whether the predecessor classification voted in the original election for the underlying craft, the Board determined that the target classification was already included in the craft or class for which the applicant was the certified representative.[297] In that case the determinative factor appears to be that the target classification, in addition to having special duties, performed the same duties as the members of the underlying craft or class.[298]

In determining whether the target classification should be accreted to another craft or class, the most important factor relied on by the Board is community of interest.[299] This issue, in turn, is determined by the employees' duties, work environment, and degree of interaction.[300] The Board also examines factors such as functional integration and the terms and conditions of employment.[301]

XII. Termination of Representation Rights

The RLA guarantees the right of a craft or class to be unrepresented.[302] Whereas the NMB has declined to create a decertification procedure as such,[303] a craft or class will become unrepresented where an individual or a union petitions the NMB for an election and less than a majority vote for representation, or an incumbent renounces representation. There is no statutory provision in the RLA that allows a carrier to invoke an NMB investigation it if doubts that an incumbent union continues to enjoy majority status.[304]

---

[297]American Airlines, 19 NMB at 117, 126.

[298]*Id.* at 126.

[299]American Airlines, 10 NMB 26 (1982).

[300]Pacific S.W. Airlines, 14 NMB 10 (1986).

[301]American Airlines, 10 NMB 26.

[302]Railway & Steamship Clerks v. Association for the Benefit of Non-Contract Employees, 380 U.S. 650, 59 LRRM 2051 (1965).

[303]*In re* Chamber of Commerce, 14 NMB 347 (1987).

[304]The issue of court enforcement of NMB certifications and the carrier's continued obligation to treat with a certified or recognized union is discussed in Chapter 4, "Negotiation of Collective Bargaining Agreements."

The NMB has no standard procedure governing cases in which employees desire to terminate their union's representative status. Decertification has typically been achieved through a "straw man" petition by one or more employees who only nominally seek to become the new representative. The straw man must present a majority showing of interest. The ensuing election could result in decertification in two ways. If a majority of the employees do not vote for any representative, the incumbent union would be decertified and the employees would become unrepresented. Alternatively, the straw man could petition for an election, win the election, and then disclaim representative status.[305]

Through the years, the NMB has varied its response to employee decertification attempts. In the early 1980s, the NMB implemented several requirements that were barriers to the straw man procedure. First, it required any would-be "representative" to comply with the organizational and reporting requirements of the Labor Management Reporting and Disclosure Act (LMRDA),[306] and the NMB amended Section 1.01 of its Representation Manual to require every applicant to meet these LMRDA requirements within 90 days of filing an application. Second, the NMB began to impose a one-year waiting period before a representative could renounce representation.[307] Third, the NMB refused to conduct an election if the applicant did not intend to represent the employees.[308] Moreover, if an election was held, and a majority did not vote, the NMB declared that the certification of the previous representative remained in effect if it concluded the applicant had no intention of being a representative.[309] Likewise, if a straw man won the election and then disclaimed representative status, the previous certification continued in effect.[310]

---

[305]*In re* Chamber of Commerce, 14 NMB 347.

[306]Lamoille Valley R.R., 8 NMB 454 (1981). The district court later refused to overturn the NMB's decision. Lamoille Valley R.R. v. NMB, 539 F Supp 237, 110 LRRM 2835 (D Vt, 1982). *See also* Air Fla. v. NMB, 534 F Supp 1, 109 LRRM 2924 (SD Fla, 1982), *dismissed*, 720 F2d 686, 114 LRRM 3064 (CA 11, 1983).

[307]Transkentucky Transp. Ry., 9 NMB 190 (1982).

[308]Atchison, T. & S.F. Ry., 8 NMB 469 (1981).

[309]Chicago Union Station Co., 8 NMB 141 (1980).

[310]Manufacturers Ry., 7 NMB 451 (1980).

In *Russell v. NMB*,[311] the Fifth Circuit held that the NMB failed to fulfill its statutory duty to investigate representation disputes when it refused to process the election petition of an individual who sought to decertify the union, rather than actually to represent the employees in the craft or class covered by the petitions.[312] The NMB argued that its actions were justified because a basic purpose of the RLA was to foster representation of employees. The Fifth Circuit concluded that employees are also given the right under the Act to reject collective bargaining: "The Act supports but does not require collective bargaining, and in our view the implicit message throughout the Act is that the 'complete independence' of the employees necessarily includes the right to reject collective representation."[313] The Fifth Circuit therefore held that the Board failed to fulfill its duty under Section 2, Ninth of the RLA by refusing to investigate a straw man application intended to achieve decertification.

Following *Russell*, the NMB declined to adopt a decertification procedure,[314] but stated that a representative would no longer need to comply with the LMRDA.[315] Since 1987, the NMB has made clear that when a challenger petitions for an election against an incumbent, and a majority of employees do not vote for any union, the craft or class is unrepresented.[316] Moreover, the NMB will allow a representative to give up its certification freely,[317] apparently no longer imposing a one-year waiting period.

---

[311]714 F2d 1332, 114 LRRM 2800 (CA 5, 1983), *cert. denied*, 467 U.S. 1204, 116 LRRM 2393 (1984).

[312]The Fifth Circuit concluded that judicial review of the NMB was available because there was a substantial showing that the Board either violated the employees' constitutional rights or acted in excess of its delegated powers. *See* United States v. Feaster, 410 F2d 1354, 71 LRRM 2218 (CA 5), *cert. denied*, 396 U.S. 962, 72 LRRM 2866 (1969).

[313]Russell v. NMB, 714 F2d 1332, 1343, 114 LRRM 2800 (CA 5, 1983), *cert. denied*, 467 U.S. 1204, 116 LRRM 2393 (1984).

[314]*In re* Chamber of Commerce, 14 NMB 347 (1987).

[315]*Id.* at 360.

[316]Swissair, 16 NMB 192 (1989); Jet Am. Airlines, 13 NMB 96 (1986); Jet Am. Airlines, 12 NMB 301 (1985); Alitalia Airlines, 10 NMB 331 (1983).

[317]Zantop Int'l Airlines, 17 NMB 243 (1990); Japan Air Lines, 17 NMB 320 (1990).

XIII. EFFECT OF CORPORATE STRUCTURE ON REPRESENTATION RIGHTS

Corporate transactions such as mergers,[318] sales,[319] or the creation of a new carrier by an existing carrier[320] may raise representation questions about the status of unions that previously represented affected employees. However, questions concerning the effect of fundamental changes in corporate structure on existing collective bargaining agreements are outside the NMB's jurisdiction.[321]

The standard NMB certification has for many years provided that the certification applied to the carrier and its "successors and assigns."[322] Nevertheless, the NMB has never defined the concept of successorship to representation rights.[323] In *Railway Labor Executives' Ass'n v. Wheeling Acquisition Corp.*,[324] a union sought a finding of successorship against a regional rail entity that had acquired a portion of a trunk line. After a court enjoined recognitional picketing by the union and refused to order the railroad to recognize the

---

[318]*See* Air Line Employees v. Republic Airlines, 798 F2d 967, 123 LRRM 2437 (CA 7), *cert. denied,* 479 U.S. 962, 123 LRRM 2984 (1986); Teamsters v. Texas Int'l Airlines, 717 F2d 157, 114 LRRM 3091 (CA 5, 1983); Machinists v. Northeast Airlines, 536 F2d 975, 92 LRRM 3057 (CA 1), *cert. denied,* 429 U.S. 961, 93 LRRM 2734 (1976); Railway & Steamship Clerks v. United Air Lines, 325 F2d 576, 54 LRRM 2774 (CA 6, 1963), *cert. dismissed,* 379 U.S. 26, 57 LRRM 2396 (1964).

[319]Railway Labor Executives' Ass'n v. Wheeling Acquisition Corp., 736 F Supp 1397, 135 LRRM 2345 (ED Va), *aff'd sub nom.* Railway Labor Executives' Ass'n v. Wheeling & L. E. Ry., 914 F2d 53, 135 LRRM 2436 (CA 4, 1990).

[320]*Compare* Air Line Pilots Ass'n v. Texas Int'l Airlines, 656 F2d 16, 19–20, 107 LRRM 3185 (CA 2, 1981) (court lacks jurisdiction to adjudicate whether Texas International violated scope clause of pilots' agreement by creating nonunion New York Air) *with* Air Line Pilots v. Transamerica Airlines, 817 F2d 510, 125 LRRM 2777 (CA 9), *cert. denied,* 484 U.S. 963, 126 LRRM 3112 (1987) (court has jurisdiction to adjudicate whether creation of related airline would violate RLA status quo requirements, where it is alleged that new carrier would replace part of existing carrier's business and operate in same market).

[321]Delta Air Lines, 14 NMB 291, 301–02 (1987).

[322]*See, e.g.,* Long Island R.R., 4 NMB 223, 224 (1963).

[323]North Carolina Ports Auth., 9 NMB 398 (1982). *See also* Fox Valley & W. Ltd., 21 NMB 112, 127 (1994) (NMB explicitly declined to decide successorship issue).

[324]Railway Labor Executives' Ass'n v. Wheeling Acquisition Corp., 736 F Supp 1397, 135 LRRM 2345 (ED Va), *aff'd sub nom.* Railway Labor Executives' Ass'n v. Wheeling & L. E. Ry., 914 F2d 53, 135 LRRM 2436 (CA 4, 1990).

union, the unions took their case to the NMB. The NMB did not consider whether the unions enjoyed representation rights automatically under the successorship doctrine, but held elections in the normal manner.[325]

In its earliest days the NMB faced issues involving the combination of formerly separate railroads into giant systems. These issues led the NMB to develop the single-carrier doctrine, which was used to determine representation patterns following mergers, acquisitions, and spin-offs of new subsidiaries. Subsequently, the NMB published Merger Procedures to be followed by the interested parties and the Board in ascertaining single-carrier status and the representation consequences of such a determination.[326] The NMB's two sets of Merger Procedures, for airlines[327] and for railroads,[328] are virtually identical. The Merger Procedures[329] provide that the NMB will decide three issues: (1) whether a single carrier will exist; (2) which unions will survive or disappear; and (3) the craft or class lines on the merged carrier.

A. Single-Carrier Test

When a representation dispute arises concerning two related corporations, which, under Section 1, First might be

---

[325]See Wheeling & L. E. Ry., 18 NMB 38 (1990); Wheeling & L. E. Ry., 18 NMB 85 (1990).

[326]A challenge to the validity of some aspects of these procedures was successful in the D.C. Circuit. See Railway Labor Executives' Ass'n v. NMB, 29 F3d 655, 146 LRRM 2897 (CA DC, 1994) (5–4 en banc decision), cert. denied, 148 LRRM 2832 (1995), discussed infra §XIII.B.

[327]NMB, Procedures for Handling Representation Issues Resulting from Mergers, Acquisitions or Consolidations in the Airline Industry, 14 NMB 388 (July 31, 1987) [hereinafter Airline Merger Procedures].

[328]NMB, Procedures for Handling Representation Issues Resulting from Mergers, Acquisitions or Consolidations in the Railroad Industry, 17 NMB 44 (Nov 27, 1989) [hereinafter Railroad Merger Procedures].

[329]Under the NMB's Merger Procedures, incumbent representatives of a carrier undergoing a merger, acquisition, or consolidation may file applications for representation investigations supported by other than authorization cards. In those circumstances, the NMB will also accept dues checkoff authorizations or seniority lists covering employees at any of the carriers involved in the merger or related transaction. The showing of interest for incumbent applicants in these instances will be 35% for 60 days following the NMB's determination of the effect of the merger on existing NMB certifications. After the 60-day period, absent unusual or

deemed a carrier either jointly or separately, the NMB must define the scope of the craft or class by determining whether the two carriers should be treated jointly or separately for representation purposes.[330]

In its First Annual Report, the Board stated:

> The Board has ruled generally that where a subsidiary corporation reports separately to the Interstate Commerce Commission, and keeps its own pay roll and seniority rosters, it is a carrier as defined in the Act, and its employees are entitled to representation separate from other carriers who may be connected with the same railroad system. If the operations of a subsidiary are jointly managed with operations of other carriers and the employees have also been merged and are subject to the direction of a single management, then the larger unit of management is taken to be the carrier rather than the individual subsidiary companies.[331]

In a number of early NMB cases, separate reporting to the ICC was held conclusive proof that the merged railroads were still separate carriers.[332] However, over time, the merger of management and employees into a single operating unit came to be determinative, and separate ICC reporting became secondary.[333] Single-carrier status was determined by looking at integrated operations, finances, schedules, and facilities; interlining or leasing agreements; interchange of personnel and maintenance work; common ownership, officers, and

---

extraordinary circumstances, the showing of interest will revert to the standard 50%+ requirement for represented crafts or classes with an agreement in effect. For the status of the Merger Procedures, see *infra* §XIII.B, notes 35–54 and accompanying text.

[330]RLA §1, First defines a "carrier" for jurisdictional purposes to include any entity that is owned or controlled by a carrier or under common control with a carrier that performs services in connection with transportation. This section does not specify whether related entities must be combined or held separate for representation purposes.

[331]NMB, FIRST ANNUAL REPORT 22 (1935), quoted in New York & L. B. R.R., 5 NMB 331, 333 (1974); Donora S. R.R., 2 NMB 80, 83 (1952); New York C. R.R., 1 NMB 197, 205 (1941), *aff'd sub nom.* Switchmen's Union v. NMB, 135 F2d 785 (CA DC), *rev'd on other grounds*, 320 U.S. 297, 13 LRRM 616 (1943).

[332]*E.g.*, St. Louis-S.W. Sys., NMB Case No. R-54 (1934); New York, C. & St. L. R.R., 1 NMB 1 (1935); Donora S. R.R., 2 NMB at 83.

[333]Maine C. R.R., 4 NMB 290 (1967); San Antonio, U. & G. R.R., 2 NMB 157, 166–67 (1950).

employees; sharing of payroll and computer facilities; and the history of collective bargaining.[334] The unification of labor policy outweighed other facts that might lead to a different conclusion, including the fact that the employees of the two consolidated companies had separate collective bargaining agreements.[335]

In *Republic Airlines*,[336] the NMB announced its policy not to foster multiple bargaining units in a deregulated airline industry if separate bargaining units would detract from rational labor–management relations. It compared the railroad industry, where a long history of mergers and acquisitions had resulted in complex railroad systems. Since the NMB's processes were not always invoked, rail employees in the same craft or class sometimes continued to have separate representatives, even if operations were integrated. The NMB stated in *Republic* that "[t]he pattern of representation which has resulted in the railroad industry has, in the Board's judgment led to uneven representation, duplication of effort, and confusion; and has significantly reduced the ability of railroads to integrate operations and manage a single rail system."[337]

Following *Republic*, the Board stated that examination of the traditional factors (ICC reporting, separate payroll, and separate seniority rosters) is only the starting point for determining the representational aspects of contemporary mergers and acquisitions. Other facts and circumstances are also relevant. In one case,[338] the only factors indicating the separate status were the maintenance of separate seniority lists and labor contracts. These factors were outweighed by the fact that labor relations were handled jointly, not locally. Consequently, the NMB found single-carrier status.[339] In other cases, however, the NMB has found that separate-carrier status remained among commonly owned rail carriers,

---

[334]Air Fla., 7 NMB 61 (1979).

[335]Airlift Int'l, Inc., 4 NMB 142 (1967); New York & L. B. R.R., 5 NMB 331 (1974).

[336]8 NMB 49 (1980).

[337]*Id.* at 54.

[338]Seaboard, 11 NMB 217 (1984).

[339]*Id. See also* National R.R. Passenger Corp., 12 NMB 80 (1985); Texas P.-M. P. T. R.R., 11 NMB 245 (1984).

even after many aspects of related railroads' operations were combined.[340]

In *Trans World Airlines/Ozark Airlines*,[341] the Board articulated the single-carrier test that it has repeated in subsequent railroad and airline single-carrier cases:[342]

> whether the two systems are held out to the public as a single carrier[;] . . . whether a combined schedule is published; how the carrier advertises its services; whether reservation systems are combined; whether tickets are issued on one carrier's stock; if signs, logos and other publicly visible indicia have been changed to indicate only one carrier's existence; whether personnel with public contact were held out as employees of one carrier; and whether the process of repainting planes and other equipment, to eliminate indications of separate existence, has been progressed.[343]

The Board also seeks to determine if the carriers have combined their operations from a managerial and labor relations perspective. The Board investigates whether labor relations and personnel functions are handled by one carrier; whether the carriers have a common management, common corporate officers, and interlocking boards of directors; whether there is a combined workforce; and whether separate identities are maintained for corporate and other purposes.

The NMB has also found a single carrier to exist despite the absence of a corporate merger. When Midway acquired

---

[340]Winston Salem Southbound Ry., 11 NMB 255 (1984). In Ogden Union Ry. & Depot Co., 12 NMB 48 (1984), and in Western P. R.R., 12 NMB 160 (1985), the Board found that subsidiaries of Union Pacific retained their identities as separate carriers, based on the fact that they had their own ICC reporting, accounting, payroll, labor agreements, and seniority rosters. Labor relations at Western Pacific were handled in the initial stages locally but at the highest levels were controlled by a single director of Union Pacific.

[341]14 NMB 218 (1987).

[342]Guilford Transp. Indus., 18 NMB 413 (1991); Burlington N. Ry., 18 NMB 240 (1991); Metroflight, Inc., 18 NMB 56 (1990); Detroit & T. Shore Line R.R., 17 NMB 282 (1990); Central R.R./Norfolk S. R.R. Subsidiaries, 16 NMB 5 (1988); USAir, Inc., 16 NMB 412 (1989); Federal Express Corp., 16 NMB 433 (1989); USAir, Inc., 15 NMB 135 (1988); Braniff, 15 NMB 294 (1988); Alaska Airlines, 15 NMB 42 (1987); Delta Air Lines, 14 NMB 291 (1987); Delta Air Lines, 14 NMB 443 (1987); American Airlines, 14 NMB 379 (1987); Missouri P. R.R. (Union Pacific), 14 NMB 417 (1987).

[343]Trans World Airlines/Ozark Airlines, 14 NMB at 236.

Air Florida,[344] Air Florida operations generally were subsumed within Midway, but the former Air Florida maintenance operation was spun off into a separately incorporated aircraft maintenance facility that marketed its services to Midway and other customers. The Board decided sua sponte to include the maintenance subsidiary as part of the single carrier along with Midway and the rest of Air Florida.

In the *Guilford* case,[345] the NMB found that a number of Guilford-owned railroads and the several small, commonly owned railroads that operated as part of the Guilford system constituted a single carrier. The NMB found that since operations were centralized, marketed, and held out as the Guilford system, that system was a single carrier.[346] Similarly, the NMB found Precision Valley Aviation and Northeast Express Regional Airlines to be a single carrier even though the carriers had not merged and were not completely commonly owned.[347] The NMB relied heavily on the centralization and combination of operations.

In *USAir/Shuttle,*[348] the NMB found that USAir and the former Trump Shuttle comprised a single carrier even though the airlines were not commonly owned, because USAir had taken over management of all aspects of the Shuttle's operations.

B. Carrier Petitions for Investigation

Unlike in all other representation disputes, which must be initiated by a labor organization, a carrier facing a relevant change in corporate structure may, according to the NMB Merger Procedures, petition for investigation of a merger representation dispute.[349] A carrier files with the Board at the time it applies to the Department of Transportation (DOT) or

---

[344]Midway Airlines, 14 NMB 447 (1987).

[345]Guilford Transp. Indus., 18 NMB 113, 18 NMB 413 (1991).

[346]The NMB subsequently invalidated the Terminal Railroad's simplified craft structure, however, and conducted elections on a multicraft basis.

[347]Precision Valley Aviation, 20 NMB 619 (1993).

[348]19 NMB 388 (1992).

[349]Airline Merger Procedures, *supra* note 327, at 393; Railroad Merger Procedures, *supra* note 328, at 53–54.

the ICC for approval of a transaction.[350] The carrier must state whether it intends to operate as a single transportation system or as separate systems. If the carrier does not intend to effect an operational merger immediately after obtaining DOT or ICC approval, but determines to do so at some later time, the carrier must again invoke the NMB's services at that later time, prior to the operational merger.

The D.C. Circuit has held that the NMB's investigation of representation matters may be commenced only at the request of employees in the applicable craft or class or by labor organizations acting on the employees' behalf.[351] Accordingly, that court concluded that the NMB's Railroad Merger Procedures are invalid to the extent that they permit representation investigations to be triggered by carrier requests or sua sponte by the NMB.[352] The District of Columbia district court previously had held that the NMB's Airline Merger Procedures (which contained provisions identical to the railroad procedures invalidated by the D.C. Circuit) were not subject to judicial review.[353]

The NMB has not determined what, if any, modifications will be made to the Railroad or Airline Merger Procedures. As a consequence, it is not currently established whether the industry merger practices in effect prior to the NMB Merger Procedures will be applicable nationwide,[354] or whether the

---

[350]As a result of transfer of statutory authority for antitrust review of airline transactions, 49 USC §1378(b), the triggering event requiring an airline petition is now uncertain.

[351]Railway Labor Executives' Ass'n v. NMB, 29 F3d 655, 146 LRRM 2897 (CA DC, 1994) (5–4 en banc decision), cert. denied, 148 LRRM 2832 (1995).

[352]29 F3d at 669.

[353]Teamsters v. NMB, 136 LRRM 2193 (D DC, 1990).

[354]Air Line Employees v. Republic Airlines, 798 F2d 967, 123 LRRM 2437 (CA 7), cert. denied, 479 U.S. 962, 123 LRRM 2984 (1986); Teamsters v. Texas Int'l Airlines, 717 F2d 157, 114 LRRM 3091 (CA 5, 1983); Air Line Pilots v. Texas Int'l Airlines, 656 F2d 16 (CA 2, 1981); Machinists v. Northeast Airlines, 536 F2d 975, 92 LRRM 3057 (CA 1), cert. denied, 429 U.S. 961, 93 LRRM 2734 (1976); Railway & Steamship Clerks v. United Air Lines, 325 F2d 576, 54 LRRM 2774 (CA 6, 1963), cert. dismissed, 379 U.S. 26, 57 LRRM 2396 (1964); Northwest Airlines, 13 NMB 399 (1986); Republic Airlines, 7 NMB 21 (1980); Pan Am. World Airways, 7 NMB 225 (1980).

NMB will treat the Merger Procedures as applicable outside the D.C. Circuit.

C. Union Certification Following a Transaction

Prior to the NMB's development of the Merger Procedures, in some transactions involving the combination of two or more carriers into a single carrier, the surviving carrier would unilaterally treat the representation certifications of the unions at the disappearing carriers as if they were extinguished by operation of law. If one of those unions wished to challenge that action by the carrier, the union's recourse was to ask the NMB to investigate a representation dispute.[355] Under the Merger Procedures, however, union certifications following a transaction are extinguished only by order of the NMB following an investigation.[356] Now, the certifications of the minority unions apparently may remain in effect until "on or after" the date of the NMB's single-carrier decision.[357] Where the size of merged employee groups is "comparable," certifications remain in effect pending the results of an election.[358]

Unions that will disappear may get an expedited election in the combined craft or class upon a 35 percent showing of interest (all employees whom the union represented prior to the merger are included automatically).[359] However, if the Board finds that two employee groups with different incum-

---

[355]*See* Air Line Employees Ass'n v. Republic Airlines, 798 F2d 967, 123 LRRM 2437; IBT v. Texas Int'l Airlines, 717 F2d 157, 114 LRRM 3091; Machinists v. Northeast Airlines, 536 F2d 975, 92 LRRM 3057; Railway & Steamship Clerks v. United Air Lines, 325 F2d 576, 54 LRRM 2774.

[356]Republic Airlines, 8 NMB 49 (1980).

[357]Airline Merger Procedures, *supra* note 327, at 391; Railroad Merger Procedures, *supra* note 328, at 51.

[358]Federal Express Corp., 16 NMB 433 (1989); USAir, Inc., 16 NMB 412 (1989). *See also* Missouri P. R.R., 15 NMB 95 (1988); Union P. R.R., 15 NMB 247 (1988) (NMB held in place certificate of two rail unions after single-carrier determination had been made, even though one of unions was as practical matter defunct).

[359]Airline Merger Procedures, *supra* note 327, at 391; Railroad Merger Procedures, *supra* note 328, at 51–52.

bent representatives are comparable in size, the Board may order an election without any showing of interest by the employees.[360] The NMB has not set a specific percentage to define comparability.[361]

D. Unresolved Issues

Even if the NMB's Merger Procedures remain in effect, they may not apply to transactions where an airline or railroad operates a second carrier separately. In two decisions predating the adoption of the Merger Procedures,[362] the NMB has decided that there is no representation issue properly before the Board in such a case unless a union representing employees on one of the carriers furnishes a showing of interest.

Another unresolved issue is the bargaining pattern that must result if different subunits of the same union represented employees prior to the single-carrier finding. Multiple general chairs or committees of the same international union have sometimes continued to represent and bargain for employees in the territories of the predecessor railroads, and affected railroads have asked the NMB to declare that the unions must act through a single representative. After finding single-carrier status in *Grand Trunk Western*[363] and *Burlington Northern*,[364] the Board resolved any representation questions where different unions represented the employees in the same craft. Where multiple general chairs of the same inter-

---

[360]The Teamsters challenged the Board's authority to forgo the showing of interest, but the NMB was upheld in Teamsters v. NMB, 136 LRRM 2193 (D DC, 1990).

[361]Comparability has not been found where one group comprised only 31% of the total. Federal Express Corp., 16 NMB at 442, 451–52 (42 Federal Express flight planners "substantially outnumber [ed]" their 19 counterparts at Flying Tigers); *compare* Command Airways, 18 NMB 372, 376 (1991) (flight attendants comparable where one group numbered 76 and the other 84) *with* Continental Airlines/Continental Express, 20 NMB 582 (1993) (flight attendants not comparable where one group numbered 6994 and the other 423) *and* Continental Airlines/Continental Express, 20 NMB 580 (1993) (flight dispatchers not comparable where one group numbered 65 and the other 26).

[362]Transamerica Airlines/Trans Int'l Airlines, 12 NMB 204 (1985); Overseas Nat'l Airlines, 12 NMB 269 (1985).

[363]Grand Trunk W. R.R., 17 NMB 282, 304 (1990).

[364]Burlington N. Ry., 18 NMB 240, 244, 261–62 (1991).

national enjoyed bargaining rights under the union constitution on a regional basis, however, the NMB refused to identify a single union "spokesperson," stating that "it is not within the purview of the Board to designate specific individuals to act on behalf of labor organizations."[365]

---

[365]Grand Trunk W. R.R., 17 NMB at 304.

CHAPTER 3

PROTECTION OF EMPLOYEES' RIGHT OF SELF-ORGANIZATION

I. STATUTORY FRAMEWORK

The Act's protection of employees' right of self-organization affects the legal relations among carriers, organizations and employees in three distinct phases: while employees are seeking to organize or to replace or displace an incumbent representative; during the ongoing relationship between a carrier, the employees and their representative; and during periods of self-help. This chapter discusses the first two of these phases. Chapter 6 deals with the ways in which the Act's prohibitions on interference affect the right to engage in self-help.

A. 1926 Act—Section 2, Third

As enacted in 1926, the RLA contained a single provision that protected the right of self-organization: Section 2, Third. This provision safeguarded the right of the "respective parties" to designate representatives in such manner as may be provided in their corporate organization or unincorporated association, or by other means of collective action, without interference, influence, or coercion exercised by either party over the self-organization or designation of representatives by the other.[1]

---

[1]Railway Labor Act, Pub. L. No. 257, 44 Stat. 577 (1926); see Texas & N.O. R.R.v. Railway & Steamship Clerks, 281 U.S. 548, 559 (1930).

In *Texas & New Orleans Railroad v. Railway & Steamship Clerks*,[2] the Supreme Court held that Section 2, Third was constitutional, and that it imposed legal obligations enforceable in the courts. The lawsuit was brought by a national rail union, which had been recognized by the carrier as the representative of its clerical employees, seeking to enjoin the carrier from interfering with the employees' choice of representative and from dealing with another organization. The lower courts found that the latter organization had been established with the assistance of the carrier in order to enable it to conclude a more favorable wage agreement than was being demanded by the national union. The Supreme Court upheld an injunction and a contempt order against the carrier, requiring it to cease from interfering with the employees' free choice of representative, to disestablish the newly created organization, and to reinstate officers of the national union and other employees who had been discharged in consequence of their activities on behalf of the national union.[3] In doing so the Court made the following observation:

> Freedom of choice in the selection of representatives on each side of the dispute is the essential foundation of the statutory scheme. All the proceedings looking to amicable adjustments and to agreements for arbitration of disputes, the entire policy of the act, must depend for success on the uncoerced action of each party through its own representatives to the end that agreements satisfactory to both may be reached and the peace essential to the uninterrupted service of the instrumentalities of interstate commerce may be maintained.[4]

B. 1934 Amendments—Statement of Purpose

In 1934, the Act was amended, in part to strengthen employees' right to organize without carrier interference[5] and

---

[2]281 U.S. 548.

[3]*Id.; see also* opinions below: Railway & Steamship Clerks v. Texas & N.O. R.R., 24 F2d 426, 25 F2d 873, 876 (SD Tex, 1928); Texas & N.O. R.R. v. Railway & Steamship Clerks, 33 F2d 13 (CA 5, 1929).

[4]Texas & N.O. R.R.v. Railway & Steamship Clerks, 281 U.S. at 569.

[5]*See* Virginian Ry. v. System Fed'n, 300 U.S. 515, 543, 1 LRRM 743, 745 (1937); Pub. L. No. 442, 48 Stat. 1185, 1187–88 (1934).

in part to "strengthen the position of the labor organizations *vis-a-vis* the carriers, to the end of furthering the success of the basic congressional policy of self-adjustment of the industry's labor problems between carrier organizations and effective labor organizations."[6]

The 1934 amendments added to the Act a statement of purposes in Section 2, including the following: "(2) to forbid any limitation upon freedom of association among employees or any denial, as a condition of employment or otherwise, of the right of employees to join a labor organization" and "(3) to provide for the complete independence of carriers and of employees in the matter of self-organization to carry out the purposes" of the Act.[7] In furtherance of these purposes, Section 2, Third was modified and expanded, and Section 2, Fourth, Fifth, Eighth, Ninth, and Tenth were added to the Act.

C. Section 2, Third

As modified by the 1934 amendments, Section 2, Third continues to prohibit "interference, influence or coercion by either party over the designation of representatives by the other."[8] It specifies that "neither party shall in any way interfere with, influence, or coerce the other in its choice of representatives." In addition, whereas the original Section 2, Third protected organizations and employers, the new provision granted a right to the carrier's employees, namely, the right to designate, without "interference, influence, or coercion" by the carrier, representatives "who or which are not employees of the carrier."

---

[6]Machinists v. Street, 367 U.S. 740, 759, 48 LRRM 2345 (1961).

[7]RLA §2(2), (3).

[8]The 1934 amendments deleted from §2, Third the earlier prohibition on interference with selection of the other party's representatives "in the manner provided" in the corporate or association governing documents. However, §2, Third continues to protect carriers from interference by unions in the carriers' choice of representatives.

D. Section 2, Fourth

Section 2, Fourth was added to the Act by the 1934 amendments. It elaborates on employees' rights, setting forth that employers may not interfere with

- employees' right to organize or to remain unorganized,
- employees' right to bargain collectively through representatives of their own choosing, and
- the right of a majority of any craft or class to select the representative of that craft or class.

Section 2, Fourth prohibits a carrier or its officers or agents from denying or in any way questioning the right of its employees to join, organize, or assist the labor organization of their choice. The section also prohibits a carrier from using its funds to maintain, assist, or contribute to a "labor organization, labor representative, or other agency of collective bargaining, or in performing any work therefor." This paragraph further provides that it is unlawful for a carrier "to influence or coerce employees in an effort to induce them to join or remain or not to join or remain members of any labor organization." A proviso states that the Act does not prohibit a carrier from permitting an employee or local representatives of employees from conferring with management during working hours or from furnishing free transportation to employees "while engaged in the business of a labor organization."[9]

E. Section 2, Fifth

Section 2, Fifth of the Act, another feature of the 1934 amendments, prohibits a carrier from requiring prospective

---

[9]As originally enacted, §2, Fourth also prohibited a carrier from collecting dues, fees, or assessments on behalf of a union: "[I]t shall be unlawful for any carrier . . . to deduct from the wages of any employees any dues, fees, assessments, or other contributions. . . ." This bar was removed with the addition of §2, Eleventh to the Act in 1951. See RLA §2, Eleventh; see also infra §X.

employees "to sign any contract or agreement promising to join or not to join a labor organization."[10]

F. Section 2, Eighth

Section 2, Eighth, also added by the 1934 amendments, requires carriers to post notices in the form specified by the NMB. These notices must set forth the provisions of Section 2, Third, Fourth, and Fifth and state that "all disputes between the carrier and its employees will be handled in accordance with the provisions" of the Act. Section 2, Eighth further provides that "the provisions of . . . [Section 2, Third, Fourth, and Fifth] are made part of the contract of employment between the carrier and each employee, and shall be binding upon the parties, regardless of any other express or implied agreement between them."[11]

G. Section 2, Ninth

Section 2, Ninth of the Act, also added in 1934, provided a new method to determine employees' choice of representatives. It charged the newly created National Mediation Board (NMB) with the duty, inter alia, to resolve disputes among a carrier's employees as to the identity of their representative. This provision obligates the carrier to "treat with the representative so certified as the representative of the craft or class for the purposes of the RLA." Section 2, Ninth authorizes the NMB "to take a secret ballot of the employees involved, or to utilize any other appropriate method of ascertaining the names of their duly designated and authorized representatives in such manner as shall insure the choice of representatives by the employees without interference, influence or coercion exercised by the carrier." The section also authorizes

---

[10]Section 3 of the Norris-LaGuardia Act, 29 USC §103, enacted in 1932, had declared such "yellow dog" contracts to be contrary to public policy and unenforceable in federal courts. Section 2, Fifth of the RLA went further by prohibiting a carrier from requiring such agreements and by mandating carriers to discard such agreements if in force as of the effective date of the 1934 amendments.

[11]See also 29 CFR §1205.1 (1994).

the Board to designate who may participate in an election and to establish the rules for an election.[12]

H. Section 2, Tenth

The 1934 amendments also added Section 2, Tenth to the RLA, creating criminal penalties on carriers and their officers or agents for "willful failure or refusal . . . to comply with the terms" of Section 2, Third, Fourth, Fifth, Seventh, or Eighth. Section 2, Tenth also imposes upon "any United States attorney to whom any duly designated representative of a carrier's employees may apply" the "duty . . . to institute in the proper court and to prosecute under the direction of the Attorney General of the United States, all necessary proceedings for the enforcement of the provisions of" Section 2 of the Act "and for the punishment of all violations thereof." This includes civil, as well as criminal, proceedings.[13]

II. PREEMPLOYMENT PROTECTION OF THE RIGHT OF SELF-ORGANIZATION

The Act affords only limited protection of the right of self-organization prior to the creation of an employer–employee relationship. Section 2, Fifth prohibits carriers from requiring "any person seeking employment to sign any contract or agreement promising to join or not to join a labor organization." Section 2, Eighth states that this provision, like several others in Section 2, is "made a part of the contract of employment between the carrier and each employee."

Section 2, Fifth, like the other 1934 additions to the Act, is intended "to advance the maintenance of effective labor organizations."[14] However, the only appellate court decisions construing Section 2, Fifth have stressed that it narrowly

---

[12]*See* Chapter 4, "Negotiation of Collective Bargaining Agreements," §I for a discussion of the obligation to "treat" or negotiate with the employees' representative.

[13]Railway & Steamship Clerks v. Florida E.C. Ry., 384 U.S. 238, 242, 62 LRRM 2177, 2178 (1966).

[14]Air Line Pilots Ass'n v. United Air Lines, 802 F2d 886, 915, 123 LRRM 2617, 2638 (CA 7, 1986), *cert. denied*, 480 U.S. 946, 124 LRRM 3192 (1987).

encompasses agreements or promises with respect to the choice of joining labor organizations and does not incorporate protections against interference in self-organization and the choice of representatives embodied in Section 2, Third and Fourth, such as the right to strike.[15]

III. JUDICIAL PROTECTION OF EMPLOYEES' RIGHT OF SELF-ORGANIZATION

A. Jurisdiction

The 1934 amendments added administrative procedures to the Act to protect employees against carrier interference with the right to organize or to refrain from organizing.[16] Nonetheless, the courts have in general continued to recognize a private right of action to enforce the right to organize without carrier interference.[17] The first such case in the Supreme Court, *Virginian Railway v. System Federation*,[18] upheld the power of the courts to compel a carrier to treat with a union certified by the NMB under the recently created procedures of Section 2, Ninth.

Subsequently, the courts have generally accepted jurisdiction of actions brought against carriers for interference with employees' rights under RLA Sections 2, Third and Fourth during union organizing drives.[19] These courts have

---

[15]*Id.*; Nelson v. Piedmont Aviation, Inc., 750 F2d 1234, 1236, 118 LRRM 2138 (CA 4, 1984), *cert. denied*, 471 U.S. 1116, 119 LRRM 2376 (1985).

[16]These were the power of the NMB to determine the employees' choice of representative "in such manner as shall insure the choice of representatives by the employees without interference, influence, or coercion exercised by the carrier" (RLA §2, Ninth) and the duty of the U.S. Attorneys to institute "necessary" court proceedings for enforcement of §2 of the Act (RLA §2, Tenth).

[17]Thus, the holding of Texas & N.O. R.R. v. Railway & Steamship Clerks, 281 U.S. 548 (1930), that the Act's protections of the right of self-organization are judicially enforceable in a private suit continues to apply after the 1934 amendments.

[18]300 U.S. 515, 1 LRRM 743 (1937).

[19]*See, e.g.*, Stepanischen v. Merchants Despatch Transp. Corp., 722 F2d 922, 924, 926, 114 LRRM 3641, 3642, 3644 (CA 1, 1983) and cases cited therein; Adams v. Federal Express Corp., 547 F2d 319, 94 LRRM 2008 (CA 6, 1976), *cert. denied*, 431 U.S. 915, 95 LRRM 2326 (1977); Burke v. Compania Mexicana de Aviacion, 433 F2d 1031, 75 LRRM 2658 (CA 9, 1970); Union of Professional Airmen v. Alaska Aeronautical Indus., 95 LRRM 2868 (D Alaska, 1977); Associated Pilots of Alaska

held or implied that neither the enforcement procedures specified in Section 2, Tenth nor the NMB's powers under Section 2, Ninth to determine the identity of the employees' representative without interference by the carrier are the exclusive means for protecting employees' rights under Section 2, Third and Fourth.[20]

Legal actions to seek relief for carrier interference with organizing activities under Section 2, Third or Fourth may be brought during the processing of representation disputes under Section 2, Ninth as well as after the dispute has been determined.[21]

B. Standing

The courts have generally recognized that individual employees may bring actions claiming interference with the right to organize under Section 2, Third and Fourth.[22] Similarly,

---

Int'l Air, Inc. v. Alaska Int'l Air, Inc., 96 LRRM 3233 (D Alaska, 1976); Kent v. Fugere, 438 F Supp 560, 96 LRRM 3267 (D Conn, 1977); Griffin v. Piedmont Aviation, Inc., 384 F Supp 1070, 87 LRRM 2764 (ND Ga, 1974). *See also* America W. Airlines v. NMB, 986 F2d 1252, 142 LRRM 2639 (CA 9, 1992) (NMB lacks power to adjudicate the legality of carrier conduct). *But see* Machinists v. Air Indies Corp., 86 LRRM 2076 (D PR, 1973) (complaint of carrier interference by union that lost NMB election within exclusive jurisdiction of NMB).

[20]In Stepanischen v. Merchants Despatch Transp. Corp., 722 F2d 922, 114 LRRM 3641, for example, the court ruled that the Act extends an implied private right of action to employees for carrier interference with their right to organize because, among other factors, the Supreme Court had recognized such a right in Texas & N.O. R.R. v. Railway & Steamship Clerks, 281 U.S. 548. The court observed that the Congress that adopted the 1934 amendments to the Act did not express an intent to overrule *Texas & N.O. R.R.* or to make proceedings by the U.S. Attorneys the exclusive means for enforcing the Act. Stepanischen v. Merchants Despatch Fed'n Corp., 722 F2d at 926–27, 114 LRRM at 3642–43.

[21]*See, e.g.*, Adams v. Federal Express Corp., 90 LRRM 2742 (WD Tenn, 1975), aff'd, 547 F2d 319, 94 LRRM 2008 (CA 6, 1976), *cert. denied*, 431 U.S. 915, 95 LRRM 2326 (1977) (action brought during organizing drive); Burke v. Compania Mexicana de Aviacion, 433 F2d 1031, 75 LRRM 2658 (action brought following organizing drive). One district court has held that the NMB's findings in a representation proceeding that employees were not discharged for engaging in organizing activities do not bar the employees from suing the carrier for wrongful discharge in violation of the Act, and the findings do not bind the court. Freiburger v. Emery Air Charter, 142 LRRM 2570 (ND Ill, 1992).

[22]*See, e.g.*, Stepanischen v. Merchants Despatch Transp. Corp., 722 F2d at 924, 926, 114 LRRM at 3642, 3644 and cases cited therein; Adams v. Federal Express Corp., 547 F2d 319, 94 LRRM 2008; Burke v. Compania Mexicana de Aviacion,

they have recognized the standing of previously recognized or certified unions to bring such actions.[23] On the other hand, in *Adams v. Federal Express Corp.*,[24] the Sixth Circuit held that a union that lost an NMB election lacked standing to join as a plaintiff in a suit by employees claiming carrier interference with the election. In several other cases, courts have adjudicated interference claims by unions seeking to be certified without discussing whether the union possessed standing to assert the claims.[25]

---

433 F2d 1031, 75 LRRM 2658; Union of Professional Airmen v. Alaska Aeronautical Indus., 95 LRRM 2868; Associated Pilots of Alaska Int'l Air, Inc. v. Alaska Int'l Air, Inc., 96 LRRM 3233; Kent v. Fugere, 438 F Supp 560, 96 LRRM 3267; Griffin v. Piedmont Aviation, Inc., 384 F Supp 1070, 87 LRRM 2764. *See also* America W. Airlines, Inc. v. NMB, 986 F2d 1252, 142 LRRM 2639 (NMB lacks power to adjudicate the legality of carrier conduct). *But see* Machinists v. Air Indies Corp., 86 LRRM 2076 (complaint of carrier interference by union that lost NMB election within exclusive jurisdiction of NMB).

People who are neither employees nor subordinate officials (e.g., supervisors and other management officials) are not protected by §2. Robinson v. Pan Am. World Airways, 597 F Supp 1063 (SD NY, 1984); Podlesnick v. Airborne Express, Inc., 627 F Supp 1113 (SD Ohio, 1986), *aff'd without opinion*, 836 F2d 550 (CA 6, 1987). *See* Chapter 1, "Introduction," for a discussion of coverage of the Act.

[23]*E.g.*, Texas & N.O. R.R. v. Railway & Steamship Clerks, 281 U.S. 548 (action by previously recognized union to prevent carrier from negotiating with company union and to protect employees from discharge because of union activities). In Railway & Steamship Clerks v. Delpro Co., 549 F Supp 780, 112 LRRM 2268 (D Del, 1982), a district court held that a certified union may not serve as a class representative to recover individual damages for violations of status quo and related obligations under the RLA, but may sue for declaratory and injunctive relief. However, in People Express Pilot Merger Comm. v. Texas Air Corp., 127 LRRM 2879 (D NJ, 1987), a district court held that a committee elected by a majority of the pilots to enforce a seniority integration agreement had standing as a representative under the RLA or as a class representative under Fed. R. Civ. P. 23(a) and (b). A substantial body of case law has also developed dealing with the ability of incumbent unions to enforce the rights of employees under §2, Third and Fourth concerning carrier actions after certification or recognition: these cases are discussed in *infra* §IX. *See, e.g.*, Air Line Pilots Ass'n v. United Air Lines, 802 F2d 886, 123 LRRM 2617 (CA 7, 1986), *cert. denied*, 480 U.S. 946, 124 LRRM 3192 (1987). In the context of a sympathy strike, a district court held that employees terminated for refusing to cross the picket line of a union that was not their representative had standing to challenge their discharge under RLA §2, Third and Fourth. Arthur v. United Air Lines, 655 F Supp 363, 126 LRRM 2082 (D Colo, 1987).

[24]547 F2d 319, 94 LRRM 2008 (CA 6, 1976), *cert. denied*, 431 U.S. 915, 95 LRRM 2326 (1977). *See also* Grosschmidt v. Chautauqua Airlines, 122 LRRM 3254 (ND Ohio, 1986).

[25]*See e.g.*, Aircraft Mechanics Fraternal Ass'n v. United Air Lines, 406 F Supp 492, 91 LRRM 2248 (ND Cal, 1976); Union of Professional Airmen v. Alaska

Section 2, Tenth of the Act authorizes U.S. Attorneys to "institute . . . and to prosecute under the direction of the Attorney General of the United States" all necessary proceedings for the enforcement of the provisions of Section 2. The Supreme Court has held that this provision confers standing on the United States to enforce Section 2 in civil proceedings.[26] Section 2, Tenth indicates that the U.S. Attorney may initiate proceedings upon application made by "any duly designated representative of a carrier's employees."

C. Forms of Prohibited Interference During Organizing

1. Discipline. The courts have adjudicated cases concerning a variety of claimed violations of employees' right to organize. The most prominent cases concern carrier discipline directed against individuals for attempting to organize. When such cases have involved a mixture of antiunion and legitimate business motives, some courts have followed the National Labor Relations Board's *Wright Line*[27] test and have

---

Aeronautical Indus., 95 LRRM 2868 (action by union on behalf of employees as to interference during organizing; no discussion of whether union had been certified).

[26]Railway & Steamship Clerks v. Florida E.C. Ry., 384 U.S. 238, 242, 62 LRRM 2177, 2178 (1966). *See supra* §1.H for a discussion of remedies under §2, Tenth. *See also* U.S. DEPARTMENT OF JUSTICE, U.S. ATTORNEYS' MANUAL 9-139.100 (Oct. 1, 1988) [hereinafter U.S. ATTORNEYS' MANUAL].

[27]Wright Line, 251 NLRB 1083, 105 LRRM 1169 (1980), *enforced*, 662 F2d 899, 108 LRRM 2513 (CA 1, 1981), *cert. denied*, 455 U.S. 989, 109 LRRM 2779 (1982); *see also* NLRB v. Transportation Mgmt. Corp., 462 U.S. 393, 403, 113 LRRM 2857, 2661 (1983) (sustaining the *Wright Line* test). In *Wright Line*, the NLRB adopted the following standard for causation and burden of proof in cases under §8(a)(1) and (3) of the National Labor Relations Act:

First, we shall require that the General Counsel make a *prima facie* showing sufficient to support the inference that protected conduct was a "motivating factor" in the employer's decision. Once this is established, the burden will shift to the employer to demonstrate that the same action would have taken place even in the absence of the protected conduct.

Wright Line, 251 NLRB at 1089, 105 LRRM at 1175.

The NLRB added the following statement in a footnote:

[W]e note that in those instances where, after all the evidence has been submitted, the employer has been unable to carry its burden, we will not seek to qualitatively analyze the effect of the unlawful cause once it has been found. It is enough that the employees' protected activities are causally related to the employer action which is the basis of the complaint. Whether that "cause" was the straw that broke the camel's back or a bullet between the eyes, if it were enough to determine events, it is enough to come within the proscription

held that the employee will not recover if, despite proof that antiunion motives played a part in the employer's actions, the employer shows that the employee would have been disciplined even if the employee "had not been involved with the union."[28] One court summarized this test, stating, "An employer will be found to have violated [the Act's prohibition on interference] if plaintiff proves that her protected conduct was a substantial or motivating factor in the discharge or other adverse job action, unless the employer proves by a preponderance of the evidence that it would have taken the same action regardless of its forbidden motivation."[29] The court went on to note that "[t]he risk that the influence of legal and illegal motives cannot be separated is thus borne by the employer."[30]

Other courts have invalidated the carrier's action where antiunion motives played "some" or "any" part in the discipline.[31]

2. Other Forms of Interference. Some court cases concern other forms of claimed carrier interference in organizing drives. For example, courts have held that Section 2, Third and Fourth prohibit employers from offering employees improved benefits or other preferential treatment that are in-

---

of the Act.
Id. n.14.

[28]Roscello v. Southwest Airlines Co., 726 F2d 217, 222–23, 119 LRRM 3372, 3376 (CA 5, 1984); *see also* Grosschmidt v. Chautauqua Airlines, 122 LRRM 3254 (ND Ohio, 1986); AFM Pilots Ass'n v. AFM Corp., 96 Lab. Cas. (CCH) ¶¶14,115 (D Mass, 1982).

[29]Grosschmidt v. Chautauqua Airlines, 122 LRRM at 3258.

[30]*Id.*, citing NLRB v. Transportation Mgmt. Corp., 462 U.S. at 405, 113 LRRM at 2861.

[31]Adams v. Federal Express Corp., 470 F Supp 1356, 1364, 101 LRRM 2543, 2547 (WD Tenn, 1979) (discipline set aside where antiunion motive played "any part"), *aff'd*, 654 F2d 452, 109 LRRM 3123 (CA 6, 1981); Hodges v. Tomerlin, 510 F Supp 1287, 1293, 107 LRRM 2282 (SD Ga, 1981) (antiunion motives played "some part"); Lum v. China Airlines Co., 413 F Supp 613, 616–17, 92 LRRM 2451, 2454–55 (D Haw, 1976) (antiunion motivation "at least to some degree"); *see also* Conrad v. Delta Air Lines, 494 F2d 914, 918, 86 LRRM 2242 (CA 7, 1974) ("[a]nti-union motivation invalidates even a discharge which could be justified on independent grounds").

tended to undermine union organizing.[32] Other courts have held that claims of interference of this type should not be considered by the courts but by the NMB in conducting representation proceedings under Section 2, Ninth, unless the conduct in question amounts to "company unionism."[33] Courts have also ruled that they lack jurisdiction to hear claims that carriers interfered with representation rights by negotiating collective bargaining agreements with incumbent unions while plaintiffs were seeking to organize the craft or class.[34] One court observed that such claims may be resolved only by the NMB, in the absence of "total company domination" of the incumbent union."[35]

Two other courts have found violations where a carrier prohibited employees from wearing union insignia during an organizing drive, in the absence of a negative impact on safety or efficiency.[36] One of these courts also held that the Act prohibits carrier interrogation or surveillance of employees to learn of union activities.[37]

D. Judicial Remedies and Procedures

1. Judicial Remedies. Several forms of relief have been awarded to employees who prevail in court cases on grounds of carrier interference with representation rights. These include orders of reinstatement, backpay, restored benefits, and

---

[32]Adams v. Federal Express Corp., 470 F Supp at 1370, 101 LRRM at 2551–52; Union of Professional Airmen v. Alaska Aeronautical Indus., 95 LRRM 2868, 2870 (D Alaska, 1977).

[33]Train Dispatchers v. Denver & R.G.W. R.R., 614 F Supp 543, 545 (D Colo, 1985); see also Aircraft Mechanics Fraternal Ass'n v. United Air Lines, 406 F Supp 492, 508–09, 91 LRRM 2248, 2259–60 (ND Cal, 1976).

[34]Texidor v. Ceresa, 590 F2d 357, 359, 100 LRRM 2477, 2478 (CA 1, 1978); Aircraft Mechanics Fraternal Ass'n v. United Air Lines, 406 F Supp at 508–09, 91 LRRM at 2259–60.

[35]Aircraft Mechanics Fraternal Ass'n v. United Air Lines, 406 F Supp at 509, 91 LRRM at 2266.

[36]Scott v. American Airlines, 488 F Supp 415, 104 LRRM 2889 (ED NY, 1980); Adams v. Federal Express Corp., 470 F Supp 1356, 1362–63, 101 LRRM 2543, 2546 (WD Tenn, 1979), aff'd on other grounds, 654 F2d 452, 109 LRRM 3123 (CA 6, 1981).

[37]Adams v. Federal Express Corp., 470 F Supp at 1369, 101 LRRM at 2551.

restored seniority.[38] Lower courts are divided on the issue of whether punitive damages are available to an employee for carrier interference with the right to organize.[39]

The Act also establishes criminal penalties against carriers and their officers and agents for willful failure to comply with Section 2, Third, Fourth, Fifth, Seventh, or Eighth of the Act.[40] There has been only one reported criminal prosecution under Section 2, Tenth.[41]

---

[38]Burke v. Compania Mexicana de Aviacion, 433 F2d 1031, 1034, 75 LRRM 2658, 2660–61 (CA 9, 1970) (damages and reinstatement); Adams v. Federal Express Corp., 470 F Supp at 1363, 1368, 101 LRRM at 2546, 2550 (reinstatement, restored seniority, and backpay); Lum v. China Airlines Co., 413 F Supp 613, 617, 92 LRRM 2451, 2455 (D Haw, 1976) (reinstatement and restored benefits); *but see* Associated Pilots of Alaska Int'l Air, Inc. v. Alaska Int'l Air, Inc., 96 LRRM 3233, 3238 (D Alaska, 1976) (on motion for preliminary injunction, court enjoined further violations of §2, Fourth but denied reinstatement of employee).

[39]Brown v. World Airways, 539 F Supp 179, 118 LRRM 3183 (SD NY, 1982) (court declined to strike claim for punitive damages, at least where employee was not represented by union); Freiburger v. Emery Air Charter, 795 F Supp 253, 260, 143 LRRM 2148, 2153 (ND Ill, 1992) (applying *Brown* to uphold claim for punitive damages by unrepresented employee); Machinists v. Northwest Airlines, 131 LRRM 2598 (D Minn, 1988) (same holding); Machinists v. Jet Am. Airlines, 115 LRRM 3283, 3284 (CD Cal, 1983) (applying *Brown* to case involving precertification conduct, where union was certified after case was filed); Belton v. Air Atlanta, Inc., 647 F Supp 28, 32, 124 LRRM 2661, 2665 (ND Ga, 1986) (following *Brown*); *but see* Brady v. Trans World Airlines, 244 F Supp 820, 822, 60 LRRM 2115, 2116 (D Del, 1965) (backpay and benefits are sole monetary remedies in action against carrier for wrongful discharge in violation of union security clause under §2, Fourth and Eleventh), *aff'd on other grounds*, 401 F2d 87, 69 LRRM 2048 (CA 3, 1968); Railway Carmen v. Delpro Co., 579 F Supp 1332, 118 LRRM 3185 (D Del, 1984) (punitive damages may not be recovered under §2, Fourth where action is brought by union); Grosschmidt v. Chautauqua Airlines, 122 LRRM 3254 (ND Ohio, 1986) (punitive damages may not be recovered in action brought by unrepresented employee); Maas v. Frontier Airlines, 676 F Supp 224, 128 LRRM 2420 (D Colo, 1987) (no punitive damages in actions under the RLA); Tipton v. Aspen Airways, 741 F Supp 1469, 1471, 135 LRRM 2151, 2153 (D Colo, 1990) (same holding).

[40]RLA §2, Tenth. The statute states that it shall be the duty of any U.S. Attorney to prosecute violations of the specified provisions of §2 and for the punishment of violations, upon application of "any duly designated representative of a carrier's employees." RLA §2, Tenth. The U.S. ATTORNEYS' MANUAL provides that "[a]s a matter of policy, prosecutions as well as requests for investigation concerning violations of [§2, Tenth] should be declined unless they contain allegations of egregious carrier interference with employee rights tantamount to actual or threatened violence, or involve prohibited payments to employee representatives." U.S. ATTORNEYS' MANUAL, *supra* note 26, at 9-139.103.

[41]United States v. Winston, 558 F2d 105, 109–10, 95 LRRM 2877, 2880–81 (CA 2, 1977) (reversing convictions of airline officials for violating §2, Tenth through discharge of union adherents in connection with organizing drive; court ruled that

2. Statute of Limitations. Two courts of appeals have addressed the question of the applicable statute of limitations in actions brought against carrier interference with organizing campaigns. The Second Circuit has ruled that this type of claim is governed by a six-month statute of limitations.[42] The First Circuit has applied the same limitations period to an action claiming wrongful discharge of an incumbent union official in violation of Section 2, Fourth.[43]

3. Right to Jury Trial. District courts have reached opposite conclusions as to the right to a jury trial in wrongful discharge cases under Section 2, Third and Fourth, as a result of differing views as to whether claims for backpay and other monetary relief are equitable or legal in nature.[44]

---

jury should have been instructed that defendants must have intended to violate a known legal duty in order to be convicted, and that in a criminal prosecution, if legitimate reasons existed for the discharge, the government must establish that such reasons alone would not have led to the discharge).

[42]Robinson v. Pan Am. World Airways, 777 F2d 84, 120 LRRM 3374 (CA 2, 1985). The court has applied the same period to all actions under §2, Third and Fourth of the Act. Gvozdenovic v. United Air Lines, 933 F2d 1100, 1107, 137 LRRM 2534, 2539 (CA 2), *cert. denied*, 112 U.S. 3, 138 LRRM 2536 (1991).

[43]Benoni v. Boston & Me. Corp., 828 F2d 52, 56, 126 LRRM 2273 (CA 1, 1987). *See also* Duncan v. Southwest Airlines, 127 LRRM 2921, 2922–23 (CA 9, 1988) (declining to apply a uniform federal six-month limitations period to a claim under §2, Fourth that was filed before the court adopted such a period for hybrid-type actions in Machinists v. Aloha Airlines, 790 F2d 727, 122 LRRM 2642 (CA 9), *cert. denied*, 479 U.S. 931, 123 LRRM 2904 (1986)).

[44]Freiburger v. Emery Air Charter, 795 F Supp 253, 143 LRRM 2148 (ND Ill, 1992) (refusing to strike claim for jury trial where plaintiffs sought legal damages for wrongful discharge for engaging in organizing activity); Machinists v. Northwest Airlines, 131 LRRM 2598 (D Minn, 1988) (upholding right to jury trial in claim for punitive damages, which is a legal claim, but not in claim for backpay, which is an equitable claim); Maas v. Frontier Airlines, 676 F Supp 224, 128 LRRM 2420 (D Colo, 1987) (striking claim for jury trial in action for wrongful discharge under RLA for engaging in picketing and related activities; equitable relief, but not legal damages, available in this type of action); Tipton v. Aspen Airway, 741 F Supp 1469, 1472, 135 LRRM 2151, 2154 (D Colo, 1990) (striking claim for jury trial in action for wrongful discharge in violation of §2, Fourth); Hodges v. Virgin Atl. Airways, 714 F Supp 75, 129 LRRM 3008 (SD NY, 1988) (same holding). In Teamsters v. Terry, 494 U.S. 558, 571, 133 LRRM 2793, 2797 (1990), the Supreme Court held that claims for backpay and benefits in a duty of fair representation action are legal in nature unless "incidental to or intertwined with injunctive relief." In Roscello v. Southwest Airlines, 726 F2d 217, 119 LRRM 3372 (CA 5, 1984), the Fifth Circuit declined to decide whether a plaintiff claiming wrongful discharge in retaliation for union activities was entitled to a trial by jury, because a jury trial was warranted

IV. ROLE OF THE NMB IN PROTECTING EMPLOYEE FREEDOM OF CHOICE

In a representation dispute properly referred to the NMB, it is the duty of the Board to ascertain the employees' representative "in such manner as shall insure the choice of representatives . . . without interference, influence, or coercion exercised by the carrier."[45] The NMB's stated test for any case of alleged interference is whether "laboratory conditions" have been "tainted."[46] For an election to be considered fair, laboratory conditions must be maintained from the time the carrier becomes aware of the employees' organizing drive until the election is completed.[47]

The Board has noted that in the context of its investigations of representation disputes, the adjudication of violations of Section 2, Fourth is not within the Board's authority.[48] Thus, the Board's determination as to whether laboratory conditions have been maintained need not include a finding that the carrier committed unlawful actions; rather, the Board's goal is to provide "an election environment in which the eligible voters [are] able to make their decision . . . with sufficient insulation from interference, influence or coercion by the carrier."[49] To make this determination, the NMB as-

---

on a companion duty of fair representation claim, and both claims were required to be submitted to the jury because they raised common questions of fact.

[45]RLA §2, Ninth. *See* USAir, Inc., 18 NMB 290, 296 (1991); USAir, Inc., 17 NMB 377, 385–86 (1990); Key Airlines, 13 NMB 153, 161–62 (1986); Laker Airways, 8 NMB 236, 243 (1982); Zantop Int'l Airlines, 6 NMB 834, 835 (1979).

[46]USAir, Inc., 18 NMB at 323; Intertec Aviation, L.P., 18 NMB 150, 158 (1991); USAir, Inc., 17 NMB at 414–15; Florida E.C. Ry., 17 NMB 177, 187–88 (1990); America W. Airlines, 17 NMB 79, 95 (1990); Key Airlines, 16 NMB 296, 308 (1989); Air Wis., 16 NMB 235, 239 (1989); Key Airlines, 13 NMB 153, 162 (1986); Laker Airways, 8 NMB at 247; Zantop Int'l Airlines, 6 NMB at 835. This test is similar to the NLRB test for "laboratory conditions;" *see* General Shoe Corp., 77 NLRB 124, 21 LRRM 1337 (1948) and discussion in THE DEVELOPING LABOR LAW 85 (Patrick Hardin ed., 3d ed. 1992).

[47]Continental Airlines/Continental Express, 21 NMB 229 (1994).

[48]Southwest Airlines, 21 NMB 332, 350 (1994); Washington C. R.R., 20 NMB 191, 230 (1993); Florida E.C. Ry., 17 NMB 177, 187 (1990); America W. Airlines, 17 NMB at 98; Key Airlines, 16 NMB 296, 310 (1989).

[49]Evergreen Int'l Airlines, 20 NMB 675, 713–14 (1993).

sesses the totality of the carrier's conduct.[50] The Board has also found that laboratory conditions may be violated by threats that are made by a third party having a relationship to the carrier, such as a potential investor in the carrier.[51] Judicial decisions finding that a carrier interfered with organizing rights may be relied upon by the NMB in deciding whether to conduct a rerun election or take other steps to ensure the employees' freedom of choice is protected during a representation dispute.[52]

Some conduct is highly likely to draw a finding that laboratory conditions were tainted. However, the NMB's overarching "totality of the circumstances" test[53] sometimes makes it difficult to isolate dispositive conduct. The following subsections discuss applications of these principles.

A. Interference With NMB Voting Procedures

The NMB has stated that "[e]mployees should be given accurate information concerning the method of voting and the consequences of voting."[54] Accordingly, a carrier runs the risk of interfering with its employees' choice of representative when it provides employees with inaccurate or misleading information about the NMB's voting procedures or about the consequences of electing a representative, even if the information is not intentionally inaccurate.[55] The following NMB findings illustrate this general principle:

---

[50]Federal Express Corp., 20 NMB 7, 43 (1992); Intertec Aviation, L.P., 18 NMB at 158; USAir, Inc., 17 NMB 377, 427 (1990); America W. Airlines, 17 NMB at 98 (1990); Dalfort Corp., 16 NMB 271, 273 (1989).

[51]Mid Pac. Airlines, 13 NMB 178, 190 (1986) (unlawful interference for potential investor to threaten that he will not invest in ailing carrier if employees continue organizing activities).

[52]See, e.g., Transkentucky T. R.R., 8 NMB 495, 497–98 (1981) (accepting district court findings that carrier discharged employees in retaliation for organizing and ordering a rerun election utilizing a remedial ballot on the basis of this and other findings of interference); Washington C. R.R., 20 NMB at 229 (citing Transkentucky T. R.R. with approval).

[53]Federal Express Corp., 20 NMB at 43.

[54]Zantop Int'l Airlines, 6 NMB 834, 835 (1979).

[55]USAir, Inc., 17 NMB 377, 421 (1990).

- A carrier interfered with an election when it gave its employees memoranda containing erroneous directions on how to mark ballots.[56]

- A carrier interfered with an election when it inaccurately told employees that a union can be voted in forever.[57]

- Carriers interfered with an election when they told employees to vote "no union" without telling them that writing "no union" on the ballot would invalidate the ballot.[58]

- A carrier interfered with an election when it disseminated inaccuracies and misstatements concerning strikes, seniority, requirements for union membership, and the payment of dues.[59]

On the other hand, the Board held in another case that providing misleading information concerning the method of voting against union representation did not constitute election interference because the statements did not "misinform employees . . . to the extent that the election results would be affected."[60] Similarly, advising employees that they can vote against a union by tearing up their ballots has been held not to constitute election interference.[61]

Carrier actions to deprive a union of authorization cards or carrier involvement with election balloting presents a high risk that the carrier will draw a finding of election interference. For example, the Board has found that carriers committed election interference when they

- instructed employees to tear up their union authorization cards,[62]

---

[56]Chicago & S. Air Lines, 2 NMB 1, 2 (1948).
[57]USAir, Inc., 17 NMB at 421.
[58]Zantop Int'l Airlines, 6 NMB at 835; Allegheny Airlines, 4 NMB 7, 12 (1962).
[59]USAir, Inc., 17 NMB at 421.
[60]USAir, Inc., 18 NMB 290, 330, 331 (1991).
[61]San Joaquin Valley R.R., 21 NMB 391, 392 (1994).
[62]Mid Pac. Airlines, 13 NMB 178, 190–91 (1986).

- seized authorization cards and union records,[63]
- accepted or retained ballots,[64]
- solicited ballots from employees,[65]
- provided a box for employees to deposit their ballots,[66] or
- provided employees with mailing envelopes to send their ballots to the carrier.[67]

The Board has found that solicitation of ballots is interference even if the carrier in fact collects no ballots.[68] Other carrier efforts to obtain information on employee voting, such as a Freedom of Information Act request for the names of those employees requesting duplicate ballots, may contribute to a finding of election interference.[69]

B. Reprisals Against Employees

The NMB has found carrier election interference when carriers

- fired employees for supporting the union;[70]
- demoted union supporters,[71] reduced their pay,[72] transferred them,[73] or forced them to resign;[74] or
- engaged in collective reprisals, such as abolishing jobs or closing a job site.[75]

---

[63]Sea Airmotive, Inc., 11 NMB 87, 90–92 (1983).

[64]Washington C. R.R., 20 NMB 191, 231 (1993) (soliciting and receiving ballots described as "gross abuse"); Laker Airways, 8 NMB 236, 250 (1981); *accord,* Rio Airways, 11 NMB 75, 78 (1983); *see also* Mercury Servs., Inc., 9 NMB 312, 323 (1982).

[65]Mercury Servs., Inc., 9 NMB at 323; Laker Airways, 8 NMB at 250; *accord,* Rio Airways, 11 NMB at 78–79; *see* Metroflight, Inc., 13 NMB 284, 290 (1986).

[66]Rio Airways, 11 NMB at 79.

[67]Laker Airways, 8 NMB at 250 (distributing such envelopes with paychecks compounds violation).

[68]Rio Airways, 11 NMB at 79.

[69]Laker Airways, 8 NMB at 236, 249 (1981).

[70]Washington C. R.R., 20 NMB 191, 233–34, (1993); Key Airlines, 16 NMB 296, 309 (1989); Sea Airmotive, Inc., 11 NMB 87, 90 (1983); Transkentucky T. R.R., 8 NMB 495, 500 (1981).

[71]Sea Airmotive, Inc., 11 NMB 87, 90 (1983).

[72]*Id.*

[73]Key Airlines, 16 NMB at 309.

[74]Key Airlines, 13 NMB 153, 162–63 (1986).

[75]Florida E.C. Ry., 17 NMB 177, 187 (1990).

C. Favoring One Representative Over Another

A carrier may interfere with an election when it discriminates in favor of one candidate over another. The NMB has held that proof of such discrimination depends on demonstrating a "pattern" of carrier support for the allegedly favored party.[76] Isolated incidents that might indicate carrier support for a union or that might indicate carrier–union collusion—such as allowing the union to use a carrier airplane to make a campaign film[77]—do not necessarily establish the requisite pattern of carrier support needed to establish carrier interference.[78] The Board has held that a carrier did not interfere with an election when it allowed a representative to exercise its rights under the collective bargaining agreement to enter the carrier's premises.[79]

A carrier may commit election interference if it encourages employees to form and join a proposed representative organization.[80] The Board has held that management generally may maintain employee committees to discuss workplace issues without interfering with laboratory conditions.[81] However, the Board may find interference if such committees are formed during an election period;[82] if the company encourages employees to join an existing committee during an election period; or if the company uses an existing committee to assist it on an antiunion effort, such as by raising new matters for committee approval during an election campaign.[83] In

---

[76]Northwest Airlines, 14 NMB 49, 56 (1986).

[77]Id.; see also Atchison, T. & S.F. Ry., 12 NMB 95, 114 (1985) (no interference where no company official was aware of or approved use of communications equipment by applicant during campaign).

[78]Denver & R.G. W. R.R., 12 NMB 303, 309 (1985) (evidence of "some interaction" between union and carrier insufficient to constitute carrier support); see, e.g., Seaboard Sys. R.R., 12 NMB 119, 120 (1985) (insufficient evidence of carrier support where carrier and potential representative both sent letters to employees, within two days of each other, telling them of their option not to return their ballots).

[79]Dalfort Corp., 16 NMB 271, 272 (1989).

[80]Evergreen Int'l Airlines, 20 NMB 675, 710, 714 (1993); Metroflight, 18 NMB 532, 544 (1991); see also Mackey Int'l Airlines, 5 NMB 220, 221 (1975) (dismissing representation application of union "fostered, assisted and dominated by the carrier").

[81]Metroflight, 18 NMB at 544; Continental Airlines/Continental Express, 21 NMB 229, 254 (1994).

[82]Federal Express Corp., 20 NMB 7, 48 (1992); Metroflight, 18 NMB at 544.

[83]See Continental Airlines/Continental Express, 21 NMB at 254.

one case, a carrier's overt expressions of favoritism toward a new organization while the organization solicited authorization cards to displace an incumbent union led the Board to dismiss the new organization's application on the ground that the authorization cards were "tainted."[84] The Board reached this result even though the applicant "did not solicit the carrier's support."[85]

The Board has also indicated that favoritism toward an organization in the form of "special access" to phone mail, providing an employee address list to one group, arranging special time off, or payment of travel expenses constitutes election interference.[86]

D. Granting or Withholding Benefits

The granting or withholding of a benefit during an organizing drive may constitute carrier interference.[87] This subject raises complex issues of proof because the issues focus in part on whether the disputed conduct would have occurred in the absence of a union organizing campaign, and findings of interference may turn on the manner and timing of the benefit changes.[88] The following benefit changes were factors in NMB findings of election interference:

- Pay raises timed to affect the outcome of an election[89]
- Merit increases granted to all employees, in a departure from existing policy, in order to "convey the idea that a union was unnecessary"[90]

---

[84]Southwest Airlines, 21 NMB 332, 350–51 (1994).

[85]*Id.* at 350.

[86]Evergreen Int'l Airlines, 20 NMB 675, 709–10 (1993).

[87]Key Airlines, 16 NMB 296, 209–10 (1989) (carrier interference to provide pay raise to all employees except those in craft or class involved in organizing drive); Laker Airways, 8 NMB 236, 251–53 (1981); America W. Airlines, 17 NMB 79, 98–99 (1990) (interference for carrier to distribute profit-sharing checks during election period).

[88]*See, e.g.,* Adams v. Federal Express Corp., 470 F Supp 1356, 1371–72, 101 LRRM 2543, 2553 (WD Tenn, 1979) (interpreting §2, Fourth) ("the guiding principle is that the employer must act as he would in the absence of a union campaign"), *aff'd on other grounds,* 654 F2d 452, 109 LRRM 3123 (CA 6, 1981).

[89]Evergreen Int'l Airlines, 20 NMB at 706–07.

[90]Laker Airways, 8 NMB at 251–53.

- A "party" held to distribute profit-sharing checks during the election period[91]
- New hotel benefits granted in response to a union campaign[92]
- An unscheduled increase in layover benefits timed to occur immediately prior to the ballot period[93]
- Paid days off provided for days on which workplace balloting was scheduled[94]
- Accelerated issuance of an employee policy manual and announcement of this change in a campaign letter[95]

In the following cases, benefit changes occurred but the Board rejected claims of carrier interference:

- The carrier provided improvements in the dental plan that had been scheduled prior to authorization of the election.[96]
- The carrier granted pay increases in accord with a historical pattern.[97]
- The carrier implemented a profit-sharing plan as scheduled 18 months before the representation application was filed.[98]
- The carrier provided transportation benefits that were planned prior to the campaign.[99]
- The carrier improved a companion pass travel program that was comparable to prior improvements and was not "part of a pattern of interference."[100]

A carrier may commit interference without actually providing a new benefit, simply by offering the benefit to employ-

---

[91]America W. Airlines, 17 NMB at 98–99.
[92]Evergreen Int'l Airlines, 20 NMB 675, 707–08 (1993).
[93]America W. Airlines, 17 NMB 79, 98 (1990).
[94]Linea Aeropostal Venezolana, 3 NMB 54, 55 (1955).
[95]Evergreen Int'l Airlines, 20 NMB at 708.
[96]USAir, Inc., 17 NMB 377, 426 (1990).
[97]Id.
[98]City of Prineville Ry., 13 NMB 63, 71 (1985).
[99]Federal Express Corp., 20 NMB 7, 46 (1992).
[100]USAir/Shuttle, 20 NMB 162, 179 (1993).

ees.[101] However, provision of a benefit may not constitute interference when the benefit is insignificant,[102] or when the carrier demonstrates that the purpose of the benefit is other than influencing the employees' choice of representative.[103]

E. Making Threats

A carrier may interfere with its employees' freedom of choice when it threatens that if the union is selected, the employees will suffer adverse consequences.[104] Examples of such threats have included the following:

- Statements that support for the union would cause employees to lose pay, benefits, or their jobs[105]
- Statements that unionization would cause the carrier to subcontract the employees' work[106] or to merge with another carrier[107]
- A statement that unionization would cause the carrier to close its facility[108]

---

[101]Sea Airmotive, Inc., 11 NMB 87, 90–92 (1983) (interference when carrier offers promotions and other advantages to employees who quit union or who do not join union); Mercury Servs., Inc., 9 NMB 312, 323 (1982) (interference when carrier offers increase in wages and benefits in exchange for ballots); Laker Airways, 8 NMB 236, 251 (1981). See also Adams v. Federal Express Corp., 470 F Supp 1356, 1370, 101 LRRM 2543, 2552 (WD Tenn, 1979) (in §2, Fourth context, carrier's promise to remedy grievances may constitute interference), aff'd on other grounds, 654 F2d 452, 109 LRRM 3123 (CA 6, 1981); Union of Professional Airmen v. Alaska Aeronautical Indus., 95 LRRM 2868, 2870 (D Alaska, 1977).

[102]City of Prineville Ry., 13 NMB at 71–72 (offering profit-sharing plan not interference when, inter alia, sum available to employees is small). See also Adams v. Federal Express Corp., 470 F Supp at 1370, 101 LRRM at 2551–52 (no interference when carrier provided employees with occasional beer parties and made membership in recreational club available).

[103]Federal Express Corp., 20 NMB at 45–46 (not interference to seek legislative changes affecting pension benefits that were not designed to affect outcome of election); USAir, Inc., 17 NMB 377, 426 (1990) (not interference to institute employee stock ownership plan designed to avoid potential hostile takeover). See also Adams v. Federal Express Corp., 470 F Supp at 1370, 101 LRRM at 2552 (in §2, Fourth context, not interference to institute incentive program intended to get aircraft loaded more promptly).

[104]See Sea Airmotive, Inc., 11 NMB at 90.

[105]Florida E.C. Ry., 17 NMB 177, 181, 187 (1990); Key Airlines, 16 NMB 296, 311 (1989); Allegheny Airlines, 4 NMB 7, 9–10 (1962).

[106]Florida E.C. Ry., 17 NMB at 181, 187; Key Airlines, 16 NMB at 311.

[107]Key Airlines, 16 NMB at 311.

[108]Florida E.C. Ry., 17 NMB at 181, 187.

The NMB has not accepted carrier claims that threats constitute constitutionally protected speech.[109]

F. Polling and Surveillance

The NMB has found that a carrier interferes with its
employees' free choice of representative when the carrier
polls the employees on whether they support the union.[110]
Examples of impermissible polling have included the following:

- Interviewing employees to determine whether they
  support the union[111]
- Holding a carrier-run "election" to determine whether
  the employees support the NMB-certified union[112]
- Circulating a petition among the employees asking the
  union to withdraw[113]

The Board has also found that a carrier interferes with
employees' freedom of choice when it collects employee ballots. As the NMB has explained, when a carrier collects the
ballots, "[e]ven employees who would otherwise simply throw
their ballots in the trash feel compelled to turn them in as
an act of 'loyalty.' "[114] Likewise, the Board has held that a
carrier's calling an employee at home to check whether the
employee received a ballot constituted election interference
because the action created the impression that the carrier was
"keeping a close watch" on the employees.[115] One court has

---

[109]Allegheny Airlines, 4 NMB at 11–12. See infra §V.

[110]Mercury Servs., Inc., 9 NMB 312, 323 (1982); Laker Airways, 8 NMB 236,
250 (1981) (polling by carrier during representation election constitutes a per se
violation).

[111]See Washington C. R.R., 20 NMB 191, 232 (1993) (supervisors asking "several" individuals whether they support "carrier" or "union" constitutes impermissible
polling); Key Airlines, 13 NMB 153, 163–64 (1986) (individual employee meetings
to determine whether employees supported union were impermissible). But see
Adams v. Federal Express Corp., 470 F Supp 1356, 1369, 101 LRRM 2543, 2551 (WD
Tenn, 1979) (carrier questioning did not violate RLA §2, Fourth when "conversations
were of a casual nature" and "the employees questioned were not intimidated"),
aff'd on other grounds, 654 F2d 452, 109 LRRM 3123 (CA 6, 1981).

[112]Machinists v. Continental Airlines, 754 F Supp 892, 894–96, 136 LRRM
2301, 2303–04 (D DC, 1990).

[113]Mid Pac. Airlines, 13 NMB 178, 190 (1986).

[114]Mercury Servs., Inc., 9 NMB at 321; Laker Airways, 8 NMB at 249.

[115]Laker Airways, 8 NMB 236, 249–50 (1981).

held that polling, like carrier threats, is not a form of constitutionally protected speech.[116]

G. Prohibiting Union Insignia

The issue of prohibiting the wearing of pro-union insignia during a representation campaign has drawn little attention in NMB cases.[117] In one case, the Board declined to rule on whether the prohibition constituted interference.[118]

H. Other Types of Carrier Interference

The Board's decisions indicate that a carrier runs a risk that the Board will find election interference when the carrier

- prohibits the posting of pro-union literature on employee bulletin boards and in employee break rooms, particularly when the carrier's restriction on use of bulletin boards is not applied evenhandedly,[119] or
- discriminates between pro-union and antiunion messages in determining whether to allow communications with employees.[120]

In other cases, the NMB has indicated that a carrier would not commit election interference if the carrier

- prohibits the posting of a union document that may have led employees to the mistaken belief that it was issued by the NMB[121] or
- regulates the form of a union's access to the carrier's premises in accordance with a provision of the applicable collective bargaining agreement.[122]

---

[116]Machinists v. Continental Airlines, 754 F Supp at 896, 136 LRRM at 2303–04.

[117]See supra §III.C.2 for a discussion of judicial treatment of union insignia issues in organizing drives.

[118]America W. Airlines, 21 NMB 293, 296 (1994).

[119]USAir, Inc., 17 NMB 377, 423 (1990).

[120]Id. (carrier commits interference when it allows employees to use telex equipment for antiunion messages but otherwise prohibits unauthorized use of equipment).

[121]USAir, Inc., 18 NMB 290, 326 (1991).

[122]See America W. Airlines, 18 NMB 140, 161 (1991).

V. CARRIER SPEECH: RESTRICTIONS ON "PERVASIVE CAMPAIGNS"

The NMB acknowledges that "carriers may communicate to employees concerning election issues" without committing election interference.[123] However, to protect the laboratory conditions in election proceedings, the Board weighs a carrier's free speech rights against employees' rights to be free from carrier interference in the election of representatives.[124]

Since the Board evaluates interference cases on the basis of the "totality of the circumstances,"[125] carrier campaign statements may or may not draw findings of election interference based upon the context in which they were made. In the following examples, carrier statements contributed to findings of election interference:

- Statements that a union could not be removed once it was certified[126]
- Misleading statements concerning the effect of unionization on seniority rights, the possibility of strikes, and the requirement for dues[127]
- Heavy criticism of the union[128]
- Inaccurate statements concerning voting procedures[129]
- Misleading statements concerning dues obligations[130]
- Correspondence from the corporate chair suggesting that the company's future depended upon his leadership (and that the employees' choice was between his leadership and the union president's), because the let-

---

[123]Federal Express Corp., 20 NMB 7, 49 (1992).

[124]*Id.*; Washington C. R.R., 20 NMB 191, 234 (1993); Allegheny Airlines, 4 NMB 7 (1962); *see also* Texas & N.O. R.R. v. Railway & Steamship Clerks, 281 U.S. 548, 571 (1930) (carriers have no constitutional right to interfere with employee freedom of choice); Machinists v. Continental Airlines, 754 F Supp 892, 896, 136 LRRM 2301, 2303–04 (D DC, 1990).

[125]Federal Express Corp., 20 NMB at 43.

[126]USAir, Inc., 17 NMB 377, 421 (1990).

[127]*Id.*

[128]America W. Airlines, 17 NMB 79, 102 (1990).

[129]Zantop Int'l Airlines, 6 NMB 834 (1979).

[130]Federal Express Corp., 20 NMB 7, 50 (1992).

ter "could be perceived as a reminder of the 'power and authority' which [the chair] exercised"[131]

- Expression of antiunion views by senior supervisors in small group meetings with employees in the carrier's office[132]
- Expressions critical of an incumbent union and favorable to an applicant[133]

The Board reviews not only the context of employer communications but also the degree of the carrier's involvement in an election campaign. In particular, the Board is critical of "pervasive" carrier campaign activity.[134] The Board has stated that the carrier's proper role in election campaigns is "far more limited" than the role of labor organizations and that there is a "level of carrier communication . . . which overwhelms an employee's right to select or not select a collective bargaining representative without carrier interference or influence."[135] Even if the content of the carrier's communication is not objectionable, the Board has considered the frequency and volume of the carrier's communications and has found that the level of communications interfered with the employees' freedom of choice.[136]

VI. Misconduct by Unions

The statutory provisions of the RLA that regulate representation proceedings do not expressly prohibit misconduct

---

[131]*Id.*

[132]Allegheny Airlines, 4 NMB 7, 13 (1962); Key Airlines, 16 NMB 296, 303–04 (1989).

[133]Southwest Airlines, 21 NMB 332, 349 (1994).

[134]USAir, Inc., 17 NMB 377, 427 (1990); Federal Express Corp., 20 NMB at 51; Southwest Airlines, 21 NMB at 349.

[135]Federal Express Corp., 20 NMB 7, 51 (1992).

[136]*Id. See also* Evergreen Int'l Airlines, 20 NMB 675, 714 (1993) (51 employee meetings in one month combined with discussion of election issues "were part of a pervasive campaign which undermined employee freedom of choice"); Washington C. R.R., 20 NMB 191, 234 (1993) ("some material, when coupled with the pervasive and sustained posture by the carrier in this case, had an adverse effect on employee free choice").

by a labor organization.[137] Nonetheless, the Act requires the NMB to investigate disputes involving representation and authorizes the Board to establish the rules governing an election. On this basis, the Board investigates allegations of union interference with employee freedom of choice as a result of objections filed by carriers[138] or other unions.[139]

In cases of alleged election interference by unions, the Board applies the same test as in cases of alleged carrier interference, namely, whether laboratory conditions have been contaminated. In both instances, the Board considers all facts and circumstances on a case-by-case basis. However, "because of the unique power and authority which carriers possess in the workplace,"[140] the application of this standard to an identical factual situation may result in different conclusions involving union versus carrier interference.[141] The Board has ordered a rerun election for union interference in only one reported case, where both the union and the carrier jointly requested the Board to a hold a rerun election.[142]

In one case, the Board rejected a union's claim that a rival union's dissemination of a sample ballot that contained an "X" in the right-hand margin to all employees, indicating a preference for the latter union, misrepresented election procedures and implied that the NMB had approved the literature.[143] The Board ruled that the distribution of one ballot did not warrant setting aside the election, since the

---

[137]RLA §2, Third, Fourth, Ninth. Section 2, Third prohibits unions from interfering with the *employer's* choice of its representatives; this provision plays no role in proceedings under RLA §2, Ninth to determine the employees' choice of representative.

[138]This is so even though a carrier is not a "party" to a representation dispute under §2, Ninth. Railway & Steamship Clerks v. Association for the Benefit of Non-Contract Employees, 380 U.S. 650, 666, 59 LRRM 2051, 2057 (1965); Horizon Air, 14 NMB 413, 414 (1987).

[139]Air Wis., 16 NMB 235 (1989); Continental Airlines, 14 NMB 131 (1987); Southwest Airlines, 13 NMB 120 (1986); Long Island R.R., 12 NMB 187 (1985).

[140]Air Wis., 16 NMB at 239–40.

[141]*Id.*; Federal Express Corp., 20 NMB 486, 526 (1993).

[142]Alia Royal Jordanian Airlines, 10 NMB 361 (1983) (carrier claim that union solicited employees to turn in their ballots to union for mailing).

[143]Long Island R.R. OBIT, 12 NMB 187 (1985).

ballot did not create the impression that the Board's impartiality had been breached.[144] In another case, the Board rejected a carrier's claim that a union had misrepresented NMB procedures, but implied that such a misrepresentation if found could be a basis for setting aside an election.[145]

The NMB has also rejected a carrier's claim that a union interfered with a fair election by mailing unsolicited, duplicate ballot request forms to employees and encouraging employees to request duplicate ballots if they had not received an NMB ballot.[146] The Board found no basis for the carrier's claim that these letters gave employees the impression that the union knew whether particular employees had voted, or that this practice caused confusion in identifying the NMB's official ballot, stating, "[N]o one except employees of the NMB knows *who* voted in the election."[147]

The NMB also rejected claims of union election interference in the following cases:

- The union photographed employees during the voting but on a floor different from the one where the polling took place.[148]
- The union photographed a flight attendant lawfully campaigning on behalf of a rival.[149]
- The union allegedly promised pay increases if it won.[150]
- Supervisors actively campaigned for the union on company time.[151]

In one case, the Board declined to set aside an election based on isolated incidents of violence and threats of union

---

[144]*Id.*

[145]Continental Airlines, 14 NMB 131, 138 (1987).

[146]Southwest Airlines, 13 NMB 120 (1986).

[147]*Id.* at 123 (quoting Mercury Servs., 9 NMB 312 (1982)). The Board's position is that so long as the request for a duplicate ballot is signed and sent by an eligible individual and is not sent by telegram or facsimile or received fewer than five calendar days before the date of the account, the integrity of the duplicate ballot process has been preserved. NMB REPRESENTATION MANUAL §12.206-1 (1995); *see also* USAir, Inc., 16 NMB 194, 203 (1989).

[148]Rio Airways, 11 NMB 160, 161 (1984).

[149]Pacific S.W. Airlines, 14 NMB 303, 324 (1987).

[150]Metroflight, Inc., 19 NMB 254, 260–61 (1992).

[151]Jet Am., Inc., 10 NMB 275, 284 (1983).

retaliation that were not specifically attributed to the labor organization.[152] In another case, the Board held that alleged coercion of employees to obtain their signatures on authorization cards does not require dismissal of an application for election, because the employees "retain the option of voting in the election should they still desire representation, or refraining from voting should they not wish to be represented."[153]

In *Air Wisconsin*,[154] the union was accused of circulating campaign literature that falsely explained employee seniority rights and thereby interfered with employee free choice during the election. The Board rejected the carrier's claims that this conduct interfered with employees' freedom of choice, observing that a competing union had had an opportunity to circulate a written response to the allegedly misleading information.[155]

In *Federal Express Corp.*,[156] the Board ruled that a union had not tainted the election's laboratory conditions by (1) urging employees to vote for a union "or tear up your ballot if that is your decision," (2) characterizing the Board's prior finding of carrier interference as citing the carrier for "coercive communications," and (3) polling employees concerning their preferences during the mail ballot period.[157] The Board noted that the polling illustrated the differences in application of its standards between carriers and organizations, since "polling by a carrier is coercive precisely because of the substantial and material ability of the carrier to act against employees," whereas "the kind of polling evidenced here did not carry with it the same threat of imminent retaliation."[158]

---

[152]Air Wis., 16 NMB 235, 237 (1989).
[153]Singapore Airlines, 9 NMB 304, 305 (1982). *See also* Fox River Valley R.R., 20 NMB 251, 259 (1993) ("Union campaign communications used in an effort to collect authorization cards do not taint the laboratory conditions."); Rich Int'l Airways, 14 NMB 66 (1986).
[154]16 NMB 235.
[155]*Id.* at 238.
[156]20 NMB 486 (1993).
[157]*Id.* at 525–35.
[158]*Id.* at 534.

VII. NMB CONDUCT

The conduct of NMB personnel in administering Section 2, Ninth proceedings may also give rise to election objections to be resolved by the Board. In a variety of contexts, both unions and carriers have attempted, mostly without success, to challenge Board conduct.

The Board has set aside an election where the incumbent labor organization was inadvertently left off the ballot.[159] The Board has also counted ballots discovered after a vote count where the ballots had been misplaced.[160] On the other hand, the Board has refused to set aside elections where unions were listed in the wrong order on the ballot,[161] where an applicant did not receive sample ballots and notice of the election,[162] where a carrier made allegations of agency bias during the proceedings,[163] where there was a challenge of improper ex parte communications,[164] and where there were allegations that the mediator did not follow the Representation Manual.[165]

VIII. REMEDIES FOR INTERFERENCE WITH LABORATORY CONDITIONS

A. Rerun Elections

If the NMB determines that an election under Section 2, Ninth was not conducted under laboratory conditions, it takes action "intended to eliminate the taint of interference on the election."[166] The Board has dismissed an application even before an election after finding that carrier interference

---

[159]Pan Am. World Airways, 5 NMB 16 (1987).
[160]Aspen Airways, 8 NMB 123 (1980); Kiamichi R.R., 19 NMB 285 (1992).
[161]Dalfort Corp., 13 NMB 40 (1985).
[162]Intertech Aviation, 19 NMB 1 (1991).
[163]Washington C. R.R., 20 NMB 191 (1993).
[164]Fox River Valley R.R., 20 NMB 251 (1993).
[165]Zantop Int'l Airlines, 21 NMB 18 (1993).
[166]Federal Express Corp., 20 NMB 7, 44 (1992).

tainted the procurement of authorization cards needed to support a showing of interest.[167]

The Board describes these actions as "remedies" but not as "sanctions."[168] The Board considers the remedies to constitute means for "meeting the Act's directive of insuring that employees are free to make their decision regarding representation" without interference.[169] For this purpose, "[r]emedies are fashioned in accord with the extent of the carrier interference found."[170]

The Board's ordinary remedy for overcoming interference in an election is to order a rerun election, conducted in the same manner as the original election.[171] In the typical rerun, the Board uses the original cutoff date and eligibility list, and the ballot contains the same candidates and permits write-in votes to the same extent as in the original.[172]

The Board has adopted ballot and procedural modifications for rerun elections in order to remedy particularly high levels of carrier interference with employees' freedom of choice. One procedure is the *Laker* ballot, which is intended to remedy "egregious" levels of interference.[173] In a *Laker* rerun election, the ballot permits employees to vote "yes" or "no" as to the applicant organization and does not provide space for write-in votes; the applicant is certified if the majority of voters favor the applicant, whether or not a majority of eligible employees vote in the election.[174] In *Laker Airways*, the NMB also utilized a ballot box rather than a mail ballot

---

[167]Southwest Airlines, 21 NMB 332, 350 (1994).

[168]Evergreen Int'l Airlines, 20 NMB 675, 715 (1993).

[169]*Id.*

[170]Federal Express Corp., 20 NMB at 44.

[171]*E.g.,* Chicago & S. Air Lines, 2 NMB 1 (1948); Universal Airlines, 4 NMB 120 (1967); Piedmont Airlines, 5 NMB 126 (1970); Houston Belt & Terminal Ry., 5 NMB 286 (1970); Auto-Train Corp., 5 NMB 343 (1975); Zantop Int'l Airlines, 6 NMB 834 (1979).

[172]America W. Airlines, 21 NMB 293 (1994).

[173]Laker Airways, 8 NMB 236, 253, 256 (1981).

[174]*Id.* at 258; *see also* Federal Express Corp., 20 NMB 7, 44 (1992) (describing *Laker* ballot). The *Laker* procedure was foreshadowed in an early case in which the Board remedied election interference by holding a rerun election based on the majority of the votes cast rather than the majority of eligible voters as in the original election. *See* System Fed'n v. Virginian Ry., 11 F Supp 621, 625–26 (ED Va, 1935), 84 F2d 641 (CA 4, 1936), *aff'd,* 300 U.S. 515, 1 LRRM 743 (1937).

to conduct the rerun and ordered the carrier "to post [prescribed] notices assuring employees of their rights" and to provide eligible employees with copies of the Board's decision.[175] The NMB has ordered several *Laker* rerun elections, basing the rerun outcome on the majority of votes cast and requiring the posting of notices and/or use of a ballot box election.[176] In one case where the election interference was not regarded as severe, the Board ordered a rerun election based on the majority of votes cast but utilizing the normal Board ballot.[177]

Another Board remedy for election interference is the *Key* ballot.[178] In that procedure, the petitioning organization is certified unless a majority of eligible voters cast ballots *against* representation by the organization.[179] As in the *Laker* ballot, no write-in space is provided; the only choice on the ballot is to vote "no," so that ballots not cast are counted for representation by the union. This remedy is reserved for "egregious" cases, where the *Laker* procedure is ineffective, against "serious and repeated carrier interference."[180] The *Key* procedure has also been utilized in a rail industry election in response to "egregious" and "offensive" carrier conduct.[181]

B. Notices

The Board also remedies carrier interference in representation elections by mailing to voters in a rerun election a copy of the Board's findings of election interference.[182] These

---

[175]Laker Airways, 8 NMB at 257.

[176]Transkentucky T. R.R., 8 NMB 495 (1981); Mercury Servs., Inc., 9 NMB 312 (1982); Rio Airways, 11 NMB 75 (1983); Sea Airmotive, Inc., 11 NMB 87 (1983); Key Airlines, 13 NMB 153 (1986); Mid Pac. Airlines, 13 NMB 178 (1986); Metroflight, Inc., 13 NMB 284 (1986); Evergreen Int'l Airlines, 20 NMB 675, 715 (1993).

[177]Florida E.C. Ry., 17 NMB 177 (1990).

[178]Key Airlines, 16 NMB 296, 313 (1989).

[179]*See* Washington C. R.R., 20 NMB 191 (1993) (election set aside on ground that nonemployees were allowed to vote); Washington C. R.R. v. NMB, 830 F Supp 1343, 1359–60, 143 LRRM 2871, 2883 (ED Wash, 1993).

[180]Key Airlines, Inc., 16 NMB at 311.

[181]Washington C. R.R., 20 NMB 191, 236 (1993).

[182]*Id.* at 239.

notices have taken a variety of forms, including statements that the carrier's conduct interfered with the initial election[183] and statements that a *Key* or *Laker* ballot was selected for the rerun in order to protect against further interference by the carrier.[184]

C. Other Remedies

Although the NMB does not generally require carriers to provide organizations with employee address lists for election campaigns,[185] the Board has required that such lists be made available for rerun elections as a remedy for election interference.[186]

The NMB has stated in several cases that it may issue certification based on a check of authorization cards as a remedy for election interference.[187] The Board has also stated that it may refer carrier election interference "to the appropriate prosecutorial authority for investigation of actions which may be criminal violations under Section 2, Tenth of the Act."[188] The Board has not taken either of these actions.

D. Judicial Review of NMB Remedies

A narrow scope of judicial review applicable to NMB representation decisions is applicable to review of the Board's choice of remedies. The Board is authorized to "investigate" a representation dispute, "to take a secret ballot of the employees involved or to utilize any other appropriate method of ascertaining the names of [the employees'] duly designated

---

[183]*See, e.g.*, Metroflight, 18 NMB 532, 548 (1991); USAir, Inc., 17 NMB 377, 430 (1990); Florida E.C. Ry., 17 NMB 177, 190 (1990); America W. Airlines, 17 NMB 79, 104 (1990).

[184]Washington C. R.R., 20 NMB at 240 (notice accompanying *Key* ballot); Evergreen Int'l Airlines, 20 NMB 675, 717 (1993) (notice accompanying *Laker* ballot).

[185]Chamber of Commerce of the United States, 14 NMB 347, 361 (1987).

[186]Washington C. R.R., 20 NMB 191, 238 (1993); USAir, Inc., NMB 290, 334 (1991); USAir, Inc., 17 NMB at 428.

[187]Washington C. R.R., 20 NMB at 237; Key Airlines, 16 NMB 296, 308 (1989); Railway & Steamship Clerks v. Virginian Ry., 125 F2d 853, 10 LRRM 316 (CA 4, 1942) (upholding use of cards to determine representative).

[188]Washington C. R.R., 20 NMB at 237.

and authorized representatives in such manner as shall insure the choice of representatives by the employees without interference, influence, or coercion exercised by carrier."[189] In addition, the Board is authorized "to establish the rules to govern" an election conducted under Section 2, Ninth.[190] Few cases have been brought to review the Board's choice of remedies in election interference cases.

Two cases have addressed the Board's use of the *Key* ballot procedure for rerun elections and have upheld the procedure as falling within the Board's authority to establish rules for elections and to respond to carrier interference.[191] In *Washington Central Railroad*,[192] the court observed that the Board could certify a union in a *Key* procedure where one-half of the eligible voters voted in favor of the union, and one-half voted against.[193]

The Board's use of a special notice in rerun elections stating that the carrier's conduct was "unlawful"[194] has drawn a mixed response from courts. In *America West Airlines v. NMB*,[195] the Ninth Circuit held that the district court did not abuse its discretion by issuing a preliminary injunction enjoining distribution of such a notice. The court determined that the notice's statement that the carrier engaged in illegal conduct improperly suggested that the Board had engaged in "adjudication" rather than an "investigation," and the court ruled that the court had no authority to "adjudicate" and thus could not issue a notice so implying."[196] However, in a subsequent case concerning the same notice, a district court in the Fifth Circuit declined to follow the *America West* decision

---

[189]RLA §2, Ninth.

[190]*Id.*

[191]Washington C. R.R. v. NMB, 830 F Supp 1343, 1360, 143 LRRM 2871, 2883 (ED Wash, 1993); Key Airlines v. NMB, 743 F Supp 34, 38, 135 LRRM 2405, 2408 (D DC, 1990).

[192]Washington C. R.R. v. NMB, 830 F Supp at 1359–60, 143 LRRM at 2883.

[193]*Id.* The court overturned the election on the ground that the Board permitted nonemployees to vote. *See* discussion in Chapter 2, "Selecting a Bargaining Representative," §X.

[194]America W. Airlines, 17 NMB 79 (1990); Metroflight, 18 NMB 532 (1991).

[195]969 F2d 777, 140 LRRM 2765 (CA 9, 1992), *modified*, 986 F2d 1252, 142 LRRM 2639 (CA 9, 1993).

[196]969 F2d at 781–83, 140 LRRM at 2769–70, 986 F2d at 1257–58.

and held that the notice lay within the Board's authority to investigate a representation dispute.[197]

IX. PROTECTION AGAINST INTERFERENCE FOLLOWING CERTIFICATION OR RECOGNITION OF A UNION

A. In General

Enforcement of Section 2, Fourth's prohibitions against carrier interference with self-organization after a union has been certified or recognized may involve different issues from enforcement of similar prohibitions during the precertification period. This difference stems in part from the interplay between the statutory protections against interference and other doctrines that limit the role of the judiciary in the administration of the Act in favor of tribunals such as the applicable Adjustment Boards.[198]

The Supreme Court has observed that the protections against interference in Section 2, Fourth address "primarily the precertification rights and freedoms of unorganized employees."[199] Nonetheless, postcertification judicial intervention to enforce the RLA's requirements remains available where in its absence "[t]here would be no remedy to enforce

---

[197]Metroflight, Inc. v. NMB, 820 F Supp 288, 291, 142 LRRM 2419, 2422 (ND Tex., 1992).

[198]RLA §2, Fourth. A related provision of the Act, §2, First, imposes on the parties the continuing duty to "exert every reasonable effort" to make agreements; this provision may also be viewed as a prohibition on interference since, as the Supreme Court observed, "The bargaining status of a union can be destroyed by going through the motions of negotiating almost as easily as by bluntly withholding recognition." Chicago & N.W. Ry. v. United Transp. Union, 402 U.S. 570, 575, 77 LRRM 2337, 2338 (1971) (quoting Archibald Cox, The Duty to Bargain in Good Faith, 71 HARV. L. REV. 1401, 1412–13 (1958). Section 2, First is discussed in Chapter 4, "Negotiation of Collective Bargaining Agreements," §II.

The relation between enforcement of statutory and contractual rights is also a prominent issue in the administration of the status quo obligations of the Act, and can arise in the administration of self-help rights. See Chapter 6, "Exercise of Economic Weapons."

[199]Trans World Airlines v. Flight Attendants (IFFA), 489 U.S. 426, 440, 130 LRRM 2657, 2662 (1989).

the statutory commands."[200] Thus, the courts have jurisdiction following certification or recognition of a representative to determine whether a carrier's actions violate the protections in Section 2, Fourth, at least where the exercise of such jurisdiction is necessary to enforce the protections in the Act.[201]

For example, the courts have jurisdiction to enforce a union's certification issued by the NMB under Section 2, Ninth, and a carrier's refusal to treat with the employees' representative violates Section 2, Third and Fourth, as well as Section 2, Ninth, of the RLA.[202] The carrier's obligation to treat with the employees' representative has also been read to include the duty not to "wrongfully destroy the effectiveness of the chosen representative."[203] Thus, in several cases the courts have adjudicated claims of interference under Section 2, Third and Fourth where the carrier's actions threatened the effective functioning of the employees' representative or were based on antiunion animus.[204]

---

[200]Trans World Airlines v. Flight Attendants (IFFA), 489 U.S. at 441, 130 LRRM at 2664 (quoting Switchmen's Union v. NMB, 320 U.S. 297, 300, 13 LRRM 616, 618 (1943)).

[201]See *supra* §III.A for a discussion of court jurisdiction over claims of precertification carrier interference.

[202]Virginian Ry. v. System Fed'n, 300 U.S. 515, 1 LRRM 743 (1937). *See also* Steele v. Louisville & N. R.R., 323 U.S. 192, 200, 15 LRRM 708, 711 (1944) (selection of representative by majority of craft or class binds entire craft); Railroad Telegraphers v. Railway Express Agency, 321 U.S. 342, 347, 14 LRRM 506, 508 (1944) (collective bargaining agreement extinguishes individual employment agreements).

[203]Railroad Trainmen v. Central Ry. Co., 305 F2d 605, 608, 50 LRRM 2586, 2588 (CA 5, 1962).

[204]Air Line Pilots v. Transamerica Airlines, 817 F2d 510, LRRM 2777 (CA 9), *cert. denied*, 484 U.S. 963, 126 LRRM 3112 (1987) (allegation that carrier created alter ego airline to transfer work away from represented pilots stated claim under §2, Fourth over which courts have jurisdiction); Virgin Atl. Airways v. NMB, 956 F2d 1245, 139 LRRM 2541 (CA 2), *cert. denied*, 141 LRRM 2408 (1992) (allegation that carrier discharged employees who struck to enforce certification and that carrier solicited signed repudiations of the union stated a claim under §2, Third and Fourth); Ruby v. TACA Int'l Airlines, 439 F2d 1359, 77 LRRM 2089 (CA 5, 1971) (relocation of pilot base in order to escape application of RLA constituted both a major dispute and a violation of §2, Fourth); Conrad v. Delta Air Lines, 494 F2d 914, 86 LRRM 2242 (CA 7, 1974) (court had jurisdiction of claim that individual pilot was discharged because of his support for incumbent union); Arcamuzi v. Continental Air Lines, 819 F2d 935, 125 LRRM 2938 (CA 9, 1987) (plaintiffs may be entitled to injunctive relief to restrain carrier from requiring them to undergo polygraph examinations as a condition of returning from strike, based on claim that polygraph requirement

For example, in *Railway Labor Executives' Ass'n v. Boston
& Maine Corp.*,[205] the First Circuit held that the district court
had jurisdiction of the union's claim that the carrier violated
Section 2, Fourth and related sections of the Act by discriminatory abolition of strikers' jobs after the strike. The court
held that "such a controversy involves the substantive rights
protected by the RLA and is within the competency of the
district courts because these are claims that cannot be resolved
by interpretation of the collective bargaining agreement."[206]
The court observed that the agreement did not, and could
not lawfully, authorize the carrier to abolish jobs in retaliation
for engaging in protected activities.[207]

The *Railway Labor Executives* court described the procedure that a court should follow where a case "presents a claim
of violation of the RLA and a defense that the challenged
action was permitted by the collective bargaining agreement."[208] In such a case, the district court *"must weigh and assess
the merits* of the parties' positions to determine the question of
its jurisdiction. . . . If the court finds merit to the claim that
substantive rights protected by the RLA are at stake, the
controversy is properly before the district court."[209]

In several other cases of alleged interference the courts
have declined to exercise jurisdiction on the ground that the

---

was motivated by antiunion animus in retaliation for striking); Railway Labor Executives' Ass'n v. Boston & Me. Corp., 808 F2d 150, 124 LRRM 2145 (CA 1, 1986),
cert. denied, 484 U.S. 830, 126 LRRM 2496 (1987) (post-strike discriminatory abolition
of strikers' jobs violated statutory rights although collective bargaining agreement
conferred on carrier unlimited right to abolish jobs); Flight Attendants (AFA) v.
Horizon Air Indus., 135 LRRM 2855, 2859 (D Or, 1990) (carrier violated §2, Third,
Fourth, and Ninth during negotiations by circulating questionnaires to represented
employees that showed an "unwillingness to deal fairly" with the union), *aff'd on
other grounds*, 976 F2d 541, 141 LRRM 2430 (CA 9, 1992); Clift v. UPS, 133 LRRM
2639 (WD Ky, 1990) (court has jurisdiction of postcertification claim that probationer
employees were discharged for engaging in union activities).

[205] 808 F2d 150, 124 LRRM 2145 (CA 1, 1986), *cert. denied*, 484 U.S. 830, 126
LRRM 2496 (1987).

[206] 808 F2d at 157, 124 LRRM at 2150.

[207] 808 F2d at 158, 124 LRRM at 2150.

[208] *Id.*

[209] *Id* (citing Machinists v. Northwest Airlines, 673 F2d 700, 109 LRRM 3124
(CA 3, 1982) (Third Circuit endorsed the concept of taking a peek at the merits to
determine whether a claim of interference really involved a relatively high level of
antiunion animus or involved issues that could be resolved in the Adjustment Board
under the collective bargaining agreement).

complaint presented a minor dispute concerning interpretation of a collective bargaining agreement[210] or a representation dispute subject to NMB jurisdiction.[211] In some cases, courts ruled against the union on the merits because of failure to demonstrate a sufficient degree of antiunion animus on the part of the carrier to justify court intervention.[212] Several of these cases take the view that, in the context of an ongoing collective bargaining relationship, if the matter raises issues that can be resolved by interpretation of a collective bargaining agreement by the applicable Adjustment Board, the court will not exercise jurisdiction unless the plaintiff comes forth with specific evidence of antiunion animus or discrimination.[213] Where the court takes this view of the case, it is likely to determine its jurisdiction after a preliminary consid-

---

[210]Machinists v. Alaska Airlines 813 F2d 1038, 125 LRRM 2102 (CA 9, 1987) (union's claims that carrier's post-strike recall plan discriminated against union supporters raised a minor dispute as to whether strike violated existing collective bargaining agreement); Flight Attendants (UFA) v. Pan Am. World Airways, 789 F2d 139, 122 LRRM 2240 (CA 2, 1986) (claim of improper suspension was a minor dispute where union failed to prove that discipline of a union representative was part of an effort to undermine union's effectiveness); Machinists v. Northwest Airlines, 673 F2d 700, 109 LRRM 3124 (court lacked jurisdiction of claims that discipline of employees was part of effort to undermine union since a peek at the merits demonstrated that discipline was undertaken for legitimate reasons and case therefore presented a minor dispute); Machinists v. Eastern Airlines, 320 F2d 451, 53 LRRM 2795 (CA 5, 1963) (claims of interference were predicated entirely on alleged violations of collective bargaining agreement and therefore raised minor dispute for determination by Adjustment Board; no charge was asserted of underlying purpose to thwart effectiveness of bargaining agent).

[211]Air Line Pilots Ass'n v. Texas Int'l Airlines, 656 F2d 16, 107 LRRM 3185 (CA 2, 1981) (interference claim concerning creation of new subsidiary airline to serve new markets created a representation dispute subject to NMB jurisdiction; claim concerning transfer of existing work to new nonunion subsidiary would state claim under §2, Third and Fourth).

[212]National R.R. Passenger Corp. v. Machinists, 915 F2d 43, 135 LRRM 2578 (CA 1, 1990) (insufficient proof of antiunion animus); Air Line Pilots Ass'n v. Eastern Air Lines, 863 F2d 891, 129 LRRM 2691 (CA DC, 1988), cert. dismissed, 112 S. Ct. 37 (1991) (plaintiff could not sustain claim that furloughs, work transfers, and downsizing by carrier violated §2, Third and Fourth; applying Wright Line test, court determined that, although carrier's actions were motivated in part by antiunion animus, carrier sustained its burden of proof, and actions would have been taken in absence of such animus. See Wright Line, 251 NLRB 1083, 105 LRRM 1169 (1980), enforcement granted, 662 F2d 899, 108 LRRM 2513 (CA 1, 1981), cert. denied, 455 U.S. 393, 403, 113 LRRM 2857, 2861 (1983); see discussion in supra §III.C.

[213]See Flight Attendants (UFA) v. Pan Am. World Airways, 789 F2d 139, 142, 122 LRRM 2240 (CA 2, 1986) and cases cited therein.

eration of whether the challenged action was motivated by antiunion animus or constituted a normal application of the carrier's rights under the collective bargaining agreement.[214]

B. Direct Dealing Between Carrier and Represented Employees

The carrier's obligation to treat or bargain with the employees' authorized representative implies the obligation to bargain only with the union and not with individuals, and failure to fulfill this obligation may violate Section 2, First through Fourth, as well as Section 2, Ninth of the Act.[215] On the basis of these obligations, one district court held that a carrier violated the Act by seeking direct input from represented employees concerning their views on subjects then in negotiation.[216] In two other cases, district courts denied union requests for injunctions against carrier communications with represented employees in which the carriers described their views of the unions' negotiating positions.[217] These courts stated that, in order to minimize judicial intrusion into the

---

[214]National R.R. Passenger Corp. v. Machinists, 915 F2d at 52–53, 135 LRRM at 2584–85 (CA 1, 1990) (claims of improper discipline of union representatives are normally minor disputes that can be resolved by the Adjustment Board; "direct proof" of antiunion animus required to support court jurisdiction); Flight Attendants (APFA) v. American Airlines, 843 F2d 209, 128 LRRM 2267 (CA 5, 1988) (union's request for an injunction under §2, Fourth requiring carrier to permit employees to wear buttons protesting a "B" scale gave rise to minor dispute, because carrier asserted arguable claim that collective bargaining agreement barred buttons); Flight Attendants (UFA) v. Pan Am. World Airways, 789 F2d 139, 122 LRRM 2240 (claim concerning discipline of union representative must be heard by Adjustment Board unless plaintiff can demonstrate that discipline was part of an effort to undermine representative's effectiveness); Machinists v. Northwest Airlines, 673 F2d 700, 109 LRRM 3124, 3131 (union seeking relief against interference must "allege that the defendant is engaged in a general campaign or effort to destroy or undermine the union's representation of its members").

[215]See, e.g., Virginian Ry. v. System Fed'n, 300 U.S. 515, 1 LRRM 743 (1937) (certification of union imposes duty to deal with no other); Railroad Telegraphers v. Railway Express Agency, 321 U.S. 342, 347, 14 LRRM 506, 508 (1944) (collective bargaining agreement extinguishes individual agreements).

[216]Flight Attendants (AFA) v. Horizon Air Indus., 135 LRRM 2855, 2859 (D Or, 1990), aff'd on other grounds, 976 F2d 541, 141 LRRM 2430 (CA 9, 1992).

[217]Flight Attendants (IFFA) v. Trans World Airlines, 94 Lab. Cas. (CCH) ¶13,635 (WD Mo, 1981); Air Line Pilots Ass'n v. Flying Tiger Line, Inc., 659 F Supp 771, 125 LRRM 2368 (ED NY, 1987).

bargaining process, such orders should be entered only where such communications are part of an effort "to disrupt negotiations or destroy the union's bargaining power"[218] or where "the communication is couched in such terms as to give the impression, explicitly or impliedly, of an unwillingness to deal fairly" with the representative.[219] Such an impression does not arise from the employer's report of its "version of what was said at the bargaining table" or a request that the employees "consider the validity of its proposals" or "suggest to their representatives the position they should take."[220] Likewise, the court held that "criticism" of the union is permitted unless it is "so virulent or extensive as to cast serious doubt on the feasibility of further good faith discourse."[221]

Direct dealing issues also arise where a carrier negotiates individual "buyout" or "separation" agreements with represented employees. Several courts of appeals have declined to exercise jurisdiction over such cases on the ground that they presented minor disputes, finding that the individual agreements arguably were authorized by the collective bargaining agreement.[222] To establish jurisdiction over this type of claim, where it otherwise presented a minor dispute, the Seventh Circuit held that the union would need to show that the individual separation agreements were part of an effort to undermine the union's representation of its members.[223]

On the other hand, two district courts have held that individual buyout agreements violate the Act's prohibition on direct dealing and, in the words of one of the courts, undermine "the very design and purpose of the Railway Labor Act which was enacted to promote and protect effective

[218]Flight Attendants (IFFA) v. Trans World Airlines, 94 Lab. Cas. ¶13,635.
[219]Air Line Pilots Ass'n v. Flying Tiger Line, Inc., 659 F Supp at 775, 125 LRRM at 2371.
[220]659 F Supp at 776.
[221]Id.
[222]Machinists v. Soo Line R.R., 850 F2d 368, 128 LRRM 2826 (CA 8, 1988), rev'g 833 F2d 730 (CA 8 1987), cert. denied, 489 U.S. 1010, 130 LRRM 2656 (1989); Railway & Steamship Clerks v. Atchison, T. & S.F. Ry., 847 F2d 403, 128 LRRM 2425 (CA 7, 1988); Railway & Steamship Clerks v. Atchison, T. & S.F. Ry., 894 F2d 1463, 133 LRRM 2761 (CA 5, 1990).
[223]Railway & Steamship Clerks v. Atchison, T. & S.F. Ry., 847 F2d at 441, 128 LRRM at 2432.

collective bargaining and representation in employment matters and to assure industrial peace."[224]

C. Carrier Support of Union

Just as the courts may hear claims that a carrier has improperly acted to undermine the effectiveness of the employees' designated representative, they may also hear claims that a carrier dominates a representative in a manner designed to interfere with the employees' freedom of choice.[225] The Ninth Circuit has held, however, that a carrier's payment of a union's costs for an employee ownership transaction did not violate Section 2, Fourth of the RLA.[226]

D. Status of "Concerted Activities"

In a few instances the courts have addressed questions concerning efforts of employees to oppose actions of their carrier. Unlike Section 7 of the National Labor Relations Act (NLRA), the RLA contains no explicit protection for such

---

[224]Southern Pac. Fed'n Co. v. Railway & Steamship Clerks, 636 F Supp 57, 58, 121 LRRM 3541–42 (D Utah, 1986) (citing J.I. Case Co. v. NLRB, 321 U.S. 332, 14 LRRM 501 (1944)); Railroad Telegraphers v. Railway Express Agency, 321 U.S. 342, 14 LRRM 506 (1944); *see also* Railway & Steamship Clerks v. Chesapeake & O. Ry., 115 LRRM 3635 (ND Ohio, 1983).

[225]Texas N.O. R.R. v. Railway & Steamship Clerks, 281 U.S. 548 (1930); Barthelemy v. Air Line Pilots Ass'n, 897 F2d 999, 133 LRRM 2812 (CA 9, 1990).

[226]Barthelemy v. Air Line Pilots Ass'n, 897 F2d at 1016, 133 LRRM at 2825. The Court observed that

> the line between cooperation and support is not an obvious one. Permissible cooperation becomes prohibited support once the union's independence is compromised. This is a subjective inquiry: the question is whether the assistance provided the union is *in fact* depriving employees [of] their freedom of choice. It is not the potential for but the reality of domination that . . . [the Act is] intended to prevent.

Id.

Such payments do not violate §302 of the Labor Management Relations Act, 29 USC §186 (1994), since that provision does not cover RLA unions. Landry v. Air Line Pilots Ass'n, 901 F2d 404, 427, 134 LRRM 2311 (CA 5), *cert. denied*, 498 US 895, 135 LRRM 2552 (1990); United States v. Davidoff, 359 F Supp 545, 547–48 (ED NY, 1973).

activities.[227] Thus, one court of appeals held that the RLA does not protect employees from alleged carrier retaliation for protesting an agreement between the carrier and the union, because the employees' "activities [bore] no relationship to establishing a union" and the employer's action bore "no relationship to undermining a union."[228] Similarly, one district court ruled that a concerted protest by unrepresented employees against management policies, unrelated to an effort to organize a union, was not protected by the RLA.[229]

Similar reasoning led the Fifth Circuit to hold that the RLA confers on unrepresented employees no right to bring coworkers with them to disciplinary meetings with management.[230] The plaintiff in that case argued that the Act conferred on employees of carriers covered by the RLA the same *Weingarten* rights as are conferred on other employees by Section 7 of the NLRA.[231] The court of appeals disagreed, observing that *Weingarten* rights are premised on the protection in the NLRA of the right "to engage in . . . concerted activities for the purpose of . . . mutual aid or protection" but that the RLA contains no comparable protection.

A district court has held that the Act prohibits a carrier from discharging nonunion employees for refusing to cross picket lines during a primary strike against their employer by unionized employees in another craft or class, unless the terminations are "necessary to prevent disruption of vital transportation services."[232]

---

[227]*Compare* RLA §2, Fourth ("Employees shall have the right to organize and bargain collectively through representatives of their own choosing.") *with* NLRA §7 ("Employees shall have the right to . . . bargain collectively through representatives of their own choosing, and to engage in other concerted activities for the purpose of collective bargaining or other mutual aid or protection.").

[228]Herring v. Delta Air Lines, 894 F2d 1020, 1023, 133 LRRM 2469, 2472 (CA 9, 1990), *cert. denied*, 494 U.S. 1016, 133 (LRRM 2744 (1990).

[229]Rachford v. Evergreen Int'l Airlines, 596 F Supp 384, 386 117 LRRM 3195–96 (ND Ill, 1984).

[230]Johnson v. Express One Int'l, Inc., 944 F2d 247, 138 LRRM 2592 (CA 5, 1991).

[231]*See* NLRB v. Weingarten, Inc., 420 U.S. 251, 88 LRRM 2689 (1975) (NLRA §7 precludes an employer from denying an employee's request for union representation at an investigatory interview that the employee reasonably believes may result in discipline).

[232]Arthur v. United Air Lines, 655 F Supp 363, 126 LRRM 2082 (D Colo, 1987).

X. UNION SECURITY AGREEMENTS

A. Historical Background

When the RLA was passed in 1926 there was no reference to union security agreements.[233] In 1934, as part of the effort to restrict carrier-sponsored unions, the Act was amended to prohibit any form of compulsory union membership.[234]

By 1950, unions advocated legislation to allow agreements requiring union membership. Extensive hearings and debate in Congress culminated in amendment of the Act in early 1951.[235] The 1951 amendment modified the prohibition of compulsory union membership and expressly authorized carriers and unions to enter union shop agreements,[236] by which a current employee may be required by the collective bargaining agreement, as a condition of employment, to pay dues, assessments, and initiation fees (but not to become a member).[237] The amendment effectively eliminated the right to be a "free rider," that is, an employee in the bargaining unit whom the union is legally required to represent, but who refuses to contribute to the cost of that representation.[238] This provision of the RLA preempts state right-to-work laws.[239]

---

[233] Act of May 20, 1926, ch. 347, §§1–11, 44 Stat. 577.

[234] Act of June 21, 1934, ch. 691, §11, 48 Stat. 1185 (repealed 1951). Section 2, Fifth of the 1934 amendments prohibits a carrier from requiring "any person seeking employment to sign any contract or agreement promising to join or not to join a labor organization." *See* Felter v. Southern P. Transp. Co., 359 U.S. 326, 332 n.6, 43 LRRM 2876 (1959). Section 2, Fourth prohibits a carrier from using its funds "in maintaining or assisting or contributing to" any labor organization.

[235] Act of Jan. 10, 1951, ch. 1220, 64 Stat. 1238; RLA §2, Eleventh.

[236] Railway Employees' Dep't v. Hanson, 351 U.S. 225, 231–32, 38 LRRM 2099, 2101 (1956).

[237] *See* Kidwell v. Transportation Communications Union, 946 F2d 283, 138 LRRM 2537 (CA 4, 1991), *cert. denied*, 140 LRRM 2120 (1992); Pilots Against Illegal Dues v. Air Line Pilots Ass'n, 938 F2d 1123, 137 LRRM 2963 (CA 10, 1991).

[238] *See* Ellis v. Railway & Steamship Clerks, 466 U.S. 435, 446, 116 LRRM 2001, 2006 (1984); Kidwell v. Transportation Communications Union, 946 F2d at 293, 138 LRRM at 2544.

[239] RLA §2, Eleventh; Railway Employees' Dep't v. Hanson, 351 U.S. at 231–32, 38 LRRM at 2101.

B. Structure of RLA Union Security Provisions

Section 2, Eleventh (a) of the Act permits the negotiation of union shop agreements that (1) allow employees at least 60 days after the date of actual employment or the effective date of the labor contract to join the union, (2) establish eligibility for membership on the same terms and conditions for all employees, and (3) limit the obligation to join the union to the payment of uniformly required dues, initiation fees, and assessments.

Section 2, Eleventh (b) authorizes dues checkoff agreements between unions and carriers, allowing a carrier to deduct from employee wages any periodic dues, initiation fees, and assessments due the union and to forward the deductions to the union, provided (1) the employee authorizes the employer in writing to make the deduction from wages and (2) the checkoff authorizations are revocable in writing after one year or on expiration of the labor contract, whichever occurs first. Dues checkoff agreements can be entered into whether or not the parties agreed to a union shop clause, and vice versa.[240]

Section 2, Eleventh (c) establishes a rail industry proviso for alternative union membership. It allows "operating" employees (i.e., engineers and train and yard service employees) in the rail industry who transfer to another craft, covered by a union security agreement, to refrain from joining the incumbent union in their new craft. Instead these employees may satisfy the union security requirement by being a member of another union that represents operating employees and is "national in scope."[241]

---

[240]Felter v. Southern P. Transp. Co., 359 U.S. 326, 43 LRRM 2876 (1959).

[241]Alternative membership is available only to employees who are engaged in employment covered by RLA §3, First (h), and the unions in which alternative membership is acceptable are limited to certain national organizations that have been identified by the Supreme Court. RLA §2, Eleventh (c); see Pennsylvania R.R. v. Rychlik, 352 U.S. 480, 39 LRRM 2421 (1957). An employee who seeks to escape the agency shop rule in §2, Eleventh by joining a union that does not qualify for alternative membership is not protected against termination. See Pigott v. Detroit, T. & I. R.R., 221 F2d 736, 35 LRRM 2562 (CA 6, 1955).

Because employees in operating crafts are subject to numerous transfers, the availability of alternative union membership to satisfy agency shop obligations permits these employees to retain their basic union membership and benefits without also having to pay dues or fees to additional unions.[242] Alternate membership status can result in dues being paid to a union that is not the employee's collective bargaining representative.[243]

C. Legal Challenge to Union Security Agreements

Employees may lawfully be terminated for not fulfilling financial obligations pursuant to a union security agreement after the 60-day grace period. Employees discharged in violation of Section 2, Eleventh (a) may sue both the union and the carrier in federal district court for a declaratory judgment or damages.[244] Lack of intent is not a defense, nor is it a defense for the employer to show that it was acting on instructions from the union.[245]

Whether exhaustion of contractual grievance procedures is a prerequisite to filing suit is unsettled. Several courts have required grievance procedure exhaustion, whereas others have excused exhaustion on the ground that utilizing a mechanism controlled by the union and the company would be futile.[246]

---

[242]*See* Pennsylvania R.R. v. Rychlik, 352 U.S. 480, 39 LRRM 2421.

[243]Felter v. Southern P. Transp. Co., 359 U.S. 326, 43 LRRM 2876; Locomotive Firemen & Enginemen v. Northern Pac. R.R., 274 F2d 641, 45 LRRM 2557 (CA 8, 1960).

[244]*See* Klemens v. Air Line Pilots Ass'n, 736 F2d 491, 115 LRRM 3537 (CA 9), *cert. denied*, 469 U.S. 1019, 117 LRRM 2936 (1984); Bagnall v. Air Line Pilots Ass'n, 626 F2d 336, 104 LRRM 2769 (CA 4, 1980), *cert. denied*, 449 U.S. 1125, 106 LRRM 2256 (1981); Brady v. Trans World Airlines, 401 F2d 87, 69 LRRM 2048 (CA 3, 1968), *cert. denied*, 393 U.S. 1048, 70 LRRM 2249 (1969); Cunningham v. Erie R.R., 358 F2d 640, 62 LRRM 2016 (CA 2, 1966).

[245]Brady v. Trans World Airlines, 401 F2d at 100–01, 69 LRRM at 2057–58; Cunningham v. Erie R.R., 358 F2d 640, 62 LRRM 2016.

[246]*Compare generally* Dean v. Trans World Airlines, 924 F2d 805, 136 LRRM 2273 (CA 9, 1991) (no duty to exhaust contractual grievance procedure in dispute over discharge for nonpayment of dues, because grievance procedure controlled by carrier and union); Klemens v. Air Line Pilots Ass'n, 736 F2d 491, 115 LRRM 3537 (exhaustion of grievance procedure unnecessary where contract allows dispute

The courts have construed the requirement of Section 2, Eleventh (a) that membership be made available to all on the same terms and conditions to require that financial conditions be uniform, but not necessarily equal. Thus, dues pegged to a percentage of earnings satisfy the statute's requirements,[247] but union rules that limit the membership rights of certain classes of employees, while exacting full dues, do not.[248] Union security agreements cannot be used to enforce fines and penalties for disciplinary purposes.[249]

Unions have been accorded some flexibility in deciding when to seek enforcement of a union security clause. For example, in one case a union was permitted to condone varying lengths of arrearages when there was a nondiscriminatory basis for distinctions in treatment.[250] But a union was not permitted to depart from its usual method of enforcing its dues delinquency policy in order to discriminate against a member who had been complaining about a perceived discrepancy in seniority.[251]

Provisions of a union's constitution and bylaws setting out terms for payment of financial obligations to the union

---

over payment of dues to be grieved only after threat of discharge); *and* Bagnall v. Air Line Pilots Ass'n, 626 F2d 336, 104 LRRM 2769 (same holding) *with* Republic Steel Corp. v. Maddox, 379 U.S. 650, 652–53, 58 LRRM 2193 (1965) (employee, at a minimum, must attempt to exhaust exclusive grievance and arbitration procedures established by a bargaining agreement before bringing action in the courts); Crusos v. United Transportation Union, 786 F2d 970, 122 LRRM 2564 (CA 9, 1986) (arbitrator was within his jurisdiction in determining wrongful discharge grievance concerning grievants' nonpayment of dues); *and* Brady v. Trans World Airlines, 401 F2d at 100–01, 69 LRRM at 2057–58 (exhaustion of grievance procedure necessary unless adequate reason is shown for failure).

[247]Bagnall v. Air Line Pilots Ass'n, 626 F2d 336, 104 LRRM 2769; *accord,* Klemens v. Air Line Pilots Ass'n, 736 F2d 491, 115 LRRM 3537.

[248]Fenderson v. Flight Attendants (IFFA), 743 F Supp 245, 135 LRRM 2185 (SD NY, 1990).

[249]Railway Employees' Dep't v. Hanson, 351 U.S. 225, 38 LRRM 2099 (1956). If a levy is equally imposed, that fact may support enforceability. In Fenderson v. Flight Attendants (IFFA), 743 F Supp 245, 135 LRRM 2185, the court held that a reinstatement fee of $250 for former members who wanted to rejoin the union was not a fine or penalty. Rather, since the reinstatement fee would apply to anybody who dropped membership, for whatever reason, and to new members, the fee was held to be a valid initiation fee that was enforceable through application of the union security clause.

[250]Hostetler v. Railroad Trainmen, 287 F2d 457, 47 LRRM 2703 (CA 4, 1961), *cert. denied,* 368 U.S. 955, 49 LRRM 2359 (1962).

[251]Cunningham v. Erie R.R., 358 F2d 640, 62 LRRM 2016 (CA 2, 1966).

may be incorporated into the union security agreement.[252] Upon incorporation, any fees or assessments contrary to the bylaws or constitution may not be used to support a discharge. In *Brady v. Trans World Airlines*,[253] the Third Circuit sustained the district court's ruling that an employee was improperly discharged for nonpayment of a reinstatement fee because the union's imposition of the reinstatement fee was inconsistent with specific provisions of the union constitution.

Minimal litigation has occurred involving Section 2, Eleventh (b)'s twofold requirement of written authorization from the employee and the opportunity to withdraw authorization after contract expiration or after one year, whichever occurs first. In the only case under Section 2, Eleventh (b) to result in a decision by the Supreme Court, the Court held that the union cannot prescribe a form that must be used by employees to revoke checkoff authorization.[254] Instead, the Court took the position that the authority of carriers and unions to enter dues checkoff agreements must be narrowly construed to preserve maximum freedom of choice for employees.

D. Objections to Union Expenditures of Funds

In a series of decisions, the Supreme Court has held that the "government's vital policy interest" in eliminating "free riders" permitted Congress to authorize unions and employers, through collective bargaining agreements, to require individuals who decline to join a union to nonetheless provide it with financial support.[255] Although objecting nonmembers are relieved from underwriting certain political or ideological

---

[252]*See, e.g.*, Brady v. Trans World Airlines, 401 F2d 87, 69 LRRM 2048 (CA 3, 1968), *cert. denied*, 393 U.S. 1048, 70 LRRM 2249 (1969).

[253]*Id.*

[254]Felter v. Southern P. Transp. Co., 359 U.S. 326, 43 LRRM 2876 (1959).

[255]Lehnert v. Ferris Faculty Ass'n, 500 U.S. 507, 137 LRRM 2321, 2325–26 (1991); Ellis v. Railway & Steamship Clerks, 466 U.S. 435, 446–48, 116 LRRM 2001, 2006–08 (1984); Machinists v. Street, 367 U.S. 740, 749, 760–64, 48 LRRM 2345, 2348, 2352–54 (1961); Railway Employees' Dep't v. Hanson, 351 U.S. 225, 235, 38 LRRM 2099 2102–03 (1956).

activities,[256] they must fund those union expenditures that are

> necessarily or reasonably incurred for the purpose of per-
> forming the duties of an exclusive representative of the em-
> ployees in dealing with the employer on labor–management
> issues. Under this standard, objecting employees may be com-
> pelled to pay their fair share of not only the direct costs of
> negotiating and administering a collective-bargaining contract
> and of settling grievances and disputes, but also the expenses
> of activities or undertakings normally or reasonably employed
> to implement or effectuate the duties of the union as exclusive
> representative of the employees in the bargaining unit.[257]

In *Lehnert v. Ferris Faculty Ass'n*,[258] the Supreme Court confirmed that so long as there is "some indication" that the activity "may ultimately enure to the benefit" of the bargaining unit, the expenses undertaken in performance of the challenged activity—even if spent on activities undertaken for employees in a different bargaining unit from that of the plaintiffs—are chargeable to objecting nonmembers.[259]

In *Chicago Teachers Union v. Hudson*,[260] the Court held that unions must establish procedures that give agency fee

---

[256]Abood v. Detroit Bd. of Educ., 431 U.S. 209, 235–36, 95 LRRM 2411, 2421 (1977); Machinists v. Street, 367 U.S. at 768–69, 48 LRRM at 2355.

[257]Ellis v. Railway & Steamship Clerks, 466 U.S. at 448, 116 LRRM at 2007; *see* Lehnert v. Ferris Faculty Ass'n, 137 LRRM at 2327–29. In *Ellis*, the Court held that unions can charge objecting nonmembers for the costs of conventions and social activities; for costs related to union publications (except to the extent they report on nonchargeable activities, such as organizing); and for litigation expenditures that relate to negotiating and administering labor contracts, resolving grievances, or any other litigation that concerns bargaining unit employees and is normally undertaken by the union. However, unions cannot charge objectors for organizing expenses. 466 U.S. at 448–53, 116 LRRM at 2007–09.

[258]500 U.S. 507, 137 LRRM 2321.

[259]137 LRRM at 2327–29; *accord*, Ellis v. Railway & Steamship Clerks, 466 U.S. at 447–48, 116 LRRM at 2007–09; Crawford v. Air Line Pilots Ass'n, 992 F2d 1295, 1299–1301, 143 LRRM 2185, 2187–88 (CA 4) (en banc), *cert. denied*, 144 LRRM 2391 (1993) (nonmember objectors lawfully charged for strike activities by pilots employed by airlines other than those by which the objectors were employed, and for a general "major contingency fund"). There was no majority position in *Lehnert* with regard to the appropriate treatment of litigation-related expenditures that were not confined to the objectors' bargaining unit.

[260]475 U.S. 292, 121 LRRM 2793 (1986).

payers (1) an adequate explanation of the basis for the fee, (2) a reasonably prompt opportunity to challenge the amount of the fee before an impartial decision maker, and (3) an escrow for the amounts reasonably in dispute while such challenges are pending.[261]

To assure that funds tendered by agency fee payers are not used to subsidize noncredentials expenditures, the escrowed funds must be deposited in interest-bearing accounts pending a determination of the chargeability of union expenditures, or the union must provide for an advance reduction of the fees arguably in dispute.[262] Unless the full amount of dues from agency fee payers is escrowed, the escrow account must be verified by an independent auditor.[263]

---

[261]475 U.S. at 310, 121 LRRM at 2800. A union has no duty to adjust fees until the nonmember submits an objection to the union's expenditures. Abood v. Detroit Bd. of Educ., 431 U.S. 209, 95 LRRM 2411 (1977); Railway & Steamship Clerks v. Allen, 373 U.S. 113, 118–19, 53 LRRM 2128, 2130–31 (1963); Machinists v. Street, 367 U.S. 740, 774–75, 48 LRRM 2345, 2357–58 (1961); Chicago Teachers Union v. Hudson, 475 U.S. 292, 121 LRRM 2793 (1986).

[262]Ellis v. Railway & Steamship Clerks, 466 U.S. 435, 116 LRRM 2001 (1984); Crawford v. Air Line Pilots Ass'n, 992 F2d 1295, 1299–1301, 143 LRRM 2185, 2187–88 (CA 4, 1993) (en banc); Pilots Against Illegal Dues v. Air Line Pilots Ass'n, 938 F2d 1123, 1133, 137 LRRM 2963, 2971 (CA 10, 1991); Andrews v. Education Ass'n, 829 F2d 335, 338–39, 127 LRRM 2929, 2931–32 (CA 2, 1987); Grunwald v. San Bernadino City Unified School Dist., 994 F2d 1370, 1374, 143 LRRM 2305, 2307 (9th Cir.), *cert. denied*, 144 LRRM 2680 (1993). *But see* Damiano v. Matish, 830 F2d 1363, 1369–70, 126 LRRM 2727, 2731–32 (CA 6, 1987) (advance fee reduction required).

[263]Chicago Teachers Union v. Hudson, 475 U.S. 292, 121 LRRM 2793. Some courts have held that a failure to implement *Hudson* safeguards deprives the union of authority to cause the termination of agency fee payers who are delinquent in the payment of dues. Dean v. Trans World Airlines, 924 F2d 805, 136 LRRM 2273 (CA 9, 1991); Tierney v. Toledo, 824 F2d 1497, 125 LRRM 3217 (CA 6, 1987).

CHAPTER 4

NEGOTIATION OF COLLECTIVE BARGAINING AGREEMENTS

I. DUTY TO TREAT WITH CERTIFIED REPRESENTATIVE

A. In General

The duty of a carrier to treat—i.e., to negotiate or otherwise deal—with the certified representative of its employees over rates of pay, rules, and working conditions arises upon the certification of the representative by the National Mediation Board (NMB) pursuant to Section 2, Ninth. That section provides that "[u]pon receipt of such certification the carrier shall treat with the representative so certified as the representative of the craft or class."[1] Although the RLA as a general rule does not prohibit a carrier from voluntarily recognizing a labor union prior to certification,[2] the carrier may not be compelled to recognize a union that has not been certified by the NMB.[3] This rule applies even though there may be independent evidence, such as membership cards, that the organization represents a majority of the employees.[4] Even though a union has received the majority of votes in an NMB

---

[1]The content of the duty to treat is discussed in *infra* §§II, III.
[2]*See* Chapter 2, "Selecting a Bargaining Representative," §IV.
[3]*Id.*
[4]Scheduled Skyways, Inc. v. NMB, 738 F2d 339, 342, 116 LRRM 3007 (CA 8, 1984). *See also* Summit Airlines v. Teamsters, 628 F2d 787, 105 LRRM 2020 (CA 2, 1980).

election, the carrier has no duty to treat until the NMB certifies the election results.[5]

The duty to treat is enforceable in federal court by injunctive relief,[6] and union self-help may also be permitted if a carrier refuses to bargain with the duly designated representative.[7] Once an employee organization has been certified, the certification remains in force until the NMB extinguishes the certification or certifies a different representative, or the representative surrenders the certificate.[8] The certification cannot be waived by a union's failure to seek negotiations or be modified by agreement.[9] A carrier's good faith belief that an organization is no longer supported by a majority of employees within the craft or class is not sufficient to relieve the carrier of its duty to treat with the representative.[10]

One circumstance in which courts have refused to enforce an existing certification is where a representation dispute exists among the carrier's employees that is within the exclusive jurisdiction of the NMB.[11] Examples of representation disputes that have resulted in such a refusal are a schism within the certified union in which two factions asserted representation rights,[12] and a merger of two carriers that resulted

---

[5]Scheduled Skyways, Inc. v. NMB, 738 F2d at 342.

[6]Virginian Ry. v. System Fed'n No. 40, 300 U.S. 515, 549–53, 1 LRRM 743 (1937).

[7]United Air Lines v. Teamsters, 874 F2d 110, 115, 131 LRRM 2329 (CA 2, 1989).

[8]Russell v. NMB, 714 F2d 1332, 114 LRRM 2800 (CA 5, 1983), *cert. denied*, 467 U.S. 1204, 116 LRRM 2393 (1984).

[9]Machinists v. Alitalia Airlines, 600 F Supp 268, 116 LRRM 3214 (SD NY, 1984), *aff'd*, 753 F2d 3, 118 LRRM 2237 (CA 2, 1985) (union's failure to negotiate for many years regarding group of employees did not modify certification).

[10]Machinists v. Alitalia Airlines, 753 F2d 3, 118 LRRM 2237. *See also* Virgin Atl. Airways v. NMB, 956 F2d 1245, 139 LRRM 2541 (CA 2), *cert. denied*, 113 S Ct 67, 141 LRRM 2408 (1992) (certification enforceable despite NMB voting rules that could have allowed less than majority to select representative); Machinists v. Continental Airlines, 754 F Supp 892, 136 LRRM 2301 (D DC, 1990) (poll designed to determine union's majority support violates RLA).

[11]*See* Switchmen's Union v. NMB, 320 U.S. 297, 13 LRRM 616 (1943).

[12]Ruby v. American Airlines, 323 F2d 248, 255, 54 LRRM 2202 (CA 2, 1963), *cert. denied*, 376 U.S. 913, 55 LRRM 2455 (1964); Pan Am. World Airways v. Teamsters, 275 F Supp 986, 994, 66 LRRM 2559 (SD NY, 1967), *aff'd per curiam*, 404 F2d 938, 70 LRRM 2384 (CA 2, 1969).

in elimination of the carrier for which the union held its certification.[13]

B. Duty to Treat With Recognized Union

Although voluntary recognition is permissible under the RLA,[14] and a number of rail and air carriers have long-standing recognition agreements, there has been scant judicial attention to the effect of such agreements on the duty to treat. In one reported decision involving a carrier's refusal to continue dealing with a voluntarily recognized union, the Second Circuit held that "we accept appellants' argument that, in the light of §2 Second, Fourth and Sixth, it is not fatal that [the union] never had been certified so as to come within the precise command of §2 Ninth that the employer 'treat with the representative so certified.'" The court dismissed the particular action on the basis that it raised a representation dispute within the jurisdiction of the NMB.[15]

C. Multiemployer Bargaining

A form of multiemployer bargaining known as "national handling" is common in the rail industry. A series of cases decided in the late 1960s and early 1970s state that national handling can be obligatory where the subject matter is practically appropriate for national resolution or there is a clear history of national bargaining.[16] More recent decisions have

---

[13]Air Line Employees v. Republic Airlines, 798 F2d 967, 123 LRRM 2437 (CA 7), cert. denied, 479 U.S. 962, 123 LRRM 2984 (1986); Machinists v. Northeast Airlines, 536 F2d 975, 92 LRRM 3057 (CA 1), cert. denied, 429 U.S. 961 (1976); Railway & Steamship Clerks v. United Air Lines, 325 F2d 576, 93 LRRM 2734 (CA 6, 1963), cert. dismissed, 379 U.S. 26 (1964). See also Western Airlines v. Teamsters, 480 U.S. 1301, 124 LRRM 3139 (1987) (O'Connor, J.).

[14]See Chapter 2, "Selecting a Bargaining Representative," §IV.

[15]Ruby v. American Airlines, 323 F2d 248, 254–55, 54 LRRM 2202 (CA 2, 1963), cert. denied, 376 U.S. 913 (1964).

[16]Railroad Trainmen v. Atlantic Coast Line Ry., 383 F2d 225, 229, 66 LRRM 2115 (CA DC, 1967), cert. denied, 389 U.S. 1047, 67 LRRM 2232 (1968); Delaware & H. Ry. v. United Transp. Union, 450 F2d 603, 76 LRRM 2900 (CA DC, 1971), cert. denied, 403 U.S. 911, 77 LRRM 2404 (1971); United Transp. Union v. Burlington N. Ry., 325 F Supp 1125, 1131, 76 LRRM 2838 (D DC, 1971); Machinists v. National R.R. Labor Conference, 310 F Supp 905, 73 LRRM 2319 (D DC, 1970), appeal dismissed, 463 F2d 872, 79 LRRM 3028 (CA DC, 1972); Chicago, B.Q. R.R. v. Railway Employees Dep't, 301 F Supp 603, 70 LRRM 3415 (D DC, 1969).

held that a carrier has no duty to enter into a new round of national handling even if the carrier has joined in previous rounds, and that the carrier need not serve Section 6 notices or otherwise negotiate over the decision to withdraw from national handling.[17] The latter decisions have rested on an interpretation of Section 2, Third that provides that collective bargaining representatives "shall be designated by the respective parties without interference, influence, or coercion by either party over the designation of representatives by the other."[18]

D. Duty Not to Negotiate With Others

The duty to treat with the certified union implies the obligation not to treat with any other purported representative over the rates of pay, rules, or working conditions of the craft or class.[19] This doctrine has been applied to invalidate an agreement with a union that was construed to regulate the terms and conditions of employment of a different craft or class.[20]

Although the Supreme Court initially asserted in *Virginian Railway v. System Federation No. 40*[21] that the duty to treat did not preclude a carrier from entering into agreements with individual employees,[22] the Court subsequently held that the RLA prohibits a carrier from negotiating directly with employees over matters that are the subject of collective bargaining.[23] The fact that individual employees are willing to

---

[17]United Transp. Union v. Grand Trunk W. R.R., 901 F2d 489, 490, 133 LRRM 2845 (CA 6), *cert. denied,* 498 U.S. 815, 135 LRRM 2463 (1990); Railway & Airline Supervisors v. Soo L. R.R., 891 F2d 675, 679, 133 LRRM 2081 (CA 8, 1989), *cert. denied,* 498 U.S. 809, 135 LRRM 2463 (1990); United Transp. Union v. Chicago & I. M. Ry., 731 F Supp 1336, 1340–41, 134 LRRM 2474 (CD Ill, 1990); United Transp. Union v. Illinois C. R.R., 731 F Supp 1332 (ND Ill, 1990).

[18]*Eg.,* United Transp. Union v. Chicago & I. M. Ry., 731 F Supp at 1340–41.

[19]Virginian Ry. v. System Fed'n No. 40, 300 U.S. 515, 1 LRRM 743 (1937).

[20]Air Line Pilots Ass'n v. UAL Corp., 874 F2d 439, 131 LRRM 2265 (CA 7, 1989).

[21]300 U.S. 515, 1 LRRM 743 (1937).

[22]300 U.S. at 549.

[23]Railway & Steamship Clerks v. Florida E. C. Ry., 384 U.S. 238, 246, 62 LRRM 2177 (1966); Railroad Telegraphers v. Railway Express Agency, 321 U.S. 342, 346–47, 14 LRRM 506 (1944).

enter into such agreements or are uniquely situated does not create an exception to this prohibition.[24] However, during a strike a carrier may enter into individual contracts with strike replacements that deviate from the collective bargaining agreement to the extent that such individual agreements are "reasonably necessary" to the carrier's continued operation during the strike.[25] Such replacements, though, still fall within the craft or class, and are subject to the union's representation rights following the strike.[26]

The prohibition against negotiations with individual employees does not prevent the carrier from communicating with its employees unless the communication gives the impression that the employer is not willing to deal in good faith with the employees' representative.[27] Thus, some courts have held that a carrier may provide its employees with either party's bargaining proposals, may question the union's proposals or negotiation strategy, and may even state that the union's position is preventing the parties from reaching an agreement, so long as the carrier does not state or imply that it is not willing to continue negotiating with the employees' representative.[28] However, one court has held that a carrier violated the RLA when it distributed questionnaires to its

---

[24]Railroad Telegraphers v. Railway Express Agency, 321 U.S. at 346–47. *See also* Melanson v. United Air Lines, 931 F2d 558, 137 LRRM 2151 (CA 9), *cert. denied,* 138 LRRM 2479 (1991); Lewellyn v. Fleming, 154 F2d 211, 17 LRRM 927 (CA 10), *cert. denied,* 329 U.S. 715, 18 LRRM 2469 (1946); Southern P. Transp. Co. v. Railway & Steamship Clerks, 636 F Supp 57, 58–59, 121 LRRM 3541 (D Utah, 1986).

[25]Air Line Pilots Ass'n v. United Air Lines, 802 F2d 886, 123 LRRM 2617 (CA 7, 1986), *cert. denied,* 480 U.S. 946, 124 LRRM 3192 (1987); Empresa Ecuatoriana de Aviacion, S.A. v. Machinists Dist. Lodge 100, 690 F2d 838, 111 LRRM 2971 (CA 11, 1982), *cert. dismissed,* 463 U.S. 1250 (1983). *See* Chapter 6, "Exercise of Economic Weapons," §V.

[26]Rakestraw v. United Air Lines, 981 F2d 1524, 1536, 142 LRRM 2054 (CA 7, 1992), *cert. denied,* 144 LRRM 2392 (1993).

[27]Flight Attendants (AFA) v. Horizon Air Indus., 976 F2d 541, 141 LRRM 2430 (CA 9, 1993); Air Line Pilots Ass'n v. Flying Tiger Line, Inc., 659 F Supp 771, 774–75, 125 LRRM 2368 (ED NY, 1987); Flight Attendants Ass'n v. Trans. World Airlines, 682 F Supp 1003, 127 LRRM 3266 (WD Mo, 1986), *aff'd,* 878 F2d 254, 131 LRRM 2785 (CA 8, 1989), *cert. denied,* 493 U.S. 1044, 134 LRRM 2480 (1990).

[28]Air Line Pilots Ass'n v. Flying Tiger Line, Inc., 659 F Supp at 774–75; Flight Attendants (IFFA) v. Trans World Airlines, 94 Lab. Cas. (CCH) ¶13,635 (WD Mo, 1981).

employees soliciting their views on the issues raised during negotiations.[29]

II. DUTY TO EXERT EVERY REASONABLE EFFORT TO MAKE AND MAINTAIN AGREEMENTS

Section 2, First of the RLA states that "[i]t shall be the duty of all carriers, their officers, agents, and employees to exert every reasonable effort to make and maintain agreements concerning rates of pay, rules, and working conditions." This duty, which the Supreme Court has called "[t]he heart of the Railway Labor Act,"[30] is a judicially enforceable obligation applicable to both carriers and unions.[31]

The duty to exert every reasonable effort to make and maintain agreements resembles the duty to bargain in good faith under the National Labor Relations Act (NLRA),[32] and the courts have generally assumed the RLA provision to be as stringent, or more so.[33] However, the Supreme Court has cautioned that under the RLA, in order to avoid governmental interference with the substantive terms of collective bargaining agreements, the courts must use "great circumspection" before finding a violation of Section 2, First in cases

---

[29]*See* Flight Attendants (AFA) v. Horizon Air Indus., 976 F2d 541, 141 LRRM 2430.

[30]Railroad Trainmen v. Jacksonville Terminal Co., 394 U.S. 369, 377–78, 70 LRRM 2961, 2964 (1969).

[31]Chicago & N.W. Ry. v. United Transp. Union, 402 U.S. 570, 578, 77 LRRM 2337, 2340 (1971); Elgin, J. & E. Ry. v. Burley, 325 U.S. 711, 723 n.12 (1945); Virginian Ry. v. System Fed'n No. 40, 300 U.S. 515, 549–53, 1 LRRM 743 (1937).

[32]29 USC §158(d) (1994). The Supreme Court has cautioned, however, that "parallels between [the two statutes] should be drawn with the utmost care and with full awareness of the differences between the statutory schemes." Chicago & N.W. Ry. v. United Transp. Union, 402 U.S. at 579 n.11, 77 LRRM at 2340, n.11.

[33]Flight Attendants (AFA) v. Horizon Air Indus., 976 F2d at 544 (duty under RLA "at least as stringent" as under NLRA); Japan Air Lines Co. v. Machinists, 389 F Supp 27, 34, 88 LRRM 2910, 2915–16 (SD NY, 1975), aff'd, 538 F2d 46, 92 LRRM 3383 (CA 2, 1976) (assuming duty under RLA is greater than under NLRA); REA Express, Inc. v. Railway & Steamship Clerks, 358 F Supp 760, 771–72 & n.43, 83 LRRM 2153, 2162 & n.43 (SD NY, 1973) (same holding); Machinists v. National R.R. Labor Conference, 310 F Supp 905, 913 & n.8, 73 LRRM 2594, 2599 & n.8 (D DC, 1970), *appeal dismissed*, 463 F2d 872, 79 LRRM 3028 (CA DC, 1972) (duties are equivalent).

where the party's behavior does not rise to a level that manifests a "desire not to reach an agreement."[34]

The courts evaluate the totality of the circumstances to determine whether a party has violated its duty under Section 2, First by "go[ing] through the motions with 'a desire not to reach an agreement.'"[35] Conduct that has been found to violate Section 2, First includes refusing to bargain over rates of pay, rules, or working conditions;[36] unilateral changes in the status quo;[37] adopting a "take-it-or-leave-it" approach to bargaining;[38] and imposing preconditions to bargaining.[39] On the other hand, courts have held that a party does not by itself breach the duty by being adamant about its proposals,[40] by sharply increasing the number of its demands,[41] or by engaging in "robust, bare-knuckled bargaining."[42]

There is limited case law concerning whether Section 2, First includes a duty to provide information to a collective

---

[34]Chicago & N.W. Ry. v. United Transp. Union, 402 U.S. at 579 n.11, 77 LRRM at 2340 n.11 (1971).

[35]402 U.S. at 578, 77 LRRM at 2340 (1971) (quoting NLRB v. Reed & Prince Mfg. Co., 205 F2d 131, 134, 32 LRRM 2225, 2228 (CA 1), cert. denied, 346 U.S. 887, 33 LRRM 2133 (1953)). See Flight Attendants (AFA) v. Horizon Air Indus., 976 F2d 541, 141 LRRM 2430 (CA 9, 1992); Flight Attendants (IFFA) v. Trans World Airlines, 682 F Supp 1003, 1020, 127 LRRM 3266, 3280 (WD Mo, 1988), aff'd, 878 F2d 254, 131 LRRM 2785 (CA 8, 1989), cert. denied, 493 U.S. 1044, 134 LRRM 2480 (1990); Railway Labor Executives' Ass'n v. Boston & Me. Corp., 664 F Supp 605, 615, 126 LRRM 2659, 2667 (D Me, 1987); REA Express, Inc. v. Railway & Steamship Clerks, 358 F Supp 760, 773, 83 LRRM 2153, 2163 (SD NY, 1973).

[36]Flight Attendants (AFA) v. Horizon Air Indus., 976 F2d 541, 141 LRRM 2430 (CA 9, 1992); Teamsters v. BIC Guardian Servs., Inc., 87 LRRM 2817, 2818 (ND Tex, 1974).

[37]Air Line Pilots v. Transamerica Airlines, 817 F2d 510, 513, 125 LRRM 2777, 2780 (CA 9), amended on other grounds, 125 LRRM 3107 (CA 9), cert. denied, 484 U.S. 963, 126 LRRM 3112 (1987).

[38]Chicago & N.W. Ry. v. United Transp. Union, 330 F Supp 646, 650, 78 LRRM 2001 (ND Ill, 1971).

[39]Teamsters v. BIC Guardian Servs., Inc., 87 LRRM 2817, 2818 (ND Tex, 1974).

[40]Flight Attendants (IFFA) v. Trans World Airlines, 878 F2d 254, 131 LRRM 2785 (CA 8, 1989), cert. denied, 493 U.S. 1044, 134 LRRM 2480 (1990); REA Express, Inc. v. Railway & Steamship Clerks, 358 F Supp 760, 771–72 n.43, 83 LRRM 2153, 2161–62 n.43 (SD NY, 1973); Erie L. Ry. v. Lighter Captains Union, 338 F Supp 955, 964, 79 LRRM 2637, 2644 (D NJ, 1972).

[41]Flight Attendants (UFA) v. Pan Am. World Airways, 624 F Supp 64, 66–67 n.1, 121 LRRM 3463, 3466 n.1 (ED NY, 1985).

[42]Trans Int'l Airlines v. Teamsters, 650 F2d 949, 958, 103 LRRM 2669, 2674 (CA 9, 1980), cert. denied, 449 U.S. 1110, 106 LRRM 2200 (1981).

bargaining counterpart. The only court of appeals decision to consider the issue held that no such duty existed with respect to information sought for grievance processing,[43] and several district courts have reached the same result with respect to information sought for bargaining and for grievance processing.[44] One district court decision, however, indicated that the court would reach the opposite result.[45]

The federal courts will typically remedy a violation of Section 2, First by ordering the party to bargain in good faith, and if appropriate, to maintain the status quo during such negotiations.[46] The Supreme Court has cautioned, however, that after exhaustion of Section 6 procedures, a strike injunction may issue as a remedy under Section 2, First only if it is "the only practical, effective means of enforcing the duty."[47]

A party need not wait until the conclusion of negotiations to bring an action under Section 2, First, but may seek relief during the negotiations.[48] Although such cases often arise during mediation, the NMB does not attempt to adjudicate

---

[43]Pacific Fruit Express v. Union P. R.R., 826 F2d 920, 126 LRRM 2221 (CA 9, 1987), *cert. denied,* 487 U.S. 1205, 128 LRRM 2664 (1988).

[44]Teamsters v. Pan Am. World Airways, 716 F Supp 726, 733, 135 LRRM 2075 (ED NY, 1989); USAir, Inc. v. NMB, 711 F Supp 285, 297–98, 132 LRRM 2395, 2404 (ED Va), *aff'd,* 894 F2d 403, 133 LRRM 2072 (CA 4, 1989); *see also* Air Line Pilots Ass'n v. Trans World Airlines, 729 F Supp 888, 134 LRRM 3285 (D DC, 1989).

[45]Flight Attendants (IFFA) v. Trans World Airlines, 682 F Supp 1003, 1020–21, 127 LRRM 3266 (WD Mo, 1988), *aff'd,* 878 F2d 254, 131 LRRM 2785 (CA 8, 1989), *cert. denied,* 493 U.S. 1044, 134 LRRM 2480 (1990) (information for bargaining sought).

[46]Flight Attendants (AFA) v. Horizon Air Indus., 976 F2d 541, 141 LRRM 2430 (CA 9, 1992); Machinists v. Transportes Aereos Mercantiles Pan Americanos, 924 F2d 1005, 1011, 136 LRRM 2686, 2691 (CA 11), *cert. denied,* 112 S Ct 167, 138 LRRM 2480 (1991); Chicago & N.W. Ry. v. United Transp. Union, 471 F2d 366, 368–69, 80 LRRM 3355, 3357 (CA 7, 1972), *cert. denied,* 410 U.S. 917, 82 LRRM 2245 (1973); Railway & Steamship Clerks v. Atlantic Coast Line R.R., 201 F2d 36, 41, 31 LRRM 2264, 2268 (CA 4), *cert. denied,* 345 U.S. 992, 32 LRRM 2246 (1953).

[47]Chicago & N.W. Ry. v. United Transp. Union, 402 U.S. 570, 583, 77, LRRM 2337, 2341 (1971).

[48]Machinists v. Transportes Aereos Mercantiles Pan Americanos, 924 F2d at 1010, 136 LRRM at 2690 (CA 11), *cert. denied,* 112 S Ct 167, 138 LRRM 2480 (1991); Air Line Pilots Ass'n v. Transamerica Airlines, 817 F2d 510, 513, 125 LRRM 2777, 2780 (CA 9, 1987), *amended on other grounds,* 125 LRRM 3107 (CA 9), *cert. denied,* 484 U.S. 963, 126 LRRM 3112 (1987).

violations of Section 2, First.[49] In the absence of a statute of limitations made expressly applicable to actions under Section 2, First, courts that have addressed the issue have "borrowed" the six-month statute of limitations applicable to unfair labor practice matters under the NLRA.[50]

III. Scope of Bargaining Obligations

A. Statutory Subjects of Bargaining

The subjects of the duty to make and maintain agreements under Section 2, First are "rates of pay, rules and working conditions." The Supreme Court has advised that these terms are to be interpreted broadly;[51] and although there has been relatively little litigation, the phrase has been held to include, inter alia, the design and operation of locomotives,[52] drug testing programs,[53] compulsory retirement age,[54] and pensions.[55] Furthermore, Section 2, Second obligates the parties to "confer" with respect to "[a]ll disputes," without limitation to "rates of pay, rules or working conditions," and Section 2, First requires the parties to attempt to "settle all disputes, whether arising out of the application of such agreements or otherwise," in order to avoid any interruptions to commerce. The courts have not been called upon to decide

---

[49]*See, e.g.,* Flight Eng'rs v. American Airlines, 303 F2d 5, 7, 50 LRRM 2453 (CA 5, 1962) (NMB delayed mediation pending resolution by "competent tribunal" of dispute over subjects for bargaining).

[50]29 USC §160(b) (1994). *See* Flight Attendants (AFA) v. Horizon Air Indus., 976 F2d 541, 547, 141 LRRM 2430 (CA 9, 1992); Flight Attendants (IFFA) v. Trans World Airlines, 682 F Supp 1003, 1021–22, 127 LRRM 3266, 3281 (WD Mo, 1988), *aff'd,* 878 F2d 254, 131 LRRM 2785 (CA 8, 1989), *cert. denied,* 493 U.S. 1044, 134 LRRM 2480 (1990).

[51]Railroad Telegraphers v. Chicago & N. W. R.R., 362 U.S. 330, 338, 45 LRRM 3104 (1960).

[52]Norfolk & W. Ry. v. Locomotive Eng'rs, 459 F Supp 136, 99 LRRM 2475 (WD Va, 1978).

[53]Machinists v. Trans World Airlines, 686 F Supp 930, 130 LRRM 3112 (D DC, 1988).

[54]Flaherty v. Kansas, O. & G. R.R., 252 F Supp 736, 62 LRRM 2149 (ED Okla, 1966).

[55]Elgin, J. & E. Ry. v. Railroad Trainmen, 302 F2d 540, 50 LRRM 2148 (CA 7), *cert. denied,* 371 U.S. 823, 51 LRRM 2222 (1962).

whether these obligations may expand the duty to bargain beyond the subjects listed in Section 2, First.

Some courts have concluded that the concepts of "mandatory" and "permissive" subjects of bargaining developed under the NLRA also apply under the RLA.[56] The NLRA distinction is that a party may properly bargain to impasse over mandatory subjects (that is, rates of pay, rules, and working conditions), whereas with respect to permissive subjects, bargaining is permitted but "parties are not free to insist upon their position to impasse without violating their good faith bargaining duty."[57] There is, however, little case law on what might constitute permissive subjects under the RLA except in the context of "management prerogatives," described in the following subsection.

Some decisions also identify impermissible subjects of bargaining under the RLA. These include attempts to bargain with respect to employees in another craft or class,[58] or seeking terms that would control the bargaining rights of employees in another craft or class.[59]

B. Duty to Bargain Over Managerial Prerogatives

Several cases have discussed the scope of the duty to bargain over so-called managerial prerogatives—principally, the decision to discontinue all, or part of, the carrier's business.

---

[56]*E.g.*, Rakestraw v. United Air Lines, 981 F2d 1524, 1536, 142 LRRM 2054 (CA 7, 1992), *cert. denied*, 144 LRRM 2392 (1993); Teamsters v. Southwest Airlines Co., 842 F2d 794, 799, 128 LRRM 2225 (CA 5, 1988), *cert. denied*, 493 U.S. 1043, 133 LRRM 2264 (1990); Air Line Pilots Ass'n v. United Air Lines, 802 F2d 886, 902, 123 LRRM 2617 (CA 7, 1986), *cert. denied*, 480 U.S. 946, 124 LRRM 3192 (1987); Japan Air Lines Co. v. Machinists, 538 F2d 46, 92 LRRM 3383 (CA 2, 1976); Transport Workers v. Argentine Airlines, 479 F Supp 625, 629–34 (SD NY, 1979).

[57]Air Line Pilots Ass'n v. United Air Lines, 802 F2d 886, 902, 123 LRRM 2617 (CA 7, 1986), *cert. denied*, 480 U.S. 946, 124 LRRM 3192 (1987).

[58]802 F2d at 902–03, 123 LRRM at 2628–29.

[59]Air Line Pilots Ass'n v. UAL Corp., 874 F2d 439, 445, 131 LRRM 2265 (CA 7, 1989). Not every term that affects persons outside the craft or class violates the RLA, however. *E.g.*, Locomotive Eng'rs v. Atchison, T. & S.F. Ry., 768 F2d 914, 120 LRRM 3022 (CA 7, 1985).

The earliest decision to consider the issue was *Railroad Telegraphers v. Chicago & North Western Railway Co.*,[60] which involved a carrier's efforts to consolidate or close certain stations and eliminate a number of jobs. When the union served a Section 6 notice proposing that no jobs be eliminated, the carrier refused to bargain, and the union struck. The court of appeals held that a district court strike injunction was proper, finding that the union's proposal "represent[ed] an attempt to usurp legitimate managerial prerogative in the exercise of business judgment with respect to the most economical and efficient conduct of its operations."[61] The Supreme Court disagreed, holding that job security is a proper subject of bargaining under the RLA, and that the Norris-LaGuardia Act therefore bars an injunction against the strike.[62] "It would stretch credulity too far," the Court stated, "to say that the Railway Labor Act, designed to protect railroad workers, was somehow violated by the union acting precisely in accordance with that Act's purpose to obtain stability and permanence in employment for workers."[63]

Following the *Telegraphers* decision, the Supreme Court decided two cases considering the scope of managerial prerogatives under the NLRA. In the first case, *Textile Workers Union v. Darlington Manufacturing Co.*,[64] the Court held that an employer under the NLRA "has the absolute right to terminate his entire business for any reason he pleases," without bargaining with the union over the decision.[65] In the second, *First National Maintenance Corp. v. NLRB*,[66] the Court held that under some circumstances there is no duty to bargain under the NLRA over the partial closure of a business. In reaching this conclusion, the Court distinguished the *Telegraphers* decision as based "on the particular aims of the Railway Labor Act and national transportation policy."[67]

---

[60]362 U.S. 330, 45 LRRM 3104 (1960).

[61]Chicago & N. W. Ry., v. Railroad Telegraphers, 264 F2d 254, 259, 43 LRRM 2708 (CA 7, 1959).

[62]362 U.S. at 339–40, 45 LRRM at 3108–09.

[63]*Id.*

[64]380 U.S. 263, 58 LRRM 2657 (1965).

[65]380 U.S. at 268, 58 LRRM at 2659.

[66]452 U.S. 666, 107 LRRM 2705 (1981).

[67]452 U.S. at 686 n.23, 107 LRRM at 2713 n.23.

In *Pittsburgh & Lake Erie Railroad v. Railway Labor Executives' Ass'n (P&LE)*,[68] the Court revisited this subject matter under the RLA.[69] The *P&LE* decision involved a carrier's decision to sell all of its rail assets to a third party. The buyer planned to operate the railroad with a greatly diminished workforce and without assuming the selling carrier's collective bargaining agreements. When the union sought to negotiate over both the decision to sell and effects of the sale, the selling carrier refused to bargain.

The Supreme Court held that there was no obligation under the RLA to bargain over the decision to go out of business, distinguishing *Telegraphers* as follows:

> In *Telegraphers* a railroad was seeking simply to eliminate or consolidate some of its little-used local stations. The railroad here, by contrast, sought to sell all its lines and go out of business. There is nothing in *Telegraphers* that forces us to reach the result, in this extreme case, that P&LE was prohibited from terminating its operations without first bargaining with the unions. Notwithstanding the policy considerations prompting the enlarged scope of mandatory bargaining under the RLA, in light of [*Darlington*],[70] . . . we are not inclined to extend *Telegraphers* to a case in which the railroad decides to retire from the railroad business.[71]

Although the *P&LE* case relied on the total nature of the asset sale as a basis for declining to require bargaining over the decision, two court of appeals decisions since *P&LE* have held that there is no duty to bargain with respect to partial asset sales.[72] Courts have also held that carriers need not

---

[68]491 U.S. 490, 131 LRRM 2611 (1989).

[69]In *P&LE*, the Court also held that the carrier had no obligation under §2, Seventh, to serve a §6 notice with respect to the sale. For a discussion of this issue, *see infra* §VIII.C.

[70]Textile Workers Union v. Darlington Mfg. Co., 380 U.S. 263, 58 LRRM 2657 (1965).

[71]491 U.S at 508 n.17, 131 LRRM at 2617–18 n.17.

[72]Chicago & N. W. Transp. Co. v. Railway Labor Executives' Ass'n, 908 F2d 144, 134 LRRM 2854 (CA 7, 1990), *cert. denied*, 498 U.S. 1120, 136 LRRM 2600 (1991); Railway Labor Executives' Ass'n v. Chicago & N. W. Transp. Co., 890 F2d 1024, 133 LRRM 2005 (CA 8, 1989), *cert. denied*, 497 U.S. 1003, 134 LRRM 2536 (1990).

A number of courts have also refused to issue injunctions against partial line

bargain over a decision to enter into a merger of two carriers[73] or a carrier's long-standing practice of subcontracting certain ground functions offshore.[74] These holdings, however, presuppose that the carrier's action does not independently violate the RLA.[75]

C. Effects Bargaining Under the RLA

In *P&LE*,[76] the Supreme Court held that although the carrier had no duty to bargain over the *decision* to go out of business, the carrier was obligated to bargain over the *effects* of the sale on employees. The full extent of the duty, however, has not been clearly delineated.

In *P&LE*, at the time the unions served their Section 6 notices, "the terms of P&LE's agreement with [the buyer] were more or less settled . . . , [so to] the extent that the union's demands could be satisfied only by the assent of the buyers they sought to change or dictate the terms of the sale and in effect challenged the decision to sell itself."[77] Under these circumstances, the Court held that the carrier was not obligated to bargain over the effects of the sale to the extent that the unions' proposals would require agreement of the buyer.

---

sales on the alternative ground that the partial sale was arguably permitted by the collective bargaining agreement, and the sale therefore created a "minor dispute" over which the court had no jurisdiction. *See* Railway Labor Executives' Ass'n v. CSX Transp., Inc., 938 F2d 224, 229, 137 LRRM 2833 (CA DC, 1991), *cert. denied*, 139 LRRM 2528 (1992); CSX Transp., Inc. v. United Transp. Union, 950 F2d 872, 139 LRRM 2061 (CA 2, 1991); Railway & Steamship Clerks v. Missouri P. R.R. Co., 944 F2d 1422, 138 LRRM 2639 (CA 8, 1991); Chicago & N. W. Transp. Co. v. Railway Labor Executives' Ass'n, 908 F2d 144, 134 LRRM 2854; Railway Labor Executives' Ass'n v. Chicago & N. W. Transp. Co., 890 F2d 1024, 133 LRRM 2005; Air Line Pilots Ass'n v. Eastern Air Lines, 889 F2d 291, 130 LRRM 2322 (CA DC, 1989).

[73]Machinists v. Northeast Airlines, Inc., 473 F2d 549, 80 LRRM 2197 (CA 1, 1972).

[74]Japan Air Lines Co. v. Machinists, 538 F2d 46, 92 LRRM 3383 (CA 2, 1976).

[75]*E.g.*, Air Line Pilots Ass'n v. Transamerica Airlines, 817 F2d 510, 125 LRRM 2777 (CA 9), *cert. denied*, 484 U.S. 963, 126 LRRM 3112 (1987) (establishment of nonunion subsidiary airline during negotiations violated §2, First, Third, and Fourth).

[76]Pittsburgh & L.E. R.R. v. Railway Labor Executives' Ass'n, 491 U.S. 490, 131 LRRM 2611 (1989).

[77]491 U.S. at 512, 131 LRRM at 2619.

The *P&LE* Court also held that the duty to bargain over effects terminated when the sale was consummated.[78] One appellate court since *P&LE* has held that this rule applies only where the carrier goes out of business entirely, and that in a partial asset sale the duty to bargain over effects continues after the sale is consummated.[79]

Another issue arising under the *P&LE* decision is the extent to which the status quo obligations apply during effects bargaining. The courts that have considered this question have held that the status quo obligation does not bar the carrier from proceeding with the transaction, because such a rule would transform effects bargaining into decision bargaining.[80]

IV. INITIATING THE BARGAINING PROCESS

Collective bargaining in the airline and railroad industries occurs on both informal and formal levels. Section 2, Second obligates the parties to "confer" with respect to "[a]ll disputes." In an established collective bargaining relationship, the parties frequently engage in informal discussions over a variety of employee-oriented subjects, sometimes merely for general informational purposes. These discussions may ultimately lead to changes in agreement or in other basic terms and conditions of employment. These informal discussions are generally viewed as not regulated by the procedural requirements of Sections 5 and 6 of the RLA unless the parties agree otherwise.

In contrast, formal bargaining to reopen agreements under the RLA is highly structured and regulated.[81] The formal

---

[78]*Id.*

[79]Railway Labor Executives' Ass'n v. Chicago & N. W. Transp. Co., 890 F2d 1024, 1025–26, 133 LRRM 2005 (CA 8, 1989).

[80]Railway Labor Executives' Ass'n v. CSX Transp., Inc., 938 F2d 224, 229, 137 LRRM 2833 (CA DC, 1991); Chicago & N. W. Transp. Co. v. Railway Labor Executives' Ass'n, 908 F2d 144, 134 LRRM 2854 (CA 7, 1990), *cert. denied,* 498 U.S. 1120, 136 LRRM 2600 (1991).

[81]*See generally* Railroad Trainmen v. Jacksonville Terminal Co., 394 U.S. 369, 378–80, 70 LRRM 2961 (1969); Teamsters Local 808 v. NMB, 888 F2d 1428, 1431–33, 132 LRRM 2913 (CA DC, 1989). For a discussion of the application of §§5 and 6 of the RLA to negotiation of an initial agreement, *see infra* §IV.B.

bargaining process is initiated when one party serves upon the other a written notice of proposed changes in rates of pay, rules, and working conditions, as provided by Section 6 of the RLA. Section 6 requires that the notice be served at least 30 days in advance of the effective date of a proposed change. In the absence of an agreement to the contrary, there is no prohibition against the serving of notices well in advance of 30 days, and such service triggers a bargaining obligation.[82] Circumstances may exist, however, where the filing of a Section 6 notice could give rise to a claim of bad faith bargaining, such as the filing of a notice the day after an agreement is signed.[83] In order to avoid continuous negotiations, airline labor and management typically include in their collective bargaining agreements provisions that restrict the filing of Section 6 notices to a designated period, typically 60 to 90 days, prior to the contract's stipulated amendable date.[84] Formal notice may be waived entirely, such as where a party has constructive notice of the proposed changes and participates in conferences.[85]

The form of a Section 6 notice may vary. No particular format is provided by the statute and there are no special requirements that a notice must meet to be valid. Frequently, Section 6 notices do not contain the proposed agreement language, or even the specific changes intended. A notice is considered "adequate if it informs a party of the purpose sought to be attained by the other party with sufficient definition to enable the former to understand the implications of the notice and proposed means adapted to the goal's attainment."[86] Because a notice need not be in any particular form, a court reviewing a Section 6 notice is likely to take a functional

---

[82]Railroad Trainmen v. Akron & B. B. R.R., 385 F2d 581, 596–97, 65 LRRM 2229 (CA DC, 1967), *cert. denied*, 390 U.S. 923, 67 LRRM 2384 (1968).

[83]*Id.*

[84]For a discussion of duration and moratorium clauses, *see infra* §X.

[85]Childers v. Railroad Trainmen, 192 F2d 956, 959, 29 LRRM 2217 (CA 8, 1951).

[86]Pullman Co. v. Railway Conductors & Brakemen, 316 F2d 556, 562, 52 LRRM 2829 (CA 7), *cert. denied*, 375 U.S. 820, 54 LRRM 2312 (1963). *See also* Railroad Trainmen v. Southern Ry., 393 F2d 303, 309, 67 LRRM 3026 (CA 5, 1968).

rather than a technical approach. In one case, the court found that the carrier's response to the union's Section 6 notice "functionally served" as a Section 6 notice in its own right.[87]

The RLA provides that upon receipt of the Section 6 notice, the parties must confer within 10 days to reach agreement about when and where to hold the first conference.[88] At a minimum, negotiations are to commence within 30 days of the notice, unless the parties expressly agree otherwise.[89]

The RLA does not limit the number of proposals that the initiating party may include in its Section 6 notice, and the proposals need not be objectively reasonable.[90] Courts have jurisdiction to assess the legality of the Section 6 notice itself, but the scope of that jurisdiction is limited. The courts are not authorized by the RLA "to dissect proposals into legal and illegal components by probing either party's motivations. Unless illegal on their face and in their entirety, opening proposals that contain bargainable subject matter are not subject to further review."[91] The proposals contained in the Section 6 notice are usually revised during negotiations, as each party reacts to the demands of the other.[92]

Once bargaining under the Section 6 procedure begins, neither party may resort to self-help until the processes of the RLA have been exhausted.[93]

---

[87]Railway & Airline Supervisors v. Soo L. R.R., 690 F Supp 802, 807–08, 129 LRRM 2905 (D Minn, 1988), aff'd, 891 F2d 675, 133 LRRM 2081 (CA 8, 1989), cert. denied, 498 U.S. 809, 135 LRRM 2463 (1990).

[88]RLA §6.

[89]See Railway Labor Executives' Ass'n v. Boston & Me. Corp., 664 F Supp 605, 611, 126 LRRM 2659 (D Me, 1987) ("[T]he requirements of Section 6 are best read as mechanisms which ensure that the parties to the dispute begin to communicate with each other. They are not inflexible deadlines incapable of modification, by express agreement, where the circumstances of the parties to the dispute mandate a different timetable.").

[90]Flight Attendants (IFFA) v. Trans World Airlines, 682 F Supp 1003, 127 LRRM 3266 (WD Mo, 1988), aff'd per curiam, 878 F2d 254, 131 LRRM 2785 (CA 8, 1989), cert. denied, 493 U.S. 1044, 134 LRRM 2480 (1990).

[91]Railway Labor Executives' Ass'n v. Boston & Me. Corp., 664 F Supp at 617–18.

[92]Trans Int'l Airlines v. Teamsters, 650 F2d 949, 103 LRRM 2669 (CA 9, 1980), cert. denied, 449 U.S. 1110, 106 LRRM 2200 (1981); Flight Attendants (UFA) v. Pan Am. World Airways, 624 F Supp 64, 121 LRRM 3463 (ED NY, 1985).

[93]For a discussion of the status quo obligation, see infra §IV.H.

V. NMB MEDIATION PROCEDURES

A. Commencement of Mediation

The RLA does not restrict or limit the duration of the bargaining period. The parties may continue to negotiate for as long as they desire, and the status quo remains undisturbed for that entire period. There is no minimum period of negotiation that must occur before mediation can be requested. The NMB assigns a docket number to all mediation requests and encourages the parties to continue direct negotiations without the aid of a mediator if it believes the request was made too soon in the negotiation process.

If conferences (i.e., bargaining) have terminated, a 10-day waiting period begins during which the status quo remains in effect.[94] If neither party formally requests mediation during this period, or the NMB does not sua sponte proffer mediation within the period,[95] the parties may resort to self-help at the end of the period.[96] So long as the request for mediation is made within the 10-day period, it is immaterial if the NMB does not docket the request until after the period has lapsed.[97]

The parties may request mediation through almost any telecommunication device (or in person), including letter, telegram, telecopy, or Form NMB 2, which is printed by the

---

[94]RLA §6.

[95]Even absent a request for mediation from the parties, the NMB may proffer mediation during negotiations or within 10 days of impasse, an action that maintains the status quo until the RLA's procedures have been exhausted. RLA §5, First.

[96]Iberia Air Lines v. NMB, 472 F Supp 104, 101 LRRM 2676 (SD NY, 1979), aff'd, 636 F2d 1201, 106 LRRM 2816 (CA 2, 1980), cert. denied, 450 U.S. 999, 106 LRRM 2817 (1981); Railway Labor Executives' Ass'n v. Boston & Me. Corp., 664 F Supp 605, 126 LRRM 2659 (D Me, 1987); Railway & Steamship Clerks v. Philadelphia, B. & N. E. R.R., 633 F Supp 371 (ED Pa, 1986). Questions are sometimes raised between the parties as to whether a termination of conferences has been reached. Where there is a question as to whether conferences have terminated, a party will often request mediation in order to avoid the lifting of the status quo 10 days after the termination of conferences, as provided by §6 of the RLA. Once mediation has been requested, either party may then raise with the Board or its agents questions regarding the appropriateness or timeliness of mediation.

[97]Railway Executives' Ass'n v. Boston & Me. Corp., 664 F Supp 605, 126 LRRM 2659 (D Me, 1987).

NMB and available through the Executive Director of the agency.[98] The Board's implementing regulations require that

1. the request for mediation and all other follow-up correspondence be submitted in duplicate;
2. the application identify the carrier and labor organization, and describe the nature of the dispute, the number of employees involved, the date of any contract between the parties, the date of the Section 6 notice, and the date of the final conference;
3. a copy of the Section 6 notice (or notices) accompany the request for mediation; and
4. the application be signed by the carrier's highest official designated to handle disputes under the RLA or by the chief executive of the labor organization, as appropriate.[99]

Upon receipt of the mediation request at the NMB's offices in Washington, D.C., the Executive Director will docket the request and assign it a case number in the NMB's "A" series. The NMB views its responsibilities in docketing mediation cases as nondiscretionary. If the application appears to be facially defective in any manner, the Executive Director will investigate and attempt to have the deficiency corrected. The Executive Director will notify both parties that the request for mediation has been received and docketed and will ask the nonmoving party for any statement that it wishes to make regarding the filing of the application. The Executive Director's notification letter will also remind the parties of their obligation to maintain the status quo, although the NMB has no role in enforcing that obligation.[100]

B. Process of Mediation

The process of mediation escapes definition, although clearly it is more "art" than "science."[101] Mediation has been

---

[98]*See* 29 CFR §1203.1 (1994).

[99]*See id.*

[100]Teamsters v. Texas Int'l Airlines, 717 F2d 157, 114 LRRM 3091 (CA 5, 1983) (NMB lacks authority to enforce labor agreements or status quo provisions of RLA).

[101]Teamsters Local 808 v. NMB, 888 F2d 1428, 1436, 132 LRRM 2913 (CA DC, 1989).

described as a catalytic process through which the disputants, with the aid of an impartial mediator, seek ways to break their bargaining impasse by identifying and isolating a common ground for agreement and settlement.[102] Mediation's ultimate success depends on a combination of factors, including (1) timing, (2) the ability of the mediator to win the parties' confidence and to determine what is at the core of their dispute, (3) the willingness of the parties to "use" the mediator and the process, (4) the mediator's skill as a persuader and influencer, (5) the balance of power between the parties, and (6) luck.[103]

The success of mediation frequently depends on the passage of time alone. Because of the mandatory and obligatory nature of the mediation process, the parties are pressured to compromise their positions even though each may believe that its original position was reasonable. As expressed by Justice Black in *Detroit & Toledo Shore Line Railroad v. United Transportation Union*,[104] the RLA's major dispute processes are designed to be "almost interminable," and that is the force that often moves the parties to compromise and settlement without strikes or other economic disruptions.[105]

The NMB has considerable flexibility to structure mediation as it sees fit, including the timing and format of meetings, the duration of mediation, the timing of a release, and any preconditions imposed on release.[106] One court has observed that the NMB's latitude in mediation includes anything "that can fairly be said to be designed to settle a dispute without a strike and does not independently offend other laws."[107]

---

[102]General Comm. of Adjustment v. Missouri-K.-T. R.R., 320 U.S. 323, 13 LRRM 627 (1943).

[103]Teamsters Local 808 v. NMB, 888 F2d at 1436–38.

[104]396 U.S. 142, 72 LRRM 2838 (1969).

[105]396 U.S. at 149, 150 ("[S]ince disputes usually arise when one party wants to change the status quo without undue delay, the power which the Act gives to the other party to preserve the status quo for a prolonged period will frequently make it worthwhile for the moving party to compromise with the interests of the other side and thus reach agreement without interruption to commerce.").

[106]Machinists v. NMB, 930 F2d 45, 48, 137 LRRM 2113 (CA DC), *cert. denied*, 112 S Ct 173, 138 LRRM 2479 (1991). The term "release" is discussed in *infra* § V.D.

[107]930 F2d at 48.

C. Proffer of Arbitration

If the NMB determines that further mediation will be unsuccessful in bringing about a settlement, the NMB is obligated to proffer binding arbitration to the parties.[108] However, the RLA does not require that the NMB issue a proffer of arbitration simply because mediation has continued for a considerable period of time.[109]

Neither party is required to accept the proffer of arbitration.[110] Indeed, the RLA does not even require a response to the proffer of arbitration, nor does the Act establish any time limits on its acceptance or rejection.[111] Acceptance or rejection of the proffer of arbitration, if made, must be in writing.

The NMB will notify the parties that arbitration has been accepted or declined by either party.[112] If either party declines, neither party may resort to self-help for a period of 30 days after the notice.[113] If both parties accept the proffer of arbitration, they agree to binding interest arbitration.[114]

An agreement to arbitrate must be in writing and must define the issues to be submitted for decision.[115] Parties may use the model NMB arbitration agreement, or may create

---

[108]RLA §5, First; Piedmont Aviation, Inc. v. Air Line Pilots Ass'n, 416 F2d 633, 636, 72 LRRM 2343 (CA 4, 1969), cert. denied, 397 U.S. 926, 73 LRRM 2537 (1970).

[109]See discussion infra §V.E; Machinists v. NMB, 425 F2d 527, 73 LRRM 2278 (CA DC, 1970); Teamsters Local 808 v. NMB, 888 F2d 1428, 1438, 132 LRRM 2913 (CA DC, 1989); Machinists v. NMB, 930 F2d 45, 137 LRRM 2113.

[110]RLA §7, First. A refusal to accept a proffer of arbitration may affect a party's ability to obtain injunctive relief. See infra §VIII.C.

[111]RLA §7, First.

[112]Id. §5, First.

[113]Id.

[114]The agreement to arbitrate may occur at a later date. See, e.g., El Al Isr. Airlines v. Machinists, NMB Case Nos. A-11266, A-11267, A-11268, A-11269, A-11270 (1980) (parties agreed to arbitrate their differences more than two years after union had struck carrier). There is no authority on the effect on the status quo obligation of a party's reversal of position and acceptance of arbitration.

If the written agreement to arbitrate is reached before the 30-day period begins or expires, the parties must maintain the status quo until the contract terms created by the arbitration board become effective. See RLA §5, First.

[115]RLA §8.

and execute their own, as long as it contains references to the RLA, the number and method of selection of the Board of Arbitration members, the issues for submission, the time frame for completion, and a reference to the RLA requirements for filing and entering judgment on the award in federal court.[116] A party may not revoke its agreement to arbitrate.[117]

D. Release From Mediation

Section 5, First provides that if one or both parties refuse arbitration, the NMB must "notify both parties in writing that its mediatory efforts have failed, and for thirty days thereafter . . . no change shall be made in the rates of pay, rules or working conditions or established practices in effect prior to the time the dispute arose." The NMB's notice pursuant to this provision is commonly referred to as a "release" from mediation, and the 30-day period thereafter is commonly called the "30-day cooling-off period."[118]

The timing of the proffer of arbitration, and hence the release from mediation, is almost entirely within the NMB's discretion, so long as the NMB does not engage in patent official bad faith.[119] The NMB considers a variety of factors, which vary with the circumstances, in its decision whether to release the parties.[120]

When the NMB is considering a proffer of arbitration because mediation has been unsuccessful, one of the three NMB board members, as opposed to one of the staff mediators, usually becomes directly active in the case. That member

---

[116]*Id.*

[117]*Id* .

[118]Chicago & N.W. Ry. v. United Transp. Union, 402 U.S. 570, 77 LRRM 2337 (1971).

[119]*See* discussion *infra* §V.E; Machinists v. NMB, 425 F2d 527, 73 LRRM 2278 (CA DC, 1970); Teamsters Local 808 v. NMB, 888 F2d 1428, 132 LRRM 2913 (CA DC, 1989); Machinists v. NMB, 930 F2d 45, 137 LRRM 2113 (CA DC), *cert. denied,* 138 LRRM 2479 (1991).

[120]Teamsters Local 808 v. NMB, 888 F2d 1428, 132 LRRM 2913.

is frequently particularly active during the final 30-day cooling-off period after the notice of release, when the NMB typically engages in public interest mediation even though it is not statutorily obligated to do so.

E. Judicial Review of the Mediation Process

The NMB has broad latitude in managing the mediation process. As a result, there have been few cases addressing the NMB's actions during mediation.[121] Most judicial inquiry has centered on the timing of the release from mediation by the NMB.[122]

In *Teamsters Local 808 v. NMB*,[123] the District of Columbia Circuit Court of Appeals confirmed that judicial review of NMB decisions is "extraordinarily limited."[124] The court stated that "[t]he NMB is entitled to as strong a presumption as the legislature that 'if any state of facts might be supposed that would support its action, these facts must be presumed

---

[121]The fact that the courts may not review the NMB's conduct during the mediation process does not preclude them from enforcing the obligations that the RLA places on the parties' conduct in the bargaining process. *See, e.g.*, Railway Labor Executives' Ass'n v. Boston & Me. Corp., 664 F Supp 605, 613, 126 LRRM 2659 (D Me, 1987) (issue of whether court might properly order NMB to terminate mediation implicates concerns about judicial interference with mediation process, whereas issue of bad faith bargaining, even after mediation process has begun, does not); Air Line Pilots Ass'n v. Transamerica Airlines, 817 F2d 510, 513, 125 LRRM 2777 (CA 9), *amended*, 125 LRRM 3107 (CA 9), *cert. denied*, 484 U.S. 963, 126 LRRM 3112 (1987) ("The question whether federal courts have jurisdiction to review Board decisions is not the same as the question whether federal courts have jurisdiction to enforce provisions of the Act.").

[122]*See, e.g.*, Teamsters Local 808 v. NMB, 888 F2d at 1434; Machinists v. NMB, 425 F2d at 541; Machinists v. NMB, 930 F2d 45, 137 LRRM 2113.

[123]888 F2d 1428, 132 LRRM 2913 (CA DC, 1989).

[124]888 F2d at 1433 (citing Machinists v. Trans World Airlines, 839 F2d 809, 811, 127 LRRM 2854 (CA DC), *amended*, 848 F2d 232 (CA DC), *cert. denied*, 488 U.S. 820, 129 LRRM 2464 (1988)). *See also* Switchmen's Union v. NMB, 320 U.S. 297, 300–05, 13 LRRM 616 (1943) (concluding that district court was without power to review NMB's issuance of certification of representation); General Comm. of Adjustment v. Missouri-K.-T. R.R., 320 U.S. 323, 336, 13 LRRM 627 (1943) (concluding that Congress fashioned exclusive administrative remedy in NMB to resolve jurisdictional disputes between unions or among groups of employees); Professional Cabin Crew Ass'n v. NMB, 872 F2d 456, 459, 131 LRRM 2034 (CA DC), *cert. denied*, 493, U.S. 974, 132 LRRM 2960 (1989).

to exist.' "[125] The court held that absent a showing of "patent official bad faith," the courts have no authority to review the NMB's decision to keep a dispute in mediation.[126]

In *Teamsters Local 808*, the court also held that a court may not make inquiries about the NMB's understanding of the parties' positions, about the basis for the NMB's belief that efforts to mediate might still be successful, or about the NMB's reasoning process. Allowance of discretion in the mediation process is necessary to protect the special role of the mediator as a confidante of both parties.[127] In evaluating the length of the mediation, the court first emphasized that it could not estimate the proper length of mediation either objectively or statistically. It then held that in evaluating whether there has been patent official bad faith[128] by virtue of the time the dispute has been in mediation, a court may not consider the time after the civil action has been filed.[129] Two years is not an unusual length of time for mediation before the NMB.[130]

---

[125]888 F2d at 1434 (quoting Machinists v. NMB, 425 F2d 527, 540, 73 LRRM 2278 (CA DC, 1970)).

[126]*Id.* at 1430.

[127]*Id.* at 1435 (citing P. PRASOW & E. PETERS, ARBITRATION AND COLLECTIVE BARGAINING 234 (1970)).

[128]The District of Columbia Circuit Court of Appeals reaffirmed the official bad faith standard for review of the NMB's process more recently in Machinists v. NMB, 930 F2d 45, 137 LRRM 2113 (CA DC), *cert. denied,* 112 S Ct 173, 138 LRRM 2479 (1991). *See also* Machinists v. NMB, 425 F2d at 537 (district court erred in directing NMB to proffer arbitration because such court direction is proper only if NMB's action in retaining parties in mediation is "completely and patently arbitrary" or withheld for period that is "completely and patently unreasonable"); Delaware & H. Ry. v. United Transp. Union, 450 F2d 603, 608, 76 LRRM 2900 (CA DC), *cert. denied,* 403 U.S. 911, 77 LRRM 2404 (1971); Machinists v. Northwest Airlines, 674 F Supp 1393, 1396, 127 LRRM 2472 (D Minn, 1987), *rev'd,* 842 F2d 206, 130 LRRM 2061 (CA 8), *vacated and dismissed as moot,* 854 F2d 1089, 130 LRRM 2063 (CA 8, 1988); Lan Chile Airlines v. NMB, 115 LRRM 3655, 3656 (SD Fla, 1984); Seaboard World Airways v. Teamsters, 501 F Supp 47, 49, 107 LRRM 2062 (ED NY, 1980); Railway & Steamship Clerks v. Florida E. C. Ry., 384 U.S. 238, 62 LRRM 2177 (1966); Electrical Workers (IBEW) v. Washington Terminal Co., 473 F2d 1156, 1171, 82 LRRM 2030 (CA DC, 1972), *cert. denied,* 411 U.S. 906, 82 LRRM 2921 (1973).

[129]888 F2d at 1438.

[130]*Id.* at 1440.

VI. EMERGENCY BOARDS

A. In General

Section 10 of the RLA provides the final statutory mechanism for resolution of major disputes under the RLA. This section provides that if the NMB determines that the dispute "threaten[s] to substantially interrupt commerce to a degree such as to deprive any section of the Country of essential transportation service," the NMB shall notify the President, who has the discretion to "create a board to investigate and report, respecting such dispute." The Emergency Board must report to the President within 30 days of its appointment, and during those 30 days and "for thirty days after such board has made its report . . . no change, except by agreement, shall be made by the parties . . . in the conditions out of which the dispute arose."[131]

Boards have been invoked principally in the railroad industry.[132] The determination whether a dispute threatens to deprive "any section of the country of essential transportation" is open to a variety of interpretations and, accordingly, it is not possible to predict whether an Emergency Board will be appointed in a given rail dispute. The first few Emergency Boards, for instance, were appointed to resolve disputes of limited geographic scope,[133] and notwithstanding congres-

---

[131]RLA §10.

[132]Since 1926, 192 Emergency Boards have been created to investigate disputes within the railroad industry, whereas only 33 Emergency Boards have been created in the airline industry. The President has not initiated the creation of an Emergency Board in the airline industry since Emergency Board 168 in 1966. In 1978, as part of the Airline Deregulation Act of 1978 (49 USC §1301 *et seq., repealed by* Act of July 5, 1994, Pub. L. No. 103-272, §7(b), 108 Stat. 1379) Congress provided for the creation of Emergency Board 189 to investigate a dispute involving pilots at Wien Air Alaska. (The subject matter formerly covered in this section of the U.S. Code is now covered generally in 49 USC §40101 *et seq.* (1994).) In 1989, President Bush vetoed legislation that would have established a commission to investigate and report on a dispute at Eastern Airlines involving the Machinists, the Air Line Pilots Ass'n, and Trans World Airlines (H.R. 1231, 101st Cong., 2d Sess.).

[133]*See* ANNUAL REPORT OF THE U.S. BOARD OF MEDIATION 56–57 (1928) (first Emergency Board was appointed to resolve disputes on single railroad with only 737 miles of track in predominantly rural area); Donald E. Cullen, *Emergency Boards Under the Railway Labor Act, in* THE RAILWAY LABOR ACT AT FIFTY 151, 159 (Charles M. Rehmus, ed., 1976) (11 of first 18 Emergency Boards dealt with disputes on single carriers, some with fewer than 737 miles of track).

sional intent to the contrary, many of these Emergency Boards also addressed individual grievances.[134] Disputes over individual grievances continued to plague Emergency Boards until 1957, when the Supreme Court ruled that courts could enjoin any work stoppage involving an individual grievance that has been submitted to arbitration.[135]

Where the NMB concludes that a dispute threatens substantially to interrupt commerce to the extent that a section of the country will be deprived of essential transportation service, the NMB recommends to the President that an Emergency Board be appointed. The Act does not define what constitutes a substantial threat to commerce. The NMB may consider such factors as the effect of a strike or shutdown on the state of the economy as a whole (i.e., strike-induced unemployment in other industries); the immediate economic impact on transportation industries, shippers, and travelers (based on reports provided by the Department of Transportation for airlines and the Federal Railroad Administration for railroads); or the effects on military logistics and transportation requirements.

The ultimate decision to create an Emergency Board rests entirely with the President. If the President refuses to create an Emergency Board, the RLA is silent as to what further measures, if any, may be taken. However, Congress retains the power to pass special legislation to resolve such disputes.[136]

---

[134]*See generally* Cullen, *supra* note 135, at 159–60; (1976); Slocum v. Delaware, L. & W. R.R., 339 U.S. 239, 243 n.5, 25 LRRM 2617 (1950); Elgin, J. & E. Ry. v. Burley, 325 U.S. 711, 726 n.22, 16 LRRM 749 (1945).

[135]Railroad Trainmen v. Chicago River & I. R.R., 353 U.S. 30, 39 LRRM 2578 (1957).

[136]*See, e.g.,* 51-52 ANNUAL REPORT OF THE NATIONAL MEDIATION BOARD 77 (1986) (Emergency Board appointed to end 620-day strike between Wien Air Alaska and the Air Line Pilots Association.) The Wien Air Alaska Emergency Board, established by legislation, has been the only Emergency Board created in the airline industry since September 1966, when President Johnson created Emergency Board 168 (David Stowe, Chair) to investigate a dispute between Pan Am and the Transport Workers. Earlier, in July 1966, Emergency Board 167 (John Dunlop, Chair) was created to investigate a dispute between American Airlines and the Transport Workers. President Johnson also created Emergency Board 166 (Sen. Wayne Morse, Chair) in April 1966, to investigate a dispute involving the Machinists and five carriers—Eastern, National, Northwest, United, and Trans World Airlines. On the

In creating an Emergency Board, the President retains discretion to determine the number of Board members (usually three)[137] and their compensation.[138] The only statutory limitations are that "no member appointed shall be pecuniarily or otherwise interested in any organization of employees or any carrier" and that a new and separate Emergency Board be created for each labor dispute.[139]

Traditionally, the NMB has played a role in advising the President on the selection of Emergency Board members. The NMB has generally encouraged the use of professional labor–management arbitrators familiar with RLA and industry practices (the NMB maintains a roster of more than 500 such arbitrators). The Department of Labor or the Department of Transportation has, on occasion, attempted to mediate an end to the dispute prior to the creation of an Emergency Board and during the status quo period following a rejection of the Emergency Board's recommendations, and has become involved, on behalf of the President, in a legislated resolution of the dispute. The labor agencies (the Department of Labor and, since 1978, the NMB) have provided Emergency Boards with professional and administrative assistance in organizing hearings and preparing reports.

As discussed earlier, once appointed, an Emergency Board has 30 days to investigate and report to the President.[140]

---

railroad side, Congress created Emergency Boards 196, 197, and 198 to investigate issues arising out of the transfer of Conrail commuter operations to the states of New York, New Jersey, and Pennsylvania, under §510 of the Rail Passenger Service Act of 1970, Pub. L. No. 91-518, 84 Stat. 1328, as amended by the Northeast Rail Service Act of 1981, Pub. L. No. 97-35, 95 Stat. 681.

[137]53-54 ANNUAL REPORT OF THE NATIONAL MEDIATION BOARD 29 (1988).

[138]RLA §10.

[139]*Id.*

[140]*Id.* The RLA does not provide for an extension of time for the Emergency Board to report to the President. However, where the parties, the Emergency Board, and the NMB concur in requesting an extension of time, it customarily has been granted. For example, Emergency Board 219, created on May 5, 1990, to investigate the disputes involving a group of the nation's major rail carriers and their unions, received three extensions of time to file its report, which was finally submitted on January 15, 1991. Several of the unions rejected its recommendations. The unions agreed to an additional 60-day status quo period, however, because of the developing Persian Gulf crisis. Although some settlements were reached through mediation during that period, Congress finally legislated an end to the dispute by imposing the Emergency Board's recommendations on the parties. In the interim, Congress

This period is frequently extended by consent of the parties and approval of the President.[141] During this period and for 30 days thereafter the parties to the dispute are obligated to maintain the "actual, objective working conditions and practices broadly conceived, which were in effect" at the time the dispute first arose[142] (even where the cooling-off period has expired and the parties have already resorted to self-help).[143] This requirement that the parties restore and maintain the status quo is enforceable by injunction.[144]

An Emergency Board is vested with the authority to "investigate and report" to the President regarding the dispute. The Emergency Board's investigation generally consists of hearings in which the affected parties testify under oath, along with briefs and submissions. Although the RLA is silent

---

mandated the creation of a special board to review and, under stringent criteria, revise Emergency Board 219's recommendations. The special Emergency Board adopted the Emergency Board 219 report in its entirety.

[141]*See, e.g.,* Delaware & H. Ry. v. United Transp. Union, 450 F2d 603, 606, 76 LRRM 2900 (CA DC), *cert. denied,* 403 U.S. 911, 77 LRRM 2404 (1971).

[142]Detroit & Toledo Shore Line R.R. v. United Transp. Union, 396 U.S. 142, 153, 72 LRRM 2838 (1969); Railway Labor Executives' Ass'n v. Boston & Me. Corp., 639 F Supp 1092, 1104, 123 LRRM 2385 (D Me), *aff'd,* 808 F2d 150, 124 LRRM 2145 (CA 1, 1986), *cert. denied,* 484 U.S. 830, 126 LRRM 2496 (1987). In the *Boston & Me. Corp.* case, the First Circuit found that the dispute before the district court (the retaliatory discharge of employees) was not a "major dispute," and that the district court thus did not have jurisdiction to enjoin the carrier's actions under the §10 status quo provision.

[143]Railway Labor Executives' Ass'n v. Boston & Me. Corp., 639 F Supp at 1104; United Transp. Union v. Long Island R.R., 634 F2d 19, 21, 105 LRRM 2465 (CA 2, 1980), *rev'd on other grounds,* 455 U.S. 678, 109 LRRM 3017 (1982); Atchison, T. & S.F. Ry. v. United States, 617 F2d 485, 487 (CA 7, 1980).

[144]Seaboard World Airlines v. Transport Workers, 425 F2d 1086, 1091, 73 LRRM 2894 (CA 2, 1970); Pullman Co. v. Railway Conductors & Brakemen, 316 F2d 556, 52 LRRM 2829 (CA 7), *cert. denied,* 375 U.S. 820, 54 LRRM 2312 (1963); Pan Am. World Airways v. Flight Eng'rs, 306 F2d 840, 846, 50 LRRM 2801 (CA 2, 1962); Alton & S. Ry. v. Railway & Steamship Clerks, 481 F Supp 130 (D DC, 1978). In Railway Labor Executives' Ass'n v. Boston & Me. Corp., 639 F Supp 1092, 123 LRRM 2385, the district court held that the Presidential Order creating the Emergency Board applied only to those parties specifically identified in the Order. In that case, the Maintenance of Way Employees struck Maine Central. Several months later, after the Maintenance of Way Employees commenced secondary activity at several other railways including the Delaware & Hudson Railway and the Boston & Maine Corp., the President created an Emergency Board. The district court determined that because only Maine Central was identified in the Order creating the Emergency Board, only Maine Central was required to restore the status quo.

as to the form and extent of the report, Emergency Boards have historically made written reports to the President that contain recommendations for settlement of the dispute.[145] The President releases the report and may request the NMB to handle the report's distribution. The President may choose not to release the report or other documents submitted to or created by the Emergency Board. The report and all related documents are considered official presidential documents and are not released by the NMB under the Freedom of Information Act, although the NMB maintains physical custody of the records.[146]

The Emergency Board's recommendations are not binding.[147] Any party to the dispute may reject them, and if the recommendations are, in fact, rejected by one or more parties, the RLA's final 30-day cooling-off period begins to run from the first rejection.[148] The NMB continues to attempt to mediate an end to the dispute during the cooling-off period, often using the Emergency Board report as a basis for negotiations. If no agreement is reached before the conclusion of this final 30-day period, Section 10 of the RLA permits the parties to resort to self-help.

Congress has, on occasion, passed special legislation further prohibiting or delaying the parties' resort to self-help. Congress has at times required the parties to submit the dispute to a second Emergency Board,[149] to submit to final and binding arbitration,[150] or to accept the Emergency Board's recommendations.[151]

---

[145]Cullen, *supra* note 135, at 157 n.7.

[146]*See, e.g.,* Exec. Order No. 12,925, 59 Fed. Reg. 45,181 (1994).

[147]51-52 ANNUAL REPORT OF THE NATIONAL MEDIATION BOARD 76 (1986).

[148]*Id.*

[149]Burlington N. Ry. v. Maintenance of Way Employees, 481 U.S. 429, 125 LRRM 2073 (1987); Maine C. R.R. v. Maintenance of Way Employees, 835 F2d 368, 369, 127 LRRM 2053 (CA 1, 1987), *cert. denied,* 486 U.S. 1042 (1988); Maine C. R.R. v. Maintenance of Way Employees, 813 F2d 484, 486, 124 LRRM 2966 (CA 1), *cert. denied,* 484 U.S. 825, 126 LRRM 2495 (1987); Delaware & H. Ry. v. United Transp. Union, 450 F2d 603, 606, 76 LRRM 2900 (CA DC), *cert. denied,* 403 U.S. 911, 77 LRRM 2404 (1971).

[150]Locomotive Eng'rs v. Chicago, R. I. & P. R.R., 382 U.S. 423, 431–33, 61 LRRM 2209 (1986); Railroad Trainmen v. Akron & B. B. R.R., 385 F2d 581, 590, 65 LRRM 2229 (CA DC, 1967), *cert. denied,* 390 U.S. 923, 67 LRRM 2385 (1968).

[151]Maine C. R.R. v. Maintenance of Way Employees, 873 F2d 425, 428, 131 LRRM 2201 (CA 1, 1989); Maine C. R.R. v. Maintenance of Way Employees, 835

B. Commuter Rail Carriers

In 1981, Congress amended the RLA to add a special procedure for major disputes involving publicly funded or operated commuter rail carriers and their employees.[152] Any major dispute in the commuter rail industry that has not been previously resolved through the RLA's major dispute procedures may be submitted to a special Emergency Board created pursuant to Section 9A of the RLA.[153]

Under Section 9A, any party to the dispute or the governor of any state through which the commuter operates may act to require the President to create an Emergency Board to investigate and report on the dispute in accordance with Section 10 of the RLA.[154] The parties to the dispute may not alter the status quo, except by agreement, for 120 days from the creation of this Emergency Board. For the first 60 days, the Section 9A Emergency Board functions like an Emergency Board appointed pursuant to Section 10 of the RLA. If the parties have not reached a settlement by the end of that 60-day period, the NMB must conduct a public hearing on the dispute "at which each party shall appear and provide testimony setting forth the reasons it has not accepted the recommendations of the emergency board for settlement of

---

F2d at 369; Maine C. R.R. v. Maintenance of Way Employees, 813 F2d at 486; Alton & S. Ry. v. Machinists, 463 F2d 872, 875, 79 LRRM 3028 (CA DC, 1972); Electrical Workers v. Washington Terminal, 473 F2d 1156, 1158–59, 82 LRRM 2030 (CA DC, 1972), cert. denied, 411 U.S. 906, 82 LRRM 2921 (1973).

[152]RLA §9A; Teamsters Local 808 v. NMB, 888 F2d 1428, 1432, 132 LRRM 2913 (CA DC, 1989).

[153]Section 9A(a) includes an express provision extending its application to "Amtrak Commuter Services Corporation." All §9A boards created to date have investigated disputes in the northeastern United States, specifically on the Long Island Railroad and the Port Authority Trans Hudson Corp. It is uncertain whether §9A (or the RLA itself) applies to other commuter lines serving cities such as San Francisco, Chicago, and Atlanta. Long Island R.R. v. United Transp. Union, 634 F.2d 19, 23 (2d Cir. 1980), rev'd and remanded, 455 U.S. 678, 683 n.4, 109 LRRM 3017 (1982). See Tri-County Community Rail Org., 17 NMB 321 (1990).

[154]Section 9A(b) provides that if the President does not create a §10 Emergency Board, then "any party to the dispute or the Governor of any state through which the service . . . is operated may request the President to establish such an emergency board." Thus, Emergency Boards may be created for commuter rail disputes under both §9A and §10. Section 9A(c)(2), however, provides that §9A provisions shall apply to Emergency Boards created by the President under §10.

the dispute."[155] For the remaining 60 days the parties are required to maintain the status quo.

At the conclusion of the latter 60-day period, if the parties still have not reached agreement, the President must, at the request of any party to the dispute or the governor of any state "through which the service that is the subject of the dispute is operated," establish a second Emergency Board.[156] Within 30 days after the creation of the second Emergency Board, the parties must submit final settlement offers to the Board,[157] and the second Emergency Board has 30 days from the submission of the parties' settlement offers to submit a report to the President setting forth its selection of the most reasonable offer.[158] Neither party is obligated to accept the recommendations of the second Emergency Board, but failure to accept the terms results in the loss of certain benefits in the event of a strike.[159] From the time a request for a second Emergency Board has been made until 60 days after the Board has made its report to the President, "no change shall be made by the parties in the conditions out of which the dispute arose."[160]

Because waiting periods attend each step, after the creation of the first Section 9A Emergency Board, resort to self-

---

[155]RLA §9A(c).

[156]*Id.* §9A(e).

[157]*Id.* §9A(f).

[158]*Id.* §9A(g). Various 9A boards have differed in their constructions of this provision. The first 9A "second" Emergency Board, Emergency Board 201, in its report of June 3, 1983, noted that "while Board No. 199 made its recommendations for settlement of the disputes on an issue-by-issue basis, this Board, after careful review of the statute has concluded that it is required to select a single 'package' offer in each dispute." In contrast, Emergency Board 207, in its report of February 15, 1985, stated, "The Board is satisfied that it may make that selection either on the basis of the entire package offer of each party or on the basis of each individual item."

[159]RLA §9A(i) (if Emergency Board accepts final offer submitted by carrier and employees of such carrier engage in subsequent work stoppage, "employees shall not be eligible . . . for benefits under the Railroad Unemployment Insurance Act"); *Id.* §9A(j) (if Emergency Board accepts final offer submitted by employees, and employees of such carrier engage in work stoppage, carrier "shall not participate in any benefits of any agreement between carriers which is designed to provide benefits to such carriers during a work stoppage").

[160]*Id.* §9A(h).

help is effectively prohibited for 240 days.[161] Once the 240-day period is over, however, either party may resort to self-help subject to the penalties described earlier.

VII. Interest Arbitration

Once parties negotiating a collective bargaining agreement have accepted a proffer of arbitration, Sections 7, 8, and 9 of the RLA set out specific, detailed rules concerning the contents of the agreement to arbitrate, the procedures by which the arbitration must be conducted, and the procedures by which disputes over the validity or meaning of the award are to be resolved.

Section 8 provides a long list of rules governing the contents of agreements to submit disputes to arbitration.[162] Once the parties enter into an agreement to arbitrate, Section 7 provides rules governing the selection of a panel and the conduct of the arbitration. According to Section 7, Second, arbitration panels may consist of three or six people. In the case of a three-person panel under Section 7, Second (a), the union and carrier must each select one arbitrator, and these two arbitrators must select a third arbitrator, and so notify the NMB. If the arbitrators chosen by the parties fail to name the third arbitrator, they must notify the NMB within five days after their first meeting and the NMB will name the third arbitrator.

A similar procedure must be followed in the case of six-person arbitration panels under Section 7, Second (b), except that the union and carrier must each select two arbitrators, and these four arbitrators must select the final two arbitrators. In addition, if the arbitrators chosen by the parties fail to name the two arbitrators within fifteen days after their first meeting, they must notify the NMB, which will name the remaining arbitrators.

---

[161]Teamsters Local 808 v. NMB, 888 F2d 1428, 1432, 132 LRRM 2913 (CA DC, 1989).

[162]*See* 45 USC §158 (1994).

Section 7, Third (d) prevents one party from challenging the other party's selection of an arbitrator on the grounds that an arbitrator has an "interest in the controversy to be arbitrated, or because of his connection with or partiality to either of the parties to the arbitration." Parties may, however, challenge the impartiality of arbitrators selected by the NMB or the other arbitrators.

Section 7, Third (e) requires that each party be responsible for compensating the members of the board of arbitration that they select. Arbitrators selected by other arbitrators or named by the NMB are compensated by the NMB at an amount fixed by the NMB together with "necessary traveling expenses and expenses actually incurred for subsistence, while serving as an arbitrator."[163]

Under Section 7, Third (g), a board of arbitration may, "subject to the approval of the Mediation Board, also employ and fix the compensation of such assistants as it deems necessary in carrying on the proceedings." The NMB usually pays the compensation of these employees and their actual expenses.

Under Section 7, Third (b), the board of arbitration must organize and select its own chair and make all necessary rules for conducting its hearings. The section limits the scope of such rules by requiring that parties to the controversy receive "a full and fair hearing, which must include an opportunity to present their case in person, by counsel, or by other representative as they may respectively elect." Furthermore, Section 7, Third (h) requires that all testimony before the board be given under oath or affirmation.

Section 7, Third (h) gives members of a board "power to require the attendance of witnesses and the production of such books, papers, contracts, agreements, and documents as may be deemed by the board of arbitration material to just determination of the matters submitted to its arbitration." The arbitrators may request the clerk of the district court to issue subpoenas necessary to enforce these powers.

---

[163]RLA §7, Third (e).

Section 7, Third (f) specifies rules for distributing the award. The board of arbitration must furnish a certified copy of its award to the respective parties, and must "transmit the original, together with the papers and proceedings and a transcript of the evidence taken at the hearings, certified by at least a majority of the arbitrators, to the clerk of the district court of the United States for the district wherein the controversy arose."[164] The board must also furnish a certified copy of its award, and the papers and proceedings, to the NMB and furnish a certified copy of the award to the Interstate Commerce Commission.

Should a dispute arise as to the meaning or application of a valid award, Section 9, Third (c) requires that the parties submit such a controversy to the arbitration board rather than to a court. Under Section 7, Third (c), the arbitration board must reconvene upon notice from the NMB that either party desires a clarification of the award. Upon reconvening, the arbitration board may rule only on the questions relating to the "meaning or application of the award which are submitted by the party or parties in writing."[165] Because the jurisdiction of a reconvened board is limited to the interpretation or construction of its original award, it may not issue a decision that is inconsistent with its original decision.[166]

Under Section 7, Third (c), a decision by a reconvened board must be acknowledged in the same manner, and "filed in the same district court clerk's office, as the original award and becomes a part of the original award."

Courts have limited jurisdiction to review the decisions of arbitration boards. Courts are prohibited from reviewing an award to resolve ambiguities[167] and may impeach an award only for one of three reasons stated in Section 9, Third. Under Section 9, Third (a), a court may impeach an award

---

[164]Unless a petition to impeach the award is filed within 10 days, the court will enter judgment on the award. *Id.* §9, Second.

[165]*Id.* §7, Third (c).

[166]Mid-Continent Airlines v. Railway & Steamship Clerks, 83 F Supp 976, 24 LRRM 2320 (WD Mo, 1949).

[167]*See* Western Air Lines v. Labor Comm'r, 167 F2d 566, 22 LRRM 2051 (CA 9, 1948).

that "plainly does not conform to the substantive requirements laid down by the chapter, or that resulted from proceedings which were not substantially in conformity" with the chapter. Under Section 9, Third (b), an award may be impeached if it does "not conform, nor confine itself, to the stipulations of the agreement to arbitrate."[168] Finally, an award may be impeached under Section 9, Third (c) where a "member of the board of arbitration rendering the award was guilty of fraud or corruption; or [where] a party to the arbitration practiced fraud or corruption which affected the result of the arbitration." Once the district court issues its decision, Section 9, Fifth gives the parties only 10 days in which to appeal.

Minor procedural variances, however, are unlikely to result in the impeachment of an award. Section 9, Third (c) specifically states that an award must be "construed liberally by the court, with a view to favoring its validity, and no award shall be set aside for trivial irregularity or clerical error, going only to form and not to substance."[169] Moreover, defects in proceedings prior to or during the arbitration are often deemed waived if a party acquiesces to the arbitration with knowledge of the defect.[170] In addition, if the impeaching party's own action contributes to a procedural defect, the party may be estopped from complaining.[171]

---

[168]Courts have held that there must be strict adherence to the essential terms of the agreement to arbitrate. Railway & Steamship Clerks v. Norfolk S. Ry., 143 F2d 1015, 14 LRRM 905 (CA 4, 1944); see also Jones v. St. Louis-S.F. Ry., 728 F2d 257, 115 LRRM 2905 (CA 6, 1984) (arbitration before Public Law Board pursuant to RLA §3).

[169]See Maine C. R.R. v. Maintenance of Way Employees, 663 F Supp 425, 126 LRRM 3158 (D Me, 1987).

[170]Railway Conductors & Brakemen v. Clinchfield R.R., 407 F2d 985, 70 LRRM 3076 (CA 6), cert. denied, 395 U.S. 841, 72 LRRM 2443 (1969); Maine C. R.R. v. Maintenance of Way Employees, 650 F Supp 615, 124 LRRM 2521 (D Me, 1986) (arbitration required by act of Congress conducted pursuant to §§7, 8, and 9); Gibbons v. United Transp. Union, 462 F Supp 838, 101 LRRM 2352 (ND Ill, 1978); see also Krieter v. Lufthansa German Airlines, 558 F2d 966, 96 LRRM 2778 (CA 9, 1977) (same holding in minor dispute arbitration).

[171]Railway Conductors & Brakemen v. Clinchfield R.R., 407 F2d 985, 70 LRRM 3076; Gibbons v. United Transp. Union, 462 F Supp 838, 101 LRRM 2352 (ND Ill, 1978).

VIII. CARRIER OBLIGATION TO MAINTAIN THE STATUS QUO

A. Scope of the Status Quo Obligation

1. Status Quo Provisions.[172] Service by either party of a notice under Section 6 seeking to modify an agreement governing rates of pay, rules, or working conditions triggers the so-called major dispute procedures of the RLA. Under the statute, there are three explicit status quo provisions—Section 5, First, Section 6, and Section 10—that obligate the parties to maintain the status quo during three consecutive stages of the major dispute procedures.[173] In addition, the duty specified in Section 2, First to "exert every reasonable effort" to settle disputes has been described by the Supreme Court as an "implicit status quo requirement."[174]

Section 6 provides that "[i]n every case where a notice of intended change has been given, . . . rates of pay, rules, or working conditions shall not be altered by the carrier until the controversy has been finally acted upon, as required by Section 5, by the Mediation Board, unless a period of ten days has elapsed after termination of conferences without request for or proffer of the services of the Mediation Board." Section 5, First provides that for 30 days following the Board's notice that mediation efforts have failed, or until an Emergency Board is created under Section 10, "no change shall be made in the rates of pay, rules, or working conditions or established practices in effect prior to the time the dispute arose." Section 10 provides that after creation of an Emergency Board, and for 30 days after its report, "no change, except by agreement, shall be made in the conditions out of

---

[172]The nature of the status quo obligation after the parties have exhausted the RLA's major dispute resolution machinery is treated in Chapter 6, "Exercise of Economic Weapons," §V.

[173]A fourth section of the RLA, §2, Seventh, is often termed a status quo provision but in fact governs a carrier's obligation to serve a §6 notice rather than the parties' obligation to maintain the status quo once such a notice is served. Detroit & T. Shore Line R.R. v. United Transp. Union, 396 U.S. 142, 72 LRRM 2838 (1969). Section 2, Seventh is discussed at *infra* §VIII.A.8.

[174]Detroit & T. Shore Line R.R. v. United Transp. Union, 396 U.S. at 151 n.18.

which the dispute arose." The Supreme Court has stated that "these provisions, together with Section 2, First, form an integrated, harmonious scheme for preserving the status quo for the beginning of the major dispute through the final 30-day 'cooling-off' period."[175]

2. *Shore Line* Standard. Although these three RLA sections use different terminology, the Supreme Court held in *Detroit & Toledo Shore Line Railroad v. United Transportation Union*[176] that "the intent and effect of each is identical so far as defining and preserving the status quo is concerned."[177] That intent is to maintain unchanged the rates of pay, rules, and working conditions that are "in effect prior to the time the pending dispute arose and which are involved in or related to that dispute."[178] The purpose is to "prevent the union from striking and management from doing anything that would justify a strike" until the parties have exhausted the negotiation and mediation procedures, or reached agreement in the meantime if that is possible.[179] As the Supreme Court stated,

> The Act's status quo requirement is central to its design. Its immediate effect is to prevent the union from striking and management from doing anything that would justify a strike. In the long run, delaying the time when the parties can resort to self-help provides time for tempers to cool, helps create an atmosphere in which rational bargaining can occur, and permits the forces of public opinion to be mobilized in favor of a settlement without a strike or lockout. Moreover, since disputes usually arise when one party wants to change the status quo without undue delay, the power which the Act gives the other party to preserve the status quo for a prolonged period will frequently make it worthwhile for the moving party to compromise with the interests of the other side and thus reach agreement without interruption to commerce.[180]

The *Shore Line* decision involved unilateral changes made by the carrier with respect to the location at which employees

---

[175]*Id.* at 152.
[176]396 U.S. 142, 72 LRRM 2838.
[177]396 U.S at 152, 72 LRRM at 2842.
[178]396 U.S. at 153, 72 LRRM at 2842.
[179]396 U.S. at 148, 150, 72 LRRM at 2840, 2841.
[180]396 U.S. at 150, 72 LRRM at 2841.

reported for duty. The subject was not addressed by the parties' written collective bargaining agreements. When the carrier announced its intent to change its practice, relying on a special Adjustment Board ruling that the agreement did not preclude the assignments, the union served a Section 6 notice seeking to prohibit such assignments, and then filed an action in federal court seeking to preserve the status quo as it existed at the time of the notice.

The issue before the Supreme Court was whether the carrier's efforts to implement the intended change despite the union's Section 6 notice violated the status quo obligation. The carrier argued that "the purpose of the status quo provisions [was] to guarantee only that existing collective agreements continue to govern the parties' rights and duties during efforts to change those agreements."[181] The Supreme Court held, however, that the status quo that the carrier is required to maintain consists of "those actual, objective working conditions and practices, broadly conceived, which were in effect prior to the time the pending dispute arose and which are involved in or related to that dispute," and that "these conditions need not be covered in an existing agreement."[182] The Court also noted that some powers of management to make unilateral changes are themselves part of the status quo, even though they are not expressly mentioned in the existing agreement. This occurs when the management practice has "occurred for a sufficient period of time with the knowledge and acquiescence of the employees to become in reality a part of the actual working conditions."[183]

The most recent Supreme Court discussion of the *Shore Line* standard is found in *Pittsburgh & Lake Erie R.R. v. Railway Labor Executives' Ass'n (P&LE)*.[184] The Court held that "[w]hatever else *Shore Line* might reach, it did not involve the decision

---

[181]396 U.S. at 147, 72 LRRM at 2840.

[182]396 U.S. at 153, 72 LRRM at 2842.

[183]396 U.S. at 154, 72 LRRM at 2842. *See* Baker v. United Transp. Union, 455 F2d 149, 157, 79 LRRM 2165, 2169 (CA 3, 1971) ("[W]hen the railroad has engaged in certain activity over a sufficient period of time for the union to become aware of it and react accordingly if it objects, such past activity by the railroad absent objection by the union can become part of the actual status quo. . . .").

[184]491 U.S. 490, 131 LRRM 2611 (1989).

to quit the railroad business, sell its assets, and cease to be a railroad employer at all."[185] The Supreme Court viewed that decision as a "management prerogative" beyond the duty to bargain under the RLA.[186] The Court stated, moreover, that *Shore Line* "extended the relevant language of [Section 6] to its outer limits, and we should proceed with care" before applying the decision beyond its facts.[187] The Court further noted that the unilateral changes that the carrier sought to make in *Shore Line* were contrary to "the unquestioned practice for many years," and that it had been "reasonable for employees to deem" that practice "sufficiently established that it would not be changed without bargaining and compliance with the status quo provisions of the RLA."[188]

3. Invocation of the Status Quo Obligation. The obligation to maintain the status quo described in *Shore Line* applies only in a major dispute.[189] In a minor dispute, absent agreement to the contrary, the carrier generally is permitted to act on its own interpretation of the contract pending resolution of the dispute by the appropriate Adjustment Board.[190] As a result, if the carrier has an arguable contractual basis to take

---

[185]491 U.S. at 507, 131 LRRM at 2617. *See supra* §III.B.

[186]491 U.S. at 507, 131 LRRM at 2617.

[187]*Id.*

[188]*Id.* Based on the *P&LE* decision, the Seventh Circuit in Chicago & N.W. Transp. Co v. Railway Labor Executives' Ass'n, 908 F2d 144, 134 LRRM 2854 (CA 7, 1990), *cert. denied*, 498 U.S. 1120, 136 LRRM 2600 (1991), found that a carrier's decision to sell part of its business was not subject to the carrier's obligation to maintain the status quo. The court of appeals also rejected the argument that the union's §6 notice froze the status quo until after the completion of effects bargaining.

[189]Railway Carmen v. Missouri P. R.R., 944 F2d 1422, 1427–28, 138 LRRM 2639, 2641–42 (CA 8, 1991); Railway Labor Executives' Ass'n v. Chesapeake W. Ry., 915 F2d 116, 120 n.4, 135 LRRM 2439 (CA 4, 1990), *cert. denied*, 499 U.S. 921, 136 LRRM 2720 (1991); United Transp. Union v. CSX R.R., 893 F2d 584, 594, 133 LRRM 2203, 2204 (CA 3, 1990); CSX Transp., Inc. v. United Transp. Union, 879 F2d 990, 997, 131 LRRM 2681, 2688–89 (CA 2, 1989), *cert. denied*, 493 U.S. 1020, 133 LRRM 2192 (1990); Locomotive Eng'rs v. Consolidated Rail Corp., 844 F2d 1218, 1220–21, 128 LRRM 2103, 2105 (CA 6, 1988). The rights of the parties to exercise economic weapons, including altering the status quo, is the subject of Chapter 6, "Exercise of Economic Weapons." The distinction between major and minor disputes is discussed in Chapter 5, "Enforcement of Collective Bargaining Agreements," §I.

[190]*Id. But see* Chapter 5, §IX, for a discussion of injunctions issued to preserve the status quo pending submission of a dispute to a system board.

the action in question, the courts have not applied the status quo obligation described in *Shore Line*.[191]

4. Restoration of the Status Quo Obligation. Under Section 6, the carrier may not unilaterally alter the status quo "unless a period of ten days has elapsed after termination of conferences without request for or proffer of the services of the Mediation Board."[192] If neither party requests, and the NMB does not offer, mediation within 10 days after conferences terminate, then the status quo period expires and the parties are free to resort to self-help.[193] There is no authority that defines when conferences are deemed to "terminate" for the purposes of this provision.

In cases where negotiation conferences have been terminated without the invocation or proffer of the NMB's mediation services, there is a split of authority over whether, after the self-help period has begun, one party may bring it to a halt by seeking the NMB's belated participation. In *Illinois Central Railroad v. Locomotive Engineers*,[194] the court held that a request for mediation by the NMB stays the use of self-help until the NMB procedures have been exhausted. Conversely, in *Iberia Air Lines v. NMB*,[195] the court held that once

---

[191]Railway Carmen v. Missouri P. R.R., 944 F2d 1422, 1427, 138 LRRM 2639, 2641–42 (CA 8, 1991); Railway Labor Executives' Ass'n v. Chesapeake W. Ry., 915 F2d 116, 120–21, 135 LRRM 2439, 2442 (CA 4, 1990), *cert. denied*, 499 U.S. 921, 136 LRRM 2720 (1991); United Transp. Union v. CSX Transp., Inc., 893 F2d 584, 589–90, 133 LRRM 2203 (CA 3, 1990); Chicago & N. W. Transp. Co. v. Railway Labor Executives' Ass'n, 908 F2d at 148, 134 LRRM at 2865; CSX Transp., Inc. v. United Transp. Union, 879 F2d at 997–98, 131 LRRM 2681, 2688–89 (CA 2, 1989), *cert. denied*, 493 U.S. 1020, 133 LRRM 2192 (1990); Teamsters v. Southwest Airlines Co., 875 F2d 1129, 1133–34, 131 LRRM 2761, 2763–65 (CA 5, 1989) (en banc), *cert. denied*, 493 U.S. 1043, 133 LRRM 2264 (1990); Air Line Pilots Ass'n v. Eastern Air Lines, 863 F2d 891, 900, 129 LRRM 2691, 2699 (CA DC, 1988), *cert. dismissed*, 112 S Ct 37 (1991); Locomotive Eng'rs v. Consolidated Rail Corp., 844 F2d 1218, 1220–21, 128 LRRM 2103, 2105 (CA 6, 1988); Railway Executives' Ass'n v. Boston & Me. Corp., 808 F2d 150, 156, 124 LRRM 2145, 2149 (CA 1, 1986).

[192]*See supra* §IV.

[193]Iberia Air Lines v. NMB, 472 F Supp 104, 108–09, 101 LRRM 2676, 2679–80 (SD NY, 1979), *aff'd mem.*, 636 F2d 1201, 106 LRRM 2816 (CA 2, 1980), *cert. denied*, 450 U.S. 999, 106 LRRM 2817 (1981); Railway & Steamship Clerks v. Philadelphia, B. & N. E. R.R., 633 F Supp 371, 373 (ED Pa, 1986).

[194]299 F Supp 1278, 71 LRRM 2035 (ND Ill, 1969), *aff'd*, 422 F2d 593, 73 LRRM 2458 (CA 7, 1970).

[195]472 F Supp 104, 101 LRRM 2676.

the status quo period has expired, a subsequent request for the mediation services of the NMB does not revive the status quo obligation.

Once the NMB has released the parties, there are few situations in which a party may be enjoined from engaging in self-help. For example, the use of self-help cannot be halted simply because the NMB has reoffered its mediatory services.[196] Courts have also rejected the argument that a new status quo obligation may be created by service of another Section 6 notice concerning the same dispute,[197] and one circuit has ruled that a party does not lose the right to engage in self-help by not doing so within a particular period of time after the commencement of the self-help period.[198] A party retains the right to engage in self-help even if negotiations have resumed during the self-help period.[199] However, where a party fails to exert every reasonable effort to make and maintain agreements during the bargaining process, an injunction may be issued if it is "the only practical, effective means of enforcing the duty."[200]

The status quo may be restored when a Presidential Emergency Board is appointed under Section 10 after the status quo periods under Sections 6 and 5, First have expired and the parties have resorted to self-help. On the other hand, because Section 10 bars changes in "the conditions out of

---

[196]Elgin, J. & E. R.R. v. Railroad Trainmen, 302 F2d 540, 50 LRRM 2148 (CA 7), *cert. denied,* 371 U.S. 823, 51 LRRM 2829 (1962).

[197]Pullman Co. v. Railway Conductors & Brakemen, 316 F2d 556, 52 LRRM 2829 (CA 7), *cert. denied,* 375 U.S. 820 (1963); Northwest Airlines v. Air Line Pilots Ass'n, 185 F Supp 77, 46 LRRM 2689 (D Minn, 1960).

[198]Pan Am. World Airways v. Teamsters, 894 F2d 36, 133 LRRM 2292 (CA 2, 1990). *See also* REA Express v. Railway & Steamship Clerks, 358 F Supp 760, 83 LRRM 2153 (SD NY, 1973).

[199]Pullman Co. v. Railway Conductors & Brakemen, 316 F2d 556, 52 LRRM 2829; REA Express v. Railway & Steamship Clerks, 358 F Supp 760, 83 LRRM 2153.

[200]Chicago & N.W. Ry. v. United Transp. Union, 402 U.S. 570, 583, 77 LRRM 2337 (1971); Piedmont Aviation v. Air Line Pilots Ass'n, 416 F2d 633, 72 LRRM 2343 (CA 4), *cert. denied,* 397 U.S. 926, 73 LRRM 2537 (1970); Pan Am. World Airways v. Railway & Steamship Clerks, 185 F Supp 350, 46 LRRM 260 (ED NY, 1960); American Airlines v. Air Line Pilots Ass'n, 169 F Supp 777, 43 LRRM 2390 (SD NY, 1958).

which the dispute arose," the courts that have considered the issue have held that when a Presidential Emergency Board has been appointed, the parties in such a case must restore the status quo that existed before they resorted to self-help.[201]

5. Agreements to Set Employment Terms During Bargaining. The parties sometimes attempt to define in their collective bargaining agreements what terms and conditions will apply during negotiations for a new agreement. The typical circumstance in which this issue arises is where the parties have executed an agreement with a so-called snapback clause, providing that upon termination of an agreement with a duration clause the existing rates of pay, rules, or working conditions will revert to different terms. This occurs, for example, when a union has granted a bargaining concession to the employer but has sought to limit its duration. The Second Circuit, in *Air Line Pilots Ass'n v. Pan American World Airways*,[202] upheld such an agreement, holding that the parties may by agreement provide that terms different from those in the collective bargaining agreement will apply during the status quo period.[203]

6. Determining the Status Quo. The employer's obligation under *Shore Line*[204] and subsequent cases is to maintain rates of pay, rules, and working conditions. To the extent that rates of pay, rules, and working conditions are defined by a collective bargaining agreement, the question arises whether, in a case where the meaning of the agreement is

---

[201]Railway Labor Executives' Ass'n v. Boston & Me. Corp., 808 F2d 150, 155, 124 LRRM 2145, 2148 (CA 1, 1986); Alton & S. Ry. v. Railway & Steamship Clerks, 481 F Supp 130, 131 (D DC, 1978).

[202]765 F2d 377, 119 LRRM 3073 (CA 2, 1985).

[203]In reaching this decision, the court distinguished Air Cargo v. Teamsters Local 851, 733 F2d 241, 246, 116 LRRM 2141 (CA 2, 1984), in which the union, having failed for a substantial period to enforce a contractual provision on weekend work schedules, instructed its members to report for work in accordance with the contract after the parties began negotiations. The Second Circuit held that practice may control over the express terms of the agreement for purposes of establishing the statutory status quo.

[204]Detroit & T. Shore Line R.R. v. United Transp. Union, 396 U.S. 142, 72 LRRM 2838 (1969).

disputed, a court or an arbitrator should interpret the agreement.

In *Machinists v. Aloha Airlines*,[205] the union filed a Section 6 notice and the bargaining agreement expired. At the time these events occurred, the employer was enjoying the benefit of a union wage concession under an interim agreement with a snap-back clause. When the employer refused to comply with the snap-back clause, the union sought to enforce the agreement in arbitration. The Ninth Circuit held that once the collective bargaining agreement had "expired," it would no longer support a demand for arbitration.[206] The status quo provisions of the RLA, not the bargaining agreement, controlled. However, in determining the status quo, the appellate court directed the district court "to review the [bargaining agreements'] terms and the intent of the parties when they agreed to those terms."[207]

7. Matters Outside the Scope of the Status Quo Obligation. The fact that the status quo obligation applies to one subject matter does not necessarily mean it applies to the parties' entire relationship. Under the *Shore Line* decision, the status quo obligation is limited to rates of pay, rules, and working conditions that are "involved in or related to" the pending major dispute.[208] Thus, in several cases courts have declined to enforce the status quo obligation with respect to conditions that were unrelated to, or only remotely related to, the subjects of the pending Section 6 notices.[209]

Likewise, matters that are not subject to the carrier's obligation to bargain with respect to rates of pay, rules, and working conditions are beyond the scope of a carrier's status

---

[205]776 F2d 812, 120 LRRM 3326 (CA 9, 1985).

[206]776 F2d at 816.

[207]*Id.* at 816–17.

[208]Detroit & T. Shore Line R.R. v. United Transp. Union, 396 U.S. 142, 153, 72 LRRM 2838, 2842 (1969).

[209]*E.g.*, Reed v. National Air Lines, 524 F2d 456, 459, 90 LRRM 3275, 3277–78 (CA 5, 1975); Baker v. United Transp. Union, 455 F2d 149, 155 n.13, 79 LRRM 2165, 2168 n.13 (CA 3, 1971). In one case the court held that a change in a working condition not covered by a §6 notice gave rise to a minor dispute. Reed v. National Air Lines, 524 F2d 456, 90 LRRM 3275 (CA 5, 1975).

quo obligations.[210] Thus, if a court determines that an action proposed by the carrier constitutes a management prerogative over which the carrier is not obligated to bargain, it will not apply the status quo obligation.[211]

8. Absence of a Section 6 Notice. The definition of the status quo obligation under *Shore Line* concerns only the carrier's duty to maintain the status quo following service of a Section 6 notice, and the Supreme Court expressly distinguishes, as a different issue, the carrier's obligation under Section 2, Seventh, which provides that "[n]o carrier, its officers or agents shall change the rates of pay, rules, or working conditions of its employees, as a class as embodied in agreements except in the manner prescribed in such agreements or in [Section 6]."[212] Whether the carrier's proposed action would "change" the rates of pay, rules, or working conditions, and thus whether it is obligated to serve a Section 6 notice before making the change, presents the question of whether the carrier's action creates a major or a minor dispute, as defined in the case law. This issue is discussed in the next chapter.

B. Prior to the Negotiation of an Initial Collective Bargaining Agreement

1. Prior to Certification of Union. If employees are not represented by any union, the Act does not limit the power of carriers and employees to enter into individual agreements, or to order their relationships without agreements, except for prohibitions against interference with the right of self-

---

[210]Chicago & N. W. Transp. Co. v. Railway Labor Executives' Ass'n, 908 F2d 144, 154, 134 LRRM 2854 (CA 7, 1990), *cert. denied*, 498 U.S. 1120, 136 LRRM 2600 (1991). *See* Pittsburgh & L. E. R.R. v. Railway Labor Executives' Ass'n, 491 U.S. 490, 512, 131 LRRM 2611, 2619 (1989).

[211]Pittsburgh & L. E. R.R. v. Railway Labor Executives' Ass'n, 491 U.S. at 512, 131 LRRM at 2619; Chicago & N. W. Transp. Co. v. Railway Labor Executives' Ass'n, 908 F2d at 154.

[212]Detroit & T. Shore Line R.R. v. United Transp. Union, 396 U.S. at 155–56, 72 LRRM at 2843 ("Section 2, Seventh . . . does not impose any status quo duties attendant upon major disputes procedures. It simply states one category of cases in which those procedures must be invoked.").

organization.[213] Accordingly, with the exception of interference cases, the status quo obligations of the statute do not prohibit a carrier from making changes in the rates of pay, rules, or working conditions of unrepresented employees.[214]

2. During Initial Round of Postcertification Bargaining. The extent to which a carrier must maintain the status quo prior to or during initial negotiations with a union that has established representation of a previously unrepresented craft or class is less settled. The issue centers on the status of *Williams v. Jacksonville Terminal Co.*,[215] in which the Supreme Court held that the status quo obligation in Section 6 does not apply prior to execution of a collective bargaining agreement covering previously unrepresented employees. The Court's rationale was that the status quo provision in Section 6 was "aimed at preventing changes in conditions previously fixed by collective bargaining agreements" and did not cover "[i]ndependent individual contracts."[216]

Subsequent Supreme Court decisions have led to questions regarding the status of *Williams*. In the *Shore Line* decision, the Court rejected the contention, made by the carrier and based in part on *Williams*, that the status quo obligation was limited to terms "covered in an existing agreement."[217] In doing so, the Court raised, without answering, the question

---

[213]These prohibitions are discussed in Chapter 3, "Protection of Employees' Rights of Self-Organization."

[214]*Cf.* Williams v. Jacksonville Terminal Co., 315 U.S. 386, 399–400 (1942) (the prohibition in §2, Seventh against unilateral changes in the terms established by agreements protects "only agreements reached after collective bargaining"). Furthermore, one court has held that §6 notices served prior to the certification of a union have no effect and do not trigger any status quo obligation even if the union serving the notice is certified subsequently. Railway Labor Executives' Ass'n v. Wheeling & L. E. Ry., 756 F Supp 249, 253–54, 136 LRRM 2756, 2759–60 (ED Va), *aff'd*, 943 F2d 49, 138 LRRM 2160 (CA 4, 1991).

[215]315 U.S. 386 (1942).

[216]315 U.S. at 402–03.

[217]Detroit & T. Shore Line R.R. v. United Transp. Union, 396 U.S. 142, 153, 72 LRRM 2838, 2842 (1969). On the question of whether the status quo encompasses conditions "objectively" in existence at the time of the §6 notice, in addition to express and implicit terms of the bargaining agreement, the Supreme Court in Pittsburgh & L. E. R.R. v. Railway Labor Executives' Ass'n, 491 U.S. 490, 131 LRRM 2611 (1989), described *Shore Line* as "extend[ing] the relevant language of §156 to its outer limits." 491 U.S. at 506.

of the "continuing vitality" of *Williams,* and distinguished *Williams* in part on the ground that in that case "there was absolutely no history of any collective bargaining or agreement at all."[218]

Several courts of appeals have addressed whether a carrier's unilateral changes in rates of pay, rules, or working conditions prior to reaching an initial agreement violated the RLA. The Second, Ninth, and District of Columbia Circuits have permitted unilateral changes, arguing that circuit courts are bound by *Williams* unless and until the Supreme Court overrules it.[219] The Eleventh Circuit held that unilateral changes made by a carrier during negotiations for an initial agreement violated Section 2, First.[220] The court distinguished *Williams* and the Ninth and D.C. Circuit Court decisions on the ground that in those cases there was "no prior history of any collective bargaining."[221]

C. Judicial Remedies for Carrier Violations

1. Status Quo Injunctions in Major Disputes. If the court concludes that a carrier has violated one of the RLA's status quo provisions, it may grant an injunction requiring the carrier to maintain or restore the status quo until the carrier either obtains an agreement authorizing the challenged action through the major dispute procedures or ex-

---

[218]396 U.S. at 153, 72 LRRM at 2842. The Court also stated that the status quo obligation commences with the "beginning of the major dispute." *Id.*

[219]Virgin Atl. Airways v. NMB, 956 F2d 1245, 139 LRRM 2541 (CA 2), *cert. denied,* 141 LRRM 2408 (1992); Regional Airline Pilots Ass'n v. Wings W. Airlines, 915 F2d 1399, 1403, 135 LRRM 2735, 2738–39 (CA 9, 1990), *cert. denied,* 501 U.S. 1251, 137 LRRM 2696 (1991); Machinists v. Trans World Airlines, 839 F2d 809, 812–14, 127 LRRM 2854, 2856–58 (CA DC), *cert. denied,* 488 U.S. 820, 129 LRRM 2464 (1988).

[220]Machinists v. Transportes Aereos Mercantiles Pan Americanos, 924 F2d 1005, 136 LRRM 2686, *cert. denied,* 138 LRRM 2480 (1991) (The employees in question had previously been represented by another union that had reached a tentative agreement with the carrier, and the court found that the carrier had represented to the successor union that the tentative agreement comprised the status quo. The court applied a status quo obligation.).

[221]924 F2d at 1008–09, 136 LRRM at 2688–89.

hausts those procedures in an effort to reach such an agreement but no agreement is reached.[222]

If the court finds a status quo violation, it may issue an injunction requiring restoration of the status quo without a finding of irreparable injury or consideration of other equitable factors.[223] There is a conflict among the courts of appeals, however, as to the standard for issuing a preliminary injunction before any violation has been conclusively established.[224] The Second and Seventh Circuits have held that a party seeking a preliminary injunction under the RLA status quo provisions must satisfy the traditional equitable factors for injunctive relief pendente lite, including a showing of irreparable harm.[225] Other courts have applied the traditional equitable relief criteria without discussion of the issue.[226] The Eighth and District of Columbia Circuits have held that no showing of irreparable harm is required for a preliminary injunction.[227] Other courts have granted preliminary status quo injunctions against carriers without making any findings

---

[222]See, e.g., Consolidated Rail Corp. v. Railway Labor Executives' Ass'n, 491 U.S. 299, 303, 131 LRRM 2601, 2602–03 (1989); Detroit & T. Shore Line R.R. v. United Transp. Union, 396 U.S. 142, 147, 72 LRRM 2838, 2839–40 (1969); Teamsters v. Southwest Airlines Co., 875 F2d 1129, 1133, 131 LRRM 2761, 2763–64 (CA 5, 1989) (en banc), cert. denied, 493 U.S. 1043, 133 LRRM 2264 (1990); Air Line Pilots Ass'n v. Eastern Air Lines, 869 F2d 1518, 1520, 130 LRRM 2895, 2896–97 (CA DC, 1989); Maintenance of Way Employees v. Burlington N. Ry., 802 F2d 1016, 1021, 123 LRRM 2593, 2596–97 (CA 8, 1986).

[223]Consolidated Rail Corp. v. Railway Labor Executives' Ass'n, 491 U.S. 299, 131 LRRM 2601.

[224]This issue arises where the court finds that the union is likely to prevail on the merits of establishing a major dispute, or at least that there are serious questions on the merits, and that the balance of hardships weighs in favor of issuance of injunctive relief. See, e.g., Teamsters Workers, Local 553 v. Eastern Air Lines, 695 F2d 668, 677, 112 LRRM 2482, 2488–89 (CA 2, 1982).

[225]695 F2d at 677, 112 LRRM at 2488–89; National R.R. Labor Conference v. Machinists, 830 F2d 741, 750 n.7, 126 LRRM 2615, 2622 n.7 (CA 7, 1987).

[226]E.g., Longshoremen v. Norfolk S. Corp., 927 F2d 900, 903, 136 LRRM 2746, 2749 (CA 6), cert. denied, 112 S Ct 63, 138 LRRM 2479 (1991); Railway & Steamship Clerks v. Railway Express Agency, 409 F2d 312, 316, 70 LRRM 3295, 3297–98 (CA 2, 1969); Consolidated Rail Corp. v. Maintenance of Way Employees, 735 F Supp 1265, 1272 (ED Pa, 1990).

[227]Maintenance of Way Employees v. Chicago & N. W. Transp. Co., 827 F2d 330, 333 n.2, 126 LRRM 2199, 2201 n.2 (CA 8, 1987), cert. denied, 485 U.S. 988, 127 LRRM 3136 (1988); Southern Ry. v. Locomotive Firemen & Enginemen, 337 F2d 127, 133–34 (CA DC 1964).

with respect to irreparable harm, and without addressing any possible distinction between preliminary and permanent injunctive relief.[228]

2. Effect of Norris-LaGuardia Act. The Norris-LaGuardia Act provides that "[n]o court of the United States . . . shall have jurisdiction to issue any restraining order or temporary or permanent injunction in a case involving or growing out of a labor dispute, except in strict compliance" with the Act's requirements,[229] and enumerates specific acts that shall not be subject to any injunctive relief, including work stoppages and picketing.[230] The courts have held that the RLA creates a limited exception to the Norris-LaGuardia Act's bar on federal court interference in labor disputes.[231] This case law holds that an injunction is permissible where the conduct violates an express statutory prohibition and an injunction is the only practical, effective means of enforcing the statute.[232] Under this rationale, the courts have held that the Norris-LaGuardia Act generally does not prohibit injunctions against conduct found to violate the status quo provisions of the RLA.[233]

Section 8 of the Norris-LaGuardia Act provides that no injunctive relief will be granted in a labor dispute to any party "who has failed to comply with any obligation imposed by law which is involved in the labor dispute in question, or who has failed to make every reasonable effort to settle such dispute either by negotiation or with the aid of any available governmental machinery of mediation or voluntary arbitration."[234] Thus, in addition to incorporating the traditional

---

[228]*E.g.*, Southern P. Transp. Co. v. Locomotive Eng'rs, 756 F Supp 1446, 1451, 136 LRRM 2677, 2680–81 (D Kan), *appeal dismissed as moot*, No. 91-3054 (CA 10, 1991).

[229]29 USC §101 (1994).

[230]*Id.* §104.

[231]Burlington N. Ry. v. Maintenance of Way Employees, 481 U.S. 429, 125 LRRM 2073 (1987).

[232]*Id.*; Chicago & N. W. R.R. v. United Transp. Union, 402 U.S. 570, 581–82, 77 LRRM 2337 (1971).

[233]Detroit & T. Shore Line R.R. v. United Transp. Union, 396 U.S. 142, 72 LRRM 2838 (1969).

[234]29 USC §108 (1994).

equitable requirement that a party seeking injunctive relief have "clean hands," this provision " 'makes it a condition precedent that every remedy must be exhausted to settle' " the labor dispute in question before injunctive relief may be granted.[235] Accordingly, the Supreme Court has held that, although neither party to a major dispute is obliged to submit it to arbitration under the RLA, a party that has refused to do so is ordinarily barred from obtaining injunctive relief under the status quo provisions.[236] That is true for both union requests for status quo injunctions and carrier requests for strike injunctions.[237] Nevertheless, a refusal of or nonresponse to the proffer of arbitration will not necessarily bar injunctive relief where the party not seeking the injunction has also rejected, or not accepted, the proffer.[238]

Some cases hold that the RLA status quo provisions may override Section 8 of the Norris-LaGuardia Act and "lack of clean hands may be overcome by a balancing of interests, particularly where it is the public interest involved."[239] The Second Circuit, however, has pointed out that Section 8 of the Norris-LaGuardia Act is "almost identical" to Section 2, First of the RLA, and has held that because the requirements of the RLA and Section 8 are "congruent," a party seeking

---

[235]Railroad Trainmen v. Toledo, P. & W. R.R., 321 U.S. 50, 60 & n.16, 13 LRRM 725, 729 & n.16 (1944) (quoting 75 CONG. REC. 5504 (1932) (statement of Rep. LaGuardia) (emphasis omitted)).

[236]321 U.S. at 62, 13 LRRM at 730.

[237]See, e.g., Air Lines Pilots Ass'n v. United Air Lines, 802 F2d 886, 901, 123 LRRM 2617, 2627 (CA 7, 1986), cert. denied, 480 U.S. 946, 124 LRRM 3192 (1987); Transport Workers Local 553 v. Eastern Air Lines, 695 F2d 668, 679, 112 LRRM 2482, 2490–91 (CA 2, 1982); Railroad Trainmen v. Akron & B. B. R.R., 385 F2d 581, 614, 65 LRRM 2995, 3001–02 (CA DC, 1967), cert. denied, 390 U.S. 923, 67 LRRM 2835 (1968).

[238]Air Line Pilots Ass'n v. United Air Lines, 610 F Supp 243, 119 LRRM 2900 (ND Ill, 1985) (union could still seek injunction, even though it did not accept proffer of arbitration from NMB, because company had previously refused proffer of arbitration); Piedmont Aviation, Inc. v. Air Line Pilots, 416 F2d 633, 636, 72 LRRM 2343 (CA 4, 1969), cert. denied, 397 U.S. 926, 73 LRRM 2537 (1970) (even though employer immediately refused proffer of arbitration, it could seek injunction because union never accepted proffer, although union never declined either).

[239]Air Line Pilots Ass'n v. United Air Lines, 802 F2d at 901, 123 LRRM at 2627; see, e.g., Illinois C. R.R. v. Railroad Trainmen, 398 F2d 973, 976, 68 LRRM 2817, 2818 (CA 7, 1968); Akron & B. B. R.R. v. Railroad Trainmen, 385 F2d at 609, 65 LRRM at 2997–98.

injunctive relief under the RLA status quo provisions must comply with Section 8.[240]

Under the Norris-LaGuardia Act and the clean hands doctrine, unlawful acts by one party do not necessarily justify acts of self-help by the other. As the Fifth Circuit stated, "the 'cooling-off' policies of the major dispute provisions cannot be effectuated by allowing both parties simply to do away with the Act."[241] In contrast, some courts have held that resort to self-help by either party may immunize retaliation by the other. Where a carrier has changed the status quo, some courts have held that a union may engage in self-help.[242] Likewise, a carrier may be free to breach the status quo in response to unlawful strikes, at least to the extent necessary to restore service.[243]

3. Noninjunctive Remedies for Status Quo Violations.

If, by the time a court finds a status quo violation, the carrier has already taken the challenged action, or if it is otherwise impractical to grant a status quo injunction prohibiting the action, a court may grant affected employees make-whole equitable relief, including reinstatement and backpay.[244] One court of appeals has allowed a union to recover damages in the amount of dues, assessments, and initiation fees it would

---

[240]Transport Workers Local 553 v. Eastern Air Lines, 695 F2d at 678–79, 112 LRRM at 2489–90.

[241]National Airlines v. Machinists, 416 F2d 998, 72 LRRM 2294, 2298–99 (CA 5, 1969).

[242]United Industrial Workers of Seafarers (SIU) v. Board of Trustees, 400 F2d 320, 324, 68 LRRM 3043 (CA 5, 1968), cert. denied, 395 U.S. 905, 71 LRRM 2254 (1969) (strike in response to carrier's sale of facilities and termination of certain employees was lawful). See also Atlanta & W. P. R.R. v. United Transp. Union, 439 F2d 73, 76 LRRM 2603 (CA 5), cert. denied, 404 U.S. 825, 78 LRRM 2464 (1971) (change must be to present working conditions, not to future working conditions).

[243]National Airlines v. Machinists, 416 F2d 998, 1002, 72 LRRM 2294 (CA 5, 1969); Empresa Ecuatoriana De Aviacion v. Machinists, Dist. Lodge 100, 690 F2d 838, 844, 111 LRRM 2971, 2975–76 (CA 11, 1982), cert. dismissed, 463 U.S. 1250 (1983).

[244]See, e.g., Railway Labor Executives' Ass'n v. Boston & Me. Corp., 808 F2d 150, 158–59, 124 LRRM 2145, 2151 (CA 1, 1986), cert. denied, 484 U.S. 830, 126 LRRM 2496 (1987); Empresa Ecuatoriana De Aviacion v. Machinists, Dist. Lodge 100, 690 F2d at 846, 111 LRRM at 2977; United Industrial Workers of Seafarers (SIU) v. Board of Trustees, 400 F2d at 327, 68 LRRM at 3047–48.

have received had the carrier not violated the status quo by improperly "blanking" jobs.[245]

4. Statute of Limitations. The question of whether a status quo case may be time-barred has seldom arisen, because typically unions file suit seeking to enjoin potential status quo violations by carriers promptly after the carrier takes or announces action. Where the question has arisen, however, courts have "borrowed" the six-month statute of limitations under Section 10(b) of the NLRA for unfair labor practices under that Act.[246]

IX. UNION'S OBLIGATION TO MAINTAIN STATUS QUO

A. Scope of Union's Obligation

1. Status Quo Obligation During Major Disputes. Although some of the status quo provisions of the RLA refer only to carriers,[247] the courts have consistently held that unions have a corollary status quo obligation to refrain from strikes or other forms of economic pressure before the exhaustion of the major dispute procedure under the statute.[248]

---

[245]Bangor & A. R.R. v. Locomotive Firemen & Enginemen, 442 F2d 812, 822, 76 LRRM 2567, 2573–74 (CA DC, 1971).

[246]*See, e.g.,* Railway Labor Executives' Ass'n v. Southern Ry., 860 F2d 1038, 1041–42, 129 LRRM 3092, 3095 (CA 11, 1988); Locomotive Eng'rs v. Atchison, T. & S.F. Ry., 768 F2d 914, 919, 120 LRRM 3022, 3025 (CA 7, 1985); Machinists v. Aloha Airlines, 790 F2d 727, 734, 122 LRRM 2642, 2647–48 (CA 9), *cert. denied,* 479 U.S. 931, 123 LRRM 2904 (1986).

[247]*See supra* §VIII.

[248]Detroit & T. Shore Line Ry. v. United Transp. Union, 396 U.S. 142, 150, 72 LRRM 2838 (1969) ("The Act's status quo requirement is central to its design. Its immediate effect is to prevent the union from striking and management from doing anything that would justify a strike."). *See also* Chicago & N. W. Transp. Co. v. United Transp. Union, 402 U.S. 570, 77 LRRM 2337 (1974); National Air Lines v. Machinists, 416 F2d 998, 1002–03, 72 LRRM 2294 (CA 5, 1969), *on remand,* 308 F Supp 179, 73 LRRM 2163 (SD Fla), *rev'd and remanded,* 430 F2d 957, 74 LRRM 2833 (CA 5), *petition for reh'g denied,* 430 F2d 957, 75 LRRM 2046 (CA 5, 1970), *cert. denied,* 400 U.S. 992, 76 LRRM 2160, *on remand,* 82 LRRM 2999 (SD Fla, 1972), *aff'd,* 478 F2d 1062, 83 LRRM 2316 (CA 5, 1973); Air Cargo v. Teamsters, 733 F2d 241, 246–47, 116 LRRM 2141 (CA 2, 1984).

Thus, the courts will ordinarily enjoin a strike prior to exhaustion of the major dispute procedures of the RLA.[249]

One circumstance in which the courts have declined to enjoin such a strike is where it was precipitated by the carrier's own violation of status quo provisions of the statute.[250] In such a circumstance, the Norris-LaGuardia Act prohibits injunctive relief because the carrier has "failed to comply with [an] obligation imposed by law."[251] The courts will issue such relief, however, once the carrier has restored the status quo.[252]

2. Status Quo Regarding Matters of Managerial Prerogatives. As outlined previously,[253] some courts have held that carriers may have no obligation to bargain over or maintain the status quo regarding matters of managerial prerogative. The question left open by the Supreme Court's decision in *Pittsburgh & Lake Erie R.R. v. Railway Labor Executives' Ass'n (P&LE)*[254] is whether the RLA allows an injunction against a union strike over such matters. The only court to consider the issue since *P&LE* has answered this question in the affirmative. In *Chicago & North Western Transportation Co. v. Railway Labor Executives' Ass'n*,[255] the Seventh Circuit held that a threatened strike over a line sale that the court found to be within the carrier's management prerogatives violated the RLA. The court's reasoning was that by acting within its management prerogatives the carrier does not alter the status quo, and that the union therefore is not permitted to do so either.[256]

---

[249]The issues of what conduct constitutes unlawful economic pressure during the status quo period, and whether injunctive relief is appropriate against the union in cases where the union denies authorization of the job action, are addressed in *infra* §§IX.B. and C.

[250]Railroad Telegraphers v. Chicago & N. W. Ry., 362 U.S. 330, 45 LRRM 3104 (1960); United Industrial Workers of Seafarers (SIU) v. Board of Trustees, 400 F2d 320, 324, 68 LRRM 3043 (CA 5, 1968), *cert. denied*, 395 U.S. 905, 71 LRRM 2254 (1969); Atlanta & W. P. R.R. v. United Transp. Union, 439 F2d 73, 76 LRRM 2603 (CA 5), *cert. denied*, 404 U.S. 825, 78 LRRM 2464 (1971).

[251]29 USC §108 (1988).

[252]Atlanta & W. P. R.R. v. United Transp. Union, 439 F2d 73, 76 LRRM 2603; National Airlines, v. Machinists, 416 F2d 998, 72 LRRM 2294.

[253]*See supra* §III.B.

[254]491 U.S. 490, 131 LRRM 2611 (1989).

[255]908 F2d 144, 134 LRRM 2854 (CA 7, 1990).

[256]134 LRRM at 2865.

B. Union Activity Affected by the Status Quo Requirement

1. Primary Strikes. The most frequent use of the status quo injunction is to stop primary strikes sanctioned by the union. The courts will enjoin such a strike prior to exhaustion of the bargaining and mediation procedures under the RLA or the minor dispute procedures of the statute.[257]

A more difficult issue arises where the union denies sanctioning the strike. Under Section 6 of the Norris-LaGuardia Act, the union cannot be held responsible for the actions of individuals absent clear proof of participation in or ratification of those actions.[258] Thus, to issue injunctive relief where the union denies sanctioning or encouraging the primary strike, the courts will require clear proof of the union's involvement.[259]

The courts have demonstrated a wide divergence of views regarding the quantum of evidence required to prove union involvement. Some courts have relied on relatively insubstantial union statements[260] or union inaction[261] to justify injunctive relief. Other courts, however, have denied injunctive relief in the absence of mass action[262] or direct evidence of union involvement.[263]

---

[257]Locomotive Engr's v. Louisville & N. R.R., 373 U.S. 33, 52 LRRM 2944 (1963); Railroad Trainmen v. Chicago River & I. R.R., 353 U.S. 30, 39 LRRM 2578 (1957).

[258]29 USC §106 (1988).

[259]Air Line Pilots Ass'n v. United Air Lines, 802 F2d 886, 905, 123 LRRM 2617 (CA 7, 1986), cert. denied, 480 U.S. 946, 124 LRRM 3192 (1987).

[260]See Long Island R.R. v. System Fed'n, 289 F Supp 119, 70 LRRM 2764, 2678 (ED NY, 1968) (finding of union involvement in a work slowdown was based on an oblique statement by a union official that "the men are sick and tired," on the sudden inability of the union to find volunteers for overtime, and on the pervasive feeling among the union members that something had to be done about their grievances).

[261]Pan Am. World Airways v. Flight Attendants (UFA), 93 Lab. Cas. (CCH) ¶13,307 (SD NY, 1981) (failure to clearly disavow widespread calls for a sick-out found to be sufficient); REA Express v. Railway & Steamship Clerks, 62 Lab. Cas. (CCH) ¶10,917 (ED NY, 1970) (international union enjoined where local officers called strike in violation of international constitution).

[262]Texas Int'l Airlines v. Air Line Pilots Ass'n, 518 F Supp 203 (SD Tex, 1981) (failure to find clear and convincing evidence of contempt of anti-slowdown order, absent mass action).

[263]REA Express v. Railway & Steamship Clerks, 53 Lab. Cas. (CCH) ¶11,338 (SD NY, 1966) (denying injunction against wildcat strike absent evidence of union involvement).

2. Honoring Picket Lines of Another Union. Unions and employees generally have the right under the RLA to honor picket lines of another union.[264] Such conduct, however, may be enjoinable in certain circumstances.[265]

3. Other Job Actions. Although most of the litigation concerning union status quo violations has involved strikes, the rules developed in those cases also apply to other concerted actions designed to exert economic pressure by interfering with the carrier's normal operations. Examples of conduct that the courts have found to violate the status quo include concerted refusal to work overtime,[266] sick-outs,[267] mass demonstrations,[268] 24-hour union meetings,[269] and slow-downs.[270]

One court concluded that a union strike over a dispute that did not encompass rates of pay, rules, or working conditions violated the union's obligations under RLA Section 2.[271] Another court has held that wildcat strike activity violates the RLA because it pressures a carrier to treat with a group other than the certified bargaining representative.[272]

On the other hand, the RLA has been interpreted not to prohibit publicity campaigns that do not curtail the carrier's operations. In *Air Line Pilots Ass'n v. United Air Lines*,[273] the Seventh Circuit rejected a carrier's claim that a union violated the RLA through a prestrike publicity program directed at

---

[264]Locomotive Firemen & Enginemen v. Florida E.C. Ry., 346 F2d 673, 59 LRRM 2476 (CA 5, 1965); *see* Chapter 6, "Exercise of Economic Weapons," §IV.

[265]*See* Chapter 6, §IV.

[266]United Air Lines v. Machinists, 54 LRRM 2154 (ND Ill, 1963).

[267]Pan Am. World Airways v. Flight Attendants (UFA), 93 Lab. Cas. (CCH) ¶13,307 (SD NY, 1981); Texas Int'l Airlines v. Air Line Pilots Ass'n, 518 F Supp 203 (SD Tex, 1981).

[268]American Airlines v. Transport Workers, 57 LRRM 2484 (SD NY, 1964).

[269]Pennsylvania R.R. v. Transport Workers, 178 F Supp 53, 44 LRRM 2986 (D Pa, 1959).

[270]Long Island R.R. v. System Fed'n, 289 F Supp 119, 70 LRRM 2764 (ED NY, 1968); Texas Int'l Airlines v. Air Line Pilots Ass'n, 518 F Supp 203.

[271]Japan Airlines v. Machinists, 538 F2d 46, 92 LRRM 3383 (CA 2, 1976); *see supra* §III.A.

[272]Louisville & N. R.R. v. Bass, 328 F Supp 732, 745, 77 LRRM 2580 (WD Ky, 1971) ("By engaging in a wildcat strike, the dissidents, in effect, ask the carrier to treat with them over the problem at hand, not with the authorized representative.").

[273]802 F2d 886, 123 LRRM 2617 (CA 7, 1986), *cert. denied*, 480 U.S. 946, 124 LRRM 3192 (1987).

travel agents because it was directed toward "undermining United's ability to continue to provide service" in a later strike, and thus differed from work stoppages or mass demonstrations which, although not strikes, "had the consequence of a strike."[274]

C. Judicial Remedies for Union Violations

1. Injunctive Relief. The most common judicial remedy for a union's violation of the status quo obligation is an injunction prohibiting the strike or other work stoppage.[275] In such a case, Section 4 of the Norris-LaGuardia Act does not prohibit an injunction, but the procedural requirements of the statute must be met.[276]

2. Monetary Damages. The Fifth and Sixth Circuits have held that a carrier may not recover damages under the RLA for unlawful strikes.[277] One district court decision, however,

---

[274]802 F2d at 906–07. *See also* KLM Airlines v. Transport Workers, 57 LRRM 2063 (ED NY, 1964) (union may engage in informational picketing during status quo period regarding airlines' decision to hire nonunion subcontractor so long as union does not imply that affected employees were employed directly by the airline).

[275]Railroad Trainmen v. Chicago River & I. R.R., 353 U.S. 30, 39 LRRM 2578 (1957) (strike over minor dispute); National Airlines v. Machinists, 416 F2d 998, 72 LRRM 2294 (CA 5, 1969) (wildcat strike); Air Cargo v. Teamsters, 733 F2d 241, 116 LRRM 2141 (CA 2, 1984); Atchison, T. & S.F. Ry. v. United Transp. Union, 734 F2d 317, 116 LRRM 2571 (CA 7, 1984) (enjoining strike over minor dispute); Pan Am. World Airways v. Flight Attendants (UFA), 93 Lab. Cas. (CCH) ¶13,307 (SD NY, 1981) (sick-outs); United Air Lines v. Machinists, 54 LRRM 2154 (ND Ill, 1963) (overtime refusals); Long Island R.R. v. System Fed'n, 289 F Supp 119, 70 LRRM 2764 (ED NY, 1968) (widespread slowdown); American Airlines v. Transport Workers, 57 LRRM 2484, 2487 (SD NY, 1964) (picketing, concerted work stoppages, mass demonstrations).

[276]Chicago & N.W. Ry. v. United Transp. Union, 402 U.S. 570, 77 LRRM 2337 (1971); Locomotive Eng'rs v. Louisville & N. R.R., 373 U.S. 33, 52 LRRM 2944 (1963); Railroad Trainmen v. Chicago River & I. R.R., 353 U.S. 30, 39 LRRM 2578; Railroad Trainmen v. Toledo, P. & W. R.R., 321 U.S. 50, 13 LRRM 725 (1944).

[277]CSX Transp., Inc. v. Marquar, 980 F2d 359, 141 LRRM 2785 (CA 6, 1992); Burlington N. Ry. v. Maintenance of Way Employees, 961 F2d 86, 140 LRRM 2395 (CA 5, 1992); Louisville & N. R.R. v. Brown, 252 F2d 149, 155, 41 LRRM 2436, 2440 (CA 5), *cert. denied*, 356 U.S. 949, 42 LRRM 2043 (1958).

has awarded a carrier damages against a union for a strike in violation of Section 3, First (p).[278]

X. MORATORIUM AND DURATION CLAUSES

A. Moratorium Clauses

In the railroad industry, contracts historically have been negotiated without fixed duration.[279] Such contracts are generally interpreted to continue in force indefinitely, and in the absence of a contractual restriction the parties may serve a Section 6 notice seeking to modify the contract at any time.[280] However, to avoid constant negotiations, most rail carriers have negotiated what are known as moratorium clauses, which prohibit either party from serving a Section 6 notice to commence negotiations before a specified date.[281] Some moratorium clauses prohibit any Section 6 notices,[282] whereas others bar only proposed changes to specified provisions in the agreement.[283] In an airline industry case involving a claim that a moratorium clause deprived employees of rights guaranteed under Section 6 of the RLA, the Second Circuit held

---

[278]*See* Denver R. G. W. R.R. v. Railroad Trainmen, 58 LRRM 2568 (D Colo, 1965), *rev'd on other grounds,* 367 F2d 137 (CA 10), *rev'd,* 387 U.S. 556, 65 LRRM 2385 (1967).

[279]*See* Railway & Airline Supervisors v. Soo L. R.R., 891 F2d 675, 678, 133 LRRM 2081 (CA 8, 1989), *cert. denied,* 498 U.S. 809, 135 LRRM 2463 (1990); Railway & Steamship Clerks v. Florida E. C. Ry., 384 U.S. 238, 62 LRRM 2177 (1966).

[280]Detroit, T. & I. R.R. v. Locomotive Eng'rs, 77 Lab. Cas. (CCH) ¶11,079 (ED Mich, 1975); Train Dispatchers v. Union P. R.R., 679 F Supp 1535, 126 LRRM 2679 (WD Mo, 1987); *see also* Railway & Steamship Clerks v. Railroad Retirement Bd., 239 F2d 37, 38 LRRM 2788 (CA DC, 1956).

[281]*Id.*

[282]Train Dispatchers v. Union Pacific R.R., 679 F Supp 1535, 126 LRRM 2679 (WD Mo, 1987).

[283]Railway & Airline Supervisors v. Soo L. R.R., 891 F2d 675, 678, 133 LRRM 2081 (CA 8, 1989); Burlington N., Inc. v. Railroad Yardmasters, 79 Lab. Cas. (CCH) ¶11797 (ND Ill, 1976); Seaboard World Airlines v. Transport Workers, 443 F2d 437, 77 LRRM 2452 (CA 2, 1971), *aff'd after remand,* 425 F2d 1086, 73 LRRM 2894 (CA 2, 1970); Flight Eng'rs v. American Airlines, 303 F2d 5, 50 LRRM 2453 (CA 5, 1962); Southern P. Transp. Co. v. BRC, 81 Lab. Cas. (CCH) ¶24,379 (ND Cal, 1975).

that such clauses are permissible, at least where they are of reasonable duration.[284]

In *Railway & Steamship Clerks v. Florida East Coast Railway Co.*,[285] the Supreme Court held that under a typical railroad agreement of indefinite duration, those portions of the agreement that were not subject to a notice of intended changes pursuant to Section 6 remain in force even after the parties have exhausted the negotiation and mediation procedure under the statute and have been released to self-help on another Section 6 notice. The effect of this ruling is to keep such agreements in effect indefinitely.

B. Duration Clauses

In the airline industry, contracts generally contain duration terms, which specify what is commonly known as the amendable date.[286] The typical clause, at least in the published decisions, provides that the agreement will "continue in full force and effect until [the amendable date] and thereafter," either indefinitely or on a year-to-year basis, "unless written notice of intended change is served in accordance with Section 6 of the Railway Labor Act" within a specified period, such as 30 to 90 days, prior to the amendable date.[287]

The courts of appeals have disagreed on the effect of such typical airline industry duration clauses. A series of decisions in the Second[288] and Ninth Circuits[289] have interpreted

---

[284]Seaboard World Airlines v. Transport Workers, 443 F2d 437, 78 LRRM 2720 (CA 2, 1971) (10-year duration); *see also* Lenfest v. Boston & Me. Corp., 537 F Supp 324, 336–37 (D Mass, 1982); Maine C. R.R. v. Maintenance of Way Employees, 873 F2d 425, 131 LRRM 2201 (CA 1, 1989), *aff'g* 663 F Supp 425, 430–32, 126 LRRM 3158 (D Me, 1987).

[285]384 U.S. 238, 62 LRRM 2177 (1966).

[286]*See* Trans World Airlines v. Flight Attendants (IFFA), 809 F2d 483, 484, 124 LRRM 2364 (CA 8, 1987), *aff'd mem. by an equally divided Court*, 485 U.S. 175, 127 LRRM 2740 (1988).

[287]*E.g., id.*; Air Line Pilots Ass'n v. Pan Am. World Airways, 765 F2d 377, 379, 119 LRRM 3073 (CA 2, 1985).

[288]Air Cargo v. Teamsters Local 851, 733 F2d 241, 116 LRRM 2141 (CA 2, 1984). A variation of this holding is Flight Eng'rs v. Eastern Airlines, 359 F2d 303, 62 LRRM 2374 (CA 2, 1966), which appears to assume that the agreement remains in effect during the status quo period, but terminates following release by the NMB, when the parties are permitted to resort to self-help.

[289]Machinists v. Aloha Airlines, 776 F2d 812, 816, 120 LRRM 3326 (CA 9, 1985); Machinists v. Reeve Aleutian Airways, 469 F2d 990, 81 LRRM 2910 (CA 9, 1972), *cert. denied*, 411 U.S. 982, 83 LRRM 2167 (1973).

these agreements to terminate or expire on their amendable date.[290] *Machinists v. Aloha Airlines*[291] held that a contract cannot be enforced during the status quo period, after the amendable date, because "[t]here is nothing in the Railway Labor Act which extends a contract beyond its termination date."[292] Under the *Aloha* rationale, the carrier's only obligation to keep the existing rates of pay, rules, and working conditions in effect following the expiration of the agreement is the status quo requirement under Section 6. Thus, any dispute over a carrier's unilateral change in working conditions following "expiration" of the contract must be determined by the court as a status quo issue, even if determining the status quo requires interpreting the parties' agreement.[293]

A contrary result has been reached in another Second Circuit case[294] and in decisions from the District of Columbia,[295] Seventh,[296] and Eighth Circuits.[297] The District of Columbia Circuit made the following conclusion:

> *Aloha* appears to ignore the purposes behind the RLA's bifurcated dispute resolution procedure. . . . The expiration of the collective bargaining agreement tells us little or nothing about the track for which the dispute is suitable. Yet the consequence of the *Aloha* rule is that after the filing of a Section 6 notice and the expiration of a bargaining agreement no dispute be-

---

[290]The closely related issue of whether the parties may dictate which employment terms apply during the status quo period is discussed in *supra* §VIII. *See, e.g.,* Air Line Pilots Ass'n v. Pan Am. World Airways, 765 F2d 377, 119 LRRM 3073 (CA 2, 1985).

[291]776 F2d 812, 120 LRRM 3326.

[292]776 F2d at 816.

[293]*Id.*

[294]*See, e.g.,* Manning v. American Airlines, 329 F2d 32, 55 LRRM 2423 (CA 2), *cert. denied,* 339 U.S. 817 (1964).

[295]Air Line Pilots Ass'n v. Eastern Airlines, 863 F2d 891, 129 LRRM 2250 (CA DC, 1988).

[296]EEOC v. United Air Lines, 755 F2d 94 (CA 7, 1985). *See also* Air Line Pilots Ass'n v. UAL Corp., 897 F2d 1394, 1398, 133 LRRM 2863 (CA 7, 1990) ("Collective bargaining agreements governed by the RLA do not expire on their expiration dates. The Act abhors a contractual vacuum. If on the date of the expiration the parties have not negotiated a replacement agreement . . . the old agreement continues in force.").

[297]Trans World Airlines v. Flight Attendants (IFFA), 809 F2d 483, 484, 124 LRRM 2364 (CA 8, 1987), *aff'd mem. by an equally divided Court,* 485 U.S. 175, 127 LRRM 2740 (1988).

tween the parties can proceed along the track devised by Congress for "minor" disputes.[298]

The Second Circuit observed that "the very purpose of Section 6 is to stabilize relations by artificially extending the lives of agreements for a limited period regardless of the parties' intentions."[299] The Seventh and Eighth Circuits examined the contractual language itself and concluded that the parties intended that the contract would continue indefinitely except insofar as a notice of intended changes was served.[300]

XI. DUTY TO BARGAIN BEFORE AMENDABLE DATE

The express purpose of a moratorium or duration clause is to prohibit the parties from serving a Section 6 notice seeking to change the agreement while the clause is in effect. Although there is extensive authority under the NLRA as to whether such provisions constitute a waiver of the employer's obligation to bargain for the term of the agreement,[301] there is no analogous body of case law under the RLA. Rather, under the RLA, the carrier's right to make changes without the union's consent during the term of an agreement typically arises as an issue of whether the employer's proposed conduct creates a major or a minor dispute under the statute.[302]

Where a carrier seeks to take some unilateral action to which the union objects, if the union believes that the matter

---

[298]Air Line Pilots Ass'n v. Eastern Airlines, 863 F2d at 899.

[299]Manning v. American Airlines, 329 F2d 32, 35, 55 LRRM 2423 (CA 2, 1964), cert. denied, 339 U.S. 817 (1964).

[300]EEOC v. United Air Lines, 755 F2d at 97; Trans World Airlines v. Flight Attendants (IFFA), 809 F2d at 488.

[301]See generally I THE DEVELOPING LABOR LAW 699–710 (Patrick Hardin ed., 3d. ed 1992).

[302]E.g., Teamsters v. Southwest Airlines Co., 875 F2d 1129, 1135–36, 131 LRRM 2761 (CA 5, 1989) (en banc), cert. denied, 493 U.S. 1043, 133 LRRM 2264 (1990). The Fifth Circuit noted in this decision that use of the major–minor dispute analysis may create substantially different results from those that would obtain in a case arising under the NLRA. Under the NLRA, the Fifth Circuit observed, the courts will find a duty to bargain during the term of agreement unless there is a "clear and unmistakable waiver" of the union's right to bargain, whereas the result under the RLA is that the employer need not bargain before acting unilaterally so long as the agreement "arguably" permits the carrier's actions.

is not covered by the existing agreement, and the union is unable to serve a Section 6 notice seeking to bargain over the subject because of a moratorium or duration clause, it will generally file a lawsuit seeking to enjoin the action on the theory that the action constitutes a change in the existing agreement, without compliance with Section 6 or the agreement, in violation of Section 2, Seventh.[303] Under the body of case law discussed in the next chapter, if the court concludes that the agreement arguably permits the carrier's actions, the court will characterize the dispute as minor and will generally refuse to enjoin the action.

---

[303]*See generally* Consolidated Rail Corp. v. Railway Labor Executives' Ass'n, 491 U.S. 299, 131 LRRM 2601 (1989).

CHAPTER 5

ENFORCEMENT OF COLLECTIVE
BARGAINING AGREEMENTS

A central purpose of the RLA is to require the parties to resolve so-called minor disputes through conferences and, if necessary, through various arbitration mechanisms known as Adjustment Boards. The RLA sets forth three types of Adjustment Boards for the rail industry: the National Railroad Adjustment Board (NRAB), Special Boards of Adjustment, and Public Law Boards.[1] Although the RLA gave the National Mediation Board (NMB) the power to create a National Air Transport Adjustment Board, it has not been established. In the airline industry, the parties have established the Adjustment Board required by Section 184, which they typically refer to as a System Board of Adjustment.[2] These arbitral mechanisms will be explained in greater detail; however, it is essential to understand which disputes must be resolved through arbitration, and the distinction between major and minor disputes.[3]

I. MAJOR AND MINOR DISPUTES

The drafters of the RLA distinguished between two types of contractual disputes: those concerning an "intended

---

[1]RLA §153.

[2]Congress put the airline industry within the jurisdiction of the RLA in 1936 pursuant to a new title II (ch. 166, 49 Stat. 1189), which provided that all the provisions of the RLA were applicable to air carriers with the exception of §153.

[3]"Major" and "minor" are two of the four kinds of disputes under the RLA. For a general introduction to statutory and representation disputes, *see* Chapter 1, "Introduction," §I.

change in agreements affecting rates of pay, rules, or working conditions,"[4] and those "arising out of grievances or out of the interpretation or application of agreements."[5] The former are subject to the notice, negotiation, and mediation process discussed in the previous chapter, with the parties ultimately able to invoke self-help; the latter are committed to the exclusive jurisdiction of the appropriate Adjustment Board established under the RLA for final and binding arbitration.[6] Although the terms are not used in the statute, the two categories have become identified universally as "major" and "minor" disputes.[7]

The first authoritative judicial definition of major and minor disputes is contained in the 1945 Supreme Court decision *Elgin, Joliet & Eastern Railway v. Burley:*[8]

> [Major disputes relate] to disputes over the formation of collective agreements or efforts to secure them. They arise where there is no such agreement or where it is sought to change the terms of one. Therefore, the issue is not whether an existing agreement controls the controversy. They look to the acquisition of rights for the future, not to the assertion of rights claimed to have vested in the past.
>
> [A minor dispute], however, contemplates the existence of a collective agreement already concluded or, at any rate, a situation in which no effort is made to bring about a formal change in terms or to create a new one. The dispute relates either to the meaning or proper application of a particular

---

[4]RLA §6. The same concept is expressed somewhat differently in *id.* §2, Seventh, as disputes concerning a "change [in] the rates of pay, rules, or working conditions of [the carrier's] employees, as a class as embodied in agreements."

[5]*Id.* §2, Sixth.

[6]Railroad Trainmen v. Chicago River & I. R.R., 353 U.S. 30, 39 LRRM 2578 (1957).

[7]The Supreme Court adopted these railroad industry terms in Elgin, J. & E. Ry. v. Burley, 325 U.S. 711, 16 LRRM 749 (1945), as a shorthand method of describing two classes of controversy. The terms have confused more than one court by suggesting that one kind of dispute is more significant than another. *See, e.g.,* Air Line Pilots Ass'n v. Trans World Airlines, 713 F2d 940, 114 LRRM 2241 (CA 2, 1983); Transport Workers, Local 553 v. Eastern Air Lines, 695 F2d 668, 112 LRRM 2482 (CA 2, 1982). In Consolidated Rail Corp. v. Railway Labor Executives' Ass'n, 491 U.S. 299, 305, 131 LRRM 2601, 2603 (1989), the Supreme Court made clear that the magnitude of the dispute has no bearing on the major/minor distinction.

[8]325 U.S. 711, 16 LRRM 749 (1945).

provision with reference to a specific situation or to an omitted case. In the latter event the claim is founded upon some incident of the employment relation, or asserted one, independent of those covered by the collective agreement, e.g., claims on account of personal injuries. In either case the claim is to rights accrued, not merely to have new ones created for the future.[9]

A. "Arguably Justified" Standard

Although the *Elgin* distinction appears clear in principle, applying it has occupied the vast majority of published decisions under the RLA. In one of the earliest and most influential decisions to address the issue, *Rutland Railway v. Locomotive Engineers,*[10] the Second Circuit rejected use of a Section 6 notice seeking to modify the agreement as the defining factor, concluding that the difference "between the interpretation and the application of an existing agreement, and ... a change in an original intended meaning is often a matter of degree."[11] The court observed that

> we must not place undue emphasis on the contentions or maneuvers of the parties. Management will assert that its position, whether right or wrong, is only an interpretation or application of the existing contract. Unions, on the other hand, will obviously talk in terms of change. Since a Section 6 notice is required by the statute in order to initiate a major dispute, the labor representatives are likely to serve such a notice in any dispute arising out of any ambiguous situation so as thereby to make the controversy appear more like a major dispute.[12]

The *Rutland* decision held that although the federal courts were not to "adjudicate the merits of the controversy," they were required to determine the nature of the parties' dispute based on their own examination of the contractual issues involved.[13]

---

[9]325 U.S. at 723, 16 LRRM at 757. That part of the quotation referring to "omitted cases" is discussed *infra* §I.B.

[10]307 F2d 21, 50 LRRM 2535 (CA 2, 1962), *cert. denied,* 372 U.S. 954, 52 LRRM 2704 (1963).

[11]307 F2d at 33, 50 LRRM at 2544.

[12]*Id.*

[13]*Id.*

In the three decades following the *Rutland* decision, virtually every circuit has adopted a variation of the same test,[14] holding that a minor dispute exists where the claim that the dispute is one of contract meaning or application is "arguable,"[15] not "obviously insubstantial,"[16] "arguably predicated on the terms of the agreement,"[17] or not "frivolous."[18]

In *Consolidated Rail Corp. v. Railway Labor Executives' Ass'n*,[19] the Supreme Court adopted the same standard: "Where an employer asserts a contractual right to take the contested action, the ensuing dispute is minor if the action is arguably justified by the terms of the parties' collective-bargaining agreement. Where, in contrast, the employer's claims are frivolous or obviously insubstantial, the dispute is major."[20] The carrier's burden in such a case, the Court stated, is "relatively light."[21]

In applying the "arguably justified" test, the courts have examined a variety of factors, including the language of the collective bargaining agreement and any relevant amendments or side letters, the negotiating history of the agree-

---

[14]*See* Southern Ry. v. Locomotive Firemen & Enginemen, 384 F2d 323, 53 LRRM 2193 (CA DC, 1967); Airlines Stewards & Stewardesses Ass'n v. Caribbean Atl. Airlines, 412 F2d 289, 71 LRRM 2896 (CA 1, 1969); Transport Workers, Local 553 v. Eastern Air Lines, 695 F2d 668, 112 LRRM 2482 (CA 2, 1982); United Transp. Union v. Penn Cent. Transp. Co., 505 F2d 542, 87 LRRM 3056 (CA 3, 1974); Kushto v. Railway & Steamship Clerks, 818 F2d 290, 125 LRRM 2268 (CA 4, 1987); St. Louis, S. F. & T. Ry. v. Railroad Yardmasters, 328 F2d 749, 55 LRRM 2583 (CA 5), *cert. denied,* 377 U.S. 980, 56 LRRM 2480 (1964); United Transp. Union, Local 1477 v. Baker, 482 F2d 228, 83 LRRM 2684 (CA 6, 1973); United Transp. Union v. Baker, 499 F2d 727, 85 LRRM 2526 (CA 7), *cert. denied,* 419 U.S. 839, 87 LRRM 2398 (1974); United Transp. Union v. Burlington N. Ry., 458 F2d 354, 80 LRRM 2127 (CA 8, 1972); Switchmen's Union v. Southern Pac. Co., 398 F2d 443, 68 LRRM 2738 (CA 9, 1968).

[15]Maine C. R.R. v. United Transp. Union, 787 F2d 780, 782, 122 LRRM 2017, 2019 (CA 1), *cert. denied,* 479 U.S. 848, 123 LRRM 2592 (1986).

[16]National Ry. Labor Conference v. Machinists, 830 F2d 741, 746, 126 LRRM 2615, 2618 (CA 7, 1987).

[17]O'Donnell v. Wien Air Alaska, Inc., 551 F2d 1141, 1146, 95 LRRM 2108, 2112 (CA 9, 1977).

[18]Machinists v. Soo L. R.R., 850 F2d 368, 376, 128 LRRM 2826, 2832 (CA 8, 1988), *cert. denied,* 489 U.S. 1010, 130 LRRM 2656 (1989).

[19]491 U.S. 299, 131 LRRM 2601 (1989).

[20]491 U.S. at 307, 131 LRRM at 2604.

[21]*Id.* (quoting Maintenance of Way Employees v. Burlington N. Ry., 802 F2d 1016, 1022, 123 LRRM 2593 (CA 8, 1986)).

ment,[22] past practice under the agreement,[23] arbitration decisions interpreting the contract,[24] arbitration decisions interpreting similar language in other bargaining agreements,[25] and contract clauses reserving to management the right to act unilaterally regarding matters not covered by the agreement.[26] The absence of contract language is not controlling; in *Consolidated Rail*, the Court held that a carrier's defense could rest "solely upon implied contractual terms, as interpreted in light of past practice."[27]

The explicit purpose of defining a dispute as major or minor is to determine whether the carrier has an obligation to bargain with the union prior to implementing a proposed change in the terms and conditions of employment. Although the narrow effect of a holding that a claim presents a minor dispute may be "to delay collective bargaining . . . until the arbitration process is exhausted,"[28] the practical effect may be to eliminate the obligation to bargain at all during the term of an agreement, or while a moratorium clause is in effect, if the union or carrier is unable to propose changes to the agreement at that time.[29]

---

[22]*E.g.*, Chicago & N.W. Transp. Co. v. Electrical Workers (IBEW), 829 F2d 1424, 126 LRRM 2462 (CA 7, 1987); Carbone v. Meserve, 645 F2d 96, 107 LRRM 2204 (CA 1), *cert. denied*, 454 U.S. 859, 108 LRRM 2559 (1981).

[23]*E.g.*, Railway & Steamship Clerks v. Atchison, T. & S.F. Ry., 847 F2d 403, 406 n.2, 128 LRRM 2425, 2428 n.2 (CA 7, 1988); Maine C. R.R. v. United Transp. Union, 787 F2d 780, 122 LRRM 2017 (CA 1, 1985), *cert. denied*, 479 U.S. 848, 123 LRRM 2592 (1986); Rutland Ry. v. Locomotive Eng'rs, 307 F2d 21, 50 LRRM 2535 (CA 2, 1962), *cert. denied*, 372 U.S. 954, 52 LRRM 2704 (1963).

[24]*E.g.*, Chicago & N.W. Transp. Co. v. United Transp. Union, 656 F2d 274, 108 LRRM 2065 (CA 7, 1981).

[25]Railway & Steamship Clerks v. Missouri P. R.R., 944 F2d 1422, 138 LRRM 2639 (CA 8, 1991).

[26]*E.g.*, Empresa Ecuatoriana De Aviacion, S.A. v. Machinists, Dist. Lodge 100, 690 F2d 838, 843, 111 LRRM 2971 (CA 11, 1982), *cert. dismissed*, 463 U.S. 1250 (1983); Railway Express Agency v. Railway & Steamship Clerks, 437 F2d 388, 392, 76 LRRM 2328 (CA 5), *cert. denied*, 403 U.S. 919, 77 LRRM 2528 (1971); Rutland Ry. v. Locomotive Eng'rs, 307 F2d at 35.

[27]Consolidated Rail Corp. v. Railway Labor Executives' Ass'n, 491 U.S. 299, 312, 131 LRRM 2601, 2606 (1989).

[28]491 U.S. at 310, 131 LRRM at 2605.

[29]*See generally* Chapter 4, "Negotiation of Collective Bargaining Agreements," for a discussion of contract moratorium and duration clauses.

B. Preemption

Although the courts also use "minor dispute" terminology in examining the preemption of state law claims by the RLA, the preemption analysis is substantially different from the major/minor dispute analysis, and the definition of minor dispute therefore is not interchangeable with that of preemption.[30] The common element in both circumstances is that the courts use the term "minor dispute" to describe the exclusive jurisdiction of an Adjustment Board over disputes "arising out of grievances or out of the interpretation or application of agreements."[31] In one situation, however, the courts are attempting to distinguish between two types of disputes under the RLA, whereas in the other the courts are determining "whether the dispute was subject to the RLA in the first place."[32]

In *Hawaiian Airlines v. Norris,*[33] a preemption case, the Court expressly disavowed a reference in the *Elgin* opinion to "omitted cases,"[34] holding that minor disputes, for the purposes of a preemption analysis, do *not* "encompass state-law claims that exist independent of the collective-bargaining agreement."[35] With respect to *Consolidated Rail*, the Court distinguished the "arguably justified" standard as appropriate "only for policing the line between major and minor disputes."[36] For preemption purposes, the Court held, the standard for preemption is identical to that employed under the NLRA in *Lingle v. Norge Division of Magic Chef,*[37] that is,

---

[30]*See* Hawaiian Airlines v. Norris, 146 LRRM 2577 (1994). For a detailed discussion of preemption, *see* Chapter 7, "Accommodating the RLA to Other Laws."

[31]RLA §2, Sixth.

[32]Hawaiian Airlines v. Norris, 146 LRRM 2577 (S. Ct. 1994). Furthermore, the policies involved are different. In the former situation, the courts apply a presumption in favor of finding a minor dispute so as to avoid disruptions to interstate commerce; in the latter situation, the courts must balance implied federal preemption with the exercise of traditional state powers.

[33]*Id.*

[34]The "omitted case" language in *Elgin* had practical import primarily in cases addressing the preemptive scope of the RLA, and was seldom, if ever, cited in cases distinguishing between major and minor disputes.

[35]146 LRRM at 2582.

[36]146 LRRM at 2585.

[37]486 U.S. 399, 128 LRRM 2521 (1988).

whether "the state-law claim is dependent on the interpretation of a collective-bargaining agreement."[38]

II. DUTY TO MEET TO RESOLVE DISPUTES

The RLA requires the parties to meet and confer for the purposes of resolving minor disputes prior to submission of disputes to the appropriate Adjustment Boards. Thus, the statutory duty to exert "every reasonable effort" to settle all disputes, specified by Section 2, First, includes the duty to confer over minor disputes.[39] Section 2, Second requires the carrier and employee representatives to meet expeditiously in conferences in order to consider and possibly to resolve disputes between the parties.

Section 2, Sixth sets forth several specific procedural requirements for minor dispute conferences. Within 10 days of receipt of a request for a conference, the parties must specify the time and place at which the conference will be held. The conference location is limited to a point on the carrier's line, unless the parties agree to the contrary. Although the date for the conference should afford the conferees a reasonable opportunity to travel, it may not be more than 20 days after receipt of the notice to confer.

Section 3, First (i) provides rules for the referral of minor disputes to the NRAB. Such disputes must be considered by the parties in the "usual manner" through the highest designated level of the carrier, and then, failing resolution, either party may invoke the jurisdiction of the appropriate division of the NRAB. The same first-stage grievance resolution procedures apply with respect to Public Law Boards, established under the second paragraph of Section 3, Second.[40] This requirement also applies to the airline industry, prior to referral of a minor dispute to an appropriate Adjust-

---

[38]Hawaiian Airlines v. Norris, 146 LRRM 2577, 2584 (S. Ct. 1994).

[39]Rutland Ry. v. Locomotive Eng'rs, 307 F2d 21, 50 LRRM 2535 (CA 2, 1962), *cert. denied*, 372 U.S. 954, 52 LRRM 2704 (1963). *See* Elgin, J. & E. Ry. v. Burley, 325 U.S. 711, 16 LRRM 749 (1945).

[40]Locomotive Eng'rs v. Denver & R. G. R.R., 411 F2d 1115, 1116–17, 71 LRRM 2690 (CA 10, 1969).

ment Board under Section 184. Thus, the RLA's prearbitration conference requirements are more than statutory guidelines.[41]

An effort to resolve a minor dispute in conferences between the parties may also be a prerequisite for entitlement to injunctive relief. Where a party has failed to comply with the RLA conferencing requirements, Section 8 of the Norris-LaGuardia Act (the "clean hands" provision), requiring that "every reasonable effort" to settle a dispute be made by the party seeking a federal court injunction in a labor dispute, may not be satisfied.[42]

The RLA does not specify the particular manner in which the parties' prearbitration conferences should be conducted. Judicial construction describes a process, short of extended formal negotiations, that includes reasonable steps toward resolution of the dispute. The process should facilitate communication of the parties' positions and avoid unfair surprise. The parties must act in good faith in a genuine attempt to resolve the dispute.[43]

Employee challenges to initial disciplinary hearings have been unsuccessful. These "on the property" conferences require only a good faith effort to resolve the disputes, consistent with the "usual and customary" procedures.[44] No specific

---

[41]Railroad Trainmen v. Chicago River & I. R.R., 353 U.S. 30, 39 LRRM 2578 (1957); Elgin J. & E. Ry. v. Burley, 325 U.S. 711, 16 LRRM 749; Machinists v. Northwest Airlines, 304 F2d 206, 50 LRRM 2499 (CA 8, 1962); Louisville & N. R.R. v. Brown, 252 F2d 149, 41 LRRM 2436 (CA 5), cert. denied, 356 U.S. 949, 42 LRRM 2043 (1958).
Efforts by one party to block referral to the NRAB by failing to cooperate in completing the RLA conferencing process have been judicially criticized. In such an instance, the other party may advance the case to the NRAB. However, the NRAB may refuse jurisdiction if it concludes that the dispute is not ripe for arbitral resolution. Railway & Steamship Clerks, Itasca Lodge 2029 v. Railway Express Agency, 391 F2d 657, 67 LRRM 2824 (CA 8, 1968).
[42]29 USC §108 (1995); see Rutland Ry. v. Locomotive Eng'rs, 307 F2d at 38–42; Butte, A. & P. Ry. v. Locomotive Firemen & Enginemen, 268 F2d 54, 44 LRRM 2184 (CA 9), cert. denied, 361 U.S. 864, 44 LRRM 3000 (1959).
[43]Rutland Ry. Corp. v. Locomotive Eng'rs, 307 F2d 21, 50 LRRM 2535; cf. Railway & Steamship Clerks v. Atlantic Coast Line R.R., 201 F2d 36, 31 LRRM 2264 (CA 4), cert. denied, 345 U.S. 992, 32 LRRM 2246 (1953); Railroad Trainmen v. Toledo, P. & W. R.R., 321 U.S. 50, 13 LRRM 725 (1944). In the railroad industry, the record is created during the "on the property" stage.
[44]See RLA §3, First (i); Edwards v. St. Louis-S.F. R.R., 361 F2d 946, 62 LRRM 2300 (CA 7, 1966).

statutory requirements are applicable to hearings associated with discipline,[45] and an employee is not afforded the right to legal counsel at the initial disciplinary hearing.[46] The Fifth Circuit has held that under the RLA an employee in a craft or class not represented by a union has no right to bring a coworker to a meeting with management that may result in the imposition of discipline.[47]

III. HISTORICAL BACKGROUND TO ADJUSTMENT BOARDS

Prior to World War I, there was limited federal involvement in the resolution of grievances or questions of contract interpretation and application.[48] During World War I, the federal government assumed control of the railroads, and the President created the U.S. Railroad Administration to

---

[45]Brooks v. Chicago R. I. & P. R.R., 177 F2d 385, 25 LRRM 2051 (CA 8, 1949).

[46]Edwards v. St. Louis-S.F. R.R., 361 F2d 946, 62 LRRM 2300 (CA 7, 1966); Broady v. Illinois C. R.R., 191 F2d 73, 28 LRRM 2444 (CA 7), cert. denied, 342 U.S. 897, 29 LRRM 2166 (1951); Butler v. Thompson, 192 F2d 831, 29 LRRM 2167 (CA 8, 1951); Brooks v. Chicago R. I. & P. R.R., 177 F2d 385, 25 LRRM 2051. When an employee in a railroad operating craft is a member of a different union from the one that represents the craft in which the member works, the representative at an investigatory conference will be determined either by the collective bargaining agreement or in the parties' usual and customary manner. Landers v. National R.R. Passenger Corp., 485 U.S. 652, 128 LRRM 2097 (1988).

[47]See Johnson v. Express One Int'l, 944 F2d 247, 138 LRRM 2592 (CA 5, 1991) (§2, Fourth does not give employee right to have coworker present during investigatory interview by employer where no union representative has been elected or recognized); Machinists v. Frontier Airlines, 664 F2d 538, 109 LRRM 2124 (CA 5, 1981) (complaints over the denial of union representation to employees being interrogated are subject to RLA's grievance and arbitration procedures).

[48]For an in-depth discussion of the history of the RLA, see Chapter 1, "Introduction." This section is a summary of articles and cases describing the various Adjustment Boards authorized by the RLA. See, e.g., THE RAILWAY LABOR ACT AT FIFTY (Charles M. Rehmus ed., 1976) [hereinafter RLA AT FIFTY]; FRANK N. WILNER, THE RAILWAY LABOR ACT AND THE DILEMMA OF LABOR RELATIONS (1991); Lloyd K. Garrison, The Railroad Adjustment Board: A Unique Administrative Agency, 46 YALE L.J. 567 (1937); Elgin, J. & E. Ry. v. Burley, 325 U.S. 711, 16 LRRM 749 (1945); Slocum v. Delaware, L. & W. R.R., 339 U.S. 239, 25 LRRM 2617 (1950); Railroad Trainmen v. Chicago River & I. R.R., 353 U.S. 30, 39 LRRM 2578 (1957); Union P. R.R. v. Price, 360 U.S. 601, 44 LRRM 2316 (1959); Locomotive Eng'rs v. Louisville & N. R.R., 373 U.S. 33, 52 LRRM 2944 (1963); Andrews v. Louisville & N. R.R., 406 U.S. 320, 80 LRRM 2440 (1972).

settle questions concerning the application and interpretation of general wage schedules. The Railroad Administration was comprised of three boards. The first had jurisdiction over the operating crafts, including engineers, conductors, and brake operators. The second board had jurisdiction over shop crafts, and the third was responsible for the maintenance of way and clerical employees. After the war, the railroads were returned to private ownership, and the Railroad Administration was abolished.

A. Transportation Act of 1920

The Transportation Act of 1920 provided for the establishment of consensual Adjustment Boards to handle grievances and disputes over working conditions.[49] These Boards could be formed at any level and involved one or more unions or carriers. Three Regional Train Service Boards of Adjustment were established to handle discipline cases. Also, approximately 300 regional and single System Boards were created pursuant to this Act. However, no means existed to break the deadlocks that often arose.

The 1920 Act also established a new federal agency, the Railroad Labor Board (RLB), with jurisdiction to settle contract negotiations, disputes over the interpretation of agreements, disputes referred from the Adjustment Boards, and disputes that did not come within the jurisdiction of the Adjustment Boards. The RLB had no authority to enforce its decisions or the decisions of the various Adjustment Boards.

B. RLA of 1926

The RLA of 1926 continued the Adjustment Boards created by the 1920 Act.[50] Nevertheless, no national Boards were established, and only one new regional Board was established in 1928, for the southwestern region, to supplement

---

[49]Transportation Act of 1920, Ch. 347, 44 Stat. 577.

[50]The Act provided that Adjustment Boards "shall be created by agreement between any carrier or groups of carriers, or the carriers as a whole, and its or their employees."

the three existing regional Boards established pursuant to the 1920 Act. The problem with deadlocks continued.[51] Moreover, there were no sanctions for a party's refusal to participate in the establishment of Adjustment Boards.

C. 1934 Amendments

Accordingly, the RLA was amended in 1934 to create a permanent NRAB.[52] Congress provided for neutral referees to break deadlocks and a method for enforcement that permitted limited judicial review.[53]

The 1934 amendments also continued the right of the parties to create their own Adjustment Boards to resolve collective bargaining disputes.[54] These Boards, called Special Boards of Adjustment (SBAs), proved to be more effective than those in existence prior to 1934, in part because they typically included neutral members to decide grievances in the event of a deadlock.

However, the 1934 amendments were not totally effective. A growing backlog of cases developed at the NRAB, particularly in the First Division, covering the operating crafts.[55] It was not uncommon to have a case pending for several years.[56] Moreover, both sides ignored the concept of stare decisis, returning repeatedly to the NRAB, "shopping"

---

[51]See RLA AT FIFTY, supra note 47, at 212.

[52]RLA §3, First, ch. 691, 48 Stat. 1185.

[53]RLA §3, First (l), (p).

[54]Id. §3, Second.

[55]By 1943, the backlog had reached 6000 cases. See RLA AT FIFTY, supra note 47, at 216.

[56]See Walker v. Southern Ry., 385 U.S. 196, 198, 63 LRRM 2491, 2492 (1966). This backlog worsened following the Supreme Court's initial decision in Elgin, J. & E. Ry. v. Burley, 325 U.S. 711, 16 LRRM 749 (1945). The Supreme Court held in Burley that, in order for a union to settle claims on behalf of its members, the members must authorize the union's action in some legally sufficient way according to the common law rules of agency. Thereafter, the carriers insisted upon written authorizations. The unions objected to such a requirement, and no cases were processed for more than a year. On rehearing, 327 U.S. 661, 17 LRRM 899 (1946), the Court resolved the issue by holding that if the employee knew the claim was submitted to the Board and made no objection, a lack of authorization defense would be waived. See THE RAILWAY LABOR ACT AT FIFTY, 218 (Charles M. Rehmus, ed., 1976) [hereinafter RLA AT FIFTY].

for a referee who they thought would render a favorable award.[57]

As the backlog grew, the carriers and the unions sought relief through the SBAs. As already noted, these Boards usually included a neutral member in order to avoid deadlocks.[58] The voluntary character of SBAs, however, limited their usefulness as a means of eliminating the backlog at the NRAB.

D. 1966 Amendments

In 1966, the RLA was amended to provide for the establishment of Public Law Boards, which can be established on a single railroad at the request of either party.[59] Procedures for the appointment of neutral members were provided, and the traditional NRAB procedural rules were relaxed.[60] Public Law Boards have helped relieve the backlog of cases at the NRAB.[61] The consensual procedure for establishing SBAs remains available and is sometimes used to resolve disputes over protective agreements involving job security issues.

E. Inclusion of Airline Industry

In 1936, a new title II was added to the RLA that made the provisions of the Act, with the exception of Section 3, applicable to the fledgling airline industry.[62] The deletion of Section 3 has created some confusion, because Section 3 contains, among other pertinent items, the standard for judicial review and the statute of limitations for enforcing

---

[57]*See* RLA AT FIFTY, *supra* note 56, at 220.

[58]*See infra* §VII for a more detailed discussion of these Boards.

[59]Pub. L. No. 89–456, 80 Stat. 208 (1966).

[60]The 1966 amendments also provided specific standards for judicial review of Board awards, limiting such review to whether (1) the Board had jurisdiction over the dispute, (2) the requirement of the RLA had been met, or (3) any person sitting on the Board had engaged in fraud or corruption. RLA §3, First (q). In addition, the 1966 amendments made all awards of Boards final and binding upon the parties, no longer subjecting monetary awards to de novo review by courts. *Id.* §3, First (m).

[61]RLA AT FIFTY, *supra* note 56, at 230–31.

[62]RLA §§201–08, ch. 166, 49 Stat. 1189.

awards.[63] Congress intended "to extend to air carriers and their employees the same benefits and obligations available and applicable in the railroad industry."[64] These "same benefits and obligations" included the duty to establish and utilize Adjustment Boards for resolution of disputes "growing out of grievances, or out of the interpretation or application of agreements concerning rates of pay, rules, or working conditions."[65]

Whereas Section 3, First of the RLA created an NRAB to serve the railroad industry, Section 205 merely authorized the NMB to create a National Air Transport Adjustment Board when, in its judgment, "it shall be necessary to have a permanent national board of adjustment."[66] The NMB has not created such a Board.

The RLA requires an air carrier and its employees, acting through their authorized representative, to establish an Adjustment Board not exceeding the jurisdiction of Adjustment Boards in the railroad industry.[67] Although the RLA authorizes the establishment of Adjustment Boards on an individual carrier, system, or group of carriers among any class or classes of employees,[68] in practice Boards have been established by a single carrier and a single union representing a particular craft or class. They are typically called System Boards of Adjustment, or simply System Boards.

IV. EXCLUSIVE JURISDICTION OF ADJUSTMENT BOARDS

A. Jurisdiction Over Minor Disputes

In the rail industry, the RLA established the NRAB to resolve minor disputes and gave the parties the right to create

---

[63]See infra §X for a discussion of judicial review and the statute of limitations.
[64]Machinists v. Central Airlines, 372 U.S. 682, 685, 52 LRRM 2803, 2804 (1963).
[65]RLA §204.
[66]Id. §205.
[67]Id. §204.
[68]Id.

additional Adjustment Boards;[69] in the airline industry, the RLA requires the establishment of Adjustment Boards.[70] The Boards have "mandatory, exclusive and comprehensive" jurisdiction over minor disputes arising over grievances or over the interpretation or application of labor agreements.[71] Congress intended the remedies provided by these Boards "to be the complete and final means for settling minor disputes."[72]

The Adjustment Board's jurisdiction to resolve minor disputes is exclusive in that neither the carrier, the labor organization, nor the affected employee may bypass the Adjustment Board and seek any other kind of judicial or administrative remedy for a minor dispute.[73] Nothing in the Act, however, prevents parties from resolving a minor dispute through a voluntary, private dispute resolution procedure.[74] Neither federal[75] nor state[76] courts may exercise jurisdiction to decide a minor dispute. Once an award has been issued, that award is judicially enforceable,[77] but Adjustment Board awards cannot be challenged except through the limited judicial review provided by the RLA. Nor may any party engage in self-help over a minor dispute[78] or over dissatisfaction with the Adjustment Board's resolution of such a dispute.[79]

---

[69]Locomotive Eng'rs v. Louisville & N. R.R., 373 U.S. 33, 36–38, 52 LRRM 2944, 2945–46 (1963); see generally Elgin, J. & E. Ry. v. Burley, 325 U.S. 711, 722–25, 16 LRRM 749 (1945).

[70]RLA §204.

[71]Locomotive Eng'rs v. Louisville & N. R.R., 373 U.S. at 38, 52 LRRM at 2946. For a discussion of what constitutes a minor dispute, see supra §I.

[72]373 U.S. at 38, 52 LRRM at 2946.

[73]Id.; Pennsylvania R.R. v. Day, 360 U.S. 548, 552–53, 44 LRRM 2325, 2327 (1959); Andrews v. Louisville & N. R.R., 406 U.S. 320, 80 LRRM 2240 (1972).

[74]The first paragraph of §3, Second provides that the parties are free to establish such voluntary Boards.

[75]Railway Conductors & Brakemen v. Pitney, 326 U.S. 561, 17 LRRM 722 (1946).

[76]Railway Conductors & Brakemen v. Southern Ry., 339 U.S. 255, 24 LRRM 2624 (1950); Slocum v. Delaware, L. & W. R.R., 339 U.S. 239, 25 LRRM 2617 (1950); Andrews v. Louisville & N. R.R., 406 U.S. 320, 80 LRRM 2240; Sheehan v. Union P. R.R., 439 U.S. 89, 99 LRRM 3327 (1978).

[77]See RLA §3, First (p).

[78]Railroad v. Trainmen v. Chicago River & I. R.R., 353 U.S. 30, 39 LRRM 2578 (1957).

[79]Locomotive Eng'rs v. Louisville & N. R.R., 373 U.S. 33, 52 LRRM 2944 (1963).

Any party to a labor agreement can insist that a minor dispute be resolved through the Adjustment Board.[80] In the railroad industry, the individual employee also has the right to pursue a dispute through the NRAB.[81]

Whether the obligation to arbitrate exists when no collective bargaining agreement is in effect remains an open question. The issue arises in two contexts: (1) prior to the negotiation of the parties' first collective bargaining agreement, and (2) after the relevant contract has been terminated or has ended or become amendable and the parties are in the process of negotiating a new agreement. Consistent with the view that minor disputes typically arise out of the interpretation of labor agreements, disputes that arise out of unilateral changes in working conditions prior to the negotiation of an initial agreement are decided under the bargaining requirements of the Act.[82] Thus, one court has held that there is no duty

---

[80]Railroad Trainmen v. Chicago River & I. R.R., 353 U.S. at 34, 39 LRRM at 2579. Although the Supreme Court initially viewed the RLA's procedures for adjustment of minor disputes as optional, in Andrews v. Louisville & N. R.R., 406 U.S. 320, 80 LRRM 2240 (1972), the Court determined that those procedures were mandatory and overruled contrary precedent.

[81]See Elgin, J. & E. Ry. v. Burley, 325 U.S. 711, 16 LRRM 749 (1945); Electrical Workers (IBEW) v. Foust, 442 U.S. 42, 49 n.11, 101 LRRM 2365, 2368 n.11 (1979); Graf v. Elgin, J. & E. Ry., 790 F2d 1341, 122 LRRM 2549 (CA 7, 1986); Masy v. New Jersey Transit Rail Operations, 790 F2d 322, 122 LRRM 2700 (CA 3), cert. denied, 479 U.S. 916, 125 LRRM 3216 (1986). See also infra §VIII for a discussion of the issue in the airline industry.

The language of §3, Second, which permits the creation of Public Law Boards, has been construed to prohibit individual employees from proceeding before such Boards without a union representative. Locomotive Eng'rs v. Denver & R. G. R.R., 411 F2d 1115, 1118, 71 LRRM 2690 (CA 10, 1969); O'Neill v. Public Law Bd. No. 550, 581 F2d 696, 692 n.7, 99 LRRM 2204 (CA 7, 1978); Chicago, R. I. & P. R.R. v. NMB, 435 F2d 339, 341, 76 LRRM 2047 (CA 7, 1970); cert. denied, 402 U.S. 944 (1971); Ruffin v. Railway & Steamship Clerks, 314 F Supp 1365, 1370, 75 LRRM 2450 (ED Pa, 1970); Antonioli v. Lehigh Coal & Navigation Co., 47 FRD 198, 200, 72 LRRM 2422 (ED Pa, 1969). The language of the first paragraph of §3, Second indicates that an employee grievance can be brought before an SBA only through a union representative: "Nothing in this section shall be construed to prevent any individual carrier, system, or group of carriers and any class or classes of its or their employees, all acting through their representatives, selected in accordance with the provisions of this chapter, from mutually agreeing to the establishment of system, group or regional boards of adjustment."

[82]Regional Airline Pilots Ass'n v. Wings W. Airlines, 915 F2d 1399, 1401, 135 LRRM 2735 (CA 9, 1990), cert. denied, 501 U.S. 1251, 137 LRRM 2696 (1991). See also Machinists v. Transportes Aeros Mercantiles Pan Americandos, S.A., 924 F2d

to arbitrate a dispute over working conditions before those conditions are set by the first agreement.[83]

When the relevant collective bargaining agreement has become amendable, the issue of whether disputes over working conditions are subject to arbitration is less clear. Typically, in the railroad industry contracts are of indefinite duration, except that the parties may serve a Section 6 notice after a certain date. A second form of duration clause provides for automatic periodic renewal unless a Section 6 notice is served by a certain date prior to renewal. Under such a provision, those contractual terms that are not the subject of a Section 6 notice continue to be enforceable.[84]

Disputes over working conditions that involve conduct that took place *before* the agreement became amendable are arbitrable.[85] Circuits are divided over disputes in the airline industry involving conduct that occurs *after* the agreement term, but during the status quo period. The Ninth Circuit has held that disputes that arise after the amendable date of the collective bargaining agreement and the filing of a Section 6 notice are major disputes not subject to the jurisdiction of

---

1005, 1007 n.3, 136 LRRM 2686, 2688 n.3 (CA 11), *cert. denied*, 138 LRRM 2480 (1991). For a more detailed discussion, *see* Chapter 4, "Negotiation of Collective Bargaining Agreements," §VIII.B.

[83]Air Line Pilots Ass'n v. Jetstream Int'l Airlines, 716 F Supp 203, 133 LRRM 2182 (D Md, 1989). The court expressly rejected the argument that there is an obligation to arbitrate disputes before any agreement is signed, citing the language of §3 that requires arbitration in disputes "growing out of grievances or out of the interpretation or application of agreements."

[84]*See* Trans World Airlines v. Flight Attendants (IFFA), 809 F2d 483, 124 LRRM 2364 (CA 8, 1987) (holding that union security clause, which was not subject of reopening by §6 notice, had not been terminated), *aff'd by an equally divided Court*, 485 U.S. 175, 127 LRRM 2740 (1988). In that case, the Eighth Circuit explicitly declined to follow Machinists v. Reeve Aleutian Airways, 469 F2d 990, 81 LRRM 2910 (CA 9, 1972) (once major dispute process has run its course, and agreement by its terms has come to end, changes in working conditions can be unilaterally imposed by carrier), *cert. denied*, 411 U.S. 982, 83 LRRM 2167 (1973). 809 F2d at 489–91,124 LRRM at 2369–70. Whether a §6 notice reopens a particular contract provision or the entire contract is treated in Chapter 4, "Negotiation of Collective Bargaining Agreements," §X.

[85]Flight Eng'rs v. Eastern Air Lines, 359 F2d 303, 310, 62 LRRM 2374, 2378–79 (CA 2, 1966). *Cf.* Nolde Bros. v. Bakery Workers Local 358, 430 U.S. 243, 94 LRRM 2753 (1977) (under National Labor Relations Act (NLRA), parties obligated to arbitrate dispute that ripens after contract's termination but concerns obligations arguably created by expired contract).

an Adjustment Board.[86] The District of Columbia Circuit rejected the notion that the amendable date of the contract and the filing of a Section 6 notice automatically make all disputes major, holding that a dispute over furloughs was a minor dispute within the exclusive jurisdiction of the Adjustment Board.[87] The Third Circuit is in accord with the District of Columbia Circuit, expressly rejecting the Ninth Circuit's view.[88]

B. Exceptions to Adjustment Board Jurisdiction

Over time the courts have created exceptions to the exclusive jurisdiction of the Adjustment Board. Courts may have jurisdiction to hear a minor dispute when (1) the employer has repudiated the grievance machinery, (2) resort to the administrative remedy would be futile, or (3) the employer

---

[86]Machinists v. Aloha Airlines, 776 F2d 812, 816, 120 LRRM 3326, 3328 (CA 9, 1985) (once contract expired and §6 notice was filed, no collective bargaining agreement existed to be interpreted and RLA itself mandated status quo), *cert. denied,* 479 U.S. 931, 123 LRRM 2904 (1986). The rule is not clear in the Second Circuit. Air Cargo v. Teamsters Local 851, 733 F2d 241, 245–46, 116 LRRM 2141, 2144 (CA 2, 1984), declared disputes to be major that began with §6 notices proposing changes in the collective bargaining agreement affecting working conditions. In a footnote, however, the Second Circuit stated that even after "one party has served a Section 6 notice indicating a desire to change a collective bargaining agreement, it is still for the district court to determine whether the dispute in question is actually over a proposed change in rates of pay, rules or working conditions, and is therefore major." 733 F2d at 247 n.6, 116 LRRM at 2145 n.6. Teamsters v. Pan Am. World Airways, 607 F Supp 609, 122 LRRM 3232 (ED NY, 1985), relied on this language in *Air Cargo* in finding a dispute that arose after exchange of §6 notices to be minor because it involved a question of contract interpretation instead of contract formation. *See also* Machinists v. British Airways PLC, 718 F Supp 134, 131 LRRM 2907 (ED NY, 1989). *Cf.* Litton Fin. Printing v. NLRB, 501 U.S. 190, 137 LRRM 2441 (1991) (declining to extend unilateral change doctrine under NLRA to impose statutory duty to arbitrate postexpiration disputes absent explicit agreement that certain benefits continue past expiration of collective bargaining agreement, unless postexpiration action involves facts and occurrences that arose before expiration; postexpiration action infringes right that accrued or vested under agreement; or, under normal principles of contract interpretation, disputed contractual rights survive expiration of remainder of agreement).

[87]Air Line Pilots Ass'n v. Eastern Air Lines, 863 F2d 891, 898–900, 129 LRRM 2691, 2697–99 (CA DC, 1988).

[88]Miklavic v. USAir, Inc., 21 F3d 551, 554–55, 146 LRRM 2001, 2003–04 (CA 3, 1994).

is joined in a breach of the duty of fair representation claim against the union.[89]

V. EFFECT OF CORPORATE RESTRUCTURING ON BARGAINING AGREEMENTS

This section addresses whether and in what form a collective bargaining agreement survives various types of corporate transactions, as well as issues related to the integration of workforces resulting from such transactions.[90]

A. Application of Contracts

In a case involving an asset acquisition, the Seventh Circuit applied National Labor Relations Act law to hold that the successor employers were not bound by the predecessor's collective bargaining agreement, absent "a near identity of employers and perfect continuity of a single enterprise."[91] The court observed that "the rail operations [were] totally altered after the transfer of ownership" and that a low percentage of the predecessor's employees were employed in the new operations.[92]

---

[89]See Czosek v. O'Mara, 397 U.S. 25, 29–30, 73 LRRM 2481 (1970); Glover v. St. Louis-S.F. Ry., 393 U.S. 324, 329–31, 70 LRRM 2097 (1969); Childs v. Pennsylvania Fed'n Maintenance of Way Employees, 831 F2d 429, 126 LRRM 2777 (CA 3, 1987); Masy v. New Jersey Transit Rail Operations, 790 F2d 322, 122 LRRM 2700 (CA 3), cert. denied, 479 U.S. 916, 125 LRRM 3216 (1986); Sisco v. Consolidated Rail Corp., 732 F2d 1188, 116 LRRM 2097 (CA 3, 1984); Raus v. Railway Carmen, 663 F2d 791, 108 LRRM 2994 (CA 8, 1981); Goclowski v. Penn Cen. Transp. Co., 571 F2d 747, 758–60, 97 LRRM 2563 (CA 3, 1977); Schum v. South Buffalo Ry., 496 F2d 328, 330, 86 LRRM 2459 (CA 2, 1974). For a discussion of duty of fair representation claims, see infra §XI.

[90]Disputes over whether the surviving entity is a "single carrier or system" and related representational questions are discussed in Chapter 2, "Selecting a Bargaining Representative," §XIII.

[91]In re Chicago, Mil., St. Paul & P. R.R., 658 F2d 1149, 1174 (CA 7, 1981) (applying NLRB v. Burns Int'l Sec. Servs., Inc., 406 U.S. 272, 80 LRRM 2225 (1972)), cert. denied, 455 U.S. 1000 (1982).

[92]Id. at 1174 n.59; see also Railway Labor Executives Ass'n v. Wheeling & L. E. Ry., 741 F Supp 595, 135 LRRM 2364 (ED Va), aff'd, 943 F2d 49, 138 LRRM 2160 (CA 4, 1990) (unpublished opinion). One court has also suggested that in the event that no union is certified to represent employees on a combined carrier, existing contracts must fail because no union remains for purposes of contract administration. Teamsters v. Texas Int'l Airlines, 717 F2d 157, 161, 114 LRRM 3091 (CA 5, 1983).

In the context of a transaction that resulted in a single carrier for representational purposes, the District of Columbia Circuit held that the terms of separate collective bargaining agreements define the status quo prior to the negotiation of an agreement between the carrier and its new employee representative. In *Flight Attendants (AFA) v. USAir, Inc.,*[93] USAir executed an agreement to manage the Trump Shuttle, and the two carriers remained legally separate corporations. The NMB found the carriers to be a single transportation system and certified one union to represent a craft or class that previously had been represented by separate unions. The court found nonetheless that the contract negotiated by the union whose certification was terminated defined the status quo for those employees previously covered by that contract.[94]

Similarly, a district court has held that an existing collective bargaining agreement survived a transaction that resulted in an increased number of unions. In *Maintenance of Way Employees v. Guilford Transportation Industries,*[95] a single holding company owned four separate railroads. After the rail lines of all four were leased to and operated by a single subsidiary, the NMB found that the four companies together constituted a single carrier. The NMB also held an election, and certified several unions to replace the one union that previously had represented the single carrier's employees. The newly certified unions sought to negotiate contracts with the railroad, but the company refused because its contract with the prior collective bargaining union contained a moratorium clause. Citing RLA cases that held that a change in representative does not void an existing labor contract,[96] as well as a case

---

[93]24 F3d 1432, 146 LRRM 2534 (CA DC, 1994).
[94]24 F3d at 1437–38.
[95]808 F Supp 46 (D Me, 1992).
[96]The court cited NMB decisions in Metro-N. R.R., 10 NMB 345, 349 (1983) and Lehigh Valley R.R., 3 NMB 225, 226 (1960), and several federal court cases: Machinists v. Northwest Airlines, 843 F2d 1119, 1123, 127 LRRM 3207, 3210 (CA 8), *vacated as moot,* 854 F2d 1088, 129 LRRM 2595 (CA 8, 1988); Teamsters v. Texas Int'l Airlines, 717 F2d at 163, 114 LRRM at 3097 (dicta); Air Transport Employees v. Western Airlines, 105 LRRM 3004 (CD Cal, 1980); Aircraft Mechanics Fraternal Ass'n v. United Airlines, 406 F Supp 492, 507 n.23, 91 LRRM 2248, 2258 n.23 (ND Cal, 1976).

honoring a moratorium clause under similar circumstances,[97] the court held that the previous contract survived the corporate restructuring.[98] As a result, the single carrier was not obligated to bargain until the moratorium clause expired.

Courts have also addressed the issue of whether a scope clause in a collective bargaining agreement permits a union to arbitrate a claim that its collective bargaining agreement with the carrier applies to a related corporate entity following a corporate restructuring of the carrier. The Second Circuit rejected such efforts in *Flight Attendants (IUFA) v. Pan American World Airways*[99] and *Flight Engineers v. Pan American World Airways*,[100] finding that the claims presented representation disputes within the exclusive jurisdiction of the NMB. A contrary result was reached by district courts in *Air Line Pilots Ass'n v. Texas International Airlines*[101] and *Flight Attendants (AFA) v. United Air Lines*,[102] in which the courts issued orders compelling arbitration. In *Flight Attendants (AFA) v. Delta Air Lines*,[103] the court declined to order specific performance over the scope clause, but did compel arbitration over a claim for damages caused by an alleged breach of the scope clause.[104]

B. Seniority Integration

Another issue that invariably arises in the context of a merger or an acquisition is the integration of seniority lists.

---

[97]Long Island R.R. v. Teamsters Local 808, 67 LRRM 2463, 2464 (ED NY, 1967).

[98]808 F Supp at 54.

[99]836 F2d 130, 127 LRRM 2284 (CA 2, 1988).

[100]896 F2d 672, 133 LRRM 2625 (CA 2), *cert. denied*, 495 U.S. 953 (1990).

[101]567 F Supp 66 (SD Tex, 1983).

[102]149 LRRM 2317 (D DC, 1994).

[103]879 F2d 906, 131 LRRM 3009 (CA DC, 1989), *cert. denied*, 494 U.S. 1065, 133 LRRM 2920 (1990).

[104]879 F2d at 912–14, 131 LRRM at 3014–16. *See also* Western Airlines v. Teamsters, 480 U.S. 1301, 1305, 124 LRRM 3139, 3140 (1987) (O'Connor, J.) ("The great weight of the case law supports the proposition that disputes as to the effect of collective bargaining agreements on representation in an airline merger situation are representation disputes within the exclusive jurisdiction of the National Mediation Board."). For a discussion of the circumstances in which corporate restructurings result in representation disputes, *see* Chapter 2, "Selecting a Bargaining Representative," §XIII.

Sharply differing views often arise as to the appropriate basis for integration.

The Interstate Commerce Commission (ICC) has a statutory responsibility to impose provisions to protect employees in the event of a merger or asset sale in the railroad industry.[105] The implementation of these provisions has resulted in complex seniority integration arrangements.

Prior to the Airline Deregulation Act of 1978 (ADA),[106] the Civil Aeronautics Board (CAB) routinely imposed labor protective provisions (LPPs) as a condition of any merger involving RLA air carriers.[107] Those provisions required fair and equitable seniority integration and provided for arbitration if an agreement could not be reached. Since the ADA was passed, however, the CAB and, subsequently, the Department of Transportation (DOT)[108] have determined to impose LPPs only where no opportunity has existed to bargain collectively over protection or where the imposition of LPPs is

---

[105]See Fox Valley & W. Ltd. v. ICC, 15 F3d 641, 644 (CA 7, 1994) (ICC is required to condition its approval of a multicarrier acquisition upon protection of the employees involved and has discretionary authority to impose LPPs in transactions in which the rail assets of a carrier are shifted to a noncarrier; see 49 USC §§11347, 10901) (1995)). Issues relating to the Interstate Commerce Act's regulation of railroad mergers and asset-transfer transactions are discussed in more detail in Chapter 7, "Accommodating the RLA to Other Laws," §II.

[106]106 Pub. L. No. 95-504, 92 Stat 1705.

[107]Air Line Pilots Ass'n v. DOT, 880 F2d 491, 493, 131 LRRM 3093 (CA DC, 1989); Air Line Pilots Ass'n v. DOT, 791 F2d 172, 174, 122 LRRM 2757 (CA DC, 1986); United-Capital Merger Case, 33 CAB 307, 323–31, 342–47 (1961).

[108]At the end of 1984, the CAB was abolished and authority over airline mergers was transferred to the DOT. 49 USC §1551(b) (1995). The ADA created an Employee Protective Program (EPP) to be available for 10 years following enactment of the ADA. 49 USC app. §1552 (1995). It authorized limited unemployment benefits to certain long-term, "protected" airline employees who suffered economically as a result of the ADA, as determined by the CAB and its successor, the DOT. In 1984, the District of Columbia Circuit held that the CAB, which had neither rejected nor granted any EPP applications before it ceased to exist, had unreasonably delayed the processing of the applications. See Air Line Pilots Ass'n v. CAB, 750 F2d 81 (CA DC, 1984). In 1993, the District of Columbia Circuit ruled that the DOT had erred two years earlier when it concluded that employee dislocations at Braniff International Airlines did not qualify under the EPP. The court remanded that case and three others that the DOT had decided at the same time. See Air Line Pilots Ass'n v. Federal Aviation Admin., 3 F3d 449, 144 LRRM 2228 (CA DC, 1993).

needed to avoid widespread labor strife.[109] Regardless, the necessity for integrating seniority lists following merger transactions continues. Where the affected employee groups have been unable to agree upon an integrated seniority list, the parties have often agreed to submit the issue to arbitration.[110]

Given the importance of seniority, it is not surprising that employees dissatisfied with the methods by which seniority is integrated have initiated litigation challenging the integration, usually on the ground of an alleged breach by their unions of the duty of fair representation. Such challenges have failed,[111] except in very limited circumstances. Courts have sustained such challenges where the union representatives of an employee group with interests "utterly hostile and adverse" to the disgruntled employees denied those employees any participation in the integration process, contrary to the union's own constitutional provisions,[112] or where employees have been denied participation in a seniority integration procedure because they were nonunionized prior to the merger.[113]

---

[109]Air Line Pilots Ass'n v. DOT, 838 F2d 563, 565, 127 LRRM 2597 (CA DC, 1988); Flight Attendants (UFA) v. DOT, 803 F2d 1029, 1032, 123 LRRM 3080 (CA 9, 1986); Air Line Pilots Ass'n v. DOT, 791 F2d at 174, 122 LRRM at 2759.

[110]See, e.g., Air Wis. Pilots Protection Comm. v. Sanderson, 909 F2d 213, 134 LRRM 3039 (CA 7, 1990), cert. denied, 498 U.S. 1085, 136 LRRM 2543 (1991); Gvozdonovic v. United Airlines, 933 F2d 1100, 137 LRRM 2534 (CA 2), cert. denied, 498 U.S. 1085, 138 LRRM 2536 (1991).

[111]Rakestraw v. United Airlines, 981 F2d 1524, 1533–34, 142 LRRM 2054 (CA 7, 1992); Gvozdenovic v. United Air Lines, 933 F2d at 1104; Air Wis. Pilots Protection Comm. v. Sanderson, 909 F2d at 216; Northeast Master Executive Council v. CAB, 506 F2d 97, 103–04, 87 LRRM 2056 (CA DC, 1974), cert. denied, 419 U.S. 1110, 88 LRRM 2235 (1975); Hyland v. United Air Lines, 254 F Supp 367, 374, 62 LRRM 2460, 2465 (ND Ill, 1966); Masy v. New Jersey Transit Rail Operations, 790 F2d 322, 327, 122 LRRM 2700, 2704 (CA 3), cert. denied, 479 U.S. 916, 125 LRRM 3216 (1986); Laturner v. Burlington N. Ry., 501 F2d 593, 602, 86 LRRM 3144, 3152 (CA 9, 1974), cert. denied, 419 U.S. 1109, 88 LRRM 2235 (1975). The duty of fair representation is discussed more fully in infra §XI.

[112]Beardsley v. Chicago & N.W. Transp. Co., 850 F2d 1255, 128 LRRM 2793, 2804 (CA 8, 1988), cert. denied, 489 U.S. 1066, 130 LRRM 2736 (1989). See also Volkman v. United Transp. Union, 724 F Supp 1282, 1329–31 (D. Kan. 1989).

[113]Bernard v. Air Line Pilots Ass'n, 873 F2d 213, 217, 131 LRRM 2206 (CA 9, 1989).

VI. NRAB

A. NRAB Structure

The NRAB is comprised of four separate divisions that, with the exception of administrative matters, generally operate independently of each other.[114] The First Division is composed of 8 members, 4 designated by labor organizations and 4 by the rail carriers. It processes disputes involving "engineers, firemen, hostlers, and outside hostler helpers, conductors, trainmen, and yard-service employees,"[115] traditionally known as "operating" employees. The Second Division has jurisdiction over the "shop craft" employees. It has 10 members, 5 from labor and 5 from management. The Third Division has jurisdiction over disputes involving a miscellany of crafts and classes. It also consists of 10 members who are divided equally among labor and management. The Fourth Division covers employees of carriers who, directly or indirectly, engage in the transportation of passengers or property by water and any other employees who are not covered by the first three Divisions. This division has 6 members, 3 selected by management and 3 by labor.

B. NRAB Jurisdiction

Section 3, First (i) of the RLA provides the NRAB with jurisdiction over disputes "growing out of grievances *or* out of the interpretation or application of agreements concerning rates of pay, rules, or working conditions."[116]

C. NRAB Procedures

Before a dispute growing out of a disciplinary grievance or the interpretation of a collective bargaining agreement can

---

[114]The NRAB is located in Chicago pursuant to RLA §3, First (s). The structure of the organization is dictated by §3, First (h). The NRAB receives technical support from the NMB.

[115]*Id.* §3, First (h).

[116]*See* Railroad Trainmen v. Chicago River & I. R.R., 353 U.S. 30, 36–37, 30 LRRM 2578 (1957). *See also* Locomotive Eng'rs v. Louisville & N. R.R., 373 U.S. 33, 52 LRRM 2944 (1963).

be presented to the NRAB, it must be handled on the property "in the usual manner up to and including the chief operating officer of the carrier designated to handle such disputes."[117] This on-the-property handling is typically begun by the local chair with the corresponding local carrier officer.[118] If they cannot resolve the dispute, the local chair will send the matter up to the next level, and it will be appealed to the corresponding carrier officer. If the parties are unable to resolve the matter by negotiation or conference, then a petition can be filed with the appropriate Division of the Board.[119] The filing of a petition may be done jointly or ex parte.[120] An employee may also file a petition.[121] The majority of submissions are filed ex parte. Matters that are not handled on the property cannot progress to the Board.[122] The administrative record is created during the initial phases of the procedure on the property. In discipline cases, the process may be more formal and include a fully transcribed hearing with witnesses and

---

[117]RLA §3, First (i).

[118]In the nonoperating crafts, there is generally a single bargaining representative, and employees may select this exclusive bargaining representative as spokesperson or may proceed on their own. In the operating crafts, employees may belong to a different operating union from the one whose collective bargaining agreement with the carrier is in dispute. Because of the constant flow between crafts by operating employees, these employees are permitted to fulfill a union shop agreement by belonging to any labor organization "national in scope, organized in accordance with this Act and admitting to membership employees of a craft or class in any of said services." *Id.* §2, Eleventh (c). *See* Chapter 3, "Protection of Employees' Right of Self-Organization," §X. However, employees have no right to representation by a union other than the collective bargaining representative at on-the-property grievance and disciplinary proceedings, unless such an option is provided by agreement or by custom. Landers v. National R.R. Passenger Corp., 485 U.S. 652, 128 LRRM 2097 (1988).

[119]RLA §3, First (i).

[120]*Id.*; NRAB, FIRST DIVISION, JOINT SUBMISSIONS TO FIRST DIVISION, CIRCULAR A (Oct. 26, 1937); NRAB, FIRST DIVISION, EX PARTE SUBMISSIONS TO FIRST DIVISION, CIRCULAR B (Oct. 14, 1949).

[121]RLA §3, First (j); Elgin, J. & E. Ry. v. Burley, 325 U.S. 711, 740 n.39, 16 LRRM 749 (1945); Landers v. National R.R. Passenger Corp., 485 U.S. at 658–69, 128 LRRM at 2099; Kaschak v. Consolidated Rail Corp., 707 F2d 902, 906, 113 LRRM 2760 (CA 6, 1983).

[122]RLA §3, First (i); 29 CFR §301.2 (1994). *See* Ryan, NRAB Award No. 20551 (1965); *see also In re* Colorado & W. Ry., Procedural Law Board No. 2827 (1981). For a discussion of this issue in the context of SBAs and Public Law Boards in the rail industry, *see infra* §VII; for System Boards of Adjustment in the airline industry, *see infra* §VIII.

documentary evidence presented to a carrier official acting as the hearing officer. Subsequent phases proceed on the basis of the record and more closely resemble an appellate proceeding in which the record is deemed to be established.

The initial step for invoking the NRAB's jurisdiction is the filing of a Notice of Intent to File a Submission with the Board's Executive Secretary, indicating the party's intention to file a submission within 30 days.[123] The letter must clearly state the claim and the particular question on which an award is desired.[124] The submission, to be filed within 30 days thereafter, must contain the names of the parties, a statement of claim by the petitioner, a statement of facts, and a statement of the position of the party.[125]

An oral hearing will be granted, if requested, and the Division will serve notice of such hearing on the parties.[126] At the hearing, employees may represent themselves[127] or be represented by counsel or their union representative. In the case of a jurisdictional dispute between two unions, notice and an opportunity to be heard must be provided to all unions who have a claim to the work in question.[128]

The NRAB is not bound by the Administrative Procedure Act[129] or the Federal Rules of Evidence.[130] The circuit

---

[123]29 CFR §301.5(g) (1994); NRAB INSTRUCTION SHEET (Jan. 1, 1988).
[124]Id.
[125]29 CFR §301.5 (1994).
[126]RLA §3, First (j); Jones v. St. Louis-S.F. Ry., 728 F2d 257, 262–63, 115 LRRM 2905 (CA 6, 1984) (right to be heard), cert. denied, 486 U.S. 1010 (1988).
[127]Elgin, J. & E. Ry. v. Burley, 325 U.S. 711, 740 n.39, 16 LRRM 749 (1945); Childs v. Pennsylvania Fed'n Maintenance of Way Employees, 831 F2d 429, 126 LRRM 2777 (CA 3, 1987).
[128]Transportation-Communication Employees Union v. Union P. R.R., 385 U.S. 157, 63 LRRM 2481 (1966).
[129]Kotakis v. Elgin, J. & E. Ry., 520 F2d 570, 576, 90 LRRM 2966 (CA 7, 1975) (citing 5 USC §551(1)(E) (1995)); Locomotive Firemen & Enginemen v. Chicago, B. & Q. R.R., 225 F Supp 11, 18, 55 LRRM 2089 (D DC), aff'd per curiam, 331 F2d 1020, 55 LRRM 2517 (CA DC), cert. denied, 377 U.S. 918 (1964); Stranford v. Pennsylvania R.R., 155 F Supp 680, 688–89 (D NJ, 1957). The Administrative Procedure Act excludes "agencies composed of representatives of the parties or of representatives of organizations of the parties to the disputes determined by them" from the definition of the term "agency" for purposes of the statute. 5 USC §551(1)(E) (1995).
[130]See Gunther v. San Diego A. & E. Ry., 382 U.S. 257, 60 LRRM 2496 (1965); Hodges v. Atlantic Coast Line R.R., 363 F2d 534, 62 LRRM 2662 (CA 5, 1966), cert. denied, 385 U.S. 1011, 64 LRRM 2108 (1967).

courts have divided, however, on the question of whether the parties are entitled to certain due process rights.[131]

A majority of the Division is required to decide an issue.[132] If the Division cannot secure a majority vote of its members, the Division can then select a neutral "referee" to sit with the Division and make an award.[133] If the Division cannot agree upon and select a referee within 10 days of a deadlock, a member of the Division or a party to the dispute may certify that fact to the NMB.[134] The NMB shall select a referee within 10 days of receiving such a certificate.[135]

The Division's decision, formally called an award, must be in writing and served upon the parties.[136] When the award is in favor of the petitioner, the Division will issue an order directed to the carrier to make the award effective and, if the award includes a monetary remedy, to pay the employee the amount due by a named date.[137] When the Division rules against the petitioner, the Division will issue an order denying the claim.[138] In the event of a dispute over the interpretation of the award, either party can request that the Division interpret the award.[139] If a carrier does not comply with the award, the petitioner or any person for whose benefit the award was made can bring an action in U.S. district court to enforce the award.[140] Reasonable attorneys' fees and costs are awarded if the petitioner prevails.[141]

---

[131]Whether Adjustment Board proceedings are subject to Fifth Amendment due process requirements is treated in *infra* §X. *See, e.g.*, English v. Burlington N. Ry., 18 F3d 741, 145 LRRM 2746 (CA 9, 1994). A frequent question arises over what constitutes proper notice to the parties. *See infra* §VII for a discussion of the conflict among the circuits on this question.

[132]RLA §3, First (n). The Division can delegate its authority to two or more members to conduct hearings and make findings. *Id.* §3, First (k).

[133]*Id.* §3, First (*l*).

[134]*Id.*

[135]*Id.*

[136]*Id.* §3, First (m); Railway & Steamship Clerks v. St. Louis S.W. R.R., 676 F2d 132, 111 LRRM 2391 (CA 5, 1982). Awards must be signed by the Division and attested to by the NRAB Secretary. 29 CFR §301.9 (1994).

[137]RLA §3, First (o).

[138]*Id.*

[139]*Id.* §3, First (m).

[140]*Id.* §3, First (p).

[141]*Id.*

Any party to an award who is aggrieved by the award can seek review in federal district court upon three narrow bases: (1) the failure of the Board to comply with the requirements of the RLA, (2) the Board's failure to conform or confine itself to matters within its jurisdiction, or (3) fraud or corruption involving a member of the Board making the award.[142] Some courts have added a fourth basis and permit review on the ground that the petitioner was denied due process.[143]

VII. SBAs and Public Law Boards in the Railroad Industry

A. Establishing SBAs and Public Law Boards

The RLA expressly permits an individual carrier, a system or group of carriers, or any class of employees acting through these representatives to agree mutually to the establishment of a system, group, or regional Board of Adjustment.[144] These SBAs are thus creatures of contract, most often between an individual railroad and a single labor organization. No statutory provision grants individual employees a right to process their grievances on their own before an SBA.[145] Adjustment Board procedures and the Board's jurisdiction over grievances are typically enumerated in the agreement creating the Board.

---

[142]RLA §3, First (q). Judicial review of Adjustment Board awards is discussed in *infra* §X.

[143]*See, e.g.,* Machinists v. Metro-N. Commuter R.R., 24 F3d 369, 146 LRRM 2086 (CA 2, 1994); Shafii v. PLC British Airways, 22 F3d 59, 62–64, 146 LRRM 2147, 2149–51 (CA 2, 1994) (discussing split between circuits concerning NRAB due process review).

[144]RLA §3, Second. For a brief discussion of the establishment of SBAs, *see* NMB, FIFTY-THIRD AND FIFTY-FOURTH ANNUAL REPORT 23 (1987–88).

[145]*Compare* RLA §3, First (j) *with id.* §3, Second. *See* Locomotive Eng'rs v. Denver & R. G. R.R., 411 F2d 1115, 1118, 71 LRRM 2692 (CA 10, 1969); *see also* O'Neill v. Public Law Bd. No. 550, 581 F2d 692, 696 n.7, 99 LRRM 2204 (CA 7, 1978).

SBAs usually consist of three members—a labor organization member, a railroad member, and a neutral chair. If the parties fail to agree on the identity of the neutral, the NMB will designate one. The partisan members of the Board are compensated by the party they represent. Although one district court has held that the NMB is not required to compensate neutrals, the NMB does so in practice except where the agreement establishing the SBA provides that the parties will pay the neutral.[146]

The procedures for establishing a Public Law Board were added to the RLA in 1966.[147] Either the union or the carrier may request in writing that the other party agree to establish a Public Law Board in order to resolve a pending collective bargaining dispute.[148] Should the other party reject a request or fail to reply within 30 days, the moving party may seek NMB intervention. Upon request, the NMB will designate an individual associated in interest with the noncompliant party to serve on the Public Law Board along with a member appointed by the moving party. Should these two members fail to agree either upon an award or the appointment of a neutral member to break the deadlock, either member may request that the NMB appoint a neutral third member to assist in the resolution of the dispute. The NMB may also be called upon to designate a neutral member to resolve procedural disputes concerning the establishment and jurisdiction of the Public Law Board. Such a "procedural neutral" is responsible for drafting the agreement establishing the Public Law Board, which is binding on the parties.[149]

---

[146]Railway Labor Executives' Ass'n v. NMB, 785 F Supp 167, 140 LRRM 2580 (D DC, 1991). For a variety of reasons, in particular the desire to obtain the services of a particular arbitrator, the parties may agree to compensate the neutral rather than have the NMB provide compensation.

[147]The procedures are set forth in RLA §3, Second. See also 29 CFR §1207 (1994).

[148]Locomotive Eng'rs v. Denver & R. G. R.R., 411 F2d 1115, 1118, 71 LRRM 2690 (CA 10, 1969). Individual employees seeking to have their grievances adjusted may not invoke the processes of a Public Law Board; only the collective bargaining representative can do this.

[149]RLA §3, Second. See also 29 CFR §1207 (1994).

B. Jurisdiction of SBAs and Public Law Boards

The jurisdiction of SBAs is determined by the agreement of the parties establishing the Board.[150] The jurisdiction of Public Law Boards is coextensive with that of the NRAB.[151] The 1966 amendments expressly state that the cases to be presented to a Public Law Board are to be defined in the agreement establishing it. Thus, the parties to a minor dispute can further restrict the jurisdiction of an SBA or a Public Law Board by setting forth specific subject area limitations in the arbitration agreement. One court has held that parties can expand the Board's authority, for example, by agreeing to submit to arbitration questions involving interpretation of the RLA.[152] In addition, through the terms of the arbitration agreement, the parties may agree that the arbitration panel is to review only certain issues framed or particular evidence submitted.[153]

In order to prevent unnecessary delay in resolving a dispute, arbitration agreements may also limit the time period in which the Adjustment Board may render an award. An SBA or a Public Law Board that fails to render a timely award will, however, not lose jurisdiction to resolve the grievance unless the arbitration agreement states unequivocally that the Board's jurisdiction terminates after a specified period of time.[154] In the absence of such an unequivocal provision, the authority of the Board will expire only after a "reasonable" time.[155]

---

[150]RLA §3, Second ¶1.

[151]Railroad Trainmen v. Chicago River & I. R.R., 353 U.S. 30, 36 n.13, 39 LRRM 2578 (1957); Consolidated Rail Corp. v. Railway Labor Executives' Ass'n, 491 U.S. 299, 131 LRRM 2601 (1989). *See also* Taylor v. Missouri P. R.R., 794 F2d 1082, 1084, 123 LRRM 2351 (CA 5), *cert. denied*, 479 U.S. 1018, 124 LRRM 3192 (1986).

[152]Richmond, F. & P. R.R. v. Transportation Communications Union, 973 F2d 276, 278–80, 141 LRRM 2115 (CA 4, 1992).

[153]United Transp. Union v. Clinchfield R.R., 427 F2d 161, 162, 74 LRRM 2318 (CA 6, 1970), *cert. denied*, 400 U.S. 824, 75 LRRM 2378 (1970).

[154]Hill v. Norfolk & W. Ry., 814 F2d 1192, 1199, 124 LRRM 3057 (CA 7, 1987); Jones v. St. Louis-S.F. Ry., 728 F2d 257, 265, 115 LRRM 2905 (CA 6, 1984), *cert. denied*, 486 U.S. 1010 (1988).

[155]Jones v. St. Louis-S.F. Ry., 728 F2d 257, 115 LRRM 2905.

Finally, the Adjustment Board has exclusive jurisdiction to decide any procedural issues relating to the arbitration proceeding.[156]

C. Procedures Before SBAs and Public Law Boards

Whereas Section 3, First of the RLA expressly provides minimum procedural standards for NRAB proceedings, Section 3, Second is virtually silent on the procedural standards applicable to proceedings before SBAs and Public Law Boards.[157] Accordingly, much litigation has arisen over whether the procedural standards enumerated in Section 3, First are applicable as a matter of law to proceedings before SBAs and Public Law Boards.

As explained more fully earlier,[158] Section 3, First (i) requires that before the NRAB can hear a dispute, the parties must first attempt to resolve it "on the property," through their own grievance mechanisms, including a determination on the matter by "the chief operating officer of the carrier designated to handle such disputes." The courts as well as the parties to minor disputes in the rail industry have assumed that this condition precedent to resolution of a grievance by the NRAB applies equally to resolution of grievances by Public Law Boards, but SBAs often consider matters on an expedited basis.[159]

Regardless of which Adjustment Board (the NRAB, an SBA, or a Public Law Board) the parties bring their grievance to, virtually all carriers and employee representatives in the

---

[156]Railway Carmen v. Atchison, T. & S.F. Ry., 956 F2d 156, 159, 139 LRRM 2596 (CA 7, 1992); Norfolk & W. Ry. v. Transportation Communications Union, 17 F3d 696, 145 LRRM 2617 (CA 4, 1994).

[157]The only procedural mandate contained in §3, First that is specifically applicable to private Adjustment Boards is that a quorum is established on a Public Law Board for the purposes of rendering a decision by the presence of any two members.

[158]See supra §II.

[159]See, e.g., Locomotive Eng'rs v. Denver & R. G. R.R., 411 F2d 1115, 1116–17, 71 LRRM 2690 (CA 10, 1969), in which the court assumed, without deciding, that the parties appropriately complied with the on-the-property requirement of §3, First (i) prior to the submission of their dispute to a Public Law Board under §3, Second.

rail industry have entered into collective bargaining agreements that establish a formal internal grievance process that must be employed prior to referral of the dispute to arbitration. The procedures followed on the property are governed by the terms of those agreements. Employees who assert that the attempt to resolve the dispute on the property denied their procedural rights mandated by the collective bargaining agreement can present this issue before the NRAB.[160] Moreover, a failure to raise those rights before the Adjustment Board may result in a waiver.[161]

Several courts have also held that the notice requirement of Section 3, First (j), which states that the NRAB "shall give due notice of all hearings to the employee or employees and the carrier or carriers involved," applies to Section 3, Second Public Law Board proceedings.[162] This provision requires at minimum that the parties receive notice of the date and time of the hearing and be given an opportunity to be heard in person or through a representative.[163] Notice must be given to all persons substantially or materially affected by a decision of the Public Law Board.[164]

The courts disagree as to whom the Public Law Board must direct notice if an employee is represented in the grievance process by a union official. The Fifth and Seventh Circuits have held that if the employee is represented by a union official, notice upon the union is sufficient to meet the minimum requirements of the statute.[165] By contrast, the Ninth

---

[160]*See, e.g.*, Edwards v. St. Louis-S.F. R.R., 361 F2d 946, 953–54 & n.19, 62 LRRM 2300 (CA 7, 1966).

[161]Hill v. Norfolk & W. Ry., 814 F2d 1192, 1198, 124 LRRM 3057 (CA 7, 1987) (failure to raise procedural rights at hearing before a Public Law Board constituted waiver of right to raise issue later).

[162]*See, e.g.*, Cole v. Erie L. Ry., 541 F2d 528, 535, 93 LRRM 2077 (CA 6, 1976), *cert. denied,* 433 U.S. 914, 95 LRRM 2765 (1977); Murray v. Consolidated Rail Corp., 736 F2d 372, 373, 116 LRRM 2810 (CA 6, 1984); Steelworkers Local 1913 v. Union R.R., 597 F2d 40, 42, 101 LRRM 2283 (CA 3, 1979); Railway & Steamship Clerks v. St. Louis S.W. Ry., 676 F2d 132, 135 n.2, 111 LRRM 2391 (CA 5, 1982), *cert. denied,* 484 U.S. 907, 126 LRRM 2946 (1987); O'Neill v. Public Law Bd. No. 550, 581 F2d 692, 695, 99 LRRM 2204 (CA 7, 1978).

[163]Steelworkers Local 1913 v. Union R.R., 597 F2d at 43.

[164]Railway & Steamship Clerks v. St. Louis S.W. Ry., 676 F2d at 135–36.

[165]O'Neill v. Public Law Bd. No. 550, 581 F2d at 694–95; Railway & Steamship Clerks v. St. Louis S.W. Ry., 676 F2d at 136.

and Sixth Circuits have held that the employee must receive actual notice, regardless of whether or not he or she is represented in the Adjustment Board proceeding by a union official.[166] The notice requirement may be waived by a party who appears at the Adjustment Board proceeding and fails to raise the procedural error at that point.[167]

The provision in Section 3, First (m) that permits the parties to request the NRAB to interpret its award in the event of a dispute over its meaning has been applied to Section 3, Second arbitration proceedings as well.[168] In addition, the enforcement provisions of Section 3, First have been applied to awards of Public Law Boards[169] and, as a practical matter, to awards issued by SBAs.[170]

VIII. Boards of Adjustment in the Airline Industry

When the RLA was amended in 1936 to cover the air transportation industry, Adjustment Boards in the airline industry were to be comparable to those in the railroad industry. Section 3, First of the RLA created the NRAB to serve the railroad industry; however, Section 205 merely authorized the NMB to create a National Air Transport Adjustment Board, which it has not done.

---

[166]English v. Burlington N. Ry., 18 F3d 741, 145 LRRM 2746 (CA 9, 1994); Cole v. Erie L. Ry., 541 F2d at 535.

[167]Railway & Steamship Clerks v. St. Louis S.W. Ry., 676 F2d 132, 136–38, 111 LRRM 2391 (CA 5, 1982); Schneider v. Southern Ry., 822 F2d 22, 24, 125 LRRM 3251 (CA 6, 1987).

[168]United Transp. Union v. Soo L. R.R., 457 F2d 285, 287, 79 LRRM 2727 (CA 7, 1972).

[169]See, e.g., United Transp. Union v. Indiana Harbor Belt Ry., 540 F2d 861, 93 LRRM 2130 (CA 7, 1976); Cole v. Erie L. Ry., 541 F2d 528, 93 LRRM 2077 (CA 6, 1976), cert. denied, 433 U.S. 914, 95 LRRM 2765 (1977); Railway & Steamship Clerks v. St Louis-S.F. Ry., 419 F2d 933, 73 LRRM 2074 (CA 8, 1969), cert. denied, 400 U.S. 818, 75 LRRM 2378 (1970); Locomotive Eng'rs v. St. Louis S.W. Ry., 757 F2d 656, 119 LRRM 2064 (CA 5, 1985).

[170]Merchants Despatch Transp. Corp. v. Systems Fed'n No. One Ry. Employees' Dep't, 551 F2d 144, 94 LRRM 3119 (CA 7, 1977); Employees Protection Ass'n v. Norfolk & W. Ry., 511 F2d 1040, 88 LRRM 2938 (CA 4, 1975); Railway & Steamship Clerks v. Jacksonville Terminal Co., 591 F2d 1387, 100 LRRM 3130 (CA 5, 1979).

Section 204 of the RLA requires an air carrier and its employees to establish a Board of Adjustment not exceeding the jurisdiction of Boards of Adjustment in the railroad industry. The duty imposed on the parties to create such Boards is "more than a casual suggestion."[171] It is a compulsory obligation that may be judicially enforced.[172]

Section 204 authorizes the establishment of Boards of Adjustment on an individual carrier, system, or group of carriers among any class or classes of employees; but in practice these System Boards of Adjustment have been established only by a single carrier and a single union representing a particular craft or class.

A. Jurisdiction of Boards of Adjustment

The establishment of Adjustment Boards is compelled by statute,[173] and their jurisdiction is defined in the collective bargaining agreement.[174] The Board's "jurisdiction must be broad enough reasonably to effectuate the purposes of the RLA."[175] One district court has held that no obligation to establish a Board of Adjustment arises until a collective bargaining agreement exists.[176]

---

[171]Machinists v. Central Airlines, 372 U.S. 682, 686, 52 LRRM 2803 (1963).
[172]Id.
[173]RLA §184.
[174]Air Line Pilots Ass'n v. Jetstream Int'l Airlines, 716 F Supp 203, 205, 133 LRRM 2182, 2184 (D Md, 1989).
[175]Id. Some courts hold that, although a collective bargaining agreement can limit a probationary employee's substantive rights with respect to discharge—for example, leaving a discharged probationary employee without much to argue before an arbitrator, Conrad v. Delta Air Lines, 494 F2d 914, 86 LRRM 2242 (CA 7, 1974)—it may not bar a probationary employee from grieving a disciplinary action or termination, Capraro v. United Parcel Serv. Co., 993 F2d 328, 335–36, 143 LRRM 2260, 2267 (CA 3, 1993) (such a collective bargaining agreement would not constitute "a permissible 'contractual limitation on grievance procedures' "). In distinguishing an employee's substantive and procedural rights, the Third Circuit harmonized its holding in Capraro with that of the Seventh Circuit in Conrad. 993 F2d at 336 n.13, 143 LRRM at 2268 n.13.
[176]Air Line Pilots Ass'n v. Jetstream Int'l Airlines, 716 F Supp at 207, 133 LRRM at 2186.

B. Procedures Before Boards of Adjustment

The procedures applicable to Boards of Adjustment also typically are set forth in the relevant collective bargaining agreement, or they may be created by the Boards acting within their authority under the agreement.[177] These procedures include requirements relating to the preliminary steps of the grievance process, usually beginning with informal conferences, the filing of a written grievance, and one or more formal meetings attended by higher-ranking union and carrier officials.[178]

Generally, Adjustment Board determination of whether there has been adequate compliance with procedural requirements is final and binding on the parties.[179] It is the Adjustment Board that "must consider equitable defenses to arbitra-

---

[177]Wells v. Southern Airways, 616 F2d 107, 110, 104 LRRM 2338 (CA 5), *cert. denied*, 449 U.S. 862 (1980); Hall v. Eastern Air Lines, 511 F2d 663, 89 LRRM 2111 (CA 5, 1975); Giordano v. Modern Air Transp., 504 F2d 882, 87 LRRM 3231 (CA 5, 1974); Rosen v. Eastern Air Lines, 400 F2d 462, 69 LRRM 2065 (CA 5, 1968), *cert. denied*, 394 U.S. 959, 70 LRRM 3195 (1969).

[178]Because §3 was expressly omitted from title II, several courts have held that the various procedural provisions of §3, First are inapplicable to the airline industry. *See, e.g.,* Air Line Pilots Ass'n v. Northwest Airlines, 415 F2d 493, 72 LRRM 2160 (CA 8, 1969) (§3, First (p), which permits the recovery of attorneys' fees by the petitioner in an action to enforce an arbitration award, is not applicable to the airline industry); Rosen v. Eastern Air Lines, 400 F2d 462, 69 LRRM 2065, 2066 (court declined to consider defendant's argument that plaintiff had failed to state a claim under §3 "since this section is not applicable to airlines"); Brady v. Trans World Airlines, 167 F Supp 469, 474 n.5, 43 LRRM 2093 (D Del, 1958) (Supreme Court's construction of a particular provision of §3, First would not be applicable to the airline industry but for the existence of identical statutory language in §204).

Courts have held, however, that airline employees have the same statutory right to take their case before a System Board of Adjustment, without a union representative, as railroad employees have to process their claims before the NRAB. *See* Miklavic v. USAir, Inc., 21 F3d 551, 146 LRRM 2001 (CA 3, 1994) (citing §3, First (j) and railroad cases, without discussing the issue of the inapplicability of that section, and those cases, to the airline industry); Carter v. Eastern Airlines, 131 LRRM 2674 (ND Ga, 1988) (same situation); Stevens v. Teamsters Local 2702, 504 F Supp 332, 109 LRRM 2712 (WD Wash, 1980).

[179]*See* Union P. R.R. v. Sheehan, 439 U.S. 89, 99 LRRM 3327 (1978); Northwest Airlines v. Air Line Pilots Ass'n, 808 F2d 76, 80, 124 LRRM 2300 (CA DC, 1987), *cert. denied*, 484 U.S. 101, 128 LRRM 2296 (1988); Air Line Pilots Ass'n v. Texas Int'l Airlines, 656 F2d 16, 20 n.6, 107 LRRM 3185 (CA 2, 1981); Rosen v. Eastern Airlines, 400 F2d at 464.

tion and determine whether the party demanding arbitration has satisfied procedural requirements."[180] Questions of "procedural arbitrability" are for the Adjustment Board, not a court.[181]

If a grievance cannot be resolved during the preliminary steps of the grievance procedure, either the union or the carrier may invoke the jurisdiction of the Adjustment Board.[182] The procedural requirements associated with submission of a grievance to the Board, as well as the procedures to be followed by the System Adjustment Board during arbitration, are set forth in the collective bargaining agreement. There are various practices with respect to the role of the neutral member. Under some agreements, the neutral sits with the other members in all of the cases before the Board. Under other agreements, the carrier and union members meet first and conduct a full evidentiary hearing. A neutral member joins the Board if the other members deadlock. Then either the case is again heard by the full Board de novo or the neutral member reviews the record and requests further testimony only if it is necessary to a decision.

IX. INJUNCTIONS DURING MINOR DISPUTES

A. Status Quo Obligation During Minor Disputes

In *Railroad Trainmen v. Chicago River & Indiana Railroad*,[183] the Supreme Court held that a union may not exercise self-help to exert pressure on the carrier in a minor dispute over contractual grievances. The Court reasoned that because such grievances are subject to the compulsory minor dispute procedures of the RLA—that is, the exclusive jurisdiction of the appropriate Adjustment Board—the courts are necessar-

---

[180]Machinists v. Republic Airlines, 761 F2d 1386, 1390, 119 LRRM 2642 (CA 9, 1985). For a discussion of the statute of limitations, *see supra* §VII. C and note 161.

[181]Larsen v. American Airlines, 313 F2d 599, 603, 52 LRRM 2411 (CA 2, 1963).

[182]RLA §184.

[183]353 U.S. 30, 39 LRRM 2578 (1957).

ily empowered to enjoin strikes designed to evade those procedures.[184] The same result has been reached in the airline industry, although airline System Boards are established pursuant to a different statutory provision.[185]

B. Status Quo Conditions on Strike Injunctions

The Supreme Court has held that strike injunctions from a federal court pending arbitration of a minor dispute are necessary to preserve the exclusive jurisdiction of the Adjustment Boards.[186] In *Locomotive Engineers v. Missouri-Kansas-Texas Railroad*,[187] *(M-K-T),* the Supreme Court held that, although there is no statutory requirement that the status quo be maintained during the pendency of a minor dispute, a court has inherent equitable discretion to condition a strike injunction upon the carrier's maintenance of, or return to, the status quo with respect to the subject matter of the strike in order to preserve the jurisdiction of the Adjustment Board "by preventing injury so irreparable that a decision of the Board in the unions' favor would be but an empty victory."[188] Subsequent decisions have held that *M-K-T* conditions may be imposed when the implementation of the change over which the strike arose "may well make pragmatically impossi-

---

[184]353 U.S. at 34–42, 39 LRRM at 2579–82. *See also* Pittsburgh & L. E. R.R. v. Railway Labor Executives' Ass'n, 491 U.S. 490, 513–514, 131 LRRM 2611 (1989); Locomotive Eng'rs v. Missouri-K.-T. R.R., 363 U.S. 528, 534, 46 LRRM 2429 (1960); Locomotive Eng'rs v. Louisville & N. R.R., 373 U.S. 33, 52 LRRM 2944 (1963); Manion v. Kansas City Terminal Ry., 353 U.S. 927, 39 LRRM 2641 (1957) (per curiam); Baltimore & O. R.R. v. United Railroad Workers Union, 271 F2d 87, 44 LRRM 2974 (CA 2, 1959).

[185]45 USC §184 (1986). *See, e.g.,* Teamsters Local 19 v. Southwest Airlines Co., 875 F.2d 1129, 131 LRRM 2761 (CA 5, 1989); Empresa Ecuatoriana De Aviacion, S.A. v. Machinists, Dist. Lodge 100, 690 F2d 838, 111 LRRM 2971 (CA 11, 1982); Trans Int'l Airlines, v. Teamsters, 650 F2d 949, 103 LRRM 2669 (CA 9, 1980).

[186]Railroad Trainmen v. Chicago River & I. R.R., 353 U.S. 30, 39, 39 LRRM 2578, 2581 (1957); Manion v. Kansas City Terminal Ry., 353 U.S. 927, 39 LRRM 2641.

[187]363 U.S. 528, 46 LRRM 2429 (1960).

[188]363 U.S. at 534, 46 LRRM at 2432; *see also* Consolidated Rail Corp. v. Railway Labor Executives' Ass'n, 491 U.S. 299, 304, 131 LRRM 2601, 2603 (1989).

ble any truly complete remedial order of the adjustment board."[189]

The Adjustment Boards have full power under Section 3 of the RLA to grant monetary relief to employees to make them whole for carrier violations of labor agreements, as well as to grant reinstatement and make necessary seniority adjustments when employees are wrongfully furloughed or discharged.[190] The courts generally do not impose *M-K-T* conditions merely because a carrier's disputed action will result in job loss or lost wages for employees.[191] In *M-K-T* itself, however, the status quo condition was justified because the carrier action in that case would, among other things, have required displaced employees to relocate from their homes,[192] a loss that may transcend economic hardship. Other lower court cases have granted *M-K-T* conditional injunctions where employees would be displaced by reason of arrangements between carriers and third parties, such as contracting out work, in circumstances where "restructuring the operation of the [carriers] to return them to what is now the status quo might well be totally unworkable."[193]

C. Status Quo Injunctions in Absence of Strike

When a court determines that a union's status quo claim presents a minor dispute because the carrier has presented

---

[189]National Ry. Labor Conference v. Machinists, 830 F2d 741, 750, 126 LRRM 2615, 2622 (CA 7, 1987); *see* Illinois C. R.R. v. Railroad Trainmen, 398 F2d 973, 979, 68 LRRM 2817, 2821 (CA 7, 1968).

[190]RLA §3, First (o). *See, e.g.*, Chicago & N.W. Transp. Co. v. Railway Labor Executives' Ass'n, 855 F2d 1277, 1288, 129 LRRM 2216, 2224 (CA 7), *cert. denied*, 488 U.S. 966, 129 LRRM 3072 (1988).

[191]*E.g.*, Chicago & N.W. Transp. Co. v. Railway Labor Executives' Ass'n, 855 F2d at 1288, 129 LRRM at 2224; Maine C. R.R. v. United Transp. Union, 787 F2d 780, 781–82, 122 LRRM 2017, 2018–19 (CA 1), *cert. denied*, 479 U.S. 848, 123 LRRM 2592 (1986).

[192]363 U.S. 528, 534, 46 LRRM 2429, 2431 (1960).

[193]*E.g.*, National Ry. Labor Conference v. Machinists, 830 F2d at 751, 126 LRRM at 2623; *but see* Chicago & N.W. Transp. Co. v. Railway Labor Executives' Ass'n, 855 F2d at 1288, 129 LRRM at 2224 (denying *M-K-T* condition prohibiting carrier from selling line and displacing all incumbent employees on that line, on ground that if sale violated any agreements Adjustment Board could subsequently make employees whole through monetary relief and seniority adjustments).

an arguable contractual justification for its challenged action, the status quo provision of the RLA do not apply and the carrier generally is permitted unilaterally to implement its interpretation of the agreement pending a decision by an Adjustment Board.[194]

The Supreme Court in *M-K-T* expressly left open the issue of whether a court may enjoin a carrier from altering the status quo pending arbitration of a minor dispute in the absence of a strike injunction.[195] More recently, in *Consolidated Rail Corp. v. Railway Labor Executives' Ass'n*,[196] the Court noted that this remains an open issue.

In *Railway & Steamship Clerks, Westchester Lodge 2186 v. Railway Express Agency*,[197] the Second Circuit held that *M-K-T* permits the federal courts to grant status quo injunctions in minor disputes to preserve the jurisdiction of the Adjustment Boards.[198] The Second Circuit reasoned that denying jurisdiction to issue status quo injunctions would cause unions to strike merely in order to obtain *M-K-T* conditions, an outcome that would be contrary to RLA's policy of preventing strikes.[199]

A number of circuit courts have followed *Westchester Lodge,* stating that a union may obtain a status quo injunction in circumstances in which the Adjustment Board's jurisdiction is threatened because it could not provide employees with a

---

[194]Consolidated Rail Corp. v. Railway Labor Executives' Ass'n, 491 U.S. 299, 304, 131 LRRM 2601, 2603 (1989); United Transp. Union, Gen. Comm. of Adjustment v. CSX R.R., 893 F2d 584, 594, 133 LRRM 2203, 2211 (CA 3, 1990); Sheet Metal Workers v. Burlington N. Ry., 893 F2d 199, 202, 133 LRRM 2296, 2298 (CA 8, 1990); Teamsters v. Southwest Airlines Co., 875 F2d 1129, 1133, 131 LRRM 2761, 2763–65 (CA 5, 1989) (en banc), *cert. denied*, 493 U.S. 1043, 133 LRRM 2264 (1990); Air Line Pilots Ass'n v. Eastern Air Lines, 869 F2d 1518, 1520, 130 LRRM 2895, 2896–97 (CA DC, 1989); National Ry. Labor Conference v. Machinists, 830 F2d 741, 749, 126 LRRM 2615, 2621 (CA 7, 1987); Maine C. R.R. v. United Transp. Union, 787 F2d at 781, 122 LRRM at 2018; Railway & Steamship Clerks v. Norfolk & W. Ry., 745 F2d 370, 375, 117 LRRM 2695, 2697–98 (CA 6, 1984); United Transp. Union v. Penn Cent. Transp. Co., 505 F2d 542, 545, 87 LRRM 3056, 3058 (CA 3, 1974).
[195]363 U.S. at 531 n.3, 46 LRRM at 2430 n.3.
[196]491 U.S. 299, 304 n.5, 131 LRRM 2601, 2603 n.5 (1989).
[197]329 F2d 748, 55 LRRM 2835 (CA 2, 1964).
[198]329 F2d at 752–53, 55 LRRM 2837.
[199]329 F2d at 752, 55 LRRM at 2837.

remedy if the status quo were altered.[200] The First Circuit, however, has rejected *Westchester Lodge,* holding that a district court does not have jurisdiction, independent of that otherwise existing, to issue a status quo injunction in a minor dispute.[201]

The standard for *Westchester Lodge* injunctions, in the circuits where such injunctions are available, has been variously stated.[202] Several decisions have held that a loss of job or wages alone will not entitle employees to a *Westchester Lodge* status quo injunction.[203]

---

[200]Allied Pilots Ass'n v. American Airlines, 898 F2d 462, 465–66, 134 LRRM 2148, 2150–51 (CA 5, 1990). *See, e.g.,* Teamsters v. Southwest Airlines Co., 875 F2d 1129, 1136, 131 LRRM 2761, 2766 (CA 5, 1989) (en banc), *cert. denied,* 493 U.S. 1043, 133 LRRM 2264 (1990); Air Line Pilots Ass'n v. Eastern Air Lines, 869 F2d 1518, 1520 n.2, 130 LRRM 2895, 2897 n.2 (CA DC, 1989) (dicta); Railway Labor Executives' Ass'n v. Norfolk & W. Ry., 833 F2d 700, 708, 126 LRRM 3121, 3126–27 (CA 7, 1987) (injunction denied); Teamsters v. Western Air Lines, 813 F2d 1359, 1363, 125 LRRM 2153, 2156 (CA 9, 1987); Maintenance of Way Employees v. Burlington N. R.R., 802 F2d 1016, 1022, 123 LRRM 2593, 2597–98 (CA 8, 1986) (dicta): Machinists v. Frontier Airlines, 664 F2d 538, 542, 109 LRRM 2124, 2127 (CA 5, 1981); United Transp. Union v. Penn Cent. Transp. Co., 505 F2d 542, 545, 87 LRRM 3056, 3058 (CA 3, 1974) (dicta, no minor dispute injunction requested).

[201]Machinists v. Eastern Air Lines, 826 F2d 1141, 1150–51, 126 LRRM 2037, 2044–45 (CA 1, 1987); Locomotive Eng'rs v. Boston & Me. Corp., 788 F2d 794, 797, 122 LRRM 2020, 2022 (CA 1), *cert. denied,* 479 U.S. 829, 123 LRRM 2592 (1986). *Accord* United Ry. Supervisors' Ass'n v. Consolidated Rail Corp., 136 LRRM 2918, 2919 (ND Ohio, 1991).

[202]*See* Teamsters v. Southwest Airlines Co., 875 F2d at 1133–34, 131 LRRM at 2763–65 (injunction may issue only if a disruption of the status quo would result in irreparable injury of such magnitude that it would render any subsequent decision meaningless); Air Line Pilots Ass'n v. Eastern Air Lines, 869 F2d at 1520 n.2, 130 LRRM at 2897 n.2 (dicta) (injunction available only when necessary to preserve the arbitrator's ability to decide the dispute); Railway Labor Executives' Ass'n v. Norfolk & W. Ry., 833 F2d 700, 126 LRRM 3121 (CA 7, 1987) (injunction denied; appropriate for a court to issue a preliminary injunction in a minor dispute only when an injunction is needed to preserve the NRAB's jurisdiction); Teamsters v. Western Air Lines, 813 F2d 1359, 125 LRRM 2153 (CA 9, 1987) (injunctive relief is appropriate to compel parties to fulfill their obligations under the RLA); Maintenance of Way Employees v. Burlington N. Ry., 802 F2d 1016, 123 LRRM 2593 (injunction may be necessary to preserve the jurisdiction of the NRAB, i.e., to keep the dispute from growing into a major one while the settlement process is under way); United Transp. Union v. Penn Cent. Transp. Co., 505 F2d 542, 87 LRRM 3056 (dicta) (injunction would only be granted to preserve the jurisdiction of the Adjustment Board).

[203]*E.g.,* Allied Pilots Ass'n v. American Airlines, 898 F2d 462, 134 LRRM 2148; Sheet Metal Workers v. Burlington R.R., 893 F2d 199, 205, 133 LRRM 2296, 2301 (CA 8, 1989); Teamsters v. Southwest Airlines Co., 875 F2d at 1133–34, 131 LRRM at 2763–65; United Transp. Union v. Penn Cent. Transp. Co., 505 F2d 542, 87 LRRM 3056.

Some courts have held that, because the district court's jurisdiction in a minor dispute is limited to preservation of the exclusive jurisdiction of the Adjustment Boards, a *Westchester Lodge* injunction cannot be issued unless the minor dispute has been submitted to an Adjustment Board.[204] Generally, however, when a minor dispute has not yet been submitted to an Adjustment Board, the courts have held that if a *Westchester Lodge* injunction is otherwise warranted it may be granted and made conditional upon submission to an Adjustment Board.[205]

X. ACTIONS TO ENFORCE OR VACATE ADJUSTMENT BOARD AWARDS

Section 3, First of the Act provides procedures for enforcing and reviewing NRAB awards. Subsection 3(p) permits the grievant, or any person for whose benefit an order of the Board is made, to seek compliance in a district court in which the petitioner resides, or in which the principal operating office of the carrier is located, or through which the carrier operates.[206] If any employee, group of employees, or carrier is aggrieved by the failure of the Board to make an award, or by any terms of an award, or by failure to include terms, then any of them may file a petition for review in district court.[207] The district court has jurisdiction to affirm the order or to set it aside in whole or in part, or the court may remand for further action that the court may direct.[208] The party

---

[204]*E.g.*, United Transp. Union v. Penn Cent. Transp. Co., 505 F2d 542, 87 LRRM 3056; Railway & Steamship Clerks, Westchester Lodge 2186 v. Railway Express Agency, 329 F2d 748, 55 LRRM 2835 (CA 2, 1964); Railway Labor Executives' Ass'n v. Metro-N. Commuter R.R., 759 F Supp 1019, 1023 (SD NY, 1990). *Cf.* Manion v. Kansas City Terminal Ry., 353 U.S. 927, 39 LRRM 2641 (1957) (per curiam) (strike injunction in minor dispute may not issue until dispute is submitted to Adjustment Board).

[205]*E.g.*, Teamsters v. Western Air Lines, 813 F2d 1359, 125 LRRM 2153 (CA 9, 1987); Railway & Steamship Clerks Local Lodge 2144 v. Railway Express Agency, 409 F2d 312, 318, 70 LRRM 3295, 3299–3300 (CA 2, 1969).

[206]RLA §3, First (p).

[207]*Id.* §3, First (q).

[208]*Id.*

seeking review or enforcement must file "within two years from the time the cause of action accrues under the award" of the Board.[209]

The first paragraph of Section 3, Second providing for the voluntary establishment of SBAs is silent regarding the enforcement of awards of such Boards, although as a practical matter the standard of review is the same as for the NRAB.[210] The second paragraph of Section 3, Second, added in 1966 to provide for the establishment of Public Law Boards, states that awards may be enforced in federal district courts on the same basis as awards of the NRAB.[211] It has been generally held that, although the statute uses only the term "enforce," it also provides for jurisdiction to review the award of a Public Law Board.[212]

Awards of System Boards of Adjustment in the airline industry are enforced and reviewed in the same manner as Adjustment Board awards in the railroad industry.[213] In the absence of express statutory language, however, the courts have articulated a greater variety of standards for review of airline awards. In practice, awards are rarely overturned. However, the limitations period for the review and enforcement of airline System Board awards has not been settled.[214]

---

[209]*Id.* §3, First (r). Section 3 does not apply to the airline industry, and the RLA does not expressly provide a statute of limitations for airline industry cases.

[210]*Id.* §3, Second. *See* Merchants Despatch Transp. Corp. v. Systems Fed'n No. One Ry. Employees' Dep't, 551 F2d 144, 94 LRRM 3119 (CA 7, 1977); Employees Protection Ass'n v. Norfolk W. Ry., 511 F2d 1040, 88 LRRM 2938 (CA 4, 1975); Railway & Steamship Clerks v. Jacksonville Terminal, 591 F2d 1387, 100 LRRM 3130 (CA 5, 1979).

[211]RLA §3, Second.

[212]*See* United Transp. Union v. Indiana Harbor Belt Ry., 540 F2d 861, 863, 93 LRRM 2130 (CA 7, 1976); Locomotive Eng'rs v. St. Louis S.W. Ry., 757 F2d 656, 660, 119 LRRM 2064 (CA 5, 1985).

[213]Machinists v. Central Airlines, 372 U.S. 682, 694–95, 52 LRRM 2803 (1963); *see also* Shafii v. PLC British Airways, 22 F3d 59, 61, 146 LRRM 2641, 2647 (CA 2, 1994); Hunt v. Northwest Airlines, 600 F2d 176, 178, 101 LRRM 2647 (CA 8), *cert. denied,* 444 U.S. 946, 116 LRRM 2288 (1979); Giordano v. Modern Air Transp., 504 F2d 882, 883, 87 LRRM 3231 (CA 5, 1974); Rossi v. Trans World Airlines, 350 F Supp 1263, 1269, 81 LRRM 2955 (DC Cal, 1972), *aff'd,* 507 F2d 404, 88 LRRM 2983 (CA 9, 1974).

[214]Flight Attendants (AFA) v. Republic Airlines, 797 F2d 352, 356–57, 123 LRRM 2110 (CA 7, 1986) (applying §3, First (r) two-year limitations period to action

The Supreme Court has held that there are reasons of policy that favor the exclusiveness and finality of Adjustment Board jurisdiction.[215] Accordingly, courts are not permitted to review the merits of System Board decisions.[216]

The scope of judicial review allowed under the RLA has been characterized as being "among the narrowest known to the law."[217] The Supreme Court confirmed this characterization in *Union Pacific Railroad v. Sheehan*:[218]

> Judicial review of Adjustment Board orders is limited to three specific grounds: (1) Failure of the Adjustment Board to comply with the requirements of the Railway Labor Act; (2) failure of the Adjustment Board to conform, or confine, itself to matters within the scope of the jurisdiction; and (3) fraud or corruption, 45 USC § 153 First (q). Only upon one or more of these bases may a court set aside an order of the Adjustment Board.[219]

The Court concluded that it had "time and again emphasized that this statutory language means just what it says."[220]

---

challenging Adjustment Board jurisdiction); Machinists v. Aloha Airlines, 790 F2d 727, 733–34, 122 LRRM 2642 (CA 9), *cert. denied*, 479 U.S. 931, 123 LRRM 2904 (1986) (applying six-month limitation to breach of collective bargaining agreement action); Vaughter v. Eastern Airlines, 619 F Supp 463, 472–73 (SD Fla, 1985), *aff'd*, 817 F2d 685 (CA 11, 1987) (applying Florida state statute of limitations); Richey v. Hawaiian Airlines, 533 F Supp 310, 313 (MD Ga, 1982) (challenge to Adjustment Board's jurisdiction was time barred because nine-month delay was too long).

[215]Slocum v. Delaware, L. & W. Ry., 339 U.S. 239, 243–44, 25 LRRM 2617, 2619 (1950) (Court has found that the expertise of the Board in railroad matters and the desirability of uniformity in the interpretation of collective agreements require that courts defer to Board jurisdiction). *See also* Order of Railway Conductors v. Pitney, 326 U.S. 561, 567, 17 LRRM 722 (1946); Union P. R.R. v. Sheehan, 439 U.S. 89, 94, 99 LRRM 3327 (1978).

[216]Gunther v. San Diego & A.E. R.R., 382 U.S. 257, 263–64, 60 LRRM 2496, 2498 (1965); Locomotive Eng'rs v. Louisville & N. R.R., 373 U.S. 33, 38, 52 LRRM 2944, 2946 (1963); Union P. R.R. v. Price, 360 U.S. 601, 617, 44 LRRM 2316 (1959); Railroad Trainmen v. Chicago River & I. R.R., 353 U.S. 30, 39 LRRM 2578 (1957).

[217]Denver & R. G. R.R. v. Blackett, 538 F2d 291, 293, 92 LRRM 3289, 3291 (CA 10, 1976); Diamond v. Terminal Ry., 421 F2d 228, 233, 73 LRRM 2230, 2233 (CA 5, 1970); Eastern Airlines v. Transport Workers, 580 F2d 169, 172, 99 LRRM 2634, 2636 (CA 5, 1978).

[218]439 U.S. 89, 99 LRRM 3327 (1978).

[219]439 U.S. at 93.

[220]*Id.* at 94.

Nonetheless, several courts have added due process as a fourth basis for reviewing Adjustment Board decisions.[221] In *English v. Burlington Northern Railroad*,[222] the Ninth Circuit held that due process requires that

> (1) the Board be presented with a "full statement of the facts and all supporting data bearing upon the disputes," 45 USC § 143 subd. 1(i), and (2) the "[p]arties may be heard either in person, by counsel, or by other representatives . . . and the . . . Board shall give due notice of all hearings to the employee." 45 USC § 153 subd. 1(j).[223]

It is clear that in order to satisfy the state action requirement of the Fifth Amendment, any due process claim must relate to the proceedings before the Adjustment Board and not an on-the-property investigation by the carrier.[224]

Finally, in reviewing awards that would result in the reinstatement of alcohol- or drug-impaired employees, the Eighth and Eleventh Circuits have held that adjustment awards are subject to public policy review.[225] In these cases, the courts found that enforcement of the award would be denied where such enforcement would contravene a "well defined and dom-

---

[221]*See, e.g.,* Shafii v. PLC British Airways, 22 F3d 59, 62–64, 146 LRRM 2147, 2149–51 (CA 2, 1994) (discussing split between circuits concerning due process review); English v. Burlington N. Ry., 18 F3d 741, 145 LRRM 2746 (CA 9, 1994); Locomotive Eng'rs v. St. Louis S.W. Ry., 757 F2d 656, 119 LRRM 2064 (CA 5, 1985); Arroyo v. Crown Air/Dorado Wings, 672 F Supp 50, 52 (D PR, 1987) (citing district court cases). *But see* Henry v. Delta Air Lines, 759 F2d 870, 873, 119 LRRM 3154 (CA 11, 1985) (Supreme Court's decision in *Sheehan* precludes due process challenges to System Board awards). The Court in Union P. R.R. v. Sheehan reversed a circuit court's holding that overruled an Adjustment Board's decision on due process grounds. Nonetheless, the Court did not specifically address whether it is proper for a district court to review a Board decision on due process grounds. 439 U.S. 89, 99 LRRM 3327.

[222]18 F3d 741, 145 LRRM 2746 (CA 9, 1994).

[223]18 F3d at 744. *See supra* §VII for a discussion of the conflict among the circuits as to what constitutes due notice.

[224]*E.g.,* 18 F3d at 744 (involving railroad Public Law Board); Elmore v. Chicago & Il. M. Ry., 782 F2d 94, 121 LRRM 2381 (CA 7, 1986) (applying rule to NRAB); Hunt v. Northwest Airlines, 600 F2d 176, 101 LRRM 2647 (CA 8) (applying rule to airline System Board of Adjustment), *cert. denied,* 444 U.S. 946, 116 LRRM 2288 (1979).

[225]Union P. R.R. v. United Transp. Union, 3 F3d 255, 144 LRRM 2027 (CA 8, 1993); Delta Air Lines v. Air Line Pilots Ass'n, 861 F2d 665, 130 LRRM 2014 (CA 11, 1988), *cert. denied,* 493 U.S. 871, 132 LRRM 2623 (1989).

inant" public policy, namely, the policy against the operation of a carrier by an employee "whose impaired judgment due to the use of drugs or alcohol could seriously threaten public safety."[226] The District of Columbia Circuit, however, declined to set aside an arbitration award reinstating an alcoholic employee on the condition that he could establish fitness for duty.[227] The court noted that the public policy basis for review is "extremely narrow," limited to awards that violate established law or compel some unlawful act.[228]

XI. Breach of Union's Duty of Fair Representation

A union with the status of exclusive bargaining agent under the RLA has the duty to represent fairly each of the employees whom it represents. This duty was first announced in an RLA case, *Steele v. Louisville & Nashville Railroad*,[229] where the Supreme Court struck down a bargaining agreement that discriminated against members of the craft or class on account of race. The Court found embedded in the principle of exclusive representation an implied obligation to represent employees fairly and without hostile discrimination. A wide range of discretion is accorded the union, but it must exercise that discretion "fairly, impartially, and in good faith."[230]

The duty of fair representation was also read into the representation provisions of the NLRA. An NLRA case, *Vaca v. Sipes*,[231] recognized the duty in a suit against a union for

---

[226]Union P. R.R. v. United Transp. Union, 3 F3d at 260–61. *Accord,* Delta Air Lines v. Air Line Pilots Ass'n, 861 F2d 665, 130 LRRM 2014.

[227]Northwest Airlines v. Air Line Pilots Ass'n, 808 F2d 76, 1214 LRRM 2300 (CA DC, 1987), *cert. denied,* 486 U.S. 1014, 128 LRRM 2296 (1988).

[228]808 F2d at 83. Those circuits that have vacated Adjustment Board awards on public policy grounds would presumably apply the same reasoning to NRAB awards. *See* Union P. R.R. v. United Transp. Union, 3 F3d 255, 144 LRRM 2027; Delta Air Lines v. Air Line Pilots Ass'n, 861 F2d 665, 130 LRRM 2014; *see also* Misco, Inc. v. Paperworkers, 768 F2d 739, 742–43, 120 LRRM 2119 (CA 5, 1985), *rev'd,* 484 U.S. 29, 126 LRRM 3113 (1987).

[229]323 U.S. 192 (1944).

[230]*Id.* at 204.

[231]386 U.S. 171, 64 LRRM 2369 (1967).

failing to take an employee's grievance to arbitration under an applicable bargaining agreement. Prohibited, according to the Court, is union conduct that is "arbitrary, discriminatory, or in bad faith."[232] In a later case, the Court held that the duty applies both to contract administration and to collective bargaining negotiations.[233]

A discussion of the contours of the union's duty of fair representation would require elaboration beyond the scope of this book.[234] This section's more modest objective is to explore a variety of issues where the duty to represent fairly and the RLA intersect.

An employee may have a claim against a union for breach of its duty of fair representation and also a dispute with the employer over the interpretation or application of a collective bargaining agreement. The issue then arises under what circumstances the courts have jurisdiction over the employer on the claim of breach of the agreement. Three Supreme Court RLA cases are of importance in answering this issue.

A. Supreme Court Cases

The first important decision on this issue under the RLA is a 1969 Supreme Court case, *Glover v. St. Louis-San Francisco Railway*,[235] in which the plaintiffs alleged that their employer and union had conspired to keep black employees from obtaining promotions to which they were entitled under the applicable collective bargaining agreement. The railroad argued that because the RLA gave the NRAB exclusive jurisdiction over the disputes "between an employee or group of employees and a carrier or carriers,"[236] the district court therefore had no jurisdiction over the carrier. The Supreme

---

[232]386 U.S. at 190.

[233]Air Line Pilots Ass'n v. O'Neill, 499 U.S. 65, 78, 136 LRRM 2721, 2726 (1991).

[234]*See generally* THE DEVELOPING LABOR LAW 1285–1358 (Patrick Hardin ed., 3d ed. 1992).

[235]393 U.S. 324, 70 LRRM 2097 (1969).

[236]RLA §3, First.

Court held that federal courts have jurisdiction over both unions and carriers, and that the jurisdiction extends to "discriminatory action in negotiating the terms of an agreement and discriminatory enforcement of terms that are fair on their face."[237] The Court explained that "although the employer is made a party to insure complete and meaningful relief, . . . in essence the 'dispute' is one between some employees on the one hand and the union and management together on the other."[238]

The railroad also argued that under the Court's 1967 decision in *Vaca v. Sipes*,[239] the action should be dismissed because the plaintiffs had failed to exhaust their remedies under the contract. The Supreme Court, however, stated that *Vaca* had identified at least two exceptions to the exhaustion doctrine, and that "the circumstances of the present case call into play another of the most obvious exceptions to the exhaustion requirement—the situation where the effort to proceed formally with contractual or administrative remedies would be wholly futile."[240] Finally, in response to the argument that in order to invoke federal court jurisdiction an employee must at least "attempt to exhaust contractual remedies," the Court held that the plaintiffs' consistent complaints to the union and to the employer had fulfilled this requirement.[241]

One year following *Glover*, in *Czosek v. O'Mara*,[242] the Supreme Court addressed the respective liability of employers and unions in a hybrid action in which the plaintiff alleged the union had breached the fair representation duty and the carrier had breached the bargaining agreement. The Court held that the union could properly be sued alone, but that the union could not be held liable for damages caused by

---

[237]393 U.S. at 329, 70 LRRM at 2099.
[238]393 U.S. at 329, 70 LRRM at 2098–99.
[239]386 U.S. 171, 64 LRRM 2369 (1967). The *Vaca* decision was decided under the NLRA, but the Supreme Court did not distinguish the case on this basis.
[240]393 U.S. at 330, 70 LRRM at 2099.
[241]393 U.S. at 331, 70 LRRM at 2099.
[242]397 U.S. 25, 73 LRRM 2481 (1970).

the employer's underlying wrongful discharge "except to the extent that its refusal to handle the grievances added to the difficulty and expense of collecting from the employer."[243] The Court declined to comment on the circumstances, if any, where an RLA employer can be made a party to such a suit:

> [W]e have no occasion to consider whether under federal law, which governs in cases like these, the employer may always be sued with the union when a single series of events gives rise to claims against the employer for breach of contract and against the union for breach of the duty of fair representation or whether, as the Court of Appeals held, when there are no allegations tying union and employer together, the union is suable in the District Court for breach of duty but resort must be had to the Adjustment Board for a remedy against the employer.[244]

Two years later, the Court held in *Andrews v. Louisville & Nashville Railroad*[245] that where the only source of a railroad employee's right not to be discharged was a collective bargaining agreement between the railroad and union, a discharged railroad employee who had not pursued the administrative remedies under the RLA could not bring an action against the railroad for damages for alleged wrongful discharge. No breach of the duty to represent fairly was presented in the case, but the emphasis on the exclusivity of the plaintiff's administrative remedies—resort to the NRAB— has been treated by some courts as of importance in deciding whether a carrier can be joined in a fair representation case.

B. Circuit Courts of Appeals Cases

Courts of appeals have varied widely in their interpretation and application of *Glover, Czosek,* and *Andrews.* The Dis-

---

[243] 397 U.S. at 29, 73 LRRM at 2482.
[244] *Id.*
[245] 406 U.S. 320, 80 LRRM 2240 (1972).

trict of Columbia,[246] Fourth,[247] and Eleventh[248] Circuits have
not recognized exceptions to the principle that railroad Adjustment Boards have exclusive jurisdiction over claims for
breach of collective bargaining agreements. The First Circuit,
although not discussing the conditions under which a federal
court has jurisdiction over a breach of contract claim against
a carrier, has held that there are strong reasons, if the plaintiff
establishes a breach of duty against the union, to remand
the claim to the Adjustment Board for consideration of the
breach of contract claim against the carrier.[249]

---

[246]Haney v. Chesapeake & O. R.R., 498 F2d 987, 991–92, 86 LRRM 2012,
2015–16 (CA DC, 1974). The court relied on the strong exclusivity policy announced
in *Andrews,* and on the fact that the plaintiff had the power to invoke administrative
remedies without the union's intervention. The court did not discuss any fair representation cases.

[247]Harrison v. United Transp. Union, 530 F2d 558, 90 LRRM 3265 (CA 4,
1975), *cert denied,* 425 U.S. 958, 92 LRRM 2168 (1976). The court stated:

[A]s a general rule, [the carrier is not] required to make certain that the union
fairly represents [the carrier's] employees. The case might be a different one
if [the plaintiff] had proved that [the carrier] and [the union] acted in concert
with the joint motive to discriminate against the employee, as was alleged in
Glover v. St. Louis-San Francisco Railway Co.

530 F2d at 561 (citation omitted).

[248]Rader v. United Transp. Union, 718 F2d 1012, 114 LRRM 3127 (CA 11,
1983). The court stated:

In this instance the only evidence of collusion that the plaintiff cites is the
failure of the Union to pursue his grievance. Since the Railway Labor Act
allows an employee to process a claim to [the] National Railway Adjustment
Board without the concurrence of the Union, this allegation is an insufficient
ground for allowing the plaintiff to avoid exhausting his administrative remedies. The *Glover* case on which the plaintiff relies may be distinguished from
the instant case as *Glover* involved systematic racial discrimination against a
group of employees by both the Union and the Railroad. We are bound by
the decision of the Supreme Court in *Andrews,* decided three years after *Glover,*
which requires an exhaustion of administrative remedies, without exception,
prior to pursuing an action in federal court.

718 F2d at 1014 (citation omitted).

Since the NRAB is not available to airline employees, this reasoning may be
inapplicable to airline carriers. No case has been found discussing this issue.

[249]Stanton v. Delta Air Lines, 669 F2d 833, 838, 109 LRRM 2739, 2742 (CA
1, 1982). The Fifth and Ninth Circuits have rejected efforts to establish jurisdiction
over the carrier on the basis that the employee had not established a breach of duty
of fair representation, without reaching when such a claim may be available. Trial
v. Atchison, T. & S.F. Ry., 896 F2d 120, 123, 133 LRRM 2868, 2870–71 (CA 5,
1990); Morales v. Southern Pac. Transp. Co., 894 F2d 743, 133 LRRM 2690 (CA
5, 1990); Bautista v. Pan Am. World Airlines, 828 F2d 546, 126 LRRM 2559 (CA
9, 1987).

Two circuits, the Eighth[250] and Tenth,[251] have held that the federal courts must take jurisdiction over a railroad employer in a hybrid action where the plaintiff alleges collusion between the employer and the union, or where the employer is "tied to" the union's breach of the duty.[252] However, the mere allegation that the employer and union have engaged in collusion does not establish federal court jurisdiction.[253] For example, the fact that the union and employer agree on an interpretation of the contract that is different from that of the employee does not constitute collusion.[254] Similarly, although some courts applying the collusion exception have expressed the concern that an employee will not receive a fair hearing from a board composed of the parties accused of colluding,[255] the fact that an Adjustment Board consists

---

[250]Raus v. Railway Carmen, 663 F2d 791, 108 LRRM 2994 (CA 8, 1981); Hunt v. Missouri P. R.R., 729 F2d 578, 115 LRRM 3388 (CA 8, 1984) (quoting *Raus*). In *Raus*, the court wrote:

> [W]here there are good faith allegations and facts supporting those allegations indicating collusion or otherwise tying the railroad and the union together in allegedly arbitrary, discriminatory or bad faith conduct amounting to a breach of the duty of fair representation, the district court has jurisdiction over the union on the fair representation claim and over the railroad on the contract violation claim.

663 F2d at 798 (footnote omitted).

[251]Hodges v. Atchison, T. & S.F. Ry., 728 F2d 414, 417, 115 LRRM 3222, 3224 (CA 10), *cert. denied*, 469 U.S. 822, 117 LRRM 2551 (1984); Richins v. Southern Pac. Co., 620 F2d 761, 762, 104 LRRM 2291, 2292 (CA 10, 1980), *cert. denied*, 449 U.S. 1110, 106 LRRM 2200 (1981). In *Richins*, the court also suggested that jurisdiction over the carrier might be warranted because "full relief in federal court" could not be secured in the carrier's absence. 620 F2d at 762, 104 LRRM 2292–93.

[252]In Steffens v. Railway & Steamship Clerks, 797 F2d 442, 123 LRRM 2065 (CA 7, 1986), the court did not reach the issue of when the carrier may be sued, but it implicitly embraced a collusion theory:

> There is disagreement over whether the plaintiff needs to allege that the employer is in some way involved in the union's breach . . .—but we need not reach this question here since the plaintiffs did allege collusion between the [carrier] and [the union] to defeat their rights under the collective bargaining agreement.

797 F2d at 445 n.2.

[253]Transport Workers v. American Airlines, 413 F2d 746, 751, 71 LRRM 2789, 2792 (CA 10, 1969).

[254]Capraro v. United Parcel Serv., 993 F2d 328, 143 LRRM 2260 (CA 3, 1993) (preemption case).

[255]Dean v. Trans World Airlines, 924 F2d 805, 136 LRRM 2273 (CA 9, 1991); Middleton v. CSX Corp., 694 F Supp 941, 948, 129 LRRM 2328 (SD Ga, 1988).

principally of company and union representatives does not by itself excuse the employee from utilizing the grievance procedure to settle a contractual dispute.[256] Finally, it has been held that the fact that the duty of fair representation claim will not survive summary judgment forecloses a claim against the carrier.[257]

Three other circuits—the Second,[258] Third,[259] and Sixth[260]—have adopted an alternative position. The Sixth Circuit in *Atkins v. Louisville & Nashville Railroad* summarized this position:

> It is clear that when arbitration is mandatory, an employee must at least attempt to use and exhaust the contractual grievance procedure before seeking judicial review of his claim. . . . However, there are several exceptions to the exhaustion requirement, as the Supreme Court first recognized in Vaca v. Sipes, 386 U.S. 171 (1967). In *Vaca*, the Court specified at least two situations in which suit could be brought by an employee despite failing to fully exhaust contractual remedies: (1) when the union has the "sole power" under the contract to invoke the upper level grievance procedures and yet prevents an employee from exhausting contractual remedies by wrongfully refusing to process the employee's grievance in violation of its duty of fair representation; and (2) when the employer's conduct amounts to a repudiation of the remedial procedures specified in the contract. . . . The Supreme Court recognized yet a third exception from the exhaustion requirement in Glover v. St. Louis-San Francisco Railway Co., 393 U.S. 324 (1969). That exception arises "where the effort to

---

[256]Atkins v. Louisville & N. R.R., 819 F2d 644, 650, 125 LRRM 2722, 2726–27 (CA 6, 1987); Haney v. Chesapeake & O. R.R., 498 F2d 987, 991–92, 86 LRRM 2012, 2015–16 (CA DC, 1974); Wells v. Southern Airways, 616 F2d 107, 110, 104 LRRM 2338 (CA 5), *cert. denied*, 449 U.S. 862 (1980).

[257]Bautista v. Pan Am. World Airlines, 828 F2d 546, 126 LRRM 2559 (CA 9, 1987).

[258]Schum v. South Buffalo Ry., 496 F2d 328, 86 LRRM 2459 (CA 2, 1974).

[259]Childs v. Pennsylvania Fed'n Maintenance of Way Employees, 831 F2d 429, 438, 126 LRRM 2777 (CA 3, 1987); Masy v. New Jersey Transit Rail Operations, 790 F2d 322, 122 LRRM 2700 (CA 3), *cert. denied*, 479 U.S. 916, 125 LRRM 3216 (1986); Sisco v. Consolidated Rail Corp., 732 F2d 1188, 1190, 116 LRRM 2097 (CA 3, 1984).

[260]Atkins v. Louisville & N. R.R., 819 F2d 644, 125 LRRM 2722; *see also* Kaschak v. Consolidated Rail Corp., 707 F2d 902, 113 LRRM 2760 (CA 6, 1983).

proceed formally with contractual or administrative remedies would be wholly futile." Id. at 330. The Court found this third exception to be applicable in the case before it since the plaintiffs had alleged racial discrimination on the part of the grievance decisionmaking body, which prevented fair resolution of their grievances.[261]

The repudiation exception, which would permit the federal courts to assert jurisdiction when the employer refuses to process a grievance through the contractual grievance procedure, has seldom been invoked.[262] Some courts have questioned whether the Adjustment Board procedures could ever be repudiated under the RLA because they are statutorily mandated.[263]

The futility exception has been infrequently invoked in circumstances not involving collusion between the union and the employer, and some cases appear to use the terms "futility" and "collusion" interchangeably.[264] Some decisions have refused to apply the futility exception where the employee could have processed his or her own grievance without assistance or approval from the union,[265] as is so with the NRAB.[266] One Third Circuit case stated that the court would find futility where there was "prejudice" or "predisposition" by the Adjustment Board;[267] however, another Third Circuit case em-

---

[261]Atkins v. Louisville & N. R.R., 819 F2d 644, 649–50, 125 LRRM 2722, 2726–27 (CA 6, 1987).

[262]The Ninth Circuit in Dean v. Trans World Airlines, 924 F2d 805, 136 LRRM 2273 (CA 9, 1991), refers to "evidence of repudiation," but the holding of the decision was that there was evidence to support a jury's finding of futility in a duty of fair representation action in which the union claimed a failure to exhaust administrative remedies to challenge a dues assessment.

[263]See, e.g., Stanton v. Delta Air Lines, 669 F2d 833, 838, 109 LRRM 2739, 2742 (CA 1, 1982).

[264]Childs v. Pennsylvania Fed'n Maintenance of Way Employees, 831 F2d 429, 438, 126 LRRM 2777 (CA 3, 1987). See also Masy v. New Jersey Transit Rail Operations, 790 F2d 322, 122 LRRM 2700 (CA 3), cert. denied, 479 U.S. 916, 125 LRRM 3216 (1986); Raus v. Railway Carmen, 663 F2d 791, 108 LRRM 2994 (CA 8, 1981).

[265]Atkins v. Louisville & N. R.R., 819 F2d at 650, 125 LRRM at 2726–27; Masy v. New Jersey Transit Rail Operations, 790 F2d 322, 122 LRRM 2700. See also Hoffman v. Missouri P. R.R., 806 F2d 800, 124 LRRM 2139 (CA 8, 1986).

[266]See 45 USC §184 (1986).

[267]Childs v. Pennsylvania Fed'n Maintenance of Way Employees, 831 F2d 429, 438, 126 LRRM 2777.

phasized that the fact that the employee will likely lose on the merits does not constitute futility for the purposes of the exception.[268] The Third Circuit has further held that where the core of the dispute between the employee, on one hand, and the employer and union, on the other, involves a question of contract interpretation, the exception does not apply at all.[269] Courts addressing the issue have imposed a burden on plaintiffs at the pleading stage to allege facts supporting the futility claim.[270]

The exception involving the union's breach of duty of fair representation has been invoked where the union has failed to process a grievance, or has done so only perfunctorily, in violation of its duty of fair representation. Some courts have applied this exception and have permitted the employee to assert a claim in federal court against the employer, even though the employer played no part in the breakdown of the administrative process,[271] but others have held that the employer must be implicated in the union's breach of duty.[272]

Certain courts have recognized a "fourth exception" in cases where the employer is not implicated, allowing the employer to be joined where it is not involved in the union's breach "but the employer's presence is necessary for complete relief."[273] One court has asserted that where no facts tie the employer to the plaintiff's claim, but the employer's presence is necessary for complete relief, it is appropriate to assert jurisdiction over the employer for the purpose of ordering

---

[268]Capraro v. United Parcel Serv., 993 F2d 328, 335 n.11, 143 LRRM 2260 (CA 3, 1993) (preemption case).

[269]Goclowski v. Penn Cent. Transp. Co., 571 F2d 747, 97 LRRM 2563 (CA 3, 1977).

[270]Hunt v. Missouri P. R.R., 729 F2d 578, 115 LRRM 3388 (CA 8, 1984); Raus v. Railway Carmen, 663 F2d 791, 108 LRRM 2994 (CA 8, 1981); Transport Workers v. American Airlines, 413 F2d 746, 751, 71 LRRM 2789, 2792 (CA 10, 1969).

[271]Schum v. South Buffalo Ry., 496 F2d 328, 332, 86 LRRM 2459, 2461–62 (CA 2, 1987).

[272]Sisco v. Consolidated Rail Corp., 732 F2d 1188, 1190, 116 LRRM 2097 (CA 3, 1984).

[273]Masy v. New Jersey Transit Rail Operations, 790 F2d 322, 327, 122 LRRM 2700 (CA 3), cert. denied, 479 U.S. 916, 125 LRRM 3216 (1986); Kaschak v. Consolidated Rail Corp., 707 F2d 902, 113 LRRM 2760 (CA 6, 1983).

arbitration, but the court should itself adjudicate the contractual dispute.[274] Other cases have allowed broader relief.[275]

The courts that have recognized exceptions to the rule requiring exhaustion of administrative remedies have frequently stated that these exceptions do not allow the employee to select the forum to process a grievance.[276] In *Glover*, however, the Supreme Court stated that where the carrier and the union are "working 'hand-in-glove,'" repeated complaints by the employees to the union will satisfy exhaustion requirements.[277] The courts of appeals have relaxed the exhaustion requirement even further.[278] Because hybrid claims depend

---

[274]Masy v. New Jersey Transit Rail Operations, 790 F2d at 327.

[275]In Kaschak v. Consolidated Rail Corp., 707 F2d 902, 113 LRRM 2760, the court of appeals stated:

If [the district] court finds that [the plaintiff] was relying upon his union to process his grievance, that such reliance was reasonable in the circumstances and that it was that reliance which caused his failure to personally present his claim to the [NRAB], the action against [the carrier] would then be properly cognizable in federal court.

707 F2d at 903.

[276]*See, e.g., id.* at 913.

[277]The full text of the Court's remarks on this point are as follows:

To process a grievance with the Company without the cooperation of the Brotherhood would be a useless formality. To take the grievance before the National Railroad Adjustment Board (a tribunal composed of paid representatives from the Companies and the Brotherhoods) would consume an average time of five years, and would be completely futile under the instant circumstances where the Company and the Brotherhood are working "hand-in-glove." All of these purported administrative remedies are wholly inadequate, and to require their complete exhaustion would simply add to plaintiffs' expense and frustration, would exhaust plaintiffs, and would amount to a denial of "due process of law," prohibited by the Constitution of the United States.

Glover v. St. Louis-S.F. Ry., 393 U.S. 324, 327, 70 LRRM 2097 (1969). The Court was also persuaded that on the facts of the case—involving racial discrimination—the NRAB lacked the power to award full relief. 393 U.S. at 329.

[278]In Kaschak v. Consolidated Rail Corp., 707 F2d 902, 113 LRRM 2760 (CA 6, 1983), the court allowed the case to proceed against the carrier and the union because the plaintiff alleged that he reasonably relied on his union to carry his grievance to the NRAB. The court did not require a showing of a "hand-in-glove" relationship, and the carrier was not involved in the failure to file the grievance. *Accord,* Schum v. South Buffalo Ry., 496 F2d 328, 86 LRRM 2459 (CA 2, 1974); Dean v. Trans World Airlines, 924 F2d 805, 810–11, 136 LRRM 2273, 2276–77 (CA 9, 1991) (repeated requests to the union sufficient, where the airline union controlled the grievance procedure). One court sustained the dismissal of an employee suit against a union and a carrier where the employees alleged the exhaustion of their contract remedies would have been futile, but the employees did not request

upon the assertion of a breach of the duty of fair representation claim against the union, several courts have held that if the claim against the union is dismissed, the claim against the employer must also be dismissed.[279]

Although most hybrid cases involve a breach of duty of fair representation claim against the union and a breach of contract claim against the employer, where the alleged breach of fair representation took place in negotiating an agreement, courts have asserted that an employer could be independently liable for "collusion" in the union's breach of duty.[280] In all of these decisions, however, the courts have dismissed the claim on the basis that the facts—in particular, the carrier's negotiation with the union—did not establish "collusion."[281]

---

the union to file a grievance on their behalf. Morales v. Southern Pac. Transp. Co., 894 F2d 743, 133 LRRM 2690 (CA 5, 1990).

[279]Bautista v. Pan Am. World Airlines, 828 F2d 546, 126 LRRM 2559 (CA 9, 1987); see also Hodges v. Atchison, T. & S.F. Ry., 728 F2d 414, 417, 115 LRRM 3222, 3224 (CA 10) (union not named a defendant and no collusion between union and carrier alleged), cert. denied, 469 U.S. 822, 117 LRRM 2551 (1984). In Kaschak v. Consolidated Rail Corp., 707 F2d 902, 113 LRRM 2760, the plaintiff alleged that the union had failed to represent him fairly by failing to file a timely grievance on his behalf, and that the carrier had breached the bargaining agreement, but the union was not made a party to the suit. The court allowed the case to go forward.

[280]E.g., Rakestraw v. United Airlines, 765 F Supp 474, 137 LRRM 2586 (ND Ill, 1991), aff'd in part and rev'd in part, 981 F2d 1524, 142 LRRM 2054 (CA 7, 1992), cert. denied, 144 LRRM 2392 (1993); United Indep. Flight Officers v. United Air Lines, 572 F Supp 1494, 1508, 114 LRRM 3347 (ND Ill, 1983), aff'd, 756 F2d 1274, 119 LRRM 2301 (CA 7, 1985).

[281]Id.

CHAPTER 6

EXERCISE OF ECONOMIC WEAPONS

The right of carriers and unions to use economic weapons before the exhaustion of the RLA's major dispute procedures is treated in an earlier chapter.[1] This chapter treats the use of economic weapons after the exhaustion of major dispute procedures.

I. PRIMARY PRESSURES BY UNIONS

Once the parties have exhausted the RLA's major dispute resolution machinery, a union can utilize the "full range of peaceful economic power [it] can muster, so long as its use conflicts with no other obligation imposed by federal law,"[2] regardless of whether the carrier has engaged in any form of self-help.[3] The Supreme Court has stated that "we should hesitate to imply limitations on all but those forms of self-help that strike a fundamental blow to union or employer activity and the collective bargaining process itself."[4]

---

[1]*See* Chapter 4, "Negotiation of Collective Bargaining Agreements," §§VIII, IX.

[2]Railroad Trainmen v. Jacksonville Terminal Co., 394 U.S. 369, 392, 70 LRRM 2961, 1969 (1969); *see also* Chapter 4, "Negotiation of Collective Bargaining Agreements," §§VIII, IX.

[3]Locomotive Eng'rs v. Baltimore & O. R.R., 372 U.S. 284, 52 LRRM 2524 (1963).

[4]Trans World Airlines v. Flight Attendants (IFFA), 489 U.S. 426, 442, 130 LRRM 2657 (1989).

Thus, the test to determine the legality of particular forms of self-help under the RLA has been whether that conduct is expressly prohibited by the RLA or some other applicable law. Withholding services and peaceful picketing are clearly permissible.[5] Some conduct that might be unlawful or unprotected under the National Labor Relations Act (NLRA) has thus been deemed lawful under the RLA (for example, certain secondary pressures).[6] Some courts have held that intermittent strikes, whereby employees withhold services for a period of time, come back to work, and then leave again sometime later, are permissible.[7] Picket line violence may be enjoined under appropriate state laws.[8]

In the railroad industry, where much of the collective bargaining is done on a national, multicarrier basis, unions sometimes engage in selective strikes against one or a small number of carriers in an attempt to obtain an agreement with all of the carriers. Such selective strikes are lawful and may not be enjoined during the self-help period unless the goal of the strikes is to get a carrier to leave an established practice of national bargaining and reach its own agreement with the organizations.[9]

---

[5]Railroad Trainmen v. Jacksonville Terminal Co., 394 U.S. 369, 70 LRRM 2961; Railway & Steamship Clerks v. Florida E. C. Ry., 384 U.S. 238, 62 LRRM 2177 (1966); Locomotive Eng'rs v. Baltimore & O. R.R., 372 U.S. 284, 52 LRRM 2524; Railroad Telegraphers v. Chicago & N. W. R.R., 362 U.S. 330, 45 LRRM 3104 (1960).

One court has held that a military no-strike clause, by which the union agrees not to strike military flights after the contract has expired and/or RLA procedures have been exhausted, is binding and valid under the RLA. Trans Int'l Airlines v. Teamsters, 650 F2d 949, 960, 104 LRRM 2619 (CA 9), amended, 104 LRRM 2619 (CA 9, 1980), cert. denied, 449 U.S. 1110 (1981). The Norris-LaGuardia Act prohibits enforcing the clause by injunction, however. Id.

[6]Railroad Trainmen v. Jacksonville Terminal, 394 U.S. at 386–90; see also infra §II.

[7]Pan Am. World Airways v. Teamsters, 894 F2d 36, 133 LRRM 2292 (CA 2, 1990); Flight Attendants (AFA) v. Alaska Airlines, 847 F Supp 832 (WD Wash, 1993).

[8]Railroad Trainmen v. Jacksonville Terminal Co., 394 U.S. 369, 385–86, 70 LRRM 2961 (1969).

[9]Deleware & H. Ry. v. United Transp. Union, 450 F2d 603, 611, 76 LRRM 2900 (CA DC), cert. denied, 403 U.S. 911, 77 LRRM 2404 (1971); Machinists v. National Ry. Labor Conference, 310 F Supp 905, 73 LRRM 2594 (D DC, 1970), appeal dismissed, 463 F2d 872, 79 LRRM 3028 (CA DC, 1972).

II. SECONDARY PRESSURES

During the self-help period, a union may exert pressure against a carrier by picketing another carrier or a non-RLA employer, or a union with a dispute with a non-RLA employer may picket a carrier. Each of these actions is referred to as "secondary activity," meaning that it is directed at an entity (the secondary employer) with which the union has no dispute. Whereas the NLRA specifically addresses secondary activity,[10] the RLA is silent on the matter.[11]

Several variables are present in the applicable cases, including (1) whether the union is an "NLRA union" or an "RLA union"; (2) whether the employer is a carrier (an "RLA employer") or a noncarrier (an "NLRA employer"); and (3) whether the challenged conduct is economic pressure, such as a strike or picketing, or the maintaining of an employer/union agreement.

A. Economic Pressure Against RLA Employers

When employees of an RLA carrier picket another RLA carrier, so long as the employees may lawfully engage in self-help against their employer, the RLA does not prohibit secondary picketing against another carrier.[12]

Before 1959, the position of the National Labor Relations Board (NLRB) was that the NLRA did not apply to secondary pressure directed by an NLRA union against an RLA em-

---

[10]NLRA §8(b)(4)(B), (e). The details of the secondary boycott sections of the NLRA are beyond the scope of this book. *See* THE DEVELOPING LABOR LAW Ch. 22 (Patrick Hardin ed., 3d ed. 1992).

[11]Burlington N. Ry. v. Maintenance of Way Employees, 481 U.S. 429, 439–40, 125 LRRM 2073 (1987).

[12]Burlington N. Ry. v. Maintenance of Way Employees, 481 U.S. 429, 125 LRRM 2073; Consolidated Rai' Corp. v. Maintenance of Way Employees, 792 F2d 303, 122 LRRM 2679 (CA 2, 1986), *cert. denied*, 481 U.S. 1036, 125 LRRM 2224 (1987); United Air Lines v. Teamsters, 874 F2d 110, 131 LRRM 2329 (CA 2, 1989); *see also* Railroad Trainmen v. Jacksonville Terminal Co., 394 U.S. 369, 70 LRRM 2961 (state court may not enjoin secondary picketing in this situation); Blyer v. Teamsters, 656 F Supp 1158, 126 LRRM 2104 (ED NY, 1987) (federal court may not invoke §10(e) of the NLRA to enjoin secondary picketing in this situation).

ployer.[13] In 1959 amendments to the NLRA, however, Congress extended the protection against secondary economic pressure by NLRA unions—picketing and the inducement of strikes—to RLA employers.[14] Absent unusual circumstances, however, the NLRA does not prevent RLA unions from bringing secondary pressure against RLA employers.[15]

B. Economic Pressure Against NLRA Employers

While the NLRA prohibits NLRA unions from bringing certain secondary pressures against both NLRA and RLA employers, the pre-1959 NLRA did not include RLA unions in its statutory definition of "union" and "labor organization," and thus the NLRA was interpreted not to apply to secondary pressures brought by RLA unions.[16] Although the definition of the target of a secondary boycott was expanded in 1959 to cover RLA employers, the definitions of "union" and "labor organization" were left unchanged.[17] The Second Circuit has held that notwithstanding the fact that the statutory definitions were left intact, the NLRA applies to secondary pressure brought by an RLA union against an NLRA employer.[18] The NLRB's General Counsel disagrees, refusing to issue second-

---

[13]International Rice Milling, 84 NLRB 360 (1949), *enforcement denied,* 183 F2d 21, 25 (CA 5), *rev'd on other grounds,* 341 U.S. 665 (1951).

[14]*See* NLRA §8(b)(4)(B); Machinists (Luftansa German Airlines), 197 NLRB 232, 80 LRRM 1305 (1972), *enforced sub nom.* Marriott Corp. v. NLRB, 491 F2d 367, 85 LRRM 2257 (CA 9), *cert. denied,* 419 U.S. 881, 87 LRRM 2397 (1974).

[15]*See* Railroad Trainmen v. Jacksonville Terminal Co., 394 U.S. 369, 377, 70 LRRM 2961 (1969). In dicta, the Court intimated the possibility that the NLRA might apply "where railway organizations act as agents for, or as joint ventures with, unions subject to the NLRA, see IBEW v. NLRB, 350 F2d 791 (CA DC, 1965); or where railway unions are engaged in a dispute on behalf of their nonrail employees; or where a rail carrier seeks a remedy against the conduct of nonrailway employees, see United Steelworkers of America v. NLRB, 376 U.S. 492, 501 (1964); IBT Local 25 v. New York, N.H. & H.R. Co., 350 U.S. 155 (1956)." *Id.*

[16]*See* Railroad Trainmen v. Jacksonville Terminal Co., 394 U.S. at 377 n.10.

[17]*Id.*

[18]Marriott In-Flight Servs. v. Transport Workers Local 504, 557 F2d 295, 95 LRRM 2609 (CA 2, 1977). In that case an RLA carrier proposed to subcontract work to an independent that had been done by its RLA employees. The union protested, but the subcontracting went forward. The union then picketed the subcontractor, an NLRA employer.

ary boycott complaints against RLA unions for engaging in secondary picketing against NLRA employers.[19]

In *Machinists (Lufthansa German Airlines)*,[20] the employer, an RLA carrier, purchased meals from an NLRA employer. When the Machinists' Union, which represented the carrier's employees, objected, the carrier signed an agreement with the union that, in effect, promised that meals would be purchased from unionized companies. The agreement was challenged under the NLRA's secondary boycott provisions,[21] and the union argued that it was an RLA union, not subject to the NLRA. The NLRB disagreed, holding that the union was subject to the NLRA because 88 percent of its members were NLRA employees, 96 percent of its bargaining agreements were with NLRA employers, and the "dispute [was] not over the terms and conditions of employment of airline employees."[22] The NLRB's General Counsel has stated that a union is not an NLRA union where 86 percent of its members are RLA employees.[23]

C. Hot Cargo Agreements

A hot cargo agreement is an agreement between an employer and a union in which the employer agrees not to do business with a second employer.[24] Prior to 1959, such an agreement was not per se unlawful,[25] but the 1959 NLRA amendments added Section 8(e) to make such employer/union agreements an unfair labor practice. The NLRB originally held that Section 8(e) applied to agreements between

---

[19]*See* Air Line Pilots Ass'n (Keg S., Inc.), Case 12-CC-1217 (Gen. Couns. Advice Mem., Dec. 27, 1990); Longshoremen (ILA) (Armco, Inc.), Case 8-CC-966 (Gen. Couns. Advice Mem. Aug. 24, 1979); Air Line Pilots Ass'n (employer), Case 7-CC-1016 (Gen. Couns. Advice Mem., July 24, 1979).

[20]197 NLRB 232, 80 LRRM 1305 (1972), *enforced subnom.* Marriott Corp. v. NLRB, 491 F2d 367, 85 LRRM 2257 (CA 9), *cert. denied*, 419 U.S. 881, 87 LRRM 2397 (1974).

[21]Section 8(e), discussed *infra* §II.C.

[22]80 LRRM at 1305, 1311.

[23]Air Line Pilots Ass'n (Keg S., Inc.), Case 12-CC-1217.

[24]*See generally* National Woodwork Mfrs. Ass'n v. NLRB, 386 U.S. 612 (1967).

[25]Carpenters Local 1976 v. NLRB, 357 U.S. 93 (1958).

an NLRA union and a non-NLRA employer, such as an RLA carrier,[26] but later reversed itself.[27]

III. Sympathy Strikes

Although neither the NLRA nor the RLA uses the term "sympathy strike," courts generally use the term in reference to concerted activity by one employee group for the purpose of aiding another employee group that is engaged in a labor dispute.[28] Sympathy strikes in which employees refuse to cross a picket line can arise in a variety of factual contexts, including where the employees engaging in the sympathy activity

- belong to the same union and work for the same carrier as the group of employees who are engaged in the primary strike,[29]

- belong to a different union or to no union at all but work for the same carrier as the picketing employees,[30]

---

[26]Machinists (Luftansa German Airlines), 197 NLRB 232, 80 LRRM 1305 (1972), *enforced sub nom.* Marriott v. NLRB, 491 F2d 367, 85 LRRM 2257 (CA 9), *cert. denied,* 419 U.S. 881, 87 LRRM 2397 (1974).

[27]Electrical Workers (IBEW) Local 3 (N.Y. Elec. Contractors Ass'n), 244 NLRB 357, 102 LRRM 1285 (1979).

[28]*See, e.g.,* Buffalo Forge Co. v. Steelworkers, 428 U.S. 397, 400, 407, 92 LRRM 3032 (1976); Trans Int'l Airlines v. Teamsters, 650 F2d 949, 954, 103 LRRM 2669 (CA 9), *cert. denied,* 449 U.S. 1110, 106 LRRM 2200 (1981); Northwest Airlines v. Air Line Pilots Ass'n, 442 F2d 246, 247–48, 77 LRRM 2102 (CA 8), *aff'd on reh'g,* 442 F2d 251, 77 LRRM 2116 (CA 8), *cert. denied,* 404 U.S. 871, 78 LRRM 2464 (1971); Railroad Trainmen v. Atlantic Coast Line R.R., 362 F2d 649, 654, 62 LRRM 2393 (CA 5), *aff'd,* 385 U.S. 20, 63 LRRM 2296 (1966); Locomotive Firemen & Enginemen v. Florida E. C. Ry., 346 F2d 673, 674–75, 59 LRRM 2476 (CA 5, 1965); Machinists v. Northwest Airlines, 304 F2d 206, 209, 50 LRRM 2499 (CA 8, 1962); NLRB v. Peter Cailler Kohler Swiss Chocolates Co., 130 F2d 503, 505–06, 10 LRRM 852 (CA 2, 1942); Eastern Air Lines v. Air Line Pilots Ass'n, 710 F Supp 1342, 132 LRRM 2127 (SD Fla), *aff'd mem.,* 136 LRRM 2392 (CA 11, 1989); Trans World Airlines v. Machinists, 629 F Supp 1554, 1556, 127 LRRM 3186 (WD Mo, 1986); Northwest Airlines v. Transport Workers, 190 F Supp 495, 496, 47 LRRM 2473 (WD Wash, 1961).

[29]*See* Trans Int'l Airlines v. Teamsters, 650 F2d 949, 103 LRRM 2669.

[30]*See* Eastern Air Lines v. Air Line Pilots Ass'n, 710 F Supp 1342, 132 LRRM 2127; Arthur v. United Air Lines, 655 F Supp 363, 126 LRRM 2082 (D Colo, 1987).

- belong to the same union as the picketing employees but work for a carrier that is a target of secondary picketing,[31] or

- belong to a different union from that of the picketing employees and work for a carrier that is a target of secondary picketing.[32]

The action of sympathy strikers is generally an expression of union solidarity stemming from the notion "that by their action each one of them assures himself, in case his turn ever comes, of the support of the one whom they are all then helping."[33] Traditionally, unions have picketed with the expectation that other union members will honor picket lines by not crossing them.[34] Employees honoring a picket line as a mere pretext for furthering their interests in a primary dispute with their employer may be engaging in unlawful self-help.[35]

The majority of the circuits to have addressed the issue have held that, notwithstanding the limitations set forth in the Norris-LaGuardia Act on the availability of injunctive relief against a strike,[36] so long as a carrier advances at least an arguable contractual basis for contending that a union

---

[31]*See* Northwest Airlines v. Machinists, 712 F Supp 732, 133 LRRM 2038 (D Minn, 1989); Western Md. R.R. v. System Bd. of Adjustment, 465 F Supp 963 (D Md, 1979).

[32]*See* Southeastern Pa. Transp. Auth. v. Railroad Signalmen, 882 F2d 778, 132 LRRM 2094 (CA 3), *cert. denied*, 493 U.S. 1044, 133 LRRM 2264 (1990); Long Island R.R. v. Machinists, 874 F2d 901, 131 LRRM 2001 (CA 2), *cert. denied*, 493 U.S. 1042, 133 LRRM 2264 (1990).

[33]NLRB v. Peter Cailler Kohler Swiss Chocolates Co., 130 F2d 503, 505, 10 LRRM 852 (CA 2, 1942).

[34]*See* Western Md. R.R. v. System Bd. of Adjustment, 465 F Supp at 975. In one case the National Railroad Adjustment Board took "official notice" of the fact that in the railroad industry, regardless of individual workers' motives, "union members will not usually cross a picket line." NRAB Second Div. Award No. 4494, at 618 (Mar. 26, 1964) (citing to, and quoting from, various treatises on labor relations and labor economics).

[35]Eastern Air Lines v. Air Line Pilots Ass'n, 710 F Supp 1342, 132 LRRM 2127 (SD Fla) (not unlawful self-help to respect picket line of a striking union when carrier did not carry its burden of establishing that union would not have honored picket line but for its own dispute with carrier), *aff'd mem.*, 136 LRRM 2392 (CA 11, 1989).

[36]29 USC §§101–15 (1988).

cannot engage in a sympathy strike, the dispute over the union's right to do so is a minor one that must first be arbitrated.[37] Other courts have reached a different result, holding that the Norris-LaGuardia Act bars injunctive relief against a sympathy strike under the RLA.[38]

IV. Implementing a Bargaining Proposal

Once the major dispute procedures have been exhausted, the obligation to maintain the status quo with respect to the matters that are in dispute[39] ceases, and the RLA permits the parties "to employ the full range of whatever peaceful economic power they can muster, so long as its use conflicts with no other obligation imposed by federal law."[40] A carrier's self-help rights in this circumstance include the power to implement unilaterally any proposed changes that were raised and exhausted through the major dispute procedures.[41]

---

[37]Southeastern Pa. Transp. Auth. v. Railroad Signalmen, 882 F2d 778, 132 LRRM 2094 (CA 3, 1989), cert. denied, 493 U.S. 1044, 133 LRRM 2264 (1990); Long Island R.R. v. Machinists, 874 F2d 901, 131 LRRM 2001 (CA 2, 1989), cert. denied, 493 U.S. 1042, 133 LRRM 2264 (1990); Trans Int'l Airlines v. Teamsters, 650 F2d 949, 104 LRRM 3142 (CA 9, 1980), cert. denied, 449 U.S. 1110, 106 LRRM 2200 (1981); Northwest Airlines v. Machinists, 442 F2d 244, 77 LRRM 2100 (CA 8, 1970); Machinists v. Northwest Airlines, 304 F2d 206, 50 LRRM 2499 (CA 8, 1962); Chicago & I. M. Ry. v. Railroad Trainmen, 315 F2d 771, 52 LRRM 2627 (CA 7), vacated as moot, 375 U.S. 18, 54 LRRM 2314 (1963); Burlington N. Ry. v. Maintenance of Way Employees, 791 F Supp 744, 143 LRRM 2293 (ND Ill, 1992). See also Wien Air Alaska v. Teamsters, 93 LRRM 2934 (D Alaska, 1976); Chicago & N. W. Ry. v. Railway & Steamship Clerks, 99 LRRM 3072 (ND Ill, 1978).

[38]Eastern Air Lines v. Air Line Pilots Ass'n, 710 F Supp 1342, 132 LRRM 2127; Locomotive Firemen & Enginemen v. Florida E. C. Ry., 346 F2d 673, 59 LRRM 2476 (CA 5, 1965); Eastern Air Lines v. Flight Eng'rs, 340 F2d 104, 58 LRRM 2174 (CA 5), cert. denied, 382 U.S. 811, 60 LRRM 233 (1965); Railroad Trainmen v. Atlantic Coast Line R.R., 362 F2d 649, 62 LRRM 2393 (CA 5), aff'd by an equally divided Court, 385 U.S. 20, 63 LRRM 2296 (1966).

[39]See Chapter 4, "Negotiation of Collective Bargaining Agreements," §VIII.

[40]Railroad Trainmen v. Jacksonville Terminal Co., 394 U.S. 369, 392, 70 LRRM 2961, 2969 (1969). See also Trans World Airlines v. Flight Attendants (IFFA), 489 U.S. 426, 442, 130 LRRM 2657, 2663 (1989).

[41]Railway & Steamship Clerks v. Florida E. C. Ry., 384 U.S. 238, 244–45, 62 LRRM 2177, 2179 (1966); Locomotive Eng'rs v. Baltimore & O. R.R., 372 U.S. 284, 291, 52 LRRM 2524, 2526 (1963).

As a general rule, unless the carrier has proposed a change pursuant to Section 6, Section 2, Seventh bars unilateral changes during self-help periods.[42] During a strike, however, a carrier's obligation under Section 2, Seventh is qualified by its duty as a common carrier to make all reasonable efforts to continue to provide transportation services.[43] Thus, during a strike a carrier, in addition to implementing unilaterally proposals that have been exhausted through the major dispute procedures, may make any other changes in conditions established by agreements that are "reasonably necessary" to continue operations.[44] The Supreme Court has emphasized, however, that this standard must be construed strictly, and that "a district court called upon to grant a carrier relief from the provisions of a collective bargaining agreement should satisfy itself that the carrier is engaged in a good faith effort to restore service to the public, and not, e.g., using the strike to curtail that service."[45]

The departures from collective bargaining agreements that have been approved under the "reasonably necessary" standard include permanent replacement of strikers where that would arguably be inconsistent with an otherwise applicable agreement,[46] paying replacements more than the applica-

---

[42]Railway & Steamship Clerks v. Florida E. C. Ry., 384 U.S. at 244–45, 62 LRRM at 2179. See also Trans World Airlines v. Flight Attendants (IFFA), 809 F2d 483, 484, 124 LRRM 2364 (CA 8, 1987), aff'd mem. by an equally divided Court, 485 U.S. 175, 127 LRRM 2740 (1988); EEOC v. United Air Lines, 755 F2d 94, 98 (CA 7, 1985); Florida E. C. Ry. v. Railroad Trainmen, 336 F2d 172, 182, 56 LRRM 3009, 3015 (CA 5, 1964), cert. denied, 379 U.S. 990, 58 LRRM 2256 (1965).

[43]Railway & Steamship Clerks v. Florida E. C. Ry., 384 U.S. at 244–45, 62 LRRM at 2179 (rail carriers); Air Line Pilots Ass'n v. United Air Lines, 802 F2d 886, 123 LRRM 2617 (CA 7, 1986) (air carriers), cert. denied, 480 U.S. 946, 124 LRRM 3192 (1987).

[44]Railway & Steamship Clerks v. Florida E. C. Ry., 384 U.S. at 248, 62 LRRM at 2180.

[45]Railway & Steamship Clerks v. Florida E. C. Ry., 384 U.S. at 248 & n.8, 62 LRRM at 2180 & n.8.

[46]E.g., Air Line Pilots Ass'n v. United Air Lines, 802 F2d at 907, 123 LRRM at 2632; Empresa Ecuatoriana De Aviacion v. Machinists Dist. Lodge 100, 690 F2d 838, 844, 111 LRRM 2971, 2975–76 (CA 11, 1982), cert. dismissed, 463 U.S. 1250 (1983). Under the Supreme Court's decision in Trans World Airlines v. Flight Attendants (IFFA), 489 U.S. 426, 130 LRRM 2657 (1989), permanent replacement of economic strikers, either by new hires or by employees who cross picket lines, may

ble collective bargaining agreement would provide for similarly situated regular employees,[47] use of supervisors to perform craft work,[48] making work assignments across craft lines,[49] changes in crew complement or consist rules,[50] and disregard of union shop agreements with respect to replacements for the duration of a strike.[51] The carrier's right to continue to implement the changes ends when the strike ends.[52]

In determining what is reasonably necessary, the courts will subject to heightened scrutiny any action that, whether intentionally or otherwise, appears to "undercut the union's ability protected by the RLA to function as an effective representative for its members."[53] Carrier actions taken out of antiunion sentiment alone cannot be justified as "reasonably necessary."[54] For this reason, courts have disapproved under the reasonably necessary standard such actions as granting permanent "superseniority" to strike crossovers[55] and promises to disregard union shop agreements after strikes end.[56] However, the mere fact that a particular change may create

---

now be among the general "economic warfare" rights of carriers upon exhaustion of the major dispute procedures, without regard to the "reasonably necessary" standard. *See infra* §V.

[47]Air Line Pilots Ass'n v. United Air Lines, 802 F2d at 909, 123 **LRRM** at 2633–34.

[48]Florida E. C. Ry. v. United States, 348 F2d 682, 684, 686, 59 **LRRM** 2854, 2856, 2857 (CA 5, 1965), *aff'd sub nom.* Railway & Steamship Clerks v. Florida E. C. Ry., 384 U.S. 238, 62 **LRRM** 2177 (1966).

[49]Florida E. C. Ry. v. Railroad Trainmen, 336 F2d 172, 181, 56 **LRRM** 3009 (CA 5, 1964), *cert. denied*, 379 U.S. 990, 58 **LRRM** 2256 (1965).

[50]Florida E. C. Ry. v. United States, 348 F2d at 684, 686, 59 **LRRM** at 2856, 2857.

[51]Florida E. C. Ry. v. Railroad Trainmen, 336 F2d 172, 56 **LRRM** 3009.

[52]Railway & Steamship Clerks v. Florida E. C. Ry., 384 U.S. at 248, 62 **LRRM** at 2180.

[53]*E.g.*, Air Lines Pilots Ass'n v. United Air Lines, 802 F2d 886, 899, 123 **LRRM** 2617, 2625, (CA 7, 1986), *cert. denied*, 480 U.S. 946, 124 **LRRM** 3192 (1987).

[54]802 F2d at 900, 123 **LRRM** at 2626.

[55]*Id.*

[56]Florida E. C. Ry. v. United States, 348 F2d 682, 684, 59 **LRRM** 2854, 2855–56 (CA 5, 1965), *aff'd sub nom.* Railway & Steamship Clerks v. Florida E. C. Ry., 384 U.S. 238, 62 **LRRM** 2177 (1966); Cox v. Northwest Airlines, 319 F Supp 92, 100, 75 **LRRM** 2542, 2549 (D Minn, 1970).

an incentive for employees to refrain from striking or to return to work does not make the measure impermissible.[57]

V. DISCHARGE, DISCIPLINE, OR REPLACEMENT OF STRIKERS

Section 2, Fourth guarantees employees "the right to organize and bargain collectively" and provides that a carrier may not "deny or in any way question the right of its employees to join, organize, or assist in organizing the labor organization of their choice." In *Trans World Airlines v. Flight Attendants (IFFA)*,[58] the Supreme Court held that although the parties' right to self-help is generally not limited under the RLA, Section 2, Fourth bars the exercise of "those forms of self-help that strike a fundamental blow to union or employer activity and the collective bargaining process itself."[59]

The most common situation in which the courts invoke Section 2, Fourth to limit the right of self-help involves the treatment of traditional economic strikers. Section 2, Fourth prohibits a carrier from discharging economic strikers[60] or abolishing the jobs held by strikers in retaliation for their actions.[61]

On the other hand, Section 2, Fourth does not prohibit a carrier from hiring permanent replacement workers for the positions held by strikers during an economic strike and retaining those workers in those positions at the conclusion

---

[57]Trans World Airlines v. Flight Attendants (IFFA), 489 U.S. 426, 443, 130 LRRM 2657, 2663 (1989).

[58]489 U.S. 426, 130 LRRM 2657 (1989).

[59]489 U.S. at 442. The Court also used the phrase "inherently destructive of union or employer activity" to designate the same standard. *Id.*

[60]*See* Air Line Pilots Ass'n v. United Air Lines, 614 F Supp 1020, 119 LRRM 3483 (ND Ill, 1985), *aff'd in part and rev'd in part*, 802 F2d 886, 123 LRRM 2617 (CA 7, 1986), *cert. denied*, 480 U.S. 946, 124 LRRM 3192 (1987). In one case, the court held that the status quo obligation under §6 of the RLA prohibits the mass discharge of wildcat strikers prior to release from mediation, but that such employees could be replaced. National Airlines v. Machinists, 416 F2d 998, 72 LRRM 2294 (CA 5, 1969), *cert. denied*, 400 U.S. 992, 76 LRRM 2160 (1971).

[61]Railway Labor Executives' Ass'n v. Boston & Me. Corp., 808 F2d 150, 124 LRRM 2145 (CA 1, 1986), *cert. denied*, 484 U.S. 830, 126 LRRM 2496 (1987).

of the strike.[62] The Supreme Court upheld this right in *TWA,* holding that a carrier was not obligated to displace either permanent replacements or crossovers (existing employees who did not join or who abandoned the strike) to make room for more strikers following termination of the strike.[63]

Whereas the Court in *TWA* recognized that such a ruling might have the effect of discouraging employees from participating in a lawful strike, it held that such a result was "a secondary effect fairly within the arsenal of economic weapons available to employers during a period of self-help."[64] The Court also rejected the argument that the carrier had, in effect, granted superseniority to the nonstrikers because the vacancies created by the strikers were filled by the nonstrikers in the manner provided by the collective bargaining agreement. Section 2, Fourth, the Court noted, grants employees the right *not* to strike, and requiring the displacement of nonstriking employees would have the "effect of penalizing those who decided not to strike in order to benefit those who did."[65]

The courts have outlined a number of rules applicable to the hiring of permanent replacement workers. Former strikers generally must be reinstated to available openings, or given a preference over other applicants for future vacancies, after an economic strike has ended.[66] One court has applied

---

[62]Air Line Pilots Ass'n v. United Air Lines, 614 F Supp 1020, 119 LRRM 3483; Machinists v. Alaska Airlines, 124 LRRM 2458 (WD Wash, 1986); Air Line Pilots Ass'n v. Southern Airways, 44 Lab. Cas. (CCH) ¶17,460 (MD Tenn, 1962). *Cf.* National Airlines v. Machinists, 416 F2d 998, 72 LRRM 1250 (CA 5, 1969) (carrier violated §6 by discharging strikers during status quo period, but may replace strikers), *cert. denied,* 400 U.S. 992, 76 LRRM 2160 (1971).

[63]Trans World Airlines v. Flight Attendants (IFFA), 489 U.S. 426, 130 LRRM 2657 (1989).

[64]489 U.S. at 438.

[65]*Id.*

[66]Eastern Air Lines v. Air Line Pilots Ass'n, 920 F2d 722, 725, 136 LRRM 2082, 2084 (CA 11, 1990), *cert. denied,* 112 S Ct 278, 138 LRRM 2479 (1991); Machinists v. Alaska Airlines, 124 LRRM 2458; Air Line Pilots Ass'n v. Southern Airways, 44 Lab. Cas. (CCH) ¶17,460. *See also* Flight Attendants (IFFA) v. Trans World Airlines, 132 LRRM 2422 (WD Mo, 1989) (carrier not required to prove that hiring permanent replacements was a business necessity because offer of permanent employment is presumptively needed to attract replacements). One court has held

this rule even though the strike itself violated the status quo provisions of the RLA.[67] As a result, when a replacement has been "hired," and whether the replacement is "permanent," have been the subject of litigation. Several decisions have held that prospective replacements who have not completed mandatory training, and entered revenue service, before a strike ends are not employees under the Act, and thus do not qualify as permanent replacements entitled to remain in their positions.[68] In order for replacements to be considered permanent, an employer must have clearly communicated that it intends to hire the replacement on a permanent basis, i.e., beyond the duration of the strike.[69] A striking employee is entitled to reinstatement to his or her former position upon making an unconditional offer to return to work if the replacement is only temporary.[70]

Under the NLRA, the Supreme Court has held that an employer who makes an offer of permanent employment to replacement employees may be sued under state law for misrepresentation or breach of contract if the employer subsequently agrees to a back-to-work agreement that displaces permanent replacements from their jobs upon the conclusion

---

that an exception to this rule applies in cases where employees engage in an intermittent strike; in those circumstances, the carrier is under no obligation to fill a vacancy created by one intermittent striker with another intermittent striker who is on a recall list. Flight Attendants (AFA) v. Alaska Airlines, 847 F Supp 832 (WD Wash, 1993).

[67]National Airlines v. Machinists, 416 F2d 998, 72 LRRM 2294 (CA 5, 1969), *cert. denied,* 400 U.S. 992, 76 LRRM 2160 (1971).

[68]Eastern Air Lines v. Air Line Pilots Ass'n, 920 F2d 722, 136 LRRM 2082; Flight Attendants (IFFA) v. Trans World Airlines, 819 F2d 839, 125 LRRM 2544 (CA 8, 1987), *cert. denied,* 485 U.S. 958 (1988); Air Line Pilots Ass'n v. United Air Lines, 802 F2d 886, 123 LRRM 2617 (CA 7, 1986), *cert. denied,* 480 U.S. 946, 124 LRRM 3192 (1992). *But see* National Air Lines v. Machinists, 430 F2d 957, 74 LRRM 2833 (CA 5, 1970) (suggesting that replacement is considered hired where employer manifests intention to bind itself to a firm commitment of employment), *cert. denied,* 400 U.S. 992, 76 LRRM 2160 (1971).

[69]Flight Attendants (IFFA) v. Trans World Airlines, 819 F2d 839, 125 LRRM 2544. *See generally* Belknap, Inc. v. Hale, 463 U.S. 491, 501, 113 LRRM 3057, 3061 (1983); Mcdallion Kitchens, Inc., 275 NLRB 58, 119 LRRM 1016, *enforced,* 806 F2d 185, 190, 123 LRRM 3153, 3156 (CA 8), *cert. denied,* 481 U.S. 1937, 125 LRRM 2152 (1987).

[70]Flight Attendants (IFFA) v. Trans World Airlines, 819 F2d 839, 125 LRRM 2544.

of a strike.[71] One state court decision has held that the same rule applies under the RLA.[72]

Some courts have held that institution of a separate training program for prospective replacements during the status quo period does not violate Section 6 of the RLA unless the program has some effect on the working conditions of current employees.[73]

Most of the case law involving striker discharge and replacement has involved traditional strike activity, in which the employees remain off the job until settlement of the dispute. As a result, there is little authority on whether Section 2, Fourth prohibits an employer from discharging or disciplining employees who engage in job actions other than a traditional strike, such as intermittent strikes or other conduct that would be considered unprotected activity under the NLRA.[74] The Second Circuit, in *Pan American World Airways v. Teamsters*,[75] held that the RLA did *not* prohibit an intermittent strike; but the court left open the issue of whether discipline or discharge of the participating employees would violate Section 2, Fourth. One district court has held that intermittent strikers may be replaced but not discharged.[76]

VI. LOCKOUTS

The only reported case to address the lawfulness of a carrier lockout did not resolve the issue. In early 1970, four

[71]Belknap, Inc. v. Hale, 463 U.S. at 501, 113 LRRM at 3061.

[72]Bubbel v. Wien Air Alaska, 682 P2d 374, 116 LRRM 2473 (Alaska, 1984) (replacement worker's state law contract claims not preempted by RLA). *See also* Air Line Pilots Ass'n v. United Air Lines, 802 F2d at 910, 123 LRRM 2617 (suggesting that rule in *Belknap* would apply under the RLA).

[73]Air Line Pilots Ass'n v. United Air Lines, 802 F2d 886, 917, 123 LRRM 2617 (CA 7, 1986), *cert. denied*, 480 U.S. 946, 124 LRRM 1318 (1987); Teamsters v. World Airways, 111 LRRM 2170 (ND Cal, 1982). *See also* Air Line Pilots Ass'n v. Eastern Air Lines, 869 F2d 1518, 130 LRRM 2895 (CA DC, 1989) (dispute over contracting out of replacement pilot training in preparation for sympathy strike raised a minor dispute).

[74]Under the NLRA, the courts have identified a range of conduct short of a traditional strike that is considered lawful but is not protected by the right to strike. *See generally* THE DEVELOPING LABOR LAW, *supra* note 10, at 1110–20.

[75]894 F2d 36, 133 LRRM 2292 (CA 2, 1990).

[76]Flight Attendants (AFA) v. Alaska Airlines, 847 F Supp 832 (WD Wash, 1993).

shop craft unions threatened to engage in whipsaw strikes against the nation's 128 Class I railroads, which in turn threatened a lockout. On January 31, 1970, a district court enjoined both parties from engaging in self-help; the court was "merely maintaining the status quo among the parties until a full adjudication of the claims of all parties can be had."[77] Five weeks later, the court issued a preliminary injunction against the strike.[78] Because the carriers had threatened the lockout only in the event of a strike, the court ruled that the unions' application for injunctive relief against the lockout became moot upon the issuance of injunctive relief against the strike. However, the court did rule that threat of a lockout under the circumstances did not violate the RLA.[79]

---

[77]Machinists v. National Ry. Labor Conference, 310 F Supp 905, 73 LRRM 2594 (D DC, 1970), *appeal dismissed*, 463 F2d 872, 79 LRRM 3028 (CA DC, 1972); Machinists v. National Ry. Labor Conference, 310 F Supp 904, 73 LRRM 2319, 2320 (D DC, 1970).

[78]Machinists v. National Ry. Labor Conference, 310 F Supp 905, 73 LRRM 2594.

[79]Under the NLRA, the Supreme Court has held that an employer may lock out its employees for the purpose of bringing economic pressure to bear on the union in support of its legitimate bargaining position. American Ship Bldg. v. NLRB, 380 U.S. 300, 58 LRRM 2672 (1965). *See also* NLRB v. Truck Drivers Union, 353 U.S. 87, 39 LRRM 2603 (1957) (not an unfair labor practice for nonstruck members of multiemployer bargaining unit to lock out their employees); NLRB v. Brown, 380 U.S. 278, 58 LRRM 2663 (1965) (employer faced with whipsaw strike can hire temporary replacements to operate business during otherwise lawful lockout).

CHAPTER 7

ACCOMMODATING THE RLA TO OTHER LAWS

I. OVERVIEW OF INTERSTATE COMMERCE ACT REGULATION OF RAIL CARRIERS

Rail carriers that transport freight or passengers in interstate commerce are subject to comprehensive regulation by the Interstate Commerce Commission (ICC) under the Interstate Commerce Act (ICA).[1] The principal purpose of ICA regulation of rail carriers is the maintenance of an adequate and efficient rail transportation system.[2] For the most part, that regulation does not address the rights of railway labor, and thus does not present potential conflicts with the RLA or other labor laws applicable to railroads that could trigger statutory accommodation issues.[3]

When rail carriers participate in transactions that result in changes in the ownership of rail lines or transfers of operating rights (such as leases and grants of trackage rights), however, there is considerable overlap between the ICA and the RLA.[4] That overlap exists because these transactions

---

[1]49 U.S.C. §§10101 et seq.

[2]ICA §§10102(20), 10501, 10101a(3), (4), (5).

[3]*See, e.g.,* Railroad Telegraphers v. Chicago & N. W. Ry., 362 U.S. 330, 342, 45 LRRM 3104, 3108–09 (1960) ("wasteful" expenditures in connection with a carrier's RLA obligations may "[run] counter" to the ICA's general statutory policy encouraging efficient railroad operations, but that does not amount to direct conflict requiring accommodation of one statute to the other).

[4]Pittsburgh & L. E. R.R. v. Railway Labor Executives' Ass'n, 491 U.S. 490, 510, 131 LRRM 2611, 2618 (1989).

usually entail operating changes that may have adverse effects upon employees, such as the loss of jobs.

Virtually all transactions affecting the ownership or operation of rail lines must be authorized by the ICC.[5] The ICA requires the ICC to impose compensatory and procedural labor protective conditions on many of the transactions the ICC authorizes,[6] and ordinarily grants the ICC discretionary jurisdiction to impose such protection even where it is not required by statute.[7] The purpose of labor protection under the ICA, the Supreme Court has said, is to serve the "public interest in the maintenance of an adequate rail transportation system" by aiding in "maintenance of a service uninterrupted by labor disputes."[8] The ICC lacks power to impose labor protection only where Congress has determined that labor protective obligations in particular transactions would be contrary to the public interest.[9] Thus, in most railroad transactions, the ICA addresses issues that ordinarily would fall exclusively under the RLA, and that overlap may lead to conflicts between the two statutes, or between the ICA and the Norris-LaGuardia Act (NLGA)[10] if railroad employees strike to protest the effects of a transaction.

A. Transactions in Which the ICA Requires Labor Protective Conditions

Under the current codification of the ICA, the ICC is required to impose labor protective conditions for the benefit of rail employees in several types of transactions.[11] The pri-

---

[5]The exceptions are transactions involving only "spur, industrial, team, switching, or side tracks," or "a street, suburban, or interurban electric railway that is not operated as part of a general system of rail transportation." ICA §10907.

[6]ICA §§10903(b)(2), 10910(e), (j), 11123(a)(3), 11125(a)(4), 11347.

[7]United States v. Lowden, 308 U.S. 225, 233 (1939); Maintenance of Way Employees v. United States, 366 U.S. 169, 173, 48 LRRM 2033, 2035 (1961).

[8]United States v. Lowden, 308 U.S. at 230, 235–36, 238.

[9]See Illinois C.G. R.R.—Abandonment—in Alexander Co., Ill., 366 ICC 911, aff'd, Simmons v. ICC, 760 F2d 126, 129–30, 118 LRRM 3099, 3101 (CA 7, 1985), cert. denied, 474 U.S. 1055, 121 LRRM 2208 (1986).

[10]29 U.S.C. §101 et seq. (1988).

[11]The ICA was recodified "without substantive change" as title 49 of the U.S. Code in 1978. Pub. L. No. 95-473, §3(a), 92 Stat. 1466 (1978). In this chapter, decisions under the ICA prior to 1978 refer to predecessors of the current recodified provisions.

mary type of transaction subject to mandatory labor protection is that governed by Section 11343, which requires ICC authorization for most transactions involving two or more established carriers.[12]

Under Section 11347, the ICC must require any rail carrier involved in a Section 11343 transaction "to provide a fair arrangement at least as protective of the interest of employees who are affected by the transaction as the terms imposed under [prior codifications of this section], and the terms established under section 405 of the Rail Passenger Service Act (45 U.S.C. 565)" for the protection of employees of Northeastern railroads affected by the formation of Amtrak. The labor protective conditions imposed under Section 11347 in the various types of Section 11343 transactions are discussed in detail in a later section.[13] The conditions all provide similar compensatory and procedural benefits, the most important of which are income protection for up to six years for employees displaced or dismissed from their jobs because of a covered transaction; compulsory expedited negotiations and, if necessary, mandatory arbitration governing each participating carrier's selection and assignment of its employees in light of a transaction; and a requirement barring participating carriers from making unilateral changes in their rates of pay, rules, working conditions, or collective bargaining agreements.[14] Thus far, the ICC has found no requirement

---

[12]The transactions enumerated in §11343(a) are as follows:

(1) consolidation or merger of the properties or franchises of at least 2 carriers into one corporation for the ownership, management, and operation of the previously separately owned properties.

(2) a purchase, lease, or contract to operate property of another carrier by any number of carriers.

(3) acquisition of control of a carrier by any number of carriers.

(4) acquisition of control of at least 2 carriers by a person that is not a carrier.

(5) acquisition of control of a carrier by a person that is not a carrier but that controls any number of carriers.

(6) acquisition by a rail carrier of trackage rights over, or joint ownership in or joint use of, a railroad line (and terminals incidental to it) owned or operated by another rail carrier.

[13]See infra §III.

[14]See New York Dock Ry.—Control—Brooklyn E.D. Terminal, 360 ICC 60 (1979) (conditions for mergers, consolidations, sales, and control transactions), aff'd

under Section 11347 that an acquiring carrier take on the transferor's employees or assume its collective bargaining agreements.[15]

Section 11347 permits rail carriers and unions to substitute negotiated protection agreements in lieu of the conditions ordinarily required by the ICC, but the ICC must approve such agreements as part of its order authorizing the transaction, and the agreements are not thereafter subject to change by agreement of the parties.[16]

B. Abandonments

When a rail carrier abandons or discontinues operations over any "part" of its lines, Section 10903(b)(2) requires the ICC to impose labor protective conditions "at least as beneficial" to employees as those imposed under Section 11347. The ICC has adopted protective conditions, similar to those imposed under Section 11347, for abandonments of lines by carriers that will continue to operate the remainder of their systems.[17] As a matter of discretion, however, the ICC has long refused to impose labor protective conditions when a carrier abandons or discontinues operation of its entire railroad, on the ground that imposing continued rail labor costs upon a company no longer in the railroad business would not be related in any way to the statutory goal of maintaining

---

sub nom. New York Dock Ry. v. United States, 609 F2d 83, 102 LRRM 2835 (CA 2, 1979); Mendocino Coast Ry.—Lease & Operate—California W. R.R., 354 ICC 732 (conditions for leases), *modified*, 360 ICC 653, *aff'd sub nom.* Railway Labor Executives' Ass'n v. United States, 675 F2d 1248, 110 LRRM 2136 (CA DC, 1982); Norfolk & W. Ry.—Trackage Rights—Burlington N. Ry., 354 ICC 605 (conditions for trackage rights), *modified*, 360 ICC 653, *aff'd sub nom.* Railway Labor Executives' Ass'n v. United States, 675 F2d 1248, 110 LRRM 2136 (CA DC, 1982).

[15]Wilmington Terminal R.R.—Purchase & Lease—CSX Transp., 6 ICC2d 799, *aff'd sub nom.* Railway Labor Executives' Ass'n v. United States, 930 F2d 511, 137 LRRM 2074 (CA 6, 1991); United Transp. Union v. United States, 905 F2d 463, 468–69, 134 LRRM 2511, 2515–16 (CA DC, 1990).

[16]Norfolk & W. Ry. v. Nemitz, 404 U.S. 37, 78 LRRM 2721 (1971).

[17]Oregon Short Line R.R.—Abandonment—Portion Goshen Branch, 354 ICC 584 (1978).

and strengthening the railroad system.[18] That policy has been upheld on judicial review under Section 10903.[19]

C. "Feeder Line" Sales

Section 10910 establishes a so-called feeder line program intended to permit shippers and governmental authorities that are dependent upon particular rail lines to acquire the lines if service deteriorates.[20] If a "financially responsible person" that is not a Class I or Class II rail carrier offers to purchase a line upon which the owner is providing inadequate service, and if the sale is likely to result in improved service, the ICC may require the owner to sell the line to that person at its "constitutional minimum value."[21] Section 10910(j) requires the ICC to impose labor protective conditions "at least as protective" as those under Section 11347 upon the seller carrier. In addition, under Section 10910(e), the ICC must require the purchaser to use the seller's employees on the line "to the maximum extent practicable." The ICC does not require, however, that the purchaser maintain the seller's wages and work rules or assume its collective bargaining agreements.[22]

D. Averting Temporary Disruptions

Sections 11123 and 11125 permit the ICC to issue orders to avert temporary disruption or interruption of service. Section 11125 applies when a rail carrier cannot transport traffic offered to it, either because its cash position makes that impossible or because a court order—generally a bankruptcy order—requires the carrier to discontinue operations. Section 11125 also applies if a carrier discontinues operations for any

---

[18]*E.g.*, Wellsville, A. & G. R.R.—Abandonment of Entire Line, 354 ICC 744, 746 (1978); Okmulgee N. Ry., Abandonment, 320 ICC 637, 646–47 (1964).

[19]Railway Labor Executives' Ass'n v. ICC, 735 F2d 691, 700–01, 116 LRRM 2937, 2945 (CA 2, 1984).

[20]*See* H.R. Conf. Rep. No. 1430, 96th Cong., 2d Sess. 124 (1980).

[21]ICA §10910(b)(1).

[22]*E. g.*, Cheney R.R.—Feeder Line Acquisition—CSX Transp. Line Between Greens & Ivalee, Ala., 5 ICC2d 250, 275–76 (1989).

reason without first obtaining ICC authority under Section 10903.[23] If any of these criteria are met, the ICC may issue a "directed service order" requiring another carrier to take over the defaulting carrier's lines. Directed service orders cannot remain in effect more than 240 days (an initial 60-day period that may be extended by the ICC for no more than 180 days).[24]

Section 11125(b)(4) requires a directed service carrier to hire the employees of the defaulting carrier that previously performed the transportation services covered by the directed service order. In addition, Section 11125(b)(4) contains a unique provision requiring the directed service carrier to assume for the duration of the order the other carrier's employment obligations and practices, including collective bargaining agreements, and any obligations under employee protective conditions that accrue during the directed service period. The directed service carrier is not, however, responsible for employment obligations of the other carrier that accrued prior to the initiation of directed service.[25]

Section 11123 applies when an equipment shortage, traffic congestion, or any "other failure in traffic movement" threatens to create an emergency with "substantial adverse effects" on rail transportation in a "substantial region" of the United States.[26] To avert such an emergency, the ICC may enter service orders to maintain rail service. The ordinary duration of such orders is 30 days, but if the emergency continues beyond that period, the ICC may, after a hearing, extend the order as necessary for the duration of the emergency.[27] Section 11123 speaks in terms of orders dealing with car service, utilization of locomotives, and joint use of facilities; one court of appeals has concluded that this provision, unlike Section 11125, does not authorize the ICC to grant one carrier temporary authority to take over the lines and

---

[23]ICA §11125(a).
[24]Id. §11125(b)(1).
[25]Id. §11125(b)(3); see Directed Serv. Order No. 1504, Supp. Order No. 3, 53 Fed. Reg. 32,117 (1988).
[26]ICA §11123.
[27]Id. §§11123(a)(1), (2).

common carrier duties of another.[28] The ICC, has, however, relied upon Section 11123 to authorize carriers to assume the operations of a bankrupt carrier.[29]

As regards labor protection, the difference between Sections 11123 and 11125 is significant. Under Section 11123, the Commission must require an emergency service carrier to retain the other carrier's employees, but only "to the maximum extent practicable;"[30] whereas Section 11125 requires retention of the other carrier's employees without the limiting proviso.[31] Moreover, Section 11123, unlike Section 11125, does not require the emergency service carrier to assume the other carrier's employment obligations or collective bargaining agreements.[32]

E. Transactions Subject to Discretionary Imposition of Labor Protection

Just as Section 11343 covers most transactions involving more than one carrier, Section 10901 covers most transactions that involve only a single carrier. That section expressly applies when a carrier constructs an extension to its line; constructs an additional rail line; or acquires, operates, or provides transportation by any means over an extended or additional line.[33] The provisions of Section 10901 pertaining to transactions in which carriers acquire rail lines or operating rights over rail lines must, however, be read in light of Section 11343, which generally governs when the transferring company is also a carrier. Thus, Section 10901 applies to such transactions only when the transferring company is a "noncarrier,"[34] that is, a company that does not operate as a carrier in interstate commerce at the time of a proposed transaction—

---

[28]Atchison, T. & S.F. Ry. v. United States, 617 F2d 485 (CA7, 1980).

[29]Serv. Order No. 1510, 55 Fed. Reg. 31,906 (1990); Serv. Order No. 1506, 54 Fed. Reg. 7293 (1989).

[30]ICA §11123(a)(3).

[31]Id. §11125(b)(4).

[32]See In re Delaware & H. Ry., 120 B.R. 772, 775 (D Del, 1990).

[33]ICA §10901(a).

[34]See 49 CFR §1150.1(a) (1994); Simmons v. ICC, 829 F2d 150, 126 LRRM 2362 (CA DC, 1987).

regardless of what it has done in the past, what it may plan to do in the future, or whether it has affiliates that are carriers.[35]

The principal importance of Section 10901, however, is as the vehicle for creation of new railroads, generally short-line and regional railroads, through transactions in which noncarriers become rail carriers by acquiring and commencing operations on lines of existing carriers or by obtaining trackage rights on such lines. Whereas the ICA does not expressly require ICC approval for those noncarrier acquisitions, the federal courts and the ICC have interpreted Section 10901, and its predecessor prior to the 1978 recodification,[36] to apply to these transactions.[37]

Section 10901 contains no provision for mandatory labor protection. Section 10901(e) permits, but does not require, the ICC to impose labor protective conditions, which may be equivalent to those under Section 11347, when an existing carrier proposes both to construct and operate a new line. As regards noncarrier acquisitions, Section 10901(c)(1)(a)(ii) authorizes the ICC to condition its authorization of any Section 10901 transaction upon any terms that it finds necessary in the public interest. That general grant of public interest authority, which applies to noncarrier acquisitions under Section 10901, provides the ICC with discretion to impose labor protective conditions if necessary to further the public interest in maintaining the rail transportation system and in pre-

---

[35]*See, e.g.,* County of Marin v. United States, 356 U.S. 412 (1958); United Transp. Union v. Bessemer & L.E. R.R., 342 ICC 849, 855 (1974).

[36]Former ICA §1(18).

[37]*See, e.g.,* Illinois v. United States, 604 F2d 519 (CA 7, 1979), *cert. denied,* 445 U.S. 951 (1980); *Ex parte* No. 392, Class Exemption for the Acquisition & Operation of Rail Lines under 49 USC 10901, 1 ICC2d 810, *review denied,* 817 F2d 145 (CA DC, 1987); Iowa Terminal R.R.—Acquisition & Operation, 312 ICC 546, 548 (1961) (noting that the ICC had "consistently entertained" applications by noncarriers to acquire and operate rail lines under §1(18)). *Cf.* Texas & N. O. R.R. v. Northside Belt Ry., 276 U.S. 475, 479–80 & n.1 (1928) (when a noncarrier "undertakes to engage in interstate commerce" as a rail carrier, "its operation becomes immediately a matter of national concern," and thus a noncarrier's application to construct and operate a railroad on a right-of-way owned, but "unused by," a railroad, was subject to ICC approval under §1(18)).

venting labor disputes over authorized transactions from interrupting rail service.[38]

In 1985, the ICC formally adopted a policy against imposition of labor protective conditions in noncarrier acquisitions under Section 10901, although the Commission retains discretion to impose such conditions when they are required by "exceptional" circumstances.[39] Since adoption of that policy, the ICC has never imposed employee protections in Section 10901 acquisitions over the opposition of the carriers involved; thus, it is not clear what circumstances the ICC would consider sufficiently exceptional to justify employee protections.[40] This policy was adopted to encourage the formation of new railroads, which the ICC determined would prevent abandonments.[41] Rail lines require maintenance and periodic rehabilitation, and if a carrier is determined to cease operating one of its lines, it may be unwilling or unable to continue to invest capital in maintenance and rehabilitation. The ICC has therefore concluded that, given a choice between transferring the line when it is fully operational, subject to labor protection, and deferring maintenance until the line becomes abandonable, many carriers would choose the latter option.[42]

F. Transactions in Which Labor Protection Is Prohibited

In one class of line transactions the ICC lacks jurisdiction to impose labor protective conditions—so-called forced sales under Section 10905. Section 10905 applies when a financially

---

[38]*See, e.g.*, ICC v. Railway Labor Executives' Ass'n, 315 U.S. 373, 376–77, 10 LRRM 378, 380 (1942); Knox & Kane R.R.—Gettysburg R.R.—Petition for Exemption, 366 ICC 439, 440 n.2 (1982).

[39]*Ex parte* No. 392, 1 ICC2d at 815. *See also infra* §III.

[40]*See infra* §III.

[41]*Ex Parte* No. 392, 1 ICC2d at 813; *see* FRVR Corp.—Exemption—Acquisition & Operation—Certain Lines of Chicago & N. W. Transp. Co.—Petition for Clarification, Fin. Docket No. 31205, slip. op. at 1–3 (served Jan. 29, 1988), *vacated on other grounds sub nom.* Railway Labor Executives' Ass'n v. ICC, 888 F2d 1227, 132 LRRM 2912 (CA 8, 1989), *cert. denied*, 494 U.S. 1079, 133 LRRM 3112 (1990).

[42]*See* Knox & Kane R.R.—Gettysburg R.R.—Petition for Exemption, 366 ICC at 444.

responsible person, which may be a carrier, offers to purchase a rail line that the ICC has approved for abandonment under Section 10903. If the owner accepts the offer, the ICC must approve the sale and dismiss the abandonment proceeding.[43] Once the sale has been approved, the parties are required to consummate it, unless the purchase offer is withdrawn within 10 days after the ICC's decision.[44]

Section 10905 contains neither an express provision for labor protection nor a general grant to the ICC of power to impose conditions in the public interest. The ICC has therefore concluded that it is neither required nor permitted to impose labor protective conditions on Section 10905 forced sales, and that decision has been upheld on judicial review.[45] In the ICC's view, the omission of labor protective jurisdiction under Section 10905 reflects a specific congressional determination that the heavy costs of labor protective conditions would defer forced sales and lead to abandonments, contrary to the public interest in maintaining an adequate rail transportation system.[46]

G. "Deregulation" Under the Staggers Rail Act of 1980

During the late 1970s, the freight railroad industry experienced several large-scale bankruptcies.[47] In 1980, Congress determined that the inflexible and comprehensive regulation of railroads under the ICA had contributed to the decline of the industry and adopted the Staggers Rail Act amendments to the ICA.[48] The principal purpose of the Staggers Act was to foster the long-standing statutory goal of maintaining a viable national rail transportation system by freeing the industry from "unnecessary regulation."[49]

---

[43]ICA §10905(e).
[44]*Id.* §10905(f)(2).
[45]Illinois C.G. R.R.—Abandonment—in Alexander Co., Ill., 366 ICC 911, *aff'd,* Simmons v. ICC, 760 F2d 126, 129–30, 118 LRRM 3099 (CA 7, 1985), *cert. denied,* 474 U.S. 1055 (1986).
[46]*Id.* at 914.
[47]*See* H.R. REP. No. 1035, 96th Cong., 2d Sess. 33–37 (1980).
[48]Pub. L. No. 96-448, 94 Stat. 1895 (1980).
[49]H.R. CONF. REP. No. 1430, 96th Cong., 2d Sess. 80 (1980).

The Staggers Act amended the ICA to establish, in Section 10101a, a new Rail Transportation Policy (RTP) containing 15 factors that the ICC must take into account in regulating the railroad industry. As pertinent to line transactions, the RTP seeks "to minimize the need for Federal regulatory control over the rail transportation system and to require fair and expeditious regulatory decisions when regulation is required," "to ensure the development and continuation of a sound rail transportation system," and "to reduce regulatory barriers to entry into and exit from the industry."[50] The RTP also requires the ICC to "encourage fair wages and safe and suitable working conditions in the railroad industry."[51]

The statutory vehicle for relaxation of regulation of rail line transactions is ICA Section 10505. As amended by the Staggers Act, Section 10505 requires the ICC to exempt a transaction from particular provisions of the ICA when the application of those provisions is not necessary to carry out the RTP, and when the transaction either is of "limited scope" or does not present a need to protect shippers from abuse of market power.[52]

The ICC has relied upon Section 10505 to grant class exemptions from several classes of transactions, substituting expedited notice and information requirements for the otherwise applicable extensive prior approval procedures. The most significant of these class exemptions provides blanket authorization for all noncarrier acquisitions under Section 10901. Noncarrier acquisitions that result in the creation of Class III railroads—those that will have no more than $10 million annual revenues from railroad operations as calculated by the ICC[53]—are authorized after 7 days' notice to the ICC, and acquisitions that result in the creation of larger railroads are authorized after 35 days' notice.[54] Other class exemptions make the 7-day notice procedure applicable to a variety of Section 11343 transactions, including carrier acqui-

---

[50]ICA §§10101a(2), (4), (7).
[51]*Id.* §10101a(12).
[52]*Id.* 10505(a).
[53]49 CFR pt. 1201, General Instruction 1.1 (1994).
[54]*Id.* §§1150.31–35.

sitions of nonconnecting lines, transactions within a corporate family, and trackage rights transactions.[55] Transactions that are not subject to class exemptions may be exempted from prior approval procedures through individual exemptions, if the participating carriers demonstrate that the Section 10505 criteria are met.

Since 1980, Section 10505 exemptions have become the "standard method used to acquire Commission approval" for transactions subject to its jurisdiction.[56] This change reflects the ICC's determination that expeditious consummation of many transactions furthers the public interest as defined in the RTP.[57]

II. ACCOMMODATION OF ICA AND OTHER LABOR LAWS

A. Accommodation of ICA and RLA

Railroad mergers or line transfers generally result in changes for railroad employees, such as job loss, transfers, or loss of seniority rights, which are often restricted to particular points or districts on a carrier.[58] As described earlier, the status quo provisions of the RLA ordinarily prevent carriers from making unilateral changes in agreements governing these issues without first exhausting the RLA major dispute procedures over the proposed changes.[59] These procedures are "purposely long and drawn out."[60] As noted previously,[61] particularly since the enactment of the Staggers Act, the ICC has specifically authorized consummation of most railroad

---

[55]*Id.* §§1180.2(d), 1180.4(g).

[56]*Ex parte* No. 392, Class Exemption for the Acquisition & Operation of Rail Lines under 49 USC 10901, 1 ICC2d 810, 811, *review denied,* 817 F2d 145 (CA DC, 1987); see Pittsburgh & L.E. R.R. v. Railway Labor Executives' Ass'n, 491 U.S. 490, 500, 131 LRRM 2611, 2614 (1989).

[57]*See, e.g., Ex parte* No. 392, 1 ICC2d at 816; *Ex parte* No. 282, Railroad Consolidation Procedures—Trackage Rights Exemption, 1 ICC2d 270, 281 (1985).

[58]*See* United States v. Lowden, 308 U.S. 225, 233 (1939).

[59]*See* Chapter 4, "Negotiation of Collective Bargaining Agreements," §VIII.

[60]Railway & Steamship Clerks v. Florida E. C. Ry., 384 U.S. 238, 246, 62 LRRM 2177, 2179 (1966).

[61]*See supra* §I.

transactions on an expedited basis. If these transactions were subjected to the notice and negotiation requirements of the RLA, they probably could not be consummated on an expeditious basis and might not be consummated at all.[62] The federal courts have also recognized this potential conflict between the ICA and the RLA in ICC-authorized transactions.[63]

Where the changes a carrier must make in connection with an ICC-authorized transaction are committed to managerial prerogative, the carrier can exercise its rights or duties under the ICC order without affecting employee rights under the RLA, and there is no conflict between the two statutes.[64] In some cases, however, conflict is unavoidable, as where a transaction entails a change that is expressly prohibited by a collective bargaining agreement. In such a case, the question of which statute overrides the other depends primarily on what provision of the ICA governs the transaction, and may depend as well on the terms of the ICC's order authorizing the transaction.

B. Section 11343 Transactions

Section 11341(a) of the ICA provides that the ICC's authority over Section 11343 transactions is "exclusive," and

---

[62]Maine C. R.R.—Georgia P. Corp., Canadian P. Ltd. & Springfield Terminal Ry.—Exemption from 49 USC 11342 & 11343, Fin. Docket No. 30532, slip op. at 7 (served Sept. 13, 1985), *aff'd mem. sub nom.* Railway Labor Executives' Ass'n v. ICC, 812 F2d 1443 (CA DC, 1987).

[63]*See, e.g.,* Norfolk & W. Ry. v. Train Dispatchers, 499 U.S. 117 136 LRRM 2727, 2733–35 (1991); Missouri P. R.R. v. United Transp. Union, 782 F2d 107, 111, 121 LRRM 2445, 2447–48 (CA 8, 1986), *cert. denied,* 482 U.S. 927, 125 LRRM 2616 (1987); Locomotive Eng'rs v. Boston & Me. Corp., 788 F2d 794, 801, 122 LRRM 2020 (CA 1), *cert. denied,* 479 U.S. 829, 123 LRRM 2592 (1986); Nemitz v. Norfolk & W. Ry., 436 F2d 841, 845, 76 LRRM 2340, 2343 (CA 6), *aff'd on other grounds,* 404 U.S. 37, 78 LRRM 2721 (1971); Locomotive Eng'rs v. Chicago & N. W. Ry., 314 F2d 424, 427–28, 52 LRRM 2595, 2596–98 (CA 8), *cert. denied,* 375 U.S. 819, 54 LRRM 2312 (1963).

[64]Pittsburgh & L. E. R.R. v. Railway Labor Executives' Ass'n, 491 U.S. 490, 131 LRRM 2611 (1989) (sale of entire railroad); CSX Transp., Inc. v. United Transp. Union, 950 F2d 872, 139 LRRM 2061 (CA 2, 1991) (sale and lease of parts of lines); M.T. Properties, Inc. v. Transportation Communications Union, 914 F2d 1083, 135 LRRM 2443 (CA 8, 1990), *cert. denied,* 499 U.S. 937, 136 LRRM 2976 (1991) (whole-line leases); *In re* Delaware & H. Ry., 120 B.R. 772 (D Del., 1990) (emergency service orders under §11123 of the ICA).

also that a carrier participating in a transaction "approved" under Section 11343 is exempt from "the antitrust laws and all other law, including State and municipal law, as necessary to let that person carry out the transaction."

The Supreme Court in *Norfolk & Western Railway* v. *Train Dispatchers*[65] held that the phrase "all other law" in Section 11343 includes the RLA and collective bargaining agreements that derive their force and effect from the RLA. The Court noted that the mandatory labor protective conditions that apply under Section 11347 to all Section 11343 transactions ensure accommodation of the interests of affected employees "to the greatest extent possible."[66] Once these interests are accounted for, however, Section 11341(a) "guarantees that ... obligations imposed by laws such as the RLA will not prevent the efficiencies of the [transaction] from being achieved."[67] Preemption of collective bargaining agreements that stand in the way of changes essential to a transaction is necessary because the "resolution process for major disputes under the RLA would so delay the proposed transfer of operations that any efficiencies the carriers sought would be defeated."[68] The Court did not address whether the scope of the override authority provided by Section 11341(a) was limited by the labor protective conditions mandated by its sister statutory provision, Section 11347; whether the standards for determining necessity before Section 11341(a) can be utilized; or whether the override authority provided by Section 11341(a) applied only to the specific transaction before the Commission for approval or extended further to foreseeable consequences of that transaction.[69]

---

[65]499 U.S. 117, 136 LRRM 2727 (1991).

[66]499 U.S. at 133.

[67]*Id.*

[68]*Id.*

[69]*Id.* (citing ICC v. Locomotive Eng'rs, 482 U.S. 270, 298, 125 LRRM 2526, *cert. denied*, 482 U.S. 927, 125 LRRM 2616 (1987)). *See also* United Transp. Union v. Norfolk & W. Ry., 822 F2d 1114, 125 LRRM 3080 (CA DC, 1987), *cert. denied*, 484 U.S. 1006, 127 LRRM 2256 (1988) (appeal of arbitrator's decision on necessity cannot be heard by district court, but must be appealed to the Commission).

Two of those issues were clarified recently in *Train Dispatchers v. ICC*,[70] in which the District of Columbia Circuit held that Section 11347 limits Section 11341 in that it protects collective bargaining agreement provisions that create "rights, privileges and benefits."[71] The court remanded the case for the ICC to define those terms. The court also held that the "necessary" language of Section 11341 requires a finding that the potentially exempt law, such as a collective bargaining agreement, is an impediment to the approved transaction.[72]

C. Conditions of Approval

Both the courts and the ICC thus far have agreed that the ICC's authorization to consummate a transaction implicitly extends changes in employee rights relating to assignment of work and reduction of forces that are inextricably linked to consummation, such as the abolishment of jobs in a consolidation or when a carrier ceases operation upon transfer of operations,[73] or changes in the pay of operating employees who are paid on a mileage basis when a carrier's route is truncated by a transaction.[74]

Whether the ICC has power to authorize changes in employee rights that are not inextricably linked to consummation is not settled. The ICC has frequently asserted power to authorize changes in employee working conditions, including the power to abrogate or modify provisions in collective bargaining agreements, when it deems such changes necessary to ensure successful and efficient operations after consummation of a Section 11343 transaction.[75] Such assertions met

---

[70]26 F3d 1157, 146 LRRM 2724 (CA DC, 1994).

[71]26 F3d at 1163.

[72]*Id.* at 1164.

[73]*See* United States v. Lowden, 308 U.S. 225, 233 (1939); Union P. Corp—Control—M.-K.-T. R.R., 4 ICC2d 409, 511 (1988).

[74]*See, e.g.,* Locomotive Eng'rs v. Boston & Me. Corp., 788 F2d 794, 796, 799, 801, 122 LRRM 2020, 2021, 2023–24, 2025 (CA 1), *cert. denied*, 479 U.S. 829, 123 LRRM 2592 (1986).

[75]*See, e.g.,* CSX Corp.—Control—Chessie Sys., Inc. & Seaboard C.L. Indus., 6 ICC2d 715, 752 (1990).

with a mixed reception in the courts of appeals prior to the Supreme Court's *Norfolk & Western Railway*[76] decision.[77] No court has addressed the question since that decision, nor has any court addressed the question of how the ICC's assertion of such power squares with requiring participating carriers to preserve the rights of employees under collective bargaining agreements, which is one of the statutory minimum protections required by Section 11347.[78] However, it is clear, as the Fifth Circuit has held, that Section 11341(a) does not give the ICC a "hunting license" to "[void] contracts that are not germane to the success of the approved transaction."[79]

D. Standard for Necessity

Section 11341(a) expressly requires that preemption of an "other law" that may apply to a Section 11343 transaction be "necessary . . . to carry out the transaction." The question of what constitutes necessity is inextricably linked to the question of what conditions the ICC may approve as part of a Section 11343 transaction (as well as the nature of the transaction and of the change sought). Necessity for preemption of the RLA is clearest when application of that statute would directly block consummation of a transaction authorized by the ICC.[80] The lower federal courts are divided on the question of whether preemption of the RLA is necessary with respect to subsequent changes in working conditions that

---

[76]Norfolk & W. Ry. v. Train Dispatchers, 499 U.S. 117, 136 LRRM 2727 (1991).

[77]*Compare* Locomotive Eng'rs v. Chicago & N. W. Ry., 314 F2d 424, 429, 52 LRRM 2595, 2598 (CA 8), *cert. denied,* 375 U.S. 819, 54 LRRM 2312 (1963) *with* Texas & N. O. R.R. v. Railroad Trainmen, 307 F2d 151, 158–59, 50 LRRM 2663, 2667–69 (CA 5, 1962), *cert. denied,* 371 U.S. 952, 52 LRRM 2122 (1963).

[78]*See* New York Dock Ry.—Control—Brooklyn E.D. Terminal, 360 ICC 60, app. III, art. 1, §2, *aff'd sub nom.* New York Dock Ry. v. United States, 609 F2d 83, 102 LRRM 2835 (CA 2, 1979); Norfolk & W. Ry.—Trackage Rights—Burlington N. Ry., 354 ICC 605, app. 1, art. 1, §2 (1978).

[79]City of Palestine v. United States, 559 F2d 408, 414 (CA 5, 1977), *cert. denied,* 435 U.S. 950 (1978).

[80]*See, e.g.,* Burlington N. R.R. v. United Transp. Union, 862 F2d 1266, 1280, 129 LRRM 3119, 3129 (CA 7, 1988); Locomotive Eng'rs v. ICC, 761 F2d 714, 723, 119 LRRM 2258, 2263–64 (CA DC, 1985), *rev'd on other grounds,* 482 U.S. 270, 125 LRRM 2526 (1987).

facilitate the goals of the transaction,[81] and the Supreme Court left that question open in its *Norfolk & Western Railway* decision.[82]

E. Application of Section 11341(a) Preemption to Exempted Transactions

The preemption of other laws under Section 11341(a) applies when a rail transaction is "approved" under Section 11343.[83] Because many Section 11343 transactions are authorized by means of exemptions under Section 10505 from the otherwise applicable prior approval procedures, the question has arisen whether these exempted transactions can qualify for immunity under Section 11341(a).

Section 10505 exemptions relieve carriers of detailed prior approval requirements specified by ICA Section 11344. Exemptions do not remove transactions from the ICC's jurisdiction under Section 11343; the requirement that all transactions enumerated in that provision receive authorization by the ICC applies regardless of what procedures the ICC adopts for granting authorization. In addition, the ICC retains continuing jurisdiction over exempted transactions and may, under Section 10505(d), revoke exemptions if that is necessary to further the RTP.[84] The ICC therefore regards Section

---

[81]*Compare* United Transp. Union v. Norfolk & W. Ry., 822 F2d 1114, 1117–18, 125 LRRM 3080, 3082–83 (CA DC, 1987), *cert. denied*, 484 U.S. 1006, 127 LRRM 2256 (1988); Missouri P. R.R. v. United Transp. Union, 782 F2d 107, 111, 121 LRRM 2445, 2447–48 (CA 8, 1986), *cert. denied*, 482 U.S. 927, 125 LRRM 2616 (1987) *and* Locomotive Eng'rs v. Chicago & N. W. Ry., 314 F2d at 429, 52 LRRM at 2598 (all recognizing preemption of RLA with respect to subsequent changes in working conditions) *with* Burlington N. R.R. v. United Transp. Union, 862 F2d at 1280, 129 LRRM at 3129; Railway Labor Executives' Ass'n v. Grand Trunk W. R.R., 737 F Supp 1027, 1028–29 (ND Ill, 1990) *and* Southern P. Transp. Co. v. Locomotive Eng'rs, 756 F Supp 1446, 1454, 136 LRRM 2677, 2682–83 (D Kan), *dismissed as moot*, No. 91-3054 (CA 10, 1991) (all limiting scope of RLA preemption to consummation of transactions).

[82]Norfolk & W. Ry. v. Train Dispatchers, 499 U.S. 117, 136 LRRM 2727 (1991).

[83]Although §11341(a) contains a reference to transactions "exempted" under §11341(e), that provision refers to certain motor carrier transactions that are exempted under §11343(e).

[84]*See* G. & T. Terminal Packaging Co. v. Consolidated Rail Corp., 830 F2d 1230, 1234 (CA 3, 1987), *cert. denied*, 485 U.S. 988 (1988).

10505 exemptions as tantamount to approval of exempted transactions.[85]

The two federal courts of appeals that have considered the question have held that exempted Section 11343 transactions are entitled to Section 11341(a) immunity from the RLA.[86] One district court has held to the contrary.[87]

F. Section 10901 and Section 10910 Transactions

Subchapter I of the ICA, which includes Sections 10901 through 10910, contains no express provision comparable to Section 11341(a) for preemption of other laws. In *Pittsburgh & Lake Erie Railroad v. Railway Labor Executives' Ass'n*,[88] the Supreme Court held that a carrier selling a line to a noncarrier under Section 10901 was obliged under the RLA to bargain over union Section 6 notices seeking protection from the effects of the sale, and the Court found nothing in Section 10901 that would relieve the carrier of that obligation.

---

[85]*E.g., Ex parte* No. 392, Class Exemption for the Acquisition & Operation of Rail Lines under 49 USC 10901, 1 ICC2d 810, 811, *review denied,* 817 F2d 145 (CA DC, 1987). On the other hand, on a different issue, the ICC has determined that exempted transactions are not eligible for antitrust immunity under §11341(a). *See Ex parte* No. 282, Railroad Consolidation Procedures—Trackage Rights Exemption, 1 ICC2d 270, 279 (1985).

[86]Railway Labor Executives' Ass'n v. Guildford Transp. Indus., 843 F2d 1383, 129 LRRM 2128 (CA 1, 1988), *aff'g* 667 F Supp 29, 126 LRRM 2670 (D Me, 1987), *cert. denied,* 492 U.S. 905, 131 LRRM 2759 (1989); United Transp. Union v. Norfolk & W. Ry., 822 F2d 1114, 125 LRRM 3080 (CA DC, 1987), *cert. denied,* 484 U.S. 1006, 127 LRRM 2256 (1988). *See also* Locomotive Eng'rs v. Boston & Me. Corp., 788 F2d 794, 122 LRRM 2020 (CA 1), *cert. denied,* 479 U.S. 829 (1986) (holding that exempted transaction was immune from RLA under §11341(a), without addressing potential differences between exempted and formally approved transactions); Pittsburgh & L. E. R.R. v. Railway Labor Executives' Ass'n, 491 U.S. 490, 501, 131 LRRM 2611, 2614 (1989) (referring to exemption rules as expedited procedure "for seeking approval" of transactions); Burlington N. R.R. v. United Transp. Union., 862 F2d 1266, 129 LRRM 3119 (CA 7, 1988) (same).

[87]Southern P. Transp. Co. v. Locomotive Eng'rs, 756 F Supp 1446, 1453, 136 LRRM 2677, 2682 (D Kan), *appeal dismissed as moot,* No. 91-3054 (CA 10, 1991).

[88]Pittsburgh & L. E. R.R. v. Railway Labor Executives' Ass'n, 491 U.S. at 514, 131 LRRM at 2620.

G. Mandatory ICC Orders Under Sections 10505, 11123, and 11125

No express provision for immunity from other laws applies to carriers subject to ICC orders compelling forced sales under Section 10505 or to emergency and directed service orders under Sections 11123 and 11125. Although directed and emergency service orders are subject to mandatory labor protection, it is unsettled whether those orders prevail over contrary obligations of carriers under the RLA. Section 10505 has been interpreted to prohibit labor protective conditions on forced sales.[89] No court has addressed the question of implied preemption of the RLA under Sections 10505, 11123, and 11125.

The collateral attack doctrine, which provides that ICC rulings may be set aside only on direct review by a court with jurisdiction to do so, and not by means of a collateral action whose effort would be to invalidate or set aside the ICC ruling,[90] has been applied to bar a request under the RLA for a status quo injunction against consummation of a forced sale under Section 10505.[91] In *Pittsburgh & Lake Erie Railroad v. Railway Labor Executives' Ass'n*,[92] the Supreme Court held that the collateral attack doctrine does not apply to actions seeking to enforce the RLA against Section 10901 transfers, because ICC orders and exemptions under Section 10901 only permit, but do not require, consummation.

H. Accommodation of the RLA and the NLGA

Questions of accommodation of the RLA and the NLGA[93] arise when unions strike or threaten to strike to

---

[89]Simmons v. ICC, 760 F2d 126, 118 LRRM 3099 (CA 7, 1985), *cert. denied*, 474 U.S. 1055, 121 LRRM 2208 (1986).

[90]Venner v. Michigan C. R.R., 271 U.S. 127 (1927); *see also* Hobbs Administrative Orders Review Act, 28 USC §2342(5) (1993 Supp. IV).

[91]Railway Labor Executives' Ass'n, v. Staten Island R.R., 792 F2d 7, 122 LRRM 2939 (CA 2, 1986), *cert. denied*, 479 U.S. 1054, 125 LRRM 3136 (1987).

[92]491 U.S. 490, 511 n.18, 131 LRRM 2611 (1989).

[93]29 USC §§101 *et seq.* (1988).

protect ICC-authorized transactions. Section 4 of the NLGA ordinarily deprives the federal courts of jurisdiction to enjoin strikes in labor disputes.[94] That provision is "accommodate[d]," however, to permit strike injunctions under other laws that are part of the pattern of federal labor legislation and that provide peaceable administrative procedures for particular labor disputes.[95] The Supreme Court has held in several cases that the ICA generally is not a labor statute to which the NLGA may be accommodated,[96] but none of these cases involved transactions in which the ICC had jurisdiction to address labor disputes or situations in which the ICA prohibited labor protection.

In *Pittsburgh & Lake Erie Railroad v. Railway Labor Executives' Assn,*[97] the Supreme Court held that the NLGA is not accommodated in Section 10901 of the ICA, which contains no provision "that imposes any duty on rail unions to participate in ICC proceedings and to seek ICC protections with which they must be satisfied."[98] The Eighth Circuit has held, however, that the NLGA must be accommodated to Section 11347 of the ICA, which provides mandatory labor protection in all Section 11343 transactions.[99] An early decision of the Fifth Circuit, while holding that, in general, ICC labor protection procedures under the predecessor of Section 11347 are not a "complete and proper channel" for labor disputes in connection with ICC-authorized transactions, stated that if the ICC determines that particular union demands were contrary to the public interest, the NLGA would have to be

---

[94] NLGA §4(a), 29 USC §104(a) (1989).

[95] Railroad Trainmen v. Chicago River & I. R.R., 353 U.S. 30, 41–42, 39 LRRM 2578, 2582 (1957).

[96] Burlington N. R.R. v. Maintenance of Way Employees, 481 U.S. 429, 435 n.3, 125 LRRM 2073, 2075 n.3 (1987); Railroad Telegraphers v. Chicago & N. W. Ry., 362 U.S. 330, 339, 342, 45 LRRM 3104, 3107, 3108–09 (1960); Railroad Trainmen v. Chicago River & I. R.R., 353 U.S. at 42, 39 LRRM at 2582.

[97] 491 U.S. 490, 131 LRRM 2611 (1989).

[98] 491 U.S. at 514, 131 LRRM at 2620.

[99] Missouri P. R.R. v. United Transp. Union, 782 F2d 107, 111–12, 121 LRRM 2445, 2448 (CA 8, 1986) (per curiam), *cert. denied*, 482 U.S. 927, 125 LRRM 2616 (1987).

accommodated to the ICA to permit an injunction against a strike over those demands.[100]

III. Labor Protective Provisions in the Railroad Industry

The first legislation specifically to protect railroad employees is found in the Emergency Railroad Transportation Act of 1933 (ERTA),[101] which was enacted to encourage railroads to take actions that would consolidate operations, avoid unnecessary duplication of services and facilities, and promote financial reorganization. Section 7(b) of ERTA required, within very limited margins, railroads consolidating or reorganizing their current number of employees, and changing compensation for such employees, to compensate employees for moving expenses and financial losses when they were transferred.[102]

One month before the expiration of ERTA, the standard railroad labor unions reached what was formally titled "Agreement of May, 1936, Washington, D.C.," but is commonly referred to in the railroad industry as the Washington Job Protection Agreement (WJPA).[103] One of the primary purposes of the WJPA was to provide partial financial compensation to railroad employees who lost their jobs[104] or suffered losses in earnings[105] as a result of a coordination by two or more railroads of facilities, operations, or services.[106] The

---

[100]Texas & N. O. R.R. v. Railroad Trainmen, 307 F2d 151, 157, 161–62, 50 LRRM 2663, 2667, 2671 (CA 5, 1962), *cert. denied*, 371 U.S. 952, 52 LRRM 2122 (1963).

[101]Act of June 16, 1933, ch. 91, §§1–17, 209, 48 Stat. 211.

[102]ERTA §7(b).

[103]This reference is a misnomer, because the WJPA does not directly protect jobs; it provides compensation for a loss of a job or for decreased earnings.

[104]WJPA §7.

[105]*Id.* §6.

[106]*Id.* §2(a) defines a "coordination" as the "joint action by two or more carriers whereby they unify, consolidate, merge or pool in whole or in part their separate railroad facilities or any of the operations or services previously performed by them through such separate facilities."

WJPA also provided notice, negotiation, and arbitration procedures[107] for protecting seniority rights and the place of work,[108] as well as compensation for moving expenses and/ or loss from the sale of a home.[109] Thus, although the WJPA did not freeze job levels as ERTA did, the WJPA did provide, for affected employees who lost their job as a result of a coordination, a choice of a one-year lump sum displacement allowance or a monthly allowance for five years,[110] as well as, for those employees still working, up to five years of coverage for diminished earnings.[111] Therefore, in many respects the WJPA mirrored those areas of employee protection afforded railroad workers under the ERTA, but at less generous levels. The WJPA has served as the blueprint from which most ICC-imposed labor protections originate.

A. ICC Implied Authority

Whereas the expiration of ERTA repealed the specific employee protections of that Act, it did not repeal the ICC's authority, derived from the Transportation Act of 1920, to condition its approval of railroad mergers upon terms and conditions that were "just and reasonable."[112] One year prior to the negotiation of the WJPA, the ICC had concluded that it had the authority to condition its approval of a railroad consolidation on the provision of certain protections for adversely affected employees.[113] That decision by the ICC ultimately reached the Supreme Court in *United States v. Lowden*,[114] where the Court unanimously affirmed the ICC's power to impose employee protections as "just and reasonable conditions" in the "public interest."[115]

---

[107]*Id.* §4.

[108]*Id.* §§5, 13.

[109]*Id.* §§10, 11.

[110]*Id.* §7(a).

[111]*Id.* §6.

[112]Act of Feb. 28, 1920, ch. 91, 41 Stat. 480, 482. Act of June 16, 1933, ch. 91, tit. II, 48 Stat. 217–20.

[113]St. Paul Bridge & T. Ry.—Control, 199 ICC 588, 596 (1934).

[114]308 U.S. 225 (1939).

[115]*Id.* at 233–34 (*citing* 49 USC §5(4), now *id.* §11347 (1988)).

Shortly after the *Lowden* decision, the Commission found that under the abandonment provisions of the Act, formerly included in Section 1(18) and now codified in Section 10903, it had no power to impose protective conditions.[116] The Commission reasoned that the term "public convenience and necessity" as found in Section 1(18) through (20) of the ICA was less broad than the term "public interest" found in Section 5(4). Therefore, the Commission could not impose conditions for the protection of employees because such protections were not included within the concept of "public convenience and necessity."[117]

The Commission's decision was appealed, and eventually the Supreme Court unanimously affirmed a lower court ruling that reversed the ICC's conclusion that it lacked power under Section 1(18) through (20) to improve conditions for the protection of employees.[118] The Court found that the term "public convenience and necessity" in Section 1(18) should be given the same meaning the Court had given the term "public interest" in the *Lowden* decision.[119] Hence, the Court found the national interest in stable labor relations that was advanced by providing labor protections in a merger, as was the case in *Lowden*, should similarly apply to abandonments.[120]

B. Transportation Act of 1940

One year after the *Lowden* decision, Congress enacted the Transportation Act of 1940,[121] which liberalized the standards for ICC approval of mergers while at the same time added for the first time *mandatory* labor protection for railroad em-

---

[116]Pacific Elec. Ry.—Abandonment, 242 ICC 9 (1940).
[117]*Id.*
[118]ICC v. Railway Labor Executives' Ass'n, 315 U.S. 373 (1942).
[119]*Id.* at 376–78.
[120]The so-called *Burlington* conditions were then developed and were first imposed in Chicago B. & Q. R.R.—Abandonment, 257 ICC 700 (1944). These conditions were essentially identical to the *Oklahoma* conditions, discussed *infra* note 127, except that under the *Burlington* conditions employees had to relocate to retain their protections, whereas such relocation was not necessary under the *Oklahoma* conditions unless required by the employee's collective bargaining agreement.
[121]54 Stat. 898, Act of September 18, 1940, ch. 722.

ployees adversely affected by such mergers.[122] Section 5(2)(f), since recodified as Section 11347, mandates that in approving any rail merger or consolidation or other transaction subject to Section 5(2), the Commission "shall require a fair and equitable arrangement to protect the interests of the railroad employees affected."

In enacting Section 5(2)(f), Congress operated under the assumption that the ICC would impose substantially the same level of protections as under the WJPA.[123] Thus, Section 5(2)(f) incorporated some, but not all, of the employee protections provided under ERTA.

Following the enactment of Section 5(2)(f), the ICC began to develop standard labor protective conditions that in usual cases would provide what the Commission considered to be the fair and equitable arrangement required by that section.[124] In unusual cases, the Commission retained the authority to adapt the employee protections to the circumstances presented. In *Oklahoma Railway Trustees—Abandonment,*[125] a Section 5(2) purchase proceeding and not an abandonment, the Commission imposed five detailed protective provisions, modeled after the WJPA and protective conditions previously imposed by the ICC as a matter of discretion, as a condition of its approval.[126] Those conditions are commonly referred to as the *Oklahoma* conditions.[127] Shortly thereafter, the Commission adopted the convention of not spelling out in each case the details of the employee protections but instead incorporating those protections by reference to the *Oklahoma* conditions.[128]

---

[122]ICC §5(2)(f).

[123]*Hearings on H.R. 2531 Before the House Comm. on Interstate and Foreign Commerce,* 67th Cong., 1st Sess. 216–17, 243 (1939).

[124]Oklahoma Ry. Trustees—Abandonment, 257 ICC 177, 198 (1944).

[125]257 ICC 177.

[126]*Id.* at 198.

[127]The *Oklahoma* conditions provided (1) a dismissal allowance for employees whose jobs were abolished and who had no seniority in other jobs; (2) a displacement allowance for employees who suffered a decrease in monthly income; (3) a compensation of benefits allowance to preserve pension, health, and related benefits; (4) a moving allowance for employees forced to relocate; and (5) protection against financial loss from the sale of a home in the event any employees were required to move. §§4, 5, 6, 7, 9. The protective period was to extend four years, or less if the employee had fewer than four years of service.

[128]Chicago & N. W. Ry.—Merger, 261 ICC 672 (1946).

In 1952, the Commission revised the *Oklahoma* conditions in the *New Orleans Union Passenger Terminal Case*.[129] The primary significance of the *New Orleans* conditions is the Commission's adoption of Sections 4 and 5 of the WJPA, which require that the parties to an ICC transaction reach an implementing agreement prior to consummation of the transaction.[130] The effect of the *New Orleans* conditions was to "superimpose the *Oklahoma* conditions upon the provisions of the Washington Agreement [i.e., WJPA]."[131] Only the implementing agreement requirement ensured that before employees were displaced by a transaction, an arrangement would be in place that would protect their interests.[132]

The *New Orleans* conditions became the basic minimum arrangement imposed by the ICC in railroad control and merger[133] cases. The ICC has imposed these conditions in consolidation[134] and reorganization[135] cases, and to a lesser extent in trackage rights[136] and lease[137] cases, where the Commission has alternately continued to impose the *Oklahoma* conditions.

C. Urban Mass Transportation Act of 1964

In 1964, Congress passed the Urban Mass Transportation Act (UMTA)[138] to provide federal financial aid to local

---

[129]282 ICC 271, 280–81 (1952).

[130]*See* New York Dock Ry. v. United States, 609 F2d 83, 92–93, 102 LRRM 2835 (CA 2, 1979).

[131]Southern Ry.—Control—Central of Ga. Ry., 331 ICC 151, 162 (1967).

[132]An implementing agreement accomplishes two primary purposes: (1) to apply the substantive protections to the particular transaction and (2) to provide the basis upon which the carrier will select and assign the affected employees as a result of the transaction (i.e., seniority issues). Ultimately, the purpose of the implementing agreement is to apportion the adverse impact of the transaction on employees on a mutually acceptable basis. Delaware & H. Ry.—Lease & Trackage Rights Exemption—Springfield T. Ry., 4 ICC 2d 322 (1988).

[133]Louisville & N. R.R. Merger, 295 ICC 457 (1957), *aff'd sub nom.* Stott v. United States, 166 F Supp 851 (SD NY, 1958).

[134]New Orleans Union Passenger Terminal Case, 282 ICC 271 (1952).

[135]Florida E. C. Ry. Reorg., 307 ICC 5 (1958).

[136]Erie R.R. Co. Trackage Rights, 295 ICC 303 (1956).

[137]St. Louis S. Ry. Lease, 290 ICC 205 (1953).

[138]Pub. L. No. 88-365, 78 Stat. 302 (1964) (codified at 49 USC §1601 *et seq.* (1988 & 1991 Supp. III)).

governments to assist them in developing and operating mass transportation systems capable of meeting the needs of urban communities.[139]

To protect displaced employees and collective bargaining rights, Section 13(c) of UMTA makes it a condition of federal assistance that the Secretary of Labor certify that a federal aid applicant has made "fair and equitable arrangements" to protect the interests of any employees who might be adversely affected by the federal grant. These arrangements could include, if applicable, provisions to (1) preserve employee rights, privileges, and benefits under existing collective bargaining agreements; (2) continue collective bargaining rights; (3) protect employees against a worsening of their employment positions; (4) ensure employment or reemployment to employees of acquired companies; and (5) provide paid employee training or retraining. Noting that a standard of protection had already been provided to railroad employees under the ICA, Congress provided in Section 13(c) that labor protective arrangements under UMTA must provide affected employees with at least the same level of benefits as those established by Section 5(2)(f) of the ICA.

D. Rail Passenger Service Act of 1970

Congress passed the Rail Passenger Service Act of 1970 (RPSA)[140] to stem the abandonment of intercity rail passenger service. Public policy was thought to require the preservation of passenger service along certain specific geographic corridors. RPSA authorized the creation of the National Railroad Passenger Corporation (Amtrak), which would be responsible for the provision of all intercity rail passenger service. Any railroad could contract with Amtrak to provide passenger services and, in doing so, would itself be relieved of any passenger service responsibilities.

---

[139]See 49 USC §§1601, 1602 (1988 & 1991 Supp. III); H.R. REP. No. 204, 88th Cong., 1st Sess. (1964), reprinted in 1964 U.S. CODE CONG. & ADMIN. NEWS 2569–74.

[140]Pub. L. No. 91-518, 84 Stat. 1327 (codified at 45 USC §501 et seq. (1988)).

Because Congress expected that the consolidation of rail passenger services brought about by RPSA would result in the loss of numerous railroad jobs, Section 405 of RPSA provided for labor protective provisions in all railroad-Amtrak contracts for employees affected by discontinuances of passenger rail service.[141] The types of labor protective arrangements required by RPSA were almost identical to those mandated under UMTA, except that in RPSA there were no required assurances of continued employment.[142] Furthermore, as in UMTA, the protections required by Section 405 were mandated to be at least equivalent to the benefits established pursuant to Section 5(2)(f) of the ICA. Finally, RPSA provided that no contract between Amtrak and a railroad could be made until the Secretary of Labor certified that the required labor protective arrangements were included in the contract.[143]

On April 16, 1971, Amtrak tendered identical contracts to all of the passenger railroads. The contracts contained employee protective provisions that had been certified by Secretary of Labor Hodgson as being "fair and equitable" as required by Section 405.[144] These labor protective arrangements became known as "Appendix C-1."[145]

In several respects, the arrangements in Appendix C-1 expanded labor protections that had been made available under the ICA and, more specifically, the WJPA.[146] Appendix C-1 extended the period of labor protection from four to six years after an employee was dismissed or displaced. It also provided for upward adjustment of benefits equivalent to general wage increases that the displaced employee would

---

[141]45 USC §565 (1988).

[142]*See id.* §565(b), and in particular *id.* §565(b)(4). Only priority for reemployment was mandated.

[143]It should be noted that, except for the requirement to maintain labor agreements, the liability for these labor protective arrangements rested with the railroad abandoning passenger service, not with Amtrak. *Id.* §565(c).

[144]Congress of Ry. Unions v. Hodgson, 326 F Supp 68, 70, 77 LRRM 2268 (D DC, 1971).

[145]*See* New York Dock Ry. v. United States, 609 F2d 83, 89, 102 LRRM 2835 (CA 2, 1979).

[146]Appendix C-1 had no application beyond the RPSA transactions and did not amend either the ICA or the WJPA.

have earned at the home railroad had he or she not been
displaced. Finally, where a railroad and an employee disputed
whether an Amtrak assumption of services resulted in the
employee's displacement, Appendix C-1 shifted the burden
of proof from the employee to the employer.

E. Regional Rail Reorganization Act of 1973

The bankruptcies of several major railroad carriers in
the Northeast and Midwest in the early 1970s spurred the
federal government again to become involved in the reorganization and consolidation of the railroad industry. The Regional Rail Reorganization Act of 1973 (3R Act),[147] which
became law on January 2, 1974, provided for the restructuring of rail service in the Northeast and Midwest and the
establishment of the Consolidated Rail Corporation (Conrail)
to operate the restructured system.

The 3R Act provided labor protective arrangements for
employees adversely affected by Conrail's assumption of private railroad operations.[148] These arrangements differed
from past legislated labor protections in two significant ways.

The first significant difference was that the 3R Act did
not merely set minimum guidelines for labor protective arrangements; it actually mandated specific terms and conditions that would be applied to affected employees. These
terms and conditions were the result of recommendations
that railroad union and carrier representatives made to Congress.[149] Certain of the labor protective provisions contained
in the 3R Act were significantly more generous than the
protections that had been extended under RPSA.[150] Most
significantly, employees adversely affected by the establishment of Conrail who had five or more years of railroad service

---

[147]Pub. L. No. 93-236, 87 Stat. 985 (1973) (codified as amended at 45 USC
§701 et seq. (1988)).

[148]See title V of the 3R Act, 45 USC §§771–80 (1988). The 3R Act was applicable
only to Conrail's system building and did not extend its mandated labor protection
to other transactions still covered by ICA §5(2)(f).

[149]See COMMENTS OF THE SECRETARY OF TRANSPORTATION ON PUB. L. No. 93-
236 (Nov. 14, 1973), reprinted in 1973 U.S. CODE CONG. & ADMIN. NEWS 3295–97.

[150]Id.

were eligible for lifetime (to age 65) income protection, in contrast to the six-year maximum period allowed under RPSA. Like the RPSA income protective arrangements, monthly income protection payments under the 3R Act would be increased as railroad wages in general increased. In addition, employees who were severed entirely from railroad employment were made eligible for severance benefits of up to $25,000. Finally, employees forced to change their residences because of the establishment of Conrail were to be reimbursed for relocation expenses.[151]

The second significant aspect of the 3R Act's labor protective provisions was that the Act provided for the unprecedented use of direct government funding to pay for the benefits. Congress appropriated $250 million in 1974 for this purpose, anticipating that this amount would be sufficient to cover the cost of labor protective benefits through the end of the century.[152] The funds were nearly exhausted by 1980.[153]

F. Railroad Revitalization and Regulatory Reform Act of 1976

As the financial decline of the railroads continued, Congress took further action in 1976 by enacting the Railroad Revitalization and Regulatory Reform Act of 1976 (4R Act).[154] The 4R Act was intended to revitalize the industry by streamlining regulation in such a manner as to allow railroads to compete with other forms of transportation, while maintaining protections for consumers of rail services.[155]

The 4R Act amended Section 5(2)(f) of the ICA to enhance labor protective provisions on certain rail transactions subject to the ICC. These provisions were to be no less protective of employee interests than the standards that had pre-

---

[151]The WJPA also served as a source of benefits for affected rail employees and, in some instances, provided greater levels of benefits.

[152]See 45 USC §779 (1988).

[153]See Henry H. Perritt, Jr., *Ask and Ye Shall Receive: The Legislative Response to the Northeast Rail Crisis*, 28 Vill. L. Rev. 326 (1983).

[154]Pub. L. No. 94-210, 90 Stat. 31.

[155]See S. Rep. No. 499, 94th Cong., 2d Sess. 1, *reprinted in* 1976 U.S. Code Cong. & Admin. News 14, 15.

viously been established by ICA Section 5(2)(f) *and* Section 405 of RPSA.[156] In addition, the 4R Act amended the ICA to make labor protection mandatory rather than discretionary in abandonment transactions.[157]

Based on the authority of the 4R Act, the ICC increased the levels of labor protection required for approved transactions. In the case of rail mergers, control and acquisition transactions, consolidations, and unifications, the ICC combined the most favorable labor protective provisions contained in Appendix C-1 and the *New Orleans* conditions.[158] These subsequently became known as the *New York Dock* conditions. In trackage rights and lease transactions, the ICC combined protections provided in Appendix C-1 with the *Oklahoma* conditions.[159] The appropriate standards for trackage rights transactions subsequently became known as the *Norfolk and Western* conditions. The standards for lease transactions became known as the *Mendocino Coast* conditions.[160] Finally, in abandonment cases, the ICC set the level of labor protective provisions as those required under Appendix C-1.[161] These subsequently became known as the *Oregon Short Line* conditions.

In general, the favorable Appendix C-1 provisions that were added to the previously effective conditions following the 4R Act were (1) the six-year period of income protection, (2) the allocation of the burden of proof to the employer to show that an employee was not displaced by the ICC ap-

---

[156]*See* §402(a) of the 4R Act.

[157]*See id.* §802.

[158]*See* New York Dock Ry.—Control—Brooklyn E. Dist. Terminal, 354 ICC 399, *modified*, 360 ICC 60, *aff'd*, 609 F2d 83, 102 LRRM 2835 (CA 2, 1979). The *New Orleans* conditions were the labor protection provisions applied to those types of transactions prior to passage of the 4R Act. Southern Ry.—Control—Central of Ga. Ry., 317 ICC 557 (1962), *modified*, 317 ICC 729 (1963) *and* 331 ICC 151 (1967).

[159]*See* Mendocino Coast Ry.—Lease & Operate—Cal. W. R.R., 360 ICC 653, *aff'd*, Railway Labor Executives' Ass'n v. United States, 675 F2d 1248 (CA DC, 1982). The ICC had applied the *Oklahoma* conditions prior to passage of the 4R Act to trackage right and lease transactions. *See* 675 F2d at 1250–51.

[160]*See* Mendoino Coast Ry.—Lease & Operate—Cal. W. R.R., 360 ICC 653.

[161]*See* Oregon Short Line R.R.—Abandonment—Portion Goshen Branch, 354 ICC 76 (1977), *modified*, 354 ICC 584 (1978) *and* 360 ICC 666 (1980).

proved-transaction, and (3) the "indexing" of benefits to wage increases negotiated during the benefit period.[162]

G. Labor Protection in the 1980s

Despite the legislative efforts of the federal government in the 1970s, the 1980s opened with the railroad industry continuing to suffer serious financial decline in the face of competition from other modes of interstate transportation. Congress again examined conditions in the industry and concluded that a major source of the industry's problems was intensive and inflexible economic regulation to which rail carriers and parties seeking to enter the industry were subjected. Congress responded by passing the Staggers Rail Act of 1980.[163]

The Staggers Act directly affected ICA labor protection requirements in several respects.[164] Labor protective conditions were made mandatory for feeder line sealers and the elimination of rate bureaus.[165] The ICC was granted discretion to impose labor protection on reciprocal switching agreements and on the construction of new rail lines.[166] Labor protective conditions were not provided for forced or involuntary sales of rail lines.

The Staggers Act's most profound effect on labor protection, though, was the combination of its rail transportation policy statements and its amendment of Section 10505 of the ICA.[167] As amended, Section 10505 provided the procedure by which the ICC could exempt rail transactions from regulation under particular ICA provisions to the extent that such regulation was "not necessary to carry out" the broad transportation policies of the Staggers Act. This exemption would apply to transactions that were limited in scope, and where

---

[162]*See* New York Dock Ry.—Control—Brooklyn E. Dist. Terminal, 354 ICC 399, *modified*, 360 ICC 60, *aff'd*, 609 F2d 83, 102 LRRM 2835 (CA 2, 1979); Mendocino Coast Ry., 360 ICC 653; Oregon Short Line R.R., 360 ICC 666.

[163]Pub. L. No. 96-448, 94 Stat. 1897.

[164]*See supra* §II.

[165]§§401 & 219.

[166]§§223 & 221.

[167]§§213 & 101.

regulation was not required to prevent a party to the transaction from abusing its market power.[168] Section 10505 was to serve as the vehicle for implementing Section 10101a's policy, and the ICC exempted several broad categories of rail transactions from labor protection under Section 10505 as the 1980s progressed. For example, in its 1982 decision in *Knox & Kane Railroad*,[169] the ICC relied on Section 10505 to exempt a transaction involving a line sale from a carrier to a noncarrier from the requirement of prior regulatory approval.

The Staggers Act amendments to Section 10905 of the ICA provided that, where a financially responsible party offered to purchase a rail line for which the ICC had (or would have) authorized abandonment, the ICC could force the owner of the line to sell it to the prospective purchaser. If an agreement on terms of the sale could not be reached, the ICC would determine those terms, including the sale price. Section 10905 was silent, though, as to whether the ICC could impose labor protective conditions.

In 1983, in *Illinois Central Gulf Railroad*,[170] the ICC determined that it had no statutory authority to impose labor protection on line sales governed by Section 10905.[171] The ICC initially noted that Section 10905 was silent concerning labor protection, whereas other Staggers Act amendments to the ICA had expressly dealt with the ICC's mandatory or discretionary authority to impose labor protective conditions on other types of transactions.[172] The ICC also concluded that forcing the imposition of labor protective conditions would likely conflict with the goal of Section 10905 to encourage sales of lines that would otherwise be abandoned by making such line sales more costly.[173]

---

[168]*See supra* §II.

[169]Knox & Kane R.R.—Gettysburg R.R.—Petition for Exemption, 366 ICC 439 (1982).

[170]Illinois C. G. R.R.—Abandonment, 366 ICC 911, *aff'd sub nom.* Simmons v. ICC, 760 F2d 126 (CA 7, 1985), *cert. denied,* 474 U.S. 1055 (1986).

[171]*Id.*

[172] *Id.* at 912–13.

[173]*Id.* at 914.

H. Exemption of Section 10901 Transactions

In 1985, after considering numerous individual cases, the ICC promulgated a rule, Ex parte No. 392,[174] which exempted from ICC regulation all acquisitions under ICA Section 10901 of rail lines by new rail carriers. In Ex parte No. 392, the Commission stated that labor protection normally would not be imposed on the exempted transactions.[175] The ICC concluded that the high cost of such provisions would discourage acquisition and continued operation of abandoned or abandonable lines, contrary to the ICC's congressionally directed policies encouraging the continuation of rail operations.[176] Moreover, the ICC noted that increased abandonments could hurt employee interests by eliminating jobs, whereas encouragement of new carriers entering the industry fostered a continuation of work and job opportunities for railroad employees.[177]

Ex parte No. 392 did not absolutely preclude the imposition of labor protective conditions for exempted Section 10901 transactions. A party seeking labor protection was permitted to file a petition with the ICC to revoke the exemption under Section 10505(d). However, the ICC stated that labor protection would be granted on such a petition only if a union could show "extraordinary circumstances" that justified protective conditions.[178] Since Ex parte No. 392, the ICC has defined the "extraordinary circumstances" required for labor protection as encompassing situations where (1) there is misuse of the ICC's rules or procedures; (2) existing contracts provide employee protections in the event of a line sale; (3) labor would suffer unique and disproportionate injuries compared to the benefits of the transaction to the transporta-

---

[174]*Ex parte* No. 392 (Sub-No. 1), Class Exemption for the Acquisition & Operation of Rail Lines under 49 USC §10901, 1 ICC2d 810, *review denied*, 817 F2d 145 (CA DC, 1987), *codified at* 49 CFR §1150.31–34 (1994).

[175]1 ICC2d at 813–14.

[176]*Id.* at 815.

[177]*Id.*

[178]*Id.*

tion system, and labor could be compensated for these injuries without terminating the transaction or substantially undoing the transaction's benefits to the transportation system; or (4) the parties to the Section 10901 transaction voluntarily agree to labor protective provisions.[179] To date, though, the ICC has imposed labor protection only in situations where parties have voluntarily agreed to such conditions.[180]

I. Noncarrier Line Transactions

Ex parte No. 392 did not remove all rail line acquisitions by noncarriers from ICC regulation and mandatory imposition of labor protection. Section 11343 of the ICA requires ICC approval for transactions in which a noncarrier acquires control of at least two carriers, or in which a noncarrier that already controls at least one carrier acquires control of another carrier. In addition, Section 11343 encompasses noncarrier acquisitions of lines where, whatever the form of the transaction, the *effect* of the transaction was to place one or more carriers in control of the acquired lines.[181] If an acquisition by a noncarrier was governed by Section 11343 rather than Section 10901, it was subject to the mandatory imposition of labor protective provisions under Section 11347 of the ICA.[182]

---

[179]*See* FRVR Corp.—Exemption—Acquisition & Operation—Certain Lines of Chicago & N. W. Transp. Co., Fin. Docket No. 31205, *vacated on other grounds sub nom.* Railway Labor Executives' Ass'n v. ICC, 888 F2d 1227, 132 LRRM 2912 (CA 8, 1989), *cert. denied*, 494 U.S. 1079, 133 LRRM 3112 (1990); P&LE Acquisition Corp.—Acquisition & Operation Exemption—Assets of the Pittsburgh & L. E. R.R., Fin. Docket No. 31607 (Apr. 3, 1990).

[180]*See* P&LE Acquisition Corp., Fin. Docket No. 31607.

[181]*See* 49 USC §11343(b). Note, however, that the ICC has permitted use of *Ex parte* No. 392 by a noncarrier that is owned by a noncarrier holding company that also owns a carrier. *E.g.*, Railway Labor Executives' Ass'n v. ICC, 914 F2d 276, 135 LRRM 2566 (CA DC, 1990), *cert. denied*, 499 U.S. 959, 136 LRRM 3024 (1991).

[182]*See* 49 USC §§11344, 11347. Section 11344 describes the procedure for authorization of a §11343 transaction. Section 11347 provides that transactions for which approval is sought under §11344 are subject to employee protective arrangements.

J. Subsequent Refinements in Employee Protections

In the wake of the numerous line sales by major Class I railroads in the late 1980s, the Commission addressed the various obligations of the purchaser and seller under the *New York Dock* protections. Primarily at issue was whether the implementing agreement required by Article I, Section 4 of the *New York Dock* conditions would be a joint agreement between the buyer, seller, and their unions, or separate implementing agreements negotiated between the seller and its unions and the buyer and its unions.

In *Brandywine Valley Railroad—Purchase,*[183] the Commission examined the issue and concluded that all parties must participate in the implementing agreement process.[184] The Commission based this finding on Sections 4 and 5 of the WJPA, which are mandated by that part of Section 11347 that states that the employee protections will be "at least as protective . . . as those imposed before February 5, 1976."

However, one year later in *Wilmington Terminal Railroad—Purchase and Lease—CSX Transportation, Inc.,*[185] the Commission reversed itself. The ICC found that the buyer need not be a party to the implementing agreement negotiations between the seller and its unions, but need only negotiate an agreement with its own unions, if any.[186] The Commission further held that the buyer was *not* required to (1) give priority rights of hire to the seller's employees displaced by the transaction; (2) assume the seller's collective bargaining agreements and associated rights, benefits, and privileges; or (3) preserve the collective bargaining rights and representatives of the seller's employees who accepted positions with the buyer.[187] In addition, the ICC concluded that the seller's obli-

---

[183]5 ICC2d 764, *petition for review dismissed,* No. 89-1503 (CA DC, 1991).

[184]*Id.* at 773–74 (quoting Delaware & H. Ry.—Lease Exemption, 4 ICC2d 322, 325 (1988)).

[185]6 ICC2d 799, *aff'd sub nom.* Railway Labor Executives' Ass'n v. ICC, 930 F2d 511 (CA 6, 1991).

[186]*Id.* at 820.

[187]*Id.* at 814–15.

gation to provide protection to its employees ceased as soon as the employees accepted employment with the buyer, even if those jobs provided a lower rate of compensation than the ones they lost, but continued if the employees elected to decline jobs with the buyer and remain in the seller's employment.[188]

K. Employee Protections Reached by Negotiations

Whereas most ICA transactions in which employee protections are required result in the imposition of the standard ICC protective arrangements, the parties are free to negotiate their own arrangement, provided it meets the minimum levels required by Section 11347. When the parties choose to negotiate their own arrangement, the ICC reviews that protective arrangement to ensure it meets these minimum levels. Beyond that, the parties are free to tailor the agreement to their own needs.

The principal exercise of this ICC authority occurred in the 1960s in connection with a number of merger and control cases that resulted in the formation of what are now the major Class I railroads. These consolidations of large railroads into even bigger rail systems had a clear impact on significant numbers of employees. The parties responded to the carrier's desire to combine facilities and consolidate operations and the employees' interests in preserving their rights under their existing collective bargaining agreements with the so-called attrition agreements.[189] Under such arrangements, the railroads provided guarantees of lifetime employment to their current employees in return for modifications in the agreements permitting them to move employees, and sometimes

---

[188]*Id.* at 815.

[189]*See* Norfolk & W. Ry.—Merger, Wilmington Terminal R.R.—Purchase & Lease—CSX Transp. Inc., Virginian Ry., 307 ICC 401, 439 (1959); Chicago & N. W. Ry.—Purchase—Minneapolis & St. L. Ry., 312 ICC 285, 296 (1960); Norfolk & W. Ry.—Merger—New York, C. & St. L. R.R., 324 ICC 1, 50 (1964); Atchison, T. & S.F. Ry.—Merger, 324 ICC 254, 255, 261 (1965); Pennsylvania R.R.—Merger—New York C. R.R., 328 ICC 304, 313 (1966); Great N. Pac.—Merger—Great N., 331 ICC 228, 277–79 (1967); Seaboard Coast Line R.R.—Merger—Piedmont & N. Ry., 334 ICC 378, 384–85 (1969).

but not always their work, throughout the merged or commonly controlled systems. In each instance, the ICC found the arrangement satisfied the requirements of the predecessor to Section 11347, Section 5(2)(f). The Commission did not modify these arrangements in any way.

What sets such agreements apart from protective arrangements negotiated under the RLA is that once they have been negotiated, Section 11347 of the ICA prevents the parties from "substantially abrogating" the benefits.[190] Although the parties can modify such arrangements by providing additional protection or by giving employees a choice between their existing protections and another arrangement, the parties must not materially reduce those benefits.[191]

IV. OVERVIEW OF FEDERAL AVIATION ADMINISTRATION REGULATION OF AIR CARRIERS

The comprehensive scheme of government regulation of the air transportation industry, which most recently was embodied in the Federal Aviation Act of 1958,[192] was first established by the Civil Aeronautics Act of 1938.[193] That Act created the Civil Aeronautics Authority, later renamed the Civil Aeronautics Board (CAB), which was charged, inter alia, with the implementation of government regulation in the areas of air carrier economic regulation and civil aeronautics safety regulation.[194] Whereas the CAB was eventually eliminated in 1985 pursuant to the Airline Deregulation Act of 1978 (ADA),[195] government regulation in these areas has continued under the authority of the U.S. Department of Transportation (DOT) and the Federal Aviation Administration (FAA).

---

[190]Norfolk & W. Ry. v. Nemitz, 404 U.S. 37, 44–45, 78 LRRM 2721 (1971).
[191]*Id.*
[192]Pub. L. No. 85-726, 72 Stat. 731 (codified at 49 USC §§40101 *et seq.* (1994)).
[193]Act of June 23, 1938, Ch. 601, 52 Stat. 973.
[194]Civil Aeronautics Act of 1938 §§401 *et seq.*, 601 *et seq.*
[195]Pub. L. No. 95-504, 92 Stat. 1705.

A. Air Carrier Economic Regulation

The Federal Aviation Act established an elaborate framework of economic regulation based on the certificate of public convenience and necessity. The CAB, through its power to impose conditions on changes in the status of such certificates, and especially through its power to impose "such terms and conditions as it shall find to be just and reasonable" on its approval of various consolidations, mergers, purchases, acquisitions of control, and other transactions in the airline industry,[196] exerted significant influence in the area of labor–management relations.[197]

Although the government's role in economic regulation of the airline industry has decreased considerably since the passage of the ADA, there are still provisions in the statutes that regulate the economic aspects of the employment relationship. Section 401(k) of the Federal Aviation Act requires that "[e]very air carrier shall maintain rates of compensation, maximum hours, and other working conditions and relations of all of its pilots and copilots . . . so as to conform with the decision numbered 83 made by the National Labor Board on May 10, 1934,"[198] which prescribed minimum wages and working conditions for pilots, including a maximum of 85 hours of flying per month.[199] There is, however, a question regarding the continued vitality of Decision No. 83 as incorpo-

---

[196]Civil Aeronautics Act of 1938 §408(b).

[197]This was the basis of the Board's imposition of the labor protective provisions discussed in *infra*. §V. The government's role in this area was by and large eliminated as a result of the passage of the ADA and the administrative interpretation thereof.

[198]Civil Aeronautics Act of 1938 §401(l)(1).

Section 401(k)(1) applies to interstate air transportation in the continental United States. Section 401(k)(2) contains a similar provision with respect to "overseas or foreign air transportation or air transportation wholly within a Territory or possession of the United States." Civil Aeronautics Act of 1938 §401(l)(2).

Pursuant to §416(b) of the Civil Aeronautics Act, the Board was allowed to grant exemptions from present §401(k) with respect to wages for daylight flying. However, exemptions were not allowed as to wages for night flying or maximum hours.

[199]*In re* Air Line Pilots' Wage Dispute, Decisions of the National Labor Board pt. II, at 21 (1934).

rated by Section 401(k).[200] There is also a private cause of action to collect the difference between actual wages and the minimum wages established in the Board's Decision,[201] but inflation since 1934 has reduced those minimums to a point where they are no longer meaningful.[202]

Section 401(k)(4) of the Federal Aviation Act provides that "[i]t shall be a condition upon the holding of a certificate by any air carrier that such carrier shall comply with Title II of the Railway Labor Act, as amended."[203] Section 401(k)(4) is not applicable to air carriers that were operating pursuant to a regulatory exemption from the certification requirement,[204] and it does not require a domestic carrier to recognize a certified union as the representative of employees who are not U.S. citizens and who work wholly outside the United States.[205]

B. Airline Safety Regulations

Pursuant to Section 601(a)(6) of the Federal Aviation Act, the FAA is required to issue "reasonable rules and regulations, or minimum standards . . . as the Secretary of Transportation may find necessary to provide adequately for na-

---

[200]The FAA's safety regulations permit a pilot to work more than 85 hours per month. *See generally* 50 Fed. Reg. 29,308 (1985) ("One commenter objected to the Part 121 monthly flight time limit of 100 hours in any calendar month on the basis that Decision 83, which was incorporated into law, is still in force. . . . Decision 83 was incorporated into Federal law in the Civil Aeronautics Act of 1938, and reenacted in both the Federal Aviation Act of 1958 and the Airline Deregulation Act of 1978. Decision 83 is incorporated into Title IV of the Federal Aviation Act, which governs economic regulation, not into Title VI, which affects safety regulations. The economic decisions in Decision 83 have never carried over to safety rules such as the monthly flight time limit."). *Accord*, Air Line Pilots v. CAB, 215 F2d 122, 124 (CA 2, 1954).

[201]Laughlin v. Riddle Aviation Co., 205 F2d 948 (CA 5, 1953).

[202]For example, Decision No. 83 imposed a minimum base salary of $1600 per year, and a minimum wage of $4 to $7.50 per hour depending on aircraft speed and day/night flying. *See In re* Air Line Pilots' Wage Dispute, pt. II, at 21.

[203]Civil Aeronautics Act of 1938 §401(l)(4). *See also* Air Line Pilots v. Southern Airways, Enforcement Proceeding, 36 CAB 430 (1962).

[204]Professional Airmen v. CAB, 511 F2d 423, 88 LRRM 3537 (CA DC, 1975).

[205]Air Line Stewards & Stewardesses Ass'n v. Trans World Airlines, 173 F Supp 369, 378–79 (SD NY), *aff'd*, 273 F2d 69 (CA 2, 1959), *cert. denied*, 362 U.S. 988 (1960).

tional security and safety in air commerce"[206] in such a manner "as will best tend to reduce or eliminate the possibility of, or recurrence of, accidents in air transportation."[207] Under this authority, the FAA licenses pilots, mechanics, dispatchers, and other employees.[208] Pursuant to the provisions of Section 601(a)(5), the FAA is mandated to promulgate "[r]easonable rules and regulations governing, in the interest of safety, the maximum hours or periods of service of airmen, and other employees, of air carriers."[209] Such regulations—now known as Federal Air Regulations (FARs)—have been promulgated setting forth yearly, monthly, and daily maximum hours, and mandatory rest periods for various types of employees, including mechanics and pilots.[210]

With respect to the pilot's certificate, Section 602(b) also provides that an applicant must be "physically able to perform the duties pertaining to the position for which the airman certificate is sought."[211] The FAA thus requires all applicants for a pilot certificate also to obtain a medical certificate. In implementing the medical certificate requirement, a number of physical conditions that could be regarded as disabilities (e.g., a history of heart trouble, drug addiction, or alcoholism) may under some circumstances result in disqualification.[212]

---

[206]Civil Aeronautics Act of 1938 §601(a)(6).

[207]*Id.* §601(b).

[208]*See* 14 CFR pts. 61, 63, 65 (1994).

[209]Civil Aeronautics Act of 1938 §601(a)(5).

[210]*See, e.g.,* 14 CFR §§121.361–525, 135.261–71 (1994). For an explanation of these regulations, *see* 50 Fed. Reg. 29,306–22 (1985).

[211]Civil Aeronautics Act of 1938, §602(b).

[212]The regulations are codified at 14 CFR pt. 67 (1994). *See generally* Schwartz v. Helms, 712 F2d 633 (CA DC, 1983) (upholding a regulation that provides for an automatic disqualification of all pilots with a history of symptomatic coronary heart disease); Day v. National Transp. Safety Bd. 414 F2d 950 (CA 5, 1969) (affirming the denial of a medical certificate to a pilot who failed to establish that he had not experienced a myocardial infarction); Meik v. National Transp. Safety Bd., 710 F2d 584 (CA 9, 1983) (affirming the denial of a certificate to a pilot who had suffered, and recovered from, a moderate cerebrovascular accident of unknown origin); Johnson v. National Transp. Safety Bd., 707 F2d 402 (CA 9, 1983) (affirming the denial of a certificate to a pilot who had a clinical history and diagnosis of alcoholism). *See also* Delta Air Lines v. United States, 490 F Supp 907, 916–18 (ND Ga, 1980) (invalidating the FAA's practice of routinely granting exemptions from the regulations requiring absolute disqualification where specified medical conditions are present).

The most controversial such regulation is the "Age 60 Rule," under which a person may not, once he or she reaches the age of 60, hold a pilot's certificate and hence may not serve as a pilot for a commercial airline operating under part 121 of the FARs.[213] The validity of this rule, and the FAA's policy of not granting exemptions regardless of the physical condition of a particular pilot, have been upheld by the courts.[214]

C. Preemption of Federal and State Law by the Federal Aviation Act

Whereas questions involving the impact of ICC approval of mergers and other transactions on railroad industry collective bargaining agreements have been extensively litigated, there are no cases deciding such questions with respect to airline mergers under the Federal Aviation Act. However, the language of the ICA exempts the participants in an approved transaction from "the antitrust laws *and from all other law*,"[215] whereas the analogous provision of the Federal Aviation Act exempts the participants only "from the antitrust laws."[216] Indeed, the Federal Aviation Act as initially enacted provided an exemption from "the operations of the 'antitrust laws' . . . and of all other restraints or prohibitions made by, or imposed under, authority of law."[217] On the other hand, one court

---

[213]*See* 14 CFR §121.383(c) (1994).

[214]*See, e.g.*, Air Line Pilots Ass'n v. Quesada, 182 F Supp 595 (SD NY), *aff'd*, 276 F2d 892 (CA 2, 1960), *aff'd on later appeal*, 286 F2d 319 (CA 2), *cert. denied*, 366 U.S. 962 (1961) (upholding the FAA's initial promulgation of the Age 60 Rule); O'Donnell v. Shaffer, 491 F2d 59 (CA DC, 1974) (upholding the FAA's decision not to revoke or amend the Age 60 Rule).

For cases upholding the FAA's no-exemption policy, *see* Starr v. FAA, 589 F2d 307 (CA 7, 1978); Rombough v. FAA, 594 F2d 893 (CA 2, 1979); Gray v. FAA, 594 F2d 793 (CA 10, 1979); Keating v. FAA, 610 F2d 611 (CA 9, 1979). *See also* Baker v. FAA, 917 F2d 318 (CA 7, 1990) (criticizing the FAA's continued adherence to the no-exemption policy, but upholding the agency's conclusion that any decrease in risk associated with the greater experience of older pilots did not compensate for the increased risk associated with physical and mental deterioration), *cert. denied*, 499 U.S. 936 (1991).

[215]49 USC §11341(a) (1994) (emphasis added).

[216]Airline Deregulation Act of 1978, §30(a), Pub. L. No. 95-504, 92 Stat. 1705, 1731 (codified at 49 USC §41308(b) (1994)).

[217]Federal Aviation Act of 1958, tit. IV, §414, Pub. L. No. 85-726, 72 Stat. 731, 770 (codified at 49 USC §1384 (1976)).

concluded in an airline merger case that "even matters which the company would otherwise have to negotiate under our interpretation of the Railway Labor Act, may be excluded from the negotiations if bargaining, with its corollary of a right to strike, would have the effect of somehow jeopardizing the merger."[218] Also, when the CAB has deemed it appropriate to impose labor protective and other conditions on its approval of an airline merger or other transaction, the courts have generally ruled that the CAB's authority to attach such conditions supersedes any contrary requirements in collective bargaining agreements.[219]

With respect to the preemption of state law, the FAA's comprehensive safety regulations have led courts to conclude that the federal government has "occupied the field" as to the regulation of job qualifications for safety-sensitive positions in the airline industry, and therefore to preclude the application of state laws relating to, inter alia, disability discrimination and employment drug testing.[220] Conversely, courts have concluded that the Federal Aviation Act's economic regulation of a carrier's operations does not preclude the application of state laws relating to employment discrimination, minimum wages, and overtime.[221]

---

[218]Machinists v. Northeast Airlines, 473 F2d 549, 560, 80 LRRM 2197 (CA 1), cert. denied, 409 U.S. 845 (1972).

[219]Those cases are discussed in infra §V.

[220]Northwest Airlines v. Gomez-Bethke, 34 FEP Cases 837, 845–46 (D Minn, 1984) (the Federal Aviation Act, and the FAA's safety regulations promulgated thereunder, precluded the application of the Minnesota Human Rights Act to a carrier's decision not to participate in a program to allow alcoholic pilots to return to work contingent on carrier-monitored continued abstinence); French v. Pan Am. Express, Inc., 869 F2d 1, 3–7 (CA 1, 1989) (the Federal Aviation Act, and the FAA's safety regulations promulgated thereunder, precluded the application of a Rhode Island statute governing drug testing in the workplace to a pilot engaged in interstate flights). In French, the court concluded: "We infer from the Federal Aviation Act an unmistakably clear intent to occupy the field of pilot regulation related to air safety, to the exclusion of state law. In our judgment, such an intent is implicit in the pervasiveness of relevant federal regulation, the dominance of the federal interest, and the legislative goal of establishing a single, uniform system of control over air safety. In this case, all flight plans lead to Washington." Id. at 6–7.

[221]See Colorado Anti-Discrimination Comm'n v. Continental Air Lines, 372 U.S. 714, 723–24 (1963) (the Federal Aviation Act does not preempt the application of a state statute prohibiting racial discrimination in hiring); Santoni Roig v. Iberia Lineas Aereas de Espana, 688 F Supp 810, 817–18, 130 LRRM 2050 (D PR, 1988)

The Federal Aviation Act also contains an express preemption provision which declares that "no State . . . shall enact or enforce any law, rule, regulation, standard, or other provision having the force and effect of law relating to the rates, routes, or services of any air carrier."[222] The extent to which this provision precludes the application of state laws regulating the employer–employee relationship is unclear. In *Morales v. Trans World Airlines*,[223] the Supreme Court adopted a broad reading of the express preemption provision, pursuant to which the application of state laws "having a connection with or reference to" the rates, routes, or services of an air carrier is precluded,[224] and held that a state's efforts to regulate the format and content of airline fare advertisements was preempted. However, the Court also noted that some state laws would have "too tenuous, remote, or peripheral" a relationship to rates, routes, or services to trigger the express preemption provision.[225] At present, the courts are divided over the applicability of the express preemption provision in the employment context.[226]

(the application of local minimum wage and overtime requirements is not precluded by §601(a)(5) of the Federal Aviation Act, which directs the FAA to promulgate "[r]easonable rules and regulations governing, in the interest of safety, the maximum hours or periods of service of airmen, and other employees, of air carriers," because no such rules have been issued as to employees who are not pilots or copilots).

[222]ADA §4(a).

[223]112 S Ct 2031 (1992).

[224]*Id.* at 2037.

[225]*Id.* at 2040.

[226]*Compare* Anderson v. American Airlines, 2 F3d 590, 597 (CA 5, 1993) ("[F]ollowing the Supreme Court's cautionary note in *Morales*," the court ruled that §1305(a) did not preclude an airline employee's claim for money damages for discrimination in retaliation for filing a worker's compensation claim); Northwest Airlines v. Gomez-Bethke, 34 FEP Cases 837, 843–44 (D Minn, 1984) (the phrase "relating to . . . services of any air carrier" in §1305(a) did not preclude the application of a state antidiscrimination statute to a carrier's policy regarding pilot qualifications; the court noted that the legislative history of §1305(a) "uses the term 'services' only when discussing regulations concerning locations which air carriers may serve and the nature of the services (i.e. passenger vs. cargo, nonstop vs. interrupted service, etc.) which they may provide" *and* Gay v. Carlson, 23 Av. Cas. (CCH) 17984, 17986–87 (SD NY, 1991) (§1305(a) did not preclude a tort action based on the plaintiff's allegations that coworkers had made false reports of safety violations to the FAA and his employer, and thereby had caused his discharge) *with* Belgard v. United Air Lines, 857 P2d 467, 471 (Colo Ct App, 1992) (§1305(a) precluded claims under a state handicap discrimination statute brought by two airline employees who were

The Omnibus Transportation Employee Testing Act of 1991 adds an express preemption provision to the Federal Aviation Act that provides that "[n]o State or local government shall adopt or have in effect any law, rule, regulation, ordinance, standard, or order that is inconsistent with the regulations promulgated under this section, except that the regulations promulgated under this section shall not be construed to preempt provisions of State criminal law which impose sanctions for reckless conduct leading to actual loss of life, injury, or damage to property."[227]

V. LABOR PROTECTIVE PROVISIONS IN THE AIRLINE INDUSTRY

Two distinct types of labor protective provisions (LPPs) have developed in the airline industry. One type, providing merger protection for airline employees, was a prerequisite for government approval of airline mergers until the mid-1980s. The government no longer mandates such LPPs, but protection may be obtained through collective bargaining. A second type of LPP, also referred to as employer protective provisions, was required by the ADA in order to protect airline employees from the adverse impact of deregulation. The historical development and current status of these two types of LPPs are discussed in the following subsections.

A. Merger Protections

The concept of merger protection for airline employees has its roots in the LPPs of the ICC, discussed earlier.[228] The

---

denied promotions to line pilot; the court reasoned that "any law or regulation that restricts an airline's selection of employees, based on their physical characteristics, must necessarily have a connection with and reference to, and therefore must be one 'relating to,' the services to be rendered by that airline"), *cert. denied,* 114 S Ct 1066 (1994).

[227]Pub. L. No. 102-143, tit. V, §3(a), 105 Stat. 917, 956, enacting, inter alia, §614(e)(1) of the Federal Aviation Act of 1958. Drug testing is discussed in Chapter 1, "Introduction," § XII.

[228]*See supra* §III.

CAB adopted the ICC's approach in the early 1950s, noting that the Board's public policy considerations under the Federal Aviation Act were similar to the ICC's.[229] The Board stated that airline mergers, which benefit shareholders and the public as a whole, impose hardships on affected employees "which should be mitigated by provisions for their benefit."[230] The Board's new LPP policy withstood judicial challenge.[231]

For several years following adoption of its LPP policy, the CAB routinely imposed LPPs tailored to the particular transaction before it. In the 1960s, the Board moved toward standardization of its merger protections,[232] and in 1972 it adopted the *Allegheny-Mohawk* formula.[233] This standard set of LPPs granted specific forms of financial aid and other rights to employees adversely affected by a Board-approved merger. The specified benefits included a monthly "displacement allowance" for employees whose compensation was reduced as a result of the merger, and a "dismissal allowance" for employees who lost their jobs.[234] Adversely affected employees were guaranteed continued access to job benefits such as health insurance.[235] Employees required to relocate were entitled to reimbursement for specified moving and traveling expenses, and for expenses and losses resulting from sale of their homes.[236] The *Allegheny-Mohawk* LPPs also provided procedures for seniority integration "in a fair and equitable manner."[237]

The *Allegheny-Mohawk* decision also created procedures to resolve disputes over the application of the protective provisions and clarified the causation requirement for LPPs. Under the dispute resolution procedures, any disputes over ap-

---

[229]United-Western, Acquisition of Air Carrier Property, 11 CAB 701, 708 (1950), *aff'd sub nom.* Western Airlines v. CAB, 194 F2d 211, 213 (CA 9, 1952); North Atl. Route Transfer Case, 14 CAB 910 (1951).

[230]*Id.*

[231]*Id.*

[232]United-Capital Merger Case, 33 CAB 307, 342–47 (1961).

[233]Allegheny-Mohawk Merger Case, 59 CAB 22 (1972).

[234]*Id.* at 31–32.

[235]*Id.* at 32.

[236]*Id.* at 47–49.

[237]*Id.* at 45.

plication of the LPPs that were not resolved "within 20 days" were to be referred to expedited arbitration before a neutral selected from a National Mediation Board panel or chosen by another agreed-upon method.[238] The Board explained that in order to trigger the LPPs, it was necessary to show that the adverse impact "resulted from the merger."[239] However, the merger did not need to be the sole cause of employee injury.[240]

In applying the *Allegheny-Mohawk* dispute resolution procedures, the CAB adopted a policy of delegation and deference to arbitral decisions. The Board recognized that it was not an agency with labor relations expertise, and its decision to delegate labor relation questions to experienced labor relations professionals was upheld on judicial review.[241] The courts upheld the Board's articulated policy to resolve doubts regarding arbitrability in favor of the party seeking arbitration and to refrain from reviewing the merits of an LPP arbitrative award.[242]

With regard to the *Allegheny-Mohawk* seniority integration procedures, the Board faced court tests in which employees or employee groups challenged integrated seniority systems as falling short of the "fair and equitable" standard. Generally, the Board was satisfied that an integration was fair and equitable if the procedure (either through negotiation or arbitration) was fair. The courts upheld the Board's policy of not imposing specific substantive standards for measuring the fairness of an integrated seniority list.[243] The courts split, however, on whether the Board's decision regarding fairness precluded federal court lawsuits to invalidate an integrated

---

[238]*Id.* at 49.

[239]*Id.* at 45.

[240]*Id.* at 36–37.

[241]*See* American Airlines v. CAB, 445 F2d 891, 77 LRRM 3089 (CA 2, 1971), *cert. denied*, 404 U.S. 1015 (1972).

[242]Pan Am. World Airways v. CAB, 683 F2d 554, 110 LRRM 3237 (CA DC, 1982); *but see* Wallace v. CAB, 755 F2d 861, 884, 118 LRRM 3175, 119 LRRM 2293 (CA 11, 1985).

[243]Cook v. Pan Am. World Airways, 771 F2d 635 (CA 2, 1985), *cert. denied*, 474 U.S. 1109 (1986); Northeast Master Executive Council v. CAB, 506 F2d 97, 87 LRRM 2056 (CA DC, 1974), *cert. denied*, 419 U.S. 1110 (1975).

seniority list. Some courts held that employee lawsuits to over-turn integrated seniority lists approved by the CAB consti-tuted impermissible collateral attacks on Board orders.[244] Other courts allowed such attacks under the duty of fair representation and under federal and state age discrimina-tion statutes.[245]

After the enactment of the ADA, the CAB announced a policy change with respect to LPPs: it would no longer require LPPs "as a matter of course," but only under "special circumstances."[246] In 1983, the Board stated that in the future, LPPs would be imposed only in "special circumstances" or when "necessary to prevent labor strife that would disrupt the nation's air transportation system."[247]

On January 1, 1985, the CAB's jurisdiction over airline mergers was transferred to the DOT pursuant to the Civil Aeronautics Board Sunset Act of 1984.[248] The DOT reiter-ated the new policy against LPPs and has consistently rejected requests for their imposition.[249] The DOT has also made it clear that under the new policy a strike against one carrier would not disrupt the national air transportation system and thus would not constitute a sufficient level of labor strife to require LPPs.[250] The DOT has repeatedly stated that manda-tory LPPs are inconsistent with deregulation and that if em-ployees want merger protections, they should obtain them through collective bargaining.[251]

The DOT's policy determination that the ADA generally made it inappropriate for the Department to determine the benefits due employees in airline mergers and acquisitions

---

[244]Carey v. O'Donnell, 506 F2d 17 (CA DC, 1974), *cert. denied,* 419 U.S. 110 (1975); Kesinger v. Universal Airlines, 474 F2d 1127, 82 LRRM 2725 (CA 6, 1973).

[245]*See* Cook v. Pan Am. World Airways, 771 F2d 635; Clayton v. Republic Airlines, 716 F2d 729, 114 LRRM 2997 (CA 9, 1983).

[246]Texas Int'l—Pan Am.—National Acquisition CAB Order Nos. 79-12-163/ 164/165 at 67 (1979).

[247]Braniff S. Am. Route Transfer Case, CAB Order No. 83-6-74 (1983).

[248]Pub. L. No. 98-443, 98 Stat. 1703.

[249]*See, e.g.,* Midway-Air Fla. Acquisition Case, DOT Order No. 85-6-33 (1985).

[250]*Id.*

[251]*Id.;* Texas Air-Eastern Acquisition Case, DOT Order No. 86-8-77 (1986); Northwest-Republic Acquisition Case, DOT Order No. 86-7-81 (1986).

has been upheld by the courts.[252] However, the DOT's view that merger protections could and should be obtained through collective bargaining was rejected by one court in the context of Texas Air Corporation's acquisition of Eastern Airlines. The District of Columbia Circuit held that the DOT had to reconsider its refusal to impose LPPs in reliance on the collective bargaining process, in light of case law indicating that such bargained merger protections might not be enforceable.[253]

Thereafter, Texas Air and Eastern stipulated that Eastern would honor any LPP obligations in its existing collective bargaining agreements even if the contracts later became unenforceable under the RLA. Based on this stipulation, the DOT ruled that the court's concern as to the maintenance of the employees' contractual LPPs was satisfied and the issue rendered moot.[254] The DOT retained jurisdiction to ensure the stipulation maintained contractual LPP benefits and imposed the stipulation as a condition of Texas Air's acquisition of Eastern.[255]

B. Deregulation Protections

The ADA provided for a new and distinct set of employee protective provisions designed to cushion the impact of deregulation on airline employees. These provisions were set forth in Section 43 of the Act, the "Employee Protection Program" (EPP).[256]

Section 43 provided for financial assistance and hiring preferences for affected employees. The financial assistance provisions provided monthly payments to "eligible protected" employees.[257] A "protected employee" was defined as one who, as of October 24, 1978, had been "employed for at least

---

[252]Flight Attendants (UFA) v. DOT, 803 F2d 1029, 123 LRRM 3080 (CA 9, 1986); Air Line Pilots v. DOT, 791 F2d 172, 122 LRRM 2757 (CA DC, 1986).
[253]Air Line Pilots Ass'n v. DOT, 838 F2d 653 (CA DC, 1988).
[254]Texas Air-Eastern Acquisition Case, Order No. 89-1-11 (Jan. 9, 1989).
[255]Id.
[256]49 USC app. §1552 (1988).
[257]Id. §1552(b).

4 years by an air carrier holding a certificate issued under Section 401 of the Federal Aviation Act."[258] An "eligible protected employee" was defined as "a protected employee who on account of a qualifying dislocation (A) has been deprived of employment, or (B) has been adversely affected with respect to his compensation."[259] A "qualifying dislocation" was defined as a "bankruptcy or major contraction" of a certificated carrier that resulted from deregulation and that occurred within 10 years of the enactment of the legislation.[260] Monthly payments would be made for 72 months or until the employee obtained employment reasonably comparable to his or her last job.[261] Financial assistance would also include moving expenses and compensation for losses incurred in the sale of a home. All the financial assistance provisions required future congressional appropriation of funds.[262] The legislation also required the Secretary of Labor to issue regulations for computing monthly assistance and other financial assistance.[263]

Section 43's hiring preference applied to any "protected employee" who was furloughed or terminated by a regulated carrier within 10 years of the enactment of the ADA.[264] The hiring preference entitled "protected employees" to "first right of hire regardless of age," "by any other certificated air carrier hiring additional employees."[265] An individual terminated "for cause" would not be entitled to the "first right of hire."[266] However, in contrast to the requirements for financial assistance, eligibility for the hiring preference would not require a showing that the furlough or termination was attributable to a bankruptcy or contraction resulting from deregulation.[267] Under Section 43, a hiring carrier could give prefer-

---

[258]*Id.* §1552(h)(1).
[259]*Id.* §1552(a).
[260]*Id.* §1552(h)(2).
[261]*Id.* §1552.
[262]*Id.* §1552g(a).
[263]*Id.* §1552(a)–(c).
[264]*Id.* §1552(d).
[265]*Id.*
[266]*Id.*
[267]*Id.*

ence to its own furloughed employees before hiring protected employees from other carriers.[268]

Since enactment of the ADA, there has been delay in the implementation of the financial assistance provisions of Section 43. Although the CAB had started to receive petitions for Section 43 benefits in 1979, by October 1983 the Board had yet to hold hearings on any of those petitions.[269] The District of Columbia Circuit found this delay to be "unreasonable" and ordered expedited processing.[270] Thereafter, the CAB, and its successor, the DOT, began to process five "lead cases" that were thought to be representative. By 1990, DOT Administrative Law Judges had made initial decisions in the lead cases, finding no "qualifying dislocations" in three cases,[271] and "qualifying dislocations" in two cases.[272] In September 1991, the DOT issued its decision on review of the cases finding no qualifying dislocations in any of them.[273] The DOT held that the bankruptcies and contractions at issue were not caused by deregulation.[274]

The DOT's decision as to Braniff International Airways employees was appealed to the District of Columbia Court, which found error in the DOT's conclusions and remanded the order to the DOT for reconsideration.[275] The court found that the DOT's definition of "major cause" was internally inconsistent, and therefore unreasonable, and that the DOT's factual findings as to Braniff were arbitrary and capricious.[276] The DOT has issued an order reopening proceedings, inviting all parties to address the issues raised by the court, and seeking comments on the lead cases in light of the court's decision.[277]

---

[268]Id.

[269]See Air Line Pilots Ass'n v. CAB, 750 F2d 81 (CA DC, 1984).

[270]Id.

[271]Air New England/Mackey Int'l Airlines, Nos. 40201, 39783 (1990); Pan Am. World Airways, No. 38883 (1990).

[272]Braniff Int'l Airlines, No. 38978. United Airlines, No. 38571 (1990).

[273]Employee Program Investigations, Order No. 91-9-20 (Sept. 11, 1991).

[274]Id.

[275]Air Line Pilots Ass'n v. FAA, 3 F3d 449, 454 (CA DC, 1993).

[276]Id.

[277]Employee Protection Program Investigations, Order No. 94-7-35 (July 26, 1994).

In addition to the fact that the DOT has not made any final conclusions with respect to qualifying dislocations, the Department of Labor has yet to issue regulations establishing the amounts of assistance payments to be made to eligible employees.

Section 43 hiring preferences also encountered a delay in implementation. Soon after the Secretary of Labor issued implementing regulations in late 1983,[278] several airlines commenced a judicial challenge to Section 43 and the regulations. Their contention that the "legislative veto" feature of the statute rendered it unconstitutional was accepted by a district court.[279] The District of Columbia Circuit reversed, holding that the legislative veto provision was a severable, nonvital feature of the ADA, whereas Congress considered the EPP to be an "important aspect" of the legislation.[280] The Supreme Court affirmed in 1987.[281]

The courts have held that there is an implied private right of action to enforce the "first right of hire."[282] The District of Columbia Circuit has held that the time limitations on financial assistance (terminating payments after 72 months or upon acquisition of a reasonably comparable position) do not apply to the hiring preference provisions of Section 43. Thus, there is no time limit on an employee's first right of hire.[283] The same court has also held that a pilot's first right of hire is not cut off when the pilot is hired by a noncertified commuter airline.[284] However, the Second Circuit has relied on the financial assistance time restrictions to limit to 72 months the period for backpay recoverable by a pilot from the airline that denied him his first right of hire.[285]

---

[278]Airline Employee Protection Program, 48 Fed. Reg. 52,854 (1983).

[279]Alaska Airlines v. Donovan, 594 F Supp 92, 116 LRRM 2491 (D DC, 1984), rev'd, 766 F2d 1550, 1565, 119 LRRM 3383 (CA DC, 1985), aff'd sub nom. Alaska Airlines v. Brock, 480 U.S. 678, 124 LRRM 2958 (1987).

[280]Alaska Airlines v. Donovan, 766 F2d at 1565.

[281]Alaska Airlines v. Brock, 480 U.S. 678, 124 LRRM 2958.

[282]Long v. Trans World Airlines, 913 F2d 1262, 1265, 135 LRRM 2409 (CA 7, 1990); McDonald v. Piedmont Aviation, Inc., 930 F2d 220, 137 LRRM 2221 (CA 2), cert. denied, 138 LRRM 2824 (1991).

[283]Crocker v. Piedmont Aviation, Inc., 933 F2d 1024, 1026, 138 LRRM 2876 (CA DC, 1991).

[284]Id.

[285]McDonald v. Piedmont Aviation, Inc., 930 F2d 220, 137 LRRM 2221.

The courts are divided on the question of the appropriate statute of limitations for a private action to enforce a Section 43 hiring preference. The Second and Ninth Circuits have rejected the six-month *DelCostello*[286] limitations period, applying instead analogous state limitations periods.[287] However, the Third Circuit has disagreed, holding that the six-month period properly balances "the national interest in deregulation, the airlines' interest in repose, and the dislocated employee's need to obtain prompt employment."[288]

VI. FEDERAL BANKRUPTCY CODE

Bankruptcy laws are based on a need to protect creditors collectively. The laws inhibit individual creditors from foreclosing on a debtor's obligations in circumstances where the debtor lacks the funds to pay all its debts as they come due. This may permit the bankrupt party to continue in business, which may benefit creditors collectively. Where the bankrupt ceases to operate, bankruptcy laws are designed to provide an efficient mechanism by which creditors can divide the often meager remaining assets. Less importantly, bankruptcy relieves, and attempts to rehabilitate, debtors by delaying, modifying, or discharging their obligations to their creditors. Debtors in possession or trustees in bankruptcy have the right to reject executory agreements. The Supreme Court held in 1984 that the unmatured collective bargaining agreement obligations of an employer to its employees were "executory" and rejectable.[289] As described in a later subsection, Congress thereafter passed legislation that restricted the ability of bankrupt employers to reject collective bargaining agreements.

---

[286]DelCostello v. Teamsters, 462 U.S. 151, 113 LRRM 2737 (1983) (applying NLRA unfair labor practice limitations period to fair representation and breach of contract action).

[287]McDonald v. Piedmont Aviation, Inc., 930 F2d 220, 137 LRRM 2221 (CA 2), *cert. denied*, 138 LRRM 2824 (1991); Gonzalez v. Aloha Airlines, 940 F2d 1312, 138 LRRM 2202 (CA 9, 1991).

[288]Haggerty v. USAir, Inc., 952 F2d 781, 788, 139 LRRM 2105 (CA 3, 1992).

[289]NLRB v. Bildisco & Bildisco, 465 U.S. 513, 115 LRRM 2805 (1984).

Specific provisions in the Bankruptcy Code and the RLA preclude rejection of collective bargaining agreements, even in bankruptcy, by rail carriers. However, air carriers are permitted to use the revised bankruptcy procedures to reject their labor agreements.

A. Statutory Scheme

The Bankruptcy Code of 1978[290] permits the trustee in bankruptcy to assume or reject any executory contract of the debtor, subject to the approval of the bankruptcy court.[291] In its 1984 decision of *NLRB v. Bildisco & Bildisco*,[292] the Supreme Court held that a collective bargaining agreement is such an executory contract. *Bildisco* also held that a collective bargaining agreement becomes unenforceable when an employer files for bankruptcy protection, and remains so until the debtor-employer formally accepts the agreement. The debtor-employer is liable, however, for damages from breach or rejection of the agreement, with the liability to be settled through bankruptcy procedures.

The collective bargaining agreement in *Bildisco* was governed by the NLRA, not the RLA. Section 1167 of the Bankruptcy Code provides that a different rule should govern collective bargaining agreements subject to the RLA:

> Notwithstanding section 365 of this title, neither the court nor the trustee may change the wages or working conditions of employees of the debtor established by a collective bargaining agreement that is subject to the Railway Labor Act (45 U.S.C. 151 et seq.) except in accordance with section 6 of such Act (45 U.S.C. 156).

The *Bildisco* Court noted that this section "expressly exempts collective bargaining agreements subject to the Railway Labor Act, but grants no similar exemption to agreements subject to the NLRA."[293]

---

[290] 11 USC §§101–1330, enacted as Pub. L. No. 95-598, 92 Stat. 2549 (1978).
[291] *Id.* §365(a).
[292] 465 U.S. 513, 115 LRRM 2805.
[293] 465 U.S. at 522, 115 LRRM at 2811.

However, the RLA exemption in Section 1167 applies only to railroads, not to airlines, because the operation of Section 1167 of the Bankruptcy Code is limited by Section 103(g) of the Code, which states that "[s]ubchapter IV of chapter 11 of this title [which includes Section 1167] applies only in a case under such chapter concerning a railroad." Therefore, railroads in bankruptcy may only change their labor agreements through normal RLA bargaining procedures, but airlines in bankruptcy may reject their labor agreements in the same way as other employers.[294]

B. Bankruptcy Amendments of 1984

In response to the *Bildisco* decision,[295] Congress passed the Bankruptcy Amendments and Federal Judgeship Act of 1984,[296] adding a new Section 1113 to the bankruptcy code. Section 1113 was designed to limit the ability of employers to rid themselves of onerous labor agreements through bankruptcy, and it applies to airlines, but not to railroads:

> The debtor in possession, or the trustee if one has been appointed under the provisions of this chapter, other than a trustee in a case covered by subchapter IV of this chapter and by title I of the Railway Labor Act, may assume or reject a collective bargaining agreement only in accordance with the provisions of this section.[297]

The "subchapter IV" and "title I" referred to by this provision deal with railroads, not airlines. Consequently, airlines may assume or reject their collective bargaining agreements according to Section 1113 of the Bankruptcy Code; but railroads, under Section 1167 of the Code, may only modify their agreements according to Section 6 of the RLA.

Section 1113 requires that, after filing a bankruptcy petition, the employer (either the debtor in possession or the

---

[294]*See in re* Continental Airlines Corp., 38 B.R. 67, 115 LRRM 2364 (Bankr. SD Tex, 1984).

[295]NLRB v. Bildisco & Bildisco, 465 U.S. 513, 115 LRRM 2805 (1984).

[296]Pub. L. No. 93-353, tit. III, subtit. J, §541(a), 98 Stat. 390 (1988 & 1993 Supp. V).

[297]11 USC §1113(a) (1988).

trustee) must complete certain prerequisites before applying for rejection of the collective bargaining agreement:

1. Based on the most complete and reliable information available, the employer must propose to the employees' representative a plan that includes the modifications to the agreement necessary for reorganization and that assures equity among all creditors, the debtor, and all affected parties.[298]

2. The employer must provide the employees' representative with information necessary to evaluate the employer's proposal, subject to protective orders as necessary.[299]

3. From the time the employer makes its proposal until the court's hearing of the application, the employer must meet "at reasonable times" with the employees' representative "to confer in good faith in attempting to reach mutually satisfactory modifications" to their agreement.[300]

The bankruptcy court grants the employer's application for rejection of the agreement only if the employer's proposal has met the statutory requirements of Section 1113(b)(1), the employees' representative has refused to accept the proposal without good cause, and the balance of the equities clearly favors rejection of the agreement.[301]

The court must schedule a hearing within 14 days after receiving an application for rejection of an agreement, subject to a 7-day extension for good cause, and additional extensions as the parties may agree.[302] The court must rule within 30 days of the hearing's commencement; if it does not do so, and if the parties have not agreed to additional time for ruling, the employer may terminate or alter the agreement's provisions pending the court's ruling.[303]

---

[298]*Id.* §1113(b)(1)(A).
[299]*Id.* §1113(b)(1)(B).
[300]*Id.* §1113(b)(2).
[301]*Id.* §1113(c).
[302]*Id.* §1113(d)(1).
[303]*Id.* §1113(d)(2).

Under Section 1113(e), the employer may seek "interim" relief from the agreement before its rejection if such relief is "essential to the continuation of the debtor's business, or in order to avoid irreparable damage to the estate." A hearing on an application under Section 1113(e) is to be scheduled in accordance with the needs of the employer.

Notwithstanding other provisions of the Bankruptcy Code, and their interpretation in *Bildisco,* an employer may not unilaterally terminate or alter a collective bargaining agreement without complying with Section 1113.[304] The effect of this restriction is to overrule the holding in *Bildisco* that, regardless of whether a collective bargaining agreement had formally been rejected, it was unenforceable against an employer in bankruptcy.[305] Also, the Sixth Circuit has held that an employer's obligations under a collective bargaining agreement continue in force in bankruptcy and must be paid until modified pursuant to Section 1113, even if the obligations could not be classified as administrative expenses under the Bankruptcy Code.[306]

C. Insurance Benefits

Congress added Section 1114 to the Bankruptcy Code, as part of the Retiree Benefits Bankruptcy Protection Act of 1988,[307] to govern the rejection by a bankrupt employer of its agreement to pay insurance benefits to retired employees. The substantive standards for rejection of retiree benefits are the same as for rejection of a collective bargaining agreement under Section 1113. One procedural difference is that the bankruptcy court has 90 days after the hearing to rule on a motion to modify retiree benefits,[308] rather than the 30 days

---

[304]*Id.* §1113(f).

[305]*See* NLRB v. Bildisco & Bildisco, 465 U.S. 513, 532, 115 LRRM 2805, 2815 (1984).

[306]*In re* Unimet Corp., 842 F2d 879, 127 LRRM 3139 (CA 6), *cert. denied,* 488 U.S. 828 (1988).

[307]Pub. L. No. 100-334, 102 Stat. 610.

[308]11 USC §1114(k)(2) (1988).

allowed for ruling on a motion to modify a collective bargaining agreement.[309]

The most important innovation in Section 1114 is its recognition that collective bargaining agreements may not always provide for retiree benefits; and that even if such benefits are provided, the divergent interests of retirees and working employees can compromise the effectiveness of the employees' union as a representative of the retirees. Section 1114, therefore, provides that a court will appoint, on motion and hearing, a committee of retired employees to represent their fellow retirees. This will be done if (1) the retirees' benefits are not provided under a collective bargaining agreement; (2) they are provided under such an agreement but the signatory labor organization elects not to represent the retirees; or (3) the court decides, on motion and hearing, that representation of the retirees by someone other than the union would be appropriate.[310]

D. Judicial Construction of Section 1113

The Tenth Circuit has observed that, "while Section 1113 created new procedural requirements, it did not overrule, but in fact codified, *Bildisco's* substantive standards" for rejection of a collective bargaining agreement.[311] The Second Circuit has noted, though, that Section 1113 both codifies *Bildisco's* equitable test and adds the new requirements that (1) contract modifications be necessary to reorganization and fair to all parties, and (2) the union has rejected the proposal without good cause.[312]

The requirement that relief be "necessary to permit the reorganization of the debtor"[313] is less strict than the requirement for interim relief that the proposed modifications be

---

[309]*Id.* §1113(d)(2).

[310]*Id.* §1114(b)–(d).

[311]*In re* Mile Hi Metal Sys., Inc., 899 F2d 887, 890 n.2, 133 LRRM 2927 (CA 10, 1990) (citing NLRB v. Bildisco & Bildisco, 465 U.S. 513, 115 LRRM 2805 (1984)).

[312]Truck Drivers Local 807 v. Carey Transp., Inc., 816 F2d 82, 88 (CA 2, 1987).

[313]11 USC §1113(b)(1)(A) (1988).

"essential to the continuation of the debtor's business."[314] Most bankruptcy courts have held that proposed modifications need not be limited to those that are absolutely necessary to the employer's reorganization.[315] The Second Circuit has held that, in evaluating the necessity of proposed modifications, the court should consider the proposal as a whole, rather than consider each element of the proposal singly.[316] However, if an element is proposed in bad faith, so as to stalemate negotiations and permit outright rejection of the agreement, then the entire proposal will not be deemed unnecessary, and rejection of the agreement will not be permitted.[317] The Second Circuit also has held that a general rejection of seniority may be "necessary," for purposes of Section 1113, "[i]n an industry where rapid change has been the rule, and where the current need for intrusion into [seniority] is well-established."[318]

A proposal for modification of a collective bargaining agreement must "[assure] that all creditors, the debtor and all of the affected parties are treated fairly and equitably."[319]

---

[314]*Id.* §1113(e); *See In re* Wright Air Lines, 44 B.R. 744, 117 LRRM 3158 (Bankr ND Ohio, 1985).

[315]*In re* Mile Hi Metal Sys., Inc., 899 F2d at 890 n.2; *In re* Big Sky Transp. Co., 104 B.R. 333 (Bankr D Mont, 1989); *In re* Texas Sheet Metals, Inc., 90 B.R. 260 (Bankr SD Tex, 1988); *In re* Amherst Sparkle Market, Inc., 75 B.R. 847 (Bankr ND Ohio, 1987); *In re* Walway Co., 69 B.R. 967 (Bankr ED Mich, 1987). *See* Truck Drivers Local 807 v. Carey Transp., Inc., 816 F2d at 88–90 ("the legislative history strongly suggests that 'necessary' should not be equated with 'essential' or bare minimum"; rather, "the necessity requirement places on the debtor the burden of proving that its proposal is made in good faith, and that it contains necessary, but not absolutely minimal, changes that will enable the debtor to complete the reorganization process successfully"); *In re* Century Brass Prods., Inc., 795 F2d 265, 273, 276, 122 LRRM 2833 (CA 2), *cert. denied,* 479 U.S. 949, 123 LRRM 2984 (1986) ("the word 'necessary' . . . emphasizes the requirement of the debtor's good faith in seeking to modify its existing labor contract"; Congress aimed at an honest compromise between labor and bankruptcy principles); *but see* Wheeling-Pittsburgh Steel Corp. v. Steelworkers, 791 F2d 1074, 1088–89, 122 LRRM 2425 (CA 3, 1986) (legislative history shows that contract modification must be necessary to avoid liquidation in short run, not just to assist rehabilitation in long run).

[316]*In re* Royal Composing Room, Inc., 848 F2d 345, 348–49, 128 LRRM 2569 (CA 2, 1988), *cert. denied,* 489 U.S. 1078, 130 LRRM 3208 (1989).

[317]848 F2d at 348; *see* Truck Drivers Local 807 v. Carey Transp., Inc., 816 F2d 82, 88 (CA 2, 1987) (statutory requirement of necessity implies requirement of good faith).

[318]*In re* Royal Composing Room, Inc., 848 F2d at 348–49.

[319]11 USC §1113(b)(1)(A) (1988).

The purpose of this requirement is "to spread the burdens of saving the company to every constituency while ensuring that all sacrifice to a similar degree."[320] Depending on the circumstances, however, the salaries and benefits of nonunion employees are not necessarily required to be reduced to the same degree that union wages and benefits are reduced.[321]

The employer must provide enough information for the employees to evaluate the employer's proposal, but the employer need not provide information wanted by the employees simply to prepare their counterproposals.[322]

Both the employer and the employees' representative are required to confer in good faith. The union must explain any opposition to a proposal under Section 1113 and negotiate to resolve any objectionable provisions.[323] "At the very least, a union's lack of participation [in good faith conference] should be considered when the court decides whether the union had good cause to reject the proposal and whether the balance of equities favors rejection of the agreement. Other responses may also be available to the bankruptcy court."[324]

The union is presumed to lack good cause to reject the proposal if, before a hearing on a Section 1113 application, the union rejects the proposal without offering a reason for doing so.[325] A union does not satisfy the good cause require-

---

[320]*In re* Century Brass Prods., Inc., 795 F2d 265, 273, 276, 122 LRRM 2833 (CA 2), *cert. denied,* 479 U.S. 949, 123 LRRM 2984 (1986).

[321]Truck Drivers Local 807 v. Carey Transp., Inc., 816 F2d at 88 (nonunion pay and benefits need not be reduced where union pay above average, nonunion pay no more than average, and nonunion workload increased by staff reductions).

[322]*In re* Salt Creek Freightways, 47 B.R. 835, 839 (Bankr D Wyo, 1985).

[323]*In re* Mile Hi Metal Sys., Inc., 899 F2d 887, 890 n.2, 133 LRRM 2927 (CA 10, 1990).

[324]899 F2d at 892 n.6 (citations omitted).

[325]The Second Circuit has stated, more strictly, that "the rejection of the proposal by the union [without negotiation] will almost always without exception be without good cause." *In re* Royal Composing Room, Inc., 848 F2d 345, 348–49, 128 LRRM 2569 (CA 2, 1988), *cert. denied,* 489 U.S. 1078, 130 LRRM 3208 (1989). The Second Circuit has similarly held that, where the proposed modifications were necessary, fair, and equitable, the union's refusal to accept them was without good cause where the union neither participated meaningfully in postpetition negotiations nor offered any reason for rejecting the proposal other than its view that the proposed modifications were excessive. Truck Drivers Local 807 v. Carey Transp., Inc., 816 F2d 82, 88 (CA 2, 1987).

ment by presenting a counterproposal if the counterproposal does not have the support of the union's members.[326] The employer does not confer in good faith when it meets with employee representatives only once, to present a proposal, and does not meet again with the representatives despite their indicated willingness to discuss the matter further.[327] Whereas the "good cause" language in Section 1113 has been interpreted to require negotiations in good faith, that requirement is not necessarily the same as the requirement of bargaining in good faith that has developed under labor law.[328]

The bankruptcy court may approve rejection of a collective bargaining agreement only if "the balance of the equities clearly favors rejection of such agreement."[329] Although *Bildisco* preceded Section 1113, "the approach to the required balancing of the equities [under Section 1113(c)(3)] should not be different from the instruction provided in *Bildisco*."[330] In *Bildisco,* the Supreme Court ruled that, in balancing the equities to determine whether labor contract rejection should be permitted,

> [t]he Bankruptcy Court must consider the likelihood and consequences of liquidation for the debtor absent rejection, the reduced value of the creditors' claims that would follow from affirmance and the hardship that would impose on them, and the impact of rejection on the employees. In striking the balance, the Bankruptcy Court must consider not only the degree of hardship faced by each party, but also any qualitative differences between the types of hardship each may face.
>
> . . . [T]he Bankruptcy Court must focus on the ultimate goal of Chapter 11 when considering these equities. The Bankruptcy Code does not authorize free-wheeling consideration

---

[326]*Id.*

[327]*In re* American Provision, 44 B.R. 907, 911, 118 LRRM 2059 (Bankr D Minn, 1984).

[328]*In re* Century Brass Prods., Inc., 795 F2d 265, 273, 276, 122 LRRM 2833 (CA 2), 479 U.S. 949, 123 LRRM 2984 (1986).

[329]11 USC §1113(c)(3) (1988).

[330]Teamsters v. IML Freight, 789 F2d 1460, 1461, 122 LRRM 3066 (CA 10, 1986); Truck Drivers Local 807 v. Carey Transp., Inc., 816 F2d 82, 88 (CA 2, 1987); *In re* Century Brass Prods., Inc., 795 F2d at 273, 276.

of every conceivable equity, but rather only how the equities relate to the success of the reorganization.[331]

From *Bildisco* and similar cases, the Second Circuit has identified six permissible equitable considerations, many of which also factor into the other substantive requirements imposed by Section 1113: (1) the likelihood and consequences of liquidation if rejection is not permitted; (2) the likely reduction in the value of creditors' claims if the bargaining agreement remains in force; (3) the likelihood and consequences of a strike if the bargaining agreement is voided; (4) the possibility and likely effect of any employee claims for breach of contract if rejection is approved; (5) the cost-spreading abilities of the various parties, taking into account the number of employees covered by the bargaining agreement and how various employees' wages and benefits compare to those of others in the industry; and (6) the good or bad faith of the parties in dealing with the debtor's financial dilemma.[332]

One court has noted that "[t]he balance of the equities nearly always will tip in favor of the party that seeks to reach a compromise and to that end negotiates in good faith."[333] An employer's proposal under Section 1113 is presumptively inequitable if the arrangements it seeks to establish would violate labor law even in the absence of a collective bargaining agreement.[334] A union must show evidence of the illegality of proposed modifications, and good cause for rejecting the proposal because of such illegality, before the employer has a burden of showing the legality of the proposed changes.[335]

Relief under Section 1113(e) may be denied unless it is necessary for continued operations of the employer,[336] but

---

[331]NLRB v. Bildisco & Bildisco, 465 U.S. 513, 527, 115 LRRM 2805, 2813 (1984).

[332]Truck Drivers Local 807 v. Carey Transp., Inc., 816 F2d at 88.

[333]*In re* Royal Composing Room, Inc., 848 F2d 345, 348–49, 128 LRRM 2569 (CA 2, 1988), *cert. denied,* 489 U.S. 1078, 130 LRRM 3208 (1989).

[334]*In re* Mile Hi Metal Sys., Inc., 899 F2d 887, 890 n.2, 133 LRRM 2927 (CA 10, 1990).

[335]899 F2d at 891–92.

[336]*In re* Wright Air Lines, 44 B.R. 744 (Bankr ND Ohio, 1984).

the employer does not have to show with absolute certainty that the business will immediately fail without the relief.[337]

E. Damages for Rejection of Labor Agreement

As a general rule, a debtor that rejects an executory contract is liable to the other party for damages from the rejection, and a debtor that accepts prerejection benefits is liable for the reasonable value of those benefits.[338] Under Section 502, applicable outside of collective bargaining contexts, damages sought by employees for termination of employment contracts are limited to the compensation provided by the contract for one year from either the petition date or the date of employment termination, whichever is earlier.[339] This rule does not limit claims for insurance benefits by retired employees.[340]

It is unclear, however, whether similar damages are available for rejection of collective bargaining agreements under Section 1113.[341] When Congress enacted Section 1113 as the exclusive means of rejecting a collective bargaining agreement, it did not enact a provision analogous to Section 502 providing for rejection damages arising out of Section 1113. In dicta, some courts have assumed that contract rejection damages under Section 1113 will be determined with reference to Section 502, treating a collective bargaining agreement as an employment contract.[342] However, the only court

---

[337]*See In re* Ionosphere Clubs, Inc., 922 F2d 984, 36 LRRM 2065 (CA 2), *amended,* Adv. Proc. No. 90-6242A at 2 (SDNY, Sept. 13, 1990) (additional §1113(e) relief granted because "the relief requested is in the best interests of [the employer]'s estate, its creditors and equity security holders"), *cert. denied,* 141 LRRM 3040 (1991).

Relief has been granted under §1113 where the employer's president gave undisputed testimony that the company could not continue business more than one week longer without the requested relief. *In re* Salt Creek Freightways, 47 B.R. 835 (Bankr D Wyo, 1985).

[338]NLRB v. Bildisco & Bildisco, 465 U.S. 513, 531, 115 LRRM 2805, 2814 (1984).

[339]11 USC §502(b)(7) (1988).

[340]*Id.* §1114(j).

[341]*In re* Cortland Container Corp., 30 B.R. 715 (Bankr ND Ohio, 1983).

[342]*Id.*

to address this issue directly held that contract rejection damages are *not* available under Section 1113 and, therefore, Section 502 does not apply in the context of collective bargaining agreements.[343] The court held that by enacting Section 1113, Congress removed collective bargaining agreements from the ambit of Sections 365 and 502, and that damages were unavailable based on the facts that Section 1113 allows rejection only if "necessary" and that requiring damages would wholly defeat the purpose of contract rejection.[344]

If such damages are available, the Bankruptcy Code establishes priorities for payment of some employee claims, and these priorities may apply in particular cases.[345] However, contract rejection damages are generally paid as prepetition claims, without priority over other such claims.[346]

F. Bankruptcy Court and Other Forums

Bankruptcy courts have broad jurisdiction over "core" bankruptcy proceedings and bankruptcy-related "noncore" proceedings.[347] Bankruptcy courts also have jurisdiction over cases involving the application of the RLA or other nonbankruptcy federal statutes, although they do not have jurisdiction over cases involving "substantial and material consideration" of nonbankruptcy federal statutes.[348]

An action such as an arbitration, which is prescribed by a collective bargaining agreement, is not subject to the Bankruptcy Code's automatic stay provision,[349] and may not be stayed by the bankruptcy court except under Section 1113.[350] However, a nonbankruptcy action to enforce a collec-

---

[343]*In re* Blue Diamond Coal Co., 147 B.R. 720 (Bankr ED Tenn, 1992), *aff'd*, 160 B.R. 574 (ED Tenn, 1993).

[344]*Id.* at 730–32.

[345]11 USC §507 (1988); *cf. In re* Ionosphere Clubs, Inc., 922 F2d 984, 36 LRRM 2065 (CA 2, 1990) (denying priority claimed by virtue of postpetition agreement regarding prepetition work), *cert. denied*, 141 LRRM 3040 (1991).

[346]11 USC §502(g) (1988); NLRB v. Bildisco & Bildisco, 465 U.S. 513, 531, 115 LRRM 2805, 2814 (1984).

[347]11 USC §157 (1988).

[348]*In re* Ionosphere Clubs, Inc., 922 F2d 984, 36 LRRM 2065.

[349]11 USC §362 (1988 & 1993 Supp. V).

[350]*In re* Ionsphere Clubs, Inc., 922 F2d at 992–93.

tive bargaining agreement, if not prescribed by the agreement, is subject to the automatic stay of Section 362 to preserve the bankruptcy court's jurisdiction. The bankruptcy court must lift the stay if necessary to provide relief.[351]

Section 105(a) of the Bankruptcy Code provides, "The court may issue any order, process or judgment that is necessary or appropriate to carry out the provisions of this title." The bankruptcy court may use its equitable power under Section 105 to protect its jurisdiction by enjoining court actions to enforce a collective bargaining agreement, if it would be appropriate to apply the automatic stay of Section 362 under the circumstances.[352] The equitable powers of a bankruptcy court under Section 105 are subject to the usual limitations on a federal court's equitable powers: "[T]he power of the bankruptcy court to grant injunctive relief is no different or greater than that of a district court."[353]

A bankruptcy court's ruling on an application to accept or reject a collective bargaining agreement is appealable to either a district court[354] or a bankruptcy appellate panel,[355] and then to a court of appeals.[356] However, an order of interim relief under Section 1113(e) of the Bankruptcy Code is not a final order, and is therefore not appealable to the court of appeals,[357] except in an extreme case upon a writ of mandamus.[358]

---

[351]*Id.; See In re* Ionosphere/Eastern Air Lines, No. 89-B-10448/49, transcript at 20–22 (Bankr SD NY, 1991) (stay of actions for injunctive and monetary relief from labor practices not lifted; decision being appealed).

[352]*In re* Ionosphere Clubs, Inc., 922 F2d at 995.

[353]Machinists v. Eastern Air Lines, 121 B.R. 428, 433, 135 LRRM 2903 (SD NY, 1990) (bankruptcy court's injunction improperly granted, where employer did not exhaust settlement efforts as required by NLGA, 29 USC §108 (1988)), *aff'd*, 923 F2d 26, 136 LRRM 2310 (CA 2, 1991) (per curiam).

[354]28 USC §158(a) (1988).

[355]*Id.* §158(b).

[356]*Id.* §158(d).

[357]*In re* Landmark Hotel & Casino, 872 F2d 857, 131 LRRM 2093 (CA 9, 1989).

[358]872 F2d at 860 n.2

VII. DRUG AND ALCOHOL TESTING REGULATIONS

A. Executive Order Number 12564

On September 17, 1986, President Ronald Reagan issued Executive Order No. 12564[359] regarding government-mandated drug testing in the transportation industry. The Executive Order proposed drug testing programs for those in sensitive positions, urged the establishment of a voluntary testing program, and authorized drug tests of federal employees as a component of the employment application process, whenever there was a reasonable suspicion of drug use, when an accident occurred, and as part of employee assistance programs. Implementation of the Order, which applies to all government agencies, was to be coordinated by the Office of Personnel Management.

B. Health and Human Services Regulations

On April 1, 1988, the Department of Health and Human Services (HHS) adopted mandatory drug testing guidelines in furtherance of the Executive Order.[360] The guidelines have wide application and required the DOT to conform its practices to the guidelines within 90 days.[361]

Under these guidelines, the affected agencies must test all applicants, and randomly test its employees, for cocaine and marijuana,[362] and may test randomly for opiates, amphetamines, or phencyclidine.[363] Agencies may also test for any drug scheduled under the Controlled Substances Act if there is a reasonable suspicion of use or following an accident,[364] and an agency may petition the Secretary for approval to add any scheduled drug to its routine test protocol.[365]

---

[359]51 Fed. Reg. 32,889 (1986); see 5 USC §7301 (1988 & 1993 Supp. V).

[360]Mandatory Guidelines for Federal Workplace Drug Testing Programs, 53 Fed. Reg. 11,970 (1988).

[361]*Id.* at 11,979, subpart A, §1.1(b) (1988).

[362]*Id.* at 11,980, subpart B, §2.1(a)(1).

[363]*Id.* subpart B, §2.1(a)(2).

[364]*Id.*, subpart B, §2.1(a)(3).

[365]*Id.*, subpart B, §2.1(b).

For the protection of the employees' privacy, the specimens collected for drug testing purposes may not be tested for any other purpose unless such additional test is otherwise authorized by law.[366] The results are confidential.[367] The agency's Medical Review Officer must review a positive result with the employee to determine whether the result could be consistent with legal drug use,[368] and, if so, may declare the test negative.[369] If the test is declared positive, the results are to be disclosed only to the agency's Employee Assistance Program and the decision-making manager.[370] Both the agency and the laboratory are required to maintain the highest regard for employee privacy.[371]

To ensure accuracy, if the initial immunoassay is positive, a confirmatory gas chromatography/mass spectrometry test is required.[372] Government agencies must use testing laboratories certified for government use.[373] The laboratory manager must be well qualified,[374] and that manager is empowered to establish standards for the laboratory employees' qualifications.[375] The laboratory is subject to specific performance standards for certification,[376] ascertained, in part, by bimonthly performance tests and semiannual inspections.[377] The certification may be revoked for cause[378] and is subject to summary suspension,[379] notably for false positive results.[380]

The collection site and chain of custody must meet certain detailed standards.[381] Privacy during delivery of the aliquot, or urine specimen, is assured unless there is "reason to believe

[366]*Id.*, subpart B, §2.1(c).
[367]*Id.* at 11,986, subpart B, §2.8.
[368]*Id.* at 11,985–86, subpart B, §2.7(b), (c), (d), (f).
[369]*Id.* at 11,985–86, subpart B, §2.7(f).
[370]*Id.* at 11,985–86, subpart B, §2.7(c).
[371]*Id.* at 11,986, subpart B, §2.8.
[372]*Id.* at 11,983, subpart B, §2.4(f)(1).
[373]*Id.* at 11,985, subpart B, §2.5(d)(1).
[374]*Id.* at 11,982, subpart B, §2.3(a).
[375]*Id.*, subpart B, §2.3(a)(4).
[376]*Id.* at 11,987, subpart C, §§3.3, 3.12.
[377]*Id.* at 11,988–89, subpart C, §§3.17, 3.20.
[378]*Id.* at 11,987, subpart C, §3.13.
[379]*Id.*, subpart C, §3.14.
[380]*Id.* at 11,987–89, subpart C, §§3.13(b)(1), 3.19(b)(1).
[381]*Id.* at 11,980–83, subpart B, §§2.2, 2.4.

a particular individual may alter or substitute the specimen to be provided."[382] The guidelines anticipate that such a "reason to believe" would be a prior history of adulterating or substituting an aliquot or an irregularity in the aliquot provided, determined by visual inspection and temperature measurement.

C. DOT Regulations

The DOT issued its final regulations for drug and urine testing by transportation employers on December 1, 1989.[383] Whereas these regulations follow the HHS guidelines in most respects, there are significant differences.

For example, in addition to testing for marijuana and cocaine, testing for opiates, amphetamines, and phencyclidine is required.[384] Step-by-step procedures for generating custody control records and ensuring specimen integrity are included.[385] Whereas HHS requires blind tests only for certification and recertification, the DOT requires quarterly blind testing of all its certified laboratories.[386] To better safeguard employee privacy, DOT regulations provide that the Medical Review Officer *may* report a positive result to the Employee Assistance Program, the decision-making manager, or both,[387] whereas HHS regulations *require* a report to both.[388]

D. FAA and Federal Railroad
Administration Regulations

The FAA and Federal Railroad Administration (FRA) followed the DOT's regulations with some of their own. FAA regulations[389] require, as a part of the certification process,

---

[382]*Id.* at 11,980, subpart B, §2.2(e).
[383]Procedures for Transportation Workplace Drug Testing Programs, 40 CFR pt. 40 (1989).
[384]49 CFR §40.21(a) (1994).
[385]*Id.* §§40.23, 50.25.
[386]*Id.* §40.31(d).
[387]*Id.* §40.33(c)(7).
[388]53 Fed. Reg. 11,985–86, subpart B, §2.7(c) (1988).
[389]14 CFR, pt. 121, app. I (1994).

drug testing consonant with DOT standards of certain employees[390] of both the carrier and its contractors.[391] All positive drug test results must be reported to the Federal Air Surgeon.[392] If the Medical Review Officer makes a determination of probable drug dependence, only the Federal Air Surgeon may authorize an employee's return to duty.[393]

The FAA regulations also address alcohol abuse. Employees cannot act as crew members of an aircraft within eight hours of consuming alcohol, while having .04 percent blood-alcohol content, or while under the influence of alcohol.[394] The Federal Air Surgeon must evaluate alcoholics, who must meet certain criteria including abstinence for two years before receiving a medical certificate.[395]

The FRA regulations, unlike the FAA regulations, provide for fines up to $20,000 for any violation of the regulations.[396] The regulations specifically prohibit the use of any nonprescribed controlled substance whether on or off duty,[397] and provide for summary suspension and a prompt postsuspension hearing if such use is suspected.[398] However, they also provide for more lenient treatment when an employee voluntarily reports for treatment[399] or is reported by a coworker.[400]

Under the FRA regulations, reasonable cause testing may be based upon observation during on-duty hours, an accident or incident,[401] or a rule violation.[402] The regulations provide detailed Breathalyzer standards[403] and rely principally on the

---

[390]Flight crew, flight attendants, flight and ground instructors, dispatchers, maintenance crew, security, and air traffic control. *Id.* pt. 121, app. I, pt. III.

[391]*See id.* §121.457.

[392]*Id.* pt. 121, App. I, pt. VII(C)(5)(d).

[393]*Id.*

[394]*Id.* §91.17(a).

[395]*Id.* §67.13.

[396]*Id.* §219.9 and App. A.

[397]*Id.* §219.102.

[398]*Id.* §219.104.

[399]*Id.* §219.403.

[400]*Id.* §219.405.

[401]An incident is an event in which damage is below a certain reporting threshold. *See Id.* §219.5.

[402]*See id.* §219.301.

[403]*Id.* §219.303.

DOT regulations for urine testing standards and procedures.[404]

All positive postaccident drug test results must be reported to the FRA Administrator for Safety,[405] but public disclosure of medically authorized drug use is prohibited.[406] Any collective bargaining provision that limits the time within which an employer may discipline an employee is overridden when drug use is involved.[407] If an accident is fatal to an employee, the regulations appear to provide for mandatory autopsy.[408] In accordance with DOT regulations, the FRA also requires preemployment[409] and random[410] drug testing.

E. Urban Mass Transportation Administration Regulations

In 1988, the Urban Mass Transportation (UMT) Administration promulgated regulations purporting to require drug testing in local transit operations. In *Transit Union v. Skinner,*[411] the District of Columbia Circuit found these regulations unconstitutional. After rejecting a challenge to the union's standing (based upon legislative history and congressional solicitude for preservation of bargaining rights throughout the UMT Administration), the court found that the funding mechanism upon which the UMT Administration relied provides only for investigation of safety hazards and withholding federal funds pending approval and implementation of a *local authority's* correction plan. The UMT Administration, the court found, was without authority to promulgate the regulations.

Apart from the UMT Administration's unsuccessful regulatory attempt, all of the other regulations have now been in full force and effect for more than four years, and in

---

[404]*Id.* §219.305, *but see id.* §219.701 *et seq.*
[405]*Id.* §299.211(b).
[406]*Id.* §219.211(c), (d).
[407]*Id.* §291.211(g).
[408]*See id.* §§219.11(f), 203(4)(ii), 207.
[409]*Id.* §219.501 *et seq.*
[410]*Id.* §219.601 *et seq.*
[411]894 F2d 1362 (CA DC, 1990).

that time, they have already led to a substantial amount of litigation, as discussed in the following subsection.

F. Constitutional Questions

Railway labor organizations promptly filed suit to enjoin enforcement of FRA regulations governing suspicionless drug and alcohol testing of railroad employees as violative of employee rights. The U.S. Supreme Court, in *Skinner v. Railway Labor Executives' Ass'n*,[412] held that whereas the Fourth Amendment does apply, drug and alcohol testing that has been mandated by government regulations is reasonable even though the regulations do not require a warrant or even a reasonable suspicion that any particular employee might be impaired. The Court reasoned that safety concerns present "special needs" outside normal law enforcement, and that the compelling government interest served by the regulations therefore outweighs the "minimal" intrusion on individual privacy.[413]

All circuits that have addressed the constitutionality of government-mandated drug testing since *Skinner* have adopted the view that, taken in conjunction with *Employees Union v. Von Raab*,[414] the *Skinner* rationale covers virtually all forms of drug testing arising in the transportation industry.[415]

---

[412]489 U.S. 602, 130 LRRM 2857 (1989).

[413]489 U.S. at 619–20, 625–26.

[414]489 U.S. 656 (1989) (suspicionless drug testing of employees applying for promotion to positions involving interdiction of illegal drugs or requiring them to carry firearms was reasonable under Fourth Amendment and did not require a warrant).

[415]*See* Transport Workers v. Southeastern Pa. Transp. Auth., 884 F2d 709, 132 LRRM 2331 (CA 3, 1988) (random testing, particularly where evidence of actual drug problem exists); Tanks v. Greater Cleveland Regional Transit Auth., 930 F2d 475 (CA 6, 1991) (postincident, even though damage was minor); Moxley v. Regional Transit Servs., 722 F Supp 977 (WD NY, 1989) (medical exam upon return to work); Holloman v. Greater Cleveland Regional Transit Auth., 741 F Supp 677 (ND Ohio, 1990) (postincident and routine medical exam, distinguishing testing of employees in safety-sensitive and non-safety-sensitive positions); Bluestein v. Skinner, 908 F2d 451, *cert. denied*, 498 U.S. 1083 (CA 9, 1990) (random testing under FAA regulations). *In* Burka v. New York City Transit Auth., 739 F Supp 814 (SD NY) (liability phase), 747 F Supp 214 (SD NY, 1990) (remedy phase), the court made a distinction between the constitutional rationale applicable to employees in safety-sensitive positions and to those who are not. Employees in safety-sensitive

G. Codification of Regulations

In October 1991, President George Bush signed an appropriations bill for the DOT[416] that incorporated the Omnibus Transportation Employee Testing Act of 1991 (the Omnibus Act).[417] The Omnibus Act established a statutory mandate for the drug testing rules issued by the DOT in 1988 for the aviation and motor carrier industries, and in 1985 and 1988 for the rail industry. In addition, it enabled the UMT Administration to restore the drug testing rules it had been forced to suspend as a result of the District of Columbia Circuit's decision in *Transit Union v. Skinner*.[418]

The Omnibus Act provides for testing for the use, when in violation of law or federal regulation, of alcohol or controlled substances by people who operate aircraft, trains, and commercial motor vehicles. It requires the Secretary of Transportation to issue rules, within 12 months of enactment, establishing drug and alcohol testing programs for certain individuals employed in safety-sensitive positions in those industries. The Omnibus Act provides for five types of testing: random, preemployment, postaccident, periodic recurring, and reasonable suspicion.

The Omnibus Act's statement of congressional findings[419] cites the dangers of drug and alcohol abuse by operators of instrumentalities of transportation and opines that increased drug testing, including random testing, is a successful means of deterring abuse of alcohol and use of illegal drugs in the transportation industry. Congress also found that adequate safeguards can be implemented to protect indi-

---

positions are subject to a "bare reasonableness" standard requiring only generalized, rather than individualized, suspicion under the *Skinner* test. 739 F Supp at 827. By contrast, the constitutional rights of employees in non-safety-sensitive positions are not attenuated by any governmental "special needs." *Id*. These employees are primarily those as to whom some circumstance, such as direct supervision, intervenes so that their work does not "directly" affect public safety. *Id*. at 821. Since the "individualized suspicion" standard remains in effect for these employees, they are not subject to random testing. *Id* at 828.

[416]H.R. 2942, 102nd Cong., 1st Sess.
[417]*Id*., tit. IV, incorporating the language of S. 676, 102nd Cong., 1st Sess.
[418]894 F2d 1362 (CA DC, 1990).
[419]H.R. 2942, §2.

vidual privacy and that rehabilitation is a critical component of any testing program.

H. Testing of Airline and FAA Employees

Section 3(a) of the Omnibus Act adds a new Section 614 to the Federal Aviation Act of 1958 (the Aviation Act). A "controlled substance" is defined as any substance under Section 102(6) of the Controlled Substances Act specified by the FAA.[420] Section 614 requires the FAA Administrator to issue regulations, within 12 months of enactment, requiring domestic air carriers and foreign air carriers operating in the United States to conduct preemployment, reasonable suspicion, random, and postaccident testing of employees responsible for safety-sensitive functions[421] for use of alcohol or controlled substances in violation of law or federal regulation.[422] The Administrator is also authorized to prescribe regulations for the conduct of periodic, recurring testing of those employees.[423] The legislative history indicates that the committee intends the Administrator to be "very selective" in extending coverage of this provision to other categories of employees.[424]

Reasonable suspicion, as contemplated by the Omnibus Act, does not require a showing of probable cause. Rather, it requires "specific, personal observations concerning the appearance, behavior, or performance of the employee."[425] With respect to random testing, the Omnibus Act gives the Administrator discretion to determine how specific programs should be handled.[426] The new Section 614 of the Aviation

---

[420]Aviation Act §614(f).

[421]This includes flight crews, flight attendants, air traffic controllers, mechanics, safety inspectors, flight dispatchers, and other employees determined by the Administrator.

[422]Aviation Act §614(a)(1).

[423]Id.

[424] REPORT OF THE SENATE COMMITTEE ON COMMERCE, SCIENCE AND TRANSPORTATION ON S. 676, REP. No. 54, 102nd Cong., 1st Sess. 18 [hereinafter REPORT ON S. 676].

[425]Id.

[426]Id.

Act also requires the Administrator to establish a program of testing for FAA employees whose duties include responsibility for safety-sensitive functions.[427] In addition, the new section provides that the Administrator shall, as the Administrator deems appropriate, require the suspension or revocation of any certificate, or the disqualification or dismissal of any individual, where a drug test confirms that an individual has used alcohol or a controlled substance in violation of law or federal regulation.[428] This subsection does not require that any employee who tests positive for drug or alcohol use be dismissed or have his or her certificate revoked. Rather, it provides the Administrator the authority to take such a step directly or to require an air carrier to do so.[429]

The Aviation Act now prohibits the use of alcohol or a controlled substance by safety-sensitive employees in violation of law or federal regulation, and prohibits an individual who has been determined to have used alcohol or a controlled substance in violation of law or regulation from serving in a safety-sensitive position until that individual has completed a program of rehabilitation described in new subsection (c).[430] This does not prevent employers from discharging employees with positive test results; it merely prevents employees from returning to safety-sensitive positions without having completed a program designed to end their drug or alcohol abuse.[431] The new section prohibits individuals who have been determined to have used alcohol or a controlled substance in violation of subsection (b)(1) from returning to their positions if they engaged in such use while on duty, had previously undertaken a rehabilitation program, refused to undertake a rehabilitation program, or failed to complete such a program.[432]

The Administrator is required under the new section to issue regulations establishing requirements for rehabilitation

[427]Aviation Act §614(a)(2).
[428]*Id.* §614(a)(3).
[429]REPORT ON S. 676, *supra* note 424, at 19.
[430]Aviation Act §614(b)(1), (2).
[431]REPORT ON S. 676, *supra* note 424, at 19.
[432]Aviation Act §614(b)(3).

programs for transportation and FAA employees in safety-sensitive positions. The Act directs the Administrator to determine the circumstances under which safety-sensitive employees will be required to participate in such a program.[433]

The Omnibus Act also requires the Administrator to develop procedures designed to safeguard individual rights in testing procedures.[434] The safeguards incorporate the HHS 1988 guidelines relating to laboratory standards and testing procedures.[435] They require testing laboratories to have the ability to perform screening and confirmation tests and require that all positive tests be confirmed by a scientifically recognized testing method providing quantitative data.[436] In addition, they require that the sample be secured and retained so that the employee has the opportunity to have an independent test at a second certified laboratory, if requested within three days.[437] Test results must remain confidential, except as necessary to impose sanctions under the Omnibus Act and to ensure that employees are impartially selected for testing.[438]

The Omnibus Act preempts state action[439] by providing that states may not adopt laws or regulations inconsistent with regulations promulgated under the Act, excepting only criminal laws that impose sanctions for reckless conduct damaging persons or property.

The Omnibus Act also states that the Administrator retains discretion to continue to enforce and to amend existing regulations relating to use of alcohol and drugs by safety-sensitive employees.[440] Further, the regulations prescribed by the Administrator with respect to foreign air carriers must be consistent with the "international obligations" of the United

---

[433]*Id.* §614(c)(1), (2).
[434]*Id.* §614(d)(1).
[435]*Id.* §614(d)(2).
[436]*Id.* §614(d)(3), (4).
[437]*Id.* §614(d)(5).
[438]*Id.* §614(d)(7), (8).
[439]*Id.* §614(e)(1).
[440]*Id.* §614(e)(2).

States, and the Administrator is directed to take into consideration the laws of foreign countries.[441]

In February 1994, the FAA promulgated regulations in order to implement the Omnibus Act.[442] These regulations amend the FAA regulations to conform with the Omnibus Act and establish the aviation industry alcohol misuse prevention program. The new regulations supplement but do not change existing regulations as to alcohol misuse.

The new regulations forbid all covered employees, defined as persons who perform directly or by contract a safety-sensitive function, from certain alcohol-related conduct.[443] An employee may not report for duty or remain on duty while having a blood-alcohol content of .04 or greater; use alcohol while performing safety-sensitive duties; use alcohol within eight hours before performing crew member or flight attendant duties or within four hours before performing other safety-sensitive duties; use alcohol within eight hours after an accident, unless he or she has been tested, or his or her performance could not have contributed to the accident; or refuse to submit to alcohol testing.[444]

The regulations add alcohol testing requirements that parallel Aviation Act drug testing requirements and require alcohol testing to be conducted in conformance with DOT alcohol testing procedures.[445] Employers are required to provide educational materials explaining both FAA requirements and the employer's policies and procedures regarding meeting those requirements.[446] Employers must also train supervisors as to when reasonable suspicion exists, and refer covered

---

[441]*Id.* §614(e)(3).

[442]Alcohol Misuse Prevention Program and Antidrug Program for Personnel and Employees of Foreign Air Carriers Engaged in Specified Aviation Activities, 59 Fed. Reg. 7380 (1994).

[443]59 Fed. Reg. 7391, §121.458 (1994). Covered safety-sensitive functions include flight crew members, flight attendants, flight instructors, aircraft dispatchers, aircraft maintenance or preventive maintenance employees, ground security coordinators, aviation screeners, and air traffic controllers. *Id.* at 7391, §121.458 and pt. 121, app. J.

[444]*Id.* at 7391, §121.458.

[445]*Id.* at 7390, §121.459 and pt. 121, app. J.

[446]*Id.* at 7394, §121.459 and pt. 121, app. J.

employees who test positively for alcohol use to substance abuse professionals for evaluation, counseling, and treatment.[447] Covered employees who test positively cannot perform safety-sensitive functions.[448]

The regulations require the employer to submit an alcohol misuse prevention program to the FAA for approval and certification. They exempt employees who are located outside the United States from alcohol misuse testing.[449]

At the same time the FAA promulgated the alcohol testing regulations, it proposed amending its drug testing and misuse regulations to conform with the Omnibus Act and to clarify drug testing requirements, including employer and Medical Review Officer (MRO) responsibilities.[450] These regulations became final in August 1994 and do not substantively change drug test procedures.[451]

I. Testing of Railroad Employees

Section 4 of the Omnibus Act amends Section 202 of the Federal Railroad Safety Act of 1970.[452] This amendment, like the amendment to the Aviation Act, requires the Secretary of Transportation to establish a program requiring railroads to conduct preemployment, reasonable suspicion, random, and postaccident testing of railroad employees in safety-sensitive positions for use of alcohol or controlled substances in violation of law or federal regulation.[453] It defines the term "controlled substance" in the same manner as the Aviation Act.[454]

The Secretary is authorized to disqualify for an established period of time or dismiss any employee determined to have used or been impaired by alcohol while on duty or

---

[447]*Id.*

[448]*Id.* at 7393, §121.459 and pt. 121, app. J.

[449]*Id.* at 7395, §121.459 and pt. 121, app. J.

[450]*Id.* at 7412.

[451]Antidrug Program for Personnel Engaged in Specified Aviation Activities, 59 Fed. Reg. 42,922 (1994).

[452]Pub. L. No. 91-458, 84 Stat. 971.

[453]Railroad Safety Act §202(r)(1)(A).

[454]*Id.* §202(r)(5).

to have used a controlled substance, whether on duty or not, except as permitted for medical purposes.[455] As with the amendment to the Aviation Act, these provisions do not require dismissal or disqualification of an employee who tests positive. Rather, they authorize the Secretary to take such a step directly or to require a railroad to do so, if the Secretary believes such action is warranted.[456] The Secretary is also authorized, as under the Aviation Act, to require railroads to conduct periodic, recurring tests of safety-sensitive employees. The Secretary's discretion to continue in force and amend existing regulations is not affected by the Act.[457]

The legislative history of the amendment to the Railroad Safety Act contains the same discussion of the definition of reasonable suspicion and the administration of random testing as is contained in the legislative history of the amendment to the Aviation Act.[458] It also requires the Secretary to establish the same safeguards for individual rights called for in the Aviation Act.[459] The amendment also contains the same rehabilitation requirements as the Aviation Act[460] and requires the Secretary to establish requirements that are consistent with the "international obligations" of the United States.[461]

Unlike the amendments to the Aviation Act, the amendment to the Railroad Safety Act does not specifically preempt state laws or regulations. The legislative history indicates that Congress considered the current preemption provision under the Federal Railroad Safety Act to be adequate.[462]

Like the FAA, the Federal Railroad Safety Act (FRA) promulgated regulations in February 1994 in order to conform to the Omnibus Act and its amendments to the Railway Act.[463] The regulations, which address both drug and alcohol

---

[455]*Id.* §202(r)(1)(B), (C).
[456]REPORT ON S. 676, *supra* note 424, at 24.
[457]Railroad Safety Act §202(r)(1).
[458]REPORT ON S. 676, *supra* note 424, at 24.
[459]Railroad Safety Act §202(r)(2).
[460]*Id.* §202(r)(3).
[461]*Id.* §202(r)(4).
[462]REPORT ON S. 676, *supra* note 424, at 28.
[463]Alcohol Testing; Amendments to Alcohol/Drug Regulations, 59 Fed. Reg. 7448 (1994).

testing, require pre-employment and random alcohol testing, and mandate the reasonable suspicion test for both drugs and alcohol.[464] The changes also reflect the DOT requirement of split sample testing and other testing procedures.[465] Unlike the FAA regulations, the FRA regulations prohibit a "covered employee"[466] from using alcohol within four hours before performing safety-sensitive functions.[467] The FRA requires each railroad with more than 400,000 employee hours to submit a report each year summarizing the results of its new alcohol misuse prevention program.[468] The new regulations also set forth record-keeping requirements.[469] Other new and amended FRA regulations duplicate FAA changes.

J. Testing to Enhance Mass Transportation Safety

Section 6 of the Omnibus Act provides for drug testing in the mass transportation industry.[470] The term "mass transportation" is defined to mean all forms of mass transportation except as the Secretary of Transportation determines are adequately covered by the Railroad Safety Act or the Commercial Motor Vehicle Safety Act of 1986.[471]

Like the amendments to the Aviation Act and the Railroad Safety Act, this section requires the Secretary to establish a program within 12 months of enactment requiring mass transportation operations that receive federal financial assistance under the UMT Administration to conduct preemployment, reasonable suspicion, random, and postaccident testing

---

[464]*Id.* at 7462, subpart F, §219.501 (pre-employment alcohol testing); 7462, subpart G, §219.601 (random alcohol testing); 7461, subpart D, §219.300 (mandatory reasonable suspicion testing).

[465]*E.g., Id.* at 7464, subpart H, §219.703 *et seq.*

[466]The FRA continues to define a coverted employee as "a person who has been assigned to perform service subject to the Hours of Service Act (45 USC 61–64b) during a duty tour, whether or not the person has performed or is currently performing such service, and any person who performs such service." 59 Fed. Reg. 7457, §219.5.

[467]*Id.* at 7459, §219.101.

[468]*Id.* at 7465, subpart I, §219.801.

[469]*Id.* at 7466, subpart J, §219.901.

[470]*See also* identical provisions at H.R. 2942, §345.

[471]RLA §6(a)(4).

of mass transportation employees in safety-sensitive positions for use, in violation of law or federal regulation, of alcohol or a controlled substance. It also authorizes the Secretary to issue regulations for the conduct of periodic recurring testing.[472]

The legislative history indicates that the Secretary may grant waivers to small transit operations located in rural areas if the Secretary determines that such a waiver would not be contrary to the public interest and would not diminish safety.[473]

The mass transportation section of the Act also requires postaccident testing of any safety-sensitive employee involved in an accident in which human life is lost or bodily injury or significant property damage occurs.[474] This section contains the same requirement that the Secretary promulgate requirements for rehabilitation programs included in the Aviation and Railroad Safety Act amendments. It also contains the same procedures designed to safeguard individual rights.

The mass transportation section preempts state action, as does the amendment to the Aviation Act.[475] It also contains the same provisions with respect to enforcement of existing regulations, the international obligations of the United States, and the definition of "controlled substance."[476]

The Secretary may require disqualification for an established period of time or dismissal of any employee determined to have used or been impaired by alcohol while on duty and may impose the same sanctions on an employee determined to have used a controlled substance, whether or not on duty, except as permitted for medical purposes.[477] Other penalties applicable to mass transportation employees under other provisions of law are unaffected.[478] Finally, an entity that is required to establish an alcohol and controlled substance testing

---

[472]*Id.* §6(b)(1).
[473]Report on S. 676, *supra* note 424, at 36.
[474]RLA §6(b)(2).
[475]*Id.* §6(e)(1).
[476]*Id.* §6(e)(2), (e)(3), (a)(1).
[477]*Id.* §6(f)(1).
[478]*Id.* §6(f)(2).

program but fails to do so is not eligible for federal financial assistance under the UMT Administration.[479]

Like the FAA and FRA, in February 1994 the Federal Transportation Administration (FTA, previously the UMT Administration) promulgated final regulations to conform with the Omnibus Act.[480] The FTA regulations require employers to establish and maintain alcohol misuse prevention programs similar to those required by the FAA and FRA regulations.[481] Employers subjected to FTA regulation may not allow safety-sensitive employees to consume alcohol for four hours before performing safety-sensitive job functions; while performing a safety-sensitive function; after a fatal accident, unless eight hours have passed or the employee has been tested; or after a nonfatal accident, if the employee's involvement is not discounted as a contributing factor, until eight hours have passed or the employee is tested.[482] The regulations require the same testing as the FAA and FRA regulations and impose the same referral, training, and information requirements.[483]

The FTA also promulgated drug testing regulations in accordance with the Omnibus Act.[484] These regulations essentially duplicate FAA and FRA regulations.

K. Procedures for Transportation Workplace Drug and Alcohol Testing Programs

At the same time that the FAA, FRA, and FTA published alcohol testing regulations, the DOT published final rules regarding the procedures required by the Omnibus Act.[485] These procedures are intended to cover all DOT operating administrations conducting alcohol testing programs and to

---

[479]*Id.* §6(g).

[480]Prevention of Alcohol Misuse in Transit Operations, 59 Fed. Reg. 7532 (1994).

[481]*Id.* at 7550, §654.1.

[482]*Id.* at 7551, subpart B, §654.21 *et seq.*

[483]*Id.* at 7555, subpart C, §654.31 *et seq.*

[484]Prevention of Prohibited Drug Use in Transit Operations, *Id.* at 7572.

[485]Procedures for Transportation Workplace Drug and Alcohol Testing Programs, *Id.* at 7340.

implement the requirements set forth in the Omnibus Act for split sample testing[486] and a variety of alcohol testing procedures based on breath tests.[487] The regulations require employers to use the DOT alcohol testing form.[488] Along with this final rule, the DOT proposed blood alcohol testing rules.[489]

The DOT published further procedural changes regarding drug and alcohol testing in August 1994.[490] The regulations conform the DOT regulations with the HHS guidelines published in June 1994.[491] The DOT began requiring employers to use standard DOT forms for their workplace drug testing programs, including a custody and control form.[492] It clarified the regulations by requiring use of a split sample collection and stating the acceptable temperature range for urine drug samples.[493] The DOT added language emphasizing that couriers do not have to make entries in the chain of custody form and laid out technical amendments aimed at clarifying the laboratory reporting procedures.[494] The DOT also lowered the initial cutoff level for marijuana metabolites.[495]

VIII. Preemption of Minor Disputes

Under the Supremacy Clause of the U.S. Constitution, federal law has the power to displace or supersede not only inconsistent state laws, but also state laws that are consistent with the federal scheme. Displaced, or preempted, state law can be statutory or judge-made. A federal statute can have a similar effect on other federal laws. These preemptive ef-

---

[486]*Id.* at 7355, subpart B, §40.25.

[487]*Id.* at 7357, subpart C, §40.51 *et seq.* and app. A.

[488]*Id.* at 7358, subpart C, §40.59.

[489]*Id.* at 7367.

[490]Procedures for Transportation Workplace Drug and Alcohol Testing Programs, *Id.* at 42,996.

[491]Mandatory Guidelines for Federal Workplace Drug Testing Programs, 59 Fed. Reg. 29,908 (1994).

[492]59 Fed. Reg. 43,000, §40.23 (1994).

[493]*Id.* at 43,000, §40.25.

[494]*Id.*

[495]*Id.* at 43,001, §40.29.

fects do not occur automatically; however, their preemptive effect turns on congressional intent.[496] Federal statutes seldom explicitly state their preemptive effect, leaving that determination to the courts. The RLA is silent on the question of preemption.

One of the most significant areas of federal preemption consists of state law claims that to some extent implicate collective bargaining agreements under the RLA. Under the RLA, a minor dispute arises where a party makes a claim that requires interpretation or application of an RLA collective bargaining agreement.[497]

A. Early Applications of Minor Dispute Preemption

Early interpretations of the RLA allowed an employee who was seeking damages, but not reinstatement, for discharge in violation of a collective bargaining agreement to sue his or her employer in state court for breach of the agreement.[498] Under these cases, so long as the employee did not seek reinstatement to the job, the System Board procedure for adjusting disputes under the RLA was viewed only as one option an employee might pursue for resolving a claim with the employer.[499] These decisions viewed claims for breach of an employment contract as a creature of state law, rather than one governed by federal principles, and therefore concluded that state tribunals were appropriate for resolving such disputes.[500]

In *Andrews v. Louisville & Nashville Railroad*,[501] the Supreme Court overruled its earlier decisions and held that a discharged employee must pursue a claim for breach of a

---

[496]Hawaiian Airlines v. Norris, 146 LRRM 2577 (1994).

[497]Disputes arising out of interpretation or application of collective bargaining agreements are defined as "minor disputes" under the RLA. Elgin, J. & E. Ry. v. Burley, 325 U.S. 711, 723 (1945). For a discussion of minor disputes, see Chapter 5, "Enforcement of Collective Bargaining Agreements," §1.

[498]Moore v. Illinois C. R.R., 312 U.S. 630 (1941).

[499]*Id.* at 635–36; Transcontinental & W. Air, Inc. v. Koppal, 345 U.S. 653, 660 (1953).

[500]Transcontinental & W. Air, Inc. v. Koppal, 345 U.S. at 656–57, 662.

[501]406 U.S. 320, 80 LRRM 2240 (1972).

collective bargaining agreement before the appropriate Adjustment Board. The Court's rationale was that wrongful discharge claims necessarily involve interpretation of the collective bargaining agreement that govern the terms and conditions of employment, and the Court had ruled in prior decisions that the Adjustment Boards had exclusive jurisdiction over "minor disputes" involving interpretation or application of such agreements.[502] The Court also noted that its prior assumption that RLA collective bargaining agreements were subject to state contract law was inconsistent with more recent cases in which it had held such claims were governed exclusively by federal labor law.[503]

Prior to *Andrews*, in *Elgin, Joliet & Eastern Railway v. Burley*,[504] the Supreme Court had described minor disputes as follows:

> [A minor] dispute relates either to the meaning or proper application of a particular provision with reference to a specific situation or to an omitted case. In the latter event the claim is founded upon some incident of the employment relation, or asserted one, independent of those covered by the collective agreement, e.g., claims on account of personal injuries. In either case the claim is to rights accrued, not merely to have new ones created for the future.[505]

Following the *Andrews* decision, the courts of appeals adopted a variety of similar tests for preemption. For example:

- "State law claims which grow out of the employment relationship can constitute 'minor disputes' under the Act, even when the claims do not arise directly from the collective bargaining agreement itself. If the state law claim is 'inextricably intertwined' with the terms and conditions of employment under the collective bargaining agreement, the claim constitutes a 'minor

---

[502] 406 U.S. at 324.
[503] *Id.* at 323. The court relied on Machinists v. Central Airlines, 372 U.S. 682 (1963).
[504] 325 U.S. 711 (1945).
[505] *Id.* at 723.

dispute' under the Act and is subject to the grievance procedures contained in the bargaining agreement."[506]

- "[A] state law claim is preempted if it 'is based on a matrix of facts which are inextricably intertwined with the grievance machinery of the collective bargaining agreement and of the RLA.'"[507]
- A state claim is preempted if the action complained of it "arguably justified by the terms of the parties' collective-bargaining agreement."[508]
- A state law claim is preempted where "the gravamen of the complaint is wrongful discharge."[509]
- A state law claim is preempted where the claim "requires interpretation of" a collective bargaining agreement.[510]

Applying such standards, the courts developed a jurisprudence of RLA preemption.

B. *Norris* Case

In *Hawaiian Airlines v. Norris*,[511] the Supreme Court again addressed RLA preemption. In that case, an aircraft mechanic refused to sign a maintenance record to certify that an airline repair had been performed satisfactorily. The mechanic was discharged. He filed a state law action alleging, inter alia, that the discharge violated the state's "Whistleblower Protection Act." The Court held the claim was not preempted.

According to the Court, the standard for determining whether a state law claim is preempted by the RLA minor

---

[506]Morales v. Southern Pac. Transp. Co., 894 F2d 743, 746 (CA 5, 1990).

[507]Magnuson v. Burlington N., Inc., 576 F2d 1367, 1369–70 (CA 9), *cert. denied*, 439 U.S. 930 (1978).

[508]Polich v. Burlington N., Inc., 942 F2d 1467, 1470, 138 LRRM 2624 (CA 9, 1991).

[509]Magnuson v. Burlington N., Inc., 576 F2d at 1369–70.

[510]Davies v. American Airlines, 971 F2d 463, 466, 140 LRRM 2986 (CA 10, 1992), *cert. denied*, 143 LRRM 2424 (1993) (citing Lingle v. Norge Div. of Magic Chef, Inc., 486 U.S. 399, 128 LRRM 2521 (1988)).

[511]146 LRRM 2577 (S Ct, 1994).

dispute provisions is the same standard that is articulated in *Lingle v. Norge Division of Magic Chef, Inc.,*[512] under Section 301 of the Labor Management Relations Act (LMRA): whether a state-law claim is dependent on the interpretation of a collective-bargaining agreement. Under this standard, the Court held, the retaliatory discharge claim under state law was not preempted because any issues that required inspection of the collective bargaining agreement—such as whether the plaintiff was discharged—were "purely factual."[513]

Several other arguments were addressed by the Court:

- The Court distinguished *Andrews v. Louisville & Nashville Railroad,*[514] reasoning that the claim there was held to be preempted not on the ground that the RLA preempts all state claims based on discharge or discipline, but because in that case the parties conceded that the employee "asserted no right independent of the agreement."[515]

- In the context of minor dispute preemption, RLA preemption is not broader than LMRA preemption; it is the same.[516]

- Even if a state claim for breach of the bargaining agreement addresses "precisely the same set of facts," preemption is not required.[517]

- The term *grievances,* as used in the definition of minor disputes for preemption purposes,[518] does not mean all employment-related disputes; it "refers to disagree-

---

[512]486 U.S. 399, 128 LRRM 2521 (1988).

[513]*Id.* at 2582. *See also* Livadas v. Aubry, 114 S Ct 2068 (1994) (state law claim for penalty payment from employer not preempted even though penalty was pegged to employee's wages, which were governed by a collective bargaining agreement; discussed in Norris, 146 LRRM 2583 n.8).

[514]406 U.S. 320, 80 LRRM 2240 (1972).

[515]146 LRRM at 2582.

[516]*Id.* at 2584. *See* Westbrook v. Sky Chefs, Inc., 35 F3d 316, 147 LRRM 2491 (CA 7, 1994).

[517]146 LRRM at 2584 (quoting Lingle v. Norge Div. of Magic Chef, Inc., 486 U.S. 399, 128 LRRM 2521 (1988)).

[518]The RLA uses the language "disputes growing out of grievances or out of the interpretation or application of [collective bargaining agreements]." 45 USC §151a (1988).

ments over how to give effect to the bargained-for agreement."[519]

- The fact the action complained of in the state claim is "arguably justified" by the collective bargaining agreement "was employed only for policing the line between major and minor disputes" and "[says] nothing about the threshold question whether the dispute was subject to the RLA in the first place."[520]

The full effect of *Norris* on preemption law under the RLA must await judicial development. Many of the RLA cases decided prior to *Norris* purported to apply the *Lingle* standard,[521] or did so in addition to one of the other tests,[522] and may remain persuasive. Other cases, such as where a plaintiff unsuccessfully relied on *Lingle* in order to defeat RLA preemption,[523] will have to be reevaluated.

---

[519]146 LRRM at 2580–81, 2584–85.

[520]*Id.* at 2585 ("Obviously, [the 'arguably justified by the existing agreement'] test said nothing about the threshold question whether the dispute was subject to the RLA in the first place."). *See* Taggart v. Trans World Airlines, 147 LRRM 2820 (CA 8, 1994).

[521]Anderson v. American Airlines, 2 F3d 590, 597 (CA 5, 1993); Davies v. American Airlines, 971 F2d 463, 466, 140 LRRM 2986 (CA 10, 1992), *cert. denied*, 143 LRRM 2424 (1993); O'Brien v. Consolidated Rail Corp., 972 F2d 1, 5, 140 LRRM 3014 (CA 1, 1992); Maher v. New Jersey Transit Rail Operations, 125 NJ 455, 138 LRRM 2253 (1991).

[522]*E.g.*, Croston v. Burlington N. R.R., 999 F2d 381, 388, 143 LRRM 2702 (CA 9, 1993); Underwood v. Venango River Corp., 995 F2d 677, 684–86, 143 LRRM 2437 (CA 7, 1993); Hubbard v. United Air Lines, 927 F2d 1094, 1099, 136 LRRM 2750 (CA 9, 1991); Beard v. Carrolton R.R., 893 F2d 117, 122, 133 LRRM 2919 (CA 6, 1989); Edelman v. Western Airlines, 892 F2d 839, 844, 133 LRRM 2212 (CA 9, 1989).

Pre-*Norris* use of the *Lingle* test does not guarantee that a precedent will survive, however. Thus, after *Norris* was decided, the Seventh Circuit, in a retaliatory discharge case, overruled the opinion in Underwood v. Venango River Corp., 995 F2d 677, 684–86, 143 LRRM 2437 (CA 7   93). Westbrook v. Sky Chefs, Inc., 35 F3d 316, 147 LRRM 2491 (CA 7, 1994). The court held that *Underwood* was incorrect in not applying the *Lingle* precedent to RLA preemption. The court did not discuss whether, under *Norris* the result in *Underwood*—preemption of Racketeer Influenced and Corrupt Organizations Act (RICO) claims—would be different. The Eighth Circuit, in Taggart v. Trans World Airlines, 147 LRRM 2820 (CA 8, 1994), declined to follow O'Brien v. Consolidated Rail Corp., 972 F2d 1, 5, 140 LRRM 3014 (CA 1, 1992), and Croston v. Burlington N. R.R., 999 F2d 381, 388, 143 LRRM 2702 (CA 9, 1993), in part on the ground that those cases were pre-*Norris*.

[523]*E.g.*, Grote v. Trans World Airlines, 905 F2d 1307, 1310, 134 LRRM 2583 (CA 9), *cert. denied*, 498 U.S. 958, 135 LRRM 2872 (1990); Henegar v. Banta, 27 F3d 223, 224, 226, 146 LRRM 2652 (CA 6, 1994).

Four courts of appeals have issued opinions in RLA pre-emption cases since *Norris*.[524] In one decision, the Fifth Circuit had previously affirmed, on preemption grounds, a lower court dismissal of a claim for intentional infliction of emotional distress from a failure to provide a work environment free from gender-based discrimination. Upon reconsideration after the Supreme Court vacated the decision in light of *Norris,* the circuit court determined that the claim was not preempted because it could be decided without reference to the collective bargaining agreement.[525] The Eighth Circuit has ruled that a state claim for handicap discrimination was not preempted where the plaintiff's claim was independent of the bargaining agreement.[526] The court held that *Norris* had rejected the "arguably justified" test of RLA preemption.[527]

C. Claims Under Federal Law

Minor dispute preemption under the RLA is not re-stricted to state law claims, but extends to federal law as well, because the exclusive jurisdiction of the Adjustment Boards to resolve disputes involving interpretation or application of a collective bargaining agreement does not depend on the source of the preempted claim.[528]

---

[524]Hirras v. National R.R. Passenger Corp., 10 F3d 1142, 145 LRRM 2137 (CA 5, 1994); Westbrook v. Sky Chefs, Inc., 35 F3d 316, 147 LRRM 2491 (CA 7, 1994); Taggart v. Trans World Airlines, 147 LRRM 2820 (CA 8, 1994); Piper v. Alaska Airlines, 34 F3d 1073 (CA 9, 1994). In addition, two district court decisions have been issued since *Norris*. Fry v. Air Line Pilots Ass'n, 147 LRRM 2789 (D Colo, 1994) (adopting judge magistrate's recommendation, reported at 147 LRRM 2787), held a claim for the intentional infliction of emotional distress was preempted. Condon v. United Air Lines, 148 LRRM 2985 (D Fla, 1994), held a breach of contract claim was preempted by *Norris*.

[525]Hirras v. National R.R. Passenger Corp., 10 F3d 1142, 145 LRRM 2137.

[526]Taggart v. Trans World Airlines, 147 LRRM 2820.

[527]*Id.* at 2824. In Westbrook v. Sky Chefs, Inc., 35 F3d 316, 147 LRRM 2491, the court held that *Norris* required the overruling of Seventh Circuit precedent on preemption of retaliatory discharge claims. Piper v. Alaska Airlines, 34 F3d 1073, held that *Norris* requires reversal of Ninth Circuit precedent on preemption of a claim of race discrimination.

[528]*See* Hawaiian Airlines v. Norris, 146 LRRM 2577 (S Ct, 1994). Although the relationship between two federal statutes is not ordinarily termed "preemption," the courts have used this term under the RLA.

Under this principle, two courts of appeals held, prior to *Norris*,[529] that claims under the Racketeer Influenced and Corrupt Organizations Act (RICO) are preempted when they involve interpretation or application of a collective bargaining agreement.[530] In an illustrative case, *Underwood v. Venango River Corp.*,[531] the plaintiffs sued their employer for fraudulently inducing them, through an alleged pattern of racketeering activity, to accept employment with a third party that had purchased the assets of their former employer. The Seventh Circuit dismissed the lawsuit, holding that a RICO claim is preempted by the RLA where it seeks to vindicate a substantive right that derives from the collective bargaining agreement, *or* where adjudication of the claim requires interpretation of the collective bargaining agreement.[532] After *Norris* was decided, the Seventh Circuit overruled *Underwood*,[533] although it did not address the issue of whether *Norris* required overruling the outcome of *Underwood*.

Several pre-*Norris* courts have also ruled that a claim under the Employee Retirement Income Security Act (ERISA) for benefits under a collectively bargained pension plan is preempted by the RLA.[534] The rationale of these decisions is that such claims require interpretation of a collective bargaining agreement, and are thus subject to the arbitration process compelled by the RLA.[535] One court also concluded that Congress did not intend by enacting ERISA to alter the

---

[529]Hawaiian Airlines v. Norris, 146 LRRM 2577.

[530]Underwood v. Venango River Corp., 995 F2d 677, 684–86, 143 LRRM 2437 (CA 7, 1993), *rationale disapproved by* Westbrook v. Sky Chefs, Inc., 35 F3d 316, 147 LRRM 2491 (CA 7, 1994); Hubbard v. United Air Lines, 927 F2d 1094, 1099, 136 LRRM 2750 (CA 9, 1991); Fry v. Air Line Pilots Ass'n, 147 LRRM 2776 (D Colo, 1994).

[531]995 F2d at 679.

[532]*Id.* at 684.

[533]Westbrook v. Sky Chefs, Inc., 35 F3d 316, 147 LRRM 2491.

[534]Long v. Flying Tiger Line, 994 F2d 692 (CA 9, 1993); Sanchez v. Eastern Airlines, 574 F2d 29, 33, 98 LRRM 2256 (CA 1, 1988); Air Line Pilots Ass'n v. Northwest Airlines, 627 F2d 272, 276, 103 LRRM 2652 (CA DC, 1980). In the *Northwest* decision, the court distinguished between a claim for benefits, which requires interpretation of the collective agreement, and a claim for breach of fiduciary duty under ERISA, which does not.

[535]Long v. Flying Tiger Line, 994 F2d at 695.

exclusive jurisdiction of System Boards over contractually based disputes.[536]

Not all federal claims that arguably require interpretation of a collective bargaining agreement are preempted by the RLA. The Supreme Court has ruled that the RLA does not preempt claims under the Federal Employers' Liability Act (FELA), which allows railroad workers to sue their employers for personal injury.[537] The Court's reasoning was that Congress enacted the FELA specifically to provoke a statutory basis for compensating injuries to railroad employees, and thus could not have intended that the RLA preempt such claims.[538]

Courts have ruled that the RLA does not preempt claims under the Rehabilitation Act.[539] The same conclusion has been reached with respect to Section 1981 of the Civil Rights Act of 1866.[540]

IX.   Preemption of State Laws Regulating Collective Bargaining

A. Bargaining Process

A second branch of preemption that has application to the RLA involves situations in which the courts have concluded that Congress intended the RLA, and not state law, to govern the subject matter exclusively. Under this theory, state laws that seek to regulate the collective bargaining pro-

---

[536]*Id.*

[537]Atchison, T. & S.F. Ry. v. Buell, 480 U.S. 557, 124 LRRM 2953 (1987).

[538]480 U.S. at 566.

[539]These cases illustrate the impact of *Norris,* even when that case does not demand a different result from precedent. In Bates v. Long Island R.R., 997 F2d 1028, 1034–35, 143 LRRM 2767 (CA 2), *cert. denied,* 144 LRRM 2872 (1993), the court reasoned that arbitration does not provide the same rights and procedures available to civil rights claimants in federal court and for that reason should not be the exclusive remedy for a claim under the Rehabilitation Act. In Degutis v. Consolidated Rail Corp., 147 LRRM 2470 (ND Ill, 1994), the court reached the same result by simply applying *Norris.*

[540]McAlester v. United Air Lines, 851 F2d 1249, 1254 (CA 10, 1988).

cess, or attempt to restrict conduct Congress intended to remain free from any regulation at all, are preempted.[541]

The leading Supreme Court decisions establishing these principles under the RLA are *United Transp. Union v. Long Island Railroad*[542] and *Railroad Trainmen v. Jacksonville Terminal Co.*[543] In these decisions, the Court held that collective bargaining by rail and air carriers is to be governed exclusively by the RLA, and that the states therefore may not regulate self-help measures, including strikes or picketing, that the parties may take after failed efforts to negotiate a collective bargaining agreement.

B. Subjects of Bargaining

The Supreme Court in *California v. Taylor*[544] held that a state could not apply to RLA employees civil service laws that fixed rates of pay and overtime; established procedures for promotions, layoffs, and dismissals; and forbade conflicting collective bargaining agreement terms. Similarly, the Eleventh Circuit has ruled that a state law that mandated longevity pay for all state workers was invalid to the extent it applied to workers covered by the RLA.[545] The rationale of this decision was that because the RLA employees were governed by a collective bargaining agreement that set their wages, any state law that attempted to enhance those wages through longevity pay would constitute an impermissible unilateral change in the terms and conditions of employment.[546]

However, in *Hawaiian Airlines v. Norris*,[547] the Court made it clear that not every state law that conflicts with a substantive

---

[541]The same doctrine has been applied under the NLRA. *See* Machinists v. Wisconsin Employment Relations Comm'n, 427 U.S. 132, 92 LRRM 2881 (1976). The concept of collective bargaining not only applies to actual negotiation of a contract, but also continues through the life of the contract, and "involves day to day adjustments in the contract and other work rules, resolution of problems not covered by existing agreements, and the protection of employee rights not clearly covered by contract." Conley v. Gibson, 355 U.S. 41, 46 (1957).

[542]455 U.S. 678, 109 LRRM 3017 (1982).

[543]394 U.S. 369, 380, 70 LRRM 2961 (1969).

[544]353 U.S. 553, 559–60 (1957).

[545]Hull v. Dutton, 935 F2d 1194, 137 LRRM 2991 (CA 11, 1991).

[546]935 F2d at 1197.

[547]146 LRRM 2577 (S Ct, 1994).

term in a collective bargaining agreement is preempted. It cited with approval earlier Supreme Court cases finding states were not preempted from

- regulating the number of workers required to operate certain equipment;[548]
- requiring cabooses on all trains, even though the collective bargaining agreement required fewer;[549] or
- "regulating sanitary facilities and conditions, safety devices and protections, purity of water supply, [and] fire protection."[550]

Other laws of general applicability have survived preemption arguments as well. The Seventh Circuit held that the RLA did not preempt a Delaware statute regulating the process that a corporate board of directors must follow before adopting antitakeover provisions, even where such provisions were negotiated as part of a collective bargaining agreement.[551] The court found that antitakeover provisions were not typically a subject of collective bargaining and that therefore it was not necessary to preempt such laws in order to further the essential objectives of the RLA.[552]

C. Individual Employment Agreements

Preemption issues also arise when a carrier seeks to negotiate individual employment contracts with employees covered by a collective bargaining agreement. The Supreme Court ruled in *Railroad Telegraphers v. Railway Express Agency*[553] that individual employment agreements with employees covered by a collective bargaining agreement are void and unenforceable unless authorized by the union. Courts have recognized that individual negotiation between a carrier and its

---

[548]*Id.* (citing Missouri P. R.R. v. Norwood, 283 U.S. 249, 258 (1931)).
[549]*Id.* (citing Terminial R.R. Ass'n v. Railroad Trainmen, 318 U.S. 1 (1943)).
[550]*Id.* (quoting Terminal R.R. Ass'n v. Railroad Trainmen, 318 U.S. 1).
[551]Air Line Pilots Ass'n v. UAL Corp., 874 F2d 439, 131 LRRM 2265 (1989).
[552]*Id.* at 2270–71.
[553]321 U.S. 342 (1944).

employees interferes with collective bargaining by permitting employers to deal directly with its employees. As the Ninth Circuit has noted, "[a]llowing an employee or employer, by virtue of an individual agreement, to establish an employment status different from that of other employees would undermine the efficacy of collective bargaining."[554]

Although the RLA generally prohibits the execution of individual employment contracts without consent of the union, a carrier may be permitted to execute individual agreements with replacements hired to work during a strike. The Seventh Circuit has held that individual agreements that guaranteed replacement workers a permanent salary that was higher than wage rates under the collective bargaining agreement did not violate Section 2, Fourth, where the agreements were necessary to operate during a strike.[555]

In several cases, unions have argued that a separation program offered by an employer to its represented employees constituted impermissible interference with the collective bargaining process. One court has held that group separation programs do impede upon the collective bargaining process and are therefore unlawful,[556] whereas another upheld such agreements provided they do not conflict with the terms of a collective bargaining agreement.[557] The latter court also found support in the text of the RLA for an employee to terminate an employment relationship on terms the employee finds acceptable.[558]

---

[554]Melanson v. United Air Lines, 931 F2d 558, 561 (CA 9, 1991); *see also* Flight Attendants (UFA) v. Pan Am. World Airways, 620 F Supp 447, 456–58 (SD NY, 1985), *aff'd*, 789 F2d 139, 122 LRRM 2240 (CA 2, 1986).

[555]Air Line Pilots Ass'n v. United Air Lines, 802 F2d 886, 909, 123 LRRM 2617 (CA 7, 1986), *cert. denied*, 480 U.S. 946, 124 LRRM 3192 (1987). *See also* Belknap, Inc. v. Hale, 463 U.S. 491, 113 LRRM 3057 (1983).

[556]Railway & Steamship Clerks v. Atchison, T. & S.F. Ry., 894 F2d 1463, 1466, 133 LRRM 2761 (CA 5), *cert. denied*, 498 U.S. 846, 135 LRRM 2464 (1990); *see also* Richmond, F. & P. R.R. v. Transportation Communications Union, 973 F2d 276, 278–81, 141 LRRM 2115 (CA 4, 1992).

[557]Machinists v. Soo L. R.R., 850 F2d 368, 375, 128 LRRM 2826 (CA 8, 1988), *cert. denied*, 489 U.S. 1010, 130 LRRM 2656 (1989). *See also* Boilermakers v. Atchison, T. & S.F. Ry., 835 F Supp 1293, 144 LRRM 2882 (D Kan, 1993).

[558]850 F2d at 375 (citing 45 USC §159, Eighth) (1988).

X. PREEMPTION OF STATE AND FEDERAL LAWS REGULATING A UNION'S DUTY OF FAIR REPRESENTATION

The courts have held that the RLA preempts state or federal law in cases alleging breach of the duty of fair representation imposed on labor unions.[559] In several cases, courts have held that state common law claims alleged by individual members against a union are preempted by the duty of fair representation.[560] These courts have held that a union's collective bargaining duties to employees are governed by federal law. Thus, union members cannot sue under state law for conduct that implicates the duty of fair representation, although the courts have not precluded the possibility that a union could undertake obligations in addition to those imposed by the duty of fair representation, and thereby expose themselves to state law claims.[561]

In one case involving preemption, an airline pilot sued his union under state law for interference with a contractual relationship and civil conspiracy, as well as breach of the duty of fair representation.[562] The gravamen of his complaint was that the union and its members had engaged in a concerted effort to have him fired from his job in retaliation for his strikebreaking activities at another carrier.[563] The court found his state law claims preempted by the duty of fair representation. As an initial matter, the court found that the state law claims involved the same conduct, and sought the same relief, as plaintiff's cause of action for breach of the duty of fair representation.[564] Because the duty of fair representation is

---

[559]The duty of fair representation prohibits unions from treating their members in a manner that is arbitrary, discriminatory, or in bad faith. Air Line Pilots Ass'n v. O'Neill, 499 U.S. 65, 136 LRRM 2721 (1991).

[560]Petersen v. Air Line Pilots Ass'n, 759 F2d 1161 (CA 4, 1985); Nellis v. Air Line Pilots Ass'n, 805 F Supp 355, 141 LRRM 2950 (ED Va, 1992), aff'd, 15 F3d 50 (CA 4, 1994), cert. denied, 147 LRRM 2448 (1994); Dunn v. Air Line Pilots Ass'n, 836 F Supp 1574 (SD Fla, 1993); Eisenberg v. Trans World Airlines, 654 F Supp 125, 128, 126 LRRM 2951 (SD Fla, 1987), aff'd, 875 F2d 872 (CA 11, 1989); Reiss v. Railway & Steamship Clerks, 629 F Supp 1029, 1030 (ED Pa, 1986).

[561]Nellis v. Air Line Pilots Ass'n, 805 F Supp at 360.

[562]Nellis v. Air Line Pilots Ass'n, 805 F Supp 355, 141 LRRM 2950.

[563]Id. at 2951.

[564]Id. at 2954.

governed by federal law, and since the state law claims were duplicative, the court held that the state law claims were preempted.[565] The court also found that the claims touched upon the union's right to engage in self-help under the RLA, and were thereby subject only to federal regulation.[566] One court has held that RICO claims against unions implicating the duty of fair representation are preempted.[567]

Other courts addressing this issue have found state law claims preempted when they are based upon conduct related to the collective bargaining process. Thus, one court held state law claims preempted by the duty of fair representation when they involved allegations that a union fraudulently induced its members to honor a picket line.[568] According to the court, such claims alleged no more than that the union treated them arbitrarily and in bad faith and therefore breached its duty of fair representation.[569] Similarly, another court held that state law tort and contract claims against a union that allegedly induced members to cross a picket line, and then reneged on assurances to help find them jobs at another carrier, were preempted.[570] The court found that the state law claims asserted violations by the union of its duty to bargain on their behalf with respect to employment. Because the duty of fair representation governs this subject, the court held that the state law claims were preempted.[571]

---

[565]*Id.*

[566]*Id* .

[567]*See* Mann v. Air Line Pilots Ass'n, 848 F Supp 990 (SD Fla, 1994), *aff'd without opinion sub nom.* Bialko v. Duffy, No. 94-4265 (CA 11, 1995).

[568]Dunn v. Air Line Pilots Ass'n, 836 F Supp 1574, 1580 (SD Fla, 1993).

[569]*Id.*

[570]Nellis v. Air Line Pilots Ass'n, 805 F Supp 355, 361, 141 LRRM 2950 (ED Va, 1992), *aff'd,* 15 F3d 50 (CA 4, 1994).

[571]805 F Supp at 360.

TEXT OF THE
RAILWAY LABOR ACT

LIST OF PARALLEL
RLA/U.S.C. SECTIONS

Title I/Subchapter I—General Provisions

Title II/Subchapter II—Carriers By Air

---

*NCP = No Code Provision

Railway Labor Act (1926)

(Act May 20, 1926; redesignated and amended, May 10, 1936; last amended by P.L. 101–239, December 19, 1989)

45 USC §§151–63, 181–88

SUBCHAPTER I—GENERAL PROVISIONS

Sec. 151.   Definitions; short title

When used in this chapter and for the purposes of this chapter—

First. The term "carrier" includes any express company, sleeping-car company, carrier by railroad, subject to subtitle IV of title 49, and any company which is directly or indirectly owned or controlled by or under common control with any carrier by railroad and which operates any equipment or facilities or performs any service (other than trucking service) in connection with the transportation, receipt, delivery, elevation, transfer in transit, refrigeration or icing, storage, and handling of property transported by railroad, and any receiver, trustee, or other individual or body, judicial or otherwise, when in the possession of the business of any such "carrier": Provided, however, That the term "carrier" shall not include any street, interurban, or suburban electric railway, unless such railway is operating as a part of a general steam-railroad system of transportation, but shall not exclude any part of the general steam-railroad system of transportation now or hereafter operated by any other motive power. The Interstate Commerce Commission is authorized and directed upon request of the Mediation Board or upon complaint of any party interested to determine after hearing whether any line operated by electric power falls within the terms of this proviso. The term "carrier" shall not include any company by reason of its being engaged in the mining of coal, the supplying of coal to a carrier where delivery is not beyond the mine tipple, and the operation of equipment or facilities therefor, or in any of such activities.

Second. The term "Adjustment Board" means the National Railroad Adjustment Board created by this chapter.

Third. The term "Mediation Board" means the National Mediation Board created by this chapter.

Fourth. The term "commerce" means commerce among the several States or between any State, Territory, or the District of Columbia and any foreign nation, or between any Territory or the District of Columbia and any State, or between any Territory and any other Territory, or between any Territory and the District of Columbia, or within any Territory or the District of Columbia, or between points in the same State but through any other State or any Territory or the District of Columbia or any foreign nation.

Fifth. The term "employee" as used herein includes every person in the service of a carrier (subject to its continuing authority to supervise and direct the manner of rendition of his service) who performs any work defined as that of an employee or subordinate official in the orders of the Interstate Commerce Commission now in effect, and as the same may be amended or interpreted by orders hereafter entered by the Commission pursuant to the authority which is conferred upon it to enter orders amending or interpreting such existing orders: Provided, however, That no occupational classification made by order of the Interstate Commerce Commission shall be construed to define the crafts according to which railway employees may be organized by their voluntary action, nor shall the jurisdiction or powers of such employee organizations be regarded as in any way limited or defined by the provisions of this chapter or by the orders of the Commission.

The term "employee" shall not include any individual while such individual is engaged in the physical operations consisting of the mining of coal, the preparation of coal, the handling (other than movement by rail with standard railroad locomotives) of coal not beyond the mine tipple, or the loading of coal at the tipple.

Sixth. The term "representative" means any person or persons, labor union, organization, or corporation designated either by a carrier or group of carriers or by its or their employees, to act for it or them.

Seventh. The term "district court" includes the United States District Court for the District of Columbia; and the term "court of appeals" includes the United States Court of Appeals for the District of Columbia.

This chapter may be cited as the "Railway Labor Act."

(May 20, 1926, ch. 347, Sec. 1, 44 Stat. 577; June 7, 1934, ch. 426, 48 Stat. 926; June 21, 1934, ch. 691, Sec. 1, 48 Stat. 1185; June 25, 1936, ch. 804, 49 Stat. 1921; Aug. 13, 1940, ch. 664, Secs. 2, 3, 54 Stat. 785, 786; June 25, 1948, ch. 646, Sec. 32(a), (b), 62 Stat. 991; May 24, 1949, ch. 139, Sec. 127, 63 Stat. 107.)

REFERENCES IN TEXT

This chapter, referred to in text, was in the original "this Act", meaning act May 20, 1926, ch. 347, 44 Stat. 577, as amended, known as the Railway

Labor Act, which enacted this chapter and amended sections 225 and 348 of former Title 28, Judicial Code and Judiciary. Sections 225 and 348 of former Title 28 were repealed by section 39 of act June 25, 1948, ch. 646, 62 Stat. 992, section 1 of which enacted Title 28, Judiciary and Judicial Procedure. Section 225 of former Title 28 was reenacted as sections 1291 to 1294 of Title 28. For complete classification of this Act to the Code, see this section and Tables.

Codification

In par. First, "subtitle IV of title 49" was substituted for "the Interstate Commerce Act [49 U.S.C. 1 et seq.]" on authority of Pub. L. 95-473, Sec. 3(b), Oct. 17, 1978, 92 Stat. 1466, the first section of which enacted subtitle IV of Title 49, Transportation.

Provisions of act Aug. 13, 1940, Sec. 2, similar to those comprising par. First of this section, limiting the term "employer" as applied to mining, etc., of coal, were formerly contained in section 228e of this title. Provisions of section 3 of the act, similar to those comprising par. Fifth of this section, limiting the term "employee" as applied to mining, etc., of coal, were formerly contained in sections 228a, 261, and 351 of this title, and section 1532 of former Title 26, Internal Revenue Code, 1939.

As originally enacted, par. Seventh contained references to the Supreme Court of the District of Columbia. Act June 25, 1936 substituted "the district court of the United States for the District of Columbia" for "the Supreme Court of the District of Columbia", and act June 25, 1948, as amended by act May 24, 1949, substituted "United States District Court for the District of Columbia" for "district court of the United States for the District of Columbia".

As originally enacted, par. Seventh contained references to the "circuit court of appeals". Act June 25, 1948, as amended by act May 24, 1949 substituted "court of appeals" for "circuit court of appeals".

As originally enacted, par. Seventh contained references to the "Court of Appeals of the District of Columbia". Act June 7, 1934 substituted "United States Court of Appeals for the District of Columbia" for "Court of Appeals of the District of Columbia".

Amendments

1940—Act Aug. 13, 1940, added last sentence of par. First, and second par. of par. Fifth.

1934—Act June 21, 1934, added par. Sixth and redesignated provisions formerly set out as par. Sixth as par. Seventh.

Restriction on Establishment of New Annuities or Pensions

Pub. L. 91-215, Sec. 7, Mar. 17, 1970, 84 Stat. 72, provided that: "No carrier and no representative of employees, as defined in section 1 of the

Railway Labor Act [this section], shall, before April 1, 1974, utilize any of the procedures of such Act [this chapter], to seek to make any changes in the provisions of the Railroad Retirement Act of 1937 [section 228a et seq. of this title] for supplemental annuities or to establish any new class of pensions or annuities, other than annuities payable out of the Railroad Retirement Account provided under section 15(a) of the Railroad Retirement Act of 1937 [subsection (a) of section 228o of this title], to become effective prior to July 1, 1974; nor shall any such carrier or representative of employees until July 1, 1974, engage in any strike or lockout to seek to make any such changes or to establish any such new class of pensions or annuities: Provided, That nothing in this section shall inhibit any carrier or representative of employees from seeking any change with respect to benefits payable out of the Railroad Retirement Account provided under section 15(a) of the Railroad Retirement Act of 1937 [subsection (a) of section 228o of this title]."

SOCIAL INSURANCE AND LABOR RELATIONS OF RAILROAD COAL-MINING EMPLOYEES; RETROACTIVE OPERATION OF ACT AUGUST 13, 1940; EFFECT ON PAYMENTS, RIGHTS, ETC.

Sections 4 to 7 of act Aug. 13, 1940, as amended by Reorg. Plan No. 2 of 1946, Sec. 4, eff. July 16, 1946, 11 F.R. 7873, 60 Stat. 1095, with regard to the operation and effect of the laws amended, provided:

"Sec. 4. (a) The laws hereby expressly amended (section 1532 of Title 26, I.R.C. 1939 [former Title 26, Internal Revenue Code of 1939] and sections 151, 215, 228a, 261, and 351 of this title), the Social Security Act, approved August 14, 1935 (section 301 et seq. of Title 42), and all amendments thereto, shall operate as if each amendment herein contained had been enacted as a part of the law it amends, at the time of the original enactment of such law.

"(b) No person (as defined in the Carriers Taxing Act of 1937 [section 261 et seq. of this title]) shall be entitled, by reason of the provisions of this Act, to a refund of, or relief from liability for, any income or excise taxes paid or accrued, pursuant to the provisions of the Carriers Taxing Act of 1937 or subchapter B of chapter 9 of the Internal Revenue Code [section 1500 et seq. of former Title 26, Internal Revenue Code of 1939], prior to the date of the enactment of this Act [Aug. 13, 1940] by reason of employment in the service of any carrier by railroad subject to part I of the Interstate Commerce Act [49 U.S.C. 10501 et seq.], but any individual who has been employed in such service of any carrier by railroad subject to part I of the Interstate Commerce Act as is excluded by the amendments made by this Act from coverage under the Carriers Taxing Act of 1937 and subchapter B of chapter 9 of the Internal Revenue Code, and who has paid income taxes under the provisions of such Act or subchapter, and any carrier by railroad subject to part I of the Interstate Commerce Act which has paid excise taxes under the provisions of the Carriers Taxing Act of 1937 or subchapter B of chapter 9 of the Internal Revenue Code, may, upon making proper application therefor to the Bureau of Internal Revenue [now Internal Revenue Service], have the amount of taxes so paid applied in reduction of such tax liability with respect to employment, as may, by reason of the amendments made by this Act, accrue against them under the provisions of title VIII of the Social Security Act [section 1001 et seq. of Title 42] or the Federal Insurance Contributions Act (subchapter A of chapter 9 of the Internal Revenue Code) [section 1400 et seq. of former Title 26].

"(c) Nothing contained in this Act shall operate (1) to affect any annuity, pension, or death benefit granted under the Railroad Retirement Act of 1935 [section 215 et seq. of this title] or the Railroad Retirement Act of 1937 [section 228a et seq. of this title], prior to the date of enactment of this Act [Aug. 13, 1940], or (2) to include any of the services on the basis of which any such annuity or pension was granted, as employment within the meaning of section 210(b) of the Social Security Act or section 209(b) of such Act, as amended [sections 410(b) and 409(b), respectively, of Title 42]. In any case in which a death benefit alone has been granted, the amount of such death benefit attributable to services, coverage of which is affected by this Act, shall be deemed to have been paid to the deceased under section 204 of the Social Security Act [section 404 of Title 42] in effect prior to January 1, 1940, and deductions shall be made from any insurance benefit or benefits payable under the Social Security Act, as amended [section 301 et seq. of Title 42], with respect to wages paid to an individual for such services until such deductions total the amount of such death benefit attributable to such services.

"(d) Nothing contained in this Act shall operate to affect the benefit rights of any individual under the Railroad Unemployment Insurance Act [section 351 et seq. of this title] for any day of unemployment (as defined in section 1(k) of such Act [section 351(k) of this title]) occurring prior to the date of enactment of this Act. [Aug. 13, 1940]

"Sec. 5. Any application for payment filed with the Railroad Retirement Board prior to, or within sixty days after, the enactment of this Act shall, under such regulations as the Federal Security Administrator may prescribe, be deemed to be an application filed with the Federal Security Administrator by such individual or by any person claiming any payment with respect to the wages of such individual, under any provision of section 202 of the Social Security Act, as amended [section 402 of Title 42].

"Sec. 6. Nothing contained in this Act, nor the action of Congress in adopting it, shall be taken or considered as affecting the question of what carriers, companies, or individuals, other than those in this Act specifically provided for, are included in or excluded from the provisions of the various laws to which this Act is an amendment.

"Sec. 7. (a) Notwithstanding the provisions of section 1605(b) of the Internal Revenue Code [section 1605(b) of former Title 26, Internal Revenue Code of 1939], no interest shall, during the period February 1, 1940, to the eighty-ninth day after the date of enactment of this Act [Aug. 13, 1940], inclusive, accrue by reason of delinquency in the payment of the tax imposed by section 1600 with respect to services affected by this Act performed during the period July 1, 1939, to December 31, 1939, inclusive, with respect to which services amounts have been paid as contributions under the Railroad Unemployment Insurance Act [section 351 et seq. of this title] prior to the date of enactment of this Act.

"(b) Notwithstanding the provisions of section 1601(a)(3) of the Internal Revenue Code [section 1601(a)(3) of former Title 26, Internal Revenue Code of 1939], the credit allowable under section 1601(a) against the tax imposed by section 1600 for the calendar year 1939 shall not be disallowed or reduced by reason of the payment into a State unemployment fund after January 31, 1940, of contributions with respect to services affected by this Act performed during the period July 1, 1939, to December 31, 1939, inclusive, with respect to which services amounts have been paid as contributions under the Railroad Unemployment Insurance Act [section 351 et seq. of this title] prior to the date of enactment of this Act [Aug. 13, 1940]: Provided, That this subsection shall be applicable only if the contributions with respect to such services are paid into the State unemployment fund before the ninetieth day after the date of enactment of this Act [Aug. 13, 1940]."

Sec. 151a. General purposes

The purposes of the chapter are: (1) To avoid any interruption to commerce or to the operation of any carrier engaged therein; (2) to forbid any limitation upon freedom of association among employees or any denial, as a condition of employment or otherwise, of the right of employees to join a labor organization; (3) to provide for the complete independence of carriers and of employees in the matter of self-organization to carry out the purposes of this chapter; (4) to provide for the prompt and orderly settlement of all disputes concerning rates of pay, rules, or working conditions; (5) to provide for the prompt and orderly settlement of all disputes growing out of grievances or out of the interpretation or application of agreements covering rates of pay, rules, or working conditions.

(May 20, 1926, ch. 347, Sec. 2, 44 Stat. 577; June 21, 1934, ch. 691, Sec. 2, 48 Stat. 1186.)

REFERENCES IN TEXT

This chapter, referred to in text, was in the original "this Act", meaning act May 20, 1926, ch. 347, 44 Stat. 577, as amended, known as the Railway Labor Act, which enacted this chapter and amended sections 225 and 348 of former Title 28, Judicial Code and Judiciary. Sections 225 and 348 of former Title 28 were repealed by section 39 of act June 25, 1948, ch. 646, 62 Stat. 992, section 1 of which enacted Title 28, Judiciary and Judicial Procedure. Section 225 of former Title 28 was reenacted as sections 1291 to 1294 of Title 28. For complete classification of this Act to the Code, see section 151 of this title and Tables.

AMENDMENTS

1934—Act June 21, 1934, reenacted provisions comprising this section without change.

Sec. 152.   General duties

First. Duty of carriers and employees to settle disputes

It shall be the duty of all carriers, their officers, agents, and employees to exert every reasonable effort to make and maintain agreements concerning rates of pay, rules, and working conditions, and to settle all disputes, whether arising out of the application of such agreements or otherwise, in order to avoid any interruption to commerce or to the operation of any carrier growing out of any dispute between the carrier and the employees thereof.

Second. Consideration of disputes by representatives

All disputes between a carrier or carriers and its or their employees shall be considered, and, if possible, decided, with all expedition, in conference between representatives designated and authorized so to confer, respectively, by the carrier or carriers and by the employees thereof interested in the dispute.

Third. Designation of representatives

Representatives, for the purposes of this chapter, shall be designated by the respective parties without interference, influence, or coercion by either party over the designation of representatives by the other; and neither party shall in any way interfere with, influence, or coerce the other in its choice of representatives. Representatives of employees for the purposes of this chapter need not be persons in the employ of the carrier, and no carrier shall, by interference, influence, or coercion seek in any manner to prevent the designation by its employees as their representatives of those who or which are not employees of the carrier.

Fourth. Organization and collective bargaining; freedom from interference by carrier; assistance in organizing or maintaining organization by carrier forbidden; deduction of dues from wages forbidden

Employees shall have the right to organize and bargain collectively through representatives of their own choosing. The majority of any craft or class of employees shall have the right to determine who shall be the representative of the craft or class for the purposes of this chapter. No carrier, its officers, or agents shall deny or in any way question the right of its employees to join, organize, or assist in organizing the labor organization of their choice, and it shall be unlawful for any carrier to interfere in any way with the organization of its employees, or to use the funds of the carrier in maintaining or assisting or contributing to any labor organization, labor representative, or other agency of collective bargaining, or in performing any work therefor, or to influence or coerce employees in an effort to induce them to join or remain or not to join or remain members of any labor organization, or to deduct from the wages of employees any dues, fees, assessments, or other contributions payable to labor organizations, or to collect or to assist in the collection of any such dues, fees, assessments, or other contributions: Provided, That nothing in this chapter shall be construed to prohibit a carrier from permitting an employee, individually, or local representatives of employees from conferring with management during working hours without loss of time, or to prohibit a carrier from furnishing free transportation to its employees while engaged in the business of a labor organization.

Fifth. Agreements to join or not to join labor organizations forbidden

No carrier, its officers, or agents shall require any person seeking employment to sign any contract or agreement promising to join or not to join a labor organization; and if any such contract has been enforced prior to the effective date of this chapter, then such carrier shall notify the employees by an appropriate order that such contract has been discarded and is no longer binding on them in any way.

Sixth. Conference of representatives; time; place; private agreements

In case of a dispute between a carrier or carriers and its or their employees, arising out of grievances or out of the interpretation or application of agreements concerning rates of pay, rules, or working conditions, it shall be the duty of the designated representative or representatives of such carrier or carriers and of such employees, within ten days after the receipt of notice of a desire on the part of either party to confer in respect to such dispute, to specify a time and place at which such conference shall be held: Provided, (1) That the place so specified shall be situated upon the line of the carrier involved or as otherwise mutually agreed upon; and (2) that the time so specified shall allow the designated conferees reasonable opportunity to reach such place of conference, but shall not exceed twenty days from the receipt of such notice: And provided further, That nothing in this chapter shall be construed to supersede the provisions of any agreement (as to conferences) then in effect between the parties.

Seventh. Change in pay, rules, or working conditions contrary to agreement or to section 156 forbidden

No carrier, its officers, or agents shall change the rates of pay, rules, or working conditions of its employees, as a class, as embodied in agreements except in the manner prescribed in such agreements or in section 156 of this title.

Eighth. Notices of manner of settlement of disputes; posting

Every carrier shall notify its employees by printed notices in such form and posted at such times and places as shall be specified by the Mediation Board that all disputes between the carrier and its employees will be handled in accordance with the requirements of this chapter, and in such notices there shall be printed verbatim, in large type, the third, fourth, and fifth paragraphs of this section. The provisions of said paragraphs are made a part of the contract of employment between the carrier and each employee, and shall be held binding upon the parties, regardless of any other express or implied agreements between them.

Ninth. Disputes as to identity of representatives; designation by Mediation Board; secret elections

If any dispute shall arise among a carrier's employees as to who are the representatives of such employees designated and authorized in accordance with the requirements of this chapter, it shall be the duty of the Mediation Board, upon request of either party to the dispute, to investigate such dispute and to certify to both parties, in writing, within thirty days after the receipt of the invocation of its services, the name or names of the individuals or organizations that have been designated and authorized to represent the employees involved in the dispute, and certify the same to the carrier. Upon receipt of such certification the carrier shall treat with the representative so certified as the representative of the craft or class for the purposes of this chapter. In such an investigation, the Mediation Board shall be authorized to take a secret ballot of the employees involved, or to utilize any other appropriate method of ascertaining the names of their duly designated and authorized representatives in such manner as shall insure the choice of representatives by the employees without interference, influence, or coercion exercised by the carrier. In the conduct of any election for the purposes herein indicated the Board shall designate who may participate in the election and establish the rules to govern the election, or may appoint a committee of three neutral persons who after hearing shall within ten days designate the employees who may participate in the election. The Board shall have access to and have power to make copies of the books and records of the carriers to obtain and utilize such information as may be deemed necessary by it to carry out the purposes and provisions of this paragraph.

Tenth. Violations; prosecution and penalties

The willful failure or refusal of any carrier, its officers or agents, to comply with the terms of the third, fourth, fifth, seventh, or eighth paragraph of this section shall be a misdemeanor, and upon conviction thereof the carrier, officer, or agent offending shall be subject to a fine of not less than $1,000, nor more than $20,000, or imprisonment for not more than six months, or both fine and imprisonment, for each offense, and each day during which such carrier, officer, or agent shall willfully fail or refuse to comply with the terms of the said paragraphs of this section shall constitute a separate offense. It shall be the duty of any United States attorney to whom any duly designated representative of a carrier's employees may apply to institute in the proper court and to prosecute under the direction of the Attorney General of the United States, all necessary proceedings for the enforcement of the provisions of this section, and for the punishment of all violations thereof and the costs and expenses of such prosecution shall be paid out of the appropriation for the expenses of the courts of the United States: Provided, That nothing in this chapter shall be construed to require an individual employee to render labor or service without his consent, nor shall anything in this chapter be construed to make the quitting of his labor by an individual employee an illegal act; nor shall any court issue any process to compel the performance by an individual employee of such labor or service, without his consent.

Eleventh. Union security agreements; check-off

Notwithstanding any other provisions of this chapter, or of any other statute or law of the United States, or Territory thereof, or of any State, any carrier or carriers as defined in this chapter and a labor organization or labor organizations duly designated and authorized to represent employees in accordance with the requirements of this chapter shall be permitted—

(a) to make agreements, requiring, as a condition of continued employment, that within sixty days following the beginning of such employment, or the effective date of such agreements, whichever is the later, all employees shall become members of the labor organization representing their craft or class: Provided, That no such agreement shall require such condition of employment with respect to employees to whom membership is not available upon the same terms and conditions as are generally applicable to any other member or with respect to employees to whom membership was denied or terminated for any reason other than the failure of the employee to tender the periodic dues, initiation fees, and assessments (not including fines and penalties) uniformly required as a condition of acquiring or retaining membership.

(b) to make agreements providing for the deduction by such carrier or carriers from the wages of its or their employees in a craft or class and payment to the labor organization representing the craft or class of such employees, of any periodic dues, initiation fees, and assessments (not including fines and penalties) uniformly required as a condition of acquiring or retaining membership: Provided, That no such agreement shall be effective with respect to any individual employee until he shall have furnished the employer with a written assignment to the labor organization of such membership dues, initiation fees, and assessments, which shall be revocable in writing after the expiration of one year or upon the termination date of the applicable collective agreement, whichever occurs sooner.

(c) The requirement of membership in a labor organization in an agreement made pursuant to subparagraph (a) of this paragraph shall be satisfied, as to both a present or future employee in engine, train, yard, or hostling service, that is, an employee engaged in any of the services or capacities covered in the First division of paragraph (h) of section 153 of this title defining the jurisdictional scope of the First Division of the National Railroad Adjustment Board, if said employee shall hold or acquire membership in any one of the labor organizations, national in scope, organized in accordance with this chapter and admitting to membership employees of a craft or class in any of said services;

and no agreement made pursuant to subparagraph (b) of this paragraph shall provide for deductions from his wages for periodic dues, initiation fees, or assessments payable to any labor organization other than that in which he holds membership: Provided, however, That as to an employee in any of said services on a particular carrier at the effective date of any such agreement on a carrier, who is not a member of any one of the labor organizations, national in scope, organized in accordance with this chapter and admitting to membership employees of a craft or class in any of said services, such employee, as a condition of continuing his employment, may be required to become a member of the organization representing the craft in which he is employed on the effective date of the first agreement applicable to him: Provided, further, That nothing herein or in any such agreement or agreements shall prevent an employee from changing membership from one organization to another organization admitting to membership employees of a craft or class in any of said services.

(d) Any provisions in paragraphs Fourth and Fifth of this section in conflict herewith are to the extent of such conflict amended.

(May 20, 1926, ch. 347, Sec. 2, 44 Stat. 577; June 21, 1934, ch. 691, Sec. 2, 48 Stat. 1186; June 25, 1948, ch. 646, Sec. 1, 62 Stat. 909; Jan. 10, 1951, ch. 1220, 64 Stat. 1238.)

REFERENCES IN TEXT

This chapter, referred to in pars. Third, Fourth, Sixth, and Eighth to Eleventh, was in the original "this Act", meaning act May 20, 1926, ch. 347, 44 Stat. 577, as amended, known as the Railway Labor Act, which enacted this chapter and amended sections 225 and 348 of former Title 28, Judicial Code and Judiciary. Sections 225 and 348 of former Title 28 were repealed by section 39 of act June 25, 1948, ch. 646, 62 Stat. 992, section 1 of which enacted Title 28, Judiciary and Judicial Procedure. Section 225 of former Title 28 was reenacted as sections 1291 to 1294 of Title 28. For complete classification of this Act to the Code, see section 151 of this title and Tables.

The effective date of this chapter, referred to in par. fifth, probably means May 20, 1926, the date of approval of act May 20, 1926, ch. 347, 44 Stat. 577.

AMENDMENTS

1951—Act Jan. 10, 1951, added par. Eleventh.

1934—Act June 21, 1934, substituted "by the carrier or carriers" for "by the carriers" in par. Second, generally amended pars. Third, Fourth, and Fifth, and added pars. Sixth to Tenth.

CHANGE OF NAME

Act June 25, 1948, eff. Sept. 1, 1948, substituted "United States attorney" for "district attorney of the United States". See section 541 of Title 28, Judiciary and Judicial Procedure, and Historical and Revision Notes thereunder.

Sec. 153.   National Railroad Adjustment Board

First. Establishment; composition; powers and duties; divisions; hearings and awards; judicial review

There is established a Board, to be known as the "National Railroad Adjustment Board", the members of which shall be selected within thirty days after June 21, 1934, and it is provided—

(a) That the said Adjustment Board shall consist of thirty-four members, seventeen of whom shall be selected by the carriers and seventeen by such labor organizations of the employees, national in scope, as have been or may be organized in accordance with the provisions of sections 151a and 152 of this title.

(b) The carriers, acting each through its board of directors or its receiver or receivers, trustee or trustees, or through an officer or officers designated for that purpose by such board, trustee or trustees, or receiver or receivers, shall prescribe the rules under which its representatives shall be selected and shall select the representatives of the carriers on the Adjustment Board and designate the division on which each such representative shall serve, but no carrier or system of carriers shall have more than one voting representative on any division of the Board.

(c) Except as provided in the second paragraph of subsection (h) of this section, the national labor organizations, as defined in paragraph (a) of this section, acting each through the chief executive or other medium designated by the organization or association thereof, shall prescribe the rules under which the labor members of the Adjustment Board shall be selected and shall select such members and designate the division on which each member shall serve; but no labor organization shall have more than one voting representative on any division of the Board.

(d) In case of a permanent or temporary vacancy on the Adjustment Board, the vacancy shall be filled by selection in the same manner as in the original selection.

(e) If either the carriers or the labor organizations of the employees fail to select and designate representatives to the Adjustment Board, as provided in paragraphs (b) and (c) of this section, respectively, within sixty days after June 21, 1934, in case of any original appointment to office of a member of the Adjustment Board, or in case of a vacancy in any such office within thirty days after such vacancy occurs, the Mediation Board shall thereupon directly make the appointment and shall select an individual associated in interest with the carriers or the group of labor organizations of employees, whichever he is to represent.

(f) In the event a dispute arises as to the right of any national labor organization to participate as per paragraph (c) of this section in the selection and designation of the labor members of the Adjustment Board, the Secretary of Labor shall investigate the claim of such labor organization to participate, and if such claim in the judgment of the Secretary of Labor has merit, the Secretary shall notify the Mediation Board accordingly, and within ten days after receipt of such advice the Mediation Board shall request those national labor organizations duly qualified as per paragraph (c) of this section to participate in the selection and designation of the labor members of the Adjustment Board to select a representative. Such representative, together with a representative likewise designated by the claimant, and a third or neutral party designated by the Mediation Board, constituting a board of three, shall within thirty days after the appointment of the neutral member, investigate the claims of the labor organization desiring participation and decide whether or not it was organized in accordance with sections 151a and 152 of this title and is otherwise properly qualified to participate in the selection of the labor members of the Adjustment Board, and the findings of such boards of three shall be final and binding.

(g) Each member of the Adjustment Board shall be compensated by the party or parties he is to represent. Each third or neutral party selected under the provisions of paragraph (f) of this section shall receive from the Mediation Board such compensation as the Mediation Board may fix, together with his necessary traveling expenses and expenses actually incurred for subsistence, or per diem allowance in lieu thereof, subject to the provisions of law applicable thereto, while serving as such third or neutral party.

(h) The said Adjustment Board shall be composed of four divisions, whose proceedings shall be independent of one another, and the said divisions as well as the number of their members shall be as follows:

First division: To have jurisdiction over disputes involving train- and yard-service employees of carriers; that is, engineers, firemen, hostlers, and outside hostler helpers, conductors, trainmen, and yard-service employees. This division shall consist of eight members, four of whom shall be selected and designated by the carriers and four of whom shall be selected and designated by the labor organizations, national in scope and organized in accordance with sections 151a and 152 of this title and which represent employees in engine, train, yard, or hostling service: Provided, however, That each labor organization shall select and designate two members on the First Division and that no labor organization shall have more than one vote in any proceedings of the First Division or in the adoption of any award with respect to any dispute submitted to the First Division: Provided further, however, That the carrier members of the First Division shall cast no more than two votes in any proceedings of the division or in the adoption of any award with respect to any dispute submitted to the First Division.

Second division: To have jurisdiction over disputes involving machinists, boilermakers, blacksmiths, sheet-metal workers, electrical workers, carmen, the helpers and apprentices of all the foregoing, coach cleaners, powerhouse employees, and railroad-shop laborers. This division shall consist of ten members, five of whom shall be selected by the carriers and five by the national labor organizations of the employees.

Third division: To have jurisdiction over disputes involving station, tower, and telegraph employees, train dispatchers, maintenance-of-way men, clerical employees, freight handlers, express, station, and store employees, signal men, sleeping-car conductors, sleeping-car porters, and maids and dining-car employees. This division shall consist of ten members, five of whom shall be selected by the carriers and five by the national labor organizations of employees.

Fourth division: To have jurisdiction over disputes involving employees of carriers directly or indirectly engaged in transportation of passengers or property by water, and all other employees of carriers over which jurisdiction is not given to the first, second, and third divisions. This division shall consist of six members, three of whom shall be selected by the carriers and three by the national labor organizations of the employees.

(i) The disputes between an employee or group of employees and a carrier or carriers growing out of grievances or out of the interpretation or application of agreements concerning rates of pay, rules, or working conditions, including cases pending and unadjusted on June 21, 1934, shall be handled in the usual manner up to and including the chief operating officer of the carrier designated to handle such disputes; but, failing to reach an adjustment in this manner, the disputes may be referred by petition of the parties or by either party to the appropriate division of the Adjustment Board with a full statement of the facts and all supporting data bearing upon the disputes.

(j) Parties may be heard either in person, by counsel, or by other representatives, as they may respectively elect, and the several divisions of the Adjustment Board shall give due notice of all hearings to the employee or employees and the carrier or carriers involved in any disputes submitted to them.

(k) Any division of the Adjustment Board shall have authority to empower two or more of its members to conduct hearings and make findings upon disputes, when properly submitted, at any place designated by the division: Provided, however, That except as provided in paragraph (h) of this section, final awards as to any such dispute must be made by the entire division as hereinafter provided.

(l) Upon failure of any division to agree upon an award because of a deadlock or inability to secure a majority vote of the division members, as provided in paragraph (n) of this section, then such division shall forthwith agree upon and select a neutral person, to be known as "referee", to sit with the division as a member thereof, and make an award. Should the division fail to agree upon and select a referee within ten days of the date of the deadlock or inability to secure a majority vote, then the division, or any member thereof, or the parties or either party to the dispute may certify that fact to the Mediation Board, which Board shall, within ten days from the date of receiving such certificate, select and name the referee to sit with the division as a member thereof and make an award. The Mediation Board shall be bound by the same provisions in the appointment of these neutral referees as are provided elsewhere in this chapter for the appointment of arbitrators and shall fix and pay the compensation of such referees.

(m) The awards of the several divisions of the Adjustment Board shall be stated in writing. A copy of the awards shall be furnished to the respective parties to the controversy, and the awards shall be final and binding upon both parties to the dispute. In case a dispute arises involving an interpretation of the award, the division of the board upon request of either party shall interpret the award in the light of the dispute.

(n) A majority vote of all members of the division of the Adjustment Board eligible to vote shall be competent to make an award with respect to any dispute submitted to it.

(o) In case of an award by any division of the Adjustment Board in favor of petitioner, the division of the Board shall make an order, directed to the carrier, to make the award effective and, if the award includes a requirement for the payment of money, to pay to the employee the sum to which he is entitled under the award on or before a day named. In the event any division determines that an award favorable to the petitioner should not be made in any dispute referred to it, the division shall make an order to the petitioner stating such determination.

(p) If a carrier does not comply with an order of a division of the Adjustment Board within the time limit in such order, the petitioner, or any person for whose benefit such order was made, may file in the District Court of the United States for the district in which he resides or in which is located the principal operating office of the carrier, or through which the carrier operates, a petition setting forth briefly the causes for which he claims relief, and the order of the division of the Adjustment Board in the premises. Such suit in the District Court of the United States shall proceed in all respects as other civil suits, except that on the trial of such suit the findings and order of the division of the Adjustment Board shall be conclusive on the parties, and except that the petitioner shall not be liable for costs in the district court nor for costs at any subsequent stage of the proceedings, unless they accrue upon his appeal, and such costs shall be paid out of the appropriation for the expenses of the courts of the United States. If the petitioner shall finally prevail he shall be allowed a reasonable attorney's fee, to be taxed and collected as a part of the costs of the suit. The district courts are empowered, under the rules of the court governing actions at law, to make such order and enter such judgment, by writ of mandamus or otherwise, as may be appropriate to enforce or set aside the order of the division of the Adjustment Board: Provided, however, That such order may not be set aside except for failure of the division to comply with the requirements of this chapter, for failure of the order to conform, or confine itself, to matters within the scope of the division's jurisdiction, or for fraud or corruption by a member of the division making the order.

(q) If any employee or group of employees, or any carrier, is aggrieved by the failure of any division of the Adjustment Board to make an award in a dispute referred to it, or is aggrieved by any of the terms of an award or by the failure of the division to include certain terms in such award, then such employee or group of employees or carrier may file in any United States district court in which a petition under paragraph (p) could be filed, a petition for review of the division's order. A copy of the petition shall be forthwith transmitted by the clerk of the court to the Adjustment Board. The Adjustment Board shall file in the court the record of the proceedings on which it based its action. The court shall have jurisdiction to affirm the order of the division, or to set it aside, in whole or in part, or it may remand the proceedings to the division for such further action as it may direct. On such review, the findings and order of the division shall be conclusive on the parties, except that the order of the division may be set aside, in whole or in part, or remanded to the division, for failure of the division to comply with the requirements of this chapter, for failure of the order to conform, or confine itself, to matters within the scope of the division's jurisdiction, or for fraud or corruption by a member of the division making the order. The judgment of the court shall be subject to review as provided in sections 1291 and 1254 of title 28.

(r) All actions at law based upon the provisions of this section shall be begun within two years from the time the cause of action accrues under the award of the division of the Adjustment Board, and not after.

(s) The several divisions of the Adjustment Board shall maintain headquarters in Chicago, Illinois, meet regularly, and continue in session so long as there is pending before the division any matter within its jurisdiction which has been submitted for its consideration and which has not been disposed of.

(t) Whenever practicable, the several divisions or subdivisions of the Adjustment Board shall be supplied with suitable quarters in any Federal building located at its place of meeting.

(u) The Adjustment Board may, subject to the approval of the Mediation Board, employ and fix the compensations of such assistants as it deems necessary in carrying on its proceedings. The compensation of such employees shall be paid by the Mediation Board.

(v) The Adjustment Board shall meet within forty days after June 21, 1934, and adopt such rules as it deems necessary to control proceedings before the respective divisions and not in conflict with the provisions of this section. Immediately following the meeting of the entire Board and the adoption of such rules, the respective divisions shall meet and organize by the selection of a chairman, a vice chairman, and a secretary. Thereafter each division shall annually designate one of its members to act as chairman and one of its members to act as vice chairman: Provided, however, That the chairmanship and vice-chairmanship of any division shall alternate as between the groups, so that both the chairmanship and vice-chairmanship shall be held alternately by a representative of the carriers and a representative of the employees. In case of a vacancy, such vacancy shall be filled for the unexpired term by the selection of a successor from the same group.

(w) Each division of the Adjustment Board shall annually prepare and submit a report of its activities to the Mediation Board, and the substance of such report shall be included in the annual report of the Mediation Board to the Congress of the United States. The reports of each division of the Adjustment Board and the annual report of the Mediation Board shall state in detail all cases heard, all actions taken, the names, salaries, and duties of all agencies, employees, and officers receiving compensation from the United States under the authority of this chapter, and an account of all moneys appropriated by Congress pursuant to the authority conferred by this chapter and disbursed by such agencies, employees, and officers.

(x) Any division of the Adjustment Board shall have authority, in its discretion, to establish regional adjustment boards to act in its place and stead for such limited period as such division may determine to be necessary. Carrier members of such regional boards shall be designated in keeping with rules devised for this purpose by the carrier members of the Adjustment Board and the labor members shall be designated in keeping with rules devised for this purpose by the labor members of the Adjustment Board. Any such regional board shall, during the time for which it is appointed, have the same authority to conduct hearings, make findings upon disputes and adopt the same procedure as the division of the Adjustment Board appointing it, and its decisions shall be enforceable to the same extent and under the same processes. A neutral person, as referee, shall be appointed for service in connection with any such regional adjustment board in the same circumstances and manner as provided in paragraph (l) of this section, with respect to a division of the Adjustment Board.

Second. System, group, or regional boards: establishment by voluntary agreement; special adjustment boards: establishment, composition, designation of representatives by Mediation Board, neutral member, compensation, quorum, finality and enforcement of awards

Nothing in this section shall be construed to prevent any individual carrier, system, or group of carriers and any class or classes of its or their employees, all acting through their representatives, selected in accordance with the provisions of this chapter, from mutually agreeing to the establishment of system, group, or regional boards of adjustment for the purpose of adjusting and deciding disputes of the character specified in this section. In the event that either party to such a system, group, or regional board of adjustment is dissatisfied with such arrangement, it may upon ninety days' notice to the other party elect to come under the jurisdiction of the Adjustment Board.

If written request is made upon any individual carrier by the representative of any craft or class of employees of such carrier for the establishment of a special board of adjustment to resolve disputes otherwise referable to the Adjustment Board, or any dispute which has been pending before the Adjustment Board for twelve months from the date the dispute (claim) is received by the Board, or if any carrier makes such a request upon any such representative, the carrier or the representative upon whom such request is made shall join in an agreement establishing such a board within thirty days from the date such request is made. The cases which may be considered by such board shall be defined in the agreement establishing it. Such board shall consist of one person designated by the carrier and one person designated by the representative of the employees. If such carrier or such representative fails to agree upon the establishment of such a board as provided herein, or to exercise its rights to designate a member of the board, the carrier or representative making the request for the establishment of the special board may request the Mediation Board to designate a member of the special board on behalf of the carrier or representative upon whom such request was made. Upon receipt of a request for such designation the Mediation Board shall promptly make such designation and shall select an individual associated in interest with the carrier or representative he is to represent, who, with the member appointed by the carrier or representative requesting the establishment of the special board, shall constitute the board. Each member of the board shall be compensated by the party he is to represent. The members of the board so designated shall determine all matters not previously agreed upon by the carrier and the representative of the employees with respect to the establishment and jurisdiction of the board. If they are unable to agree such matters shall be determined by a neutral member of the board selected or appointed and compensated in the same manner as is hereinafter provided with respect to situations where the members of the board are unable to agree upon an award. Such neutral member shall cease to be a member of the board when he has determined such matters. If with respect to any dispute or group of disputes the members of the board designated by the carrier and the representative are unable to agree upon an award disposing of the dispute or group of disputes they shall by mutual agreement select a neutral person to be a member of the board for the consideration and disposition of such dispute or group of disputes. In the event the members of the board designated by the parties are unable, within ten days after their failure to agree upon an award, to agree upon the selection of such neutral person, either member of the board may request the Mediation Board to appoint such neutral person and upon receipt of such request the Mediation Board shall promptly make such appointment. The neutral person so selected or appointed shall be compensated and reimbursed for expenses by the Mediation Board. Any two members of the board shall be competent to render an award. Such awards shall be final and binding upon both parties to the dispute and if in favor of the petitioner, shall direct the other party to comply therewith on or before the day named. Compliance with such awards shall be enforcible by proceedings in the United States district courts in the same manner and subject to the same provisions that apply to proceedings for enforcement of compliance with awards of the Adjustment Board.

(May 20, 1926, ch. 347, Sec. 3, 44 Stat. 578; June 21, 1934, ch. 691, Sec. 3, 48 Stat. 1189; June 20, 1966, Pub. L. 89-456, Secs. 1, 2, 80 Stat. 208, 209; Apr. 23, 1970, Pub. L. 91-234, Secs. 1- 6, 84 Stat. 199, 200.)

REFERENCES IN TEXT

This chapter, referred to in par. First, (q), and par. Second, was in the original "this Act", meaning act May 20, 1926, ch. 347, 44 Stat. 577, as amended, known as the Railway Labor Act, which enacted this chapter and amended sections 225 and 348 of former Title 28, Judicial Code and Judiciary. Sections 225 and 348 of former Title 28 were repealed by section 39 of act June 25, 1948, ch. 646, 62 Stat. 992, section 1 of which enacted Title 28, Judiciary and Judicial Procedure. Section 225 of former Title 28 was reenacted as sections 1291 to 1294 of Title 28. For complete classification of this Act to the Code, see section 151 of this title and Tables.

Amendments

1970—Par. First, (a). Pub. L. 91-234, Sec. 1, substituted "thirty-four members, seventeen of whom shall be selected by the carriers and seventeen" for "thirty-six members, eighteen of whom shall be selected by the carriers and eighteen".

Par. First, (b). Pub. L. 91-234, Sec. 2, provided that no carrier or system of carriers have more than one voting representative on any division of the National Railroad Adjustment Board.

Par. First, (c). Pub. L. 91-234, Sec. 3, added "Except as provided in the second paragraph of subsection (h) of this section" preceding "the national labor organizations", and provided that no labor organization have more than one voting representative on any division of the National Railroad Adjustment Board.

Par. First, (h). Pub. L. 91-234, Sec. 4, decreased the number of members on the First division of the Board from ten to eight members, with an accompanying decrease of five to four as the number of members of such Board elected respectively by the carriers and by the national labor organizations satisfying the enumerated requirements, and set forth the provisos which limited voting by each labor organization or carrier member in any proceedings of the division or in the adoption of any award.

Par. First, (k). Pub. L. 91-234, Sec. 5, added "except as provided in paragraph (h) of this section" after the proviso.

Par. First, (n). Pub. L. 91-234, Sec. 6, added "eligible to vote" following "Adjustment Board".

1966—Par. First, (m). Pub. L. 89-456, Sec. 2(a), struck out from the second sentence the concluding words ", except insofar as they shall contain a money award".

Par. First, (o). Pub. L. 89-456, Sec. 2(b), added provision for a division to make an order to the petitioner stating that an award favorable to the petitioner should not be made in any dispute referred to it.

Par. First, (p). Pub. L. 89-456, Sec. 2(c), (d), substituted in second sentence "conclusive on the parties" for "prima facie evidence of the facts therein stated" and inserted in last sentence reasons for setting aside orders of a division of the Adjustment Board, respectively.

Par. First, (q) to (x). Pub. L. 89-456, Sec. 2(e), added par. (q) and redesignated former pars. (q) to (w) as (r) to (x), respectively.

Par. Second. Pub. L. 89-456, Sec. 1, provided for establishment of special adjustment boards upon request of employees or carriers to resolve disputes otherwise referable to the Adjustment Board and made awards of such boards final.

1934—Act June 21, 1934, amended the provisions comprising this section generally.

FEDERAL RULES OF CIVIL PROCEDURE

Costs, see rule 54 and notes of Advisory Committee under the Rule, Title 28, Appendix, Judiciary and Judicial Procedure.

Federal Rules of Civil Procedure as governing the procedure in all suits of a civil nature whether cognizable as cases at law or in equity, see rule 1.

Mandamus as abolished but relief yet available by appropriate action or motion under Federal Rules of Civil Procedure, see rule 81 and Notes of Advisory Committee under the rule.

One form of action, see rule 2.

Pleadings allowed, see rule 7.

Sec. 154.   National Mediation Board

First. Board of Mediation abolished; National Mediation Board established; composition; term of office; qualifications; salaries; removal

The Board of Mediation is abolished, effective thirty days from June 21, 1934, and the members, secretary, officers, assistants, employees, and agents thereof, in office upon June 21, 1934, shall continue to function and receive their salaries for a period of thirty days from such date in the same manner as though this chapter had not been passed. There is established, as an independent agency in the executive branch of the Government, a board to be known as the "National Mediation Board", to be composed of three members appointed by the President, by and with the advice and consent of the Senate, not more than two of whom shall be of the same political party. Each member of the Mediation Board in office on January 1, 1965, shall be deemed to have been appointed for a term of office which shall expire on July 1 of the year his term would have otherwise expired. The terms of office of all successors shall expire three years after the expiration of the terms for which their predecessors were appointed; but any member appointed to fill a vacancy occurring prior to the expiration of the term for which his predecessor was appointed shall be appointed only for the unexpired term of his predecessor. Vacancies in the Board shall not impair the powers nor affect the duties of the Board nor of the remaining members of the Board. Two of the members in office shall constitute a quorum for the transaction of the business of the Board. Each member of the Board shall receive necessary traveling and subsistence expenses, or per diem allowance in lieu thereof, subject to the provisions of law applicable thereto, while away from the principal office of the Board on business required by this chapter. No person in the employment of or who is pecuniarily or otherwise interested in any organization of employees or any carrier shall enter upon the duties of or continue to be a member of the Board. Upon the expiration of his term of office a member shall continue to serve until his successor is appointed and shall have qualified.

All cases referred to the Board of Mediation and unsettled on June 21, 1934, shall be handled to conclusion by the Mediation Board.

A member of the Board may be removed by the President for inefficiency, neglect of duty, malfeasance in office, or ineligibility, but for no other cause.

Second. Chairman; principal office; delegation of powers; oaths; seal; report

The Mediation Board shall annually designate a member to act as chairman. The Board shall maintain its principal office in the District of Columbia, but it may meet at any other place whenever it deems it necessary so to do. The Board may designate one or more of its members to exercise the functions of the Board in mediation proceedings. Each member of the Board shall have power to administer oaths and affirmations. The Board shall have a seal which shall be judicially noticed. The Board shall make an annual report to Congress.

Third. Appointment of experts and other employees; salaries of employees; expenditures

The Mediation Board may (1) subject to the provisions of the civil service laws, appoint such experts and assistants to act in a confidential capacity and such other officers and employees as are essential to the effective transaction of the work of the Board; (2) in accordance with chapter 51 and subchapter III of chapter 53 of title 5, fix the salaries of such experts, assistants, officers, and employees; and (3) make such expenditures (including expenditures for rent and personal services at the seat of government and elsewhere, for law books, periodicals, and books of reference, and for printing and binding, and including expenditures for salaries and compensation, necessary traveling expenses and expenses actually incurred for subsistence, and other necessary expenses of the Mediation Board, Adjustment Board, Regional Adjustment Boards established under paragraph (w) of section 153 of this title, and boards of arbitration, in accordance with the provisions of this section and sections 153 and 157 of this title, respectively), as may be necessary for the execution of the functions vested in the Board, in the Adjustment Board and in the boards of arbitration, and as may be provided for by the Congress from time to time. All expenditures of the Board shall be allowed and paid on the presentation of itemized vouchers therefor approved by the chairman.

Fourth. Delegation of powers and duties

The Mediation Board is authorized by its order to assign, or refer, any portion of its work, business, or functions arising under this chapter or any other Act of Congress, or referred to it by Congress or either branch thereof, to an individual member of the Board or to an employee or employees of the Board to be designated by such order for action thereon, and by its order at any time to amend, modify, supplement, or rescind any such assignment or reference. All such orders shall take effect forthwith and remain in effect until otherwise ordered by the Board. In conformity with and subject to the order or orders of the Mediation Board in the premises, [and] such individual member of the Board or employee designated shall have power and authority to act as to any of said work, business, or functions so assigned or referred to him for action by the Board.

Fifth. Transfer of officers and employees of Board of Mediation; transfer of appropriation

All officers and employees of the Board of Mediation (except the members thereof, whose offices are abolished) whose services in the judgment of the Mediation Board are necessary to the efficient operation of the Board are transferred to the Board, without change in classification or compensation; except that the Board may provide for the adjustment of such classification or compensation to conform to the duties to which such officers and employees may be assigned.

All unexpended appropriations for the operation of the Board of Mediation that are available at the time of the abolition of the Board of Mediation shall be transferred to the Mediation Board and shall be available for its use for salaries and other authorized expenditures.

(May 20, 1926, ch. 347, Sec. 4, 44 Stat. 579; June 21, 1934, ch. 691, Sec. 4, 48 Stat. 1193; Oct. 28, 1949, ch. 782, title XI, Sec. 1106(a), 63 Stat. 972; Aug. 31, 1964, Pub. L. 88-542, 78 Stat. 748.)

REFERENCES IN TEXT

This chapter, referred to in pars. First and Fourth, was in the original "this Act", meaning act May 20, 1926, ch. 347, 44 Stat. 577, as amended, known as the Railway Labor Act, which enacted this chapter and amended sections 225 and 348 of former Title 28, Judicial Code and Judiciary. Sections 225 and 348 of former Title 28 were repealed by section 39 of act June 25, 1948, ch. 646, 62 Stat. 992, section 1 of which enacted Title 28, Judiciary and Judicial Procedure. Section 225 of former Title 28 was reenacted as sections 1291 to 1294 of Title 28. For complete classification of this Act to the Code, see section 151 of this title and Tables.

The civil service laws, referred to in par. Third, are classified generally to Title 5, Government Organization and Employees. See, particularly, section 3301 et seq. of that Title.

CODIFICATION

In par. First, provisions that prescribed the basis compensation of members of the Board were omitted to conform to the provisions of the Executive Schedule. See sections 5314 and 5315 of Title 5, Government Organization and Employees.

In par. Third, "subject to the provisions of the civil service laws, appoint such experts and assistants to act in a confidential capacity and such other officers and employees" was substituted for "appoint such experts and assistants to act in a confidential capacity and, subject to the provisions of the civil-service laws, such other officers and employees". All such appointments are now subject to the civil service laws unless specifically excepted by such laws or by laws enacted subsequent to Executive Order 8743, Apr. 23, 1941, issued by the President pursuant to the Act of Nov. 26, 1940, ch. 919, title I, Sec. 1, 54 Stat. 1211, which covered most excepted positions into the classified (competitive) civil service. The Order is set out as a note under section 3301 of Title 5.

In par. Third, "chapter 51 and subchapter III of chapter 53 of title 5" were substituted for "the Classification Act of 1949, as amended" on authority of Pub. L. 89-554, Sec. 7(b), Sept. 6, 1966, 80 Stat. 631, the first section of which enacted Title 5.

Amendments

1964—Par. First. Pub. L. 88-542 inserted sentences providing that each member of the Board in office on Jan. 1, 1965, shall be deemed to have been appointed for a term of office which shall expire on July 1 of the year his term would have otherwise expired, and that upon the expiration of his term of office a member shall continue to serve until his successor is appointed and shall have qualified, and eliminated provisions which related to the terms of office of members first appointed.

1949—Par. First. Act Oct. 15, 1949, increased the basic rate of compensation for members of the board to $15,000 per year.

Par. Third. Act Oct. 28, 1949, substituted the "Classification Act of 1949" for the "Classification Act of 1923".

1934—Act June 21, 1934, amended section generally.

Repeals

Act Oct. 28, 1949, ch. 782, title XI, Sec. 1106(a), 63 Stat. 972, cited as a credit to this section, was repealed (subject to a savings clause) by Pub. L. 89-554, Sept. 6, 1966, Sec. 8, 80 Stat. 632, 655.

Sec. 155. Functions of Mediation Board

First. Disputes within jurisdiction of Mediation Board

The parties, or either party, to a dispute between an employee or group of employees and a carrier may invoke the services of the Mediation Board in any of the following cases:

(a) A dispute concerning changes in rates of pay, rules, or working conditions not adjusted by the parties in conference.

(b) Any other dispute not referable to the National Railroad Adjustment Board and not adjusted in conference between the parties or where conferences are refused.

The Mediation Board may proffer its services in case any labor emergency is found by it to exist at any time.

In either event the said Board shall promptly put itself in communication with the parties to such controversy, and shall use its best efforts, by mediation, to bring them to agreement. If such efforts to bring about an amicable settlement through mediation shall be unsuccessful, the said Board shall at once endeavor as its final required action (except as provided in paragraph third of this section and in section 160 of this title) to induce the parties to submit their controversy to arbitration, in accordance with the provisions of this chapter.

If arbitration at the request of the Board shall be refused by one or both parties, the Board shall at once notify both parties in writing that its mediatory efforts have failed and for thirty days thereafter, unless in the intervening period the parties agree to arbitration, or an emergency board shall be created under section 160 of this title, no change shall be made in the rates of pay, rules, or working conditions or established practices in effect prior to the time the dispute arose.

Second. Interpretation of agreement

In any case in which a controversy arises over the meaning or the application of any agreement reached through mediation under the provisions of this chapter, either party to the said agreement, or both, may apply to the Mediation Board for an interpretation of the meaning or application of such agreement. The said Board shall upon receipt of such request notify the parties to the controversy, and after a hearing of both sides give its interpretation within thirty days.

Third. Duties of Board with respect to arbitration of disputes; arbitrators; acknowledgment of agreement; notice to arbitrators; reconvening of arbitrators; filing contracts with Board; custody of records and documents

The Mediation Board shall have the following duties with respect to the arbitration of disputes under section 157 of this title:

(a) On failure of the arbitrators named by the parties to agree on the remaining arbitrator or arbitrators within the time set by section 157 of this title, it shall be the duty of the Mediation Board to name such remaining arbitrator or arbitrators. It shall be the duty of the Board in naming such arbitrator or arbitrators to appoint only those whom the Board shall deem wholly disinterested in the controversy to be arbitrated and impartial and without bias as between the parties to such arbitration. Should, however, the Board name an arbitrator or arbitrators not so disinterested and impartial, then, upon proper investigation and presentation of the facts, the Board shall promptly remove such arbitrator.

If an arbitrator named by the Mediation Board, in accordance with the provisions of this chapter, shall be removed by such Board as provided by this chapter, or if such an arbitrator refuses or is unable to serve, it shall be the duty of the Mediation Board, promptly, to select another arbitrator, in the same manner as provided in this chapter for an original appointment by the Mediation Board.

(b) Any member of the Mediation Board is authorized to take the acknowledgement of an agreement to arbitrate under this chapter. When so acknowledged, or when acknowledged by the parties before a notary public or the clerk of a district court or a court of appeals of the United States, such agreement to arbitrate shall be delivered to a member of said Board or transmitted to said Board, to be filed in its office.

(c) When an agreement to arbitrate has been filed with the Mediation Board, or with one of its members, as provided by this section, and when the said Board has been furnished the names of the arbitrators chosen by the parties to the controversy it shall be the duty of the Board to cause a notice in writing to be served upon said arbitrators, notifying them of their appointment, requesting them to meet promptly to name the remaining arbitrator or arbitrators necessary to complete the Board of Arbitration, and advising them of the period within which, as provided by the agreement to arbitrate, they are empowered to name such arbitrator or arbitrators.

(d) Either party to an arbitration desiring the reconvening of a board of arbitration to pass upon any controversy arising over the meaning or application of an award may so notify the Mediation Board in writing, stating in such notice the question or questions to be submitted to such reconvened Board. The Mediation Board shall thereupon promptly communicate with the members of the Board of Arbitration, or a subcommittee of such Board appointed for such purpose pursuant to a provision in the agreement to arbitrate, and arrange for the reconvening of said Board of Arbitration or subcommittee, and shall notify the respective parties to the controversy of the time and place at which the Board, or the subcommittee, will meet for hearings upon the matters in controversy to be submitted to it. No evidence other than that contained in the record filed with the original award shall be received or considered by such reconvened Board or subcommittee, except such evidence as may be necessary to illustrate the interpretations suggested by the parties. If any member of the original Board is unable or unwilling to serve on such reconvened Board or subcommittee thereof, another arbitrator shall be named in the same manner and with the same powers and duties as such original arbitrator.

(e) Within sixty days after June 21, 1934, every carrier shall file with the Mediation Board a copy of each contract with its employees in effect on the 1st day of April 1934, covering rates of pay, rules, and working conditions. If no contract with any craft or class of its employees has been entered into, the carrier shall file with the Mediation Board a statement of that fact, including also a statement of the rates of pay, rules, and working conditions applicable in dealing with such craft or class. When any new contract is executed or change is made in an existing contract with any class or craft of its employees covering rates of pay, rules, or working conditions, or in those rates of pay, rules, and working conditions of employees not covered by contract, the carrier shall file the same with the Mediation Board within thirty days after such new contract or change in existing contract has been executed or rates of pay, rules, and working conditions have been made effective.

(f) The Mediation Board shall be the custodian of all papers and documents heretofore filed with or transferred to the Board of Mediation bearing upon the settlement, adjustment, or determination of disputes between carriers and their employees or upon mediation or arbitration proceedings held under or pursuant to the provisions of any Act of Congress in respect thereto; and the President is authorized to designate a custodian of the records and property of the Board of Mediation until the transfer and delivery of such records to the Mediation Board and to require the transfer and delivery to the Mediation Board of any and all such papers and documents filed with it or in its possession.

(May 20, 1926, ch. 347, Sec. 5, 44 Stat. 580; June 21, 1934, ch. 691, Sec. 5, 48 Stat. 1195; June 25, 1948, ch. 646, Sec. 32(a), 62 Stat. 991; May 24, 1949, ch. 139, Sec. 127, 63 Stat. 107.)

REFERENCES IN TEXT

This chapter, referred to in text, was in the original "this Act", meaning act May 20, 1926, ch. 347, 44 Stat. 577, as amended, known as the Railway Labor Act, which enacted this chapter and amended sections 225 and 348 of former Title 28, Judicial Code and Judiciary. Sections 225 and 348 of former Title 28 were repealed by section 39 of act June 25, 1948, ch. 646, 62 Stat. 992, section 1 of which enacted Title 28, Judiciary and Judicial Procedure. Section 225 of former Title 28 was reenacted as sections 1291 to 1294 of Title 28. For complete classification of this Act to the Code, see section 151 of this title and Tables.

CODIFICATION

As originally enacted, par. Third (b) contained a reference to the "circuit court of appeals". Act June 25, 1948, as amended by act May 24, 1949 substituted "court of appeals" for "circuit court of appeals".

AMENDMENTS

1934—Act June 21, 1934, amended generally par. First and par. Second (e) and (f).

Sec. 156. Procedure in changing rates of pay, rules, and working conditions

Carriers and representatives of the employees shall give at least thirty days' written notice of an intended change in agreements affecting rates of pay, rules, or working conditions, and the time and place for the beginning of conference between the representatives of the parties interested in such intended changes shall be agreed upon within ten days after the receipt of said notice, and said time shall be within the thirty days provided in the notice. In every case where such notice of intended change has been given, or conferences are being held with reference thereto, or the services of the Mediation Board have been requested by either party, or said Board has proffered its services, rates of pay, rules, or working conditions shall not be altered by the carrier until the controversy has been finally acted upon, as required by section 155 of this title, by the Mediation Board, unless a period of ten days has elapsed after termination of conferences without request for or proffer of the services of the Mediation Board.

(May 20, 1926, ch. 347, Sec. 6, 44 Stat. 582; June 21, 1934, ch. 691, Sec. 6, 48 Stat. 1197.)

Amendments

1934—Act June 21, 1934, inserted "in agreements" following "intended change" in text, struck out provision formerly contained in text concerning changes requested by more than one class, and substituted "Mediation Board" for "Board of Mediation" wherever appearing.

Wage and Salary Adjustments

Ex. Ord. No. 9299, eff. Feb. 4, 1943, 8 F.R. 1669, provided procedure with respect to wage and salary adjustments for employees subject to this chapter.

Sec. 157. Arbitration

First. Submission of controversy to arbitration

Whenever a controversy shall arise between a carrier or carriers and its or their employees which is not settled either in conference between representatives of the parties or by the appropriate adjustment board or through mediation, in the manner provided in sections 151—156 of this title such controversy may, by agreement of the parties to such controversy, be submitted to the arbitration of a board of three (or, if the parties to the controversy so stipulate, of six) persons: Provided, however, That the failure or refusal of either party to submit a controversy to arbitration shall not be construed as a violation of any legal obligation imposed upon such party by the terms of this chapter or otherwise.

Second. Manner of selecting board of arbitration

Such board of arbitration shall be chosen in the following manner:

(a) In the case of a board of three the carrier or carriers and the representatives of the employees, parties respectively to the agreement to arbitrate, shall each name one arbitrator; the two arbitrators thus chosen shall select a third arbitrator. If the arbitrators chosen by the parties shall fail to name the third arbitrator within five days after their first meeting, such third arbitrator shall be named by the Mediation Board.

(b) In the case of a board of six the carrier or carriers and the representatives of the employees, parties respectively to the agreement to arbitrate, shall each name two arbitrators; the four arbitrators thus chosen shall, by a majority vote, select the remaining two arbitrators. If the arbitrators chosen by the parties shall fail to name the two arbitrators within fifteen days after their first meeting, the said two arbitrators, or as many of them as have not been named, shall be named by the Mediation Board.

Third. Board of arbitration; organization; compensation; procedure

(a) Notice of selection or failure to select arbitrators

When the arbitrators selected by the respective parties have agreed upon the remaining arbitrator or arbitrators, they shall notify the Mediation Board; and, in the event of their failure to agree upon any or upon all of the necessary arbitrators within the period fixed by this chapter, they shall, at the expiration of such period, notify the Mediation Board of the arbitrators selected, if any, or of their failure to make or to complete such selection.

(b) Organization of board; procedure

The board of arbitration shall organize and select its own chairman and make all necessary rules for conducting its hearings: Provided, however, That the board of arbitration shall be bound to give the parties to the controversy a full and fair hearing, which shall include an opportunity to present evidence in support of their claims, and an opportunity to present their case in person, by counsel, or by other representative as they may respectively elect.

(c) Duty to reconvene; questions considered

Upon notice from the Mediation Board that the parties, or either party, to an arbitration desire the reconvening of the board of arbitration (or a subcommittee of such board of arbitration appointed for such purpose pursuant to the agreement to arbitrate) to pass upon any controversy over the meaning or application of their award, the board, or its subcommittee, shall at once reconvene. No question other than, or in addition to, the questions relating to the meaning or application of the award, submitted by the party or parties in writing, shall be considered by the reconvened board of arbitration or its subcommittee.

Such rulings shall be acknowledged by such board or subcommittee thereof in the same manner, and filed in the same district court clerk's office, as the original award and become a part thereof.

(d) Competency of arbitrators

No arbitrator, except those chosen by the Mediation Board, shall be incompetent to act as an arbitrator because of his interest in the controversy to be arbitrated, or because of his connection with or partiality to either of the parties to the arbitration.

(e) Compensation and expenses

Each member of any board of arbitration created under the provisions of this chapter named by either party to the arbitration shall be compensated by the party naming him. Each arbitrator selected by the arbitrators or named by the Mediation Board shall receive from the Mediation Board such compensation as the Mediation Board may fix, together with his necessary traveling expenses and expenses actually incurred for subsistence, while serving as an arbitrator.

(f) Award; disposition of original and copies

The board of arbitration shall furnish a certified copy of its award to the respective parties to the controversy, and shall transmit the original, together with the papers and proceedings and a transcript of the evidence taken at the hearings, certified under the hands of at least a majority of the arbitrators, to the clerk of the district court of the United States for the district wherein the controversy arose or the arbitration is entered into, to be filed in said clerk's office as hereinafter provided. The said board shall also furnish a certified copy of its award, and the papers and proceedings, including testimony relating thereto, to the Mediation Board to be filed in its office; and in addition a certified copy of its award shall be filed in the office of the Interstate Commerce Commission: Provided, however, That such award shall not be construed to diminish or extinguish any of the powers or duties of the Interstate Commerce Commission, under subtitle IV of title 49.

(g) Compensation of assistants to board of arbitration; expenses; quarters

A board of arbitration may, subject to the approval of the Mediation Board, employ and fix the compensation of such assistants as it deems necessary in carrying on the arbitration proceedings. The compensation of such employees, together with their necessary traveling expenses and expenses actually incurred for subsistence, while so employed, and the necessary expenses of boards of arbitration, shall be paid by the Mediation Board.

Whenever practicable, the board shall be supplied with suitable quarters in any Federal building located at its place of meeting or at any place where the board may conduct its proceedings or deliberations.

(h) Testimony before board; oaths; attendance of witnesses; production of documents; subpoenas; fees

All testimony before said board shall be given under oath or affirmation, and any member of the board shall have the power to administer oaths or affirmations. The board of arbitration, or any member thereof, shall have the power to require the attendance of witnesses and the production of such books, papers, contracts, agreements, and documents as may be deemed by the board of arbitration material to a just determination of the matters submitted to its arbitration, and may for that purpose request the clerk of the district court of the United States for the district wherein said arbitration is being conducted to issue the necessary subpoenas, and upon such request the said clerk or his duly authorized deputy shall be, and he is, authorized, and it shall be his duty, to issue such subpoenas.

Any witness appearing before a board of arbitration shall receive the same fees and mileage as witnesses in courts of the United States, to be paid by the party securing the subpoena.

(May 20, 1926, ch. 347, Sec. 7, 44 Stat. 582; June 21, 1934, ch. 691, Sec. 7, 48 Stat. 1197; Oct. 15, 1970, Pub. L. 91-452, title II, Sec. 238, 84 Stat. 930.)

REFERENCES IN TEXT

This chapter, referred to in pars. First and Third (a), was in the original "this Act", meaning act May 20, 1926, ch. 347, 44 Stat. 577, as amended, known as the Railway Labor Act, which enacted this chapter and amended sections 225 and 348 of former Title 28, Judicial Code and Judiciary. Sections 225 and 348 of former Title 28 were repealed by section 39 of act June 25, 1948, ch. 646, 62 Stat. 992, section 1 of which enacted Title 28, Judiciary and Judicial Procedure. Section 225 of former Title 28 was reenacted as sections 1291 to 1294 of Title 28. For complete classification of this Act to the Code, see section 151 of this title and Tables.

CODIFICATION

In par. Third (f), "subtitle IV of title 49" was substituted for "the Interstate Commerce Act, as amended [49 U.S.C. 1 et seq.]" on authority of Pub. L. 95-473, Sec. 3(b), Oct. 17, 1978, 92 Stat. 1466, the first section of which enacted subtitle IV of Title 49, Transportation.

AMENDMENTS

1970—Par. Third, (h). Pub. L. 91-452 struck out the provisions authorizing the board to invoke the aid of the United States courts to compel witnesses to attend and testify and to produce such books, papers, contracts, agreements, and documents to the same extent and under the same conditions and penalties as provided for in the Interstate Commerce Act.

1934—Act June 21, 1934, substituted "Mediation Board" for "Board of Mediation" where appearing.

Effective Date of 1970 Amendment

Amendment by Pub. L. 91-452 effective on the sixtieth day following Oct. 15, 1970, see section 260 of Pub. L. 91-452, set out as an Effective Date; Savings Provisions note under section 6001 of Title 18, Crimes and Criminal Procedure.

Savings Provisions

Amendment by Pub. L. 91-452 not to affect any immunity to which any individual is entitled under this section by reason of any testimony given before the sixtieth day following Oct. 15, 1970, see section 260 of Pub. L. 91-452, set out as an Effective Date; Savings Provisions note under section 6001 of Title 18, Crimes and Criminal Procedure.

Work Rules Dispute

Pub. L. 88-108, Aug. 28, 1963, 77 Stat. 132, provided:

"[Sec. 1. Settlement of disputes]. That no carrier which served the notices of November 2, 1959, and no labor organizations which received such notices or served the labor organization notices of September 7, 1960, shall make any change except by agreement, or pursuant to an arbitration award as hereinafter provided, in rates of pay, rules, or working conditions encompassed by any of such notices, or engage in any strike or lockout over any dispute arising from any of such notices. Any action heretofore taken which would be prohibited by the foregoing sentence shall be forthwith rescinded and the status existing immediately prior to such action restored.

"Sec. 2. [Arbitration board]. There is hereby established an arbitration board to consist of seven members. The representatives of the carrier and organization parties to the aforesaid dispute are hereby directed, respectively, within five days after the enactment hereof [Aug. 28, 1963] each to name two persons to serve as members of such arbitration board. The four members thus chosen shall select three additional members. The seven members shall then elect a chairman. If the members chosen by the parties shall fail to name one or more of the additional three members within ten days, such additional members shall be named by the President. If either party fails to name a member or members to the arbitration board within the five days provided, the President shall name such member or members in lieu of such party and shall also name the additional three members necessary to constitute a board of seven members, all within ten days after the date of enactment of this joint resolution [Aug. 28, 1963]. Notwithstanding any other provision of law, the National Mediation Board is authorized and directed: (1) to compensate the arbitrators not named by the parties at a rate not in excess of $100 for each day together with necessary travel and subsistence expenses, and (2) to provide such services and facilities as may be necessary and appropriate in carrying out the purposes of this joint resolution.

"Sec. 3. [Decision of board]. Promptly upon the completion of the naming of the arbitration board the Secretary of Labor shall furnish to the board and to the parties to the dispute copies of his statement to the parties of August 2, 1963, and the papers therewith submitted to the parties, together with memorandums and such other data as the board may request setting forth the matters with respect to which the parties were in tentative agreement and the extent of disagreement with respect to matters on which the parties were not in tentative agreement. The arbitration board shall make a decision, pursuant to the procedures hereinafter set forth, as to what disposition shall be made of those portions of the carriers' notices of November 2, 1959, identified as 'Use of Firemen (Helpers) on Other Than Steam Power' and 'Consist of Road and Yard Crews' and that portion of the organizations' notices of September 7, 1960, identified as 'Minimum Safe Crew Consist' and implementing proposals pertaining thereto. The arbitration board shall incorporate in such decision any matters on which it finds the parties were in agreement, shall resolve the matters on which the parties were not in agreement, and shall, in making its award, give due consideration to those matters on which the parties were in tentative agreement. Such award shall be binding on both the carrier and organization parties to the dispute and shall constitute a complete and final disposition of the aforesaid issues covered by the decision of the board of arbitration.

"Sec. 4. [Award]. To the extent not inconsistent with this joint resolution the arbitration shall be conducted pursuant to sections 7 and 8 of the Railway Labor Act [this section and section 158 of this title], the board's award shall be made and filed as provided in said sections and shall be subject to section 9 of said Act [section 159 of this title]. The United States District Court for the District of Columbia is hereby designated as the court in which the award is to be filed, and the arbitration board shall report to the National Mediation Board in the same manner as arbitration boards functioning pursuant to the Railway Labor Act [this chapter]. The award shall continue in force for such period as the arbitration board shall determine in its award, but not to exceed two years from the date the award takes effect, unless the parties agree otherwise.

"Sec. 5. [Hearings]. The arbitration board shall begin its hearings thirty days after the enactment of this joint resolution [Aug. 28, 1963] or on such earlier date as the parties to the dispute and the board may agree upon and shall make and file its award not later than ninety days after the enactment of this joint resolution [Aug. 28, 1963]: Provided, however, That said award shall not become effective until sixty days after the filing of the award.

"Sec. 6. [Collective bargaining for issues not arbitrated]. The parties to the disputes arising from the aforesaid notices shall immediately resume collective bargaining with respect to all issues raised in the notices of November 2, 1959, and September 7, 1960, not to be disposed of by arbitration under section 3 of this joint resolution and shall exert every reasonable effort to resolve such issues by agreement. The Secretary of Labor and the National Mediation Board are hereby directed to give all reasonable assistance to the parties and to engage in mediatory action directed toward promoting such agreement.

"Sec. 7. [Considerations affecting award; enforcement.]

"(a) In making any award under this joint resolution the arbitration board established under section 2 shall give due consideration to the effect of the proposed award upon adequate and safe transportation service to the public and upon the interests of the carrier and employees affected, giving due consideration to the narrowing of the areas of disagreement which has been accomplished in bargaining and mediation.

"(b) The obligations imposed by this joint resolution, upon suit by the Attorney General, shall be enforcible through such orders as may be necessary by any court of the United States having jurisdiction of any of the parties.

"Sec. 8. [Expiration date]. This joint resolution shall expire one hundred and eighty days after the date of its enactment [Aug. 28, 1963], except that it shall remain in effect with respect to the last sentence of section 4 for the period prescribed in that sentence.

"Sec. 9. [Separability of provisions]. If any provision of this joint resolution or the application thereof is held invalid, the remainder of this joint resolution and the application of such provision to other parties or in other circumstances not held invalid shall not be affected thereby."

Federal Rules of Civil Procedure

Subpoena, see rule 45, Title 28, Appendix, Judiciary and Judicial Procedure.

Cross References

Immunity of witnesses, see section 6001 et seq. of Title 18, Crimes and Criminal Procedure.

Sec. 158.   Agreement to arbitrate; form and contents; signatures and acknowledgment; revocation

The agreement to arbitrate—
(a) Shall be in writing;

(b) Shall stipulate that the arbitration is had under the provisions of this chapter;

(c) Shall state whether the board of arbitration is to consist of three or of six members;

(d) Shall be signed by the duly accredited representatives of the carrier or carriers and the employees, parties respectively to the agreement to arbitrate, and shall be acknowledged by said parties before a notary public, the clerk of a district court or court of appeals of the United States, or before a member of the Mediation Board, and, when so acknowledged, shall be filed in the office of the Mediation Board;

(e) Shall state specifically the questions to be submitted to the said board for decision; and that, in its award or awards, the said board shall confine itself strictly to decisions as to the questions so specifically submitted to it;

(f) Shall provide that the questions, or any one or more of them, submitted by the parties to the board of arbitration may be withdrawn from arbitration on notice to that effect signed by the duly accredited representatives of all the parties and served on the board of arbitration;

(g) Shall stipulate that the signatures of a majority of said board of arbitration affixed to their award shall be competent to constitute a valid and binding award;

(h) Shall fix a period from the date of the appointment of the arbitrator or arbitrators necessary to complete the board (as provided for in the agreement) within which the said board shall commence its hearings;

(i) Shall fix a period from the beginning of the hearings within which the said board shall make and file its award: Provided, That the parties may agree at any time upon an extension of this period;

(j) Shall provide for the date from which the award shall become effective and shall fix the period during which the award shall continue in force;

(k) Shall provide that the award of the board of arbitration and the evidence of the proceedings before the board relating thereto, when certified under the hands of at least a majority of the arbitrators, shall be filed in the clerk's office of the district court of the United States for the district wherein the controversy arose or the arbitration was entered into, which district shall be designated in the agreement; and, when so filed, such award and proceedings shall constitute the full and complete record of the arbitration;

(l) Shall provide that the award, when so filed, shall be final and conclusive upon the parties as to the facts determined by said award and as to the merits of the controversy decided;

(m) Shall provide that any difference arising as to the meaning, or the application of the provisions, of an award made by a board of arbitration shall be referred back for a ruling to the same board, or, by agreement, to a subcommittee of such board; and that such ruling, when acknowledged in the same manner, and filed in the same district court clerk's office, as the original award, shall be a part of and shall have the same force and effect as such original award; and

(n) Shall provide that the respective parties to the award will each faithfully execute the same.

The said agreement to arbitrate, when properly signed and acknowledged as herein provided, shall not be revoked by a party to such agreement: Provided, however, That such agreement to arbitrate may at any time be revoked and canceled by the written agreement of both parties, signed by their duly accredited representatives, and (if no board of arbitration has yet been constitued under the agreement) delivered to the Mediation Board or any member thereof; or, if the board of arbitration has been constituted as provided by this chapter, delivered to such board of arbitration.

(May 20, 1926, ch. 347, Sec. 8, 44 Stat. 584; June 21, 1934, ch. 691, Sec. 7, 48 Stat. 1197; June 25, 1948, ch. 646, Sec. 32(a), 62 Stat. 991; May 24, 1949, ch. 139, Sec. 127, 63 Stat. 107.)

References in Text

This chapter, referred to in par. (b), was in the original "this Act", meaning act May 20, 1926, ch. 347, 44 Stat. 577, as amended, known as the Railway Labor Act, which enacted this chapter and amended sections 225 and 348 of former Title 28, Judicial Code and Judiciary. Sections 225 and 348 of former Title 28 were repealed by section 39 of act June 25, 1948, ch. 646, 62 Stat. 992, section 1 of which enacted Title 28, Judiciary and Judicial Procedure. Section 225 of former Title 28 was reenacted as sections 1291 to 1294 of Title 28. For complete classification of this Act to the Code, see section 151 of this title and Tables.

Codification

As originally enacted, par. (d) contained a reference to the "circuit court of appeals". Act June 25, 1948, as amended by act May 24, 1949, substituted "court of appeals" for "circuit court of appeals".

Amendments

1934—Act June 21, 1934, substituted "Mediation Board" for "Board of Mediation" wherever appearing.

Sec. 159.   Award and judgment thereon; effect of chapter on individual employee

First. Filing of award

The award of a board of arbitration, having been acknowledged as herein provided, shall be filed in the clerk's office of the district court designated in the agreement to arbitrate.

Second. Conclusiveness of award; judgment

An award acknowledged and filed as herein provided shall be conclusive on the parties as to the merits and facts of the controversy submitted to arbitration, and unless, within ten days after the filing of the award, a petition to impeach the award, on the grounds hereinafter set forth, shall be filed in the clerk's office of the court in which the award has been filed, the court shall enter judgment on the award, which judgment shall be final and conclusive on the parties.

Third. Impeachment of award; grounds

Such petition for the impeachment or contesting of any award so filed shall be entertained by the court only on one or more of the following grounds:

(a) That the award plainly does not conform to the substantive requirements laid down by this chapter for such awards, or that the proceedings were not substantially in conformity with this chapter;

(b) That the award does not conform, nor confine itself, to the stipulations of the agreement to arbitrate; or

(c) That a member of the board of arbitration rendering the award was guilty of fraud or corruption; or that a party to the arbitration practiced fraud or corruption which fraud or corruption affected the result of the arbitration: Provided, however, That no court shall entertain any such petition on the ground that an award is invalid for uncertainty; in such case the proper remedy shall be a submission of such award to a reconvened board, or subcommittee thereof, for interpretation, as provided by this chapter: Provided further, That an award contested as herein provided shall be construed liberally by the court, with a view to favoring its validity, and that no award shall be set aside for trivial irregularity or clerical error, going only to form and not to substance.

Fourth. Effect of partial invalidity of award

If the court shall determine that a part of the award is invalid on some ground or grounds designated in this section as a ground of invalidity, but shall determine that apart of the award is valid, the court shall set aside the entire award: Provided, however, That, if the parties shall agree thereto, and if such valid and invalid parts are separable, the court shall set aside the invalid part, and order judgment to stand as to the valid part.

Fifth. Appeal; record

At the expiration of 10 days from the decision of the district court upon the petition filed as aforesaid, final judgment shall be entered in accordance with said decision, unless during said 10 days either party shall appeal therefrom to the court of appeals. In such case only such portion of the record shall be transmitted to the appellate court as is necessary to the proper understanding and consideration of the questions of law presented by said petition and to be decided.

Sixth. Finality of decision of court of appeals

The determination of said court of appeals upon said questions shall be final, and, being certified by the clerk thereof to said district court, judgment pursuant thereto shall thereupon be entered by said district court.

Seventh. Judgment where petitioner's contentions are sustained

If the petitioner's contentions are finally sustained, judgment shall be entered setting aside the award in whole or, if the parties so agree, in part; but in such case the parties may agree upon a judgment to be entered disposing of the subject matter of the controversy, which judgment when entered shall have the same force and effect as judgment entered upon an award.

Eighth. Duty of employee to render service without consent; right to quit

Nothing in this chapter shall be construed to require an individual employee to render labor or service without his consent, nor shall anything in this chapter be construed to make the quitting of his labor or service by an individual employee an illegal act; nor shall any court issue any process to compel the performance by an individual employee of such labor or service, without his consent.

(May 20, 1926, ch. 347, Sec. 9, 44 Stat. 585; June 25, 1948, ch. 646, Sec. 32(a), 62 Stat. 991; May 24, 1949, ch. 139, Sec. 127, 63 Stat. 107.)

References in Text

This chapter, referred to in pars. Third (a), (b) and Eighth, was in the original "this Act", meaning act May 20, 1926, ch. 347, 44 Stat. 577, as amended, known as the Railway Labor Act, which enacted this chapter and amended sections 225 and 348 of former Title 28, Judicial Code and Judiciary. Sections 225 and 348 of former Title 28 were repealed by section 39 of act June 25, 1948, ch. 646, 62 Stat. 992, section 1 of which enacted Title 28, Judiciary and Judicial Procedure. Section 225 of former Title 28 was reenacted as sections 1291 to 1294 of Title 28. For complete classification of this Act to the Code, see section 151 of this title and Tables.

Codification

As originally enacted, pars. Fifth and Sixth contained references to the "circuit court of appeals". Act June 25, 1948, as amended by act May 24, 1949, substituted "court of appeals" for "circuit court of appeals".

FEDERAL RULES OF CIVIL PROCEDURE

Application of rules, see rule 81, Title 28, Appendix, Judiciary and Judicial Procedure.

Sec. 159a. Special procedure for commuter service

(a) Applicability of provisions

Except as provided in section 590(h) of this title, the provisions of this section shall apply to any dispute subject to this chapter between a publicly funded and publicly operated carrier providing rail commuter service (including the Amtrak Commuter Services Corporation) and its employees.

(b) Request for establishment of emergency board

If a dispute between the parties described in subsection (a) of this section is not adjusted under the foregoing provisions of this chapter and the President does not, under section 160 of this title, create an emergency board to investigate and report on such dispute, then any party to the dispute or the Governor of any State through which the service that is the subject of the dispute is operated may request the President to establish such an emergency board.

(c) Establishment of emergency board

(1) Upon the request of a party or a Governor under subsection (b) of this section, the President shall create an emergency board to investigate and report on the dispute in accordance with section 160 of this title. For purposes of this subsection, the period during which no change, except by agreement, shall be made by the parties in the conditions out of which the dispute arose shall be 120 days from the day of the creation of such emergency board.

(2) If the President, in his discretion, creates a board to investigate and report on a dispute between the parties described in subsection (a) of this section, the provisions of this section shall apply to the same extent as if such board had been created pursuant to paragraph (1) of this subsection.

(d) Public hearing by National Mediation Board upon failure of emergency board to effectuate settlement of dispute

Within 60 days after the creation of an emergency board under this section, if there has been no settlement between the parties, the National Mediation Board shall conduct a public hearing on the dispute at which each party shall appear and provide testimony setting forth the reasons it has not accepted the recommendations of the emergency board for settlement of the dispute.

(e) Establishment of second emergency board

If no settlement in the dispute is reached at the end of the 120-day period beginning on the date of the creation of the emergency board, any party to the dispute or the Governor of any State through which the service that is the subject of the dispute is operated may request the President to establish another emergency board, in which case the President shall establish such emergency board.

(f) Submission of final offers to second emergency board by parties

Within 30 days after creation of a board under subsection (e) of this section, the parties to the dispute shall submit to the board final offers for settlement of the dispute.

(g) Report of second emergency board

Within 30 days after the submission of final offers under subsection (f) of this section, the emergency board shall submit a report to the President setting forth its selection of the most reasonable offer.

(h) Maintenance of status quo during dispute period

From the time a request to establish a board is made under subsection (e) of this section until 60 days after such board makes its report under subsection (g) of this section, no change, except by agreement, shall be made by the parties in the conditions out of which the dispute arose.

(i) Work stoppages by employees subsequent to carrier offer selected; eligibility of employees for benefits

If the emergency board selects the final offer submitted by the carrier and, after the expiration of the 60-day period described in subsection (h) of this section, the employees of such carrier engage in any work stoppage arising out of the dispute, such employees shall not be eligible during the period of such work stoppage for benefits under the Railroad Unemployment Insurance Act [45 U.S.C. 351 et seq.].

(j) Work stoppages by employees subsequent to employees offer selected; eligibility of employer for benefits

If the emergency board selects the final offer submitted by the employees and, after the expiration of the 60-day period described in subsection (h) of this section, the carrier refuses to accept the final offer submitted by the employees and the employees of such carrier engage in any work stoppage arising out of the dispute, the carrier shall not participate in any benefits of any agreement between carriers which is designed to provide benefits to such carriers during a work stoppage.

(May 20, 1926, ch. 347, Sec. 9A, as added Aug. 13, 1981, Pub. L. 97-35, title XI, Sec. 1157, 95 Stat. 681.)

References in Text

This chapter, referred to in subsecs. (a) and (b), was in the original "this Act", meaning act May 20, 1926, ch. 347, 44 Stat. 577, as amended, known as the Railway Labor Act, which enacted this chapter and amended sections

225 and 348 of former Title 28, Judicial Code and Judiciary. Sections 225 and 348 of former Title 28 were repealed by section 39 of act June 25, 1948, ch. 646, 62 Stat. 992, section 1 of which enacted Title 28, Judiciary and Judicial Procedure. Section 225 of former Title 28 was reenacted as sections 1291 to 1294 of Title 28. For complete classification of this Act to the Code, see section 151 of this title and Tables.

The Railroad Unemployment Insurance Act, referred to in subsec. (i), is act June 25, 1938, ch. 680, 52 Stat. 1094, as amended, which is classified principally to chapter 11 (Sec. 351 et seq.) of this title. For complete classification of this Act to the Code, see section 367 of this title and Tables.

EFFECTIVE DATE

Section effective Aug. 13, 1981, see section 1169 of Pub. L. 97-35, set out as a note under section 1101 of this title.

Sec. 160.   Emergency board

If a dispute between a carrier and its employees be not adjusted under the foregoing provisions of this chapter and should, in the judgment of the Mediation Board, threaten substantially to interrupt interstate commerce to a degree such as to deprive any section of the country of essential transportation service, the Mediation Board shall notify the President, who may thereupon, in his discretion, create a board to investigate and report respecting such dispute. Such board shall be composed of such number of persons as to the President may seem desirable: Provided, however, That no member appointed shall be pecuniarily or otherwise interested in any organization of employees or any carrier. The compensation of the members of any such board shall be fixed by the President. Such board shall be created separately in each instance and it shall investigate promptly the facts as to the dispute and make a report thereon to the President within thirty days from the date of its creation.

There is authorized to be appropriated such sums as may be necessary for the expenses of such board, including the compensation and the necessary traveling expenses and expenses actually incurred for subsistence, of the members of the board. All expenditures of the board shall be allowed and paid on the presentation of itemized vouchers therefor approved by the chairman.

After the creation of such board and for thirty days after such board has made its report to the President, no change, except by agreement, shall be made by the parties to the controversy in the conditions out of which the dispute arose.

(May 20, 1926, ch. 347, Sec. 10, 44 Stat. 586; June 21, 1934, ch. 691, Sec. 7, 48 Stat. 1197.)

This chapter, referred to in text, was in the original "this Act", meaning act May 20, 1926, ch. 347, 44 Stat. 577, as amended, known as the Railway Labor Act, which enacted this chapter and amended sections 225 and 348 of former Title 28, Judicial Code and Judiciary. Sections 225 and 348 of former Title 28 were repealed by section 39 of act June 25, 1948, ch. 646, 62 Stat. 992, section 1 of which enacted Title 28, Judiciary and Judicial Procedure. Section 225 of former Title 28 was reenacted as sections 1291 to 1294 of Title 28. For complete classification of this Act to the Code, see section 151 of this title and Tables.

Amendments

1934—Act June 21, 1934, substituted "Mediation Board" for "Board of Mediation" wherever appearing.

Sec. 161.   Effect of partial invalidity of chapter

If any provision of this chapter, or the application thereof to any person or circumstance, is held invalid, the remainder of the chapter, and the application of such provision to other persons or circumstances, shall not be affected thereby.

(May 20, 1926, ch. 347, Sec. 11, 44 Stat. 587.)

References in Text

This chapter, referred to in text, was in the original "this Act", meaning act May 20, 1926, ch. 347, 44 Stat. 577, as amended, known as the Railway Labor Act, which enacted this chapter and amended sections 225 and 348 of former Title 28, Judicial Code and Judiciary. Sections 225 and 348 of former Title 28 were repealed by section 39 of act June 25, 1948, ch. 646, 62 Stat. 992, section 1 of which enacted Title 28, Judiciary and Judicial Procedure. Section 225 of former Title 28 was reenacted as sections 1291 to 1294 of Title 28. For complete classification of this Act to the Code, see section 151 of this title and Tables.

Separability; Repeal of Inconsistent Provisions

Section 8 of act June 21, 1934, provided that: "If any section, subsection, sentence, clause, or phrase of this Act [amending sections 151 to 158, 160, and 162 of this title] is for any reason held to be unconstitutional, such decision shall not affect the validity of the remaining portions of this Act.

All Acts or parts of Acts inconsistent with the provisions of this Act are hereby repealed."

Sec. 162. Authorization of appropriations

There is authorized to be appropriated such sums as may be necessary for expenditure by the Mediation Board in carrying out the provisions of this chapter.

(May 20, 1926, ch. 347, Sec. 12, 44 Stat. 587; June 21, 1934, ch. 691, Sec. 7, 48 Stat. 1197.)

REFERENCES IN TEXT

This chapter, referred to in text, was in the original "this Act", meaning act May 20, 1926, ch. 347, 44 Stat. 577, as amended, known as the Railway Labor Act, which enacted this chapter and amended sections 225 and 348 of former Title 28, Judicial Code and Judiciary. Sections 225 and 348 of former Title 28 were repealed by section 39 of act June 25, 1948, ch. 646, 62 Stat. 992, section 1 of which enacted Title 28, Judiciary and Judicial Procedure. Section 225 of former Title 28 was reenacted as sections 1291 to 1294 of Title 28. For complete classification of this Act to the Code, see section 151 of this title and Tables.

AMENDMENTS

1934—Act June 21, 1934, substituted "Mediation Board" for "Board of Mediation".

Sec. 163. Repeal of prior legislation; exception

Chapters 6 and 7 of this title, providing for mediation, conciliation, and arbitration, and all Acts and parts of Acts in conflict with the provisions of this chapter are repealed, except that the members, secretary, officers, employees, and agents of the Railroad Labor Board, in office on May 20, 1926, shall receive their salaries for a period of 30 days from such date, in the same manner as though this chapter had not been passed.

(May 20, 1926, ch. 347, Sec. 14, 44 Stat. 587.)

REFERENCES IN TEXT

Chapters 6 and 7 of this title, referred to in text, were in the original references to the act of July 15, 1913, and title III of the Transportation Act, 1920, respectively.

This chapter, referred to in text, was in the original "this Act", meaning act May 20, 1926, ch. 347, 44 Stat. 577, as amended, known as the Railway Labor Act, which enacted this chapter and amended sections 225 and 348 of former Title 28, Judicial Code and Judiciary. Sections 225 and 348 of former Title 28 were repealed by section 39 of act June 25, 1948, ch. 646, 62 Stat. 992, section 1 of which enacted Title 28, Judiciary and Judicial Procedure. Section 225 of former Title 28 was reenacted as sections 1291 to 1294 of Title 28. For complete classification of this Act to the Code, see section 151 of this title and Tables.

Sec. 164.   Repealed. Oct. 10, 1940, ch. 851, Sec. 4, 54 Stat. 1111

Section, act Feb. 11, 1927, ch. 104, Sec. 1, 44 Stat. 1072, related to advertisements for proposals for purchases or services rendered for Board of Mediation, including arbitration boards. See section 5 of Title 41, Public Contracts.

SUBCHAPTER II—CARRIERS BY AIR

Sec. 181.   Application of subchapter I to carriers by air

All of the provisions of subchapter I of this chapter except section 153 of this title are extended to and shall cover every common carrier by air engaged in interstate or foreign commerce, and every carrier by air transporting mail for or under contract with the United States Government, and every air pilot or other person who performs any work as an employee or subordinate official of such carrier or carriers, subject to its or their continuing authority to supervise and direct the manner of rendition of his service.

(May 20, 1926, ch. 347, Sec. 201, as added Apr. 10, 1936, ch. 166, 49 Stat. 1189.)

Sec. 182.   Duties, penalties, benefits, and privileges of subchapter I applicable

The duties, requirements, penalties, benefits, and privileges prescribed and established by the provisions of subchapter I of this chapter except section 153 of this title shall apply to said carriers by air and their employees in the same manner and to the same extent as though such carriers and their employees were specifically included within the definition of "carrier" and "employee", respectively, in section 151 of this title.

(May 20, 1926, ch. 347, Sec. 202, as added Apr. 10, 1936, ch. 166, 49 Stat. 1189.)

Sec. 183. Disputes within jurisdiction of Mediation Board

The parties or either party to a dispute between an employee or a group of employees and a carrier or carriers by air may invoke the services of the National Mediation Board and the jurisdiction of said Mediation Board is extended to any of the following cases:

(a) A dispute concerning changes in rates of pay, rules, or working conditions not adjusted by the parties in conference.

(b) Any other dispute not referable to an adjustment board, as hereinafter provided, and not adjusted in conference between the parties, or where conferences are refused.

The National Mediation Board may proffer its services in case any labor emergency is found by it to exist at any time.

The services of the Mediation Board may be invoked in a case under this subchapter in the same manner and to the same extent as are the disputes covered by section 155 of this title.

(May 20, 1926, ch. 347, Sec. 203, as added Apr. 10, 1936, ch. 166, 49 Stat. 1189.)

Sec. 184. System, group, or regional boards of adjustment

The disputes between an employee or group of employees and a carrier or carriers by air growing out of grievances, or out of the interpretation or application of agreements concerning rates of pay, rules, or working conditions, including cases pending and unadjusted on April 10, 1936 before the National Labor Relations Board, shall be handled in the usual manner up to and including the chief operating officer of the carrier designated to handle such disputes; but, failing to reach an adjustment in this manner, the disputes may be referred by petition of the parties or by either party to an appropriate adjustment board, as hereinafter provided, with a full statement of the facts and supporting data bearing upon the disputes.

It shall be the duty of every carrier and of its employees, acting through their representatives, selected in accordance with the provisions of this subchapter, to establish a board of adjustment of jurisdiction not exceeding the jurisdiction which may be lawfully exercised by system, group, or regional boards of adjustment, under the authority of section 153 of this title.

Such boards of adjustment may be established by agreement between employees and carriers either on any individual carrier, or system, or group of carriers by air and any class or classes of its or their employees; or pending the establishment of a permanent National Board of Adjustment as hereinafter provided. Nothing in this chapter shall prevent said carriers by air, or any class or classes of their employees, both acting through their representatives selected in accordance with provisions of this subchapter, from mutually agreeing to the establishment of a National Board of Adjustment of temporary duration and of similarly limited jurisdiction.

(May 20, 1926, ch. 347, Sec. 204, as added Apr. 10, 1936, ch. 166, 49 Stat. 1189.)

References in Text

This chapter, referred to in text, was in the original "this Act", meaning act May 20, 1926, ch. 347, 44 Stat. 577, as amended, known as the Railway Labor Act, which enacted this chapter and amended sections 225 and 348 of former Title 28, Judicial Code and Judiciary. Sections 225 and 348 of former Title 28 were repealed by section 39 of act June 25, 1948, ch. 646, 62 Stat. 992, section 1 of which enacted Title 28, Judiciary and Judicial Procedure. Section 225 of former Title 28 was reenacted as sections 1291 to 1294 of Title 28. For complete classification of this Act to the Code, see section 151 of this title and Tables.

Sec. 185. National Air Transport Adjustment Board

When, in the judgment of the National Mediation Board, it shall be necessary to have a permanent national board of adjustment in order to provide for the prompt and orderly settlement of disputes between said carriers by air, or any of them, and its or their employees, growing out of grievances or out of the interpretation or application of agreements between said carriers by air or any of them, and any class or classes of its or their employees, covering rates of pay, rules, or working conditions, the National Mediation Board is empowered and directed, by its order duly made, published, and served, to direct the said carriers by air and such labor organizations of their employees, national in scope, as have been or may be recognized in accordance with the provisions of this chapter, to select and designate four representatives who shall constitute a board which shall be known as the "National Air Transport Adjustment Board." Two members of said National Air Transport Adjustment Board shall be selected by said carriers by air and two members by the said labor organizations of the employees, within thirty days after the date of the order of the National Mediation Board, in the manner and by the procedure prescribed by section 153 of this title for the selection and designation of members of the National Railroad Adjustment Board. The National Air Transport Adjustment Board shall meet within forty days after the date of the order of the National Mediation Board directing the selection and designation of its members and shall organize and adopt rules for conducting its proceedings, in the manner prescribed in section 153 of this title. Vacancies in membership or office shall be filled, members shall be appointed in case of failure of the carriers or of labor organizations of the employees to select and designate representatives, members of the National Air Transport Adjustment Board shall be compensated, hearings shall be held, findings and awards made, stated, served, and enforced, and the number and compensation of any necessary assistants shall be determined and the compensation of such employees shall be paid, all in the same manner and to the same extent as provided with reference to the National Railroad Adjustment Board by section 153 of this title. The powers and duties prescribed and established by the provisions of section 153 of this title with reference to the National Railroad Adjustment Board and the several divisions thereof are conferred upon and shall be exercised and performed in like manner and to the same extent by the said National Air Transport Adjustment Board, not exceeding, however, the jurisdiction conferred upon said National Air Transport Adjustment Board by the provisions of this subchapter. From and after the organization of the National Air Transport Adjustment Board, if any system, group, or re-gional board of adjustment established by any carrier or carriers by air and any class or classes of its or their employees is not satisfactory to either party thereto, the said party, upon ninety days' notice to the other party, may elect to come under the jurisdiction of the National Air Transport Adjustment Board.

(May 20, 1926, ch. 347, Sec. 205, as added Apr. 10, 1936, ch. 166, 49 Stat. 1190.)

REFERENCES IN TEXT

This chapter, referred to in text, was in the original "this Act", meaning act May 20, 1926, ch. 347, 44 Stat. 577, as amended, known as the Railway Labor Act, which enacted this chapter and amended sections 225 and 348 of former Title 28, Judicial Code and Judiciary. Sections 225 and 348 of former Title 28 were repealed by section 39 of act June 25, 1948, ch. 646, 62 Stat. 992, section 1 of which enacted Title 28, Judiciary and Judicial Procedure. Section 225 of former Title 28 was reenacted as sections 1291 to 1294 of Title 28. For complete classification of this Act to the Code, see section 151 of this title and Tables.

FEDERAL RULES OF CIVIL PROCEDURE

Application of rules, see rule 81, Title 28, Appendix, Judiciary and Judicial Procedure.

Effect of rules on this section, see note by Advisory Committee under rule 81.

Sec. 186.   Omitted

CODIFICATION

Section, act May 20, 1926, ch. 347, Sec. 206, as added Apr. 10, 1936, ch. 166, 49 Stat. 1191, transferred certain pending cases before the National Labor Relations Board to the Mediation Board.

Sec. 187. Separability of provisions

If any provision of this subchapter or application thereof to any person or circumstance is held invalid, the remainder of such sections and the application of such provision to other persons or circumstances shall not be affected thereby.

(May 20, 1926, ch. 347, Sec. 207, as added Apr. 10, 1936, ch. 166, 49 Stat. 1191.)

Sec. 188. Authorization of appropriations

There is authorized to be appropriated such sums as may be necessary for expenditure by the Mediation Board in carrying out the provisions of this chapter.

(May 20, 1926, ch. 347, Sec. 208, as added Apr. 10, 1936, ch. 166, 49 Stat. 1191.)

REFERENCES IN TEXT

This chapter, referred to in text, was in the original "this Act", meaning act May 20, 1926, ch. 347, 44 Stat. 577, as amended, known as the Railway Labor Act, which enacted this chapter and amended sections 225 and 348 of former Title 28, Judicial Code and Judiciary. Sections 225 and 348 of former Title 28 were repealed by section 39 of act June 25, 1938, ch. 646, 62 Stat. 992, section 1 of which enacted Title 28, Judiciary and Judicial Procedure. Section 225 of former Title 28 was reenacted as sections 1291 to 1294 of Title 28. For complete classification of this Act to the Code, see section 151 of this title and Tables.

NATIONAL MEDIATION BOARD RULES

Source: Code of Fed. Regs., Title 29, Chapter X.

CHAPTER X—NATIONAL
MEDIATION BOARD

Abbreviation: The following abbreviation is used in this chapter: NMB = *National Mediation Board.*

PART 1200—MINIMUM STANDARDS OF CONDUCT FOR EMPLOYEES OF THE NATIONAL MEDIATION BOARD

Subpart A—Introduction

Subpart B—Ethical Conduct and Responsibilities of Employees

Subpart C—Board Regulations Governing Ethical and Other Conduct and Responsibilities of Special Government Employees

Subpart D—Board Regulations Governing Statements of Employment and Financial Interests

AUTHORITY: E.O. 11222 of May 8, 1965, 30 FR 6469, 3 CFR, 1965 Supp.; 5 CFR 735.104.

SOURCE: 32 FR 15827, Nov. 17, 1967, unless otherwise noted.

Subpart A—Introduction

§ 1200.735-1   General.

(a) The promulgation of these minimum standards of ethical conduct for employees and special Government employees of the National Mediation Board has as its objective the maintaining and reaffirming of the public's confidence in the activities of their Government. The regulations in this part are intended to act as the board moral and ethical guideposts for employees of the Board and to supplement and verbalize the individual ethic and integrity of the employees affected. The avoidance of misconduct and conflict of interest on the part of Government employees and special Government employees through informed judgment is indispensable to the maintenance of these standards.

(b) The elimination of conflicts of interests in the Federal service is one of the most important objectives in establishing general standards of conduct. A conflict-of-interest situation may be defined as one in which a Federal employee's private interest, usually of an economic nature, conflicts or raises a reasonable question of conflict with his public duties and responsibilities. The potential conflict is of concern whether it is real or only apparent.

(c) The failure of an employee to observe the basic principles of good conduct, ethics, and integrity will result in immediate adverse or disciplinary action of a severity in keeping with the offense committed and in accordance with equitable administrative practice.

(d) These standards are established in conformity with Part 735 of Title 5 of the Code of Federal Regulations.

§ 1200.735-2   Interpretation and advisory service.

It shall be the practice of the National Mediation Board to appoint as counselor for the agency one of the members of the Board itself. Based upon the experience, usually legal, and position of such individual, employees of the Board will more naturally express complete personal confidence in such a counselor. This individual shall coordinate the Board's counseling services, which services shall be brought to the attention of the Board's employees and special Government employees within 90 days after the approval of the agency's regulations by the Commission. In the case of new employees, notification of the availability of counseling services shall be effected upon their entrance on duty.

§ 1200.735-3 Reviewing statements and reporting conflicts of interest.

(a) When a statement submitted or information from other sources indicates a conflict between the interests of an employee or special Government employee and the performance of his services for the Government, and when the conflict or appearance of conflict is not resolved at a lower level, the information concerning the conflict or appearance of the conflict shall be reported to the Board through the counselor for the Board.

(b) The employee or special Government employee concerned shall be provided an opportunity to explain the conflict or appearance of conflict.

§ 1200.735-4 Disciplinary and other remedial action.

(a) A violation of the regulations in this part by an employee or special Government employee may be cause for appropriate disciplinary action which may be in addition to any penalty prescribed by law.

(b) When after consideration of the explanation of the employee or special Government employee the Board decides that remedial action is required, immediate action shall be taken to end the conflicts or appearance of conflicts of interest. Remedial action may include, but is not limited to:

(1) Change in assigned duties;

(2) Divestment by the employee or special Government employee of his conflicting interest;

(3) Disciplinary action; or

(4) Disqualification for a particular assignment.

(c) Remedial action, whether disciplinary or otherwise, shall be effected in accordance with any applicable laws, Executive orders, and regulations.

Subpart B—Ethical Conduct and Responsibilities of Employees

§ 1200.735-20 Proscribed actions.

(a) An employee shall avoid any action, whether or not specifically prohibited by this subpart, which might result in or create the appearance of:

(1) Using public office for private gain;

(2) Giving preferential treatment to any person;

(3) Impeding Government efficiency or economy;

(4) Losing complete independence or impartiality;

(5) Making a Government decision outside of official channels; or

(6) Affecting adversely the confidence of the public in the integrity of the Government.

§ 1200.735-21   Gifts, entertainment, and favors.

(a) An employee shall not solicit or accept, directly or indirectly, any gift, gratuity, favor, entertainment, loan, or any other thing of monetary value from a person who:

(1) Has, or is seeking to obtain, contractual or other business of financial relations with the Board;

(2) Conducts operations or activities that are regulated by the Board; or

(3) Has interests that may be substantially affected by the performance or nonperformance of his official duty.

(b) The restrictions set forth in paragraph (a) of this section do not apply to:

(1) Obvious family or personal relationships when the circumstances make it clear that it is those relationships rather than the business of the persons concerned which are the motivating factors;

(2) The acceptance of food and refreshments of nominal value on infrequent occasions in the ordinary course of a luncheon or dinner meeting or other meeting or during an investigation where an employee may be properly in attendance;

(3) The acceptance of loans from banks or other financial institutions on customary terms to finance proper and usual activities of employees, such as home mortgage loans; and

(4) The acceptance of unsolicited advertising or promotional material, such as pens, pencils, note pads, calendars, and other items of nominal intrinsic value.

(c) [Reserved]

(d) An employee shall not solicit a contribution from another employee for a gift to an official superior, making a donation as a gift to an official superior, or accept a gift from an employee receiving less pay than himself (5 U.S.C. 7351). However, this paragraph does not prohibit a voluntary gift of nominal value or donation in a nominal amount made on a special occasion such as marriage, illness or retirement.

(e) An employee shall not accept a gift, present, decoration, or other things from a foreign government unless authorized by Congress as provided by the Constitution and in Pub. L. 89-673, 80 Stat. 952.

(f) Neither this section nor § 1200.735-22 precludes an employee from receipt of bona fide reimbursement, unless prohibited by law, for expenses of travel and such other necessary subsistence as is compatible with this part for which no Government payment or reimbursement is made. However, this paragraph does not allow an employee to be reimbursed, or payment to be made on his behalf, for excessive personal living expenses, gifts, entertainment or other personal benefits, nor does it allow an employee to be reimbursed by a person for travel on official business under

Board orders when reimbursement is proscribed by Decision B-128527 of the Comptroller General dated March 7, 1967.

§ 1200.735-22   Outside employment and other activity.

(a) An employee shall not engage in outside employment or other outside activity not compatible with the full and proper discharge of the duties and responsibilities of his Government employment. Incompatible activities include but are not limited to:

(1) Acceptance of a fee, compensation, gift, payment of expense, or any other thing of monetary value in circumstances in which acceptance may result in, or create the appearance of, conflicts of interest; or

(2) Outside employment which tends to impair his mental or physical capacity to perform his government duties and responsibilities in an acceptable manner.

(b) An employee shall not receive any salary or anything of monetary value from a private source as compensation for his services to the Government.

(c) Employees are encouraged to engage in teaching, lecturing and writing that is not prohibited by law, the Executive Order, or the Board regulations. However, an employee shall not, either for or without compensation, engage in teaching, lecturing, or writing, including teaching, lecturing, or writing for the purpose of the special preparation of a person or class of persons for an examination of the Commission or Board of Examiners for the Foreign Service, that depends on information obtained as a result of his Government employment, except when that information has been made available to the general public or will be made available on request, or when the Board gives written authorization for use of nonpublic information on the basis that the use is in the public interest. In addition, an employee who is a Presidential appointee covered by section 401(a) of Executive Order 11222 shall not receive compensation or anything of monetary value for any consultation, lecture, discussion, writing, or appearance, the subject matter of which is devoted substantially to the responsibilities, programs, or operations of the Board, or which draws substantially on official data or ideas which have not become part of the body of public information.

[32 FR 15827, Nov. 17, 1967, as amended at 33 FR 11816, Aug. 21, 1968]

§ 1200.735-23   Financial interests.

(a) An employee shall not:

(1) Have a direct or indirect financial interest that conflicts substantially, or appears to conflict substantially, with his governmental duties and responsibilities; or

(2) Engage in, directly or indirectly, a financial transaction as a result of, or primarily relying on, information obtained through his Government employment.

(b) An employee is not precluded from having a financial interest or engaging in financial transactions to the same extent as a private citizen not employed by the Government so long as it is not prohibited by law, the Executive Order or the Board regulations in this part.

§ 1200.735-24   Use of Government property.

An employee shall not directly or indirectly use, or allow the use of, Government property of any kind, including property leased to the Government, for other than officially approved activities. An employee has a positive duty to protect and conserve Government property, including equipment, supplies, and other property entrusted or issued to him.

§ 1200.735-25   Misuse of information.

For the purpose of furthering a private interest, an employee shall not, directly or indirectly use, or allow the use of, official information obtained through or in connection with his Government employment which has not been made available to the general public.

§ 1200.735-26   Indebtedness.

An employee shall pay each just financial obligation in a proper and timely manner, especially one imposed by law such as Federal, State, or local taxes. A "just financial obligation" means one acknowledged by the employee or reduced to judgment by a court, and "in a proper and timely manner" means in a manner which the Board determines does not, under the circumstances, reflect adversely on the Government as his employer. In the event of dispute between an employee and an alleged creditor, the Board is not required to determine the validity or amount of the disputed debt.

§ 1200.735-27   Gambling, betting, and lotteries.

An employee shall not participate, while on Government owned or leased property or while on duty for the Government in any gambling activity including the operation of a gambling device, in conducting a lottery or pool, in a game for money or property, or in selling or purchasing a numbers slip or ticket.

§ 1200.735-28   General conduct prejudicial to the Government.

An employee shall not engage in criminal, infamous, dishonest, immoral, or notoriously disgraceful conduct, or other conduct prejudicial to the Government.

§ 1200.735-29   Miscellaneous statutory provisions.

Each employee shall acquaint himself with each status that relates to his ethical and other conduct as an employee of the Board and of the Government. The following statutory provisions are to be noted:

(a) House Concurrent Resolution 175, 85th Congress, 2d session, 72 Stat. B12, the "Code of Ethics for Government Service."

(b) Chapter 11 of the title 18, U.S.C., relating to bribery, graft, and conflicts of interest, as appropriate to the employees concerned.

(c) The prohibition against lobbying with appropriated funds (18 U.S.C. 1913).

(d) The prohibitions against disloyalty and striking (5 U.S.C. 7311, 18 U.S.C. 1918).

(e) The prohibition against the employment of a member of a Communist organization (50 U.S.C. 784).

(f) The prohibitions against:

(1) The disclosure of classified information (18 U.S.C. 798, 50 U.S.C. 783), and

(2) The disclosure of confidential information (18 U.S.C. 1905).

(g) The provisions relating to the habitual use of intoxicants to excess (5 U.S.C. 7352).

(h) The prohibition against the misuse of a Government vehicle (31 U.S.C. 638a(c)).

(i) The prohibition against the misuse of the franking privilege (18 U.S.C. 1719).

(j) The prohibition against the use of deceit in an examination of personnel action in connection with Government employment (18 U.S.C. 1917).

(k) The prohibition against fraud or false statements in a Government matter (18 U.S.C. 1001).

(l) The prohibition against mutilating or destroying a public record (18 U.S.C. 2071).

(m) The prohibition against counterfeiting and forging transportation requests (18 U.S.C. 508).

(n) The prohibitions against:

(1) Embezzlement of Government money or property (18 U.S.C. 641);

(2) Failing to account for public money (18 U.S.C. 643); and

(3) Embezzlement of the money or property of another person in the possession of an employee by reason of his employment (18 U.S.C. 654).

(o) The prohibition against unauthorized use of documents relating to claims from or by the Goverment (18 U.S.C. 285).

(p) The prohibition against prescribed political activities in Subchapter III of Chapter 73 of Title 5, United States Code and 18 U.S.C. 602, 603, 607, and 608.

(q) The prohibition against an employee acting as an agent of a foreign principal registered under the Foreign Agents Registration Act (18 U.S.C. 219).

Subpart C—Board Regulations Governing Ethical and Other Conduct and Responsibilities of Special Government Employees

§ 1200.735-30   Special provisions of Board regulations.

Special Government employees, including those individuals categorized as WAE (When as employed), shall be put on actual notice regarding section 5, Third (a), and 7, Third (d) of the Railway Labor Act, 45 U.S.C. Chapter 8, which provide that arbitrators appointed by the Board shall be impartial without bias and disinterested. These Board appointed arbitrators or neutrals shall be further notified of the intent of Executive Order 11222 governing conflict of interests and ethical standards of Government employees.

§ 1200.735-31   Use of Government employment.

A special Government employee shall not use his Government employment for a purpose that is, or gives the appearance of being, motivated by the desire for private gain for himself or another person, particularly one with whom he has family, business, or financial ties.

§ 1200.735-32   Outside activities of special Government employees.

Special Government employees may teach, lecture, or write in a manner not inconsistent with § 1200.735-22(c) governing other employees.

§ 1200.735-33   Use of inside information.

A special Government employee shall not use inside information obtained as a result of his Government employment for private gain for himself or another person whether by direct action on his part or by counsel, recommendation, or suggestion to another person, particularly one with whom he has family, business, or financial ties. For the purpose of this section, "inside information" means information obtained under Government authority which has not become part of the body of public information.

§ 1200.735-34   Coercion.

A special Government employee shall not use his Government employment to coerce or give the appearance of coercing, a person to provide financial benefit to himself or another person, particularly one with whom he has family, business, or financial ties.

§ 1200.735-35   Gifts, entertainment, and favors.

(a) A special Government employee, while so employed or in connection with his employment, shall not receive or solicit from a person having business with the Board anything of value as a gift, gratuity, loan, entertainment, or favor for himself or another person, particularly one with whom he has family, business or financial ties.

(b) The exceptions enumerated under § 1200.735-21(b) are applicable to special Government employees.

Subpart D—Board Regulations Governing Statements of Employment and Financial Interests

§ 1200.735-40   Form and content of statements.

The statements of employment and financial interests required for use by employees and special Government employees shall contain, as a minimum, the information required by the formats prescribed by the Commission in the Federal Personnel Manual.

§ 1200.735-41   Employees required to submit statements.

The Board shall require statements of employment and financial interests from the following employees: Board's Executive Secretary.

§ 1200.735-41a   Employee's complaint on filing requirement.

Any employee required to submit statements pursuant to § 1200.735-41, who believes his inclusion under Board regulations is improper, may file a complaint directed to the Ethical Conduct Counselor of the National Mediation Board.

§ 1200.735-42   Employees not required to submit statements.

A statement of employment and financial interests is not required of Board members. These Board members are subject to separate reporting requirements under section 401 of Executive Order 11222.

§ 1200.735-43   Time and place for submission of employees' statements.

An employee required to submit a statement of employment and financial interests under the regulations in this part shall submit that statement to the Counselor of Ethical Standards not later than:

(a) Ninety days after the effective date of the Board regulations in this part if employed on or before that effective date; or

(b) Thirty days after his entrance on duty, but not earlier than 90 days after the effective date, if appointed after that effective date.

§ 1200.735-44   Supplementary statements.

Changes in, or additions to, the information contained in an employee's statement of employment and financial interests shall be reported in a supplementary statement as of June 30 each year, except when the Civil Service Commission authorizes a different date on a showing by the Board of necessity therefor. If no changes or additions occur, a negative report is required. Notwithstanding the filing of the annual report required by this section, each employee shall at all times avoid acquiring a financial interest that could result or taking an action that would result, in a violation of the conflicts-of-interest provisions of section 208 of title 18, United States Code, or Subpart B of this part.

§ 1200.735-45   Interests of employees' relatives.

The interest of a spouse, minor child, or other member of an employee's immediate household is considered to be an interest of the employee. For the purpose of this section, "member of an employee's immediate household" means those blood relations who are residents of the employee's household.

§ 1200.735-46   Information not known by employees.

If any information required to be included on a statement of employment and financial interests or supplementary statement, including holdings placed in trust, is not known to the employee but is known to another person, the employee shall request that other person to submit information in his behalf.

§ 1200.735-47   Information prohibited.

This section does not require an employee to submit on a statement of employment and financial interests or supplementary statement any information relating to the employee's connection with or interest in, professional society or a charitable, religious, social, fraternal, recreational, public service, civic, or political organization or a similar organization not conducted as a business enterprise. For the purpose of this section, educational and other institutions doing research and development or related work involving grants of money from or contracts with the Government are deemed "business enterprises" and are required to be included in an employee's statement of employment and financial interests.

§ 1200.735-48   Confidentiality of employees' statements.

The Board shall hold each statement of employment and financial interests, and each supplementary statement, in confidence. To ensure this confidentiality, the Board shall designate which employees are authorized to review and retain the statements. Employees so designated are responsible for maintaining the statements in confidence and shall not allow access to, or allow information to be disclosed from, a statement except to carry out the purpose of this part. The Board shall not disclose information from a statement except as the Civil Service Commission or the Board may determine for good cause shown.

§ 1200.735-49 Effect of employees' statements on other requirements.

The statements of employment and financial interests and supplementary statements required of employees are in addition to, and not in substitution for or in derogation of, any similar requirement imposed by law, order, or regulation. The submission of a statement or supplementary statement by an employee does not permit him or any other person to participate in a manner in which his or the other person's participation is prohibited by law, order, or regulations.

§ 1200.735-50 Specific provisions of Board regulations for special Government employees.

(a) Each special Government employee appointed by the National Mediation Board shall file a statement of employment and financial interests on a form to be furnished by the Board. However, the following special Government employees are not required to file a statement of employment and financial interests: Neutrals, referees, and arbitrators, who are exempted due to the fact that the duties of the positions held by these employees are of such a nature and at such a level of responsibility that the submission of such a statement is not necessary to protect the integrity of the Government.

(b) It shall be the duty of the National Mediation Board to notify each of its special Government employees of the specific requirements of the Railway Labor Act and Executive Order 11222 concerning impartiality, integrity, and conflicts of interest.

(c) The statement of employment and financial interests required in this section shall be submitted not later than the time of employment of the special Government employee as provided in the Board's regulations in this part. Each special Government employee shall keep his statement current throughout his employment with the Board by the submission of supplementary statements.

PART 1201—DEFINITIONS

1201.5   Exceptions.
1201.6   Representatives.

Authority: 44 Stat. 577, as amended; 45 U.S.C. 151-163.

Source: 11 FR 117A-922, Sept. 11, 1946, unless otherwise noted. Redesignated at 13 FR 8740, Dec. 30, 1948.

§ 1201.1   Carrier.

The term "carrier" includes any express company, sleeping car company, carrier by railroad, subject to the Interstate Commerce Act (24 Stat. 379, as amended; 49 U.S.C. 1 et seq.), and any company which is directly or indirectly owned or controlled by or under common control with any carrier by railroad and which operates any equipment or facilities or performs any service (other than trucking service) in connection with the transportation, receipt, delivery, elevation, transfer in transit, refrigeration or icing, storage, and handling of property transported by railroad, and any receiver, trustee, or other individual or body, judicial or otherwise, when in the possession of the business of any such "carrier."

§ 1201.2   Exceptions.

(a) The term "carrier" shall not include any street, interurban, or suburban electric railway, unless such railway is operating as a part of a general steam-railroad system of transportation, but shall not exclude any part of the general steam-railroad system of transportation now or hereafter operated by any other motive power.

(b) The term "carrier" shall not include any company by reason of its being engaged in the mining of coal, the supplying of coal to carrier where delivery is not beyond the tipple, and the operation of equipment or facilities therefor or any of such activities.

§ 1201.3   Determination as to electric lines.

The Interstate Commerce Commission is hereby authorized and directed upon request of the Mediation Board or upon complaint of any part interested to determine after hearing whether any line operated by electric power falls within the terms of this part.

§ 1201.4   Employee.

The term "employee" as used in this part includes every person in the service of a carrier (subject to its continuing authority to supervise and direct the manner of rendition of his service) who performs any work defined as that of an employee or subordinate official in the orders of the Interstate Commerce Commission now in effect, and as the same may be amended or interpreted by orders hereafter entered by the Commission pursuant to the authority which is hereby conferred upon it to enter orders amending or interpreting such existing orders: *Provided, however,* That no occupational classification made by order of the Interstate Commerce Commission shall be construed to define the crafts according to which railway employees may be organized by their voluntary action, nor shall the jurisdiction or powers of such employee organizations be regarded as in any way limited or defined by the provisions of this Act or by the orders of the Commission.

§ 1201.5 Exceptions.

The term "employee" shall not include any individual while such individual is engaged in the physical operations consisting of the mining of coal, the preparation of coal, the handling (other than movement by rail with standard locomotives) of coal not beyond the mine tipple, or the loading of coal at the tipple.

§ 1201.6 Representatives.

The term "representative" means any person or persons, labor union, organization, or corporation designated either by a carrier or group of carriers or by its or their employees, to act for it or them.

PART 1202—RULES OF PROCEDURE

AUTHORITY: 44 Stat. 577, as amended; 45 U.S.C. 151-163.

SOURCE: 11 FR 177A-922, Sept. 11, 1946, unless otherwise noted. Redesignated at 13 FR 8740, Dec. 30, 1948.

§ 1202.1   Mediation.

The mediation services of the Board may be invoked by the parties, or either party, to a dispute between an employee or group of employees and a carrier concerning changes in rates of pay, rules, or working conditions not adjusted by the parties in conference; also, concerning a dispute not referable to the National Railroad Adjustment Board or appropriate airline adjustment board, when not adjusted in conference between the parties, or where conferences are refused. The National Mediation Board may proffer its services in case any labor emergency is found by it to exist at any time.

§ 1202.2   Interpretation of mediation agreements.

Under section 5, Second, of Title I of the Railway Labor Act, in any case in which a controversy arises over the meaning or application of any agreement reached through mediation, either party to said agreement, or both, may apply to the National Mediation Board for an interpretation of the meaning or application of such agreement. Upon receipt of such request, the Board shall, after a hearing of both sides, give its interpretation within 30 days.

§ 1202.3   Representation disputes.

If any dispute shall arise among a carrier's employees as to who are the representatives of such employees designated and authorized in accordance with the requirements of the Railway Labor Act, it is the duty of the Board, upon request of either party to the dispute, to investigate such dispute and certify to both parties, in writing, the name or names of individuals or organizations that have been designated and authorized to represent the employees involved in the dispute, and to certify the same to the carrier.

§ 1202.4   Secret ballot.

In conducting such investigation, the Board is authorized to take a secret ballot of the employees involved, or to utilize any other appropriate method of ascertaining the names of their duly designated and authorized representatives in such manner as shall ensure the choice of representatives by the employees without interference, influence, or coercion exercised by the carrier.

§ 1202.5   Rules to govern elections.

In the conduct of a representation election, the Board shall designate who may participate in the election, which may include a public hearing on craft or class, and establish the rules to govern the election, or may appoint a committee of three neutral persons who after hearing shall within 10 days designate the employees who may participate in the election.

§ 1202.6   Access to carrier records.

Under the Railway Labor Act the Board has access to and has power to make copies of the books and records of the carriers to obtain and utilize such information as may be necessary to fulfill its duties with respect to representatives of carrier employees.

§ 1202.7   Who may participate in elections.

As mentioned in § 1202.3, when disputes arise between parties to a representation dispute, the National Mediation Board is authorized by the Act to determine who may participate in the selection of employees representatives.

§ 1202.8   Hearings on craft or class.

In the event the contesting parties or organizations are unable to agree on the employees eligible to participate in the selection of representatives, and either party makes application by letter for a formal hearing before the Board to determine the dispute, the Board may in its discretion hold a public hearing, at which all parties interested may present their contentions and argument, and at which the carrier concerned is usually invited to present factual information. At the conclusion of such hearings the Board customarily invites all interested parties to submit briefs supporting their views, and after considering the evidence and briefs, the Board makes a determination or finding, specifying the craft or class of employees eligible to participate in the designation of representatives.

§ 1202.9   Appointment of arbitrators.

Section 5, Third, (a) of the Railway Labor Act provides in the event mediation of a dispute is unsuccessful, the Board endeavors to induce the parties to submit their controversy to arbitration. If the parties so agree, and the arbitrators named by the parties are unable to agree upon the neutral arbitrator or arbitrators, as provided in section 7 of the Railway Labor Act, it becomes the duty of the Board to name such neutral arbitrators and fix the compensation for such service. In performing this duty, the Board is required to appoint only those whom it deems wholly disinterested in the controversy, and to be impartial and without bias as between the parties thereto.

§ 1202.10   Appointment of referees.

Section 3, Third, (e) Title I of the act makes it the duty of the National Mediation Board to appoint and fix the compensation for service a neutral person known as a "referee" in any case where a division of the National Railroad Adjustment Board becomes deadlocked on an award, such referee to sit with the division and make an award. The National Mediation Board in appointing referees is bound by the same requirements that apply in the appointment of neutral arbitrators as outlined in § 1202.9

§ 1202.11   Emergency boards.

Under the terms of section 10 of the Railway Labor Act, if a dispute between a carrier and its employees is not adjusted through mediation or the other procedures prescribed by the act, and should, in the judgment of the National Mediation Board, threaten to interrupt interstate commerce to a degree such as to deprive any section of the country of essential transportation service, the Board shall notify the President, who may thereupon, in his discretion, create an emergency board to investigate and report to him respecting such dispute. An emergency board may be composed of such number of persons as the President designates, and persons so designated shall not be pecuniarily or otherwise interested in any organization of employees or any carrier. The compensation of emergency board members is fixed by the President. An emergency board is created separately in each instance, and is required to investigate the facts as to the dispute and report thereon to the President within 30 days from the date of its creation.

§ 1202.12   National Air Transport Adjustment Board.

Under section 205, Title II, of the Railway Labor Act, when in the judgment of the National Mediation Board it becomes necessary to establish a permanent national board of adjustment for the air carriers subject to the act to provide for the prompt and orderly settlement of disputes between the employees and the carriers growing out of grievances, or out of the application or interpretation of working agreements, the Board is empowered by its order made, published, and served, to direct the air carriers and labor organizations, national in scope, to select and designate four representatives to constitute a Board known as the National Air Transport Adjustment Board. Two members each shall be selected by the air carriers and the labor organizations of their employees. Up to the present time, it has not been considered necessary to establish the National Air Transport Adjustment Board.

§ 1202.13   Air carriers.

By the terms of Title II of the Railway Labor Act, which was approved April 10, 1936, all of Title I, except section 3, which relates to the National Railroad Adjustment Board, was extended to cover every common carrier by air engaged in interstate or foreign commerce, and every carrier by air transporting mail for or under contract with the United States Government, and to all employees or subordinate officials of such air carriers.

§ 1202.14   Labor members of Adjustment Board.

Section 3, First, (f) of Title I of the Railway Labor Act relating to the settlement of disputes among labor organizations as to the qualification of any such organization to participate in the selection of labor members of the Adjustment Board, places certain duties upon the National Mediation Board. This section of the act is quoted below:

(f) In the event a dispute arises as to the right of any national labor organization to participate as per paragraph (c) of this section in the selection and designation of the labor members of the Adjustment Board, the Secretary of Labor shall investigate the claim of such labor organization to participate, and if such claim in the judgment of the Secretary of Labor has merit, the secretary shall notify the Mediation Board accordingly, and within 10 days after receipt of such advice the Mediation Board shall request those national labor organizations duly qualified as per paragraph (c) of this section to participate in the selection and designation of the labor members of the Adjustment Board to select a representative. Such representatives, together with a representative likewise designated by the claimant, and a third or neutral party designated by the Mediation Board, constituting a board of three, shall within 30 days after the appointment of the neutral member investigate the claims of the labor organization desiring participation and decide whether or not it was organized in accordance with section 2, hereof, and is otherwise properly qualified to participate in the selection of the labor members of the Adjustment Board, and the findings of such boards of three shall be final and binding.

§ 1202.15   Length of briefs in NMB hearing proceedings.

(a) In the event briefs are authorized by the Board or the assigned Hearing Officer, principal briefs shall not exceed fifty (50) pages in length and reply briefs, if permitted, shall not exceed twenty-five (25) pages in length unless the participant desiring to submit a brief in excess of such limitation requests a waiver of such limitation from the Board which is received within five (5) days of the date on which the briefs were ordered or, in the case of a reply brief, within five (5) days of receipt of the principal brief, and in such cases the Board may require the filing of a summary of argument, suitably paragraphed which should be a succinct, but accurate and clear, condensation of the argument actually made in the brief.

(b) The page limitations provided by this section (§ 1202.15) are exclusive of those pages containing the table of contents, tables of citations and any copies of administrative or court decisions which have been cited in the brief. All briefs shall be submitted on standard 8½ × 11 inch paper with double spaced type.

(c) Briefs not complying with this section (§ 1202.15) will be returned promptly to their initiators.

[44 FR 10601, Feb. 22, 1979]

PART 1203—APPLICATIONS FOR SERVICE

Sec.

1203.2   Investigation of representation disputes.
1203.3   Interpretation of mediation agreements.

Authority: 44 Stat. 577, as amended; 45 U.S.C. 151-163.

Source: 11 FR 177A-923, Sept. 11, 1946, unless otherwise noted. Redesignated at 13 FR 8740, Dec. 30, 1948.

§ 1203.1   Mediation services.

Applications for the mediation services of the National Mediation Board under section 5, First, of the Railway Labor Act, may be made on printed forms N.M.B. 2, copies of which may be secured from the Board's Secretary. Such applications and all correspondence connected therewith should be submitted in duplicate. The application should show the exact nature of the dispute, the number of employees involved, name of the carrier and name of the labor organization, date of agreement between the parties, if any, date and copy of notice served by the invoking party to the other and date of final conference between the parties. Application should be signed by the highest officer of the carrier who has been designated to handle disputes under the Railway Labor Act, or by the chief executive of the labor organization, whichever party files the application. These applications, after preliminary investigation in the Board's officer, are given docket number in series "A" and the cases are assigned for mediation to Board members or to mediators on the Board's staff.

§ 1203.2 Investigation of representation disputes.

Applications for the services of the National Mediation Board under section 2, ninth, of the Railway Labor Act to investigate representation disputes among carriers' employees may be made on printed forms NMB-3, copies of which may be secured from the Board's Executive Secretary. Such applications and all correspondence connected therewith should be filed in duplicate and the applications should be accompanied by signed authorization cards from the employees composing the craft or class involved in the dispute. The applications should show specifically the name or description of the craft or class of employees involved, the name of the invoking organization, the name of the organization currently representing the employees, if any, and the estimated number of employees in each craft or class involved. The applications should be signed by the chief executive of the invoking organization, or other authorized officer of the organization. These disputes are given docket numbers in series "R".

[43 FR 30053, July 13, 1978]

§ 1203.3   Interpretation of mediation agreements.

(a) Applications may be filed with the Board's Secretary under section 5, Second, of the Railway Labor Act, for the interpretation of agreements reached in mediation under section 5, First. Such applications may be made by letter from either party to the mediation agreement stating the specific question on which an interpretation is desired.

(b) This function of the National Mediation Board is not intended to conflict with the provisions of section 3 of the Railway Labor Act. Providing for interpretation of agreements by the National Railroad Adjustment Board. Many complete working agreements are revised with the aid of the Board's mediating services, and it has been the Board's policy that disputes involving the interpretation or application of such agreements should be handled by the Adjustment Board. Under this section of the law the Board when called upon may only consider and render an interpretation on the specific terms of an agreement actually signed in mediation, and not for matters incident or corollary thereto.

PART 1204—LABOR CONTRACTS

Sec.
1204.1   Making and maintaining contracts.
1204.2   Arbitrary changing of contracts.
1204.3   Filing of contracts.

AUTHORITY: 44 Stat. 577, as amended; 45 U.S.C. 151-163.

SOURCE: 11 FR 177A-924, Sept. 11, 1946, unless otherwise noted. Redesignated at 13 FR 8740, Dec. 30, 1948.

§ 1204.1   Making and maintaining contracts.

It is the duty of all carriers, their officers, agents, and employees to exert every reasonable effort to make and maintain contracts covering rates of pay, rules, and working conditions.

§ 1204.2   Arbitrary changing of contracts.

No carrier, its officers, or agents shall change the rates of pay, rules, or working conditions of its employees, as a class as embodied in agreements except in the manner prescribed in such agreements or in section 6 of the Railway Labor Act.

§ 1204.3   Filing of contracts.

Section 5, Third, (e) of the Railway Labor Act requires all carriers to file with the National Mediation Board copies of all contracts in effect with organizations representing their employees, covering rates of pay, rules, and working conditions. Several thousand of such contracts are on file in the Board's Washington office and are available for inspection by interested parties.

PART 1205—NOTICES IN RE: RAILWAY LABOR ACT

AUTHORITY: 44 Stat. 577, as amended; 45 U.S.C. 151-163.

SOURCE: 11 FR 177A-924, Sept. 11, 1946, unless otherwise noted. Redesignated at 13 FR 8740, Dec. 30, 1948.

§ 1205.1 Handling of disputes.

Section 2, Eighth, of the Railway Labor Act provides that every carrier shall notify its employees by printed notices in such form and posted at such times and places as shall be specified by order of the Mediation Board and requires that all disputes between a carrier and its employees will be handled in accordance with the requirements of the act. In such notices there must be printed verbatim, in large type, the third, fourth, and fifth paragraphs of said section 2, Eighth, of the Railway Labor Act.

§ 1205.2 Employees' Bill of Rights.

The provisions of the third, fourth, and fifth paragraphs of section 2 are by law made a part of the contract of employment between the carrier and each employee and shall be binding upon the parties regardless of any other express or implied agreements between them. Under these provisions the employees are guaranteed the right to organize without interference of management, the right to determine who shall represent them, and the right to bargain collectively through such representatives. This section makes it unlawful for any carrier to require any person seeking employment to sign any contract promising to join or not to join a labor organization. Violation of the foregoing provisions is a misdemeanor under the law and subjects the offender to punishment.

§ 1205.3 General Order No. 1.

General Order No. 1, issued August 14, 1934, is the only order the Board has issued since its creation in 1934. This order sent to the President of each carrier coming under the act transmitted a sample copy of the Mediation Board's Form MB-1 known as "Notice in re: Railway Labor Act." The order prescribes that such notices are to be standard as to contents, dimensions of sheet, and size of type and that they shall be posted promptly and maintained continuously in readable condition on all the usual and customary bulletin boards giving information to employees and at such other places as may be necessary to make them accessible to all employees. Such notices must not be hidden by other papers or otherwise obscured from view.

§ 1205.4   Substantive rules.

The only substantive rules issued by the National Mediation Board are those authorized under section 2, Ninth, of the Railway Labor Act to implement the procedure of determining employee representation.

[12 FR 2451, April 16, 1947. Redesignated at 13 FR 8740, Dec. 30, 1948]

PART 1206—HANDLING REPRESENTATION DISPUTES UNDER THE RAILWAY LABOR ACT

AUTHORITY: 44 Stat. 577, as amended; 45 U.S.C. 151-163.

SOURCE: 12 FR 3083, May 10, 1947, unless otherwise noted. Redesignated at 13 FR 8740, Dec. 30, 1948.

§ 1206.1   Run-off elections.

(a) If in an election among any craft or class no organization or individual receives a majority of the legal votes cast, or in the event of a tie vote, a second or run-off election shall be held forthwith: *Provided,* That a written request by an individual or organization entitled to appear on the run-off ballot is submitted to the Board within ten (10) days after the date of the report of results of the first election.

(b) In the event a run-off election is authorized by the Board, the names of the two individuals or organizations which received the highest number of votes cast in the first election shall be placed on the run-off ballot, and no blank line on which voters may write in the name of any organization or individual will be provided on the run-off ballot.

(c) Employees who were eligible to vote at the conclusion of the first election shall be eligible to vote in the run-off election except (1) those employees whose employment relationship has terminated, and (2) those employees who are no longer employed in the craft or class.

§ 1206.2   Percentage of valid authorizations required to determine existence of a representation dispute.

(a) Where the employees involved in a representation dispute are represented by an individual or labor organization, either local or national in scope and are covered by a valid existing contract between such representative and the carrier a showing of proved authorizations (checked and verified as to date, signature, and employment status) from at least a majority of the craft or class must be made before the National Mediation Board will authorize an election or otherwise determine the representation desires of the employees under the provisions of section 2, Ninth, of the Railway Labor Act.

(b) Where the employees involved in a representation dispute are unrepresented, a showing of proved authorizations from at least thirty-five (35) percent of the employees in the craft or class must be made before the National Mediation Board will authorize an election or otherwise determine the representation desires of the employees under the provisions of section 2, Ninth, of the Railway Labor Act.

§ 1206.3   Age of authorization cards.

Authorizations must be signed and dated in the employee's own handwriting or witnessed mark. No authorizations will be accepted by the National Mediation Board in any employee representation dispute which bear a date prior to one year before the date of the application for the investigation of such dispute.

§ 1206.4   Time limits on applications.

Except in unusual or extraordinary circumstances, the National Mediation Board will not accept an application for investigation of a representation dispute among employees of a carrier:

(a) For a period of two (2) years from the date of a certification covering the same craft or class of employees on the same carrier, and

(b) For a period of one (1) year from the date on which:

(1) The Board dismissed a docketed application after having conducted an election among the same craft or class of employees on the same carrier and less than a majority of eligible voters particpated in the election; or

(2) The Board dismissed a docketed application covering the same craft or class of employees on the same carrier because no dispute existed as defined in § 1206.2 of these Rules; or

(3) The Board dismissed a docketed application after the applicant withdrew an application covering the same craft or class of employees on the same carrier after the application was docketed by the Board.

[44 FR 10602, Feb. 22, 1979]

§ 1206.5 Necessary evidence of intervenor's interest in a representation dispute.

In any representation dispute under the provisons of section 2, Ninth, of the Railway Labor Act, an intervening individual or organization must produce proved authorization from at least thirty-five (35) percent of the craft or class of employees involved to warrant placing the name of the intervenor on the ballot.

§ 1206.6 Eligibility of dismissed employees to vote.

Dismissed employees whose requests for reinstatement account of wrongful dismissal are pending before proper authorities, which includes the National Railroad Adjustment Board or other appropriate adjustment board, are eligible to participate in elections among the craft or class of employees in which they are employed at time of dismissal. This does not include dismissed employees whose guilt has been determined, and who are seeking reinstatement on a leniency basis.

§ 1206.7 Construction of this part.

The rules and regulations in this part shall be liberally construed to effectuate the purposes and provisions of the act.

§ 1206.8 Amendment or recission of rules in this part.

(a) Any rule or regulation in this part may be amended or rescinded by the Board at any time.

(b) Any interested person may petition the Board, in writing, for the issuance, amendment, or repeal of a rule or regulation in this part. An original and three copies of such petition shall be filed with the Board in Washington, D.C., and shall state the rule or regulation proposed to be issued, amended, or repealed, together with a statement of grounds in support of such petition.

(c) Upon the filing of such petition, the Board shall consider the same, and may thereupon either grant or deny the petition in whole or in part, conduct an appropriate hearing thereon and make other disposition of the petition. Should the petition be denied in whole or in part, prompt notice shall be given of the denial, accompanied by a simple statement of the grounds unless the denial is self-explanatory.

PART 1207—ESTABLISHMENT OF SPECIAL ADJUSTMENT BOARDS

1207.3   Compensation of neutrals.
1207.4   Designation of PL Boards, filing of agreements, and disposition of records.

AUTHORITY: 44 Stat. 577, as amended; 45 U.S.C. 151-163.

SOURCE: 31 FR 14644, Nov. 17, 1966, unless otherwise noted.

§ 1207.1   Establishment of special adjustment boards (PL Boards).

Pub. L. 89-456 [80 Stat. 208] governs procedures to be followed by carriers and representatives of employees in the establishment and functioning of special adjustment boards, hereinafter referred to as PL Boards. Pub. L. 89-456 requires action by the National Mediation Board in the following circumstances:

(a) *Designation of party member of PL Board.* Pub. L. 89-456 provides that within thirty (30) days from the date a written request is made by an employee representative upon a carrier, or by a carrier upon an employee representative, for the establishment of a PL Board, an agreement establishing such a Board shall be made. If, however, one party fails to designate a member of the Board, the party making the request may ask the Mediation Board to designate a member on behalf of the other party. Upon receipt of such request, the Mediation Board will notify the party which failed to designate a partisan member for the establishment of a PL Board of the receipt of the request. The Mediation Board will then designate a representative on behalf of the party upon whom the request was made. This representative will be an individual associated in interest with the party he is to represent. The designee, together with the member appointed by the party requesting the establishment of the PL Board, shall constitute the Board.

(b) *Appointment of a neutral to determine matters concerning the establishment and/or jurisdiction of a PL Board.* (1) When the members of a PL Board constituted in accordance with paragraph (a) of this section, for the purpose of resolving questions concerning the establishment of the Board and/or its jurisdiction, are unable to resolve these matters, then and in that event, either party may ten (10) days thereafter request the Mediation Board to appoint a neutral member to determine these procedural issues.

(2) Upon receipt of this request, the Mediation Board will notify the other party to the PL Board. The Mediation Board will then designate a neutral member to sit with the PL Board and resolve the procedural issues in dispute. When the neutral has determined the procedural issues in dispute, he shall cease to be a member of the PL Board.

(c) *Appointment of neutral to sit with PL Boards and dispose of disputes.* (1) When the members of a PL Board constituted by agreement of the parties, or by the appointment of a party member by the Mediation Board, as described in paragraph (a) of this section, are unable within ten (10) days after their failure to agree upon an award to agree upon the selection of a neutral person, either member of the Board may request the Mediation

Board to appoint such neutral person and upon receipt of such request, the Mediation Board shall promptly make such appointment.

(2) A request for the appointment of a neutral under paragraph (b) of this section or this paragraph (c) shall;

(i) Show the authority for the request—Pub. L. 89-456, and

(ii) Define and list the proposed specific issues or disputes to be heard.

§ 1207.2   Requests for Mediation Board action.

(a) Requests for the National Mediation Board to appoint neutrals or party representatives should be made on NMB Form 5.

(b) Those authorized to sign request on behalf of parties:

(1) The "representative of any craft or class of employees of a carrier," as referred to in Pub. L. 89-456, making request for Mediation Board action, shall be either the General Chairman, Grand Lodge Officer (or corresponding officer of equivalent rank), or the Chief Executive of the representative involved. A request signed by a General Chairman or Grand Lodge Officer (or corresponding officer of equivalent rank) shall bear the approval of the Chief Executive of the employee representative.

(2) The "carrier representative" making such a request for the Mediation Board's action shall be the highest carrier officer designated to handle matters arising under the Railway Labor Act.

(c) Docketing of PL Board agreements: The National Mediation Board will docket agreements establishing PL Board, which agreements meet the requirements of coverage as specified in Pub. L. 89-456. No neutral will be appointed under § 1207.1(c) until the agreement establishing the PL Board has been docketed by the Mediation Board.

§ 1207.3   Compensation of neutrals.

(a) *Neutrals appointed by the National Mediation Board.* All neutral persons appointed by the National Mediation Board under the provisions of § 1207.1 (b) and (c) will be compensated by the Mediation Board in accordance with legislative authority. Certificates of appointment will be issued by the Mediation Board in each instance.

(b) *Neutrals selected by the parties.* (1) In cases where the party members of a PL Board created under Pub. L. 89-456 mutually agree upon a neutral person to be a member of the Board, the party members will jointly so notify the Mediation Board, which Board will then issue a certificate of appointment to the neutral and arrange to compensate him as under paragraph (a) of this section.

(2) The same procedure will apply in cases where carrier and employee representatives are unable to agree upon the establishment and jurisdiction of a PL Board, and mutually agree upon a procedural neutral person to sit with them as a member and determine such issues.

§ 1207.4   Designation of PL Boards, filing of agreements, and disposition of records.

(a) *Designation of PL Boards.* All special adjustment boards created under Pub. L. 89-456 will be designated PL Boards, and will be numbered serially, commencing with No. 1, in the order of their docketing by the National Mediation Board.

(b) *Filing of agreements.* The original agreement creating the PL Board under Public Law 89-456 shall be filed with the National Mediation Board at the time it is executed by the parties. A copy of such agreement shall be filed by the parties with the Administrative Officer of the National Railroad Adjustment Board, Chicago, Ill.

(c) *Disposition of records.* Since the provisions of section 2(a) of Public Law 89-456 apply also to the awards of PL Boards created under this Act, two copies of all awards made by the PL Boards, together with the record of proceedings upon which such awards are based, shall be forwarded by the neutrals who are members of such Boards, or by the parties in case of disposition of disputes by PL Boards without participation of neutrals, to the Administrative Officer of the National Railroad Adjustment Board, Chicago, Ill., for filing, safekeeping, and handling under the provisions of section 2(q), as may be required.

PART 1208—AVAILABILITY OF INFORMATION

Sec.
1208.1   Purpose.
1208.2   Production or disclosure of material or information.
1208.3   General policy.
1208.4   Material relating to representation function.
1208.5   Material relating to mediation function—confidential.
1208.6   Fees—duplication costs and search.
1208.7   Compliance with subpoenas.

AUTHORITY: 44 Stat. 577, as amended; 45 U.S.C. 151-163.

SOURCE: 39 FR 1751, Jan. 14, 1974, unless otherwise noted.

§ 1208.1   Purpose.

The purpose of this part is to set forth the basic policies of the National Mediation Board and the National Railroad Adjustment Board in regard to the availability and disclosure of information in the possession of the NMB and the NRAB.

§ 1208.2   Production or disclosure of material or information.

(a) *Requests for identifiable records and copies.* (1) All requests for National Mediation Board records shall be filed in writing by mailing the request or delivering it to the Executive Secretary, National Mediation Board, Washington, D.C. 20572, except that requests for records of the National Railroad Adjustment Board shall be in writing and addressed to the Administrative Officer, National Railroad Adjustment Board, 220 South State Street, Chicago, Illinois 60604.

(2) The request shall reasonably describe the records being sought in a manner which permits identification and location of the records.

(i) If the description is insufficient to locate the records, the National Mediation Board will so notify the person making the request and indicate the additional information needed to identify the records requested.

(ii) Every reasonable effort shall be made by the Board to assist in the identification and location of the records sought.

(3) Upon receipt of a request for records the Executive Secretary shall maintain records in reference thereto which shall include the date and time received, the name and address of the requester, the nature of the records requested, the action taken, the date the determination letter is sent to the requester, appeals and action thereon, the date any records are subsequently furnished, the number of staff hours and grade levels of persons who spent time responding to the request and the payment requested and received.

(4) All time limitations established pursuant to this section with respect to processing initial requests and appeals shall commence at the time a written request for records is received at the Board's offices in Washington, D.C., except for requests directed to the National Railroad Adjustment Board pursuant to § 1208.2(a)(1) in which case the time limit shall commence when the request is received at the NRAB's office in Chicago.

(i) An oral request for records shall not begin any time requirement.

(b) *Processing the Initial Request.* (1) Time limitations. Within 10 working days (excepting Saturdays, Sundays, and working holidays) after a request for records is received, the Executive Secretary shall determine and inform the requester by letter whether or the extent to which the request will be complied with, unless an extension is taken under paragraph (b)(3) of this section.

(2) Such reply letter shall include:

(i) A reference to the specific exemption or exemptions under the Freedom of Information Act authorizing the withholding of the record, a brief explanation of how the exemption applies to the record withheld.

(ii) The name or names and positions of the person or persons, other than the Executive Secretary, responsible for the denial.

(iii) A statement that the denial may be appealed within thirty days by writing to the Chairman, National Mediation Board, Washington, D.C. 20572, and that judicial review will thereafter be available in the district in which the requester resides, or has his principal place of business, or the district in which the agency records are situated, or the District of Columbia.

(3) Extension of time. In unusual circumstances as specified in this paragraph, the Executive Secretary may extend the time for initial determina-

tion on requests up to a total of ten days (excluding Saturdays, Sundays, and legal public holidays). Extensions shall be granted in increments of five days or less and shall be made by written notice to the requester which sets forth the reason for the extension and the date on which a determination is expected to be dispatched. As used in this paragraph "unusual circumstances" means, but only to the extent necessary to the proper processing of the request:

(i) The need to search for and collect the requested records from field facilities or other establishments that are separate from the office processing the request;

(ii) The need to search for, collect, and appropriately examine a voluminous amount of separate and distinct records which are demanded in a single request; or

(iii) The need for consultation, which shall be conducted with all practicable speed, with another agency or another division having substantial interest in the determination of the request, or the need for consultation among components of the agency having substantial subject matter interest therein.

(4) Treatment of delay as a denial. If no determination has been dispatched at the end of the ten-day period, or the last extension thereof, the requester may deem his request denied, and exercise a right of appeal, in accordance with § 1208.2(c). When no determination can be dispatched within the applicable time limit, the responsible official shall nevertheless continue to process the request; on expiration of the time limit he shall inform the requester of the reason for the delay, of the date on which a determination may be expected to be dispatched, and of his right to treat the delay as a denial and to appeal to the Chairman of the Board in accordance with § 1208.2(c) and he may ask the requester to forego appeal until a determination is made.

(c) *Appeals to the Chairman of the Board.* (1) When a request for records has been denied in whole or in part by the Executive Secretary or other person authorized to deny requests, the requester may, within thirty days of its receipt, appeal the denial to the Chairman of the Board. Appeals to the Chairman shall be in writing, addressed to the Chairman, National Mediation Board, Washington, D.C. 20572.

(2) The Chairman of the Board will act upon the appeal within twenty working days (excluding Saturdays, Sundays and legal public holidays) of its receipt unless an extension is made under paragraph (c)(3) of this section.

(3) In unusual circumstances as specified in this paragraph, the time for action on an appeal may be extended up to ten days (excluding Saturdays, Sundays and legal public holidays) minus any extension granted at the initial request level pursuant to § 1208.2(b)(3). Such extension shall be made by written notice to the requester which sets forth the reason for the extension and the date on which a determination is expected to be dispatched. As used in this paragraph "unusual circumstances" means, but only to the extent necessary to the proper processing of the appeal:

(i) The need to search for and collect the requested records from field facilities or other establishments that are separate from the office processing the request;

(ii) The need to search for, collect, and appropriately examine a voluminous amount of separate and distinct records which are demanded in a single request; or

(iii) The need for consultation, which shall be conducted with all practicable speed, with another agency or another division having substantial interest in the determination of the request or the need for consultation among components of the agency having substantial subject matter interest therein.

(4) *Treatment of delay as a denial.* If no determination on the appeal has been dispatched at the end of the twenty-day period or the last extension thereof, the requester is deemed to have exhausted his administrative remedies, giving rise to a right of review in a district court of the United States as specified in 5 U.S.C. 552(a)(4). When no determination can be dispatched within the applicable time limit, the appeal will nevertheless continue to be processed; on expiration of the time limit the requester shall be informed of the reason for the delay, of the date on which a determination may be expected to be dispatched, and of his right to seek judicial review in the United States district court in the district in which he resides or has his principal place of business, the district in which the Board records are situated or the District of Columbia. The requester may be asked to forego judicial review until determination of the appeal.

(d) *Indexes of Certain Records.* (1) The National Mediation Board at its office in Washington, D.C. will maintain, make available for public inspection and copying, and publish quarterly (unless the Board determines by order published in the FEDERAL REGISTER that such publication would be unnecessary or impracticable) a current index of the materials available at the Board offices which are required to be indexed by 5 U.S.C. 552(a)(2).

(i) A copy of such index shall be available at cost from the National Mediation Board, Washington, D.C. 20572.

(2) The National Railroad Adjustment Board at its offices in Chicago, Illinois will maintain, make available for public inspection and copying, and publish quarterly (unless the Board determines by order published in the FEDERAL REGISTER that such publication would be unnecessary or impracticable) a current index of the materials available at the Board offices which are required to be indexed by 5 U.S.C. 552(a)(2).

[42 FR 43627, Aug. 30, 1977]

§ 1208.3   General policy.

(a) Public policy and the successful effectuation of the NMB's mission require that Board members and the employees of the NMB maintain a reputation for impartiality and integrity. Labor and management and other interested parties participating in mediation efforts must have assurance, as must labor organizations and individuals involved in questions of representation, that confidential information disclosed to Board members and employees of the NMB will not be divulged, voluntarily or by compulsion.

(b) Notwithstanding this general policy, the Board will under all circumstances endeavor to make public as much information as can be allowed.

§ 1208.4 Material relating to representation function.

(a) The documents constituting the record of a case, such as the notices of hearing, motions, rulings, orders, stenographic reports of the hearings, briefs, exhibits, findings upon investigation, determinations of craft or class, interpretations, dismissals, withdrawals, and certifications, are matters of official record and are available for inspection and examination during the usual business hours at the Board's offices in Washington.

(b) This part notwithstanding, the Board will treat as confidential the evidence submitted in connection with a representation dispute and the investigatory file pertaining to the representation function.

§ 1208.5 Material relating to mediation function—confidential.

(a) All files, reports, letters, memoranda, documents, and papers (hereinafter referred to as confidential documents) relating to the mediation function of the NMB, in the custody of the NMB or its employees relating to or acquired in their mediatory capacity under any applicable section of the Railway Labor Act of 1926, as amended, are hereby declared to be confidential. No such confidential documents or the material contained therein shall be disclosed to any unauthorized person, or be taken or withdrawn, copied or removed from the custody of the NMB or its employees by any person or by any agent of such person or his representative without the explicit consent of the NMB.

(b) However, the following specific documents: Invocation or proffer of mediation, the reply or replies of the parties, the proffer of arbitration and replies thereto, and the notice of failure of mediatory efforts in cases under section 5, First of the Railway Labor Act, as amended, are matters of official record and are available for inspection and examination.

(c) Interpretations of mediation agreements by the NMB, arising out of section 5, Second, of the Railway Labor Act, as amended, are public records and are therefore open for public inspection and examination.

§ 1208.6 Fees—duplication costs and search.

(a)(1) Unless waived in accordance with the provisions of § 1208.62, the following fees shall be imposed for the reproduction of any record disclosed pursuant to this part.

(i) *Copying of records.* Fifteen cents per copy of each page.

(ii) *Copying of microfilm.* Fifty cents per microfilm frame.

(iii) *Clerical searches.* $1.80 for each one quarter hour spent by clerical personnel searching for and producing a requested record, including time spent copying any record.

(iv) *Non-clerical searches.* $4.10 for each one quarter hour spent by professional or managerial personnel searching for and producing a requested record, including time spent copying any record.

(v) *Certification or authentication of records.* $1.00 per certification or authentication.

(vi) *Forwarding material to destination.* Postage, insurance and special fees will be charged on an actual cost basis.

(2)(i) No charge shall be assessed for time spent in resolving legal or policy questions relating to the documents or in examining records for the purpose of deleting nondisclosable portions thereof.

(ii) No charge shall be assessed for time spent in monitoring an individual who examines documents at the Board's offices.

(3) Payment shall be made by check or money order payable to "United States Treasury."

(b)(1) No fee shall be charged for disclosure of records pursuant to this part where:

(i) The cost of providing the records is less than $5.00.

(ii) The records are requested by a congressional committee or subcommittee, a Federal court, a Federal department or agency, or the General Accounting Office.

(2)(i) The Executive Secretary may waive payment of fees, in whole or in part, when he determines that the person making the request is indigent.

(ii) A person seeking such a determination shall petition the Executive Secretary in writing stating the reasons therefore.

(iii) Determinations made pursuant to this provision will be made within the discretion of the agency.

(3)(i) The Executive Secretary may reduce or waive payment of fees in whole or in part when he determines that such reduction or waiver is in the public interest because furnishing the information can be considered as primarily benefiting the general public.

(ii) Determinations pursuant to this provision shall be made within the discretion of the agency.

(4) No fee shall be charged if a record requested is not found or for any record that is determined to be totally exempt from disclosure.

[42 FR 43628, Aug. 30, 1977]

§ 1208.7   Compliance with subpoenas.

(a) No person connected in any official way with the NMB shall produce or present any confidential records of the Board or testify on behalf of any party to any cause pending in any court, or before any board, commission, committee, tribunal, investigatory body, or administrative agency of the U.S. Government, or any State or Territory of the United States, or the District of Columbia, or any municipality with respect to matters coming to his knowledge in his official capacity or with respect to any information contained in confidential documents of the NMB, whether in answer to any order, subpoena, subpoena duces tecum, or otherwise without the express written consent of the Board.

(b) Whenever any subpoena or subpoena duces tecum calling for confidential documents, or the information contained therein, or testimony as described above shall have been served on any such person, he will appear in answer thereto, and unless otherwise expressly permitted by the Board, respectfully decline, by reason of this section, to produce or present such confidential documents or to give such testimony.

PART 1209—PUBLIC OBSERVATION OF NATIONAL MEDIATION BOARD MEETINGS

Sec.
1209.01   Scope and purpose.
1209.02   Definitions.
1209.03   Conduct of National Mediation Board business.
1209.04   Open meetings.
1209.05   Closing of meetings; reasons therefor.
1209.06   Action necessary to close meetings; record of votes.
1209.07   Notice of meetings; public announcement and publication.
1209.08   Transcripts, recordings or minutes of closed meetings; retention; public availability.
1209.09   Requests for records under Freedom of Information Act.
1209.10   Capacity of public observers.

Authority: 5 U.S.C. 552b(g), 44 Stat. 577, as amended (45 U.S.C. 151 et seq.)

Source: 42 FR 60739, Nov. 29, 1977, unless otherwise noted.

§ 1209.01   Scope and purpose.

(a) The provisions of this part are intended to implement the requirements of section 3(a) of the Government in the Sunshine Act, 5 U.S.C. 552b.

(b) It is the policy of the National Mediation Board that the public is entitled to the fullest practicable information regarding its decisionmaking processes. It is the purpose of this part to provide the public with such information while protecting the rights of individuals and the ability of the agency to carry out its responsibilities.

§ 1209.02   Definitions.

For purposes of this part:
(a) The terms "Board" or "Agency" mean the National Mediation Board, a collegial body composed of three members appointed by the President with the advice and consent of the Senate.

(b) The term "meeting" means the deliberations of at least two members of the Board where such deliberations determine or result in the joint conduct or disposition of official agency business, but does not include deliberations required or permitted or with respect to any information proposed to be withheld under by 5 U.S.C. 552b(d) or (e)/5 U.S.C. 552b(c).

§ 1209.03   Conduct of National Mediation Board business.

Members shall not jointly conduct or dispose of agency business other than in accordance with this part.

§ 1209.04   Open meetings.

Every portion of every Board meeting shall be open to public observation except as otherwise provided by § 1209.05 of this part.

§ 1209.05   Closing of meetings; reasons therefor.

(a) Except where the Board determines that the public interest requires otherwise, meetings, or portions thereof, shall not be open to public observation where the deliberations concern the issuance of a subponea, the Board's participation in a civil action or proceeding or an arbitration, or the initiation, conduct or disposition by the Board of any matter involving a determination on the record after opportunity for a hearing, or any court proceeding collateral or ancillary thereto.

(b) Except where the Board determines that the public interest requires otherwise, the Board also may close meetings, or portions thereof, when the deliberations concern matters or information falling within the scope of 5 U.S.C. 552b (c)(1) (secret matters concerning national defense or foreign policy); (c)(2) (internal personnel rules and practices); (c)(3) (matters specifically exempted from disclosure by statute); (c)(4) (trade secrets and commercial or financial information obtained from a person and privileged or confidential); (c)(5) (matters of alleged criminal conduct or formal censure); (c)(6) (personal information where disclosure would cause a clearly unwarranted invasion of personal privacy); (c)(7) (certain materials or information from investigatory files compiled for law enforcement purposes); or (c)(9)(B) (disclosure would significantly frustrate implementation of a proposed agency action).

§ 1209.06   Action necessary to close meetings; record of votes.

A meeting shall be closed to public observation under § 1209.05, only when a majority of the members of the Board who will participate in the meeting vote to take such action.

(a) When the meeting deliberations concern matters specified in § 1209.05(a), the Board members shall vote at the beginning of the meeting, or portion thereof, on whether to close such meeting, or portion thereof, to public observation, and on whether the public interest requires that a meeting which may properly be closed should nevertheless be open to public observation A record of such vote, reflecting the vote of each member of the Board, shall be kept and made available to the public at the earliest practicable time.

(b) When the meeting deliberations concerns matters specified in § 1209.05(b), the Board shall vote on whether to close such meeting, or portion thereof, to public observation, and on whether the public interest requires that a meeting which may properly be closed should nevertheless be open to public observation. The vote shall be taken at a time sufficient to permit inclusion of information concerning the open or closed status of the meeting in the public announcement thereof. A single vote may be taken with respect to a series of meetings at which the deliberations will concern the same particular matters where subsequent meetings in the series are scheduled to be held within one day after the vote is taken.

(c) Whenever any person whose interests may be directly affected by deliberations during a meeting, or a portion thereof, requests that the Board close that meeting, or portion thereof, to public observation for any of the reasons specified in 5 U.S.C. 552b(c)(5) (matters of alleged criminal conduct or formal censure), (c)(6) (personal information where disclosure would cause a clearly unwarranted invasion of personal privacy), or (c)(7) (certain materials or information from investigatory files compiled for law enforcement purposes), the Board members participating in the meeting upon request of any one member of the Board, shall vote on whether to close such meeting, or any portion thereof, for that reason. A record of such vote, reflecting the vote of each member of the Board participating in the meeting, shall be kept and made available to the public within one day after the vote is taken.

(d) After public announcement of a meeting as provided in § 1209.07 of this part, a meeting, or portion thereof, announced as closed may be opened or a meeting, or portion thereof, announced as open may be closed, only if a majority of the members of the Board who will participate in the meeting determine by a recorded vote that Board business so requires and that an earlier announcement of the change was not possible. The change made and the vote of each member on the change shall be announced publicly at the earliest practicable time.

(e) Before a meeting may be closed pursuant to § 1209.05 the General Counsel of the Board shall certify that in his or her opinion the meeting may properly be closed to public observation. The certification shall set forth each applicable exemptive provision for such closing. The certification shall be retained by the agency and made publicly available as soon as practicable.

§ 1209.07   Notice of meetings; public announcement and publication.

(a) A public announcement setting forth the time, place and subject matter of meetings or portions thereof closed to public observation pursuant to the provisions of § 1209.05(a) of this part, shall be made at the earliest practicable time.

(b) Except for meetings closed to public observation pursuant to the provisions of § 1209.05(a) of this part, the agency shall make public announcement of each meeting at least 7 days before the scheduled date of the meeting. The announcement shall specify the time, place and subject matter of the meeting, whether it is to be open to public observation or closed, and the name, address and phone number of an agency official designated to respond to requests for information about the meeting. The 7 day period for advance notice may be shortened only upon a determination by a majority of the members of the Board who will participate in the meeting that agency business requires that such meeting be called at an earlier date, in which event the public announcement shall be made at the earliest practicable time. A record of the vote to schedule a meeting at an earlier date shall be kept and made available to the public.

(c) Within one day after a vote to close a meeting, or any portion thereof, pursuant to the provisions of § 1209.05(b) of this part, the agency shall make publicly available a full written explanation of its action closing the meeting, or portion thereof, together with a list of all persons expected to attend the meeting and their affiliation.

(d) If after a public announcement required by paragraph (b) of this section has been made, the time and place of the meeting are changed, a public announcement of such changes shall be made at the earliest practicable time. The subject matter of the meeting may be changed after public announcement thereof only if a majority of the members of the Board who will participate in the meeting determine that agency business so requires and that no earlier announcement of the change was possible. When such a change in subject matter is approved a public announcement of the change shall be made at the earliest practicable time. A record of the vote to change the subject matter of the meeting shall be kept and made available to the public.

(e) All announcements or changes thereof issued pursuant to the provisions of paragraphs (b) and (d) of this section, or pursuant to the provisions of § 1209.06(d), shall be submitted for publication in the FEDERAL REGISTER immediately following their release to the public.

(f) Announcement of meeting made pursuant to the provisions of this section shall be posted on a bulletin board maintained for such purpose at the Board's offices, 1425 K Street, N.W., Washington, D.C. Interested individuals or organizations may request the Executive Secretary, National Mediation Board, Washington, D.C. 20572 to place them on a mailing list for receipt of such announcements.

§ 1209.08 Transcripts, recordings or minutes of closed meetings; retention; public availability.

(a) For every meeting or portion thereof closed under the provisions of § 1209.05, the presiding officer shall prepare a statement setting forth the time and place of the meeting and the persons present, which statement shall be retained by the agency. For each such meeting or portion thereof there also shall be maintained a complete transcript or electronic recording of the proceedings, except that for meetings closed pursuant to § 1209.05(a) the Board may, in lieu of a transcript or electronic recording, maintain a set of minutes fully and accurately summarizing any action taken, the reason therefor and views thereof, documents considered, and the members' vote on each roll call vote.

(b) The agency shall maintain a complete verbatim transcript, a complete electronic recording, or a complete set of minutes for each meeting or portion thereof closed to public observation, for a period of at least one year after the close of the agency proceeding of which the meeting was a part, but in no event for a period of less than two years after such meeting.

(c) The agency shall make promptly available to the public copies of transcripts, electronic recordings or minutes maintained as provided in paragraphs (a) and (b) of this section, except to the extent the items therein contain information which the agency determines may be withheld pursuant to the provisions of 5 U.S.C. 552b(c).

(d) Upon request in accordance with the provisions of this paragraph and except to the extent they contain information which the agency determines may be withheld pursuant to the provisions of 5 U.S.C. 552b(c), copies of transcripts or minutes, or transcriptions of electronic recordings including the identification of speakers, shall be furnished subject to the payment of duplication costs in accordance with the schedule of fees set forth in § 1208.06 of the Board's Rules, and the actual cost of transcription. Requests for copies of transcripts or minutes, or transcriptions of electronic recordings of Board meetings shall be directed to the Executive Secretary, National Mediation Board, Washington, D.C. 20572. Such requests shall reasonably identify the records sought and include a statement that whatever costs are involved in furnishing the records will be acceptable or, alternatively, that costs will be acceptable up to a specified amount. The Board may determine to require prepayment of such costs.

§ 1209.09 Requests for records under Freedom of Information Act.

Requests to review or obtain copies of agency records other than notices or records prepared under this part may be pursued in accordance with the Freedom of Information Act (5 U.S.C. 552). Part 1208 of the Board's Rules addresses the requisite procedures under that Act.

§ 1209.10 Capacity of public observers.

The public may attend open Board meetings for the sole purpose of observation. Observers may not participate in meetings unless expressly invited or otherwise interfere with the conduct and disposition of agency business. When a portion of a meeting is closed to the public, observers will leave the meeting room upon request to enable discussion of the exempt matter therein under consideration.

NATIONAL MEDIATION BOARD
REPRESENTATION MANUAL

NATIONAL MEDIATION BOARD

REPRESENTATION MANUAL

NOTICE

This manual provides general procedural guidance to the NMB's staff with respect to the processing of representation cases before the National Mediation Board. Such procedural guidance is not required by or subject to the Administrative Procedure Act. The provisions of this manual are neither obligatory upon the Members of the Board nor do they constitute the exclusive procedure for the NMB's investigation of representation matters pursuant to the Railway Labor Act.

Stephen E. Crable
Chief of Staff

This manual is effective November 1, 1995 and will replace all previous versions of the manual as of that date.

Representation Manual
Table of Contents

SECTION

1.0 INITIAL NMB PROCESSING

Upon receipt of an "Application for Investigation of Representation Dispute" (Form NMB-3), the Board's office staff will assign an appropriate identification number and initiate any necessary preliminary correspondence.

1.1   *Ex Parte Communications*

1.101   Certain *ex parte* communications to the NMB in connection with pending representation matters are prohibited by this Section. The specific scope of these prohibitions is defined and specified in Subsections 1.102 through 1.104.

1.102   An "*ex parte* communication" is an oral communication to the NMB in which all participants in the particular representation matter are not present at the time it is made, or it is a written communication to the NMB not served simultaneously on all participants in that proceeding.

1.103   A "representation matter" is any proceeding filed with the NMB pursuant to Section 2, Ninth of the Railway Labor Act. A representation matter ceases to be "pending" for purposes of Section 1.1 when final agency action has been taken and the time period for filing a motion for reconsideration under Section 15.0 has expired.

1.104   No *ex parte* communications subject to this Section may be conducted with the Members of the Board or their Confidential Assistants. No *ex parte* communications subject to this Section involving substantive matters may be conducted with the Hearing Officer assigned to the particular case or proceeding which is the proposed topic of the communications.

1.2   *Communication Guidelines Generally*

1.201   General information on representation matters not pending with the NMB is available to the public through sources established by the Chief of Staff's Office.

1.202   The Chief of Staff's Office is the contact point for representation matters filed with the Board. The Chief of Staff, may at his/her discretion, designate an NMB employee for further contacts in a particular case on a basis which is not inconsistent with Section 1.1. Likewise, the Mediator may, at his/her discretion, designate another NMB employee to perform certain tasks on a basis that is not inconsistent with Section 1.1.

1.203   Within five (5) working days of the date of the NMB's Docketing letter, the representatives of the participants must file a Notice of Appearance with the Board, including name, title, address, telephone and FAX number(s). Notices of Appearance will be accepted from no more than three (3) individuals representing the same participant.

1.204   Copies of Notices of Appearance and all other submissions to the NMB, except privileged documents, shall be simultaneously served on all other participants by the same method as used for service on the NMB, if available, or by a substantially similar method. All submissions must be accompanied by a signed certificate of service. When the Mediator is the addressee of correspondence, a copy also should be simultaneously served on the Chief of Staff. Submissions not in compliance with the foregoing simultaneous service provisions will not be considered except in extraordinary circumstances.

2.0 MEDIATOR'S INVESTIGATION

2.1   *Mediator's Objective*

During the processing of a representation case, the Mediator's function is to investigate any question concerning representation in accordance with the instructions of this manual and such directives as the Board may issue. The carrier is not a party to a representation dispute and has no right to participate as a party in the investigation of such a dispute. However, the carrier is a participant and has obligations under the Act to provide information and documentation to the Board. It is necessary that the investigation be conducted with extreme impartiality, thoroughness and accuracy. Detailed reporting is normally required in all cases.

2.2   *Intervention*

The deadline for requests for intervention and all supporting authorizations is the same time and date established for the applicant's final submission of authorizations in that case (see Section 6.3).

2.3   *Review and Maintenance of Loan File*

A loan file will be sent to the Mediator when a representation case is assigned for investigation. This file should be thoroughly reviewed by the Mediator before the initial contact with the participants. If the file indicates potential craft or class and/or eligibility issues, the Mediator should reexamine previous relevant NMB cases.

During the Mediator's investigation, the loan file should be kept current chronologically, and all investigative materials gathered should be contained in this file.

2.4   *Mediator Reporting*

The Mediator should communicate reports on a basis current enough that the Board will be sufficiently and timely apprised of all relevant information such as, "Official Eligibility List", challenges or objections, Mediator decisions including rationale, appeal deadlines and any unusual developments.

3.0 COMMENCING THE INVESTIGATION

In every case, the Chief of Staff and Mediator will confer to determine whether an investigation will be conducted on-site or off-site or both.

When an on-site investigation is conducted, separate or joint meetings may be held at the Mediator's discretion.

3.1   *Access to Books and Records*

The NMB has a right by statute to have access to, and the power to make copies of, the books and records of carriers. The Mediator should always be aware of this right and in appropriate cases should advise carriers of this right and the Mediator's intention of using it, if necessary.

3.2   *Preliminary Information*

The Mediator should describe the procedures in processing a representation application to the participants, and the Mediator should also describe the scope of the application. The Mediator should determine whether the participants intend to raise any relevant issues concerning the application. All such issues should be reduced to writing by the participants and submitted within a time limit established by the Mediator.

3.3   *Additional Information*

The Mediator should, on a confidential basis, determine from the applicant and intervenor, if any, whether there are additional authorizations to be submitted.

3.4   *Statutory Jurisdiction*

Objections to statutory jurisdiction should be raised at the earliest possible stage of the investigation. If an issue is presented as to whether or not the company involved falls within the definition of a "carrier", the Mediator should investigate that issue. The Mediator should determine, and require supporting documents which show: (1) whether the company reports to or is regulated by the Interstate Commerce Commission or the Department of Transportation and/ or the Federal Aviation Administration; (2) the extent of the company's involvement in interstate as opposed to intrastate commerce; (3) whether the company engages in private as opposed to common carriage; (4) if it is a subsidiary involved in either rail or air transportation, the organizational and operational relationships between the subsidiary and the parent company; (5) whether, if an airline, U.S. mail is carried; (6) whether, if an airline, it engages in scheduled air transportation; (7) whether, if an airline, it interlines with a carrier covered by the RLA; (8) whether, if an airline, it provides substitute air service for a carrier covered by the RLA; (9) whether it holds a contract with a carrier covered by the RLA for the performance of services relating to air transportation; and (10) any other relevant facts regarding the company's operations. A determination of Railway Labor Act jurisdiction can only be made by the Board itself, not a Mediator.

3.5   *Cut-Off Date*

The cut-off date is the last day of the last payroll period ending prior to the date of receipt at the NMB's offices of the "Application for Investigation of Representation Dispute" (Form NMB-3).

If there are multiple payroll periods for the same craft or class (such as monthly, bimonthly, etc.) , the cut-off date will be the last day of the last payroll period ending prior to the receipt of the application.

3.6   *List of Potential Eligible Voters*

The carrier will be requested to prepare a system-wide alphabetical list of potential eligible voters. The carrier must provide three (3) copies to the Chief of Staff and serve a copy on each representative of the other participants. The list of potential eligible voters should include all individuals within the craft or class with an employee-employer relationship as of the cut-off date.

The list of potential eligible voters must identify each employee by full name, job classification or title, duty station or location and employer identification number. If no employee identification numbers exist, the list must include social security numbers.

3.7   *Forms Used to Check Validity of Authorizations*

Signature Samples: The carrier will be requested to provide forms or legible copies thereof, bearing the employees' signatures which may be used in verifying the authenticity of the authorizations.

The tax-withholding form may be preferred due to its ready accessibility and because it frequently bears the employee's most current signature on file with the carrier. Employment and insurance applications are examples of other acceptable forms.

The signature samples must be in the same order as the names on the list of potential eligible voters.

Delivery of Documents: The list of potential eligible voters and the signature samples should be delivered to the NMB's offices by the deadline set by the Board. If there is an on-site investigation, the list and signature samples should be submitted to the Mediator upon arrival on the carrier's property.

4.0   FILING AND CONTENT OF CHALLENGES AND OBJECTIONS DURING THE INVESTIGATION

The Mediator should inform the participants in writing that they may raise challenges or objections during the investigation. A challenge is defined as a question regarding the eligibility of an individual or individuals, other than status changes. Status changes are governed by Section 11.3. Any issue not dealing with eligibility is an objection. Objections dealing with jurisdiction and carrier interference can only be decided by the Board and should be referred to the Chief of Staff.

4.1   *Challenges or Objections*

All challenges or objections must be filed in writing, initially with the Mediator, with a copy to the Chief of Staff. The Mediator should require that all challenges or objections be supported by substantive evidence and argument. The Mediator should advise participants that unsupported allegations will be insufficient to overcome presumptions of eligibility or ineligibility as reflected by the list of eligible voters. In addition, when craft or class issues are involved, the Mediator should require that the objection be supported by NMB case citation.

4.2   *Timeliness*

It is within the discretion of the Mediator as to when the participants will be allowed to file challenges or objections. Due to variables such as the size of the electorate and/or the availability of information, no specific time limit will be prescribed herein. The Mediator will set a reasonable deadline for challenges or objections which will allow sufficient time for the filing of appeals of Mediator's decisions to the Board and for Board decisions before the date of the count. Except for changes in eligibility status occurring after the deadline, challenges or objections not presented by the deadline will be untimely. Changes in eligibility status occurring after the deadline will be handled as status changes subject to Section 11.3.

The Mediator may establish a deadline within which the participants can provide a response to challenges or objections filed by another participant.

4.3   *Rejection of Challenges or Objections*

Challenges or objections not supported by substantive evidence and argument will be rejected by the Mediator. Challenges or objections not provided to the Mediator by the deadline set by the Mediator will be rejected. Challenges or objections which do not meet the simultaneous service requirements of Section 1.204 will be rejected.

4.4   *Mediator's Decision on Challenges and Objections*

It is the Mediator's responsibility, based upon the information available, to issue written decisions, with a copy to the Chief of Staff, resolving properly filed challenges or objections and setting the deadline for appeal.

4.5   *Finality of Mediator's Decision*

If a Mediator's decision with regard to a challenge or objection has not been appealed to the Board within the prescribed time limit, the Mediator's decision is final.

4.6   *Appeals of Mediator's Decisions*

The Mediator's decision letter should advise the participants of their right to appeal the decisions in writing to the NMB. The decision letter should further state that appeals from any source will be denied as untimely unless received at the NMB's offices on or before the date specified within the letter. No participant shall be given more than ten (10) calendar days from the date of the decision letter for the receipt of their appeals by the NMB, unless specifically authorized by the Chief of Staff. Absent extraordinary circumstances, evidence submitted on appeal will not be considered by the Board unless it has been submitted to the Mediator initially.

4.601   *Submissions on Appeal*

The moving participant may file one initial position statement. The responding participant may file one response to the initial position statement. In addition, participants may request the opportunity to file rebuttal statements. No further submissions will be considered by the Board unless the Board determines that there are extraordinary circumstances.

4.602   *Extensions of Deadlines*

The Chief of Staff may consider granting extensions of deadlines for position statements described above, if these requests for extensions are submitted in writing and supported by good cause. Each participant will be limited to one extension of time, no greater than 10 days from the original deadline, in the course of the appeal process.

5.0 DETERMINATIONS

The Mediator should gather and evaluate pertinent information and make determinations concerning issues which may arise during the course of the investigation. In making such determinations, the Mediator should be guided by the principles outlined below as well as applicable Board precedent.

5.1   *Craft or Class*

In determining craft or class issues the Board gives consideration to all relevant elements, most important of which is the intent of the Railway Labor Act in settling disputes and promoting stable labor relations. The Mediator must consult with the Chief of Staff on all craft or class issues prior to issuing a decision. The Mediator's decision may be appealed to the Board pursuant to Section 4.6. Individual cases require consideration of facts peculiar to particular situations, but, in addition, there are general factors to be considered. These may include, among others, the composition and relative permanency of employee groupings along craft or class lines; the functions, duties, and responsibilities of the employees; the general nature of their work; and the extent of community of interest existing between job classifications. Previous decisions of the Board which bear upon the issues of the particular dispute should also be taken into account. Prior decisions of the Board in regard to craft or class on the same carrier shall be binding upon the Mediator.

5.2   *Classifications*

The Mediator will identify all job classifications which should be included in the craft or class. Careful consideration will be given to the functions, duties and responsibilities of the employees.

5.3   *Eligibility of Individuals*

5.301   *Part-Time Employees*

When investigating the eligibility of a part-time employee, the Mediator should determine (a) if the employee works an identifiable schedule during a specified time period; (b) whether the employee regularly relieves other employees; (c) what benefits the employee receives; (d) what deductions are taken from the employee's pay; and, (e) any other relevant facts which would indicate whether the employee has a regular part-time or a casual part-time employer-employee relationship.

The Mediator's determination of eligibility regarding part-time employees must take into consideration the varied operating practices on different carriers. If the individual's employment is casual, that is, where the employee has neither a regular employee-employer relationship nor scheduled work assignments, then the employee is ineligible.

5.302   *Temporary Employees*

It is established NMB policy that only those employees with a present interest regarding the craft or class in dispute are eligible to vote in an NMB representation election. Such policy is implemented with respect to temporary employees by examining whether or not the employees in question have a reasonable expectation of continued employment or re-employment in the craft or class.

5.303   *Working Regularly in the Craft or Class*

Absent unusual circumstances, employees who are working regularly in the craft or class at issue on and after the cut-off date are eligible to participate in the craft or class. Employees who leave the craft or class prior to the ballot count are not eligible. However, it is the Board's policy not to permit an employee to vote in more than one craft or class at the same time.

5.304   *Discharged Employees*

Ordinarily, discharged or terminated employees shall be ineligible unless the discharge is being appealed through the applicable grievance procedure or an action for reinstatement has been filed before either a court or a government agency of competent jurisdiction. An individual shall not be considered eligible if the grievance or court action has been finally acted upon and the discharge has been upheld prior to the count of ballots (see NMB Rules, Part 1206.6).

5.305   *Furloughed Employees*

Furloughed employees are eligible in the craft or class in which they last worked provided they retain an employee-employer relationship and have a reasonable expectation of returning to work. However, a furloughed employee regularly working in another craft or class is ineligible in the craft or class from which the employee is furloughed.

5.306   *Leave of Absence*

An employee on authorized leave of absence, including military leave, from the craft or class in dispute who is neither working in another craft or class, working for the carrier in an official capacity nor working for another carrier, is eligible in the craft or class involved in the investigation. For example, an employee on authorized leave of absence for labor organization activities is eligible, as well as an employee who is on authorized sick leave. Where the question of leave of absence is contested, the Mediator should require supporting documents to verify that a bona fide leave of absence is in effect.

5.307   *Probationary Employees*

Employees in the craft or class who are in probationary status are eligible.

5.308   *Working For Another Carrier*

An employee who would otherwise be eligible to vote under Section 5.304, 5.305, 5.306, or 5.311 who is working for a carrier other than the carrier involved in the dispute is ineligible.

5.309   *Contractor's Employees*

Individuals working for an independent subcontractor not part of the transportation system comprising the system of the carrier are ineligible.

5.310   *Individuals Based in Foreign Countries*

Only employees based within the United States and/or its possessions are subject to Railway Labor Act jurisdiction.

5.311   *Retired Employees*

Employees who have retired are ineligible to participate. However, an employee receiving physical disability payments is eligible if the employee retains an employee-employer relationship and has a reasonable expectation of returning to work.

An individual who has filed for and is receiving a disability annuity under the provisions of the Railroad Retirement Act shall *not* be an eligible voter.

5.312   *"Management Officials"*

If an individual is determined to be a management official, the individual is ineligible. The Mediator shall consider, in the investigation, whether the involved individual has the authority to discharge and/or discipline employees or to effectively recommend the same; the extent of supervisory authority; the ability to authorize and grant overtime; the authority to transfer and/or establish assignments; the authority to create carrier policy; the authority and the extent to which carrier funds may be committed; whether the authority exercised is circumscribed by operating and policy manuals; the placement of the individual in the organizational hierarchy of the carrier; and, any other relevant factors regarding the individual's duties and responsibilities.

5.313   *Preponderance*

On many carriers, employees may hold seniority rights or work regularly in more than one craft or class and work back and forth between these crafts or classes. Employees regularly assigned on the "cut-off date" to an extra board or bulletined position within the craft or class involved, will be automatically considered eligible to participate in the election. Employees performing emergency services in the craft or class involved will not be automatically considered eligible to participate in the election. Additionally, when the Mediator finds that employees not considered eligible by virtue of their assignment on the cut-off date, do work a preponderance of the time in the craft or class involved, a preponderance check may be used to resolve any uncertainty. In order to be added to the list of eligible voters, an employee must have worked the preponderance of the time during the specified period in the craft or class covered by the application.

Criteria credited for compensation but not actually worked should not be used in determining preponderance of work, i.e., vacation, holiday pay, as well as arbitraries paid for, but not worked, should be eliminated from consideration. In many instances, a 60-day checking period, dating back from the date of the payroll period used to determine eligibility of regularly assigned employees should suffice. In others, a 30 or even a 90-day checking period may be acceptable. A period of less than 30 days, or longer than 90 days, should not be used unless there are unusual circumstances. The period for checking should be clearly understood by the contending parties and specifically stated. The criteria upon which the preponderance is based should be determined by the Mediator and clearly explained before the check is begun.

6.0 EVIDENCE OF DISPUTE—AUTHORIZATIONS

6.1   *Form and Content of Authorizations*

There is no prescribed or acceptable form for authorizations which the NMB suggests or requires. (Petitions are not accepted.)

Requirements

Any type of authorization is sufficient if it includes the applicant's name and indicates that the employee either desires representation by the applicant for purposes of collective bargaining or desires a representation election. Any authorization card that is not signed and dated in the employee's own handwriting will not be counted towards the showing of interest. An employee's signature or mark in his/her own handwriting will be considered the employee's signature if it corresponds with the signature sample.

Recommendations

It is recommended that the authorization card include job title and employee number. If the carrier does not utilize employee identification numbers, the card should include social security numbers. The authorization card should provide a space to print the employee's name as well as a space for the employee's signature.

To facilitate implementation of card check procedures, all authorization cards submitted to the NMB by any organization or individual must be in alphabetical order on a system-wide basis. Duplicate authorization cards should not be submitted. Substantial failure to provide authorization cards in alphabetical order on a system-wide basis may result in return of authorization cards to the submitter.

6.2   *Age of Authorizations*

NMB Rules require that authorizations will be considered void if they are dated more than one year before the date on the application invoking the NMB's services.

6.3   *Acceptance of Additional Authorizations*

An applicant or intervenor may present the Mediator or the Chief of Staff with additional authorizations up to the deadline for receipt of such authorizations as specified below. The deadline for receipt of additional authorizations shall be the same for both the applicant and any intervenors.

Where the investigation is conducted off-site, additional cards should be delivered to the Chief of Staff by 5:00 p.m. the day the Chief of Staff receives the applicable list and signature samples.

When there is an on-site investigation, authorization cards not submitted with the application must be delivered to the Mediator on the property by 5:00 p.m. local time the day the Mediator receives from the carrier the applicable list of eligible employees and the signature samples.

A list of potential eligible voters which is not a system-wide alphabetical list or which fails to include full name, job title or classification, or duty station or location, when required by Section 3.6, shall not be deemed an "applicable list" for purposes of this Section. Lists furnished by the carrier after 3 P.M. shall be treated as having been received on the next calendar day. A list which is not provided for the Mediator to keep and utilize according to this manual shall not be deemed an "applicable list" for purposes of this Section.

6.4   *Cancellation or Revocation of Authorizations*

The Mediator will neither accept nor honor proposed cancellations or revocations of authorizations. Individuals seeking to revoke their authorizations should process such proposed revocations with the party to whom the original authorizations were furnished.

6.5   *Confidentiality of Authorizations*

Authorization cards or other evidence of a representation dispute should not be entrusted to any person other than an NMB representative.

It is the Mediator's responsibility to treat as confidential the names of individuals who have signed authorizations as well as the number of authorizations submitted by applicants or intervenor. The carrier or opposing party or parties should not be privy to the number or percentage of authorizations involved.

Checklists, tally sheets or markings on potential lists of eligible voters, which are used by the Mediator in determining percentages of authorizations, are also confidential.

6.6   *Initial Check of Alphabetized Authorizations*

The Mediator should compare the list of potential eligible voters with the names of the employees who signed authorizations to determine if a sufficient percentage of authorizations has been submitted to require checking the validity of the authorizations. Should the total number of authorizations submitted be insufficient prior to checking their validity, that fact should be reported to the NMB. However, if in the professional judgment of the Mediator, there appears to be a reasonable possibility that adjustments to the list may result in a sufficient showing of interest, the validity of all authorizations should be checked by comparison with carrier records.

6.601   *Percentage of Authorizations Required*

If the craft or class involved in the investigation is represented for Railway Labor Act purposes and is covered by a valid existing contract between such representative and the carrier, the application must be supported by a majority (more than 50%) of valid authorizations from individuals in the craft or class. In all other circumstances, an application must be supported by at least 35% of valid authorizations from the individuals in the craft or class. The Board's Merger Procedures are not affected by this Section.

A craft or class shall be deemed to be unrepresented for purposes of this section if the incumbent organization represents less than the full craft or class, e.g., a voluntary recognition covering part of the craft or class.

6.7   *Resolving Discrepancies in Authorizations—(Potential List of Eligible Voters)*

If, during the check of authorizations against the list of potential eligible voters, certain names cannot be located, the Mediator should attempt to resolve this discrepancy using methods as are available and necessary. The Mediator should avoid divulging to the carrier the names of the individuals who cannot be located on the list.

6.8   *Where Showing of Interest May Not Be Met*

Where it appears that the showing of interest requirement will not be met, the Mediator should notify the Chief of Staff and allow the parties to review the eligibility list before the Mediator makes the required recommendation to the Board concerning the showing of interest.

7.0 MEDIATOR'S REPORT RE CHECK OF AUTHORIZATIONS

7.1   *Contents of Reports*

After a check of authorizations has been completed, the Mediator must inform the Chief of Staff promptly of the results. The quickest method of notifying the Chief of Staff should be utilized. Any oral reports must be followed immediately with a written report in the form of either a telegram or a Mediator's report.

If more than one craft or class is involved, the Mediator's report should identify each separate craft or class, the number of eligible voters, the number of valid authorizations submitted by the applicant organization and/or intervenor(s), the percentage of valid authorizations submitted, the cut-off date for purposes of eligibility, the preponderance, if any, and any unusual facts developed by the investigation.

The Mediator must either recommend that the Board find a dispute to exist or dismiss the application. For example, "Re: NMB Case No. R-(number). Investigation developed that 400 potential eligible voters are involved. Applicant (name) submitted 300 valid authorizations for a 75% showing of interest. Intervenor (name)-submitted 204 valid authorizations for a 51% showing of interest. Recommend all mail ballot election with count in Washington, D.C., using August 4, 1977, as the cut-off date."

7.2   *Confidentiality of Report*

The contents of the Mediator's report are not to be revealed to the organization(s), the carrier, or any individual not employed by the NMB.

8.0 FINDING OF DISPUTE—AUTHORIZATION TO PROCEED BY NMB

The election will not proceed until authorized by the NMB.

The authorization from the NMB will be confirmed in writing and will indicate that the NMB has found a dispute to exist in the subject craft(s) or class(es). The authorization will establish the manner of resolving the dispute. Copies of this authorization will be sent to the involved carrier and organization(s).

9.0 DISPOSITION OF DISPUTE BY VOLUNTARY RECOGNITION

If during the Mediator's investigation, it is determined that the carrier is willing to recognize the invoking organization; that the employees involved are an unrepresented craft or class; and, there are no contesting representatives, the Mediator should report these facts to the NMB.

The Mediator should also determine if the applicant desires to be recognized rather than to have its application processed further. If the organization desires recognition and the carrier is willing to recognize the applicant, then the applicant should furnish a statement withdrawing its application. This withdrawal will be the basis for the NMB's closing of its case file.

10.0 DISPOSITION OF DISPUTES BY NMB

10.1   *Statutory Authorization*

Section 2, Ninth, of the Railway Labor Act authorizes the NMB to investigate a representation dispute and to take a secret ballot of the employees or to utilize any other appropriate method of ascertaining the names of the representatives of the employees involved.

10.2   *Elections*

In most instances where a dispute has been found to exist, the NMB will authorize an election exclusively by mail ballot. In some instances the NMB may authorize a ballot box election.

10.3   *Certification on the Basis of Check of Authorizations*

A certification on the basis of a check of authorizations may be appropriate when the employees involved in the craft or class are unrepresented and only the applicant organization is involved. Under such circumstances and where the participants agree in writing to certification on the basis of a check of authorizations, the Mediator should inform the Chief of Staff and obtain authorization from the Chief of Staff to proceed with the check of authorizations in lieu of an election.

10.4   *"Other Appropriate Methods"*

In cases where the Mediator is unable to secure information either from an incumbent or the carrier, the Mediator should report this fact to the NMB and suggest some other method, such as direct contact with the involved employees, by which the NMB may resolve the representation dispute.

11.0 PREPARATIONS FOLLOWING AUTHORIZATION OF ELECTION

11.1   *Designation of the Official Eligibility List*

The "List of Potential Eligible Voters" previously obtained from the carrier and corrected, if necessary, by the Mediator constitutes the "Official Eligibility List" following an election authorization. The Mediator shall designate the list by writing "Official Eligibility

List" on the first page and initialing the list and changes thereon. The Mediator should retain a copy of the list and loan file until the Mediator has ruled on all outstanding challenges and objections. The Mediator should notify in writing the participants, as well as the Chief of Staff, of the changes, if any, to the list of potential eligible voters that are reflected in the "Official Eligibility List." In addition, the Mediator should timely apprise the participants and the Chief of Staff in writing of any changes in the "Official Eligibility List" prior to the ballot count so that they may finalize their copies of the list.

11.2   *Address List*

Should the Board authorize an election, the carrier shall furnish to the Chief of Staff, upon request, system-wide alphabetized peel-off gummed labels and/or an appropriately formatted ascii or dbase diskette bearing the full names and current addresses of all employees on the list of potential eligible voters. The labels shall be furnished upon request, but no later than five (5) calendar days after the authorization of the election.

Labels or diskettes or their contents, will not be copied or entered into the NMB's system of records. Diskettes or unused labels will be returned or destroyed.

11.3   *Changes in Employee Status*

During the election period, the Mediator should advise the participants to send a copy of any changes in employee status during the election period to the Chief of Staff. Status changes will be handled by the Mediator. Status changes which do not meet the requirements listed below will not be considered.

Changes in employee status include, but are not limited to: death, retirement, promotion to management official, transfer out of craft or class, resignation, working for another carrier.

This information should include the effective date of the change and supporting documentation.

The Mediator is not obligated to accept any allegations of changes in employee status, absent extraordinary circumstances, if this information is provided less than 7 days before the scheduled count. Concurrence of the participants is not necessarily determinative of the Mediator's ruling.

12.0 ELECTIONS

12.1   *Preparation of Documents*

All NMB election materials should state the craft or class exactly as determined by the Board in the NMB's authorization.

12.101   *The Notice and Rules of Election*

12.101-1   *Contents of Notice*

In every case where the NMB has authorized an election, a notice will be prepared advising employees of the rules governing the election.

Form NMB-R-1, Notice and Rules of Election, is to be used in all election cases. It is incumbent upon the Mediator to carefully review the notice of election so that certain variables (e.g., craft or class involved, the time, and the place of election) are provided for in the particular circumstances involved.

12.101-2   *Posting of Notice*

The NMB will provide copies of the notice (with Form NMB-R-2, ballot marked "SAMPLE" attached) to the carrier at least five (5) calendar days before the beginning of the election period. The notice must be promptly posted by the carrier on carrier bulletin boards and in other appropriate locations, at least one per station, so that all eligible employees will be advised of the election in a timely manner.

12.102   *The Ballot*

12.102-1   *Form*

The NMB's official ballot, Form NMB-R-2, shall be reviewed by the Mediator.

12.102-2   *Places on the Ballot*

It is NMB practice to list the incumbent, the applicant, and then the intervenor in descending order on the ballot. The final line on the ballot will provide a box for write-in votes.

If there is no incumbent, and more than one applicant, the Mediator should determine the method for placement of contesting organization names on the ballot and inform the Chief of Staff. For example, the earliest date of application may be appropriate. In the event that multiple applicants applying on the same date will appear on the ballot, a method of random selection will be employed.

12.102-3   *Name on Ballot*

It is NMB practice that the national name of the organization and not that of a local union or a division is required to appear on the ballot. A reasonable abbreviation or designation may appear in parenthesis following the national name of the organization.

12.102-4   *Seal of NMB*

The ballots will normally be overprinted with a non-reproducible NMB seal. When a hand seal is used, only ballots distributed to eligible employees should be sealed.

12.102-5   *Color of Ballots*

In cases where two or more crafts or classes are being voted simultaneously on the same carrier, different colored ballots for each craft or class will be provided.

12.103   *Location and Time of Count*

The count shall be set for 2 p.m., at the NMB's office in Washington, D.C. unless otherwise directed by the Chief of Staff.

12.104   *Foreign Language Notice of Election, Ballots and Instructions*

In cases where the electorate is composed of individuals who may be unable to read English, the Mediator should notify the Chief of Staff so that the use of approved foreign language notices of election, ballots and voting instructions may be considered.

12.2   *Mail Ballot Elections*

In cases where the NMB has authorized an election exclusively by mail ballot, the following procedures will apply:

12.201   *Schedule for Voting*

The Chief of Staff, in consultation with the Mediator, will establish a time period for mail ballot voting of no less than 28 days between the date of mailing of ballots to voters and the return of ballots to the NMB. Factors such as size of the electorate, number of stations involved, and geographical distribution of the voters should be considered in determining the appropriate voting period. Sufficient time should be provided for receipt and return of ballots by those employees who desire to participate.

12.202   *Ballot Sets*

The "ballot set" consists of the ballot and Notice of Election, mailing envelope, and the prepaid postage ballot return envelope.

The NMB will ensure, to the extent possible, that every eligible voter is mailed a ballot set. The return ballot envelope shall include the case number and key number and shall be addressed to the NMB, Washington, DC 20277-4491.

Die cut window envelopes in which the case number and the key number on the ballot return envelope is visible will be used for mailing election material.

12.203   *Key Numbering*

A unique key number will be placed on each return ballot envelope and noted on the "Official Eligibility List" next to the name of each voter. This number will be used to determine the location of the returned ballot envelope on the eligibility list. This key number will be kept confidential.

The key number provides a means of controlling the integrity and security of the election. It is confidential and is devised in such a way as to eliminate the possibility of introduction into the election of additional unauthorized ballots. The key numbering system should vary from case to case in order to avoid establishing a predictable pattern.

12.204   *Handling of Ballot Materials*

Only the Mediator(s) or NMB agent(s) should actually be involved in the physical handling of material to be mailed to the voters.

12.205   *Challenged Ballots*

All individuals whose eligibility or ineligibility has been challenged and a final decision has not yet been made, will be sent challenged ballots. All challenged ballots should be marked with the letter "C" on the return ballot envelope. The eligibility list will be marked with a "C" next to the employee's name to indicate that this individual's eligibility to receive a ballot has been challenged.

If a Mediator's decision with regard to a challenge or objection has not been appealed to the Board within the prescribed time limit, the Mediator's decision is final.

When a final Board decision on eligibility is made, or if the appeal deadline has passed and an appeal has not been received, the list shall be corrected accordingly.

12.206   *Procedures Regarding Duplicates and Undeliverables*

12.206-1   *Duplicate Ballots*

When a request for a duplicate ballot is received, the eligibility list will be checked to determine if the individual is entitled to a ballot.

Only a request for a duplicate ballot signed and sent by the individual eligible employee will be honored. Requests sent by other than individual eligible employees will not be honored. A request for a duplicate ballot sent by telegram or facsimile or received less than five calendar days before the date of the count will not be honored. A request for a duplicate ballot dated or received prior to the mailing of ballots will not be honored.

The name of any individual requesting a duplicate ballot will be treated as confidential. The individual eligible voter entitled to a duplicate ballot will be sent a complete ballot set including the case number and the same key number as originally designated. However, the return ballot envelope should be clearly marked "duplicate". Notations should be made on the eligibility list indicating that a duplicate has been mailed and the date mailed.

12.206-2   *Undeliverable Ballots*

When a ballot is returned as undeliverable, the accuracy of the address will be checked using whatever method is deemed necessary. If a new address or the correction to the address is obtained at least five (5) calendar days prior to the date of the count, the ballot will be mailed to the new or corrected address.

12.3   *The Ballot Count*

Absent any unusual circumstances, the ballot count will be conducted as provided on the Notice of Election.

12.301   *Requests to Postpone the Ballot Count*

Absent extraordinary circumstances, requests to postpone the ballot count and impound the ballots must be submitted in writing, no later than two working days before the scheduled count, directed to the Chief of Staff, and must be supported by substantive evidence. The Chief of Staff will consider granting such requests only in extraordinary circumstances.

12.302   *Initial Preparations for Count of Ballots*

12.302-1   *Obtaining Ballot Envelopes From NMB Office*

The Mediator may arrange to have organization(s) and carrier representatives observe the Mediator collect the ballot envelopes from the NMB Office at the appropriate date and time.

The Mediator assigned to the count should verify that all ballots returned in the case have been delivered to his or her custody.

12.302-2   *Adjustments to the "Official Eligibility List"*

Prior to commencing the ballot count, the Mediator should adjust the "Official Eligibility List" by: (1) clearing challenges and objections; (2) accounting for undeliverable ballots; and (3) adjusting for changes in employee status.

Prior to the counting and tabulating of ballots, the Mediator should review the eligibility list and loan file to determine if the list is accurate with respect to eligibility. The ultimate decision as to eligibility must be made before commencing the ballot count.

Mediator's Decisions Not Appealed

If a Mediator's decision has not been appealed to the Board within the prescribed time limit, the Mediator assigned to the count should verify that the list reflects the Mediator's decisions.

Appeals

If an appeal has been made, the Mediator should correct the list, if necessary, to reflect the Board's rulings.

Undeliverable Ballots

The Mediator shall remove from the list of eligible voters the name of any employee a) for whom a valid mailing address has not been obtained at least five (5) working days prior to the time of the count; or b) whose ballot was returned as undeliverable within five (5) working days of the count.

Status Changes

The list should be corrected, if necessary, to reflect any status changes.

12.302-3   *Report of Election Results*

The Report of Election Results form will be prepared prior to the count for completion at the count.

12.303   *Commencing the Count*

12.303-1   *Mediator's Authority to Count*

The Mediator should not begin the counting or tabulating procedures before all timely challenges or objections with regard to eligibility or other substantive issues have been resolved. In addition, when a timely filed appeal is pending before the NMB the count should not commence.

Absent the foregoing circumstances, unless the Mediator is officially advised by the NMB to defer or cancel the ballot count, the Mediator shall complete the ballot count and overrule requests of participants either to defer or to cancel the count, even when the applicant desires to withdraw the application.

12.303-2   *Mediator's Control of Election Proceedings*

Admission To Ballot Count

It is the Mediator's responsibility to ensure that the observers neither interfere with the Board's counting procedures nor compromise the secrecy of the ballots.

It is NMB practice to allow a reasonable number of observers representing contesting organizations, as well as carrier observers, to be present during the ballot count.

Should employees on the eligibility list request the opportunity to be present during the ballot count, the Mediator may admit such observers. However, these practices are subject to the Mediator's discretion and the Mediator may limit the number of observers or, in appropriate circumstances, allow no observers since admission to the ballot count is a privilege and not a right.

Control of Election Materials: All materials which might disclose whether particular employees cast ballots or refrained from voting must be secured from the view of observers at all times. Such materials include ballot envelopes, marked eligibility lists, requests for duplicate ballots, etc. All ballots should be mixed thoroughly before unfolding and commencing the actual count.

12.303-3   *Handling of Returned Mail Ballots*

As a priority matter, the Mediator must ensure that all observers are located where they cannot determine which employees cast ballots or refrained from voting. Only the Mediator should have knowledge of which employees returned ballot envelopes.

The returned mail ballot envelopes should be compared with the list of eligible voters and, if identifiable, a check mark made next to the name of the individual who returned the ballot.

12.4   *Ballot Determinations—Invalid, Void or Valid*

12.401   *Invalid Ballot Return Envelopes*

Invalid ballot envelopes are those envelopes which can be determined on the face of the envelope not to be valid for inclusion in the ballot count. Examples of invalid ballot envelopes include unidentifiable, incomplete and returned envelopes from individuals not on the "Official Eligibility List." All ballot envelopes ruled invalid shall not be opened and shall be marked "Invalid" with reason, if appropriate. All invalid ballot envelopes shall be tabulated at the end of the ballot count and recorded on the Report of Election Results.

12.401-1   *Incomplete Returned Mail Ballot Envelope*

Returned mail ballot envelopes lacking a properly executed attest shall be ruled invalid.

If the returned ballot envelope does not contain the key number and/or the case number, and in the Mediator's judgment, the reasons for these missing identifications are not clerical error, these returned ballot envelopes shall be ruled invalid.

12.401-2   *Challenged Ballot Envelopes*

Challenged ballot envelopes from individuals who have been determined to be ineligible shall be ruled invalid.

12.401-3   *Original and Duplicate Ballot Envelopes Both Returned*

When an eligible voter returns both the original and a duplicate ballot envelope, the original shall be opened and tabulated and the duplicate ballot envelope shall be ruled invalid and marked to show why it has not been opened.

12.402   *Void Ballots*

A void ballot is a ballot cast and rejected for the reasons such as those described below. All ballots ruled void shall be tabulated and recorded on the Report of Election Results.

12.402-1   *Ballot Cast For Carrier or Carrier Official*

Ballots cast for a carrier or a carrier official shall be ruled void since a carrier or carrier official is not qualified to be an employee representative.

12.402-2   *Marks In More Than One Square*

A ballot marked in more than one square, where the intent of the voter as to choice of organization or individual is not clear, shall be ruled void.

12.402-3   *Ballot Marked "No", "No Union" or Unmarked*

A ballot marked negatively, indicating no desire for representation, shall be ruled void. A blank ballot shall be ruled void.

12.402-4   *Ballot Disclosing the Voter's Identity*

A ballot which has been signed or clearly identifies the individual voter shall be ruled void, unless the voter has placed his/
her name in the write-in space on the ballot and is not identified
elsewhere on the ballot.

12.403   *Valid Ballots*

Where the voter's intent is clear to the Mediator and the ballot
is not void, the ballot shall be ruled valid and shall be tabulated
and recorded on the Report of Election Results.

12.403-1   *Write-In Ballots*

A write-in ballot which clearly indicates the employee's desire
for representation shall be ruled valid.

13.0 TABULATION AND REPORT OF ELECTION RESULTS

The Mediator shall complete the count, tabulate the results and record them on the Report of Election Results. The form will show the
number of eligible employees, the number of invalid ballot envelopes,
void ballots, valid ballots and the organization or individual to whom
they were attributed. The Mediator shall sign the Report of Election
Results. Participants observing at the count should be requested to
voluntarily witness the Report of Election Results Copies of this report
should be provided to the participants.

13.1   *Submission of Report of Election Results*

The Mediator shall promptly deliver the completed Report of Election Results to the Chief of Staff.

14.0 ALLEGATIONS OF ELECTION INTERFERENCE

Allegations of election interference must be received in writing at
the Board's offices no later than 4:00 p.m. two (2) working days after
the date of the count. Initial filings received beyond this deadline
will not be considered timely absent extraordinary circumstances.
Allegations of election interference must be accompanied by substantive evidence. The allegations and supporting evidence must present
a *prima facie* case, otherwise the Chief of Staff will find an insufficient
basis for further investigation absent extraordinary circumstances
which justify an exception to this standard procedure. Absent extraordinary circumstances, the count will take place as scheduled and
unless a *prima facie* case is established a certification or dismissal will
be issued.

If a *prima facie* case is established, the moving party will have an
additional ten (10) working days after notification by the Chief of
Staff to supplement its initial filing. The responding party will have
ten (10) working days to file a response. The moving party will then

have five (5) working days to rebut the response, and the responding party will have five (5) working days to file a sur-rebuttal. If the Board is able to make a determination on the basis of written submissions, it will do so. In certain cases, however, the Board will conduct further investigation, either through confidential interviews, Board hearings (in camera and/or public), or otherwise.

15.0 MEDIATOR'S FINAL REPORT

Upon completion of the ballot count, the Mediator shall timely prepare the Mediator Election Report. This report should indicate, in detail, all activities and should highlight, if necessary, any actual or possible challenges or objections which have been made or could be raised.

This report, together with the loan file, including the ballots and ballot envelopes, should be promptly submitted to the Chief of Staff

16.0 RUN-OFF ELECTIONS

The procedures for run-off elections are prescribed by Section 1206.1 of the NMB Rules. All requests for run-off elections should be directed to the attention of the Chief of Staff. Only upon a written authorization of the Board will a run-off election be conducted.

A written request by an individual or organization entitled to appear on the run-off ballot must be submitted to the Board within ten (10) days after the date of the report of results of the first election.

In the event a run-off election is authorized by the Board, the name of the two (2) individuals or organizations which received the highest number of votes cast in the first election shall be placed on the run-off ballot, and no blank lines on which voters may write in the name of any organization or individual will be provided on the run-off ballot.

Employees who were eligible to vote the first election shall be eligible to vote in the run-off election, except those employees who are no longer employed in the craft or class.

17.0 BARS TO REPRESENTATION APPLICATIONS

The NMB's representation bar procedures are set forth in Part 1206.4 of the NMB Rules, revised effective February 22, 1979.

17.1   *Applicable Board Rules*

NMB Rules, Part 1206.4, governing representation bar procedures provide as follows:

Except in unusual or extraordinary circumstances, The National Mediation Board will not accept an application for investigation of a representation dispute among employees of a carrier:

(a) For a period of two (2) years from the date of a certification covering the same craft or class of employees on the same carrier, and

(b) For a period of one (1) year from the date on which:

(1) The Board dismissed a docketed application after having conducted an election among the same craft or class of employees on the same carrier and less than a majority of eligible voters participated in the election; or

(2) The Board dismissed a docketed application covering the same craft or class of employees on the same carrier because no dispute existed as defined in (1206.2 of these Rules); or

(3) The Board dismissed a docketed application after the applicant withdrew an application covering the same craft or class of employees on the same carrier after the application was docketed by the Board.

18.0 MOTIONS FOR RECONSIDERATION

Motions for Reconsideration of Board decisions concerning jurisdiction, craft or class, challenges or objections or election interference will be given consideration only upon the following circumstances: 1) the motion (original and one (1) copy) is received by the Chief of Staff within five (5) working days of the decision's date of issuance; 2) the motion is accompanied by a certificate of service which attests to its simultaneous service on the designated participants in the proceeding; and 3) the motion states with particularity the points of law or fact which the movant believes the NMB has overlooked or misapplied and the detailed grounds for the relief sought. Upon consideration of a Motion for Reconsideration, the NMB will decline to grant the relief sought absent a demonstration of material error of law or fact or under circumstances in which the NMB's exercise of discretion to modify the decision is important to the public interest. The mere reassertion of factual and legal arguments previously presented to the NMB generally will be insufficient to obtain relief. Reconsideration may not be sought from the Board's certification or dismissal.

Form NMB-3
(Revised 6-94)

OMB No. 3140-0002

NATIONAL MEDIATION BOARD

APPLICATION FOR INVESTIGATION OF REPRESENTATION DISPUTE

TO THE NATIONAL MEDIATION BOARD
Washington, D.C. 20572

A dispute has arisen among the employees of . . . .
(Name of Carrier)

. . . .
(Address of Carrier)

. . . .
(City, State and Zip)

as to who are the representatives of these employees designated and authorized in accordance with the requirements of the Railway Labor Act. The undersigned, one of the parties to the dispute, hereby requests the National Mediation Board to investigate this dispute, and to certify the name or names of the individuals or organizations authorized to represent the employees involved in accordance with Section 2, Ninth, of the Act.

. . . .
(Petitioning organization or representative)

**Parties to
Dispute**

. . . . Date . . . . . .
(Organization holding existing agreement, if any, and date thereof)

. . . .
(Other organizations or representatives involved in dispute)

If more than one craft or class, list separately	Estimated Number of Employees
1.	. . . .
2.	. . . .
3.	. . . .
4.	. . . .
5.	. . . .
6.	. . . .
7.	. . . .

**Craft or
class of
employees
involved**

Use separate line for each craft or class

**Evidence of
representation**

This application is supported by (check applicable box):
☐ At least a majority, if the employees are represented and
    there is a valid collective bargaining agreement.
☐ At least 35%, if the employees are unrepresented.

Signed at . . . . this . . . . day of . . . . , 19. . . .

Name . . . .
(Signature of applicant)

Title . . . .

. . . .
(Address)

. . . .
(City, State and Zip)

(File this application in duplicate)
(If necessary, use and attach additional sheets)

Form NMB-R-1
Rev. 7/89

**UNITED STATES OF AMERICA
NATIONAL MEDIATION BOARD
NOTICE OF ELECTION**

_____

_____

(NMB Case No.)   (Location)

TO ALL CONCERNED:

This will notify you of an election presently being held under the Railway Labor Act involving the following:

SOUGHT TO BE REPRESENTED BY:

AND PRESENTLY

This election is being conducted by Mediator

_____   ).
(Signature)   (Print Name)

Section 2, Fourth, of the Railway Labor Act, provides that "The majority of any craft or class of employees shall have the right to determine who shall be the representative of the craft or class for the purposes of the Act."

The Railway Labor Act further provides that elections shall be free from interference, influence or coercion, and that it is unlawful for a carrier to interfere with the organization of its employees.

Violations should be reported immediately to the Board Representative in care of the NATIONAL MEDIATION BOARD, Washington, D.C. 20572.

DATE OF MAILING OF BALLOTS _____

DATE AND PLACE OF COUNT OF BALLOTS: _____

_____

_____

THIS IS THE ONLY OFFICIAL NOTICE OF THE ELECTION AND MUST NOT BE DEFACED BY ANYONE.

Form NMB-R-1

UNITED STATES OF AMERICA
NATIONAL MEDIATION BOARD
RULES OF ELECTION

BALLOTING

In the event the election is conducted by United States Mail, official secret ballots will be mailed by the Mediator to the eligible voters. SHOULD ANY ELIGIBLE VOTER FAIL TO RECEIVE A BALLOT WITHIN A REASONABLE TIME AFTER THE DATE OF THE MAILING OF THE BALLOTS, SUCH VOTER MAY REQUEST A DUPLICATE BALLOT FROM THE NATIONAL MEDIATION BOARD. This request must be signed by the eligible individual and forwarded to THE NATIONAL MEDIATION BOARD, WASHINGTON, D.C. 20572. NO REQUEST WILL BE HONORED IF RECEIVED AFTER_____.

ELIGIBILITY

All employees in the craft(s) or class(es) referred to in this NOTICE OF ELECTION who appear on the payroll of the carrier during the designated period and who retain an employment relationship with the carrier on the date the vote is taken are eligible to vote.

SUPERVISION OF ELECTION

Only the Mediator or Board Representative and an individual voter will be allowed to handle the ballot in order to maintain its secrecy. The Mediator will interpret and apply the rules governing the election and shall decide on all challenged votes.

ELECTION RESULTS

The Mediator will count and tabulate all ballots at the designated time and place and report the results to the National Mediation Board.

CERTIFICATION

Certification of the organization or individual that has been designated and authorized to represent the employees involved in this dispute will be made by the National Mediation Board.

INSTRUCTIONS (MAIL BALLOT)

An Official Ballot and a return-addressed mailing envelope (no postage required) are enclosed herewith. To vote, mark an "X" in the square of your choice, fold and place the ballot in the mailing envelope. PRINT your name on the first line under the attest on the back of the envelope, and SIGN your name on the second line. Deposit this envelope in the U.S. Mail so as to reach the designated location for the count prior to the time and date indicated on the NOTICE OF ELECTION.

After the envelope has been checked against the eligibility list, your ballot will be removed and thoroughly mixed with other ballots before being unfolded and counted by the Mediator, thus insuring complete secrecy.

By order of the NATIONAL MEDIATION BOARD.

U.S. GPO: 1989—248-340

Form NMB-R-2(c)
Rev. 7/89

UNITED STATES OF AMERICA

OFFICIAL BALLOT OF NATIONAL MEDIATION BOARD

Involving

CASE NO. _____

an accretion to the craft or class of

Employees of

_____

A dispute exists among the above named craft or class of employees as to who are the representatives of such employees designated and authorized in accordance with the requirements of the Railway Labor Act. The National Mediation Board is taking a SECRET BALLOT in order to ascertain and to certify the name or names of the organizations or individuals designated and authorized for purposes of the Railway Labor Act.

INSTRUCTIONS FOR VOTING

No employee is required to vote. If less than a majority of the employees cast valid ballots, no representative will be certified. Write-in ballots are *not* permitted in this case.

If you desire to be represented by:

Mark an "X" in this square ....

NOTICE

1. This is a SECRET BALLOT. DO NOT SIGN YOUR NAME.
2. Do not cut, mutilate or otherwise spoil this ballot. If you should accidentally do so, you may return the spoiled ballot at once to the Mediator and obtain a new one.

Form NMB-2
(Revised 6-94)

NATIONAL MEDIATION BOARD

OMB No. 3140-0001

APPLICATION FOR MEDIATION SERVICES

TO THE NATIONAL MEDIATION BOARD
Washington, D.C. 20572

A dispute has arisen between the parties shown below which has not been adjusted between them, and the services of the National Mediation Board under Section 5, First, of the Railway Labor Act, are hereby invoked on specific questions set forth below. The approximate number of employees involved is _____ in the craft or class of _____.

THE SPECIFIC QUESTION IN DISPUTE

_____

_____

_____
(if necessary extend question on additional sheet or attach exhibit)

PARTIES TO DISPUTE

(Name of Carrier)	(Name of Organization or Individual)
(Labor Relations Officer)	(Organization Official)
(Address)	(Address)
(City, State and Zip)	(City, State and Zip)

WORKING AGREEMENT

If an agreement governing rates of pay, rules, or working conditions is in effect, give name of parties thereto and date thereof. If there is no such agreement, so state _____ .

COMPLIANCE WITH RAILWAY LABOR ACT

1. If this dispute involves change in the above-mentioned agreement, attach copy of the 30-day notice served by party desiring change and insert date of notice here _____ .

2. If this dispute involves the negotiation of a new or supplemental agreement, attach copy of request made by party desiring same and insert date of request here _____ .

3. If there has been a refusal to confer, so state and give reason; otherwise, give date of last conference here _____ .

Signed at . . . . this . . . . day of . . . . , 19. . . .

Name . . . .
(Signature of Carrier Official)

Name . . . .
(Signature of Organization Official)

Title . . . .

Title . . . .

(File this application in duplicate)
(If necessary, use and attach additional sheets)

TABLE OF CASES

Cases are referenced to chapter and footnote number(s): e.g., *2:* 135 indicates the case is cited in Chapter 2, footnote 135. Alphabetization is letter-by-letter: e.g., Airborne precedes Air BP.

INDEX

This index is alphabetized word-by-word (i.e., Union shops precedes Unions).

591

C

S